The Translators and Editor

RENATE BLUMENFELD-KOSINSKI is Professor of French and Italian at the University of Pittsburgh. She has also taught at Columbia University. She is the author of *Not of Woman Born: Representations of Caesarean Birth in Medieval and Renaissance Culture*; *The Writings of Margaret of Oingt, Medieval Prioress and Mystic*; and *Reading Myth: Classical Mythology and Its Interpretations in Medieval French Literature*. Among her coedited works are *Images of Sainthood in Medieval Europe, Translatio Studii: Essays by His Students in Honor of Karl D. Uitti for His Sixty-Fifth Birthday*, and *The Politics of Translation in the Middle Ages and the Renaissance*.

KEVIN BROWNLEE is Professor of Romance Languages at the University of Pennsylvania. He previously taught at Dartmouth College. He is the author of *Discourses of the Self: Autobiography and Literary Models in Christine de Pizan* and *Poetic Identity in Guillaume de Machaut*. His edited works include *Rethinking the "Romance of the Rose"; Text, Image, Reception; The New Medievalism*; and *Discourses of Authority in Medieval and Renaissance Literature*.

THE SELECTED WRITINGS OF CHRISTINE DE PIZAN

NEW TRANSLATIONS
CRITICISM

A NORTON CRITICAL EDITION

THE SELECTED WRITINGS OF CHRISTINE DE PIZAN

NEW TRANSLATIONS
CRITICISM

Translated by

RENATE BLUMENFELD-KOSINSKI
UNIVERSITY OF PITTSBURGH

and

KEVIN BROWNLEE
UNIVERSITY OF PENNSYLVANIA

Edited by

RENATE BLUMENFELD-KOSINSKI

W. W. NORTON & COMPANY · *New York* · *London*

Copyright © 1997 by W. W. Norton & Company, Inc.

The text of this book is composed in Electra
with the display set in Bernhard Modern.
Composition by the Maple-Vail Composition Services.
Manufacturing by the Maple-Vail Book Manufacturing Group.
Cover illustration: Fra Filippo Lippi, *Portrait of a Man and a Woman at a
Casement.* Tempera on wood. The Metropolitan Museum of Art, Gift of Henry G.
Marquand, 1889. Marquand Collection. Reproduced by permission.

Library of Congress Cataloging-in-Publication Data

Christine, de Pisan, ca. 1364–ca. 1431.
[Selections. English. 1996]
The selected writings of Christine de Pizan : new translations,
criticism / translated by Renate Blumenfeld-Kosinski . . . [et al.] ;
edited by Renate Blumenfeld-Kosinski.
p.   cm. — (A Norton critical edition)
Includes bibliographical references.
ISBN 0-393-97010-8 (pbk.)
1. Christine, de Pisan, ca. 1364-ca. 1431 — Translations into
English.   2. Christine, de Pisan, ca. 1364-ca. 1431 — Criticism and
interpretation.   I. Blumenfeld-Kosinski, Renate, 1952–
II. Title.
PQ1575.A23   1996
841'.2 — dc20   96-12764

W. W. Norton & Company, Inc., 500 Fifth Avenue, New York, N.Y. 10110
www.wwnorton.com

W. W. Norton & Company Ltd., Castle House, 75/76 Wells Street,
London W1T 3QT

7 8 9 0

Contents

List of Illustrations ix

Introduction xi

The Selected Writings of Christine de Pizan

From One Hundred Ballads and Other Ballads 5

The God of Love's Letter 15

From The Letter from Othea 29

From The Debate on the *Romance of the Rose* 41

From The Tale of the Shepherdess 45

From The Path of Long Study 59

From The Book of Fortune's Transformation 88

A Letter to Eustache Morel (February 10, 1404) 109

Morel's Answer 112

From The Book of the Deeds and Good Conduct of the Wise
King Charles V 113

From The Book of the City of Ladies 116

From The Book of the Three Virtues 155

From Christine's Vision 173

From The Book of the Body Politic 201

From One Hundred Ballads of a Lover and a Lady 216

The Lamentation on the Evils That Have Befallen France 224

From The Book of Peace 229

From The Letter on the Prison of Human Life 248

The Tale of Joan of Arc 252

Criticism

Jacqueline Cerquiglini • The Stranger 265

Beatrice Gottlieb • The Problem of Feminism in the Fifteenth
Century 274

Renate Blumenfeld-Kosinski • Christine de Pizan and the
Misogynistic Tradition 297

Sheila Delany • "Mothers to Think Back Through": Who Are
They? The Ambiguous Example of Christine de Pizan 312

Patricia A. Phillippy • Establishing Authority: Boccaccio's *De
Claris Mulieribus* and Christine de Pizan's *Le livre de la cité
des dames* 329

Joel Blanchard • "Vox poetica, vox politica": The Poet's Entry
into the Political Arena in the Fifteenth Century 362

Kevin Brownlee • Structures of Authority in Christine de
Pizan's *Ditié de Jehanne d'Arc* 371

Selected Bibliography 391

List of Illustrations

Christine working on *The Book of Fortune's Transformation*   3

Christine in the hall of Fortune's castle   4

Miniature from *The Book of the City of Ladies*   116

Lady Justice welcomes the Virgin Mary   117

Introduction

Christine de Pizan, the first professional woman writer in Europe, was born in Venice around 1364. Her father, Thomas of Pizan, came originally from Pizzano, a small town near Bologna.[1] He was a well-known physician and astrologer whose fame caused him to be appointed to the court of the French king Charles V. He left Italy when Christine was still an infant, and his family followed him in 1368. In her *Vision* of 1405 the adult Christine describes how they arrived in Paris in their elaborate Italian clothes, how welcome everyone made them feel, and how privileged they felt. The fortunes of Christine's family depended on the benevolence of the king who was a patron of the arts and fostered an intense intellectual life at his court.

But as the arts flourished, the political situation became more and more unstable: the Hundred Years' War (1337–1453), which pitted England against France over the succession to the French throne, had already taken its toll on the French in the disastrous battle of Crecy (1346).[2] When Charles V acceded to the throne in 1364, the English were in control of large parts of southwestern France. In addition, through the rivalries between the French nobles a civil war erupted in the first years of the fifteenth century, which marked Christine's life and work for decades.

For a long time Christine's life was like a beautiful voyage, as she described it herself in the *Livre de la mutacion de Fortune* [Book of Fortune's transformation] of 1404. Around 1379 she was married to Etienne de Castel, a notary and secretary at the royal court. Unlike many arranged medieval marriages, this was a love match. In one of her ballads, *Other Ballads "26,"* she called marriage a "sweet thing" and described how loving and considerate her husband was on their wedding night. Within a few years she had three children: two sons and a daughter, born between 1381 and 1385. But then disaster struck. King Charles V died in 1380, and his successor Charles VI did not behave as generously toward Christine's family. Both her husband and her father lost much of their pay, and Thomas of Pizan died sometime between 1384 and 1389 without leaving much of an inheritance. But Christine's greatest misfortune was the premature death of her husband in 1389 in an epidemic: she was left an almost destitute widow at twenty-

---

1. For the most complete treatment of Christine's life, see Charity Cannon Willard, *Christine de Pizan, Her Life and Works* (New York: Persea, 1984). Although Christine wrote her own name with a z, in the sixteenth century it was changed by various printers into an s, and Christine's father was believed to be from Pisa. Only recently has her name regained the z. (In older criticism one finds her name still spelled with an s.) For details on Christine's works, see the headnotes to each selection in this edition.

2. For a concise history of the Hundred Years' War, see Desmond Seward, *The Hundred Years War. The English in France, 1337–1453* (New York: Atheneum, 1978). Another fundamental work is Edouard Perroy, *The Hundred Years War*, trans. W. B. Wells (London: Eyre & Spottiswoode, 1951).

five with three small children, her mother, and a niece to support.

Forced by circumstances to "become a man," as she puts it in the *Mutacion de Fortune*, she began to write and look for patrons. This was an extraordinary step for a woman at this time. Most widows remarried or entered convents, but Christine was determined to support her family by the work of her pen. In this period even male writers did not live exclusively from their writings. Most had appointments at the court or in the Church that would provide them with a regular salary. But Christine, as a woman, could not hope to be appointed to any such positions. Her decision to turn herself into a professional writer was thus extremely unusual and daring.

Learning had always been her great love, though she describes her education several times as "crumbs I gathered from my father's table." Since the universities were closed to women, Christine's instruction depended entirely on her father. In the *Livre de la cité des dames* [Book of the city of ladies] she makes it clear that the intellectual differences between boys and girls are the result not of differing intellects but of the obstacles put into the path of girls' education. While her father furthered her ambitions of learning, her mother considered them unsuitable for a girl, and so her education never reached the level she had hoped for. Nonetheless, her knowledge of the major works of her times was impressive, and she made good use of the many compilations of historical and theological texts available in the royal and ducal libraries.

She began her literary career by writing love poetry, a genre much in demand from her patrons but not her first choice of subject matter, as she makes clear. Yet, she was very good at it, writing in different voices of men and women and constructing already in her first cycle of one hundred ballads sequences of poems that could be put together into a story, something she perfected later with her *Cent ballades d'amant et de dame* [One hundred ballads of a lover and a lady]. There are also many poems of widowhood, a new topic for lyric poetry, where she expresses the sorrow over a lost husband. Modern readers tend to read these poems as her most personal.

Christine also wrote some devotional texts, expressing her deeply held Christian faith. In the *Prieres à Notre Dame* [Prayers to our Lady] (1402–03) she addressed the Virgin in prayers for all parts of French society. In the *Sept Psaumes allegorisés* [Seven allegorized Psalms] (1409) she meditated on and interpreted Psalm 102, and in the *Heures de contemplation de la Passion de Notre Seigneur* [Hours of the contemplation of the Passion of our Lord] (ca. 1422) she seeks to comfort the French in their misfortune by recalling Christ's sufferings.[3]

But Christine's most profound love belonged to the texts she called "more subtle and more useful." Her first nonlyric work was the *Epistre d'Othéa* [Letter from Othea] of 1400, where she invented a goddess of wisdom, Othea, who uses lessons drawn from mythological stories to give advice to

---

3. Excerpts from these three texts have been translated in Charity Cannon Willard, ed., *The Writings of Christine de Pizan* (New York: Persea, 1993), 318–37 (including an appreciation of Christine's spiritual life). For another spiritual text see the *Epistre de la prison de vie humaine* [Letter on the prison of human life] on p. 248.

the Trojan prince Hector on the chivalric and spiritual life. She dedicated the different copies of this text to several high nobles and thus laid her first claim to a political voice that became more and more urgent as the situation in France deteriorated.[4] Before her more overtly political texts, Christine composed many lyrical works: love debates and complaints; more ballads and rondels; and the long poem *Dit de la pastoure* [Tale of the shepherdess] (1403), which reexamines the traditional poetic genre of the pastoral from a woman's perspective. An especially well-regarded work is her long narrative poem *Le Livre du duc des vrais amants* [The Book of the duke of true lovers] (1403–05), which combines prose and verse and explores the sentimental life of courtly lovers.[5]

In the first years of the new century (1401–02) Christine became a public player in an intellectual debate on the *Romance of the Rose*, one of the best-known texts of the Middle Ages. Composed by two different authors, Guillaume de Lorris and Jean de Meun, between 1228 and 1270, it was an allegory of love, depicting the amorous adventures of a young man as the quest for a rose bud. In the much longer second part, Jean de Meun invented various characters, such as the Jealous Husband, who spouted tirades against women.[6] When one well-known intellectual, Jean de Montreuil (1354–1418), provost of the city of Lille, felt compelled to circulate a little treatise praising the *Romance of the Rose*, Christine reacted violently. Her letters and the texts by her ally Jean Gerson (1363–1429), chancellor of the University of Paris, and by her opponents (in addition to Jean de Montreuil there were the brothers Pierre and Gontier Col) were collected in a dossier that Christine presented to the queen, Isabeau of Bavaria. This debate made Christine known and staked out her position as a defender of women. She had first taken up an explicit pro-woman position in the *Epistre au dieu d'amours* [The god of love's letter] in 1399, which accused men of maligning and mistreating women for no good reason.

In the next few years she wrote an extraordinary fifteen major works (by her own count in the *Vision*), among them four long works that combined allegory with autobiographical and political elements: *Le Livre du chemin de long estude* [The path of long study] (1402–03), the *Livre de la mutacion de Fortune* (1403), and then in a switch from verse to prose *Le Livre de la cité des dames* (1404–05), and *Lavision Christine* [Christine's Vision] (1405). She had also been commissioned by the duke of Burgundy, Philip the Bold (1342–1404), to write an official biography of his late brother, Charles V. This was the *Livre des fais et bonnes meurs du sage roy Charles V* [The book of the deeds and good conduct of the wise king Charles V] (1404). In those same years she also wrote the *Livre des trois vertus* [Book of the three virtues] (1405–06), a handbook for women's conduct in society, and a treatise on military art, *Le Livre des fais d'armes et de chevalerie* [The

4. On the political context of the *Letter from Othea*, see Sandra L. Hindman, *Christine de Pizan's "Epistre Othéa": Painting and Politics at the Court of Charles VI* (Toronto: Pontifical Institute of Mediaeval Studies, 1986).
5. See Thelma Fenster, trans. (with lyrics trans. Nadia Margolis), *The Book of the Duke of True Lovers* (New York: Persea, 1991).
6. See Charles Dahlberg, trans., *The Romance of the Rose* (Princeton, N.J.: Princeton University Press, 1971; rept. Hanover, N.H.: University Press of New England, 1983).

Book of the deeds of arms and chivalry] (1410), based on a French translation of the Roman writer Vegetius.

Christine also became involved in the production and illustration of her
own manuscripts: she would gather together a number of texts and have
them bound to present to a wealthy patron, and she would give detailed
instructions to artists concerning the content of the illuminations she
wanted in her works. This kind of close involvement in the actual manufacturing and distribution of manuscripts was extremely unusual for an author
in the Middle Ages.

Christine's extraordinary burst of literary activity in the first decade of the
century came to an end as the situation in France worsened. Charles VI
(1368–1422) was twelve when his father died in 1380, and Louis of Anjou,
his uncle, became regent. Shortly after Charles reached majority at age
fourteen, he married the Bavarian princess Isabeau. Beginning in 1392 the
king's frequent bouts of insanity required that someone govern in his stead,
but the question of who this someone should be created great troubles.
Should it be the queen, the king's uncles, or his brother, the duke of
Orléans? A constantly changing balance of power finally resulted in such
tensions between the houses of Orléans and Burgundy that on a dark
November night in 1407 Louis of Orléans was treacherously killed by his
own cousin, John the Fearless, duke of Burgundy. This murder would not
be avenged until 1419 when John was killed just as treacherously. The consequences of this assassination were disastrous for France. Two factions
formed: the Burgundians and the Armagnacs, named after Bernard d'Armagnac, the father-in-law of Louis of Orléans's son Charles. What the
English had not done to the French psyche and prosperity was accomplished by the ensuing civil war: disorder reigned; marauding bands of soldiers destroyed crops and property, causing poverty and distress; rebellions
weakened the monarchy; and a general breakdown of the spirit spread
through France.

It was this political and spiritual climate that marked Christine's last
works before her flight from Paris in 1418 to the "closed abbey" she
describes at the opening of her very last work, the *Ditié de Jehanne d'Arc*
[Tale of Joan of Arc] (1429). In her desperation over the collapse of France
she attempted to intervene by addressing the powerful people of her time.
Her hope was concentrated on the dauphin, Louis of Guyenne, born in
1397. In the *Livre du corps de policie* [Book of the body politic] (1404–07)
she laid out the principles for a just government; in the *Lamentations sur
les maux de France* [Lamentation on the evils that have befallen France]
(1410) she cried out at the sight of France in ruins and exhorted the warring
internal factions to make peace in order to defend against the outside
enemy, England; the same message was at the center of her *Livre de la paix*
[Book of peace] (1412–13); finally, in the aftermath of the disastrous battle
of Agincourt in 1415, the *Epistre de la prison de vie humaine* [Letter on the
prison of human life] (1418) turned to a Christian message of hope for
the afterlife, the liberation from the prison of our earthly bodies. As for the
political, earthly life, Christine seemed to have given up on it for a time.
We hear nothing from her for the eleven years she spent in seclusion, most

likely at the abbey of Poissy where her daughter was a nun. Her one son who survived infancy, Jean de Castel, died in 1425.

But toward the end of her life a shining light of hope appeared on the horizon: Joan of Arc. After the death of Charles VI in 1422, the English king Henry VI had become the nominal king of France, despite the presence of Charles VII, officially king of France. It was Joan's mission, inspired by a divine voice, as she stated, to crown Charles VII. This she accomplished on July 17, 1429, and only two weeks later Christine wrote her celebration of Joan's life. The young peasant girl from Domremy embodied everything Christine had prayed for: a woman was given a divine mission to restore peace in France and give the country back to the French. Most likely Christine did not live to see the terrible end of Joan, betrayed by the Burgundians and burned at the stake on May 30, 1431. It would take another two decades to chase the English from French territory.

Christine's reputation did not die with her. In 1440–42 Martin le Franc composed a work in defense of women, *Le Champion des dames* [The Champion of ladies] in which he called her the "valiant Christine" who knew Latin and Greek (she did not know Greek) and whose name would never die. Between 1545 and 1795 there are dozens of references to her,[7] always as an extraordinary learned woman. Jean de Marconville, for example, in his book on women's good and bad characteristics (1564) praised her to the skies as the wisest woman ever. Johann Eberti, a German scholar, put her into his encyclopedia of more than five hundred learned women in 1706. He singled out her *Livre du chemin de long estude* and the *Livre des trois vertus* as particularly successful.[8] But not every scholar was an admirer of Christine. Thus for Gustave Lanson, an influential educator in late-nineteenth-century France, she was an unbearable bluestocking whose works were as numerous as they were mediocre.[9]

In our own time Christine de Pizan has been rediscovered mostly as the author of the *City of Ladies*. As more and more of her works are being studied, questions on her "feminism" must be reconsidered. She certainly was the first writer to address the tradition of misogyny prevalent in both the society and the literature of her time from a female perspective. She made herself a champion for women by illustrating their achievements in culture and history and by emphasizing their intellectual equality. She created new bases for a female authority of writing by emphasizing her subjectivity as a learned woman whose affective and intellectual lives could not be separated and found literary expression in her many works. But she never advocated a change in the structures of her society.[1] Given her upbringing and social background, revolutionary ideas had to remain totally foreign to her. She

7. See Glenda McLeod, ed., *The Reception of Christine de Pizan from the Fifteenth through the Nineteenth Centuries: Visitors to the City* (Lewiston, Queenston, Lampeter: Edwin Mellen, 1992), appends. 1–2, 127–32.
8. Jean de Marconville, *De la bonté et mauvaiseté des femmes*, (Paris: Côté femmes, 1991), 60–61. Johann Caspar Eberti, *Eröffnetes Cabinet des gelehrten Frauenzimmers*, ed. Elisabeth Gössmann (Munich: iudicium, 1986), 96–97.
9. Gustave Lanson, *Histoire de la littérature française* (Paris: Hachette, 1909), 167.
1. Two articles reprinted here specifically address the problem of Christine's feminism (see pp. 274 and 312).

did not think much of the common people and would have never wanted to upset the hierarchies that shaped the society of her time. Her dearest wishes were that women should be recognized for their true worth and be treated well, that people should treasure learning, and that France should present a unified front to its long-standing enemy, England. She worked hard for these goals, in a "joyful and voluntary solitude," as she put it, and it is up to us to assess the results.

THE SELECTED WRITINGS
OF CHRISTINE DE PIZAN

This miniature shows Christine working on *The Book of Fortune's Transformation.* Her little dog is at her feet. This manuscript was one of the many presentation copies Christine had prepared for her wealthy patrons. Munich, Staatsbibliothek, gall. II, folio 2.

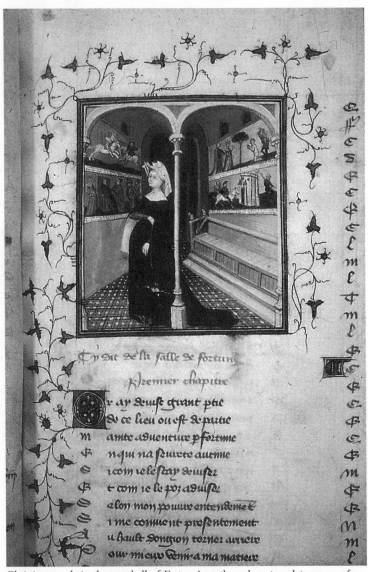

Christine stands in the vast hall of Fortune's castle and contemplates scenes from ancient history that she then transcribes for her readers. Munich, Staatsbibliothek, gall. II, folio 53.

FROM ONE HUNDRED BALLADS AND OTHER BALLADS

[Between 1393 and 1412 Christine wrote about three hundred ballads, and many shorter poems.[1] The *One Hundred Ballads* were completed before 1402 when Christine assembled her first collected works. She may have been inspired by the admired poet Eustache Deschamps who had also written *One Hundred Ballads* and by another such collection that circulated under the name of Jean le Sénéchal.[2] Christine created coherent thematic groups within the cycle: poems of widowhood; the development of a love relationship from the point of view of the lady; and another love story where both knight and lady speak, a device that announces her later *One Hundred Ballads of a Lover and a Lady*.[3] Some poems deal with mythological topics, give some sort of moral instruction or accuse false lovers; some allude to current events or are addressed to a specific patron. Many of the themes of her later works are thus already present in this first collection.

Interestingly, Christine realizes that some people may misread the love poems and confuse the poetic *I* with Christine herself. She cautions her audience to this effect in ballad "50." Her poems of widowhood, on the other hand, are generally considered to be more autobiographical, perhaps because the love poems often follow an established tradition of love poetry while there were no models for the poems of widowhood.

The formal intricacy of her poems cannot be adequately reproduced in English but was very important to Christine, as she offers a large number of different formal arrangements in her many poems.

Translated by Renate Blumenfeld-Kosinski from Maurice Roy, ed., *Oeuvres poétiques de Christine de Pisan*, vol. 1 (Paris: Firmin Didot, 1886).]

From One Hundred Ballads

14

Alone and in great suffering in this
deserted world full of sadness has my
sweet lover left me. He possessed my
heart, in greatest joy, without grief.
Now he is dead; I'm weighed down by   5

---

1. For details see the introduction to Kenneth Varty, ed., *Christine de Pisan's Ballades, Rondeaux, and Virelais. An Anthology* (Leicester: Leicester University Press, 1965), xxvii–xxviii. The ballad was originally a dance song, usually consisting of three couplets with the same rhyme and a refrain repeated after each couplet. In the fourteenth and fifteenth centuries, the ballad usually had three stanzas, ending with a refrain, and followed by a fourth shorter stanza called the *envoi*, often addressed to a prince or other patron.
2. Charity Cannon Willard, *Christine de Pizan: Her Life and Works* (New York: Persea, 1984), 59.
3. See Charity Cannon Willard, "Lover's Dialogues in Christine de Pizan's Lyric Poetry from the *Cent Ballades* to the *Cent Ballades D'Amant et de Dame*," *Fifteenth Century Studies* 4 (1981), 167–80.

grievous mourning and such sadness has
gripped my heart that I will always weep
for his death.

What can I do? It's not surprising that I
weep and sigh, with my dear lover dead.   10
For when I look deeply into my heart and
see how sweetly and without hardship I
lived from my childhood and first youth
with him, I am assailed by such great
pain that I will always weep for his   15
death.

I'm like a turtle dove without its mate,
who turns away from greenery and heads
toward aridity; or like a lamb the wolf
attempts to kill, which panics when its   20
shepherd leaves it. Thus I am left in
great distress by my lover, which gives
me so much pain that I will always weep
for his death.

17

If all my writings are about sadness,
it's no surprise, for a heart in mourning
cannot have joyous thoughts. Asleep or
awake, every hour finds me in sadness. To
find joy is difficult for a heart that   5
lives in such sadness.

I can never forget this great,
incomparable suffering which brings my
heart to such torment, which puts into my
head such grievous despair, which   10
counsels me to kill myself and break my
heart. To find joy is difficult for a
heart that lives in such sadness.

I cannot write sweet things. Whether I
want to or not, I must complain bitterly   15
about the evil which I must bemoan. It
makes me tremble like a leaf, this pain
that attacks me. To find joy is difficult
for a heart that lives in such sadness.

18

Some people keep on asking me why I am so
melancholic and why they don't see me
anymore singing or laughing but rather
behave simply like a nun—me who used
to be so gay and joyful. But there is a   5
good reason why I do not sing any longer,
for grievous mourning has taken
possession of my heart.

Fortune has done all this, may God
recognize this. She has changed into   10
mournful ways my games and my laughter.
Thus I have chosen mourning as my comfort
and the saddest life. I have grounds to
be depressed and lost in thought; I have
no hope that I will ever recover, for   15
grievous mourning has taken possession of
my heart.

It's no wonder that my joy has vanished;
for no pleasant thought, nor any other
pleasure that might bring me joy is left   20
within me. Thus the despair of my life
weighs on me and makes me hard and
ungracious. And if I'm sad, I can't help
it, for grievous mourning has taken
possession of my heart.   25

[Poems 21 to 49 chronicle the beginning and the end of a love affair
recounted in the first-person voice of a courtly lady. The next poem comments on this.]

50

Some people could misjudge the fact that
I write love poems about myself. They may
say that I know too well the risks of
love and write about its tricks, and say
how can I speak about it so true to life   5
without having experienced it myself?
But, with all due respect to those who
say this, I draw my information from the
knowledgeable poets.

For whoever wants to write beautiful and   10
pleasant poems, whether long or short,
must know that the lightest and most
pleasing inspiration comes from love,
there is no other way to compose them
well and sweetly. And without love, there   15
is no pleasing way of life: I draw my
information from the knowledgeable poets.

Whoever had these thoughts[1] should get
rid of them, for in truth my ambitions
lie elsewhere. I do not say this to   20
excuse myself or to pretend I'm pure—
better people than I have been in love.
But love gives me neither joy nor pain.
But even those whose hearts dwell
elsewhere can speak of love for their   25
enjoyment: I draw my information from the
knowledgeable poets.

53

Wise are those who know how to guard
against false lovers who have the habit
of ceaselessly betraying women with their
words. They complain about the force of
love which holds them prisoner like a   5
bird in a cage, and pretend they're all
pale with love. But I am firmly convinced
that he who complains the most is not
necessarily the sickest person.

When you hear them swear and carry on,   10
pretending to be more submissive than a
page at court, go about, reflect and look
around—and when they talk they twist
their tongue in order to deceive, and
hardly any one is the wiser when they   15
complain with such charm and grace! But
one can well judge by their faces: he who
complains the most is not necessarily the
sickest person.

May God correct such lovers. Sadly, there   20
are many of them, I believe, who go

1. I.e., the suspicious thoughts of the first stanza.

around asking the ladies for grace and
mercy, and who send messages with the
only aim of gaining advantage. This is
why my ballad says that in this case, be   25
he ever so highly placed, he who
complains the most is not necessarily the
sickest person.

[Poems 65 to 88 develop a love story. Sometimes the lady speaks and sometimes the lover.]

67

Dearest lady, truly I could never thank
you enough for the noble gift your sweet
heart bestows on me, your faithful
servant:[2] to give me your love
wholeheartedly, you whom I love and desire   5
to serve. Oh, may God give me the power
to deserve this!

Now you have filled my poor heart with
joy and taken away the torment I suffered
because of you such a long time. You have   10
rewarded me much too richly. You thought
of my advantage, to shower me with all
good things. Oh, may God give me the
power to deserve this!

Now I will be happier than I used to be,   15
and it's only just that I should live
joyfully. For it pleases me so much that
your love is mine, that even if all the
world could belong to me I'd rather lose
it entirely than your love to which I   20
will devote myself. Oh, may God give me
the power to deserve this!

69

This lovesickness hurting you so much
has taken you quite by surprise! You do
not want be faulted for being lazy in
asking for my love. I am not an expert in
love and people would call me silly, Sir,   5
if I began to love you so quickly.

2. The word in French is *ligement,* a term designating the obligation of faith between feudal lord
and vassal.

I believe that a lady sins against honor
and noble thought if she gives so quickly
what is so valuable. For those who desire
it there are no other riches, no other   10
joy. I wouldn't let you starve enough,
Sir, if I began to love you so quickly.

And you have to merit the goods of love
with great travails; you have to suffer
cold and heat before being rewarded   15
generously. You'd consider me a fool and
you'd have to blame me yourself, Sir, if
I began to love you so quickly.

78

What are we going to with this jealous
husband? I pray to God that we could just
skin him. He keeps such watch over us
that we cannot come near each other. If
we could only tie him with a filthy rope,   5
the dirty, vile, villainous man,
disfigured by gout, who angers and annoys
us so much!

If only his body could be strangled by
wolves—for what good is he, except to   10
be a hindrance! What is he good for, this
old man with his cough, except to argue,
grimace, and to spit? Not even the devil
could hold him dear, I hate him, broken,
old and coming apart, who angers and   15
annoys us so much!

Ha, he deserves to be beaten, the baboon,
who does nothing but spy around his
house! And what a house! Shake him down a
little so that he will go to bed, or make   20
him go down the stairs without walking!
Give it to him, this villain who lies in
wait for us, who angers and annoys us so
much!

79

Alas, my lady! Love made me say it. What
I said was crude and not appropriate. I

spoke as a man in pain and anger. By God,
please do not take seriously what I said,
sweetest, most prized lady. For I know   5
that I spoke crudely, and I humbly beg
your forgiveness.

A heart in the grip of jealousy does not
always turn to reason, for there is no
greater pain, no worse malady. And people   10
said to me, as I wrote to you the other
day, that you have begun to love someone
else. That's the reason for my crazy
talk, and I humbly beg your forgiveness.

But I beg you that I may be enough as   15
lover for you, though there are many of
greater renown and it may well be that I
am the worst. Don't despise my loyal
heart, overcome with love for you. I
called you false! I lied! I humbly beg   20
your forgiveness.

From Other Ballads

5

Worldly goods and all the things around
them, everyone sees well they're vain and
fallible. We're mad to leave for
transitory things eternal joys God gives
to peaceful innocents who do not care for   5
any treasure. In order not to praise
things that don't last, let us remember
that we must die.

What has become of the great men whose
histories we read, who suffered great and   10
heavy pains, so as to gain praise, honors
and victories? Are they not dead, as we
see so well? Do we not see all things
pass, whether sensible or not? Everything
must rot. Unless we believe in things   15
impossible, let us remember that we must
die.

Let us not lose God for those things, as
worthless as a pear, that will not save

us but only do us harm; let us not lie   20
just to accomplish hideous and horrible
sins, to gain delights of vanity, ugly
and not worth any praise; for God knows
all: we cannot hide from Him; to escape
His terrifying vengeance, let us remember   25
that we must die.

Princes and wise clerks, we do not want
to perish by our own evil deeds, let's be
intent on our salvation and let us
remember that we must die.   30

7

If I could only get closer to Pallas, I'd
never lack in joy and all good things;
she'd lead me on the path of comfort and
help me carry the load Fortune has made
too heavy for me.   5
But I am too weak to carry such a heavy
load, if she does not take one side of it
and helps me with her greatest effort.
May God grant it, for from Juno I will
have no comfort.   10

Pallas, Juno, and Venus wanted long ago
to plead before Paris[3] the wrong done do
them; each one said that in her opinion
she was the most beautiful and that her
powers far surpassed the others' in all   15
things. They would leave it up to Paris
who then judged Venus the most beautiful
and powerful. He said: "My lady, I would
like you to stay with me, for from Juno I
will have no comfort."   20

Because she got the golden apple, Venus
then aided him with Helen which brought

3. The son of the Trojan king Priam and his wife, Hecuba, had been given away to live as a
shepherd after a frightening prophecy. He is called on to judge who is the most beautiful
goddess: Venus, Pallas, or Juno. Each goddess offers him a bribe. Venus promises him the most
beautiful woman on earth, Helen, the wife of Menelaus; Pallas offers triumph in warfare, and
Juno riches. Paris chooses Venus's bribe, declares her the most beautiful, and hands her the
prize, a golden apple. Paris's subsequent abduction of Helen was the cause of the Trojan War.
For the importance and the many permutations of this story in the Middle Ages see Margaret
J. Ehrhart, *The Judgment of the Trojan Prince Paris in Medieval Literature* (Philadelphia: University of Pennsylvania Press, 1987). Christine returns to the judgment in many different contexts.

him death and destruction. I don't care
for her, but my heart would be overjoyed
if the valiant Pallas, who undoes all   25
wrongs and procures all good things,
would retain me as her servant: then I
would no longer need to desire future
boons, for from Juno I will have no
comfort.   30

These three powerful goddesses make the
world go round, despite their discord.
But may God recommend me to Pallas, for
from Juno I will have no comfort.

32

When I see these lovers being so sweet to
each other, giving each other deep and
sweet glances, laugh sweetly, move away
from each other and carry on—my heart
is about to break.   5

For then, because of them I think of him;
my heart is with him though I wish it
could be free. But the sweet and charming
man is far away, I am overcome with pain—
my heart is about to break.   10

My heart will languish in this grief,
filled with painful thoughts until the
moment when he returns, he whom love
makes so pleasant to me. But for now,
from the illness that brings me down my   15
heart is about to break.

Princes, I cannot be silent when I see
people walk in pairs—they are full of
joy. As for me, my heart is about to
break.   20

50

Noble sir, who wants to acquire prowess,
listen to this; hear what you must do:
you must fight in many lands; be fair to
your enemy; not flee from battle, nor
escape; fear God; speak boldly; be   5

skillful when attacking; not incur blame
for cowardice; be learned when it comes
to arms; love your prince; be loyal to
your leader; possess a strong courageous
heart; listen to advice; keep your word;   10
if you do this you'll be valiant and
wise.

Be thoughtful in the event of war; travel
must delight you; you must seek out
foreign courts and princes, learn all   15
about them and their affairs; please them
through wise words; never speak against
reason; don't malign a living soul; honor
the valiant and revered; frequent good
people; don't despise the poor; shirk no   20
pain while gaining honor; do not be
greedy, but give freely of your
possessions; may your words be truthful
and not vain; if you do this you'll be
valiant and wise.   25

Don't ask for assistance in war without
good counsel, and if it's necessary for
your honor, clamp shut your mouth and
teeth, nothing should come forth that
should be kept silent; speak gladly of   30
others' virtuous deeds but conceal the
good you've done; do not seek leisure but
temperance; shun hastiness; flee and
disdain all vice; bring to completion all
your enterprises; be not proud nor   35
boastful; in looks be sure of yourself,
don't growl, carry yourself well wherever
you may go; if you do this you'll be
valiant and wise.

Noble prince, this without doubt is the   40
way to gain the highest honor; noble sir,
follow it, I ask you: if you do this
you'll be valiant and wise.

53

My bad Fortune, I believe, will not let
me acquire any good. She's attacked me
for a long time now, this is her habit.

And however hard I try, it's in vain.
She, the disloyal one, quickly destroys   5
all that I have and brings me only evil.
Whenever happiness comes my way, bad luck
chases it away.

Nothing ever goes right for me; where I
hope to find help, whatever I seek—no   10
road leads there: I have to stay as I am
forever, that's why I weep so often, when
I see, no matter what I do, whenever
happiness comes my way, bad luck chases
it away.   15

And since Fortune thus opposes any
happiness and takes away my comfort, I
lose all hope of happiness and rest from
the evil that assails me. For I know that
whenever happiness comes my way, bad luck   20
chases it away.

Princes, thus I must languish with my
heart darker than a blackberry; the winds
throw me off my track. Is this not the
worst misfortune that attacks me? For   25
whenever happiness comes my way, bad luck
chases it away.

THE GOD OF LOVE'S LETTER

[Dated May 1, 1399, *The God of Love's Letter* is one of the longer literary
works that first established Christine's reputation as a professional woman
of letters (along with the *One Hundred Ballads* and the *Letter from Othea*),
after the debut constituted by the various short lyric pieces of her earlier
literary apprenticeship. Its form is that of the epistle, here, one dictated by
Cupid, in his capacity as king of the court of love, to all loyal lovers everywhere, his special constituency. At the same time, Christine's poem is part
of her extended polemic against what she perceived to be the fundamental
misogyny of the *Romance of the Rose*.[1] It should thus be read as already
participating in (or perhaps prefiguring) the "Debate on the *Romance of the
Rose*" that was to dominate the Parisian literary scene during 1400–02. In
this context, Christine's Ovidian Cupid figure displaces the Cupid of the

---

1. For a detailed consideration of Christine's polemic responses to the *Rose*, see K. Brownlee,
   "Discourses of the Self: Christine de Pizan and the *Romance of the Rose*," in K. Brownlee and
   S. Huot, eds., *Rethinking the "Romance of the Rose": Text, Image, Reception* (Philadelphia:
   University of Pennsylvania Press, 1992), 234–61.

Romance of the Rose, who had served, within the fiction of that text, to authorize both the courtly and the clerkly[2] discourses of what Christine considered to be the *Rose*'s predominant misogyny.

The *Letter* presents itself as a response by the god of love to a series of complaints that he has received from ladies, and a careful rhetorical structure is in evidence throughout. Cupid first responds to complaints about faulty courtly lovers who deceive women. He then turns to faulty clerkly writers who defame women. While the first category of offenders involves an implicit attack on the *Rose* of Guillaume de Lorris, the second category involves an explicit attack on the *Rose* of Jean de Meun. Christine's clerkly pro-feminist critique singles out by name Ovid's *Ars amatoria* [Art of love] and *Remedia amoris* [Love's remedies] as well as Jean de Meun's *Rose*. Her aggressive strategy for defending women in the learned, clerkly context, leads Christine to a new "feminist" biblical exegesis in which Eve is presented as free of original sin. The poem concludes as Christine-author uses the framework of her fiction playfully to display her mastery of mythographic learning and thus to reaffirm her authority as female writer.

Translated by Kevin Brownlee from Maurice Roy, ed., "L'epistre au Dieu d'Amours," in *Œuvres poétiques de Christine de Pisan*, vol. 2 (Paris: Firmin Didot, 1891), 1–26.[3]]

Here begins the God of Love's Letter.

From Cupid, king by the grace of himself, god of lovers, ruling in the shining sky with no one's help, son of the powerful goddess Venus, lord of love and all its objects, to all our loyal, obedient servants, HEALTH, LOVE, INTIMACY. (1–7)

We make it publicly known that complaints and piteous accusations have been made before us at our court by all ladies, married and unmarried, noblewomen, middle-class women, and young girls. All these women have together humbly requested our help, without which they will all be robbed of their honor and deeply shamed. And the above-mentioned ladies complain of the great crimes, the accusations, the slanders, the betrayals, the great outrages, the deceptions, and the many other pains that they receive every day from disloyal men, who blame, defame, and deceive them. They complain about France more than any other country, France which used to be their shield and protection, which used to defend them against all threats, as it is only right, and as must be the case in a noble country ruled by courtliness. But now, in this kingdom that used to honor them so much, they are more than anywhere else dishonored by deceivers and even by the noblemen who used to protect them, which they lament most piteously. For at present,

---

2. The learned, bookish language of the medieval clerk, which treated moral, philosophical, theological, political, and historical topics on the basis of the Latin writings of the classical and Christian canonical authors.
3. See also the admirable new edition and translation of Thelma S. Fenster and Mary Carpenter Erler, *Poems of Cupid, God of Love* (Leiden: Brill, 1990), 34–75.

there are many ill-trained knights and squires who regularly betray them by using pretty blandishments. They pretend to be loyal lovers, and cover their intentions with varied disguises. Thus they say that they suffer intensely because of their love for the ladies, which possesses them completely: one man complains of this; another says his heart is in pain; yet another gives the appearance of crying and sighing; another pretends that he is in great suffering, that he is pale from loving so much, almost dead, languishing; and they all swear and make lying promises to be loyal and discreet, and then go bragging about their exploits. They take great trouble to go often to churches, keeping their eyes open as they walk up and down; they kneel at the altars in order to give the false impression of piety: there are many like this. Through the streets they spur their horses, gay and glamorous with their ringing steps; many pretend to be very busy with all this; they do not spare their mules or their horses. They are very diligent in requesting information; they often ask where weddings and feasts are held, then show up at them, looking elegant and stylish, in order to pretend that they suffer from their unrequited love, giving the impression that they can scarcely endure our arrows. Others take great trouble, using messengers or acquaintances in common, in order to obtain what their false hearts desire. By such means, in more than a thousand disguises, these false lovers conceal their true natures: that is, the disloyal ones who hate faith and loyalty, who desire to deceive. (8–66)

But the loyal lovers are not part of this group; they should be loved and made much of, for they would not wish to deceive in any way: I forbid it to them; and therefore I consent that they have the sweet, savory goods of love in abundance, for I dispense generously to my true followers. These follow my true commandments, my just, loyal, and good teachings. I prohibit them from acting churlishly or committing misdeeds; I require them to pursue true honor; to be loyal, discreet and truthful, generous, courtly and unassociated with slanderers, humble and sweet, handsome and well turned out, strong and honest; eager for esteem; ready for the feats of arms necessary to acquire fame. I assert truly that whoever measures up to this standard cannot fail to receive a beautiful, beloved lady; for when I am served in this way, I give out appropriate rewards. And if by chance false lovers obtain some success, then it is not true success, even if I put up with it, for the prize is worth little if won without desire or appetite. What are fine foods and spiced wines to the indifferent palate, which takes little or no pleasure in them? But if the man who truly desires some good bread (or even a loaf of white bread) actually obtains it, then he slices it with joy and eats it with gusto, for he desires it above all else! (67–98)

Thus if they are not careful, ladies are often deceived, for they are trusting and only see the good side of things. Because of this, whether they want to or not, it often happens that they fall in love with deceivers,

and are betrayed before they become aware of what is happening. And
when they have been completely taken in by the disloyal lovers who
have tricked them, listen to how these lovers behave toward them: it is
not enough for them to have betrayed the ladies; they have companions
in their wicked behavior. There is no deed or promise that they do not
recount to one another, nor do they neglect to exaggerate their amorous
successes: they brag that they live in the bedrooms of the ladies who
love them; then they swear body and soul that this is the truth, and
tell how they lay naked in their ladies' arms. They tell their drinking
companions; and the noblemen gossip together in ducal or royal courts,
or elsewhere; these are the kinds of lessons they teach. There are many
who should be using their words to recount true and valuable stories,
chivalric exploits; but instead, comfortably relaxing in front of a warm
fire of an evening, they tease each other, and reproachfully say to one
another: "I know how you work, Lady X is your lover, and you play the
gay blade for the sake of her love; but many share in it; she receives you
after having just dismissed your predecessor!" Thus envious men
defame the fair lady, with no grounds, without knowing anything negative about her. And the one who is teased pretends to be hurt by this,
but in fact he is very pleased with this treatment. And, he speaks many
blameful words, although he makes apologies for this: in making his
apologies he names and thus accuses the lady; he pretends to conceal
and to hide that which he is delighted to tell and to reveal. (99–140)

There are others who provoke teasing against themselves, in order to
get their companions to chide them into recounting what they in fact
want everyone to know. They laugh off the chiding by naming ladies'
names, and thereby excuse themselves in a cowardly way. (141–46)

And there are others who have taken great trouble to succeed in love,
but have failed. They are ashamed because they have been refused.
They do not want others to think that they have wasted their time, and
therefore they brag about things that have never occurred. If they have
visited the lady's house for any reason whatsoever, they recount every
detail of how the household functions in order to support their boasts.
Many ugly things are said in this context; and he who does not want to
express himself explicitly uses innuendo to make his point. Thus women
are often very slanderously identified and blamed without justification;
even certain very elevated ladies, both blonds and brunettes. God, what
speakers! God, what encounters where the honor of ladies is stolen
away! (147–64)

And how does this kind of defamation profit those who should arm
themselves in order to guard and to protect women's honor? For every
man should be well disposed toward women, who are the mothers of all
of them, nor are they bitter or fickle toward their offspring, but rather
soothing, sweet, and friendly. They are responsive and helpful to the
needs of their sons; they have done and continue to do so many good

things for their sons: they consider any activity good which leads to the
gentle nourishment of man's body. At his birth, during his lifetime, at
his death, women are helpful and useful to him—understanding, sweet,
and obliging. The man who slanders women is self-centered, rude, and
full of ingratitude. Furthermore, I say that a man behaves unnaturally
when he defames, or slanders, or reproaches woman, by blaming her,
whether it is a question of one, or two, or of all women generally. (165–
84)

Even granting that some women are foolish, or full of every kind of
vice, or faithless in love and lacking all loyalty, or proud, wicked, cruel,
or inconstant, fickle, changeable, or crafty, false hearted and deceptive—should all women therefore be put in the same category, with not
a single exception? When God on high created the angels, the cherubim, the seraphim, and the archangels, were there not some who acted
badly? Should all angels be deemed wicked because of this? The man
who knows an evil woman should be on his guard against her, not
defame a third or a quarter of all of womankind, slandering every sort of
feminine behavior. For there have been, are, and shall be many women
worthy of praise for goodness and graciousness, in whom virtue and
beauty abide, whose good sense and morality have withstood the test.
And those men who blame women who are less than perfect are, I
repeat, in error, if they name them, or tell who they are, or where and
how they live. (185–209)

For God tells us not to defame sinners, nor to slander them in public.
Vices and sins should be strongly condemned, but without naming
those who are tainted with them, or defaming anyone. Thus I read what
Scripture tells us. There are many who speak without heeding this
advice, and it is shameful that such a vile practice persists among gentle-
men. I am speaking to those men who are tainted with this practice, not
to those who have not sinned in this way. For there are many noblemen
who are so worthy that they would prefer to lose their wealth rather than
to be reproached at all for such behavior, or to be caught doing it. But
the wicked men whom I am here discussing, who have neither good
deeds nor good intentions, do not take as an example Hutin de Vermeilles whose goodness was such that no one could ever reproach him,
nor did he hold with slander. He considered honoring ladies to be his
highest obligation; he would not allow them to be blamed or defamed
in his presence. He was a valiant knight, wise and well beloved; for these
reasons he was and shall be renowned. The good and valiant knight
Oton de Grandson,[1] who excelled at arms so much during his lifetime,
was held to be courtly, noble, powerful, handsome and gracious, may

---

1. Well-known lyric poet (c. 1345–1397), who had the reputation of being exemplary in courtliness as in chivalry. This reputation was shared by Hutin de Vermeilles, a knight who served as
   chamberlain to the French king Charles V. Christine also pairs Oton and Hutin as courtly
   exemplars in her *Débat de deux amants* [Debate between two lovers].

God have his soul in heaven! For he was a very true knight. Whoever
speaks ill of him commits a sin in my opinion, in spite of the fact that
Fortune was not favorable to him, since it often happens that she harms
the good. In any case, I declare that he was loyal, more valiant at arms
than Ajax,[2] Telemon's son. It never pleased him to defame anyone; he
sought to serve ladies, to prize and to love them. Many others have been
good and valiant and should be taken as examples by the men who are
flawed. There are now quite a number (as well there should be) who
follow the good lead of the exemplary ones. Honor leads them, prowess
shows them the way; they strive to acquire fame and praise; their noble
characters shine, and are apparent through their noble deeds, in this
kingdom, elsewhere, and overseas. But I shall now be silent and not
name them, so that it cannot be said that I merely flatter them, or that
what I say can be turned into boasting. Such men are truly noble, otherwise nobility would not exist. (210–58)

In addition, the above-mentioned ladies complain of the many clerks
who accuse them in prose and verse books, defaming their morals in
varied words; and they give these books as school texts to their young,
beginning students, by way of example and doctrine, to be retained into
adulthood. Some tell in verse how Adam, David, Samson, and many
other men were deceived by women both early and late: what living
man will escape? Others say that women are very deceitful, crafty, false,
and worthless. Still others say that they are highly untruthful, changeable, inconstant, and flighty. Yet others accuse them of many terrible
vices, and cast much blame on them, while excusing them for nothing.
Thus the clerks write their verses both morning and evening, now in
French, now in Latin, basing themselves on who knows what books that
repeat more lies than a drunkard. (259–80)

Ovid said much evil of women (which I consider to be a misdeed) in
a book he wrote which he called Love's Remedies,[3] in which he accused
them of dishonorable, filthy, ugly, uncouth behavior. I deny that they
possess such vices, and I stand ready to do battle on this issue with
anyone who wants to throw down the gauntlet—of course, I mean honorable women; I am not concerned with the worthless ones. Clerks are
taught this book from their earliest youth, in their beginning grammar
classes, and they teach it to others, so that none will undertake to love a
woman. They are, however, foolish and waste their time in this
endeavor; it is useless to try to prevent love in this way. For as long as
the world lasts we will never allow—my lady Nature and myself—that

2. A Greek hero during the Trojan War; see Ovid's *Metamorphoses* 13.1–398 and *Ovide moralisé*
13.1–1335.
3. Publius Ovidius Naso (43 B.C.–A.D. 17) was, beginning in the late twelfth century, the single
most influential classical Latin poet for medieval French literature. His *Remedia amoris*
[Love's remedies], widely read in the Middle Ages, is a mock recantation of his earlier *Ars
amatoria* [Art of love].

women not be cherished and loved, in spite of all those who would like
to condemn them. They will steal away and capture the hearts of many
who most blame them. By our commandments, without fraud or extortion, men will no longer be so instructed by subtle clerks, nor by their
writings, despite the fact that many books treat the topic of women and
condemn them as being worth little. And if anyone says that we should
believe these books which were written by men of great renown and
wisdom, who would not have deigned to lie, books which prove wom-
en's evil nature, I answer that those who wrote these things in their
books were (in their lives) only interested in deceiving women. They
could never possess enough women; every day they wanted new ones,
without being loyal even to the most beautiful. How did David or King
Solomon[4] behave? They angered God who punished their transgressions. Many others have been like this, including even Ovid, who
desired so many of them, then tried to defame them. And all the clerks
who have spoken so much about women were much more obsessed
with them than were other people, not with one woman only, but with
a thousand. (281–325)

Now, such behavior would not be surprising if these men had mistresses or wives who did not want to do their bidding, or who tried to
deceive them. For there is no doubt that when a man stoops to such
baseness he does not seek out worthy ladies or good and highly esteemed
women. He is not acquainted with such, nor does he have anything to
do with them. He only wants those who are at his own level: he shows
off lower-class tarts. Is it right for a skirt chaser to have a noble woman,
when he adds all women to his list, then thinks that he can cover up his
shame in impotent old age by blaming them with his subtle reasonings?
But to blame only those women who are given over to wicked vices, and
to advise them not to continue such a life would be a very good and
reasonable thing, a worthy instruction, just and laudable, without
defaming all women in general. (326–47)

With regard to deception, I do not know how to imagine or to conceive how woman can deceive man. She does not go looking for him,
or asking after him, or seeking for him at his home; nor does she think
of him, or remember him, when he comes to deceive and to tempt.
How does he tempt her? Truly in such a way that no trouble is too much
for him, no burden too heavy. He enjoys nothing except using his heart,
body and wealth in order to deceive her. And this torment and pain
continue for a long time, and are repeated many times, despite the fact
that men very often fail in their quest, no matter how hard they try. Ovid

---

4. For Solomon's relation with the queen of Sheba, see 1 Kings 10:1–13 and 2 Chronicles 9:1–
   12. Solomon's numerous "foreign wives" turned him to foreign gods in his old age, thus pro-
   voking God's wrath, as recounted in 1 Kings 11:1–13. For David's affair with Bathsheba, see 2
   Samuel 11:3–26.

speaks of these men in his treatise on *The Art of Love:* [5] because of his great pity for them he compiled a book in which he wrote and openly taught them how to deceive women, and how to win their love through dissembling; and he called the book *The Art of Love*; but it does not teach the condition or the ways of loving well, but rather the contrary. For he who wants to act according to this book will never love, no matter how much he is loved. And for this reason the book is badly named, for it is the book of *The Art of Great Deceit and of False Appearance*, such is the name I give it. (348–78)

Why then if women are weak and flighty, and easily manipulated, silly and lacking self-control, as some clerkly authors say, why do those who pursue them have any need of ruse? And why do women not give in at once, without requiring that strategies and tricks be used to catch them? For it is not necessary to go to war for a castle that is already captured. And even a poet as subtle as Ovid, who was later exiled,[6] and Jean de Meun in the *Romance of the Rose:* What great exertion! What an elaborate enterprise! And what great learning, both accessible and obscure, what adventures he described there! And how many people are entreated and begged, and how much effort and trickery is there in order to accomplish nothing more than the deception of a maid through fraud and cunning, for that is the ultimate goal! Does a weakly fortified place require such an assault? How can one try so hard for so easy a prize? I do not understand or believe that such great effort is needed to capture a weakly fortified place, nor scheming, nor ingenuity, nor great subtlety. It is necessary to conclude that, since scheming, great ingenuity and great effort are required to deceive a noble or a low-born women, they are not so fickle as is said, nor is their behavior so changeable. (379–406)

And if anyone says to me that books are full of such fickle women (a charge made by many, and one that I dislike), I answer that women did not write the books, nor did they put into them the things one reads there against women and their behavior. Thus do male authors write to their hearts' delight their descriptions of women; these authors show no mercy when they plead their own cases, happy to yield in nothing and to take for themselves the spoils of victory: for aggressive people quickly attack those who do not defend themselves. But if women had written

---

5. Ovid's *Art of Love* was a centrally important base text for the medieval literature of courtly love, including its various didactic forms; see also n. 3, p. 20. From Christine's point of view, it is particularly significant that Guillaume de Lorris in the prologue to the *Romance of the Rose* presents his work as a new and complete "art of love," thus, from the outset, establishing the Ovidian text as key model; see also p. 16. Guillaume explicitly names his new work: "The *Romance of the Rose* Where the Art of Love Is Entirely Enclosed," verses 37–38. Ernest Langlois, ed., *Le roman de la rose par Guillaume de Lorris et Jean de Meun, publié d'après les manuscrits,* 5 vols. (Paris: Didot/Champion, 1914–24).
6. Ovid was exiled from Rome in A.D. 8 to Tomis, a remote town on the Black Sea, at the very edge of the Roman world, where he would live out the rest of his life. While the full reasons behind his exile remain unknown, it seems, from Ovid's treatment of the issue in his *Tristia,* that the *Art of Love* played a role against him.

the books, I know for a fact that they would have been written differently, for women well know that they are wrongly condemned. The parts are not fairly distributed, for the strongest take the largest pieces, and the one who divides up the pieces takes the best for himself. Furthermore, the wicked slanderers who despise women say that they are all false, always have been and always will be;[7] that none have ever had any loyalty, and that he who loves any woman whatsoever finds that they are all like this when he tries them out. They are put in the wrong in every case; no matter who has acted badly, the blame is placed on women. (407–30)

But this is a wicked lie; the contrary is true. For as far as love is concerned, many women have been, are, and will be loyal, in spite of their having been treated falsely, treacherously, deceitfully, and mendaciously. How did Medea act toward the false Jason?[8] She was very loyal, and through her subtle cleverness, she enabled him to win the Golden Fleece, for which he was more famous than a hundred thousand other men. Because of her, his renown was greater than anyone else's, and he promised her that he would be her sweet, loyal love, belonging only to her; but he broke his word, left her for someone else, and departed. How did Dido act toward Aeneas,[9] when she was queen of Carthage, filled with great love and loyalty, and he was an exile from Troy, sailing wearily, dejectedly, and unhappily, having almost perished along with his men? He was taken in when he was in great need by that beautiful woman whom he falsely deceived. For she received him and his followers with very great honor and did much good for him; and afterward he behaved very badly toward her. Despite the fact that he had pledged his faith and his love to her (truly, as a deception), he then left her never to return and placed his love elsewhere. As a result, she died of grief for love of him, in a very piteous way. Anyone who wanted to tell all the trials of Penelope,[1] Ulysses's wife, would have much to say about her

7. This recalls a famous charge made by one of the *Rose*'s archmisogynists, the Jealous Husband, who states that "all you women are, will be, and have been whores, in fact or in desire" (Langlois, ed., *Rose*, verses 9,155–56).
8. Jason's betrayal of Medea after her crucial help in his conquest of the Golden Fleece is a standard example of masculine faithlessness in the Middle Ages (see Ovid's *Metamorphoses* 7.1–158, 7.350–403 and *Ovide moralisé* 7.273–1508). See also Dante's *Inferno* 18.83–99, where Jason is punished for his betrayal of women in the First Bolgia of the Eighth Circle, among the Panderers and Seducers. Particularly significant for Christine in the present passage is the fact that Jason's betrayal of Medea is twice mentioned by the Old Woman, a major character in the *Romance of the Rose*, to illustrate male deceitfulness (Langlois, ed., *Rose*, verses 13,229–64; 14,404–05).
9. For Aeneas's betrayal of Dido, see Virgil's *Aeneid* 4. See also Ovid's *Metamorphoses* 14.76–84 (and *Ovide moralisé* 14.302–526), which includes a lengthy, interpolated complaint by Dido, of which certain elements are taken from *Heroïdes* 7. The Old Woman in the *Rose* also recounts the story of Dido's abandonment (Langlois, ed., *Rose*, verses 13,174–210) to illustrate the maxim that "no woman can come to a good end" (verse 13,173). Thus the Medea-Jason story and the Dido-Aeneas story, referred to in sequence here, occur in close proximity and in the same sequence in the *Rose*.
1. Her uxorial fidelity in waiting chastely for the return of her far-wandering husband served as an antimisogynist medieval example of woman's loyalty (see Ovid's *Metamorphoses* 14.671 and Langlois, ed., *Rose*, verses 8,606–07).

goodness which is irreproachable: She was very beautiful, sought after, and well beloved, noble, wise, courageous, and famed. Many other women, so many that they cannot be counted, have been, are, and will be in this category. But I will now be silent concerning them, for it would take a very long time to tell their stories. (431–70)

Thus women are not as disloyal as some claim, rather, many of them are loyal; but it happens rather frequently that they are deceived and betrayed in love. And when they find themselves thus deceived the most intelligent women withdraw from love, and in doing this, they act very wisely. Should they be blamed for reacting in this way? And if God were to give you bad health, foolishness, treachery or deceit? It is certainly wise to withdraw in this fashion. But I know and perceive truthfully that if lovers maintain truth, faith, loyalty, equanimity toward their ladies, and if they do their duty as lovers should do according to their valid obligations, I think that few women, or none, would deceive, and that every woman would be loyal. At least those with the most self-control would not fail; for no good thing exists without some flaw. But because many men deceive and lie, and are disloyal, some women deceive them, and it is quite right: they are obliged to eat the same bread they prepared for others. There are some men who were formerly my servants, but they became weary of love either through old age or lack of courage, and they do not want to love again at any price, and they are pleased to deny me in every respect, and reject and deny my power, like wicked and rebellious servants. And such people recount their opinions to everyone, condemning and blaming me and my activities; defaming women because they can no longer pursue them, or because they want to empty their hearts of me. And they think that they can make others dislike women by blaming them, but this they cannot do. (471–508)

I certainly hate such people more than anything, and I often pay them back as they deserve. For despite their slanderous words, I make them fall hopelessly in love with foolish women, who are dishonorable, wicked, and of ill repute: with such women are they besotted. And they end up by being picked clean, for such women know well how to look after themselves. Thus those men who thought that they had escaped from love are surprised and smitten. Such men must be led along the proper path, and it is good for them to endure misfortune. What is even worse is that those men who most frequently pursue women with great deception, and who work hardest at this, do not care what it costs them or what they pay or the amount of trouble they have to endure in order to impose laboriously their will on women, to the point where they exert themselves so much in tested strategems, in false deceptions, in deceptive appearances that they attract many women through their tricks and false plots. Afterward, they make fun of the women and boast, saying that women give their consent easily and lightly, from weakness, and that no one should have confidence in them. It is a bad judgment

and a wicked decision to place all women in the same category. It is no
surprise that some women indeed act in this way too! (509–37)

Was not the great city of Troy, which had been so gloriously strong,
captured long ago through deceptions, false counsel, clever treachery,
mendacious speeches, tricks, and broken promises; and burned to the
ground? And are not kings and kingdoms betrayed every day by tricks
and plots? Books and romances are full of stories of how effectively
deceptive beautiful blandishments are; it is therefore not surprising that
working hard at lying and conniving leads to victory over something as
simple as an ignorant little woman. And if she is sneaky and cunning, is
it not because she is under the control of a malicious, sharp-eyed man,
who uses against her all the pain with which he is filled? In these ways
are women defamed and wrongly blamed by many men; this is how,
both in speech and in writing, whether true or not, women are depicted.
(538–58)

I do not, however, find this in any book or writing (in spite of what
has been slanderously spoken or written) about the life of Jesus or about
his death, effected through envy. Similarly, neither the deeds of the
Apostles who underwent much hardship for the faith nor the Gospels
show women in a bad light. On the contrary, much good is said there
concerning women: they are shown as having a very high calling, great
prudence, much sense and constancy, perfect love, great firmness of
faith, great charity, strong willpower, strong hearts entirely fixed on serving God, and they gave clear evidence of this, for they never abandoned
Him either alive or dead. Sweet Jesus, when wounded, injured, and
dead, was abandoned by all except women. The entirety of the faith
remained in a single woman. Therefore anyone who defames women is
extremely foolish, if only because of the reverence required by the
Queen of Heaven, in memory of her goodness, which was so noble and
worthy that She was elected to carry the son of God. God the Father
conferred great honor on women by choosing a woman to be his wife
and mother, God's temple joined to the Trinity. Women should thus be
joyous and gay, for they have the same form as She; God never created
anything else of comparable dignity or goodness, excepting only the
person of Jesus. (559–88)

Thus he who mocks women is very foolish, when a woman is seated
on the highest throne, next to her son, at the right hand of the Father:
this is a great honor for women's maternity. And we can find no instance
where the good Jesus reproached women; rather, he loved them and
valued them. God formed women in his worthy image and gave to her
knowledge, awareness, and the gift of understanding, so that she might
save herself. He gave her a very noble form and created her out of the
most noble material, for He did not make her out of mud and earth, but
only out of man's rib, man's body being the most noble of terrestrial
creations. And the ancient true stories of the Bible, which cannot ever

lie, tell us that in the Earthly Paradise woman was created first, not man.[2] And, concerning the deception because of which God sent us bitter consequences, for which lady Eve, our mother, is blamed, I say in truth that she did not deceive Adam, but simply repeated to him the words that the Devil had said to her, believing them to be sincere and true. Thus it was not fraud or deception, for innocence, with no concealed malice, should not be called deception. Without intending to deceive others, one cannot deceive them, for this is not true deception. Of what great evils can women thus be accused? Do not women have Paradise as their reward? Of what crimes can one accuse them? And if some foolish men wish to amuse themselves with love (may they be cursed for this), they cannot succeed; let wise men refrain from this; he who, having planned deceit, is himself deceived has no one but himself to blame. (589–628)

If I wanted to tell the whole truth about this, I would provoke the wrath of some; for very often speaking the truth causes hostility and opposition. Because of this I do not want to make comparisons: such speech often is merely hateful. Thus I am content to praise without blaming; for one can certainly call something good without condemning something else as bad or worse: he who blames others in order to promote himself sometimes undermines his own position; it is better to refrain from speaking. For this reason, I remain silent; and let everyone judge my case, and equitably make a decision according to the truth. (629–42)

He shall find, if he judges correctly, that women's greatest faults cause very little damage: they do not kill people, or wound, or maim; nor do they undertake and pursue treachery; they do not burn out or disinherit people; they do not poison or steal gold or silver; they do not cheat people out of their wealth or their inheritances through false contracts; nor do they damage kingdoms, duchies, or empires. Disaster rarely follows, even from the worst women. In general, one woman's behavior does not establish a rule for all. And whoever wants to cite historical or biblical examples against me, of one woman, or two, or several who were condemned for wickedness would be citing exceptions. For I am speaking about the average woman, and there are very few who resort to wicked ways. (643–60)

And if someone were to say to me that women's nature and characteristics do not incline them in this direction, or toward giving battle, or killing people, or making torches to set fires, or any such things; and for

---

2. Various Church Fathers and theologians said that Eve was the first to be created within the Earthly Paradise, but their interpretations varied: Ambrose in the late fourth century stated that given this advantage, one would expect woman to be superior to man, but she is not. The twelfth-century theologian Peter Abelard, by contrast, saw "a certain dignity enhancing woman's creation, since she was made in paradise but man outside it." For these passages see Alcuin Blamires, *Woman Defamed and Woman Defended: An Anthology of Medieval Texts* (Oxford, UK: Clarendon Press, 1992), 61, 235–36.

this reason that women do not and should not deserve any special fame, praise or credit for refraining from these activities, I reply (with all due respect) that indeed women are not inclined in this direction, or toward cruelty. For woman's nature is mild, very piteous, fearful and hesitant, humble, sweet, calm and very charitable, loveable, devout, modest in peace, fearful in war, unpretentious and pious, with an anger that is quickly appeased, unable to bear the sight of cruelty or suffering: these are, in sum, the natural attributes of women. And those who through some accident do not possess them act against nature; for cruelty in women is a fault, and only women's gentleness deserves to be prized. (661–84)

Since women are neither accustomed nor inclined to shed blood or to kill, they do not commit other ugly and horrible capital sins, indeed, great and enormous sins, of which they are thus free and innocent. Each human being is stained with some vice, but women cannot thereby be guilty of wicked actions in which they are not implicated. They will thus not be punished or held guilty for them, since they did not commit them. Thus I can say (without being accused of heresy) that God on high behaved with great courtliness toward women, when He created them without the predispositions which push people to commit great transgressions: for from desires result the deeds that blemish the souls of many people. It is therefore better not to have desires whose fulfillment often leads to death. Only a heretic would want to maintain that there is no merit in abstaining from sin because one feels no temptation. Such reasoning cannot be defended, for we see the contrary in the lives of the saints: St. Nicholas was incapable of sinning; he never sinned, nor was he ever tempted to do so; and many other saints did not have the desire to sin. I am speaking of mortal sins, since they could commit venial sins; but all of the saints are rightly called the chosen ones, pre-destined and elected by God. (685–714)

For all these reasons I conclude by wanting to prove that women's behavior is to be greatly approved and praised; and to recommend their nature which is not oriented toward the vices that spoil human nature and make people suffer. Through these just and true arguments, I con-clude that all reasonable men must prize, cherish and love women; nor should they want to denigrate those through whom every man is born. Let them not return evil for the good they have received, for woman constitutes the single best and most natural object in the world for men's love. It is therefore quite despicable and very shameful to blame the thing that one should love most which brings the greatest joy to every man. There is no joy in a natural man's life without woman: she is his mother, his sister, his beloved; it is very rare that she is his enemy. It is right for her to be compatible with him, the thing that is most pleasing to him; any man who condemns women cannot win fame or praise, but only great condemnation. There is no blame so vile and harmful as being considered a slanderer, and most especially in defaming women as a group: this is a contemptible and wicked act of villainy. I forbid it to any man whom I love. Let all noble hearts, therefore, keep away from it, for it leads to nothing good, but rather to great harm, shame, spite and all vile things. A man with such a vice has no place in my service. (715–48)

I have now concluded all my arguments, well and truly. May they not displease any man, for if women are good and worthy, this does not constitute anything shameful or demeaning for men: he is born and constructed of the same material. If she is bad, then he can be worth nothing: good fruit cannot come from a bad tree; he must needs resemble her as she is, and if she is good, then he will be worth more, for sons certainly resemble their mothers. And if I have spoken much good of women, and praised them according to the truth, I have not done so in order to flatter them or to make them more prideful, but, rather, in order to encourage them always to strive to become more worthy, avoiding the vices that people should not have; for whoever has great virtue and goodness is of necessity less prideful, since the virtues displace the vices. And if some women are foolish, then let this *Letter* instruct them: may they faithfully take the good as their doctrine, and abandon the bad; and may my *Letter* encourage good women eagerly to persevere in their goodness. I dare say that, if they do so, they will have renown, great honor, joy and praise, and, finally, a place in Heaven. (749–74)

Thus, I definitively conclude that punishment be meted out to the wicked: those who slander, defame, and accuse women; and those who use false, disloyal appearances to deceive them. May they all be driven out of our court, banished, dismissed, condemned, and excommunicated; and may all our goods be denied to them, for it is quite just that I excommunicate them. (775–83)

And WE COMMAND explicitly to our household in general and, in particular, to our officers, our sergeants, all our quartermasters, our provosts, and mayors and bailiffs and vicars, that all such be severely ill-treated and vilified, chastised, shamefully punished, taken, and bound over to justice. We shall no longer suffer any crimes of this kind, nor shall any further offense be brooked. So do we wish, and right is on our side. Let it be accomplished without delay. (784–95)

WRITTEN in our great palace in the heavens, on the solemn festival of May Day, when lovers make many requests to us, in the year of grace, one thousand three hundred ninety-nine, in the presence of gods and divinities. (796–800)

FROM THE GOD OF LOVE, the powerful one, to more than one hundred gods, of great power, in order to confirm our wishes: Jupiter, Apollo, and Mars; Vulcan, who burned up Phaeton; Mercury, god of speech; Aeolus, who holds the winds bound up; Neptune, god of the sea; Glaucus, who makes the sea foam; the gods of the valleys and of the mountains, of the great forests, and of the fields; and the gods who go by night in search of adventures; Pan, god of shepherds; Saturn, our mother the great Venus, Pallas, Juno, and Latona; Ceres, Vesta, Antigone, Aurora, Thetis, Arethusa who accused the god Pluto, Minerva the female warrior, and Diane the huntress; and our counselors, the other gods and goddesses numbering more than a thousand. (801–24)

Signed by CUPID, THE GOD OF LOVE, TO WHOM LOVERS ADDRESS THEIR COMPLAINTS. (825–26)

Here ends the God of Love's Letter.

FROM THE LETTER FROM OTHEA

[A few years after writing the *Letter from Othea* Christine realized that this work marked a turning point in her literary production. In 1399, she later writes in her *Vision* (book 3, chapter 10), she turned from the "pretty things" of her poetry to more subtle and noble subject matters. The *Letter* is indeed an intricate and extremely learned text in the tradition of the "mirror of princes" or courtesy books, but it is also full of original features. Each chapter is divided into three parts: text, gloss, and allegory. For the first two parts Christine draws on Ovidian mythology (via the fourteenth-century *Ovide moralisé* [Moralized Ovid] and on the *Histoire ancienne jusqu'à César* [Ancient history up to Julius Caesar], a source for many of her later works. The *Manipulus florum* [Sheaf of flowers] by Thomas Hibernicus furnished most of the quotes of ancient philosophers and Church Fathers in each allegory, but a number of the writers she cites had also been translated, and she may have consulted their works directly.[1]

There was much interest in ancient mythology at the time: the *Ovide moralisé*,[2] totaling some seventy thousand lines, had been written in the first half of the fourteenth century, probably by a Franciscan friar; it became the source for Ovidian tales for writers like Machaut, Deschamps, and Froissart. In the 1370s Boccaccio[3] had finished his *On the Genealogy of the Gods*, a vast encyclopedic work on the pagan gods in which he also developed his theories on the hidden religious and moral meanings of pagan fables.

In the *Letter* Christine presents each fable in a succinct four lines and then explains its plot or contents in a literal or historical interpretation.[4] Then she draws a moral on correct chivalric behavior from each story.

1. See Percy G. C. Campbell, *L'Epitre d'Othéa. Etudes sur les sources de Christine de Pisan* (Paris: Champion, 1924).
2. Cornelis De Boer, ed., *Ovide moralisé* in *Verhandelingen der Koninklijke Akademie van Wetenschapen, Afdeeling Letterkunde* 15, 21, 30, 36, 37, 43 (1915–38).
3. For Boccaccio's poetic theories see C. G. Osgood, *Boccaccio on Poetry* (Princeton, N.J.: Princeton University Press, 1930).
4. This way of interpreting mythological fables was very common in the Middle Ages. It dates back to the antique writer Euhemerus, who had explained that the gods were really humans who were considered divine because of their achievements. See J. D. Cooke, "Euhemerism: A Medieval Interpretation of Classical Paganism," *Speculum* 2 (1927), 396–410.

Finally, the allegory speaks of the soul and the spiritual lessons that can be learned from each fable. This structure imitates glossed manuscripts where medieval writers would comment on ancient texts in the margins by giving geographical and historical details or even moral explanations. Indeed, one of the manuscripts of the *Letter* reproduces this impression in the layout, where the text is in the center and gloss and allegory surround it in the margins.[5] But, of course, Christine was the author of all three elements! It is important to see that the whole text is structured not by the fables but by the allegories, which, at least initially, follow the scheme of series, such as the Seven Deadly Sins or the Twelve Articles of the Creed. This arrangement shows that the spiritual level of the allegory was the most important.

Othea, Christine's own invention of a goddess of wisdom or prudence, addressed her letter to the legendary prince Hector of Troy, but it was certainly meant to teach contemporary princes behavior appropriate for their public roles.[6] Interestingly, Christine presented her work to four different patrons: the dukes of Orleans, Berry, and Burgundy and to the French king. Each manuscript had a slightly different program of illustrations, supervised by Christine herself and particularly meaningful for each patron.[7]

With this work then, Christine entered a new phase in her work. Lyric poetry was now eclipsed by more serious interests. The concern for contemporary politics was to become a guiding thread in her subsequent works, and her fascination with mythological fables and the wisdom of the ancients would lead to the composition of several major texts, such as *Le Livre de la mutacion de Fortune* [The Book of Fortune's transformation] and *Le Livre du chemin de long estude* [The path of long study].

Translated by Renate Blumenfeld-Kosinski from Halina D. Loukopoulos, "Classical Mythology in the Works of Christine de Pisan, with an Edition of 'L'Epistre Othéa,' from the Manuscript Harley 4431" (diss., Wayne State University, 1977).]

Prologue to the Letter from Othea

[Christine de Pizan addresses the French king Charles VI. After praising his illustrious origins,[1] she speaks of herself.]

> Moved by humble desire, I, poor creature,
> Ignorant woman, of little importance,

---

5. See Mary Ann Ignatius, "Christine de Pizan's 'Epistre Othéa': An Experiment in Literary Form," *Medievalia et Humanistica*, n.s. 9 (1979), 127–42.

6. For the political aspects of the text see Sandra L. Hindman, *Christine de Pizan's "Epistre Othéa": Painting and Politics at the Court of Charles VI* (Toronto: Pontifical Institute of Mediaeval Studies, 1986). On the name of Othea see *ibid.*, 40–43.

7. The manuscript used for the edition translated here contains a dedication to the king, Charles VI. Hindman has studied the miniatures in the different manuscripts that show Christine presenting her book to the different patrons; see Hindman, *Christine de Pizan's "Epistre Othéa."*

1. Christine insists on the king's Trojan origins, a common theme at the time. See Colette Beaune, *The Birth of an Ideology: Myths and Symbols of Nation in Late-Medieval France*, trans. Susan Ross Huston (Berkeley: University of California Press, 1991), chap. 8.

Daughter of the philosopher and doctor of yore,
Who was the counselor and humble servant
Of your father—God be merciful to him—   5
And who came long ago from Bologna[2] "the wealthy,"
Where he was born, by his order,
Master Thomas of Pizan, also
Called and surnamed of Bologna,
Who was renowned as an eminent scholar.   10
Desiring, if I only knew how,
To make a pleasant thing that would lead you
To some pleasure, I would consider this to be to my glory;
For this reason I presently have undertaken
—from an untrustworthy memory—to rhyme this work,   15
My respected lord, to send it to you
On the first day the year renews itself;
For its subject matter is all new,[3]
Though it is unpolished in its thought, for I am not well
grounded in reason. In this I do not resemble my good father,   20
except in so far as one
Steals grains of wheat while gleaning during the harvest,
In the fields and along the bushes;
Or as one picks up the crumbs falling from the
High table, when the dishes are worthy of note.   25
I did not gather anything else[4]
Of his great sense, of which he had gathered plenty.
Please do not show contempt for my work,
My respected lord, humane and wise,
Because of the lack of merit of my ignorant person,   30
For a little bell makes a great sound,
Which, very often, wakes up the most wise
And advises them to study hard.
For this reason, most praiseworthy and benign prince,
I, named Christine, unworthy woman,   35
But having the judgment to undertake such a work,
Will begin to rhyme and tell about
A letter that was sent to Hector of Troy,
Just as the history books inform us;
If not the exact one, then a very similar one.   40
And in it there will be many verses and memorable deeds,
Pleasant to hear and even better to understand.
Now I approach the beginning.
May God let me compose to His glory

---

2. On the circumstances of her father's arrival in France see *Christine's Vision* on p. 173.
3. This statement may strike us as strange, given that almost the entire text was drawn from existing sources and that originality was not valued in the Middle Ages. Christine means "new" in the sense of putting existing materials together in a new way.
4. The theme of Christine's inadequate learning is often expressed in similar terms; see also p. xii.

All the deeds, tales, and things that could please you,   45
My respected lord, for whom I undertake all this,
And I humbly supplicate, in case I commit an error,
The generosity of your great nobility,
That it may forgive me, if I, of no worth in wisdom,
Am too bold in writing to you, a most worthy person.   50

So that those who are not learned poets can understand quickly the meaning of the stories in this book, it should be known that wherever the images are surrounded by clouds, it means that these are the figures of the gods and goddesses of whom the text that follows in the book speaks, according to the manner of the ancient poets. And because deity is a spiritual thing and elevated above the earth, the images are shown in clouds, and the first is the goddess of wisdom.[5]

Here begins the Letter of the goddess Othea that she sent to Hector of Troy[6] when he was fifteen years old.

[In text 1 of chapter 1 Othea identifies herself as goddess of prudence. She addresses Hector, calling him the son of Mars and Minerva, rather than that of Hecuba and Priam, his human parents. Othea has the gift of prophecy and, in her letter, wants to teach Hector valuable lessons.]

Gloss

Othea in Greek can mean the wisdom of woman, and as the ancients, not having the light of the true faith, adored several gods—and in this religion the greatest realms that ever existed in this world passed, like the kingdom of Assyria, of Persia, the Greeks, the Trojans, Alexander, the Romans and many others, and also all the greatest philosophers—because God had not yet opened the door of His mercy. At the present time, we Christians, by God's grace illuminated by the true faith, can interpret morally the opinions of the ancients, and many beautiful allegories can be constructed on this topic. And because the ancients had the custom of adoring everything that seemed blessed beyond the common level of things, they called several wise women who existed in their time goddesses. And it is true, according to the history books, that at the time when the great Troy flourished and had such a high reputation, a very wise woman, called Othea, thinking about the lovely youth of Hector of Troy, who already had plenty of virtues pointing to the graces that he would possess in the future, sent him several beautiful and remark-

5. Or Othea, Christine's creation. This passage shows Christine's involvement with the illustrations of her manuscripts and her concern that they should be interpreted correctly; see also p. xiv. On the manuscripts of this text and their illustrations see Sandra L. Hindman, *Christine de Pizan's "Epistre d'Othéa."*
6. The son of the Trojan king Priam and queen Hecuba.

able gifts, like the beautiful steed called Galathea, who had no equal in the world. And because all the earthly graces that a good man should possess existed in Hector, we can say morally that he acquired them through the counsel of Othea, who sent him this letter. By Othea we mean the virtue of prudence and wisdom with which he himself was adorned. And because the four cardinal virtues are necessary for good rule, we will discuss them next. And to this first virtue we have given a name and spoken about her in a poetic manner and, in deference to the true history and in order to give more coherence to our subject matter, we use to our purpose several authoritative texts of the ancient philosophers. Thus we say that the above-mentioned lady gave and sent this present to the good Hector, who can likewise stand for all those who desire goodness and wisdom. And because the virtue of wisdom is most commendable, the prince of philosophers, Aristotle says, "Because wisdom is nobler than anything else, it must be demonstrated through the best reasoning and in the most appropriate manner."

Prologue to the Allegory

In order to allegorize the gist of our subject matter we will apply Holy Scripture to our texts for the edification of the soul in this miserable world.

Since all things were created through the supreme wisdom and eminent power of God, it stands to reason that all must have their end in Him, and because our soul, which God created in His image, is—after the angels—of all created things the most noble, it is fitting and necessary that it should be adorned with the virtues through which it can be led to the purpose for which it exists. And because it can be prevented from this by the traps and attacks of the enemy from hell, who is its mortal enemy and often leads it away from achieving its beatitude, we can refer to human life as "true chivalry," as says Scripture in several places. And because all earthly things are fallible, we must continually keep in mind the future which is without end. And because this is the highest and most perfect chivalry, to which none other can be compared and with which the victorious will be crowned in glory, we will adopt a way of speaking about the chivalrous spirit and may this be done principally for the glory of God and for the profit of those who will read the present work.

Chapter 13: Minerva[7]

Text

Armors of all sorts,
Good and strong, to arm you,
Will your mother deliver to you,
Minerva, who has no bitter feelings toward you.

Gloss

Minerva was a very wise lady and she invented the art of making armor, for before that people only armed themselves with boiled leather. And because this lady possessed such great wisdom, people called her a goddess. And because Hector was very knowledgeable in using armors, and this was his true profession, Othea called him the son of Minerva, although he was the son of Queen Hecuba of Troy: and all lovers of arms can be called by a similar name. And on this topic says an authority: "Knights devoted to arms are subject to her."[8]

Allegory

By what is said about the mother who will deliver sufficient good and strong arms to the knight, we can understand the virtue of faith, which is a theological virtue and the mother of the good spirit. And that she will deliver sufficient arms, Cassiodorus[9] says in the *Exposition of the Creed* that faith is the light of the soul, the door of paradise, the window of life and the foundation of eternal salvation, for without faith no one can please God. And on this topic the apostle St. Paul says: "Without faith it is impossible to please Him" (Hebrews 11:6).

Chapter 22: Pygmalion

Text

Do not becomme besotted by the image
of Pygmalion, if you are wise,

---

7. Or Pallas Athene; Christine's special patron goddess. She addressed her in *Other Ballads* "7" (see p. 12) and identified with her as another Italian when she said: "Pallas, like you, I am an Italian woman" (see her *Livre des fais d'armes et de chevalerie*, ms, Bibliothèque Nationale, French 603, folio 2v.). She also devotes a long passage to her in the *Book of the City of Ladies* (see p. 116).
8. I.e., Minerva.
9. A Roman statesman and author (ca. 490–583). After retiring from public office, he founded two monasteries.

For with such an adorned image
Beauty is bought too dearly.

Gloss

Pygmalion was a very skilled craftsman who made images.[1] A fable
tells that he disdained women because of the great vileness he saw in
the women of Sidon and said that he would create an image that no
one could find fault with. He crafted an image of a woman of sovereign
beauty. When he had finished it, Love who knows how to enrapture
hearts with great skill, made him fall in love with his image for which
he was afflicted with love sickness, and he uttered complaints and cries
and pitiful sighs in front of it. But the image, which was of stone, did
not hear him. Pygmalion went to the temple of Venus and prayed and
cried to her with such devotion that the goddess had pity on him: and
to demonstrate her pity she grasped the torch that was near her and lit
it. Because of this sign, the lover was joyful and went to see his image.
He took it into his arms and warmed it up so much through his bare
flesh that the image came to life and began to speak. And thus Pygmalion had recovered his joy. This fable has several interpretations, just like
other fables of this kind. And poets created them so that the understanding of men could be sharpenend and made more subtle by finding different interpretations. It can be interpreted that Pygmalion despised the
vileness of frivolous women and fell in love with a maiden of great
beauty who would or could not hear his pitiful complaints, not that she
was of stone. He had made the image; this means that he fell in love by
thinking of his pretty beauties. Finally, he beseeched her so much and
kept so close to her that the maiden loved him the way he wanted and
accepted him in marriage. And like this, the image that was as hard as
stone received life through the goddess Venus. This means that the good
knight should not be besotted by such an image in such a way that he
abandons the practice of arms to which he is obliged by the order of
chivalry. And on this topic says Apthalin: "It is offensive when a prince
becomes besotted with something that leads to reproach."

Allegory

The image of Pygmalion, with which the good knight should not
become besotted, stands for the sin of lechery, against which the chivalrous spirit should guard his body. St. Jerome says of lechery in a letter:
"O fire of hell of which the wood is gluttony, the flame is pride, the
sparks are corrupt words, the smoke is bad reputation, the ashes are
poverty, and the end is the torment of hell." On this topic says the apos-

1. This story is in Ovid's *Metamorphoses* 10. Christine took the story from book 10 of the *Ovide moralisé*.

tle St. Peter: "[And shall receive the reward of unrighteousness,] as they
that count it pleasure to riot in the day time. Spots they are and blem-
ishes, sporting themselves with their own deceivings while they feast
with you" (2 Peter 2:13).

Chapter 64: Arachne

Text

Do not boast; for evil ensued from it
For Arachne, who so misjudged things
That she boasted against Pallas
For which the goddess put a spell on her.

Gloss

Arachne, so says a fable,[2] was a young woman who was very skilled in
the art of weaving and spinning, but she was too presumptious in her
knowledge and boasted to Pallas which made Pallas furious at her; and
because of this boasting she changed her into a spider. And she said:
"Because you boasted so much of your spinning and weaving, from now
on you will spin and weave work of no value." And this is where spiders
came from who still do not cease to spin and weave. So it could be that
a woman boasted to her mistress and some evil followed from it. For this
reason she[3] says to the good knight that he should not boast for it is an
ugly thing for a knight to be boastful and this could lower the esteem of
his goodness. And similarly Plato says: "When you do one thing better
than someone else, be sure not to boast of it, for your worth would be
diminished by this."

Allegory

That he should not boast, we can say that this means that the good
spirit should guard against boastfulness. For about boasting says St.
Augustine in the twelfth book of the *City of God*[4] boasting is not a vice
of human praise but a vice of the perverse soul which loves human
praise and despises the true testimony of its own conscience. On this
topic the sage says: "What has pride profited us or what advantage has
the boasting of riches brought us?" (Wisdom 5:8)[5]

---

2. Her story is in Ovid's *Metamorphoses* 6 and in the *Ovide moralisé*.
3. I.e., Othea.
4. Augustine, *City of God*, trans. Henry Bettenson (Harmondsworth: Penguin, 1984), 481.
5. The Book of Wisdom is one of the Apocryphal books of the Old Testament of the Bible.

Chapter 71: Achilles

Text

If you want to recognize true knights,
And were they enclosed in a cloister,
The test that Achilles was put to
Will teach you how to recognize them.

Gloss

Achilles, so tells a fable, was the son of the goddess Thetis and since, as a goddess, she knew that if her son used arms he would die, she, who loved him very dearly, disguised him with the clothes of a maiden and had him veiled like a nun; Achilles was hidden for a long time in the abbey[6] of the goddess Vesta until he was sufficiently matured. And the fable says that there he impregnated the daughter of king Hysirus who brought forth the most chivalrous Pirrus. Then the great Trojan wars began and the Greeks learned through their oracles that they needed Achilles; he was searched for everywhere, but no news could be had of him. Ulysses, who was full of great malice and looked for him everywhere, came to the temple, but when he could not perceive the truth, he maliciously thought of a ruse. Then he took rings, wimples, belts and all sorts of feminine jewelry, and with this he took knightly arms, beautiful and ornamented, and threw everything in the middle of the courtyard in presence of the ladies and said that each should take what she liked best at her pleasure. And then, as each thing tends to its own nature, the ladies ran toward the jewels and Achilles seized the arms; thereupon Ulysses rushed to him to embrace him knowing that he was the one he was looking for. And by showing that knights should be more inclined to arms than to dainty ornaments, which appertain to ladies, the authority wants to say that by this fact you can recognize the true knight. On this topic says Leginon: "The knight is known only through arms." And Hermes says: "Put men to a test before you trust them."

Allegory

The place where it is said "If you want to recognize a true knight," we can take to mean that the knight of Jesus Christ should be known through the arms of good works, and that such a knight should have the reward that is due good people. St. Jerome says in a Letter that just as

6. This kind of Christian vocabulary to designate elements of pagan religion was common in the Middle Ages. The *Ovide moralisé* (12.1104) also called the temple an *abbaie de nonains* ("abbey for nuns"). The story of Achilles' disguise is in Ovid's *Metamorphoses* 13 and in book 12 of the *Ovide moralisé*.

God's justice leaves no evil unpunished, it leaves no good unrewarded; so to the good no effort should seem hard, or any time long, when they await everlasting glory. Therefore Holy Scripture says: "Be ye strong therefore, and let not your hands be weak: for your work shall be rewarded" (2 Paralipomenon [Chronicles] 15:7).

Chapter 74: Fortune

Text

Do not trust in Fortune
The great goddess, or in her promise;
For in little time she changes,
She often throws the most exalted into the mire.

Gloss

Fortune, according to the manner of speaking of the poets, may well be called the great goddess, for through her we see governed the course of worldly things. And because she promises to many people much prosperity, and indeed gives it to some and takes it back quickly as it pleases her,[7] says to the good knight that he should not trust her promises nor despair in adversity. And Socrates says: "The actions of Fortune are like deceptions."

Allegory

That he should not trust in Fortune, we can take to mean that the good spirit should flee and count for nothing the pleasures of this world. Apropos of this says Boethius,[8] in the third *Book of Consolation*, that the happiness of the Epicureans should be called unhappiness, for it is the true, full, and perfect happiness that can make man properly mighty, devout, solemn, and joyous; the things into which the worldly people place their happiness do not bring these qualities. Therefore God says through the prophet: "O my people, they which lead thee cause thee to err, and destroy the way of thy paths (Isaiah 3:12).

---

7. I.e., Othea.
8. An important public figure under the emperor Theodosius and a philosopher and translator of Aristotle (ca. 475–525); he was executed in prison. His *The Consolation of Philosophy* was extremely popular in the Middle Ages and one of Christine's favorite books. The work involves coming to terms with extreme misfortune through the teachings of Lady Philosophy, who demonstrates that true happiness cannot by definition reside in any good that is under Fortune's control.

Chapter 98: Circe[9]

Text

You should avoid the port of Circe
Where Ulysses's knights
Were changed into pigs.
Remember her ways.

Gloss

Circe was a queen who had her kingdom on the Italian sea, and she was a great enchantress and knew much about oracles and witchcraft.[1] And when Ulysses, who traveled by sea after the destruction of Troy since he planned to return to his country after great and dangerous torments he had suffered, arrived at the port of this land, he asked the queen through his knights whether he could safely land in her port. Circe received the knights, and in a show of courtesy, she had them served with a drink that was delicious; but the potion had such power that suddenly the knights were transformed into pigs. Circe can be understood in several ways. She can stand for a land or a country where the knights where put into a dirty and vile prison. And she can represent a lady full of idleness by whom several knights errant, that is knights who took up arms, and who were among Ulysses's followers, that is, malicious and crafty, were made to stay as pigs. And for this reason [Othea] says to the good knight that he should not linger at such a sojourn. And Aristotle says: "He who is all inclined toward fornication cannot in the end be praised."

Allegory

We can interpret the port of Circe as hypocrisy which the good spirit should avoid above all other things. And against the hypocrites St. Gregory[2] says in his *Morals* that the life of the hypocrites is nothing but a fantastic vision and an imaginary fantasy that shows through an outward image what is not inside in true reality. On this topic says Our Lord in the Gospels: "Woe unto you, scribes and Pharisees, hypocrites! for ye

---

9. Her story is in Ovid's *Metamorphoses* 14 and the *Ovide moralisé*. Her story is also the subject of *Other Ballads* "17" and is told in *The Book of Fortune's Transformation* and *The Book of the City of Ladies*.
1. The word in French is *mioultemens*, not otherwise known. The fifteenth-century translation uses "wychecraft." See James D. Gordon, ed., *The Epistle of Othea to Hector. A "Lytil Bibell of Knyghthood"* (Philadelphia: University of Pennsylvania, 1942), 142.
2. St. Gregory the Great was pope from 590 to 604. In addition to the *Morals* he wrote saints' lives and his famous *Dialogue on Miracles*.

are like unto whitened sepulchres which indeed appear beautiful out-
wardly, but are within full of dead men's bones" (Matthew 23:27).

Chapter 100: The Sibyl[3] of Cumae

Text

I wrote one hundred authorities to you;
May you not despise them,
For Augustus[4] learned from a woman
Who reprimanded him for being worshiped.

Gloss

Caesar Augustus was the emperor of the Romans and of the entire
world; and because at the time he reigned there was peace[5] throughout
the world and he governed peacefully, foolish and impious people
maintained that peace existed because of the good that came from him;
but this was not so, for it existed because of Jesus Christ who was born
from the Virgin Mary and already lived on earth; and as long as he lived
there was peace in the entire world. But they wanted to worship Caesar
as God. But then the Sibyl of Cumae told him not to let himself be
worshiped and that there was only one God who had created everything.
And then she led him to a high mountain outside of the city, and in the
sun, by the will of Our Lord, appeared a Virgin holding a Child. The
Sibyl showed this to him and told him that this one was the true God
who should be worshiped; and the Caesar worshiped him. And because
Caesar who was the ruler of the entire world learned to recognize God
and the true faith through a woman, one can cite on this topic the
authority of Hermes: "It should not be shameful to you to hear the truth
and good teaching from whoever may pronounce it; for the truth
enobles the person who tells it."

Allegory

The place where Othea says that she wrote one hundred authorities
to him and that Augustus learned from a woman means that good words
and good teaching are praiseworthy for whoever may have said them.

---

3. Prophetic woman; there were ten Sibyls. Christine speaks of all of them at the beginning of
   book 2 of the *Book of the City of Ladies*. On their importance for the Middle Ages see Bernard
   McGinn, "*Teste David cum Sibylla:* The Significance of the Sibylline Tradition in the Middle
   Ages," in Julius Kirshner and Suzanne F. Wemple, eds., *Women of the Medieval World*
   (Oxford, UK: Basil Blackwell, 1985), 7–35.
4. Caesar Augustus (63 B.C.–A.D. 14).
5. The *Pax Augusta*, or Augustan Peace, was declared in 17 B.C.

Regarding this, Hugh of St. Victor says in his book called *Didascalion*[6] that the wise man listens gladly to everyone and learns gladly from each, and reads gladly all kinds of teachings; he does not despise Scripture; he does not despise the person; he does not despise doctrine; he searches equally everywhere and everything he sees for that which he lacks; he does not consider who speaks but rather that which is said; he does not pay attention to how much he knows, but to what he does not know. On this topic says the wise man: "A good ear should hear wisdom with all its desire" (Ecclesiasticus 3:29).[7]

Here ends the Letter from Othea.

FROM THE DEBATE ON THE *ROMANCE OF THE ROSE*

[The *Romance of the Rose* was one of the most popular texts of the Middle Ages. It began as a love allegory (a young man falling in love with a rose in a beautiful garden), written by Guillaume de Lorris around 1230. About forty years later the scholar and poet Jean de Meun added seventeen thousand lines to the first four thousand and expanded the love story to encyclopedic proportions. He invented many different speakers who, while giving advice to the lover, discussed a huge number of different subjects, including love, sexuality, and procreation. Around 1400 Jean de Montreuil, provost of Lille, circulated a little treatise (now lost) praising the romance. This provoked a literary debate in which Christine played a major role. On the pro-*Rose* side were Jean de Montreuil; Pierre Col, canon of Paris and Tournay; and his brother Gontier Col, secretary and notary to the French king. On the other side were Christine de Pizan and the theologian Jean Gerson, chancellor of the University of Paris.

By the end of the debate in 1402 the number of documents in the debate had risen to more than twenty, most of them letters, but also sermons and various polemical treatises. In 1401, Christine had gathered the first group of letters into a manuscript she presented to the French queen Isabeau of Bavaria with a letter of explanation and dedication, thus taking control of the first phase of the debate.

The principal arguments against the *Rose* were that this text spoke ill of women, used obscene expressions, and was generally a harmful and useless text. The topics discussed included the question whether an author can be blamed for the arguments he has his characters make, whether explicit sexual terms are appropriate in a literary (as opposed to, say, a medical) text, and whether a literary work can cause people to do harmful acts. Christine believes that bad examples have never taught anyone anything useful and

---

6. On this book see Ivan Illich, *In the Vineyard of the Text: A Commentary on Hugh's Didascalion* (Chicago: University of Chicago Press, 1993).
7. Ecclesiasticus, or the Wisdom of Sirach, is one of the Apocryphal books of the Old Testament.

that an author cannot hide behind his characters when he maligns women, for example. As for obscene terms, they have no place in a literary work. The opponents of the *Rose* believed that a reader may well get violent and misogynistic ideas from this text (the character of the Jealous Husband, for example, speaks of the beating of wives) and act on them. Thus the debate not only addressed literary topics but extended to moral concerns on the role and function of literature in society.

The passage reprinted here is the end of Christine's last letter, a long response to a letter by Pierre Col. Her summary and refutation of Col's arguments are a subtle mixture of claims to authority, feigned references to her intellectual inadequacy, and the unmistakable intention of ending the debate because she has more important things to do. And indeed, Col's response to this letter remained unanswered. Christine presents herself here as an intellectual figure who participates in and controls a public debate that involved some of the preeminent intellectuals of her time.

Translated by Renate Blumenfeld-Kosinski from Eric Hicks, ed., *Le Débat sur le Roman de la Rose* (Paris: Champion, 1977).]

I do not know why we debate these questions so much, for I do not believe that either you or I intend to change our minds: you say he[1] is good; I say he is bad. You will convince me that he is good when you and your accomplices will have debated—with all your subtle reasoning—and will have found that bad is good: then I will believe that the *Romance of the Rose* is good! But I know well that this opinion is characteristic of those who want to lead an evil life and who want to be on their guard against other people rather than have other people be on their guard against them. But for those who want to live well and simply, without being too much wrapped up in wordly licentiousness, and who do not wish to deceive anyone or be deceived themselves, this book has no use. And truly I would much rather belong to the party of its opponents than to that of its supporters, for I am of the opinion that the wolf profits less; and as the good gentleman said who composed the above plaidoyer: "May it please God that such a Rose will never be planted in the garden of Christendom."[2] And I don't care whether you call yourself one of its disciples. If you want to be one, be one; as for me, I reject its lessons, for I am concerned with others that I believe to be more profitable and which I find more agreeable. And I am not alone in holding this opinion and I don't know why you disciples[3] attack me so much more than others: it is hardly honorable to attack the weakest party. There are so many wise learned men worthy of being believed and filled with knowledge, and truly there are so many great princes of this king-

---

1. Genius, a character from the *Rose*.
2. A reference to the long treatise against the *Romance of the Rose* by Jean Gerson that was part of the *Debate*. See the complete translation by Joseph L. Baird and John R. Kane, *La Querelle de la Rose: Letters and Documents* (Chapel Hill: University of North Carolina, Department of Romance Languages, 1978), 70–91.
3. Of the *Rose*.

dom, knights, nobles, and so many others, who are of the same opinion as I and who think that this is useless and dishonorable reading. Why do you not then break the thick stem of the tree, from which issue forth the sap and juices, until it is dried and torn up instead of taking on the little branches above which have no strength? In order to eradicate everything you attack me who is nothing but the voice of a little grasshopper who beats his wings and makes a lot of noise, and who is nevertheless nothing compared to the grand chanting of the gracious birds.

But you say that you "cannot be surprised enough how someone can blame not only him[4] but also those who appreciate and love his book on the *Rose*." Answer: I can only be surprised how someone dares to praise this book in which there are so many things that horrify the human heart and lead it to damnation.

You say that as far as you are concerned you "prefer to be blamed for appreciating and loving a book rather than be one of those subtle blamers." You resemble Heloise of the Paraclete who said that she would rather be called *meretrix* by Master Abelard than be a crowned queen.[5] This shows very well that those wishes that please most are not always the most reasonable.

You say that everyone knows "that there are still seven thousand people . . . who are more than ready to defend it." Answer: it is a general rule that bad sects grow easily, just like weeds, but there are cases where greater numbers do not mean that their cause is better. And may it please God that there will never be such a group assembled; it is not an article of faith: may everyone have his own opinion.

[Christine states that the great theologian Gerson, attacked by Col, has no desire for this book.]

As far as I am concerned, despite my ignorance, I assure you I have no desire for it either. And why would I? It makes me neither hot nor cold, it gives me or takes from me neither anything good nor anything bad; I have no cause to be indignant, for it does not speak about my way of life, since I am not married or hope to be, nor am I a nun, nor does he[6] say anything that touches me personally: I am not Fair Welcome nor do

---

4. I.e., Jean de Meun.
5. Heloise was the mistress and later wife of her professor, Peter Abelard, in twelfth-century Paris. She believed that learning was incompatible with marriage and children and at first refused to marry Abelard, who was later castrated by her uncle's henchmen. "The Paraclete": the convent of which she was the abbess after her entry into the religious life. "*Meretrix*": whore. For the passage Christine refers to see Charles Dahlberg, trans., *The Romance of the Rose* (Princeton, N.J.: Princeton University Press, 1971), 160–61. For the history of the reception of Heloise see Barbara Newman, "Authority, Authenticity, and the Repression of Heloise," in her *From Virile Woman to WomanChrist: Studies in Medieval Religion and Literature* (Philadelphia: University of Pennsylvania Press, 1995), 46–75. Newman suggests that Christine read Heloise "through misogynist lenses" (*ibid.*, 68).
6. I.e., Jean de Meun.

I fear the Old Woman, nor do I have any buds to guard.[7] And I assure you that I love beautiful and subtle books and treatises, and I seek them out and look for them and read them gladly, though I can understand them only on a simple level. And if I do not love this book of the *Rose* the reason is simply and absolutely because it gives very bad advice and is dishonest reading and fills people's hearts with more bad than good things. In my judgment it can be the cause of damnation and of leading a worse life: I swear on my soul and my faith that this is my only motivation. And what you say later, namely that perhaps we blame the book so that people will have a greater desire to see it, and thus our opinion would be positive, you can be certain that this is not our motivation.

[Christine now responds to some of Col's rather rude accusations of presumption.]

I do not consider my deeds or my knowledge to be a great thing. The only fact is—and I can say this honestly—that I love learning and a solitary life. It is possible that in pursuing that life I picked the lower flowers of the delicious garden and did not climb the high trees in order to gather their beautiful perfumed and savory fruits[8] (not that I did not have the desire and the will, but my weak understanding did not permit it). And as far as the fragrance of the little flowers is concerned of which I fashioned dainty garlands, those who wanted them—that is, those to whom I did not dare or could not deny them—marveled at my labor, not for its greatness but for the novelty to which they were not accustomed.[9]

And I ask of you and of those who hold your opinions: do not resent me for writing in this current debate on the *Romance of the Rose*. For its beginning was accidental and not at all a conscious proposition, whatever opinion I may have uttered, as you can see in a little treatise where I spoke of the first and last issues of our debate. And I would suffer too much to be constrained in such servitude that I could not answer someone with the truth according to my conscience in a matter that one cannot hold against me.

*   *   *

And it means nothing when you say that the Holy Church, where there are so many worthy men, from its beginning tolerated it[1] for so long without reproach (it waited for me and the others to come and

---

7. References to the *Rose*. Fair Welcome was a character representing the lady's positive response to the lover. The Old Woman exhorted women to fleece their lovers. The rose bud represented the young virginal woman.
8. Note that these themes, including the image of garlands to denote learning, will be worked out later in *The Path of Long Study* and *The Book of Fortune's Transformation*.
9. Christine refers to her patrons here. See *Christine's Vision* (p. 173) for remarks on people's reactions to the novelty of a woman writing learned texts.
1. The *Rose*.

accuse it!): for you know that everything comes to a head at a certain
point, and nothing is long across the expanse of years; and it often happens that a little pointed instrument cures a big boil. How could the
Church tolerate for so long the opinion on the conception of Our
Lady—something worthier of note—without accusing anyone?[2] And
sometimes things which were not debated for a long time come to the
forefront through a great uprising; and this is not an article of faith, and
neither is our matter: may everyone believe whatever he wants and what
pleases him most. As for me, I will write nothing further on this subject,
whoever may write to me, for I have not undertaken to drink the entire
Seine: what I have written is written. I will not be silent because I doubt
my opinions—however much my lack of ingenuity and knowledge prevent me from having a beautiful style—but I prefer to devote myself to
other matters that please me more.

I beg all those who will see my little writings, that they may overlook
the defects of my learning in view of my person and take everything
with a good end in mind and a pure intention—without which it would
not be worth to present anything. Thus I end my writing about the
debate which was never spiteful but was begun, pursued, and ended as
a pastime and not to reproach anyone. I pray to the Holy Trinity, perfect
and complete wisdom, that It may illuminate you and especially all
those who love knowledge and the nobility of good conduct, with true
light so that they can be led to heavenly joy.

Amen.

Written and completed by me, Christine de Pizan, the second day of
October in the year 1402.

> Your well-wishing friend of learning,
> Christine de Pizan

FROM THE TALE OF THE SHEPHERDESS

[The Dit de la pastoure [Tale of the shepherdess] was written in May 1403.
Christine received a commission from an unidentified person, which she
considered a diversion, since her real interests and concerns lay elsewhere
by that time. Christine gives a number of twists to the familiar genre of the
pastoral poem. Most often such poems are told from the perspective of a
knight who sees a beautiful shepherdess, desires her, seduces (or rapes) her,
and leaves.[1] Christine's tale is written in the first-person voice of the shep-

2. A reference to the debate at the time on the Immaculate Conception of the Virgin (i.e., the
question of whether she was born without original sin).
1. See Kathryn Gravdal, *Ravishing Maidens: Writing Rape in Medieval French Literature* (Philadelphia: University of Pennsylvania Press, 1991). For a different view see William D. Paden,
"Christine de Pizan as a Reader of the Medieval Pastourelle," in Keith Busby and Norris Lacy,
eds., *Conjunctures: Medieval Studies in Honor of Douglas Kelly* (Amsterdam: Faux Titre,
1994), 387–405.

herdess herself and thus her inner conflicts become clearer. There is also an unusual emphasis on the professional aspects of shepherding, which were discussed in technical books such as Jean de Brie's *Le bon berger* [The good shepherd], which Christine probably knew.[2] Another striking feature is the learned context which Christine establishes in the prologue, suggesting that the *Tale* has a deeper meaning, similar to that she found in ancient fables in the *Letter from Othea*. And the shepherdess herself, together with her friend Lorete, displays a surprising knowledge of classical literature and its lessons for the lovelorn!

In many ways, then, Christine's shepherdess is an original creation: she displays psychological astuteness and continues the critique of conventional courtly behavior Christine had begun in the *God of Love's Letter*. She also exemplifies the troubles of any young woman who falls in love with someone she considers above her and that her friends think is unsuitable for her.

Translated by Renate Blumenfeld-Kosinski from Maurice Roy, ed., *Oeuvres poétiques de Christine de Pisan*, vol. 2 (Paris: Firmin Didot, 1891).]

Here begins the Book of the Shepherdess.

I, of little wisdom, have already several times undertaken to write tales about various subjects, although I do not really know how to do this. But I do it in order to lighten the weight that makes me so uncomfortable and that will stay with me to the end of my life. For it is impossible for me to forget the sweet and peaceful man from whom death separated me; this pain will always be with me. I wrote this tale in leonine rhymes,[1] as best I could, at the request of a certain person famous throughout the world, who is in a position to order something from me at his will. So I am doing it and am writing my rhymes in this month of May 1403. And it seems to me that if one looks very closely, one can understand that there is another purpose to the text than the obvious one, for one often hides in a covered parable some matters that are not understandable to everyone, and it seems to be nonsense or a fable, but in it lies a valuable lesson.[2] So I will express these ideas by beginning my rhymes:

The Shepherdess

Listen to this adventure of mine, true lovers, you've never heard one like it. If you listen carefully, you will see how Love knows how to act skillfully in order to attract and make subject to him the hearts of those

2. See Charity Cannon Willard, *Christine de Pizan: Her Life and Works* (New York: Persea, 1984), 69.

1. In English, internal rhymes in which the words before the caesurae (breaks in the verse) rhyme with the final words in the line. It was named after an otherwise unknown medieval poet named Leo or Leonius. Christine's tale, which is translated in prose, features a rhyme where the two last syllables of every rhyme pair have the same sound, for example, *pesance/mesaisance* or *saison/maison*.

2. Interestingly, Christine uses a learned vocabulary here, similar to her *Letter from Othea*.

he has captured in his traps. I am a shepherdess who complains; in my amourous plaint I want to tell about my sickness—I simply have to. Since love compels me and holds me by his force, I will tell how I was captured by the god who conquers hearts and brings them good and evil. May this story be an exemplar to the ladies who swear that they will never love. See how Love undoes all good intentions—whether weak or strong—with his great power.

I was a very young girl and spent my time in the woods and on the wild plains to feed my father's sheep in the meadows. As you can see, I spent many years to lead them around, and I grew up without a single day off from my work of being a shepherdess, which I liked. I had to get up early in the morning and cared for nothing else but to get out into the fields and forests, where I often heard the sweet song of the birds. There were no other people but shepherdesses and shepherds.

I was an expert in the profession of shepherding: to take care of lambs in the huts, to put hay into the manger, to cover the roofs with fresh straw; to separate out the sheep and cover them with ointments; to milk sheep and give the lambs to their mothers to suckle at the right time and to spread their fodder with a rake; there was no one better to do all this or to be an expert in this profession. I knew how to mix bran and oats to give strength to the sheep who had just had young ones, and I knew how to shear sheep, sitting in the pleasant shade on May mornings and evenings; and I knew how to bring grass from the meadow to the lambs in order to whet their appetite, if they were born in the season where one keeps them at home. And I could bring back from the fields misbehaving sheep, or those that were old and losing the wool on their backs. And if a sheep had a lamb out in the fields, I would bring it back in my arms to protect it from mange. There was no job too difficult for me to master. I was a skilfull shepherdess. (1–112)

[She now describes the pleasant lives of the shepherds and shepherdesses and their games and entertainments. She describes the nice outfit she was wearing. (113–356)]

I was very pretty and plump; I laughed in a low and friendly voice, so people said. Many a young man loved me dearly, but I was proud and did not condescend to loving any of them. Many a shepherd came to me with an embittered heart, crying and asking for my love, but none could obtain it. And although I saw my friends having fun with their dear boyfriends in the fields, no one could move my heart to love him and to learn another way of life than the one I had learnt. I did not know how to love, nor did I want to learn how. Nothing mattered to me but the care of my sheep. (357–77)

For a long time I lived this way, refusing love and being proud toward everyone. Be they ever so hardy, beautiful, or friendly, I did not listen to their entreaties. People called me "the proud one in matters of love" at that time. But I will tell you how Love finally took revenge on me. He changed my intentions. However beautiful a man's face and body were, however valorous he was, it seemed great folly to me to love someone and to have sweet and bitter feelings. Now I will tell you what happened to me, not twenty years ago, but rather four years ago—I wish it were even longer ago!

One day I sat in the shade of an oak tree, wearing a pretty green hat on my curly hair, near a beautiful fountain. I was rebelling against love and wanted to be alone. It was a very pretty place, leafy woods all around, grass up to my waist, but dense and low in places. There were masses of flowers of all kinds growing around the fountain. And there were beautiful trees, giving wonderful shade so that the sun was not bothersome. I was sitting there, guarding my sheep, looking at the flowers I had picked and was keeping wet in the fountain, singing with a happy voice so loud that the edge of the forest resounded with my song.

At this moment, a large group of people who had heard the melody and words of my song passed on beautiful and gentle horses on the road that had been laid through the forest. Now they stopped and some of them entered the forest, following the sound of the song. They were looking around the woods but could not right away find me because the leaves barred their view. But I, alone and fearful, heard the noise of the horses which were rushing through the forest and were already near me, although they didn't see me yet. Then I trembled with fear, held myself completely still, and stopped singing.

After a while these people, who wished me no ill, found me near the fountain. I did not quickly find my voice to greet them, but rather, without moving, remained seated and painfully shy but also joyful. I trembled and blushed when I saw them, for I had no experience in seeing such noble people: golden reins, saddles covered with white, green, and multicolored fabrics decorated with their coats of arms. The noblemen were mounted on beautiful large horses and Spanish jennets,[3] more elegant than any hunting falcon. They wore rich long cloaks, very becoming, some embroidered with gold, others with silk, with banderoles showing their coats of arms in gold and silver. They had beautiful saddlebags that looked great on them and of which the little bells sounded throughout the forest. Pretty hats covered their faces to the eyes in order to protect them from the sun. They were well outfitted, these lovely noble people, just as one would want them, gracious and with friendly faces.

Now the group assembled, jumping over many a hedge, to come to

3. Small horses.

the meeting place, where I was so troubled without any reason. Then, gladly and without any pride they all descended to the meadow. I was very surprised and already thought I was dead or about to be kidnapped. Together they walked quickly in my direction and said to me with friendly faces: "God be with you, sweet shepherdess."

And I got up—ashamed and trembling like a coward. And I finally returned their greeting, although it was very brief. In this courtly group was one knight who surpassed all the others—even if there had been a thousand—in valor, good sense, and merit. Surely everyone must have heard good things about him. He was beautiful and gentle, handsome and straight, above all the others, and it seemed to me that all the others called him "Monseigneur," which showed me that he was the grandest with the greatest authority.

Then a noble knight came forward and said to me: "Shepherdess, do not be afraid or angry, for from us you will receive only good things." Then he named the one who was above all the others and said: "Monseigneur, whom you see here, passed through here with his companions. You were singing, it seems to me, beautifully and melodiously with an unrestrained loud voice. Because of this, he desired very much to see your joyful face and to sit next to you to hear your sweet song. You cannot get away: you have to sing; nothing bad will come of it."

Then he led me to the one, whom God may protect, and I bowed down humbly and greeted him in a soft voice. But he right away took a great step toward me and lifted me up, laughing sweetly. He said graciously: "By our Savior, here is a joyful adventure!" Then he sat down on the tender grass and gave me his naked hand and made me sit next to him. There is no one who would not have wanted to sit down right away. More than six times he asked me to sing loudly and clearly. I should fear nothing, he said. But I made excuses for a long time, for I did not dare.

He said: "Sweet shepherdess, please don't be upset by my arguments, just sing the song you sing most often." When I saw their great courtesy, the fear I had was quieted. I was reassured and said to him who was smiling gently and asking me to sing, that I would quickly sing, following his command, but that he should be indulgent because my singing left a lot to be desired. Then I began to sing the song that I considered the newest and the one I liked best. I will tell you the song of which they also heard the melody:

The Little Shepherdess

There is no better job
Than to lead little lambs
Out to pasture on the meadows.
I never want to do anything else.

Whoever could see these little
Shepherdesses and pretty shepherds
Be in love with each other,
And make garlands of flowers,
Would say that there is no other
Way of life that is so pure,
He would not wish for any other way,
If he knew this one.
There is no other job as nice as this.

These herdsmen with their little goats,
Accompanied by bird song,
Tell you these shepherds' tales
And sing beautiful new motets.
And they love with all their heart;
They dance to the song of the turtledove
As long as summer lasts.
They care for no other joy.
There is no other job as nice as this.

Thus I ended my song, and I bowed down in front of the one who had asked me to sing. (433–651)

[She then sings another song.]

   Then I told him who sat next to me in a low voice: "Monseigneur, I have tarried too long; if it pleases you I will take my leave so that I will not be scolded. It is late and almost completely dark. It is time for me to get my sheep under a roof and to cover up my lambs in our little stables." So I got up and he did not forbid my taking leave, on the contrary, he agreed willingly. He accompanied me out of the forest, and certainly did not value me little.
   I began to call my animals and he helped me to gather my flock. I began to laugh and said to him with a smile: "Monseigneur, by St. Leger! It suits you well to be a shepherd; I have never seen such a pretty shepherd around here." Then he began to laugh and I took my leave. He left me, but he would not let me kneel down, neither to take my leave nor to ask for a favor. All of them shook my hand and said: "May God give you, sweet shepherdess, that which you hold dearest." And so they left. (687–723)

[She returns home. The next morning she puts on her best outfit and her friends make fun of her.]

   "How come, Marotele,[4] that you put on your beautiful little dress with the pretty belt? Has you father given you a fiancé or do you have

4. The diminutive of Marote.

some new ideas? We never saw you yesterday. Where were you hiding? People were asking about you, just ask Houdee." (766–75)

Then I called my best friend, Lorete, and said to her softly: "I certainly was not lost, rather I found more pleasant company than you; they were very sweet and friendly, and I fell in love. They were not shepherds but people knowledgeable in matters of courtesy and honor. There was no one lower in rank than a knight or a noble squire, son of a baron. They found me singing and picking flowers near the fountain in the woods where I often go alone. There they greeted me, attracted by my song. When I saw them I was dumbfounded because I thought I'd be shamed and dishonored, but there was no need to worry, because as God is my witness, I never saw more courtly people. Without any commotion they saluted me graciously, descended from their horses and sat down next to me. But above them all, there was one they called Monseigneur; he was gentle and pleasant and asked me to sing and inquired very gently about who I was and what I was doing in this forest where I was having a good time. He insisted so long that I was not afraid any more and sang a song or two. They thanked me and were very nice to me. And then it was already dark when I left them." (814–60)

[Marote now says that her nobleman will be back to see her and will love her without villainy. He will desire nothing but that they sing together!]

"God, what a nice dream!" Lorete answered. "By God who hangs on the cross, it is a bad idea to leave your circle of friends and give up your profession in order to get to know such people. Leave all this alone, you silly thing. Is this for a shepherdess who has to guard animals? You have to look out for your honor which undoubtedly you would lose very soon; then it would be better for you to be dead. Are these your kind of people? Soon they will lead you to shame and do evil things to you. It won't matter much to them. Do you need a count's son in order to fall in love? Certainly, everyone who wants to enjoy love should put his heart into the right place. There are so many good-looking young men who guard sheep and who go crazy for love of you, and serve you and praise you. Choose one of them if you want to love and do not let yourself be blamed by those who would love you frivolously, shepherdess."

Then I answered: "Sister, I certainly only want to love someone truly, this is no lie, but there is this one among a thousand whom I like for his pleasant and athletic body. Nonetheless, I'm not planning to embark on a life of love. May God keep me from getting into this! But I must admit that I want to enjoy myself and play without villainy. Just looking at what I like doesn't cost me anything, and one cannot blame me if I want to love him decently for the good that resides in him. Many noble people are loved this way for their great goodness, as I have heard." (883–933)

[Lorete insists once more that Marote will not escape love and that it is wrong to love someone who is not a shepherd but a nobleman. Marote suggests that Lorete should secretly come with her into the forest and see for herself. This is what they do.]

Soon I heard the horses, for I was all ears. I immediately jumped out onto the path to see whether it was the one that my heart was intent on. When I saw him approach from afar, I blushed all over my face and I changed color without feeling any pain. He was the third rider, the beautiful and gentle one, and there were no others. He did not bring as many people as last time.

My companion who saw him, began to tremble with fear and was deadly white in the face. She said to me with great fear: "I'm dying of fear. We will soon be put to shame, you are crazy to begin an acquaintance with such a nobleman. Let's get out of here, it will be better for us to flee and to escape under cover of these leaves into the woods. Come with me if you like, I am leaving. I'd rather lose an arm than to have found you tonight in such company."

"God, how fearful you are," said I, "Lorete, look how he laughs. You don't have to worry: he is not the kind of man who will do us any harm." He rode toward us, and I ran down toward him. He descended from his horse and I bowed down and greeted him as his high rank required.

But he raised me up immediately and said: "May God protect this gentle shepherdess, so devoted to guarding her lambs." Then he took my hand and I led him toward the green woods to sit by the fountain. He said sweetly: "Little Marote, I wanted to see you very badly, nothing held any interest for me than coming back here, for I have never seen a shepherdess, as far as I remember, who pleases me so much, or one whose singing I liked so much, or one who knew how to sing so well. Please do not refuse me the pleasure of hearing you sing without further ado. But tell me, sweet thing, is this your little companion whom I see sitting there all alone under this thatched roof?"

I began to answer the knight I liked so much, in a low voice and without a pause, for I was afraid to say something wrong: "Monseigneur, I am very glad that what I do pleases you. Surely, this is due to your goodness and not to any value I may possess. I was born under a good sign when God let me please such a knight who is known everywhere for his great renown and valiance. Without fail, I want to be yours in all honor, for I know very well that you would never want to do anything dishonorable to me, you would never condescend to that. So command whatever you like, be it a song or some tale. I will never contradict you, but obey you in all things, Monseigneur. But my companion whom you see there is not at all reliable."

Then he said: "Come here, my friend, do not be afraid of me, for I plan to do nothing that may be disagreeable to you."

"This is my friend and confidante whom I love and cherish, Monseigneur, be kind to her," I said.

Then she[5] came toward us with her head lowered, looking very modest; she took off her hat, which had no wimple, and kneeled down next
to him who gave her his hand and said: "May God protect you, sweet
shepherdess, do not be afraid of me who am your friend, but sit down
next to me. Tell me what's new with the two of you, dear shepherdesses,
for we are also shepherds, and your dear friends and your men." (989–
1,103)

[She now describes the elegant outfits of these so-called shepherds. She
sings for them again and soon it is evening. They say good-bye and Marote
sings to herself.]

> How is it possible that I
> Have to love in spite of myself?
> I never thought that love
> Was like that,
>
> I was simple, without love
> or any worrisome thought,
> I played and sang,
> I had no other desires.
>
> Now, I do nothing but think,
> Nothing means anything to me
> But to see the one who possesses
> My heart, as I swear to him.
> How is this possible?
>
> It seems to me that I see nothing
> But his gentle body and kind face,
> No matter where I am.
> I want to know nothing else.
>
> Alas, I feel the sting
> Of Love who has captured me so well
>
> That I have no more sense or reason,
> So occupied am I with love.
> How is this possible?

In the morning at daybreak I got up thinking of love and left with my
sheep in the direction of the forest. My companion followed me rather
closely, and I was very happy as soon as I heard her. She nodded to me
from afar and when she came closer we sat down by the fountain; it was

5. I.e., Lorete.

not very far. Then I thoughtfully said to her: "Tell me, Lorete, sweet friend, have I ever lied to you? Is he not beautiful, the knight you saw yesterday? Is he not graceful and kind, and pleasant to everyone? Are shepherds like this? You'd have to have a twisted mind or be blind in both eyes if he did not please you better than a shepherd, be he ever so educated. What am I doing wrong if he pleases me? I'm getting no wrong ideas and offend no one."

Lorete answered right away: "He certainly is handsome and graceful, truly there's nothing missing or wrong with him, and I can see that you will love him, and that you're still blaming yourself. But even if he surpasses all others, what good is it to you who will always remain a shepherdess? The more valor there is in him, the less he will love you. You would really be crazy to let yourself be taken over by love for him. He undoubtedly loves some beautiful and famous lady. And you think you could be loved by him, crazy and naive girl? Just watch out that he does not dishonor you, for you will never have his love. And do not trust his sweet and straightforward glances. Everybody would consider you a simpleton for expecting his love. Believe me and get away from this forest before you come to harm, and make sure you stay away before crazy love makes you commit an even greater folly. For that person shows good sense who gets away from mischief before it comes to a head. But I can talk all I want, for until now you do not even have an ounce of his love, not even one little bit. (1,218–302)

"It would be better, and I'm not joking, to love someone on a lower level rather than aiming so high that one will eventually be despised. Don't you remember, Marote, that your father, John Burote, a wise man among a thousand—there is no one like him in our town—owns many beautiful romances that speak of times past. The other day he was sitting under the elm tree and was reading. As I remember, this romance was telling the story of some lovers. It speaks of the son of a king and it seems to me that the tale says that the father was called the king of Troy.[6]

"It happened that the queen dreamed a marvelous dream—which was not a lie—when she was pregnant with this son. She dreamed that she had given birth to a huge firebrand which burned down the fortifications of the town. The city was completely destroyed, and so were the whole country and the kingdom. The king ordered the child killed after he was born, but the queen asked that he be given to a shepherd and not cut up by knives, for he was a beautiful little child. So he was brought up in the manner of a shepherd in a big forest, and he was believed to be the son of the shepherd, born in this rural village.

6. The story of Troy appears in many of Christine's works. It was known primarily through Benoit de Sainte-Maure's *Roman de Troie* [Romance of Troy] (twelfth century) and the *Histoire ancienne jusqu'à César* [Ancient history up to Julius Caesar], dating from the early thirteenth century. On the medieval use of the stories of classical lovers see Katherine Heinrichs, *The Myths of Love: Classical Lovers in Medieval Literature* (University Park: Pennsylvania State University Press, 1990).

"He was handsome, friendly and gentle, pleasant to everyone. He revealed his true nature, for although he took care of sheep and drank milk and ate ordinary bread, he was courtly and pleasing, skillful and considerate. He was a gentle shepherd. He walked through many a forest and garden while letting his sheep graze. A young girl, the most beautiful of the region, was passing by, leading her sheep to pasture, and saw the young man with his inborn nobility. The girl had a bright face, a beautiful body and bearing, and I believe her name was Oenone. He gave his heart to her because he was so enchanted by her sweet laughter.

"The gentle shepherd Paris, as one knows, was then named Alexander; there was no shepherd around who resembled him. So pleasant and amiable was he that Oenone loved him dearly and called him her sweet friend. The two lovers had a good time together, so I understand. They made themselves a bed with a baldachin from green leaves where they lay arm in arm without any cover other than branches and greenery—they needed nothing else.

"Paris promised his beloved that he would love her always and never leave her; his heart would be with her and he would not stop loving her unless a great river would run backwards. They made an agreement and he wrote something to remember this by into a tree with his knife, with which he had carved many a whistle. He said that this tree was the witness of their agreement.

"But it happened differently, for he was told where he came from and from which family he was born. This made Oenone unhappy, for he left right away and no longer guarded the sheep. Instead, he returned to Troy, which made his parents very happy. He forgot his poor beloved (who was extremely angry at this) and then loved Queen Helen, which brought him great pains and suffering.

"So you can see very well that everyone should give his heart according to his station, for Oenone did not manage to please him, whatever she tried, once he found out that he was not a shepherd but rather of royal lineage. For that reason, he wanted to love a queen, which had very bad consequences for him. And thus, I swear to you, you can see and learn that one should choose one's equal if one wants to enjoy love and have less grief.

"I think I have given you sincere advice; since we are loyal friends we cannot for any reason let the other one get into something that is not good for her, if it can be prevented by us or our friends."

I answered my friend who had given me this sermon: "Lorete, I am really surprised that you advise me not to love because I am a simple shepherdess, without fancy clothes or a wimple and that you tell me that he would never give me his heart because we are not from the same class.

"You want me to look at the example of Oenone whom Paris quickly forgot. You are right, but there is another book that speaks of Hercules who was so chivalrous and so lucky in his feats of arms that no one was better than he. Through his skill with arms he advanced so much that he became king and the ruler of a great kingdom. But Love captured him and humiliated him so much that it was not unpleasant for him to card wool with his beloved. And he, who was so valorous that he conquered lions, was subject to a woman whom he served as his lady. There is no such greatness that would not subject itself for love to the heart where it wants to lodge."

This is what I answered Lorete, and I also said that she should not think that my heart would be so flighty that it would do something crazy in this love I was enjoying so much, but that I simply had to love. (1,320–487)

[Lorete promises her support and the two young women take pleasure in talking about love. Marote's beloved joins them often.]

I don't know how to speak of the glances, the sweet words, the coming and going, the sweet laughter, our looks and our talk of love. My delightful friend, for whom I had waited many a day, sat down next to the place where I was lying stretched out on the grass. I held his head in my lap and stroked his hair and then put my arms around his neck and embraced him. Imagine our pleasure and all the sweet words that I will not tell about. And you should know that this went on for a long time without him asking me for my love. But he did not have to ask for it, for he could know for certain that he had it entirely. (1,597–624)

[He also declares his love and promises that he will never do anything that would jeopardize her honor. Now she openly speaks of her love for him.]

"Monseigneur, my love reveals itself in my face. I do not have to hide it, I know well that you see it, for Love shows it to you. Whether you like it or not, I do not believe that you don't have a lady and beloved somewhere else who speaks to you and is more of a lady than I am. You must not ask for another's love or look around elsewhere if you want to be loyal. My heart would hurt too much—though I am only a poor woman—if another lady took her pleasure with you while I get only the anger. Let's agree on this, for you should know that I love you so much that I do not wish to love another, whether our love turns out sweet or bitter. But from you I want no other promise: it is enough for me that I see you and that I get to love half of you, for you are another's friend. And I can assure you that I will do nothing crazy, I'd rather die. I don't know if you have the same intentions but I swear to you by the saints that I will never do any harm to my honor, not for a noble or for a common man."

He answered right away: "And who asks this of you? I do not have to refuse to do any of this, for by my soul I never thought of doing any-thing, in word or deed, that would cause you to be blamed or be detri-mental to your honor. Rather, I want to increase your honor. I will never ask you for anything but your love in good faith and a trusting sweet kiss. No woman should find excuses and refuse this to her beloved, by my soul! This is not asking too much, fair lady. I do not wish for any-thing else, is this too outrageous for a lover? I stake my head on it—I won't request anything further."

I laughed and said: "Who could refuse you such a courtly request? I grant it, whatever may happen, for I feel my heart breaking in two, I can no longer defend it."

Then he embraced me and kissed me sweetly, sighing with pleasure, and then he thanked me humbly. But this kiss betrayed me:[7] for my heart gave itself over completely and was struck by the arrow of Love. We were both in a state where this became all our pleasure: without tiring, we embraced and kissed—with long breaths—without any vil-lainous thoughts. Thus, in this leafy forest, I got to know my beloved and changed completely. I became estranged from the shepherds with whom I used to spend my time and began to sing other songs than those I had learned earlier. And I learned this ballad which I will now tell you and which expressed my thoughts:

Ballad

Oh, the sweetest being ever created,
The most pleasant any woman ever knew,
The most perfect in goodness,
The most beloved any woman ever loved!
The most delicious meal for my true heart,
Everything I love, my amorous desire,
My only beloved, my paradise on earth,
My eyes' most perfect pleasure,
Your sweetness makes it hard for me.

Your pain has truly invaded my heart
Which never thought it would be in
Such straits, but burning desire has so
Inflamed it that it will not survive
Unless sweet thoughts comfort it.
But memory comes and settles down with it.
In my thoughts I embrace you and hold you close,
But when I cannot get hold of the sweet kiss,
Your sweetness makes it hard for me.

7. This line (*ce baisier m'a trahy*, line 1738) recalls the famous line from the *Romance of the Rose*: "*Cis miröors m'a deceü*" (this mirror has deceived me, line 1609). Daniel Poirion, ed., *The Romance of the Rose* (Paris: Garnier Flammarion, 1974). See also p. xiii.

My sweet friend, beloved with all my heart,
No thought can banish from my heart
The sweet glance your eyes hold enclosed.
Nothing will banish it, not words
Or the gracious touch of sweet hands,
Which, without any displeasure,
Want to search around everywhere,
But when I cannot see you with my eyes,
Your sweetness makes it hard for me.

Most fair and good man who has captured my Heart, do not
forget what I ask from you,
For when I cannot see you at my leisure,
Your Sweetness makes it hard for me. (1,669–788)

[After this elaborate poem Marote realizes that she no longer keeps company with her old companions. She has become solitary. The other shepherds begin to fear for her honor.]

At the beginning I felt great joy, but not for long, and I will explain why. At that time I often saw my sweetest friend in secret. He certainly knew the way to me, and he did his duty so well that I was very satisfied. With him I found sweetness, peace, and good love. Without hesitation he gave me every pleasure he could in all things, so that I could ask for nothing else. It is true, I must admit, that once I was a bit jealous and saw him somewhat changed. I don't know whether he wanted to test me to see how much I cared about him. Or perhaps I was suspicious without a reason, for a heart in the grip of love fears to lose the one it loves. Suffering from this illness of jealousy, I sang another ballad. (1,896–921)

[Her beloved swears that he loves no one else. But he leaves quickly without saying good-bye, which pains Marote greatly. His departures become more frequent, but each time he promises to return. She sings a ballad with the refrain "My heart is about to break." She fears he has forgotten her; great ladies are surely in love with him. Yet he returns.]

I stretched out my arms and ran toward him and wept with great joy without saying anything. But the sweet man said to me: "What is wrong, my fair gracious love? Are you not happy about the return of your friend? Let's sit down on this grass and show me a happy face, my sweet darling—I wanted to see you so much!"

I cannot tell you the joy we had then. We held each other so tightly that Tristan, who was so crazily in love, never held Yseut, who brought him certain death, so tightly when she caused his death.[8] We did not

---

8. This story, first told in French in the twelfth century, was extremely popular in the Middle Ages. Tristan fell in love with his uncle's wife, Yseut, and the two had a long adulterous relationship. It ended with their deaths in each other's arms.

get tired of kissing, or of sighing sweetly. We couldn't get tired of it for we were doing it without interruption! It did not seem a long time to us.

In this love united in two hearts there was nothing evil or dishonorable, nor will there ever be. It will never abate, for when we are dead and our bodies have perished, our spirits will still love each other and will be together. Thus my pleasure lasted as long as I could be near the sweet and comely man. Love made me know him so well! To be near him was for me the earthly paradise, I could not ask for anyone or anything else.

But this time did not last long, for his stay in the region was short. My poor heart got as dark as a blackberry as soon as he told me: "My love, I have to leave immediately on a journey." (2,142–91)

[Marote exclaims that she will die of sorrow. But her beloved promises to be back soon. That was a year ago. Marote laments.]

This is how love hurts those men and women who serve him. They feel pain and don't deserve it. These things can happen. It would be better for me to be still on the pasture taking care of my sheep and to stay away from love than to love such a man who, although he is better than I, has caused me such suffering. If God does not bring him back soon, he'll be my ruin. For without him I have no desire to live. He is the pasture without which I do not want to live. I pray to God to bring him back and that he may still love me as much as I love him. His sweet eyes lodge in my heart forever. I beseech you, courtly lovers all, on naked knees and in penitential garb, pray for him. I swear to you that he is a good man, valiant and beloved by heroes.

Here ends the Tale of the Shepherdess.

From THE PATH OF LONG STUDY

[*The Path of Long Study*, written during 1402–03, is the first of Christine's first-person allegorical visions. It recounts an extended journey undertaken by Christine-protagonist under the guidance of the Cumaean Sibyl. The journey itself (like the *Romance of the Rose*) takes place within the frame of a dream that Christine-protagonist is presented as having had on the night of October 5, 1402. While the poem is initially dedicated primarily to King Charles VI of France, the first completed manuscript was presented to the duke of Berry on March 30, 1403;[1] copies were also given to the dukes of Burgundy and Orléans, all of whom are referred to in the second part of the "Prologue."

The plot line opens with Christine-protagonist lamenting the sad state of

---

1. See C. C. Willard, *Christine de Pizan: Her Life and Works* (New York: Persea, 1984), 100.

destructive warfare that engulfs the earth as a whole, and the kingdom of France in particular. Alone in her study, Christine is temporarily cheered by a rereading of Boethius's *Consolation of Philosophy*, but her initial depression over the state of the world returns to haunt her as she tries to go to sleep. No sooner has she finally fallen asleep than the figure of the Sibyl comes to her in a dream-vision and announces that she has been chosen to make a special journey (lines 451–712). This journey begins with Mount Parnassus, where Christine sees the abodes of the great philosophers (including her own father) and poets (lines 714–1170). A trip to the Holy Land ensues, followed by a tour of the Mideast and of Central Asia. This terrestrial journey ends before the boundaries of the Earthly Paradise, which Christine cannot enter (lines 1171–1568). At this point, the Sibyl leads Christine up the ladder of "speculation" to visit the celestial spheres, concluding with the travelers' arrival at the fifth heaven, the "Firmament" (lines 1569–1780). Here the Sibyl provides an astronomical/astrological tour for her charge, before leading her back down to the first heaven (Air) where the rest of the plot will take place.

Here Christine-protagonist functions primarily as a silent witness to a debate in which the allegorical figure of the Earth begs Lady Reason to stop the destruction of universal war. Reason asks the advice of Wealth, Nobility, Chivalry, and Wisdom, who are seated around her; and each of them presents the ideal qualities of her candidate for the office of world emperor, who could resolve humankind's conflicts. At the end of the debate, the allegorical figures decide that the final choice must be made at the court of France, and at the Sibyl's request, Christine is dispatched as messenger. As she is descending the ladder to return to Earth, her dream ends as she is awakened by her mother knocking loudly at her bedroom door. The dream-vision is over.

The key literary model for Christine-protagonist's journey in the *Path* is Dante's *Divine Comedy* (c. 1307–20), which Christine both rewrites and regenders. The *Path*'s Sibyl restores the guide of *Aeneid* 6; while the first-person female protagonist of Christine's poem replaces Dante-protagonist. It is important to note that the *Path* is the very first literary work in French that is explicitly based on Dante's *Comedy*.

Translated by Kevin Brownlee from Robert Püschel, ed., *Christine de Pisan. Le Livre du chemin de long estude*, 2nd ed. (Berlin: Hettler, 1887; repnt. Genève: Slatkine, 1974). The translator would like to thank Professor Andrea Tarnowski for letting him consult the manuscript version of her excellent modern French translation of Christine's *Chemin de long estude*, forthcoming in the series "Lettres gothiques" at "Livre de Poche," Paris.]

Prologue

Very excellent, redoubtable Majesty; illustrious in honor, exalted in dignity, worthy of royalty by the grace of God, all accede to your valorous power; most worthy lily, of magnificent splendor, you are pure and devout and sanctified by God who is the glorious source of all grace.

May He prize you and increase your lineage. Charles the sixth[1] of that venerable name, the good and great king of France, may God keep you in happiness and health. It is to you first of all that I offer my little poem. Although it is not worthy to be held by such hands as yours, I hope that my goodwill allows this offering to be considered a good deed. (1–14)

And next I offer it to you, exalted and magnificent dukes,[2] sprung from the flower whose splendor extends over the entire earth; your honor brings glory to France. Offspring of this beloved flower whose perfume pervades the world, may praise, glory and value always be yours, until you win a place in paradise. (15–22)

Most high princes, I present myself to you with extreme and heartfelt humility, in order to implore you very sincerely not to take as presumptuous the fact that I, an unworthy woman, write to such worthies as you. May it please you, rather, to accept my desire to serve you or to give you some pleasure, you whose nobility is so exalted and so well merited; and please excuse my simplemindedness if I have made any mistakes through ignorance, and focus instead on the loyalty embodied in my project. In order to provide you with some diverting food for thought, I have composed this poem, which I have here written down. In the following text you will hear the different participants in a celestial dispute, who have appealed to you for a resolution, using me as their messenger, I who will recount to you directly and in a poetic manner how the problem came up. For because I have written it down, I remember it. Thus judgment will be rendered by you on this great debate in which several disputants participated, for they have commanded me to present myself before you, as before a living fountain of supreme wisdom; and these disputants are so noble that they should be helped. So please do not disdain to render judgment because of the unworthiness of the messenger who transmits this debate to you: truth and reason can well be transmitted through a simple person. (23–54)

Powerful princes, do not despise my little poem because I am worth little. Now it is time to begin my work; I will recount what happened without further ado. May it please you to listen to it and to understand it: please take note of where it happened, of what and how it was. (55–60)

Here Begins the Book of the Path of Long Study

Since perverse Fortune has long been hostile to me, she cannot now cease from continually harming me through her tricks which kill many, and which have completely defeated me. Because of them, I am often

1. His reign began in 1380. In 1392 the king suffered his first attack of the madness that was to plague the rest of his reign, in increasingly longer fits of increasing severity.
2. The dukes of Berry, Orléans, and Burgundy.

in excessive pain, solitary and thoughtful; I regret the happy past that is now denied me by Fortune and a death whose memory torments me, as I constantly remember the man[3] because of whom (and of no other) I used to lead a joyous—even glorious—life, until Death snatched him away. In my opinion, he was without equal in the world; I could not have wished for anyone more wise, prudent, handsome and good than he was, in all respects. He loved me, and that was right, for I was given to him when I was young. Our love and our two hearts were completely in accord; much more than between brothers and sisters, our two wills were one, whether it was a question of joy or of sorrow. His company was so pleasing for me that when he was near me, there was no living woman more overwhelmed with the good things of life; for he showered upon me, to the best of his ability, every pleasing, delightful and enjoyable thing. It is right that he used to please me—no more, alas! In truth he pleased me so much that if I devoted all my time to praising him, I do not think that I could say enough good about him. (61–104)

Since we have been separated, I have never had another mate, nor have I ever wanted one, no matter how much wisdom or money he had. My husband stayed with me for a while, but Fortune ended up by taking his life. I think she envied the joyous, happy life he gave to me. It was a bitter misfortune to lose him whom I loved more than any other thing in this mortal world. A deep sadness then took hold of me, I became like a recluse: sad, gloomy, alone, and weary. I could not take a single step without tears filling my eyes, showing my profound mourning. (105–25)

Misfortune struck me harshly then, and has not left me alone for a single day since, although thirteen full years have elapsed. It is thus not a recent event, but my grief is fully renewed every day, as if the loss occurred only one year, or less, ago. For the great love that linked our hearts together does not allow me to forget him, although my body is weakened and my energy depleted by my past sadnesses, even though I put on a happy face before other people, and pretend that I do not remember the pain, no matter what happens. (126–44)

The one who laughs and amuses himself can be the saddest of all. Thus came the beginning of my decline, caused by Fortune's assault; since then she has continued to attack me so much that my heart and body have been stripped of joy and good luck and all possessions; through misfortune, bad luck, and unhappiness, I have long been robbed of all happiness, so that I am the lowest of all; and my complaints are useless, since Fortune has undertaken to kill or imprison my heart: it is imprisoned in such tight bonds that it is weary of struggling against them. Thus I have good reason to lament, though this does me little good. And because I have been reduced to this state by Fortune,

---

3. I.e., Christine's husband (see pp. xi–xii).

who wounds me so, I willingly choose solitude, for I must hide my mourning from other people; I grieve alone. (145–69)

One day, in order to lament alone in this fashion, joyless, I shut myself away in a little study, where I often enjoy myself by reading texts recounting various adventures. I looked through one or two books, but quickly tired of this, for I found nothing of substance that could comfort me in my state of despair; I would willingly have turned away from the thoughts that so preoccupied me. The date of this painful experience was October 5, 1402. Whether my actions were foolish or wise I do not know, but no one would have perceived them or known of them, since I would have kept my composure, no matter how strongly I was moved by love or hatred: to show one's heart is not always advantageous. (170–94)

I remained there until night fell, at which point I sent for a lamp to see whether by browsing in some book, I could free myself from the grief that oppressed me or, at the very least, make the time pass. And then I found a book which I loved very much, for it took me out of my state of dismay and desolation: it was Boethius's[4] profitable and celebrated book, *On Consolation*. I then began to read, and as I read, the grief and pain that so weighed on me were dissipated, when I learned from the book of the punishments suffered by Boethius in Rome, and put myself in his place, for a good example is very helpful in achieving comfort and removing displeasure. He was an extremely virtuous and valiant man, who was wrongly exiled for having given good advice and helped the common good. It is nothing new that those who support righteousness are rewarded harshly. (195–225)

In his service to the common good, Boethius sought no other reward than that given by God to those who try to do His will. But he was badly treated and cheated of this prize, by the false envy of those who hate good, true, and honest people, and who wickedly try to harm them. But he who trusts in God is wise, for Philosophy, about whom Boethius had learned in his studies, did not despise him because of his exile, or his troubles, or his misfortunes; rather, she came to comfort him; and spoke to him so much that she demonstrated to him through logic that earthly happiness is nothing but transitory joy: where there is no certainty, there can be no happiness; transitory things cannot make one happy. (226–50)

Happiness can only result from a goodness which cannot fail. No one should complain about having lost benefits that have been distributed by Fortune, who gives them and takes them away according to her whim. The virtues are the only good things that always keep their powers; Fortune cannot take them away, although she can remove material riches. He who is rich in virtue will never be obliged to endure pain,

---

4. See n. 8, p. 38.

no matter what happens to him. There is no other wealth that is certain, or happiness that is lasting. (251–66)

Philosophy demonstrated to Boethius, through rigorous reasoning, that good fortune is less certain and less profitable than bad fortune, no matter how unpleasant it might be. By means of effective syllogisms, she made him solve for himself a series of problems that she presented to him. As the priest absolves the sinner who makes his confession, so Boethius makes his confession at the close of his work, for he understood that what Philosophy taught him was true and good. Philosophy's exhortations consoled him for the misfortunes he had experienced, as he recounts in his treatise, which I read for that entire evening. (267–85)

If I had been able to stay up later I would have been happy to have done so, for I was enjoying myself so much, and found the subject matter of the book both pleasing and consoling. Thus I took Boethius into account, and thought that he who is truly virtuous need never worry: his sorrows will be turned into joys. My earlier melancholy was thus somewhat relieved, and I appreciated that book more and understood it better than I ever had before. For although I had read it previously, I had never seen so well how to draw consolation from it: there is a good side to the suffering that teaches us something. (286–302)

I therefore had good reason to value Boethius's book, but it was time to go to bed, for midnight had already passed. Feeling somewhat cheered up, I lay down in bed as the late hour required. After having said my prayers, I expected to fall asleep quickly, but instead I abandoned any thought of sleep, for I fell into a deep meditation: I do not know how it happened, but I could not detach myself from it, no matter how hard I tried. I began to consider how the world is empty, transitory, full of sorrow, uncertain, and unkind; how even the most powerful are not protected from fortune and unhappiness; how the world is so corrupt that it contains scarcely any good people. I considered the ambitions, the wars, the afflictions, the betrayals, the deceitful traps that are found everywhere in the world, and the great wrongs that people commit there: it is very harmful that sinning is so little feared. I marveled at why peace cannot be maintained. War is found everywhere under the heavens, not only on earth where people fight so fiercely, but even in the air there is conflict: birds of prey hunt and kill other birds, who have a natural fear of the predators and timorously flee from them. The misfortunes on earth, however, involve wars in which everyone is implicated: the more wealthy people are, the less they care for their relatives, and the more they mount armed attacks against them with lances held at the ready; or else, they launch assaults on their neighbors. And even among the Saracens we see the Sultan fight against Tamerlane [5] — may it please God that they destroy each other, so that Christians have noth-

5. A Mongol (or Turkish) conqueror who between 1380 and 1400 gained control of the Mideast, before moving on to invade Anatolia (1402), where he defeated the Osmali Sultan and

ing to do with them. It is, however, sad to state that Christians kill each other in deadly wars, because of greed for power or for newly conquered lands. (303–54)

It is pitiable that mortal man is so consumed by such greed that he is prepared to spill so much blood; and one must either render unto Caesar[6] or suffer execution—otherwise the Scriptures would lie, and they do not. And death quickly comes to those who are not careful, at which point they need no other possession than a length of earth. If one has done evil, then comes the punishment; if one has done good, he is rewarded. Earthly conquests will be useless after death: thus whoever wickedly acquires them is a fool, given how little they will finally amount to. God's Church is injured, more saddened than ever before; her pastors are now wounded, and their scattered and bewildered flocks lose their way, which causes many to be lost.[7] Thus things become worse than ever. But I do not know if mortal man will ever see the world choose a better path. May God grant that it quickly improve, before He imposes a heavy punishment upon it. (355–82)

In this state of mind I thought about the origin of this sad condition, and how it could be that even the dumb animals, whether on earth or in the air, fight with each other, kill and slaughter each other. All animals, both great and small, are motivated by a perverse desire to mistreat each other, to wound and destroy each other. And one can often see the fish in the sea arm themselves, bristling with spikes, in order not to be swallowed up by the bigger fish who want to kill and eat them. Everywhere there is violence, and not only among men: all living creatures struggle against each other, as do even the elements. (383–404)

Let anyone who might want to accuse me of lying simply consider air and earth: there is such a conflict between them that they cannot stand one another, and thus they flee from each other, earth below, air above: they have never been united or mixed together since God created them out of chaos. Fire and water hate one another and try to destroy each other. The simple truth about the cause of this hatred is that they are by nature discordant: it is impossible to make peace between two contrary things. (405–18)

Thus, since our body is composed of the elements, it is in a state of agitation; for what Nature makes out of one element, another element opposes. This opposition does not surprise me at the level of the four elements, but I am absolutely astonished by the fact that human nature

---

reached the Aegean Sea. After his death in 1405, his empire quickly broke up. He was a devout Muslim, and Christian Europe viewed with fascination his conquests at the expense of other Muslim rulers.

6. Recalling the words of Christ in Matthew 22:21: "Render therefore unto Caesar the things which are Caesar's; and unto God, the things that are God's." See also Mark 12:17 and Luke 20:25.

7. A reference to the Great Schism (1378–1417), during which there were two (and from 1409, three) competing popes.

makes fellow human beings similarly antagonistic. The Scriptures (which do not lie) tell us that the rebel angels, in a similarly antagonistic manner, wanted long ago to start a war in heaven, but God expelled them from paradise for their pride. And since that expulsion, He has never since allowed any angel to have the desire to sin, so that there has never again been any sin committed in heaven, after that initial misdeed. (419–36)

I thought of all these things, and of many others, saying to myself that God in heaven allows such discord on earth for the profit of mortal man. For when man sees the earth in such a sorry state, he is led to desire heaven where there are neither bad deeds nor bad speech, but peace, joy, concord, love, the loss of which is never to be feared. By making a small effort to struggle against the world, one can obtain this great glory: anyone who seeks after any other glory is a fool. (437–50)

With such thoughts in my mind, I went to bed; yet I was scarcely asleep before I had a strange vision that was not an illusion, but rather a reliable presentation of very true and certain things. Just at the threshold of sleep, it seemed to me that I saw a lady of great stature, with a very virtuous and wise appearance, and a dignified manner. She was neither young nor pretty, but aged and very calm. She did not wear a crown, for she was no crowned queen; rather, she was simply coiffed with a veil tied around her head, and she wore, according to the old-fashioned manner, a wide tunic. She gave the impression of strength and durability. This lady seemed to me to be an honorable, calm, temperate, and very wise woman—the mistress of all her powers. As she advanced toward me I was not afraid, since she reminded me of the goddess of wisdom, famed for her vast knowledge, whom Ovid teaches us is named Pallas.[8] However, I suspected that she was not this goddess, since I noticed that she did not wear a crown. When this lady stopped beside my bed, I was delighted with her arrival. (451–88)

Having reached me, she spoke as follows: "Daughter, may God grant that you continue to have a peaceful soul and conscience, and that you remain devoted to your love of learning, to which your temperament inclines you. And before your life is over, you will so rejoice in learning that your name will be resplendent long after your death; and because of the goodness of your memory, whose conceptual ability is powerful, I love you and want you to learn part of my secret knowledge before I leave you. If you learn even a little of my knowledge, your intellectual powers will be greatly expanded. (489–504)

"And in order for you to follow me better, I want you to know who I am. In ancient times I was a very learned women, born in the city of Cumae, situated in the lands of Romagnia, that is called the great Campania: My name was Almethea. I do not want to conceal from you how

8. See Ovid's *Metamorphoses* 5.

I acquired the knowledge of how to predict the future truly. From all sides people used to come to me in order to learn whether peace or war awaited them. During that time (and I do not say this merely to boast) no one besides me knew what was going to happen, although I had had predecessors. Six wise women had been so perfect that they became by the grace of God prophetesses, and they spoke about the most exalted secrets, and I was seventh in this line. Three others were born after me who prophesied as long as they lived. And all ten of us prophesied the coming of Jesus Christ,[9] and we dared to tell that of a perfectly sinless virgin a man would be born who would save the world and redeem Adam's sin and misdeed, although the faith was at that time not yet fully revealed; for, more than a thousand years before the coming of Jesus Christ, we assured grieving humanity that this father of all justice would come to redeem them. We composed many beautiful verses and completed many great volumes about future events, for those who knew how to understand them. (505–46)

"I lived in the world for a long time, and I will recount to you how I obtained the gift of longevity. Thus is it written in a book:[1] When I was a young and tender maid, Phoebus tried very hard to find a way to gain my favor, and to make me aware that he loved me perfectly. He greatly desired me and tried hard through gifts and beautiful language to take my virginity. But I was able to refuse him: nothing he could say or do would allow him to win me, either with his intelligence or with his riches. When he saw that he was gaining nothing, and that he was completely wasting his time, and that I would not yield to him under any conditions, then he told me to request a gift from him of something I wanted, and he would not fail to grant it. At that point, in order to request this new gift from the god, I bent down, and—like an ill-bred girl—picked up a handful of dust, and asked him that I live (without being seized by death) for as many years as there were particles of earth in my closed fist. The god willingly granted my request. And in my hand there was not a quarter or a third of a particle, or one, or two particles, but there were neither more nor less than a thousand particles of earth that I had picked up from the dust on the ground in front of me. Thus I lived for a thousand years: and now I have told you how and because of whom. (547–82)

"I became, however, so weak and aged before my life was over that I regretted this gift. For my body completely wasted away to the point where people barely could see it; but they did hear my voice which greatly pleased them because it always told them the truth. Thus I acquired age and wisdom; but if I had also requested from Phoebus

9. The medieval tradition of the Cumaean Sibyl's prophecy of the coming of Christ is based on Virgil's *Eclogue* 4.4–10. It appears in Dante's *Purgatorio* 22.64–73 and elsewhere in Christine's oeuvre, where it is used to demonstrate the value of women. See, e.g., the *Letter from Othea*, chap. 100, and the *City of Ladies* 2.3.
1. See Ovid's *Metamorphoses* 14.129–53 and *Ovide moralisé* 14.1067–716.

force and vigor for the duration of my life, I would have had it. I was not, however, shrewd enough to ask for this. (583–95)

"In order that you have even more credence in what I am telling you, let me say that I am she who long ago led Aeneas, the exiled Trojan; with no other guide or means I conducted him through hell,[2] then I led him into Italy. And I am the one who revealed the marvels to him, showed him his own future, and explained to him how he had to come to Italy where he was to marry a lady, through which union a line of princes would be born who would hold the entire world in their power. I predicted the foundation of Rome to this man, who would be its source. My mouth spoke this prophecy to him. In hell, I showed him his father, Anchises, and the soul of his mother, and other notable marvels, the exposition of which is profitable; and I led him safe and sound back to earth. I was then seven hundred years old; I still had quite a bit of time left to live. (596–620)

"Several years later, I carried to Rome nine volumes of books on Roman laws, customs, and secrets, at the time when Tarquin Priscus[3] reigned wisely there. By this time my body was in a very weakened condition. Virgil, who came after me, long remembered my verses, for he was well acquainted with them. He spoke of me in his poetry, saying: 'Now has come (as I see and understand) the time that the Cumaean Sibyl had predicted.' Thus he wrote in his poem.[4] (621–34)

"Now I have revealed myself to you whom I see ready to understand, even if you do not yet possess the full results of serious study. Because of this I have appeared here, for you seem to me to be more committed to study than other people. And I know that just a little while ago you were plunged deep in thought, and it seemed to you that this imperfect and vile world contained nothing but pestilence and wickedness. If, however, you wish to follow my flag, I will lead you into another, more perfect, world where you can much better learn than in this one the things that are truly important, agreeable, and profitable, in which there is no vileness and pain. If you make me your mistress, I will show where all the misfortune that affects this world comes from." (635–58)

When I realized that this was the Cumaean Sibyl, who was so gifted for prophecy during her time on earth, I joyfully gave thanks to God that He had revealed her to me, for I had heard much about her. And when I knew who she was, I answered her as follows: "Ah! Most beloved and unique lover of wisdom, member of the learned school of women who prophesied by divine grace and who, as the scribes of God's secrets, articulated many mysteries! Whence comes such humility to you that

---

2. Recounted in Virgil's *Aeneid* 6. Virgil himself becomes the guide for the analogous underworld journey of Dante, the new Aeneas, in the *Inferno*.
3. Or Tarquinius Priscus; according to tradition, the fifth king of Rome (616–579 B.C.). See N. G. L. Hammond and H. H. Scullard, eds., *The Oxford Classical Dictionary*, 2nd ed. (Oxford, UK: Clarendon, 1970), 1038.
4. See Virgil's *Eclogue* 4.4.

you should so beneficently reveal your pleasure to me? I understand that it is much more on account of my aspirations than of my knowledge. I do not possess enough knowledge for my understanding to be worthy of your benevolent offer to guide me as you did him whom it pleased you to show the painful spectacle of hell, where you were willing to lead the noble knight Aeneas. For being willing to guide me into a less quarrelsome and more pleasing place, for this honor I thank you. And even if my understanding were less than it is, it would still be sufficient since you are willing to guide me. Thus I desire to follow you on any path: for I well know (as God is my witness!) that you would not lead me to any place that was not good for me. I am, therefore, your humble chambermaid. Proceed ahead! I will follow after you. Now I must quickly get ready."[5] (659–99)

Then I put on my clothes, dressing myself in a simple manner. I arranged my hair and put on a veil because the October wind is more harmful to the eyes than the summer sun. Then I quickly tied my dress with a belt so that it would not prevent me from walking easily. Still, I would not have been able to follow her on foot, if it had not been that the way I had undertaken was pleasing to me, and a path that does not displease is not difficult even if there is wind or rain. We thus started out on our journey together, but I do not know what route we took, nor would I be able to describe it. (700–15)

I do know, however, that we quickly arrived in a field that was covered with flowers and green with thick grass, like colorfully variegated green meadows are during the month of May. In fact, the mild weather gave me the impression that the sweet month of May had returned. I was about to see marvelous things. From this lovely, fresh, well-maintained place, we entered a wide, straight pathway, such that more than twenty others (along with us) would have easily passed abreast through it; it was so wide and straight. From this lovely, well-made place, many pathways led out; a third of them were very narrow, some more than others. By twisting and turning in every direction, they traversed the beautiful roads which give access to all good and also to all bad places, for those who do not adhere to the straight way, as they should. But the one on which we found ourselves is safe: travelers there need not fear misfortune, or thieves, or robbers. Neither wolves nor bears live there, nor anything that can injure people, for misdeeds are prohibited there; any person can travel safely there. (716–47)

But I would not be able adequately to recount the beauty of these fair pathways; even if I wrote for a full hundred years, I would not be able to describe everything about them. For one sees and hears there every enjoyable beauty that can delight the human heart or imagination. There you would have seen pathways covered by tall trees in full green

5. This speech recalls and condenses Dante's hesitation and remotivation in regard to his journey in *Inferno* 2.

leaf, laden with flowers and fruit, where birds make such a lovely sound that the place seems to be (to tell you the truth) the Earthly Paradise. The trees are so numerous, and planted in such a way, that neither the harsh summer sun, nor the cold of winter can trouble those who travel there. The taste of these elegant fruits is even more precious than the fruits are beautiful for whoever picks them when they are ripe in order to enjoy them. Every human heart can here freely eat its fill without begging; there is room for people of all ranks. And fragrant little flowers are thickly planted along the way. Indeed, believe me when I tell you that the entire place is planted with all of the most beloved, beautiful flowers, roses, violets and lilies, flowering herbs and other delights; with all medicinal plants, useful herbs, flowers and roots; with pennyroyal, hyssop, and mint; all well ordered and arranged. (748–86)

How the Sibyl Showed to Christine the Fountain of Wisdom

Thus, burning with curiosity, I went about looking at all the aspects of this beautiful place. If I could have done it well, I wanted to study everything, but that would have taken more than a thousand years. Then, as I turned my gaze to the right, I saw the summit of a mountain, so high that it appeared to touch the clouds: I truly think that it reached them. There I saw a clear, bubbling fountain, streaming out of the large spring that fed it. No mason had ever built anything there, but the place, the site, and the entire area were so beautiful that this fountain surpassed every other fountain in the world in taste and in virtue—it was so pure, clear, and deep. This one surpassed all the others in terms of health, flavor, freshness, refinement, and clarity. I therefore stopped to look at what I am about to tell you: I saw nine ladies bathing nude in the fountain; they truly seemed to have great authority, worth, and wisdom. I very much wanted to learn more about them. Then I saw a great winged horse in the air above the rock, flying over the ladies. I marveled greatly at this spectacle, and I was more attentive than ever to the spaces and paths around the fountain, covered with flowers, greener and more beautiful than all others. (787–827)

It seemed to me, however, that very few people lived there, at the highest point of this site, because the grass showed very little sign of having been walked on. And from this great fountain, through more than a thousand little openings, lovely little streams ran down over the rock, flowing in their bright stone beds. To the eye, this flowing water seemed like shining silver in the sunlight, and its burbling made such a sweet sound that it completed the perfection of the place. Think what a pleasure it was for me then to hear Zephyr blowing melodiously through the trees, and to hear the nightingales who sweetly recited their lessons, and a hundred thousand other birds, and the sound of the running water that flowed downstream without ever pausing, and irrigated all the pathways—indeed, the water kept them always green, protecting them from drought and heat. (828–52)

The time had come for me to speak before I went on any farther, for I very much desired to know the entire truth concerning the status of this place. For this reason, I turned toward my guide and said to her: "Sweet mistress, guide on the route that I have long desired to take, now I beg you in the name of your love of knowledge, most learned lady, that you enlighten me without delay as to where I am, in what country, and the status of this place and this road; for I have great confidence in you. As we continue on our way without pausing, I would like you to please make clear to me the name of this location and its full significance. Tell me also the unvarnished truth about these verdant pathways, about these trees laden with fruit so sweet and pleasing to the taste, about this delightful fountain where I see such a distinguished company, and about the various surrounding pathways, lovely and green, and about all the precious things I see here, so well ordered that I do not believe there to be a more pleasing Earthly Paradise in this world." (853–82)

The renowned lady then replied to me: "Well beloved daughter, I am quite pleased to expound the whole truth to you, and to answer your request. Know that this pleasant pathway leads to all the places in the world. These transverse roads that you see (that only the wise are allowed to utilize) lead everywhere under the sun that people travel. And those two extremely narrow roads that you see, where the trees are thicker and the flowers and greenery more abundant and long-lived than elsewhere, those lead the person who rightly follows them all the way to heaven, although they are high and narrow. The straighter of the two, as you can see, which is also the more narrow and green, reveals the face of God to whoever follows it to the end. The road that is shorter and broader, which runs beside the other one, goes (I guarantee it to you) as high as the firmament for whoever knows how to hold to the right way, and follow the straight path. Although other roads lead there, this one is more certain, for it is the road of knowledge. The first is the road of the imagination: we will have to bypass it, for this narrow road would be too difficult for you to follow. It is thus necessary for you to follow the other one, which is beautiful for those who have taken it, who have not learned how to follow the first road. (883–922)

"These roads, these lovely passages of which, as you can see, one is wider than the other, are reserved for the most subtle minds according to their various impulses: the narrower you see them to be, the more delectable and straight they are, and the fewer the people who are allowed upon them. Diligence is thus necessary for anyone who wants to follow this road. But this other road upon which we have entered, which unfolds as easily as parchment does, is reserved for the learned who wish to pass through the world without searching for a more profound route: for he who ventures into a deep sea often drowns or loses his way. Here the lazy are excluded, for this place is restricted to those who are eager to understand and who delight in learning. Other people would not be able to perceive the great joy that this sweet place holds: for such people it is entirely hidden. (923–47)

"Look into the distance at the shadowy roads that turn off from here and lead to the bad highway! Do you see it there, dark and obscure? Whoever enters upon it is led to hell with no hope of return. It is full of devils, and he who follows it is mad. But you and I will not be taking this road, for it is inimical to the wise. Rather, we will follow the straight road, for I never take any other.[6] These tall trees that you see, which provide birdsong, fruit, flowers, and green shade against the heat of the sun—all this is in place for the comfort of tired travelers, for they can ease their way and restore their strength with the fruit. Some travelers try the fruit because of its delectable taste; others eat it for nourishment, making a meal of it for themselves and their entourage. There is no vice in any of these things, but you[7] are not yet shrewd enough to nourish yourself with this fruit. Your pleasure is simply to pass through these beautiful places; it is enough for your intelligence to profit from this experience. (948–76)

"The mountain upon which you gaze is called Parnassus; or, as many people also call this noble height, Mount Helicon.[8] The fountain that you see up there is so renowned for its nobility that it is named the Fountain of Wisdom, whose lovely streams irrigate the little green branches that keep the world in verdure and whose fruit smells so sweetly. And I want you to know the names of the ladies whose bathing you observe so attentively: they are called the nine muses. They control the fountain which is so beautiful, clear, and healthy. And they hold their holy school there, which is enclosed by great learning. The flying horse that you see truly constructed this school long ago,[9] for the fountain resulted from a powerful blow of his foot when he kicked backwards against the high, proud rock. You can now understand the nature of this place, because a subtle mind that knows how to interpret does not require a great commentator to elucidate an author's words. (977–1,006)

"These green pathways that you see, where the babbling brooks flow,

---

6. For the importance of the differences between Christine's journey and that of her Dantean model, see K. Brownlee, "Literary Genealogy and the Problem of the Father: Christine de Pizan and Dante," *Journal of Medieval and Renaissance Studies* 23 (1993), 365–87.

7. I.e., Christine.

8. In Ovid's *Metamorphoses*, the favorite haunts of the Muses are Mount Parnassus and Mount Helicon, where their sacred springs are Hippocrene and Aganippe; Christine seems to conflate these two locations.

9. For Pegasus as the creator of the Fountain of Helicon, see Ovid's *Metamorphoses* 5.254–68 and *Ovide moralisé* 5.1648–762.

high above in the most beautiful places, these are the pathways where in times past the philosophers used to speak to the muses, when they wanted to slake their thirst in the sweet water that kept them wise.[1] Do you see that flowery spot, crowned with the laurel trees that indicate its significance? That is where the prince of learning used to live, on that high hill, where he used to fill himself with the fountain's water: this was the philosopher Aristotle.[2] And you can see the beautiful and gracious places all around where the other philosophers used to live, on the heights. You see the beautiful, pure places which Socrates and Plato, Democritus and Diogenes used to frequent. The great philosopher Hermes used to delight in these spots. If you raise your eyes you will see where Anaxagoras used to be; Empedocles and Heraclitus often used to enjoy themselves there. Dioscorides the observer, Seneca, Tully, Ptolemy used to come to this beloved school beside the rippling water. The geometrician Hippocrates, Galen, Avicenna, and many other great philosophers used to gather together around the fountain where they equipped themselves with knowledge. They all used to pass through here. Your own father[3] knew this place very well, and he certainly should have, because he often spent time here, and carried away great learning. Likewise the poets: you can see where Virgil,[4] a little lower down, used to walk among these lovely fields, before the Gospel was sung. There the poets used to gather together and sing sweet songs, accompanied by their pipes, before the muses, who enjoyed them so very much that they would lovingly weave pretty crowns of flowers for the poets: Homer, the sovereign poet, who used to gather many a branch from the trees out of which he made elegant flutes from which issued sweet melodies; Ovid, and Horace the satirist, Orpheus.[5] (1,007–66)

"But I would take up too much time by naming the entire series of those who have loved this beautiful place which gave them so much honor. In addition, there were and there still are innumerable scholars[6] who refresh themselves in the shade of the trees, and students who take the water of the fountain in order to instruct themselves and to learn. (1,066–74)

"In olden times, Cadmus put forth great effort to tame, below the

1. What follows is a reworking of Dante's Limbo (*Inferno* 4.67–147), where the great pagan poets, heroes, and philosophers live in the Dantean version of the Elysian Fields.
2. Greek philosopher (384–322 B.C.), whose influence during the High Middle Ages was dominant. He (referred to as "the master of those who know" in the *Inferno* 4.131) is the first philosopher encountered by Dante in Limbo. The ensuing list (*Inferno* 4.134–44) provides the model for Christine.
3. For more on Christine's father, see p. xi. His presence provides a direct, as it were, genealogical link between Christine and the philosophers of antiquity.
4. This mention of Virgil (70–19 B.C.) initiates Christine's treatment of the great classical poets encountered by Dante in Limbo, which is closely modeled on *Inferno* 4.79–102.
5. This is Christine's version of the celebrated Dantean *bella scuola* ("beautiful school") of poetry (*Inferno* 4.88–90). In her list of poets, however, Christine substitutes Orpheus (who in Dante's Limbo was found among the philosophers, *Inferno* 4.140) for Dante's Lucan (*Inferno* 4.90).
6. *Docteurs* in the original.

fountain, a snake who had multiple heads, each one with a gilded crest.[7] This is the same serpent who still prevents many people from joining this special group. You who are now passing by here, you see the fountain pouring out the gushing water; but even if you cannot be part of this noble school,[8] at least you will dip your bucket into the streams; and you will bathe there when you want to, no matter who might object. Now I have instructed you concerning the truth of this beautiful place, and of the enclosure of the Fountain of Learning where one learns astrology, and where philosophy lives. (1,075–93)

"Formerly this was the habitation of Pallas,[9] and I think she is still here, for she does not change with the passage of time: it is the same with all forms of learning, which wise men spread throughout the world. Concerning, however, the path which we are now following, I could not recount all its virtues to you even if I had your entire lifetime; but I will tell you its name: know that it is called Long Study. No illiterate is allowed to enter it, and no bumpkins may set foot here: know that I love it for these reasons. It is reserved for those of noble heart and subtle mind." (1,094–108)

I was delighted to hear that Long Study was the name of our route. I then knew very well where we were, for I was already well acquainted with it, even though the Sibyl was pointing it out to me. I had followed it in the past, but I had never gone so high before. Then I began to smile a little, and to say to myself: "Am I mad? By St. Mary! I am like a cow from Barbary who does not recognize her own calves!" I had formerly seen these splendid places, without, however, being so attracted to them; on the contrary, I used to consider them of little value. (1,109–24)

In any case, I had never learned the name of this pleasant route, except in so far as I remember that Dante of Florence records it in the book he composed in such a beautiful style.[1] When he had entered the wild wood, and was completely overcome by fear, at the moment when Virgil appeared to help him, Dante exclaimed with great enthusiasm: "May the long study that has made me pour over your volumes, through which we first came to know each other, now avail me."[2] At that point I knew that with these words, neither silly nor frivolous, the valiant poet Dante, whose taste for learning was fierce, had embarked upon this path when he encountered Virgil, who afterward led him into hell, where he saw chains much stronger than iron. I thereupon declared that I would

---

7. See Ovid's *Metamorphoses* 3.29–94 and *Ovide moralisé* 3.1–272.
8. It is important to note that while Christine here excludes herself from full membership in the group of canonical classical poets, Dante represents himself as a member of their "beautiful school."
9. See Ovid's *Metamorphoses* 5.254–68 and *Ovide moralisé* 5.1648–762.
1. This first explicit reference to Dante's *Divine Comedy* makes use of his words to describe what Virgil had taught him: how to compose in the "beautiful style" (*bello stilo*) (*Inferno* 1.87).
2. Christine here translates directly into French Dante's appeal to Virgil for help in *Inferno* 1.83–84. The title of Christine's book is thus shown to be derived from Dante's model text.

not forget this phrase, but would use it instead of the Gospel or the sign of the Cross when I encountered various dangers and perils. In my opinion, it served me well in such cases. But I had reflected too much on what I am now in the process of recounting. (1,125–54)

I joyously answered the Sibyl: "Oh, gracious companion, highly learned lady, you who have instructed me and who led me into a place where there is neither evil nor heresy, you have done me a great favor by taking me to Long Study, for I am fated to practice it for my entire life; I will never desire to leave this path which leads me to all that is comforting. I do not wish any other perfection, this path constitutes my entire desire in this world; from my perspective there is nothing more delightful." (1,155–70)

In this way we continued our journey, and I was so absorbed in our conversation that a full day seemed to me to be no more than an hour: I paid no attention to the passage of time, and I continued on this fore-shortened road without impediment or problem or obstruction, without having to wake up too early, with nothing to reproach myself for, so that I suddenly found myself overseas, without having taken a ship or a boat, without having been uncomfortably lodged. I was thus astonished to discover where I was, and my guide, seeing that I was a little disoriented, said to me: "Daughter, do not be afraid; rest assured that I will lead you on the right way, and that I will show you many notable places which you will be delighted to see, and whose memory will provide you with joy for your entire life." (1,171–90)

Thus the Sibyl reassured me as we continued our journey, until we unproblematically arrived at the great and noble city called Constantinople, which was formerly the capital of Greece. We then entered the city, since the Sibyl wanted to show me all the marvelous things therein, which have been described in many places. I saw the marble city walls, high, strong, and of great extent, many impressive palaces, many houses with marble walls, many grand and beautiful buildings, many high pillars and many private little rooms very subtly decorated, many lovely and strange images—I assure you that they were extraordinary—and the church of the Hagia Sophia, remarkably big, and containing many marvels. I took great pleasure in visiting everything at my leisure, for it seemed to be a monument constructed by powerful and wise people. I thus praised the ancients who had sufficient talent to make such impressive work, while I lamented the bad state of the ruins of this city, where there had formerly been more than a thousand places with high walls which had tumbled to the ground because of misfortune and the long wars which the inhabitants have always had with the Saracens, who lived much too close to them. Because of this the city, formerly full of treasure and people, is now depopulated. I saw all of the fields and the vineyards within Constantinople, which provide sufficient produce for the city to be governed. The lady who accompanied me showed me all of these things. (1,191–234)

After having left this city, we traveled upward as we approached the Holy Land, but before arriving there I saw many marvels. When we reached it I was overjoyed: I wanted to visit the glorious city of Jerusalem as quickly as I could, in order to see its holy places. When the lady who was leading me heard my heartfelt desire and saw my devotion, she directed us in the right direction and showed me all the places where Jesus had been, either alive or dead. In Egypt I saw all the places where Our Lord had stayed; I saw Nazareth where he arrived from Bethlehem, his birthplace. We passed through all these places: where he was born, where he was led during the holy time of His Passion. I spent the most time observing and visiting Jerusalem, more time than in any other place on my journey. I saw the Holy Sepulcher, kissed it, and rested there a while. After I had made my oblations and said my prayers, I observed its semicircular form and measured its height and width: I still have these measurements. (1,235–68)

Having accomplished these things, we departed and climbed the Mount of Calvary where Jesus climbed with the Cross. There I saw Golgotha, where God's Holy Cross was placed. I carefully observed the place, the space, and the layout; then we descended for we had to travel elsewhere. I saw many marvelous things in Judea, as I had in Jerusalem, which I will be silent about because normally people go there as pilgrims, and this route is sufficiently well known. We left Judea and continued our journey, always heading east; but first the wise Sibyl showed me more than a thousand marvelous things, every one of which she wanted to explain to me without delay. (1,269–89)

I saw the castle of the island of Tenedos where the sea (called St. George's arm) strikes the land with great force. I saw the famous expanse of territory that used to be called Phrygia. Then she who wanted to show me everything that lay on our path said to me: "Look! There stood Troy, the city of such great renown; now all you can see are ruins, though you can still make out where the city walls (high, long, and sturdy) ran along the seacoast." (1,290–1,300)

We passed the island of Rhodes where we found many marvels, though we scarcely stopped there. We continued straight to the elevated place I desired to see, where the virgin St. Catherine is honored and adored.[3] My devotion to her cult motivated me, and for this reason the Sibyl took me there. And then she showed me, continuing on our way, the great city of Babylon.[4] Because there are so many widely dissemi-

---

3. The Monastery of St. Catherine on the slopes of Mount Sinai. See Willard, *Christine de Pizan*, 103; and Paget Toynbee, "Christine de Pizan and Sir John Maundeville," *Romania* 21 (1892), 228–39.
4. This appears to be a reference to what the Middle Ages called the "Egyptian Babylon," i.e., Cairo.

nated stories about it, she wanted me to pass through it to see the land of the Sultan, who does so much harm to Christians. Afterward I saw the city of Cairo that is larger than any four other cities; I saw the Nile that rose and fell; I saw the plain where balm grows; I saw how Babylon is well situated in a lovely area that suits it well. Above the Gion River I looked out over the entire region, including the court of that emperor whose great power horrifies us,[5] even though it is said that his war with Tamerlane will destroy him. (1,301–30)

Having seen all of this we left Babylon behind and entered the Arabian desert where we reached Mount Sinai in less than the twelve days it normally takes to get there. Even though no one can journey there without loading his provisions onto camels, we made the trip without hunger or thirst, and without carrying any money with us: it was not a difficult passage for us. And we ascended the mountain where there is a very beautiful cloistered abbey, which is not overrun with snakes or other harmful creatures. We arrived there without problems, and I said my prayers in the abbey's church, as was fitting. There are many lamps and candles there; and I kissed the head of the Virgin, and I was given, by the abbot himself, the oil which comes from her precious bones. (1,331–52)

After having done all of this, we descended the mount and turned toward the east, as it pleased she who led me; for she wanted to take me there before our voyage ended. We thus traversed many diverse countries, entering them and leaving them, but no matter how marvelous they were, they never posed any danger to me, because of the guide who led me. And she continually taught me the names of the places through which I passed, and explained to me everything I wanted to know. I am obliged, however, to give only an abridged account of what I saw; it would be boring if I were to recount everything that I saw, and, in any case, this is not my intention: many others have spoken at length about these places; I do not seek to make a new book on this subject. (1,353–72)

After a short voyage we passed through the entire territory of the Sultan, and found ourselves crossing that of the Grand Khan, where we feared but little the different kinds of serpents, spitting horrible and dangerous fire, crocodiles, dragons, and vipers, bears and rabid lions, unicorns, elephants, panthers, and more than ten thousand pairs of such strange, fierce beasts. And they would have very quickly devoured me if I had stayed among them without the guide who was leading me; but right away I remembered the good phrase that is effective in such a case, for when I was in a tight spot which would have been difficult to get out

---

5. The Turkish Sultan Bayazid I Yilderim ("the lightning"), who crushed the French- and Burgundian-led Crusaders at the key battle of Nicopolis in 1396 and who was in turn defeated by Tamerlane in 1402.

of, I escaped safely and without hindrance by saying "May long study avail me!" (1,373–94)

In spite of the harshness of the land and the great heat of the sun, we traversed Tartary and the great land of Syria and the rich island of Cathy, where I saw (but did not buy) much silk, gold, silver, spices, and all the things that bring good fortune. In Arabia I saw the Phoenix, the only bird who after dying of fire enables another to rise out of its ashes. Then, continually traveling east, we entered Greater India where I saw the many different kinds of pepper vines. We encountered many strange peoples and passed through many different places where I observed diverse, deformed monsters, multiple legal systems, and varied customs. And we saw in many of the places that we visited horribly big giants, pygmies, and frighteningly ugly people; many strange islands, diverse countries, diverse cities. I saw the Fortunate Isles where the country abounds in all the good things that one can buy in the world. I was in the kingdom of Brahmania,[6] where the people are good by nature, and do not commit sins or crimes. In all of my travels I did not see anything as great as this. (1,395–428)

I saw the four rivers that flow from the Earthly Paradise and keep an enormous territory fertile: the noble river of Phison flows through India; in it are found genuine precious stones throughout its length; then there is the Gion, which flows through Ethiopia, Egypt, Greater and Lesser Armenia; the Tigris does not irrigate any less territory, for it flows through Persia; nor does the Euphrates possess less: it flows through Armenia, Persia, and Media; its waters were shown to me along with its many diverse lakes, its many wondrous springs, many dangerous valleys, and many mountains so high and forbidding that we thought they reached to the sky, until we had actually crossed them. Because of its great height, my mistress wanted to show me Mount Olympus, at the entrance to Macedonia, which is encircled by many other mountains. And without my becoming tired, we traveled through the great Atlas mountain in Ethiopia, a mountain whose summit is so high that certain poets have maintained that it supported the sky. We went through the great mountains of Armenia where the well-stocked ark of Noah stopped after the flood. I was also on Mount Souffin the site of a well-constructed city where the prophet Samuel was born. I saw the mountains of Caspia where Gog and Magog are well enclosed: they will come forth at the arrival of the Antichrist,[7] against the law of Christ. (1,429–70)

I saw great mountains of gold and silver, where few people enter because they are guarded by serpents who would be very hard on travelers there: it is much better to keep one's distance from them. In a beautiful church in India I saw the body of St. Thomas; then I traversed the

---

6. Appears to designate south India, with the Brahmins as the ruling class. See Toynbee, "Christine de Pizan," 234–35.
7. See 1 John 2:18–22, 4:3 and 2 John 1:7. "Gog and Magog": see Revelation 20:8.

frontier province that Prester John[8] rules, where there are so many marvels that no one has ever seen any to match them, unless he went there.
The gold and silver and goods, the precious stones and the riches, the
marvels, the valuable objects that are there, all this I saw in great profu-
sion piled up in the rooms of the royal palaces: there is no similar treasure in the world. To summarize: I saw so many wondrous things there
that one hundred years would not be sufficient to recount them all, if I
lived that long. And if anyone does not believe me, let him go see it on
the route that I did, which I completed without weariness. (1,471–96)

Do not think that on this delectable route I became lazy in regard to
learning much and to thinking, for the Sibyl made me learn the natures
of all the plants, and as we walked she described to me the natures of
all living creatures and all nonrational beasts. There is nothing that
rational man can conceptualize or understand that she did not take the
trouble to teach me, and she named the properties of all that she
described for me. We continued to talk in this way as we approached
the east. We had already traveled so far, through great and wide regions,
through frighteningly narrow places, marvelous and incredible, that I
was able to see with my naked eye the trees of the moon and of the sun[9]
that spoke to Alexander when he and his men went there, and they
replied to his question. I, however, did not ask them anything but rather
maintained such great reserve that I did not deign to worship them, for
one should not give the honor of worship to anything except God alone.
The Sibyl spoke to me at length about them and their location, but she
never thought less of me for my having refused to worship them. (1,497–
531)

Thus we did not remain there, but rather we departed, we left the
trees, and continued until we reached the Pillars of Hercules,[1] that he
had placed there in order to show that it was the end of the world. Then
we turned a little to the right, in the direction of the Earthly Paradise;
and we went so far that before our journey was over we could hear the
noise of the waters that roar at the foot of the mountains that surrounded
the place. And then my mistress began to speak and said: "We are not
allowed, fair daughter, to go any farther; to approach closer would cost
us dearly. Let us rather climb this mountain, my friend, and you will
see (with God's help) what I have promised you. This water that is here
audible is so harsh on the hearing that the people of this country are
deaf by nature, I assure you truthfully. Just as the Ethiopians are colored
black because of the heat in their country, so these people here are deaf
as posts because they live close to such noise. The Earthly Paradise is

8. Legendary Christian ruler of parts of India.
9. It is interesting to note that Mandeville explicitly states that he was unable to see these trees.
   See Toynbee, "Christine de Pizan," 237.
1. Gibraltar and Jebel Musa, the points of land on either side of the Straight of Gibraltar. For the
   Middle Ages, this boundary between the Mediterranean and the Atlantic represented the frontier of the known world.

enclosed there, guarded by a wall of fire; we will not go in, for an angel
guards the entrance. Rather, we must go far away from it, and climb up
this mountain, and there make our way to a less savage place." (1,532–
68)

How the Sibyl Led Christine to the Heavens

Straightaway we climbed to a high place, and, having arrived there,
we rested for a moment; I (somewhat frightened by this turn of events)
considered very carefully what the Sibyl wanted to do. She bent down
a little, then cried out with a very loud voice, but I do not know what
name she pronounced, for she called out in the Greek language.
She was apparently heard for quite soon a strange figure—but not at
all an ugly one—issued from the sky. It asked what the Sibyl wanted,
she who had called for it in an unusually loud voice. And the Sibyl
replied: "Listen, and then tell me if we can mount on high, for this
young lady who is a student in our subtle school would like to spend
a little time up there; and if it seems to you that she can ascend as
she desires, make for her an appropriate ladder to go there, a ladder
reasonably proportioned to what you can see to be her body weight."
(1,569–95)

We did not wait there a very long time before we saw projecting out
of the firmament the tip of a long ladder, which quickly extended to the
ground. I looked closely at the ladder, marveling at its workmanship, for
it seemed to me to be very subtly made. It was light and portable, so
that whoever wanted to could fold it up and carry it anywhere with no
difficulty, no problems, no damage. It was not made of rope, nor of any
other kind of twine, nor of wood; I was not familiar with the material,
but the ladder was long, strong, and light. After I had examined it, I
could not restrain myself from asking, before we proceeded any farther,
about the mystery of this ladder; for I had not learned how to keep silent
with my guide, when any kind of doubt or question occurred to me.
And so I asked her to tell me, to make me understand, what she had
called forth that had been hidden in the sky, where this long and beautiful ladder came from, and what it was called. (1,596–625)

She thereupon answered me as follows: "Beloved daughter, I have no
wish to avoid teaching you anything that can be useful to you, and I
very much want you to understand this matter so that you can climb on
high. Know that when I spoke so loudly just now, I was calling out in
Greek to him who comes to me when he hears my summons; and the
word I spoke has a meaning equivalent to 'imagination.' This is what
transported the ladder down here, this is what inspired us to want to
acquire that which we will have to search for above. The material out
of which this ladder that ascends to the heavens is made is called 'specu-

lation,' beloved by all subtle intelligences. You will be more worthy if
you climb it. And there is not one step from heaven down to earth
which does not contain a singular mystery. I also want you to know (in
order for you to avoid ignorance) that this same material, according to
the degree to which one loves subtlety, is used to make many ladders
that are climbed in noble enterprises. These ladders are not, however,
all the same: some are lighter and more subtly made, others are more
crude and less perfect. The former are given to people of subtlety, and
constructed for those who wish to attain the heights. The length of these
ladders is proportional to the motivation of the people. But you have
already advanced far by God's grace and your own powers, for you have
the authorization to ascend to the heavens. By this ladder you will go to
no higher place than the firmament. (1,626–69)

"The route that we first took will not lead you there, but this one will,
my friend. You must ascend to the firmament, although others may
ascend higher. You, however, do not have the stamina required for a
higher ascent. I realize that this is not your fault, but your lack of sufficient intellectual power results from the fact that you were a latecomer
to my school. Now, daughter, take hold of this ladder; I will go first and
will lead you well. Climb up now, you have sufficient strength; and try
to understand the beautiful things that you will see, for you will go to a
country that is new to you." (1,670–86)

Then, in order to climb to the heavens I crossed myself with my right
hand, for the journey seemed to me strange and very dangerous; I was,
however, eager to see everything. With the Sibyl leading and me following, step by step we climbed into the heavens so high that when I looked
down it seemed to me (I assure you) that I saw the entire earth as a little
sphere, as round as a ball.[2] It frightened me to find myself in so terrifying a place, and I felt such an intense heat that I was afraid I would die
of the pain; and the air was so hot that I feared devils would carry me
off.[3] I then spoke fearfully, saying: "Blessed lady, you who have led me
as far as this, I feel that I am being cooked in this great heat. For the
love of God, consider my weakness, because my heart is beginning to
fail me. Lady, you who have taken charge of me, I know that you are
not worried about perishing here, for you do not have a perishable body,
but it is impossible for me with my all-too-material body.[4] For the love
of God, let us descend now, and let no shame be imputed to me for
having abandoned a perilous ascent. Consider my weakness and the

2. The notion that the earth was a sphere goes back to the ancient Greeks. This passage recalls
Dante's two earthward glances during his trip through the heavens. See especially *Paradiso*
22.134–35 and 27.77–87. For the Middle Ages, the single most important instance of a heavenly traveler looking back toward earth was Cicero's *Scipio's Dream*, read along with Macrobius's famous *Commentary*.
3. Cf. Dante's encounter with the sphere of fire at the end of the first Purgatorial dream, *Purgatorio* 9.30–33.
4. Cf. Dante's passage through the wall of fire that separates the seventh Purgatorial terrace from
the Earthly Paradise, in *Purgatorio* 27.16–60.

heat that is already hurting me, and please do not let me suffer so much that I become like Icarus, who fell because he had climbed too high. It went very badly for him when he flew so high that the wax with which his father had constructed his wings melted. Thus he paid very dearly for his presumption, for he perished in the sea, with bitter suffering."[5] (1,687–732)

The Sibyl answered me as follows: "I certainly understand how and for what reason all things derive their qualities from their nature. It is thus right for the feminine sex always to be fearful and afraid. Thus my words and the things that I show you please you so little that only with a great effort do you believe me. You will not fall like Icarus, for you do not wear wings attached with fragile wax: do not be afraid that you will fall. It is not presumption that leads you into this exalted region, rather it is your great desire to see beautiful things that impels you. Continue your voyage confidently and without fear, for I will guide you carefully, and I will take you back to earth." (1,733–52)

Thus was I reassured by the Sibyl more than a thousand times both here and elsewhere. And my body became more skillful and capable in ascending higher, in spite of the horrible heat. (1,753–58)

We thus continued to ascend without stopping until we had traversed the first heaven, which is that of air. Then we arrived at the one adjacent to the heaven of fire: it takes its illumination from this latter because they are contiguous, and the great light which issues from this second heaven shines very brightly. It is called the heaven of ether. Directly above it is the third heaven, that of fire. Keeping to the same route, we then climbed to the fourth heaven, whose great beauty we remarked on: it is called Olympus. We then continued traveling until we reached the fifth heaven which is beautiful, clear, shining and most exalted: this is the firmament. And this was where our ladder abruptly stopped, the ladder that was not made of rope or of anything that can unravel. (1,759–80)

The Beautiful Things That Christine Saw in the Firmament under the Guidance of the Sibyl

When I saw myself in this exalted place, I thanked God with all my heart, and felt an appropriately great joy, for I had never before seen such beauty. But my body, my limbs, my eyes would never have been able to bear the great shining brightness of this place which hurt my eyes, or its intense light which would have blinded me when I looked

---

5. Cf. Dante's fearful self-comparison to Icarus (and Phaeton) during his flight on Gerione's back in *Inferno* 17.106–14. See Ovid's *Metamorphoses* 8.183–235 and *Ovide moralisé* 8.1579–708.

into it, had it not been for the supplementary force that came from my guide to invigorate my body. But because of her I had sufficient force and power, and I was so determined to see that the great heat and light of the sun hurt neither my body nor my eyes. My worries disappeared when I saw myself in this beautiful, celestial world, so clear and pure, where all beauty was revealed and so many marvels represented. I had to thank the one who had guided me here, and so I did, as she had taught me well. I was so desirous to know, to understand, and to perceive all the aspects of this heaven that I would have liked, if it were possible, for all my bodily parts to be transformed into eyes, in order better to observe the beautiful things that I could see, that God had arranged there according to a hierarchized order. (1,781–814)

I was then inspired to observe the beautiful houses of the planets, and how they are divided into seven areas—no one has ever seen such delightful arrangements. Indeed, I then looked and saw the stars in the firmament; I saw how they were ordered, and how they moved across the heavens. And she who guided me showed me everything, explaining the names and the powers of each planet, trying hard to instruct me concerning the movements of the wandering and the positions of the fixed stars. She thus told me of their properties, the effects they produce, their oppositions, their powers, their influences, and their varied groupings. She explained to me the nature of each planet, and the movements and eclipses of the sun and the moon, and how the sun ascends across the celestial orbits and travels annually through the twelve signs of the zodiac, and across the sky every day and night, without ever stopping. The Sibyl taught and explained everything to me, but I do not think that I should speak about all that she described, because it is not appropriate that I associate myself with this kind of knowledge: I did not learn the science of astrology at school. Although I may be reproached for this lack, I can, on the other hand, recount my general impressions of what I saw. (1,815–52)

I can certainly tell how I observed the stars, one after the other, in their stable orbits in the firmament, where they were placed, one higher, one lower, in perfectly proportioned relations. I saw how the sovereign Father has ordered the sphere of the sky, which turns continually and regularly on its oblique axis situated between the two poles; and how with its rotating movement, it carries the stars, which are fixed in it, around in their orbits. From east to west it turns them, not by chance, but according to natural law, and then, it turns them back in the opposite direction, from west to east, without impediments; so that within the space of twenty-four hours they pass from one end of the sky to the other, and back again. Then I saw how the beautifully and faultlessly ordered planets move in their orbits in such a way as to slow down the movement of the celestial firmament. God made them like this so that the sky would move more quickly without disturbing the movements of the planets. (1,853–84)

Then I saw the two hemispheres of the sky, which cannot be seen together at the same time from down on earth. I saw the routes of each one's zodiacal signs, and I saw the five circles, equidistant from one another. I saw how each one begins, starting out in a fixed pattern at the north pole, and how each turns in the same way an eternally rotating wheel would; then each one moves back in the other direction to its initial starting point, once it has made a complete circuit. Then I saw in this splendidly beautiful place the circle called "austral" which is the horizon. I saw the great, wide central circle which delimits that part of the zodiac where the sun is located, equidistant between east and west. (1,885–909)

I did not waste my time at this point, since I then saw the extremely beautiful circle that, with its shining whiteness, lords it over all the others. The poets described it in their works as the way which the gods used to travel. It is called the Galaxy: it is grand and beautiful and wide. Many have called it the Milky Way because of its whiteness. From earth its traces are visible at night when the sky is cloudless and the weather fine. I saw how it starts out in the east, following over the length of the sky a path marked out by certain constellations. It reaches its limit in the north, then turns back on its tracks, thus delimiting its bright borders. I saw the twelve signs of the zodiac following their orbits in the distant skies, in two pairs of six they are set in the four parts of the sky. (1,910–32)

I saw how these signs are the houses for the planets, and how the orbits of these latter, perfectly round, are fixed in a hierarchy according to an unchangeable order. There she who had taught me the true path revealed to me, with her great wisdom, the entire mystery of the planets; and she taught me how the height of each one's orbit was determined by its motion. I tried very hard to understand, for I greatly desired to learn. But I have not undertaken to recount everything that I learned there about these things; for this would not be in accord with my project to recount what I have in mind. I saw the sun move and then repeat its beautifully ordered movement; I saw it continually follow its path, in order to illuminate the sky and the earth. I saw its chariot and its light, which seemed to me to be extremely beautiful. I saw all the movements around it, and how they elegantly divide time into years and months and weeks, days and hours, and lunar cycles. For I saw that the circle of the moon is lower and is so configured that it receives light exclusively from the sun, when it lights up the moon with its eye. (1,933–64)

In front of the sun I saw the four movements, which the poets, to amuse themselves, called the four beloved horses that maintained the chariot of the sun, and whose body and flesh is fire. The first is named

Pirus (which means "fire"); the second is Eos, as white as shining silver; the third is Ethon, gleaming like refined gold; the fourth, Phaeton, red and blazing. The chariot is all covered with finely worked gold, as Ovid describes it,[6] who has written of it very well. (1,965–78)

Thus I observed all of these marvels, and burned with desire to understand, if possible, everything that I saw in this place. I was lost in the contemplation of this beautiful and noble artifact that fulfilled its true function so well, moved by the swift ordering required by such a beautiful, unified composition, completely contained in a delimited space. Linked to the great pleasure which enchanted my eyes, there was my aural pleasure: no one could imagine or describe (even if he spoke unceasingly) the melody and the sweet sound, the harmony and the beautiful singing made by these beautiful celestial movements, by the turning of these bright, well-defined circles which are so well proportioned and ordered that there emerges from them a sweet sound, calm, measured and perfect, so that it constitutes the sovereign music that contains all the perfect chords. Thus I regarded these beautiful celestial bodies; I concentrated all my attention on them; and I praised the Creator who had made them of such perfect beauty, both in goodness and in light. They are there in such great quantity (though this does not impinge upon the space available) that no one can count them; no one knows how many there are, except Him who knows the quantities of all things. And all of them, insofar as they have being, possess very great attributes. (1,979–2,016)

And as I was thus contemplating these celestial objects and patterns, concentrating my entire mind on learning about them, but able to understand their grandeur only inadequately, despite all my intellectual effort, because my mind was too coarse, at that moment the wise Sibyl came to me and said: "Daughter, even if you were to spend a thousand years here, I do not think, my friend, that you would become bored. It is now necessary, however, for us to descend from here, for I want to have you learn about other things. Follow me, come, I am leaving, for you will not be going any higher than this: you are not allowed to advance a single step beyond this heaven; as long as you have your body, these doors will be closed to you. The Crystalline Sphere is up there, and beyond it, above everything, is the highest heaven, wherein abide the saints and the angels who are enclosed in glory, intimately beloved by God, arranged in nine orders. Above them all is the majesty of God, the sovereign power, surrounded by seraphim and cherubim,[7] perfect and beautiful." (2,017–44)

---

6. See Ovid's *Metamorphoses* 2.107–10 and *Ovide moralisé* 2.207–19.
7. The two highest of the nine categories of angels (see Dante, *Paradiso* 28.98–139). It is also important to note that Dante, in contradistinction to Christine, does experience both the Crystalline Sphere and the Empyrean, culminating in his vision of God "face to face." Christine thus seems here to be drawing an important distinction between herself and her Dantean model.

[Christine is led by the Sibyl back down to the First Heaven (Firmament), where most of the ensuing plot events take place. She is shown by the Sibyl an allegorical geography in which Lady Reason sits upon a central throne, surrounded by four chairs upon which are seated Ladies Wealth, Nobility, Chivalry, and Wisdom (2,253–554). Earth comes to petition Reason for help in ending the world's destructive cycle of wars (2,595–702). Reason asks advice of the four seated ladies (2,703–3,072), each of whom presents in abstract terms her candidate for the post of "emperor of the world," who would be able to impose peace and order (3,073–445). At Reason's request, these four allegorical ladies proceed to elaborate arguments in support of their choices, beginning with the first three (3,450–4,068). By far the longest presentation is by Wisdom, who claims to incorporate the virtues of the other three (4,080–6,072). The debate concludes with general agreement that the new world emperor should be chosen at the court of France. We reenter the text as Christine-protagonist witnesses this decision, beginning in line 6,250.]

I heard them reject many different courts, but once they had considered all possibilities, they decided unanimously that they would submit to the judgment of the princes of France, whose court is sovereign, and whose reputation is know throughout the entire world, embodying wisdom, honor, eloquence, generosity, and nobility. Wisdom agreed to this, and so did the others, and Reason as well. Thus they concluded their discussion, but they remained uncertain about how to make their debate known to the French princes, so that they could reconcile the various parties in the argument, by making a just decision. (6,250–69)

And as they were discussing whom to choose as an appropriate messenger, someone wise and well spoken, the Sibyl, my mistress, who had guided me, stepped forward and presented herself to Reason. She was not slow to speak, and said: "Respected Lady, I have listened carefully to the various sides of the present argument, and I come before you to propose someone good and appropriate to be your messenger. If you decide to choose her, you can be certain that she will not fail you. In addition, she fits your needs, for she (who is a handmaiden of our school) lives in France and was taken there when she was very young, although like me she was born in Italy, in a well-beloved city which has armed many a warship."[8] Thus the Sibyl in her goodness was pleased to speak about me, and praised me more than was necessary: she told how I had arrived there in the Firmament, how I had traversed the length and breadth of the entire earth, without becoming tired at all. She told Reason all about me, my behavior, my preferences, my emotions, without concealing anything. (6,270–303)

And when Reason had heard these things, she was very pleased: they made her very happy. And my gracious mistress signaled to me to approach; and I who was never slow in obeying her virtuous desires,

8. I.e., Venice, Christine's birthplace.

stepped forward, eager to hear what was to be requested of me, and to obey, if this court wanted to command me to do anything. When I arrived before Reason, she greeted me as warmly as is allowed for a poor, ignorant person like myself, and I was well satisfied with this. She questioned me in detail, made many inquiries about me, and taught me many wise sayings which will continually improve me, as long as I keep them in mind. Then she said to me: "Christine, dear friend who loves knowledge, you will report our debates, just as you have heard them, down on earth to the great French princes. First, you will greet them on our behalf; then you will tell them for us that we present this debate to them, as to the world's sovereign assembly: they must judge honestly which has the right, the honor, the prerogative and the superlative praise to govern the world. Is it high nobility, or chivalry, or wisdom, or great wealth? And may it please them to judge among these four after they have, to their own satisfaction, made sufficient inquiries to choose rightly; may their choice thus resolve the debate. But who knows how to put all the terms of this debate into writing, to organize everything so well that nothing is left out?" (6,304–46)

I then replied that I had written it all down, everything that I had seen, found, and discovered on my journey, without adding anything mendacious. I had thus not forgotten to write down, word for word, this debate whose unfolding had not at all annoyed me. Reason was quite happy with this, and I, in order to please her even more, took out my transcriptions of the debate. I showed them to her in order to see if there was anything that needed to be cut or revised. But I heard her say, because of her beneficence, that there were no corrections to be made, and that she was quite happy with my text. With that, I wanted to take my leave, but first she gave me some of her jewels, then ordered and commanded me to be diligent in explaining the situation to my noble earthly audience, people who had been elected judges and lawyers. I promised her that I would do this without fail, as soon as I could. Then I thanked her humbly, not just for this single gift, but for her many gifts to me, and I took my leave of her and of this worthy court, to which I sincerely commended myself. (6,347–77)

The Sibyl wanted to lead me back, just as she had promised. We started out upon the route and descended the ladder that I had climbed, which I found still in place. As we traveled I did not stop thanking Lady Sibyl who had revealed more than a thousand pleasures to me. It seemed that I had already descended quite a way, when I was called by the mother who had carried me in her womb, and who knocked on my bedroom door, astonished that I was still asleep, since it was late; and I awakened. (6,378–92)

FROM THE BOOK OF FORTUNE'S TRANSFORMATION

[Christine's *Book of Fortune's Transformation* tells us that the work was finished on November 18, 1403. Copies were presented, early in the following year, to the dukes of Burgundy and Berry, with a third manuscript almost certainly prepared for Charles VI, king of France.[1] By far the longest work that Christine had written to date, the *Transformation* involves an extended presentation of human history as a function of the operation of Fortune, a figure Christine derives from Boethius's *Consolation of Philosophy* and Jean de Meun's *Romance of the Rose*. The work is in seven parts. Parts 2 and 3, and the beginning of part 4, present a detailed "anatomy" of Fortune in allegorical terms; the conclusion of part 4, as well as parts 5, 6, and 7, contain a universal history, from the creation of the world down to the establishment of the Roman Empire, and to Christine's own time. This universal history is preceded in part 1 by a personal history: an allegorical autobiography in miniature, which traces Christine's development into the author of the present book. Of central importance in the story of this progressive discovery and acceptance of her identity as an author is the death of Christine's husband in 1390, and the subsequent transformations in all aspects of the life of the twenty-five-year-old widow. Part 1, translated here in full, gives particular importance to models explicitly provided by Ovid's *Metamorphoses*, for the representation of what is conceived of as nothing less than a gender change in the newly widowed Christine, whose masculinized persona becomes the author of the present book.

Part 2 (verses 1,461–4,272) involves an elaborate description of Fortune's Castle, based, to an important degree, on the analogous description by the character Reason in Jean de Meun's *Romance of the Rose*. In part 3 (4,273–7,052) a description of the inhabitants of Fortune's Castle leads to a philosophical and theological definition of Fortune, which stresses the particularly vulnerable position of women. Part 4 (7,053–8,748; plus 14 prose paragraphs) presents the marvelous central circular hall in Fortune's Castle, into which Christine-protagonist enters and observes the extensive wall paintings[2] that depict, first, the hierarchical relation of Philosophy to the other branches of human learning and, second, the sequential portraits of the periods of human history, starting with Genesis and the history of the Jews. Part 5 (8,749–13,456) recounts how the histories of Assyria, Persia, Greece, and Thebes are depicted on the walls. Part 6 recounts the history of the Amazons, Hercules, and the Trojan War (14,059–8,244). Part 7 begins with the history of Rome from Aeneas to Caesar (18,245–22,058); then recounts the history of Alexander the Great (22,091–3,276),[3] before

---

1. See C. C. Willard, *Christine de Pizan: Her Life and Works* (New York: Persea, 1984), 107.
2. For the importance of this configuration in Christine's self-presentation both as author and as protagonist, see K. Brownlee, "The Image of History in Christine de Pizan's *Livre de la Mutacion de Fortune*," in Daniel Poirion and Nancy Freeman Regalado, eds., "Contexts: Style and Values in Medieval Art and Literature," *Yale French Studies*, special issue (1991), 44–56.
3. The principal source for Christine's historical narrative in parts 4 to 7 is the *Histoire ancienne jusqu'à César* [Ancient history up to Julius Ceasar]. See Suzanne Solente, ed., *Le Livre de la mutacion de Fortune par Christine de Pisan*, vol. 1 (Paris: Picard, 1959–66), lxiii–xcii.

88

turning to contemporary Europe (23,277–594), and ending with the author's conclusion in the present of the time of writing (23,595–636), with which the selection printed here concludes.

Translated by Kevin Brownlee from Suzanne Solente, ed., *Le Livre de la mutacion de Fortune par Christine de Pisan*, 4 vols. (Paris: Picard, 1959–66). Part 1 is found in vol. 1, 7–55; the conclusion of the contemporary history sequence, followed by the author's epilogue, are found in vol. 4, 78–80.]

1.1 Here Begins the Book of Fortune's Transformation

How will it be possible for me, being simple and of small intelligence, to express adequately that which cannot be well expressed or well understood? No, no matter now much learning a man might have, he could not fully describe what I would wish to write. There is such great variety in the particular adversities, and so many different aspects of the heavy burdens that the changeable influence of deceitful Fortune effects, through the action of her great turning which is truly unfathomable. Thus I am necessarily inadequate to undertake such a great work as the description of the dark operations of her trickery. It would be difficult for me to speak properly now of these things, with the small understanding that I possess, when the many great men who have written about them have failed to record all that can be said about Fortune; but I will nevertheless not give up. Fortune has served me so many of her dishes that I have sufficient knowledge to speak about her. Thus I will not be silent about the good or the bad things I have to say, I will tell all that there is to tell about what I understood of her activities when I learned of her tricks through diverse experiences which happened to me because of her, through which my mind became much more subtle than it had been in the past; if these things had not happened to me, I would not have known, nor perceived so much about her activity. For this reason, it is well said that misfortune is sometimes good for something, for it teaches at the same time that it hurts. Thus I do not think I am speaking foolishness to the person who is able, with an open mind, to understand the true goal toward which I wish to strive. (1–50)

1.2 Here the Person Who Wrote This Book Tells How She Served Fortune, as She Will Explain

Now I want to recount an adventure which will perhaps seem unbelievable to many; but, although some may not believe it, it is nevertheless tested truth, perceived and experienced by me, to whom it happened. I was about twenty-five years old; what happened to me was not a dream, and I will recount, without lying, a great marvel which should, however, surprise no one, for Fortune who disguises everything, and creates or destroys at her pleasure, brought about the entire transformation which I will describe here. And, since it was brought about by her, no one should marvel at it, for, although she knows how to deceive, everyone can clearly see that she has the power to rule whatever happens in the world. Although she is vain and impure, she holds the entire world in her hand, insofar as impermanent things are concerned. She can bestow losses and victories, honor, possessions, or the opposite; and she can unexpectedly accomplish things which seemed impossible, and eliminate what had seemed probable. She often brings chains of events to contradictory conclusions, and, what is even more marvelous, she can transform unexpectedly the shapes of bodies. The changes she effects are seen everywhere. She has infinite power over everything that exists in finite time. (51–88)

Thus I will recount how I saw Fortune (who is different for each person) clearly visible to the eye, although she is invisible, and how I lived with her and suffered many disasters, for she is a great, crowned queen, and more feared than any other thing alive. Thus she has a great and very powerful court, inhabited by people of great variety; and, if one wishes to, one can learn much there, and take the good as well as the bad. One becomes wise through learning well and one advances by serving: Scripture says that to serve is to rule by paying attention to serving God;[1] the person who serves well deserves praise and honor, and by serving one becomes a master. Thus it is good to serve if it happens that through serving well one can merit praise and a good reward, or a good friend, male or female; but with me it did not at all turn out this way. I do not know if I made a mistake in serving, for I have received very little praise for it. Rather I had from it a variety of sufferings and many difficult weeks, painful and troublesome work, without at all bettering my lot. But I suspect that it is possible that the defect lies in the master, for he who serves a good master acquires good wages. (89–122)

Now I will tell how, through the efforts of my closest relations, I was placed in Fortune's court, where I stayed for a long time. And I intend to tell you where her strangely constructed domicile is located, to describe its imperfect ways and activities, just as I saw them for as long as I was at her court, where many adventures occur; what I learned there; what happened to me there; and how Fortune remembered me when it pleased her to help me quickly in my great need; and the kind of help she gave me, which was scarcely sufficient. (123–38)

But in order better to enable you to understand the goal of my project, I will tell you who I am, I who am speaking, I who was transformed

---

1. Psalm 101:23 Vulgate.

from a woman into a man by Fortune who wanted it that way. Thus she transformed me, my body and my face, completely into those of a natural man. And I who was formerly a woman, am now in fact a man (I am not lying, as my story will amply demonstrate), and, if I was formerly a woman, my current self-description is the truth. But I shall describe by means of fiction the fact of my transformation, how from being a woman I became a man, and I want people to name this poem, once the story becomes known, *Fortune's Transformation*. (139–56)

1.3 Here the Author Tells Who Her Father Was and What Sort of Wealth He Possessed

A person who desires to be known well must first of all say what nation he is from and what his extraction is, who his parents are or were, whether he is poor or well provided for, if he is worthy of renown, and then he must give his name; and it is thus appropriate that I recount all of this:

I was born near Lombardy, in a city of great renown—many pilgrims know its name![2] It was founded long ago by the Trojans; it is well and nobly situated. I was the child of a noble and renowned man, who was known as a philosopher; he was rich and had great learning, and his possessions were marvelous![3] Many have heard tell of this since he did not try to hide his treasure, for such possessions are worthy of praise; his treasure had such a power that I affirm that all the thieves ever born could never succeed in stealing a bit of it from him. He never had to worry, fear or tremble, nor be afraid that anyone would steal his treasure, as happens to many rich men who are killed and murdered for their wealth. Many die because of their wealth; it would be much better for them to have less! But my father's wealth, which I am now telling you about, is worthy of being deeply cherished, for one is never troubled by it, and it cannot be stolen by anyone. Furthermore, there is another positive attribute of this wealth (I guarantee this to you), for whoever has much of it, if he gives away piles of it continuously, the more he gives away, the more remains with him. There is thus no need for avarice resulting from the fear of having lost the treasure, for it is a streaming fountain: the more it pours forth, the more comes out of it; and, in addition, this treasure is of such a nature that no one who is rich with it will ever find that it fails him; no matter what misfortune befalls him, whether he is traveling forth or coming home, nothing can impoverish him: he can open his treasure anywhere. (157–210)

2. I.e., Venice.
3. For more on Christine's father, Thomas de Pizan, see p. xi.

1.4 Here She Tells of the Precious Stones Which She Had from Her Father

With such a treasure was my father rich; he possessed many precious stones, very noble and very powerful, stones that he had taken (and which he long kept) from the fountain on Mount Parnassus, created by a blow from Pegasus's foot, where the nine Muses[4] make merry, they who instruct many a worthy student. My father worked at the fountain so diligently that he earned the treasure that I have mentioned and which is worth more than a county, and he earned many other valuable things which are there in abundance. And among the rich treasures which my father had in his treasury there were two precious stones of great value,[5] which I highly prize; they are without a doubt worth more than any carbuncle or valuable ruby; and one of these stones had so much power that no king or emperor, since the time of King Arthur, has had one of more value. It shone with a noble brightness and gave more light than a candle; its color made it seem like a star. It was beautiful and captivating, and extremely valuable, but it was very difficult to find. The stone was scarcely possible to locate in the fountain, but if someone searched the fountain with great diligence, one of the Muses would give him instructions that would indicate its place to him, and he deserved much praise for this. And do you know what this stone can do? He who keeps it carefully and does not lose it, who always carries it with him, receives such knowledge that he can foretell future events. The stone gives celestial powers to him who has rightfully found it (this is no mere fiction) and enables him to climb to the stars and to the celestial regions. My father, who knew all its powers, most certainly had this stone, and he used it so well that he was often able to advise the great princes who rule the earth about the future occurrence of either lasting peace or great war, of winds or of torrential rains, of death, of famine; or what the weather would be. Whenever he thought it necessary, he was able, through this stone, to inhabit the sky, where the planets rotate. Thus he knew how they return on their orbits with the signs of the zodiac behind them; and he knew perfectly the power and the light of each one, and how much higher one was than another. And he knew all about the courses of the stars; he knew all of their names. This made him so famous that everyone truly believed that he inhabited the firmament, and because of this he was honored and valued, God be praised! Among the princes he was welcomed, loved, and valued because of the power of this stone, which was worth more than gold, by St. Peter! (211–88)

---

4. For more on Mount Parnassus and the nine Muses, see n. 8, p. 72.
5. They represent Thomas de Pizan's mastery of, respectively, astrology and medicine.

More on This Same Topic

As I said to you just now, my father had in his treasury another stone, valuable and more fine than refined gold ever was, no other stone was worth as much as it. This stone was of great value to many people and saved their lives. Everyone should strongly desire to acquire such a stone, but many people fear to search for it. This stone cures all illnesses, it even makes crazy people who are bound hand and foot become sane; it cures them completely; he who knows how to use it correctly without abusing its powers, can cure every other disease. I do not know what else to tell you about it, for there is no leper no matter how putrid who cannot be cured by this stone in the hands of a person who knows its properties well and uses it correctly; there is no painful gout no matter how stubborn, or any other illness that cannot be cured by the stone. He who knows how to utilize the powers of the stone, without making any mistakes, could just about revive the dead. My father had found this stone and had used it many times, with the result that many whom Death had almost taken escaped its clutches. What more can I tell you? It would be tiresome to my readers and listeners alike, if I explicitly enumerated all the powers of the jewels that my virtuous father had; and I do not say this to praise him but in order to speak the truth without dissembling: he found them all in the deep, clear and very exalted fountain. I do not know why I should name any more of them; rather, I will summarize: he was so rich with this treasure that he would not have given two loaves of bread for all the wealth of Octavius Caesar; he valued more the knowledge of Galen[6] which he possessed; he had no desire for other riches. (289–338)

1.5 Here Her Mother Is Described

My mother who was great and grand and more valorous than Penthesilea[7] (God had made her well!), surpassed my father in knowledge, power, and value, despite the fact that he had learned so much. She was a crowned queen from the moment that she was born. Everyone knows of her power and strength. It is clear that she is never idle, and, without being overbearing, she is always occupied with many, diverse tasks: her impressive works are found everywhere; every day she creates many beautiful ones. Whoever wanted to count all that she has done and continues to do would never finish. She is old without being aged, and her life cannot end before Judgment Day. God gave her the task of

6. Famous Greek doctor and writer on medical topics (c. 130–c. 200); his authority in medicine was without peer during the Middle Ages. Octavius Caesar (63 B.C.–A.D. 14), the first Roman emperor who ruled under the name of Augustus.
7. Amazon warrior queen who came to Troy to avenge Hector's death.

maintaining and increasing the world as He had made it, in order to sustain human life: she is called Lady Nature.[8] She is the mother of every person: God thus calls us all brothers and sisters. (339–68)

Now that I have told you clearly who my very illustrious parents are, I will tell you what my name is, whether you want me to or not. Even though my name is not well known, in order for me to be correctly named, just add the letters I, N, E to the name of the most perfect man who ever lived; no other letter is necessary.[9] (369–78)

1.6 Here It Is Told How She Gathered Nothing but Scraps from Her Father's Treasure

My father, whom I have already mentioned here, very strongly desired and wished for a male child who could be his heir and inherit his riches, which do not decrease no matter how generously dispersed, as I well remember him saying. He and my mother together conceived me with this hope, but he failed in his intention, for my mother, who had much more power than he, wanted to have for herself a female child resembling her, thus I was in fact born a girl; but my mother did so much for him that I fully resembled my father in all things, only excepting my gender: in manner, body, face, we so resembled each other that you would have thought that we had them in common. Thus I was called daughter and well cared for and well loved by my joyful mother who loved me so much and held me so dear that she nursed me herself as soon as she gave birth to me, and she treated me tenderly during my childhood, and because of her I grew bigger. At that time she had no other concern than that I play normally with children my own age, nor was anything else then necessary for me. But because I was born a girl, it was not at all ordained that I should benefit in any way from my father's wealth, and I could not inherit, more because of custom than justice, the possessions that are found in the very worthy fountain. If justice reigned, the female would lose nothing in this regard, nor would the son, but I am entirely certain that custom is stronger than justice in many places, and because of this, I lost through lack of learning any chance of taking this very rich treasure. Thus this custom displeases me, for if it were otherwise, I assume that I would have been extremely rich with the treasure that comes from the fountain. For I was well inclined in this direction, and I still have great desire (which does not date from yesterday) to draw deeply from the fountain. I desire this more than any earthly thing, but my desire is worthless because of the above-mentioned custom, may God curse it! And so I

8. A corrected version of the figure of Lady Nature in Jean de Meun's *Romance of the Rose*.
9. Thus the root of her name is presented as "Christ," to which is added the feminine diminutive "ine." Cf. the links she establishes with St. Christine in the *City of Ladies* 3.10.

am like the ardent and desirous lovers who cannot see or hear that which they wish to enjoy; I resemble them in this, for I desire what I do not have, namely the treasure which great learning gives to those who want to have it, and although I was born female, because of which (as I said above) I could not have it, still I am inclined toward my true condition and to be like my father; I was not able to prevent myself from stealing scraps and flakes, small coins and bits of change, that have fallen from the great wealth that my father had a great amount of. And although I have only a little of it in contrast to my great appetite, I gained nothing except furtively, and I have acquired a poor hoard, as is well evident in my work. What I have of this wealth is still very helpful to me and does me much good, no other wealth can be said to be truly mine, for no matter what treacherous Fortune has caused me to lose, this at least has remained with me, and will not fail me until I die. (379–468)

1.7 Here Is Told How She Was Put into Fortune's Service

My beautiful mother Nature cared for me until she saw that I had become a big girl, then she wanted to consider carefully my possibilities for advancement, since I had nothing of what can be taken from the treasure of knowledge. In order for me to be able to look after myself, she wanted to place me in the service of a lady of high birth, who was slightly related to her, although they did not look at all like each other, and they were not cut from the same cloth: their faces, their deeds, their morals, their natures were much too dissimilar. Although this lady is of foreign origin, she is an exalted and powerful queen; she is named Lady Fortune, and she has warped many a cloth for many people, so tightly that they could not weave it themselves, nor could they escape from it. My mother at that time placed me at Fortune's court. Lady Fortune was not changeable or cruel toward me, but rather she received me well as soon as she saw me. So I was placed with my Lady Fortune, but I was not so importunate as to request favors quickly from her, for I was concerned with nothing except playing, since I was young, and I did not see or perceive in any way that I was aware of, nor did I understand at all how that court was organized, a court where joy and happiness are of very short duration. Thus, even though there is little joy there, there is no other way to achieve advancement or acquire possessions, except through the operations of Fortune's court, and because of this I was placed there and submitted completely to her will. I was cared for there during my childhood, without receiving reproaches or insults. Then I began to grow up and desired to know how I could please my lady by following her wishes. But my very good and tender mother, who was never harsh with me, did not forget me in my hour of need, rather, she quickly came to visit me and saw clearly that she had to think of my well-being. Since it was time for me to be advanced, or married, or affianced, my gracious, joyful mother wanted to make me pretty, and therefore gave me some of her jewels. There are none, no matter how choice, that can equal those of the above-mentioned fountain, but he who can possess both of them cannot fall short in knowledge. They are very beautiful together, but the ones my mother gave me are, it seems to me, given freely, without being sought after; the fountain's two stones are, on the contrary, only acquired by great effort. (469–534)

1.8 Here Is Described the Crown Her Mother Sent Her

She who had done many good things for me placed upon my head a noble crown of great value; I love and value it more than any other. My mother had it made of pure gold in her goldsmith's workshop; it was rich in fine, precious stones; with such things and even more beautiful ones, my mother, who gave it to me, finished the crown. In my opinion it was very beautifully made, and I should be satisfied with it. However, I do not mean that I would not have desired better, or many more of her possessions, but that I should praise her and thank her for her gifts and favors to me, for it is because of her generosity (as derived from God) that I thank her. The crown, which adorned me, shone with its jewels. Such a crown suits a young girl well, and because of it I became more beautiful, better mannered, and much more considerate, and, in every way more attractive. It would take a long time to count the jewels and recount their wondrous powers, and for this reason I will briefly list the powers of only four of them, no more, and I will name the most important ones, whose shining could be seen from far away, those which made the lesser stones shine. (535–66)

1.9 Here Are Recounted the Properties of the Stones of the Above-Mentioned Crown

The first, set on the front of the crown, makes the wearer reflective, well behaved, temperate, and well spoken, and restrains anger; the wearer will never lose control, and he will surpass all others in goodness. There is truly no duchy or county, or rich kingdom, or empire which is worth as much as this stone; and it is worth more than all the wealth in the world. It is named Discretion. Next to it Consideration was well set right in the middle of the crown. Although it is necessary to possess it also, this stone is not worth as much as the first, and is more common; but a thousand other stones are not worth as much as one of the kind I have named, which is very famous. One cannot put too high a price on it, for it is not too expensive for anyone, since it appears in diverse forms; it is not the same for every person. Discretion, however, is not a friend to everybody; all people do not possess it; but Consideration is worth little without Discretion. A fool may have Consideration alone, but he is the opposite of a wise man who knows well how to extract profit and honor from it; but it seems to me that whoever has both of these stones cannot be treated badly, or fail to attain great riches. Opposite Consideration, and facing it, my mother very carefully set another stone that one cannot praise too highly. No one can sell it or rent it; only my mother can bestow it. (Such a crown with such choice jewels should be well beloved!). This last-mentioned stone, worthy of much praise, gives the power to retain that which one has heard and felt and seen, and all that which the heart has conceived. Thus, its name is Recollection. Never can an overly hasty person rightly possess this stone, so well does it function. There was another stone on the back of the crown; it was very beautiful, and contained much good. This stone enabled one to have a memory of all of the past, whatever one has heard or seen, or heard tell of, or read, whether in science or in history. It is, therefore, called Memory, in which many important things are hidden and often revealed. (No wise man despises it!). It and Recollection were well set, and, if a clever person had both of them, I truly think (according to my understanding of them) that he would acquire honor and good sense, if he did what he should. These two stones certainly go together, and also resemble each other quite a bit. (567–640)

On This Same Subject

Now I have told you about the powerful and beautiful crown that my mother sent to me—she who reserved so many good things for me. However, if I praise it, let no one believe that I am bragging that I have more of Nature's goods than any other creature, or that I possess the powers I have named, which should be loved by everyone, for I know well that I have just a small part of them. Nature has, however, given me enough of her gifts so that I can speak, reason, and understand what is right—not as well as I would like, or as much as I need to, but enough for me to use them well, and not to abuse her kindness. Thus I do not have a beautiful or agile body, or the understanding of the Sibyl, but what I have is sufficient for me; I am grateful to God for what he has made for me; and the powers that I have mentioned which are not dispersed everywhere, even though I said just now that Nature sends them to us, in fact she does not give them to us, no matter how much she is our mother or our friend; it is, rather, God who through His grace gives them to us. Nature, however, orders the body and readies it to receive the soul (which can conceptualize everything), but God Himself creates the soul, He who so values Nature that He has given her the power to make and unmake material forms. The soul, however, is celestial, a light, invisible spirit, very aware and attentive. Thus these are the undeniable, functional powers of the soul which are arranged by Nature within the body, but created by the work of God: understanding, memory, and discreet judgment, and other powers which are there, and all of which come from the soul. And why, therefore, do some people have a greater quantity of these goods and powers, than others who have less? As I understand it, there is no better explanation than the following: the body of the man who thinks better and understands more must be better organized, more dense, better devised and of better proportions (although we do not know what they are) than the body of the one who lacks awareness. I have therefore proven my argument that Nature allows or denies to us the opening of the body to the goods of the soul, according to the diverse capacities of the body to receive them, although God sends the soul into the body. Now it is time that I turn back to the original argument and subject matter that I had begun earlier. May God grant that it be advanced and completed according to His sweet will, in its original terms or in a better way; this is what I desire! (641–714)

On This Same Topic

Thus as you have heard my good mother gladdened my heart by giving me so many of her jewels that they ought to be enough for me, although she had better ones, and more beautiful ones, and more valuable ones, jewels that are worth more than rings or buckles, that she dispenses to her children. She gives these to her most beloved children, but without offending anyone, for she distributes them so that each child has his share, more to some, less to others, but they all pass through her hands. And she gave me this little crown to wear upon my curly hair, a crown that was as beautiful as my station required, and I received it with great gratitude. Its stones were very well chosen, but it was nonetheless small, for if it had been larger, it would have troubled her that the crown would have been too heavy for me to bear, for I was young and did not need weighty responsibilities. Wearing the jewels given by Nature constitutes, however, a marvelous experience, for if there is no illness that by harming and weakening the body rejects the jewels, they have the capacity to increase greatly their powers as the body grows, and to become more beautiful, and to shine with a brighter light. The body is governed by them, as are, indeed, empires and kingdoms, and even the entire world for as long as it exists; and if this is not the case, then it should be, for God in heaven ordained it this way. For this reason Nature gives and disperses them to each person, but I think that people very rarely utilize this grace infused by God, for the powers are often inverted and turned from virtues into vices. Nevertheless we all have these virtues and if we do not make use of them it is entirely our own fault. (715–62)

On This Same Topic

I thus passed out of childhood when I was adorned with the crown; and I began to know reason, in which I was very adept. I made her acquaintance through my crown, and she who disputes with foolish people was eager to instruct me, and she kept me from many follies. (763–70)

1.10 Here It Is Told How Fortune Sent Her to Deliver a Message

Hear how my lady Fortune behaved toward me, when she saw that I was beginning to learn and understand how reason operates: in order for me to know and understand better her activities, she decided to have me deliver a message for her, although I was still rather young; and she granted me a great honor and benefit as you will now hear. This lady had a rather close relative, to whom many people go with good intentions, because my mother puts men and women to the test in order to expand the population of Fortune's kingdom, where everyone works to make their houses stronger, houses which are not built of bricks and mortar. And in order that these people not become lost on the way, Law and Reason have found the right way to this relative of Fortune, to whom I was sent, very nobly conveyed. My lady Fortune, however, according to whether she wishes good or ill to befall people, assigns and sends them a good or a bad consignment of her goods, and assigns them either good or evil, sadness or joy. To this relative my lady wanted to send me. And so she ordered a ship and had it fitted out with all that is needed for a long sea voyage; and she wanted my trip honorably provided with everything required for sailing the sea. Thus the ship was quickly readied, because my lady, who had assigned her message to me, was in a hurry. And so I took leave of my friends, who wept at my departure; I also wept, but I had to obey the command of my lady, whom no one can contradict. The companions I had were good and honest, courteous, peaceful, and untroubled in their dealings with me; and all of us, honorable men and women, were launched onto the sea together. In a short while we were far from port. The sailors worked hard to take advantage of this route; eager to return to land, they headed toward the ancient Hymen,[1] for this is the name of the one to whom I was going; he is not bald or white-haired, though he is very old. Hymen is a god who, according to the poets, has at his court many servants from all the different social levels: there are many emperors, kings, and princes there, and an infinite number of commoners, and all are his servants; some complain about his service, and some are proud of it. The fault, however, lies in those who follow bad advice, or in my Lady who punishes them harshly, from which many arguments arise. As for Hymen himself, he has a good character and wants to do good for everyone. There he is served with great attentiveness, but he is not concerned with ecclesiastics who would never take a step toward him. I do not want to lie to you, but, although I have heard tell that there were Spaniards in Hymen's company, I never saw even one of them at his court, nor among all the arrivals there did I notice any canons or priests; he keeps all of them very far away from him. We thus sailed day and night, without encountering any problems, until, with great joy and celebration, our ship arrived at Hymen's port. With a great feast we gave thanks to God who had led us there without any storms. (771–856)

The ladies who had conducted me there had instructed me well concerning how I should behave in front of this very wise god, and they took me off to a secluded place, where they dressed me richly as befits a maid; they put a rich and beautiful crown, entirely made of jewels and gold, on my curly, auburn hair; around my neck I had a spotless, white silk cloak, with a hanging train, fastened with a beautiful, rich clasp; a noble buckle on my chest; a belt and all the accoutrements that are required for the adornment of a maid, who has such a message to give, according to her family rank. And it was done so well that whoever would have seen me would, without a doubt, have thought and said that I looked like the messenger from an exalted, dearly beloved lady. I was flanked by two barons, and accompanied by nobles; there were many ladies and damsels there, nobly bejeweled and beautifully dressed; there were trumpets, musicians, drums, more than two pair of horns that made everything resound. (857–87)

Thus, without saying another word, we disembarked from our ship. We went off toward the city of Hymen, but he already knew which people were to come before him, which made him very joyous. He, therefore, left his palace in order to come to meet us. This god of very great worth knew well how to behave politely. He led a noble crowd of people, all dressed in the same color, and each one showing his or her joy. There was a great sounding of instruments; it was cause for rejoicing to be in that place at that moment! The god was right in front of the door; when he and I met, we had not yet entered the palace, and he took me by my bare hand and said: "Welcome! Daughter! From now

1. The god of marriage, named as such in Ovid's *Metamorphoses* and *Ovide moralisé* 6.2232–33.

on I count you as a member of our court, which I rule." (888–910)

I greeted him humbly. I delivered my message well, as I had been charged; I think that I discharged this commission in such a way that he was satisfied. He held out to me a ring of refined gold, and with great courtliness he placed it on my finger, and took me into his service, for it is his way and his custom that when a woman comes before him with a message, whether she be poor or rich, he slips a ring on her finger, if he wants her to stay in his court (911–23)

Hymen had brought a handsome, pleasing youth with him. Then the god joyfully conferred me to the protection of the youth, and commanded that he faithfully take care of me in sickness and in health, that he not leave me for another for as long as I should remain at his court, and that he should treat me as one of his own family. Then the youth promised by his faith to be a true lover and loyal companion, as was fitting; and I found his company pleasing, for he was handsome of body and of face.[2] (924–38)

Then Hymen led me into the hall, where people were rejoicing, where so many musicians were sounding their horns that you could not have heard God's thunder; a priest—who was not from that court—hurried to put on his vestments; and he sang to us a mass that we willingly listened to; and then I received beautiful, rich presents from all sides, and both great and humble honored me greatly. Afterward we sat down at tables where there were many notable personages; we were served many delicious courses, as well as lovely, tasty side dishes; and I must joyously praise this event. Many joyous words were spoken there, and after dinner the dancing began with great sprightliness, with many a new motet sung, and many instrumental concerts performed; there one could see who danced well. But why should I make you a long story of this? There is no need for me to recount to you all the details of the happy moments which were spent in that place, for to listen to everything would be tiresome, and thus let me just say, briefly, that everyone was so pleased and so comported themselves according to their wishes, that I must praise that place to which Fortune wanted to send me. I no longer want to recount to you at length everything that happened to me during that time. I thus acquired, in that youth, a new master, but all was under the power of Fortune, who had raised me for joy, pleasure, and amusement, and my heart was not for a single day weary with being there, rather, the time passed very quickly for me. (939–81)

Hymen kept me for ten years at his great court, where I enjoyed all pleasures and shared my desires. Hymen gave me a good and well-trained household and attendants: four handsome squires, three beautiful ladies-in-waiting, with whom I considered myself well fitted out; but I was above all honored by him into whose keeping I had been given,

2. For more on Christine's marriage, see pp. xi–xii.

who worked hard for me so that, experiencing no difficulties, I felt very comfortable at that court. And he was so faithful to me, and so good that, by my soul, I could not praise highly enough the good things that I received from him. He was handsome and good under all circumstances, wise, courtly and upright, and he greatly valued nobility and learning; and with his great knowledge of navigation, he could very competently steer a ship in any weather. He was a very knowledgeable master of a vessel and knew very well how to direct it, just as he should. And he had learned this skill because he needed to, for the country of Hymen (where many people have had many misfortunes, whether they liked it or not) is close to the sea; whoever wants to achieve great prominence there must frequent the sea and know well how to lead and direct ships and vessels, both in good weather and in storms. In all of these things my master was so adept that he had saved me from many dangers by his subtle knowledge of that great oceanic sea full of ancient adventures. (982–1,024)

1.11 Here Is Told of Several Miracles Which Ovid Recounts about His Gods

It is now time for me to recount the strange case, the unusual account (as I had promised at the beginning of this book, where I placed my name) of how, when I returned to Fortune, I was changed from woman to man, which is a very marvelous thing. And it is not a lie or a fable to speak according to metaphor which does not exclude truth. For Fortune has enough power over those whom she rules to effect much greater miracles and often transforms animals into lords who are obeyed by everyone, when it pleases her; and she can change knights into animals when she wishes. This was quite evident when she had Ulysses land at Circe's[3] port long ago during his sea voyage. Circe, pretending to welcome his knights, had them served a drink which caused them to fall to the ground as if they were ill, and they were turned into pigs. My Lady Fortune herself prepared the drink which trapped them and made them eager to arrive there, in order to deliver them to misfortune. She well knows how to do such deeds that many suffer harsh difficulties! (1,025–56)

She accomplishes an infinite number of more wondrous miracles every day, with no hesitation. And she can easily do this for her power is much greater than the two serpents which Ovid tells us about in his book, where he recounts how a man, whom he names, became a

---

3. Christine's model text of the Ulysses and Circe episode is found in Ovid's *Metamorphoses* 14.248–307 and *Ovide moralisé* 14.2363–562.

woman[4] through an incident that occurred. His case, in my opinion, was as follows: This man found two serpents living together face to face in a wood through which he was traveling. He took a stake and struck them with it, thinking that they would kill him quickly; but there befell him no other misfortune than that he saw that his entire body was transformed, he was immediately changed into a completely formed woman, and such (s)he was in every situation which (s)he experienced. The young man, whose name was Tiresias, was completely astonished. And in this condition he remained for seven years during which he sewed and labored at women's tasks. At the end of this time, he went back into the deep forest and there, by chance, as the written text bears witness, he found the two serpents together. He again took a stake, it seems to me, and said that he wanted to see right away whether he could recover the form he used to have; then he struck them and immediately his complexion was changed, and all his feminine ways; and his body turned into a man's, as it had been before, so says Ovid (1,057–93).

Ovid also tells us of a king of Lydia who hated women so much that he ordered (under threat of death) the queen, his wife, who was pregnant and ready to give birth, that if she had a daughter she should burn her or have her killed quietly, for he had no desire to have a daughter, but if she had a son she should keep and protect him. The queen gave birth to a daughter, and did not have her put to a cruel and bitter death; her maternal nature prevented her from doing this. Rather, she had her daughter nursed as a son, and had the news announced everywhere that she had had a beautiful baby boy; and the king believed her. The daughter was attractive in body and in face, and her name was Iphis, a name used for both girls and boys. She soon grew big and strong, but dressed as a boy; her mother denied that Iphis was a girl, for fear that her father (who wanted a speedy marriage for his offspring) would exile her. The mother said that it was too soon for marriage, but after a long argument, it was settled; she could not change his decision. Then the queen was dumbfounded; then her life was hateful to her, for she no longer saw any means, any strategy for hiding her daughter's gender. Then she felt sure to be shamed, she did not know how she could deny the facts, and she wept softly, in private. (1,094–131)

She went to the temple of Vesta,[5] where she knelt before the goddess, moistening the floor with her tears. She made the goddess offerings and oblations, candles and prayers, wax and incense, and vows; she sacri-

---

4. The story of Tiresias's transformation is from Ovid's *Metamorphoses* 3.322–331 and *Ovide moralisé* 3.1022–49.
5. The Roman goddess of marriage, whom Christine substitutes for Ovid's Isis (an Egyptian goddess with transgressive and erotic connotations), who is depicted as the agent of transformation in both the *Metamorphoses* and the *Ovide moralisé*. The story of the transformation of Iphis from a woman into a man can be found in Ovid's *Metamorphoses* 9.667–797 and *Ovide moralisé* 9.2763–3112.

ficed heifers and oxen, on her bare knees she beat her breast. She prayed and beseeched the goddess to help her in her need, which had brought her close to death. She prayed so devoutly and so much that the goddess took pity on her, and showed this by means of a sign. The queen then took comfort, and rushed out of the temple doors. Iphis's father had rushed things so that her wedding preparations were all completed. There was joy and great celebrating which were brought about in the following way: the goddess effected a great miracle there, for that night she filled with joy both the mother and her daughter Iphis, who became a son, through the subtle goddess Vesta, who undid her woman's body and made her a son. (1,132–58)

1.12 Here Is Told How She Lost the Master of Her Ship

Ovid recounts these miracles, but it is now fitting that I tell you of my own transformation, I who by the visitation of Fortune was changed, transformed from woman to man. (1,159–64)

I continued to live with Hymen and to work at his tasks, and happily spent my time in this way, but I truly believe that Fortune came to envy the wonderful comfort in which I was living. She became aware of it and sent for me; thus I was obliged to leave my comfortable life, I could not disobey her. (1,165–72)

Hymen then prepared a large, well-furnished, swift ship and gave it to my master; he placed my household and him and me inside, and then, by his leave we departed, without considering the matter any further. In a short time we had embarked on the high seas, without having encountered at all any unfavorable wind or storm, and, if we had, my master was so wise that he well knew how to steer the ship in any kind of weather and to lead her straight. For several days the knowledgeable navigator thus steered us with the wind, he who knew well how to interpret the Pole Star and how to trim the sails the right way in order to keep on a straight course, with no problems or troubles: thus we continually advanced. (1,173–92)

Alas! Now it is time for me to tell about the grief that triumphed over my joy, the grief which overcame me at this point, nor am I ever able to forget it. Thus as we were continuing on our way, sailing by sea, I saw the sky darken and the clouds thicken so much that we could scarcely see anything. The master who saw me worried and fearful that a contrary wind or storm might abruptly harm us, went up onto the poop deck and took care to see from which direction the wind was blowing, shouting and calling to the sailors for someone to climb up to the crow's nest to see if we were close to land, so that we might be able to leave the high seas before the storm broke. One shouted, another asked questions, and to yet another he instructed and commanded that he should pull the ropes and raise the sails, according to how the wind was blowing, or release or lower the top, or let out or take in the sails in accord with what his great wisdom considered to be the best way to set them for the storm which was beginning and which quickly reached us.[6] (1,193–222)

Oh! God! I do not know how I can recount the pain which still torments me (for tears and sighs disfigure my heart and my face, and my sadness is doubled by the remembered words which recall the event which was so painful for me), but I must continue for a bit. As he was looking straight ahead, standing on the ship's poop deck, shouting that every sailor should pull ahead for the nearby land, at that moment a sudden and powerful wind started up; the whirlwind was twisted like a corkscrew, and it struck against the ship and hit our good master so violently that it took him very far out to sea; then I wished to be dead! (1,223–40)

There was no way to help. The wind struck our ship such a blow that I thought it would sink, but death was not bitter to me when I heard the sailors shout and loudly cry out, when they saw him sink into the sea, he who used to guide the ship night and day through all encumbrances and difficulties (1,241–50)

When, under the poop deck, I realized that what I feared had happened, I stood up like a mad woman, climbed up to the deck, and would have thrown myself into the sea, and I would not have failed, no matter who tried to hold me back I would have jumped in; nor did Alcyone jump more quickly into the sea when she lost Ceyx,[7] whom she used to love so well, than I would have fallen into the sea, which would have taken me away, but I was held back by my household, which quickly came running and crying to restrain me, although my heart was ready to faint. (1,251–64)

You would say that the very air trembled with the shouts, the yells, the bitter lamentations, the deep sufferings, the outbursts from me and from my entire household. Alas! We appropriately mourned him who had governed us, who was such a good pilot that he had saved many from death; and he had been such a loyal lover to me that there would never be another like him, or even resembling him in any way. And it should not be surprising that, having seen him die at sea, I felt a grief beyond compare. I thought that there was no way that the ship could have returned to a safe port, and I certainly thought many times that it would entirely perish in this storm. But the intense grief I had for him

6. For more on the death of her husband, see pp. xi–xii.
7. For the Ceyx and Alcyone story, see Ovid's *Metamorphoses* 11.384–748 and *Ovide moralisé* 11.42996–3787. It is important to note that Christine's self-comparison to Alcyone involves a key contrast: Christine-protagonist does not commit suicide in order to remain with her drowned husband, as the Ovidian heroine did. Christine's citation of the Ovidian model text thus presents her as a "corrected" version of Alcyone.

removed all fear from me; my heart did not suffer from anything else. (1,265–86)

I lay fully extended there wishing for death; and expecting it I cried out so violently that you must believe that my voice, which was not silent, pierced the clouds and the heavens; nor was there any consolation for me, since I was so devastated by my loss. In this state I remained for a long time, refusing all pleasures, hopeless of ever regaining any earthly solace or, to tell the truth, joy; and our desolated ship was blown here and there, all winds were harmful to her, for there was no one who could have set her onto her proper course. I truly thought that I could never again navigate anywhere else except on that sea, which changed joy into mourning. I thought that I would be there for my entire life, on the wrong side of happiness, who hated me because I had once been cheerful. (1,287–310)

But it did not stay like this, I have since been on land for quite some time. To summarize in a few words, my mourning was so intense and my eyes cried so much that Fortune took pity on my unhappiness, and wanted to show her friendship with me, like a good mistress, and help me in my time of trouble: but her help was a marvel! And I do not know if it was more of a danger. (1,311–20)

Wearied by long crying, I remained, on one particular occasion, completely overcome; as if unconscious, I fell asleep early one evening. Then my mistress came to me, she who gives joy to many, and she touched me all over my body; she palpated and took in her hands each bodily part, I remember it well; then she departed and I remained, and since our ship was following the waves of the sea, it struck with great force against a rock. I awakened and things were such that, immediately and with certainty, I felt myself completely transformed. I felt my limbs to be stronger than before, and the great pain and lamentation which had earlier dominated me, I felt to be somewhat lessened. Then I touched myself all over my body, like one completely bewildered. Fortune had thus not hated me, she who had transformed me, for she had instantly changed the great fear and doubt in which I had been completely lost. Then I felt myself much lighter than usual and I felt that my flesh was changed and strengthened, and my voice much lowered, and my body harder and faster. However, the ring that Hymen had given me had fallen from my finger, which troubled me, as well it should have, for I loved it dearly. (1,321–55)

Then I stood up easily; I no longer remained in the lethargy of tears which had been increasing my grief. I found my heart strong and bold, which surprised me, but I felt that I had become a true man; and I was amazed at this strange adventure. Then I raised my eyes by chance and saw the sail and the mast completely broken up, for the bad weather had equally smashed the ropes and the tops to such an extent. Our ship was seriously broken and there were cracks everywhere through which water was streaming, and the ship was already so weighed down with water that if it had stayed any longer on the rocks which it had struck, it would have sunk to the bottom of the sea. When I saw this danger, I set out to repair the ship; with nails and pitch and strong hammering I stopped up the holes; I went gathering moss among the rocks, and put it into the holes in the ship in great quantity, until I had made it sufficiently watertight and rejoined the broken edges. I had the hold drained; to make a long story short, I was able to utilize whatever was necessary to drive a ship; and as soon as I learned how to direct the bailing out, I became a good master, and it was absolutely necessary that I be one in order to help myself and my people, if I did not want to die there. Thus I became a true man (this is no fable), capable of taking charge of the ship. Fortune taught me this trade and I set myself to work in this context. (1,356–94)

As you have heard, I am still a man and I have been for a total of more than thirteen full years, but it would please me much more to be a woman, as I used to be when I used to talk with Hymen, but since Fortune has transformed me so that I shall never again be lodged in a woman's body, I shall remain a man, and with my Lady Fortune I shall stay, although in her service I have found so many hardships that I am undone by them; but until death I must continue my life, may God deliver me safely from it! I extricated myself from the rocks, prepared my ship, and set off toward the place from which I had started out, at the beginning of this part, there where my lady had her dwelling. And I arrived there in a very short time, although before doing so I encountered many problems, which I did not resolve quickly. (1,395–416)

1.13 Here Is Told How She Returned Back to Where She Had Been before Becoming a Messenger

Thus I returned back to the place from which a while before I had departed, but I now understood the status of the place, and what sorts of things might happen there, much better than I had during my childhood; and notwithstanding the great injury I had so bitterly received, my mother, who had always cared for me, never forgot me: for never had sleep, or vigil, or my transformation, or any difficulty or pain caused to me by Fortune, or long sorrow or brief happiness, or any ornament that might have been given to me, or any crown that might have been placed upon my head, ever made the cap disappear, the cap that was part of my mother's legacy, that she had placed upon my head and which suited me so well, as I have recounted earlier, when I told the story of my relations with my mother. But the precious stones have since been often much disturbed and coated with the dust that results from the grief breathed out by frivolous Fortune; but the stones have nevertheless remained more clear than ever, and they grew much bigger at the moment when I became a man; and it is certain that I was able to arrive at port through their power, to learn how to navigate the ship into the enclosure in which it remains, which purges the whole world of happiness. (1,417–50)

Then it was time for me to perceive and to know the status and the appearance of the court into which I had been placed, more than I had done in times past. Thus I will tell you what I saw there and everything that I thought about it: the place where my Lady Fortune lives (she who does not remain in the same position for a single hour), her habits and her conditions, and her great transformations. (1,451–60)

[After Christine's elaborate presentation of Fortune, first allegorically (through an extended description, in parts 2 through 4), then historically (through a sequential narrative, in parts 4 through 7), she closes the *Book of Fortune's Transformation* with a brief epilogue, concluding with a final authorial self-portrait.]

7.57 Here Is Found the Conclusion of the Book

Now I have sufficiently described what I have found and seen and understood during my long stay in the place which is harmful to many. I am still there today, where I continue in the same style to serve my mistress Fortune, although I remain the object of her spite. Therefore she repays my service with great suffering, and no service or merit of which I am capable can win me any advantage, for she breaks with her false arm everything that I build or touch. Indeed, she behaves this way with many people. (23,595–609)

O you highly placed princes, consider at least for a moment whether or not there is any safety for human beings who serve in such a dangerous situation. Can they find secure lodgings there? Taking into account all that I have recounted, can Fortune's transformations be thought of as small? Should man thus be proud of achievements that can quickly disappear? Certainly not! For there is nothing certain except unhappiness. (23,610–20)

St. Paul speaks of Fortune's castle, using different terms, when he says in his Epistle: "there are great perils in every set of circumstances: on land, on sea, alone, with others, and in studying, and in all the different human conditions, the banners of Peril are raised; there is nothing certain."[8] (23,621–29)

8. Cf. 2 Corinthians 11:26–27.

And because Unhappiness is everywhere, I have chosen as my sole joy, in order to have less suffering in spite of the constant presence of Unhappiness—whatever joy others may have, this is mine—peace, voluntary solitude, and a retiring and solitary life. (23,630–36)

Here ends the Seventh and Last Part of the *Book of Fortune's Transformation*. Thanks be to God.

A LETTER TO EUSTACHE MOREL

(February 10, 1404)[1]

[This letter to the famous poet Eustache Deschamps (1346–1406 or 1407), also known as Eustache Morel, expresses Christine's feeling about the decay she sees everywhere in her society. It also shows that she was intent on intellectual networking by keeping in touch with the notables of her time. Deschamps, who was almost twenty years her senior, answered this letter courteously, displaying some sensitivity toward her views of these troubled times and showing a high regard for her learning and literary accomplishments.

Translated by Renate Blumenfeld-Kosinski from Maurice Roy, ed., *Oeuvres poétiques de Christine de Pisan*, vol. 2 (Paris: Firmin Didot, 1891).]

To the most accomplished Eustache Morel, famous bailiff of Senlis, author of many well-known poems.

Your great reputation has encouraged me, dear master and friend, to send you this letter, written in verse,[1] though compared to your works it is nothing, I know it well. But we read that the wise man teaches his disciples to be friends with the wise if they want to learn anything. Your wisdom has made me send this letter on its way. I humbly beg you to accept this letter kindly and not to be displeased that I address you in the singular, for I learned this from the clerical style which is used by learned men.[2] I would very much like to see your virtuous works, and beg you humbly to share with me your valuable treasure—which you have so expanded and which you have drawn from the lap of Science. Do not despise my feminine understanding, even if I have my failings; rather take into account the great love I have for knowledge, as I make known to you. And if you would like to see examples of my little under-

---

1. The date Christine gives is 1403. Until the late sixteenth century, the new year started at Easter, thus February 1403 is 1404 for us.
1. The letter was written in the classic form of lines of eight syllables with paired rhymes. It is translated in prose.
2. I.e., she says *tu* instead of *vous*. Christine makes the same remark in the *Book of Peace* (see p. 229). On the clerical style see J. D. Burnley, "Christine de Pizan and the So-Called *Style Clergial*," *Modern Language Review* 81 (1986), 1–6.

standing in my works, you can order them, without special inquiries, for I'm looking for your comments. And because I am certain of your good sense, I am sending you a complaint about certain unpleasant things, as I will explain.

Sad and in tears I see that the world is badly governed; it seems to me that it is going from bad to worse. And I know that you are saddened by the same evil, for every right-thinking person wants to be governed justly. Oh, master, how hard is it to see in our present times lies and fraud so common in the cities, the castles, at princely courts and everywhere, with nobles, common people, the clergy, and in law courts. Truth has no chance, it is hidden away somewhere and does not reveal itself. Everyone tries hard to amass possessions with great covetousness, malicious fraudulence, and eagerness to deceive—and no one cares about acquiring virtuous profits. They are only intent on gaining vain riches which lead to vice, this is the only interest of these worldly people.

Do you remember, my dear sir, how Philosophy recommends honey more than wax, as Boethius proves in his beautiful and famous book, which gives us consolation?[3] He despises the worldly goods that people praise above any other grace. Better than Heaven, they love the fat earth, dotted with dung heaps and filth. One finds here and there in books that in ancient times wise philosophers were elected counselors of their cities, and also of kings, and by their good sense useless and disorderly people were confounded, just as in ancient times the pride of King Emirades was confounded by the valiant philosopher Philometor, as I have recently read, who devoted his body and soul to the common good. The good sages always benefited people by destroying this unpleasant filth, but today there is hardly anyone who desires to do anything for the common good; people only think about their gain. Public affairs are no longer taken care of, instead people feel no shame in committing the most horrible acts in public; even Nature is ashamed. Voluptuousness captures people, and they are not getting tired of it. People do not consider their own faults. All good customs fall into oblivion, for virtues do not count anymore. Knowledge, which was a principle of government in the past, is not prized at all. Then there was justice in the world, but now there are few decent people. Then there was the Golden Age, which is now all finished.[4]

Princes possessed knowledge; they must be the pillars and masts to support justice, they must govern the people by law and reason. Then the noblemen were striving to give comfort to the people through eloquence and true wisdom, exhorting them to perfect morals, by advice

3. This is a reference to one of Christine's favorite books, Boethius's *Consolation of Philosophy*, written before his execution in 525. See also n. 8, p. 38.
4. All this comes from Boethius.

and example. Though the work was often back-breaking, they labored for virtue which people today do no longer care about. Just see whether those people who should delight in pursuing noble deeds actually do so: if there are any of this kind left, let us praise God for it, as I do.

Dear brother, can one even count the number of those who are boastful and haughty, sporting exaggerated outfits, or those who have acquired riches maliciously and to the detriment of others, so that they can enjoy honors and a high estate? Do you see any who are like that in the crowds of wordly people? I am certain you do: I have no doubt that they think themselves to be gods, what do you think? Is this not a road that morally leads astray, that is unhealthy? We even see stupid people and those who do not possess many justly acquired goods become more and more proud. Why should I go on about all this? For it is certain that these people form a long, long line, and by their error faith is destroyed in this world. We hardly see anyone acquire good morals.

Judges, in order to do you injustice, do evil outside of the law, dear brother and friend: take care that people always observe justice. Oh, most select Justice, how remarkably are you read and taught in the texts that are supposed to teach just treatments! Do you actually see the favor of the law extended to poor orphans and tired widows, still crying all the time? What do you think? Is it so? I do not think so. It seems rather that the world is so perverted that all their possessions are taken from them. And I know this for certain, for I know what is what, since Fortune has made me a master of this kind of knowledge for which I have the proofs. As soon as I was in her snares, no one came to me with a friendly face to offer me comfort with good intentions. She tempted me as one tempts the simpleminded in order to deceive them. I truly can say that all my adversities have turned out the same way, and they continue. I have had more than my share of misfortune, since I gave your friend my true and loyal share. He was the one, as I tell about elsewhere. And I still have these troubles, and I beg you heartily to pray to God to give me patience, for I do not always have the strength to live with patience, which gives comfort.

I pray to God that He may protect your life in this world and in eternity. I wrote this alone in my study, diligently and with great care, on the tenth day of February 1403.[5]

> Christine de Pizan, servant of knowledge, who valiantly labors in this occupation, your well-meaning disciple.

---

5. See n. 1 to headnote, page 109.

MOREL'S ANSWER

[Eustache Morel (or Deschamps) replied to her letter with a ballad.[6]]

Eloquent muse among the nine, Christine,
I know of no one like you today,
who could equal you in learning,
you received knowledge from God, no one else;
your letters and books, which I have read   5
here and there, filled with great philosophy,
and also what you wrote to me recently,
convince me of the great abundance
of your knowledge, constantly growing.
Your achievements stand alone in the French realm.   10

God gave you the gift of Solomon,
your heart is given to teaching—as God demanded
from him; you are devoted to study, and thus follow
in the footsteps of the good master Thomas of
Bologna, whom I knew, I remember it well. Your   15
father was a doctor of astronomy; Charles V by no
means forgot him, but commended him for his great
abilities—and you followed him in the seven
learned arts.[7] Your achievements stand alone in the
French realm.   20

Ah, what a worthy honor among women and men. I am
coming to you to learn, you who complains so much
over the deceptive root whose fruit troubles
everyone.[8] I can see it by your letter, which I
received with great joy, and for which I thank you a   25
hundred times. But you will learn more about my
opinions which agree with yours in all things. May
your painful malady find a remedy. Your achievements
stand alone in the French realm.

6. This ballad is number 1,242 in volume 6 of the *Oeuvres complètes* of Deschamps, edited by
   the Marquis Queux de Saint-Hilaire and G. Raynaud (Paris: Société des Anciens Textes Français, 1878–1904). Renate Blumenfeld-Kosinski translated from this edition.
7. A reference to the seven liberal arts: the *trivium*, consisting of the verbal arts of grammar,
   rhetoric, and dialectic, and the *quadrivium* or mathematical arts, consisting of arithmetic,
   music, geometry, and astronomy. See David L. Wagner, ed., *The Seven Liberal Arts in the
   Middle Ages* (Bloomington: Indiana University Press, 1983).
8. We saw that in her letter Christine complained that her society lacked the solid foundation of
   sound moral values. Deschamps sees this as the root of current troubles.

Envoi

Oh, sweetest sister, I, Eustache, beg you to be   30
allowed to be in your company, as a serf, to learn
about your studies. I could spend my life on nothing
better, for I look to you as to Boethius in Pavia.[9]
Your achievements stand alone in the French realm.

FROM THE BOOK OF THE DEEDS AND GOOD CONDUCT OF THE WISE KING CHARLES V

[Christine's biography of her family's benefactor, Charles V, marks a turning point in her career. For the first time she was summoned by a powerful patron, the duke of Burgundy, to his palace and received a precise commission: to write about the life and deeds of the duke's brother to whom he owed a good part of his fortune. Charles had given him the immense duchy of Burgundy, which came to include Flanders when Philip married Margaret of Flanders.

When Philip approached Christine, Charles had been dead for twenty-four years. Her father and husband had worked at his court and presumably had known him well. Christine, too, had been acquainted with him personally and was able to draw on various eyewitness accounts as well as on written sources.[1] She cites passages from the *Grandes Chroniques de France* [Great Chronicles of France] frequently and also used the *Flores chronicorum* [Flowers of chronicles] by Bernard Gui, which had been translated into French in the fourteenth century. Other sources include an anonymous account of the death of Charles V and Henri de Gauchi's translation of Egidio Colonna's *De regimine principum* [On the conduct of rulers], which she also used for the *Book of the Body Politic*. The *Manipulus florum* [Sheaf of flowers], a collection of sayings culled from the Church Fathers and ancient authors by Thomas Hibernicus—much used in her *Letter from Othea*—is also a source.

The biography was not meant to be an objective evaluation of Charles's life but rather a celebration of his extraordinary qualities. Yet, as other accounts of the period testify, it is accurate, since Charles V truly was a superior ruler, especially when compared with Charles VI, who led the country into disarray. The biography contains many moving and well-observed passages, but it is also a "mirror for princes," extolling Charles's leadership and skillful rule and presenting him as a model for others. In this role he reappears in the *Book of the Body Politic* and the *Book of Peace*.

Our brief selection shows how Christine is drawn into the orbit of the

---

9. Deschamps could probably pay no greater compliment to Christine than to compare her to her hero Boethius. The term *serf* can be interpreted as a feudal term used in the context of courtly love.
1. For details, see Solente's edition, xxxii–lxxx.

duke of Burgundy to whom she had presented a copy of her *Fortune's Trans-formation* on New Year's Day 1404. Through this skillful move she garnered a major commission. In the "Prologue" we see her embark on a new kind of work, written entirely in prose, not concerned with antiquity but with the recent past. This work made her even better known and greatly enhanced her reputation.

Translated by Renate Blumenfeld-Kosinski from Suzanne Solente, ed., *Le livre des fais et bonnes meurs du sage roy Charles V*, 2 vols. (Paris: Champion, 1936–40).]

1. Here Begins the First Part of the *Book of the Deeds and Good Conduct of the Wise King Charles V*, and First of All the Prologue

Lord God, open my lips,[1] illuminate my thoughts, enlighten my understanding so that ignorance no longer weighs down my senses, preventing them from explicating the things I conceived in my memory. May the beginning, middle, and end be in praise of You, sovereign power, ungraspable dignity which the human spirit cannot comprehend!

The things that are necessary for the building of a good character and that are generally praiseworthy, we see remembered and brought back from memory by wise men in their writings, instructing us on a virtuous life. It is a worthy thing that they make their points forcefully by true and well-known examples and tell us how to conduct ourselves. For this reason I, Christine de Pizan, a woman in the shadow of ignorance seeking clear understanding, but endowed by God and Nature with the desire to give myself to the love of learning, follow the style of my predecessors, whom we owe the development of good conduct, and begin at present, by God's grace and His help in my thoughts, a new compilation, written in prose and quite different from my previous works.

I was moved to this when I was informed that it would please the most solemn and revered prince, the Duke of Burgundy, Philip, son of John, by the grace of God King of France,[2] by whose commandment I have undertaken this work. I ask his worthy and virtuous humility that he may overlook the defect of my weak knowledge, since I am not officially learned in any discipline, which could have improved my understanding and made me achieve a certain eloquence. May my simple[3] style be to the honor of the most honored and worthy Crown of France, whose light illuminates the universe, and may it please the human dignity of its most solemn princes, to whom I commend myself with humble reverence and recommendation. I present my small and insufficient

---

1. Psalm 51:15: "O Lord, open thou my lips." This is the opening of the Hours of the Virgin in contemporary Books of Hours.
2. Philip's father was John II (Jean le Bon), who reigned from 1350 to 1364.
3. Christine uses the term *rural* here. See also n. 1 on p. 233.

work to them, and to all those noblemen who love wisdom, and I announce my new polemical[4] work, in which I hope treat the virtues and qualities of nobility of heart, chivalry, and wisdom, and what good results from them. Thus my work will be divided into three parts, which will center on one topic: on the singular person of the illustrious, noble, and most praised prince, the deceased wise King Charles, fifth of that name, in reverence to whom the present work is undertaken, remembering his life, his praiseworthy virtues and his conduct, worthy of being recalled forever.

2. Here She Tells Why and By Whose Command This Book Was Made

Because people often wonder about hidden reasons and the motives for which things were done, I will recount truthfully and without showing off the beginning and development of this little compilation. In truth, in this present year 1403 I offered one of my volumes, called the *Mutacion de Fortune* to the worthy prince, my Lord of Burgundy, as a gift for the first of January, which we call Year's Day.[5] In his gracious humility he accepted it most amiably and with great joy, and it was reported to me by Monbertaut, this lord's treasurer, that he would like me to compile a treatise about a certain subject matter, which he would fully explain to me, so that I would understand what exactly the prince wanted. For this reason I, moved by a desire to accomplish his wishes as far as my understanding would permit it, went with my servants to the palace of the Louvre in Paris, where he then found himself. Once informed of my presence, he asked me by his good grace, to come before him and I was led to him most courteously by two squires named Jean de Chalon and Toppin de Chantemerle. I found him in his private quarters, with very few people, in the company of his son, my lord Antoine, Count of Rethel.[6] When I was before him and had greeted him appropriately I explained the reason for my coming and my desire to serve and please his Highness, if I was worthy to do so, and that I might to be informed by him as to the manner of the treatise he wished me to work on. Then he, in his gracious humility, thanked me much more than my lowliness deserved and explained the manner and the subject on which I should work. After having received many proofs of his goodness I took my leave, happy with my commission which I considered an order much more honorable than I was worthy or able to accomplish.[7]

4. The original term was *invective*, which today has a negative connotation.
5. Or January 1, 1404; see n. 1 to the headnote, p. 109.
6. Antoine (1384–1415) became duke of Brabant in 1405.
7. In the next chapter, Christine explains that she consulted both chronicles of the period and eyewitnesses in order to compose her book.

This manuscript was put together by Christine for the French queen Isabeau of Bavaria. John, duke of Bedford, who was then the regent of France, acquired it toward the end of the Hundred Years' War (between 1425 and 1430), and thus it began its lengthy journey to Edward Harley in England, whose wife brought it into his famous collection in 1713. The opening miniature of *The Book of the City of Ladies* shows us Christine welcoming the three allegorical ladies, Reason, Rectitude, and Justice, in her study on the left. Each holds her attribute: Reason a mirror, Rectitude a ruler, and Justice a golden measuring vessel. On the right, Christine begins the construction of the city with the help of Lady Reason. London, British Library Harley 4431, folio 290.

FROM THE BOOK OF THE CITY OF LADIES

[*The Book of the City of Ladies* responds to Christine's complaint in the *God of Love's Letter* that women had not written books about themselves and were, therefore, represented unfairly over many centuries. As Christine peruses books in her own library, she becomes painfully aware of the bad treatment women had experienced at the hands of the authors and even begins to believe them.[1] At this point three allegorical ladies, Reason, Rectitude, and Justice, appear to her and make her realize her error: she will now be charged with establishing a new written tradition of women by building the City of Ladies, where the debris that needs to be cleared from the building site stands for the writings of the antifeminists, where every stone is a celebrated woman of learned or military achievement, and where the inhabitants are women of impeccable virtue.

Within the polemical framework of refuting the misogynistic tradition,

---

1. It is remarkable how the opening scene of reading misogynistic authors recalls Virginia Woolf's foray into the British Library in search of writings about women—which are all by men. See *A Room of One's Own*, especially chaps. 1 and 2.

Lady Justice welcomes the Virgin Mary, who leads the procession of the saints into the completed City of Ladies. London, British Library Harley 4431, folio 361.

Christine works as a compiler of exemplary stories whose function it is to give counterexamples to all the reproaches leveled against women by male authors. One model may have been Jean Le Fèvre de Resson's *Livre de leesce* [Book of joy], written in the 1370s, designed to celebrate women and defend them against the misogynist attacks of Matheolus,[2] the very author who upset Christine at the beginning of the *City of Ladies.* Most of the stories come from Boccaccio's *Concerning Famous Women*, translated into French in 1401. Christine also translated a number of stories from the *Decameron*.[3] For Boccaccio, famous women were women of some achievement but not necessarily virtuous, and he certainly dwells on the crimes of Medea and the notoriousness of Cleopatra. He also states that saintly women have no place in his text, since they should not be in the company of pagan women and since there are special texts devoted to them. But Christine, like Jean Le Fèvre, includes female saints and devotes her whole book 3 to them. Her source was the *Speculum historiale* (Historical mirror) by Vincent of Beauvais[4] in the French translation made by Jean de Vignay in the late 1320s.

Women's achievements as depicted in books 1 and 2 cover all areas of learning: science, poetry, painting, agriculture, and military arts; some are even prophets. Their deeds illustrate the virtues of filial piety, devoted motherhood, marital love, chastity, constancy, and honesty. The saints of book 3 are almost all martyrs and thus are exemplars of these same virtues in a religious context.[5]

Christine's mission has been accomplished at the end of the *City of Ladies:* women now have a strong and durable refuge against slander. They will be recognized for their true worth, and their history will finally take its place alongside that of men.

In Christine's own time, the *City of Ladies* was not her most successful work, since it was often considered to be a mere translation of Boccaccio. And while a Flemish translation was made in 1475 and the first English version was printed in 1521,[6] it was not really rediscovered until the 1980s. Today, the *City of Ladies* is Christine's most frequently read text because it speaks to our modern concerns of recognizing and celebrating women's contributions throughout history.

Translated by Renate Blumenfeld-Kosinski from Maureen Curnow, "The 'Livre de la Cité des dames' of Christine de Pisan: A Critical Edition," 2 vols. (Ph.D. diss., Vanderbilt University, 1975). For easy reference, the paragraphs have been numbered as in the Curnow edition.]

2. Ed., A.-G. van Hamel *Les Lamentations de Matheolus et Le Livre de leesce de Jehan Le Fèvre de Ressons*, 2 vols. (Paris: Emile Bouillon, 1892–1905). On Matheolus, see Katharina M. Wilson and Elizabeth M. Makowski, *Wykked Wyves and the Woes of Marriage: Misogamous Literature from Juvenal to Chaucer* (Albany: State University of New York Press, 1990), 139–42. Excerpts are translated in Alcuin Blamires, ed., *Woman Defamed and Woman Defended* (Oxford, UK: Clarendon Press, 1992), 177–97.
3. Boccaccio, *Concerning Famous Women*, trans. Guido Guarino (New Brunswick, NJ: Rutgers University Press, 1963), and *The Decameron*, trans. G. H. McWilliam (Harmondsworth, UK: Penguin Books, 1972).
4. Vincent of Beauvais, *Miroir historial*, trans. Jean de Vignay (Paris: Verard, 1495–96). The Latin text was finished around 1258.
5. See R. Blumenfeld-Kosinski, " 'Femme de corps et femme par sens': Christine de Pizan's Saintly Women," *Romanic Review* 87 (1996), 157–75.
6. See Curnow's edition, 300–45.

Here Begins the Book of the City of Ladies, the First Chapter of Which Tells Why and for What Reason This Book Was Made

These are my habits and the way I spend my life: studying literature. One day, doing just that, I was sitting in my study surrounded by several volumes on a variety of topics; at that moment my mind was occupied with the weighty opinions of various authors that I had studied for a long time. I looked up from my book, wondering whether I should leave alone for now these subtle problems and enjoy myself by looking at some cheerful poetry. And as I was looking around for some small book of that kind, I came across a strange book that did not belong to me but which had been given to me for safekeeping. When I opened it I saw on the title page that it was by Matheolus.[1] Then I smiled, for although I had never seen it, I had heard people say that it, like other books, spoke well and with reverence of women, and so I thought that I would take a look at it to enjoy myself. But I had looked at it only for a moment when my good mother called me to supper—for it was that time already—and I put down the book with the intention of looking at it the next day.

The next morning, again sitting in my study as usual, I did not forget that I had wanted to look at this book by Matheolus; so I began reading it and made a little progress. But since the subject matter did not seem very agreeable to people who do not enjoy slander, and since it did not contribute anything to the building up of virtue or good manners, in view of its dishonest themes and subject, I read a little bit here and there and looked at the end, and then put it down in order to devote myself to the study of higher and more useful things. But the sight of this book, although it was of no authority, made me think along new lines which made me wonder about the reasons why so many different men, learned and nonlearned, have been and are so ready to say and write in their treatises so many evil and reproachful things about women and their behavior. And not just one or two, and not just this Matheolus, who has no particular reputation and writes in a mocking manner, but more generally it seems that in all treatises philosophers, poets, and orators, whose names it would take too long to enumerate, all speak with the same mouth and all arrive at the same conclusion: that women's ways are inclined to and full of all possible vices.

Thinking these things over very deeply, I began to examine myself and my behavior as a natural woman, and likewise I thought about other women that I see frequently, princesses, great ladies as well as a great many ladies of the middle and lower classes who were gracious enough to tell me their private and hidden thoughts. From all this I hoped that

1 la lb

1. *The Lamentations of Matheolus*, written in the late thirteenth century. It was edited together with its refutation *Le Livre de leesce* [The Book of joy] by Jean Le Fèvre. See also n. 2, p. 118.

I could judge in my conscience, without prejudice, whether these things, to which so many notable men bear witness, could be true. But according to everything I could know about this problem, however I looked at it and peeled away its various layers, it was clear to me that these judgments did not square with the natural behavior and ways of women. Nevertheless, I argued strongly against women, saying that it would be unlikely that so many famous men, such solemn scholars of such vast understanding, so clear-sighted in all things as these men seemed to be, could have lied in so many places that I could hardly find a book on morals, no matter who was its author, in which, even before finishing it, I would not find some chapters or certain sections speaking ill of women. This reason alone, in short, made me conclude that, although my intellect in its simplicity and ignorance did not recognize the great defects in myself and in other women, it must nonetheless be so. And thus I relied more on the judgment of others than on what I myself felt and knew.

I was so deeply and for such a long time transfixed by this thought   1c
that I seemed to be in a trance; and a large number of authors on this subject passed through my mind, one after the other, just like a gushing fountain. And eventually I concluded that God made a vile thing when He formed woman, wondering how such a worthy artisan could have stooped to making such an abominable piece of work which is the vessel, as they say, as well as the hiding-place and shelter of every evil and vice. As I was thinking this, a great unhappiness and sadness rose up in my heart, and I despised myself and the entire feminine sex, just as if it were a monstrosity in nature. And in my grief I spoke the following words:

"Oh, God, how can this be? For lest I be mistaken in my faith, I am   2
not allowed to doubt that Your infinite wisdom and perfect goodness created anything that is not good. Did not You Yourself form woman in a very singular way, and did You not give her all those inclinations which it pleased You she should have? And how could it be that You should have erred in anything? And nevertheless, here are all the great accusations against them, all judged, determined, and concluded. I cannot understand this hostility. And if this is so, dear Lord God, that it is true that all these abominations abound in the feminine sex—as so many testify—and if You Yourself say that the testimony of more than one witness should be believed, why should I doubt that this is true? Alas, God, why did You not let me be born into this world as a man, so that I would be inclined to serve you better and so that I would not err in anything and be of such perfection as man is said to be? But since Your kindness does not extend to me, forgive my negligence in Your service, good Lord God, and let it not displease You: for the servant who receives fewer gifts from his lord is less obliged to be of service to him."

In my grief I spoke these words and many more to God for a very long time, and in my folly I behaved as if I should be most unhappy because God had made me exist in this world in a female body.

Here Christine Tells How Three Ladies Appeared to Her, and How the One Who Was in Front Addressed Her First and Comforted Her in Her Unhappiness

Lost in these painful thoughts, my head bowed in shame, my eyes full of tears, my hand supporting my cheek and my elbow on the pommel of my chair's armrest, I suddenly saw a ray of light descending onto my lap as if it were the sun.[2] And as I was sitting in a dark place where the sun could not shine at this hour, I was startled as if awakened from sleep. And as I lifted my head to see where this light was coming from, I saw standing before me three crowned ladies of great nobility. The light coming from their bright faces illuminated me and the whole room. Now, no one would ask whether I was surprised, given that my doors were closed, and nevertheless they had come here. Wondering whether some phantom had come to tempt me, in my fright I made the sign of the cross on my forehead.

Then the first of the three began to address me as follows: "Dear daughter, do not be afraid, for we have not come to bother or to trouble you but rather to comfort you, having taken pity on your distress, and to move you out of the ignorance that blinds your own intelligence so that you reject what you know for certain and believe what you do not know, see, and recognize except through a variety of strange opinions. You resemble the fool in that funny story who was dressed in a woman's dress while he slept in a mill. When he woke up those who made fun of him told him that he was a woman and he believed their lies more readily than the certainty of his own being.[3]

"Fair daughter, what has happened to your good sense? Have you forgotten that when fine gold is tested in the furnace, it does not change or vary in strength, but rather gets purer the more it is hammered and handled in various ways? Do you not know that the best things are those that are most debated and argued about? If you just look at the highest things, which are ideas and celestial things, try to see whether the greatest philosophers, those whom you use to argue against your own sex, have ever determined what is false and contrary to the truth and whether they have not contradicted and blamed each other. You have seen this

---

2. Christine's posture expresses melancholy. The ray of light evokes the scene of the Annunciation to the Virgin. This question has been explored by V. A. Kolve, "The Annunciation to Christine: Authorial Empowerment in the *Book of the City of Ladies*," in Brendan Cassidy, ed., *Iconography at the Crossroads* (Princeton, N.J.: Index of Christian Art, Department of Art and Archaeology, 1993), 171–96.
3. This story and variations on it are well known in the folkloric tradition.

yourself in the *Metaphysics*,[4] where Aristotle argues against some opinions and speaks of Plato and others in this way. And note, moreover, how Saint Augustine and other doctors of the Church have criticized certain places in Aristotle even though he is called the prince of philosophers and was a supreme master of both natural and moral philosophy.

"And it seems that you think that all the words of the philosophers   4a
are articles of faith and that they cannot be wrong. And as for the poets of whom you speak, don't you know that they have spoken of many things in fables,[5] and that many times they mean the opposite of what their texts seem to say? And one can approach them through the grammatical figure of *antiphrasis*, which means, as you know, that if someone says this is bad, it actually means it is good and vice versa. I therefore advise you to profit from their texts and that you interpret the passages where they speak ill of women that way, no matter what their intention was. And perhaps this man who called himself Matheolus understood things in his own book in this way: for there are many things in it which, if taken literally, would be pure heresy. And as for the accusations against the holy estate of marriage ordained by God, put forth not only by him and others but even by the *Romance of the Rose* to which people give greater credence because of its author's great authority,[6] it is clearly proved by experience that the contrary of the evil that they say exists in this estate through the fault of women is true. For where has there ever been a husband who would permit his wife to dominate him in such a way that she could have the right to abuse and insult him, as those who speak of women claim? I believe that, no matter what you have seen written, you will never with your own eyes see such a husband; these lies are painted too badly. I tell you in conclusion, dear friend, that simplicity has brought you to your current opinion. Come back to yourself, recover your good sense and do not bother yourself anymore with these absurdities. For you should know that all evil things that are said about women in such a general way only hurt those who say them, and not women themselves."

---

4. Suzanne Solente has shown that Christine was familiar with St. Thomas's thirteenth-century commentary on the *Metaphysics*. See her edition of the biography of Charles V, *Le Livre des fais et bonnes meurs du sage roy Charles V*, 2 vols. (Paris: Champion, 1935–41), 1:lxvi–vii. Christine mentions St. Thomas in part 3, chapter 68 of the biography and in *Christine's Vision*.
5. As in the *Letter from Othea* and at the beginning of *The Tale of the Shepherdess*, Christine emphasizes that certain stories, or fables, can have a hidden meaning.
6. Christine's opinion on the *Romance of the Rose* became clear in *The Debate on the Romance of the Rose* (see p. 41).

Here Christine Tells How the Lady Who Had Addressed Her
Told Her Who She Was, Her Character and Her Purpose,
and Announced to Her How She Would Build a City
with the Help of the Three Ladies

The renowned lady spoke these words to me. I do not know which   5
one of my senses was more engaged in her presence: my hearing, by
listening to her worthy remarks, or my sight, by looking at her great
beauty, her attire, her dignified bearing and her most honorable countenance. And the same applied to the others, for I did not know which
one to look at, for the three ladies resembled each other so much that
one could hardly tell them apart, except that the last one, though of no
less authority than the others, had such a fierce look on her face that
whoever looked into her eyes, be he ever so bold, would not commit
any misdeed, for it seemed that she always threatened the evildoers.

I was standing before them, having risen to show my respect, and
looked at them speechlessly, just like someone who is too dumbfounded
to utter a word. And I felt great admiration in my heart, wondering who
they could be and how much I would like, if I only dared, to ask their
names and who they were; and to ask about the significance of the
different scepters that each one carried in her right hand, which were
of great richness, and to ask why they had come here. But since I considered myself unworthy to address such questions to such high ladies as
they appeared to me, I did not dare, but rather continued to look at
them, half afraid and half reassured by the words I had heard which had
made me move away from my first ideas. But the wise lady who had
addressed me and who knew in her mind what I was thinking, just like
someone who is clearsighted in everything, responded to my thoughts
as follows:

[The lady informs Christine that they are the daughters of God who have
come to this world to bring order and to advise humans. The mirror the
lady carries signifies self-knowledge. Her sisters will explain themselves in
an instant.]

"But now I will explain the reason for our coming. I want to make   6a
known to you that we do nothing without good cause and that our
appearance here is not in vain. For, although we are not common to
many places and our knowledge does not come to all people, nevertheless you, for the great love you have for inquiring into the truth of things
through long and continuous study, for which reason you are here alone
and separated from the world, you have earned to be visited and consoled by us as our dear friend, in your trouble and sadness, so that you
might have a clear vision into the things that contaminate and trouble
your heart.

"There is another greater and more special reason for our coming   7
which you will learn from what we tell you: you should know that we
have come to remove from the world the same error into which you
have fallen, so that from now on ladies and all valiant women may have
a refuge and a defensive enclosure against so many different assailants.
These ladies have been abandoned for so long, exposed like a field without a hedge, without finding a champion who would appear for their
defense, notwithstanding the noble men who by order and right should
defend them, but who through negligence and lack of interest have let
them be mocked. It is therefore no wonder that their envious enemies
and the outrageous villains, who have attacked them with various weap-
ons, have won the war against the defenseless ladies.

"Where is there a city, be it ever so strong, that could not be taken if
no one showed resistance, or a cause, be it ever so unjust, that cannot
be won by someone who pleads without opposition? And the simple
good ladies, following the example of suffering that God commands,
have gladly suffered the great offenses that, by speaking and by writing,
have wrongfully and sinfully been done to them by those who claim to
have the right to do so from God. But now it is time that their just cause
be taken from Pharaoh's hands, and this is why we three ladies, that you
see here, moved by pity, have come to you to announce a certain edifice
built like the wall of a city, with strong stones and well constructed,
which you are predestined and made to build with our help and counsel, and where no one will live except all ladies of renown and worthy
of praise: for to those who are without virtue the walls of our city will be
closed."

*Here [Christine] Tells More about the Lady and How She Speaks
to Christine about the City She Has Been Commissioned to Build
and How She Will Help Her Build the Wall and the Enclosure
That Goes around, and Then the Lady Tells Her Her Name*

"Thus, fair daughter, you have been given the prerogative among   8
women to construct the City of Ladies, for whose foundation and completion you will take and draw from the three of us fresh water as from
clear fountains, and we will give you plenty of material, stronger and
more durable than marble, even if it were cemented. Thus your city
will be incomparably beautiful and will last forever in the world.

"Have you not read how King Tros founded the great city of Troy   9
with the help of Apollo, Minerva, and Neptune, whom the people of
that time believed to be gods, and also how Cadmus founded the city of
Thebes by order of the gods?[7] And yet in the course of time these cities

---

7. As in the *Letter from Othea* and *The Book of Fortune's Transformation* Christine draws on the
thirteenth-century compilation of ancient history known as the *Histoire ancienne jusqu'à César*
[Ancient history up to Julius Caesar] for information on these ancient kingdoms, including the
Amazons and others she treats in these opening chapters.

have fallen and have turned into ruins. But I prophesy to you, as a true sibyl,[8] that this city which you will found with our help, will never be destroyed, nor will it fall: it will forever prosper in spite of all its jealous enemies. Although it will be attacked in many assaults, it will never be taken or vanquished.

"A long time ago the Amazon kingdom was founded by the order and enterprise of several courageous women who despised servitude, as you have learned from the testimony of history books. And for a long time afterwards they maintained it under the rule of several queens, most noble ladies whom they themselves elected, who governed them very well and who kept up the rule with great strength. Nonetheless, although they were strong and powerful and during their reign conquered a large part of the Orient and terrified all the neighboring lands, and although the Greeks feared them, who were then the flower of the world's countries, nonetheless, after a time the power of this kingdom failed, so that, as it happens with all earthly reigns, nothing but the name has survived to the present time.

"But you will build a much stronger edifice in this city that you must fashion. In order to begin its construction I have been commissioned, through the deliberations of us three, to deliver to you durable mortar, without any blemish, to lay the strong foundation and to raise the wide walls around, high and thick, with huge towers and strong bastions with moats around, fortified by block houses, as is fitting for a city with a strong and lasting defense. And, following our design, you will lay them deep, so that they will last longer, and then you will raise the walls above them so high they will fear no one.

"Daughter, now I have told you the reasons for our coming, and so that you will lend more credence to my words, I want to tell you my name, by whose sound alone you will be able to understand and know that, if you want to follow my orders, you have in me someone who will administer your work in such a way that you will be unable to make a mistake. I am called Lady Reason; now you see that you have good guidance. For now, I will say nothing more."

[Now the other two ladies identify themselves. The second lady's name is Rectitude. More of heaven than of the earth, she upholds the rights of the poor and the innocent. She holds a ruler in her hand with which she separates right from wrong and which will serve to measure the walls of the city. She declares herself Christine's assistant. The third lady is called Justice. She resides in heaven, on earth, and in hell, meting out what everyone deserves. She carries a gold vessel adorned with the fleur-de-lys, or lily of the Trinity. All virtues come from her. She will help Christine complete the

---

8. The ten Sibyls were wise women, able to predict the future. Boccaccio speaks of them in *Concerning Famous Women*. They appear at the beginning of book 2 of the *City*. See E. J. Richards's complete translation of *City* (New York: Persea, 1982), 99–104.

city and bring in its population of worthy ladies and the queen. She will then hand over the keys of the city to Christine.]

Here Christine Tells How She Spoke to the Three Ladies

When the three ladies had finished their speeches, to which I had listened intently and which had taken away from me all the unhappiness I had felt before their arrival, I immediately threw myself at their feet, not just on my knees but completely stretched out because of their great excellence. Kissing the earth around their feet, adoring them like goddesses of glory, I began to pray to them: "Oh ladies of the highest dignity, lights of the heavens and illumination of the earth, from where did your highnesses receive such humility that you deign to descend from your pontifical seats and shining thrones to come to the troubled and dark tabernacle of this simple and ignorant student? Who could be sufficiently grateful for such a privilege? You have already penetrated and moistened the dryness of my mind with the rain and dew from your sweet words that have descended on me; it now feels ready to germinate and bring forth new plants prepared to bear fruits of profitable virtue and delectable savor. How will such grace be given to me that I should have the privilege, according to your words, to build and fashion a new city that will exist from now on in this world?

"I am not St. Thomas the apostle, who through divine grace built a rich palace in heaven for the king of India,[9] nor does my feeble sense know the crafts, nor the measures, nor has it studied the theory and practice of stonework. And even if through the possibility of study these things were to become comprehensible to me, from where would my feeble feminine body take sufficient strength to undertake such a huge project? But nevertheless, my most respected ladies, although I am stunned by this news, I know well that nothing is impossible for God, and I cannot doubt that whatever is undertaken with your counsel and help should not come to a good end. Thus I praise God with all my strength and also you, my ladies, who have so honored me that now I am set up in this noble commission, which I accept with great joy. Here I am as your handmaiden, ready to obey. Command and I will obey, and may it be done to me according to your words."[1]

Here Christine Tells How, by Reason's Commandment and Help, She Began to Dig into the Earth in Order to Lay the Foundation

Then Lady Reason answered and said: "Up and about now, daughter! Let us go without delay to the field of letters: there the City of Ladies

13

13a

14

---

9. This story appears in the *Acts of Thomas*, one of the Apocryphal books of the New Testament and also in book 9, chapter 65 of Vincent of Beauvais's *Speculum historiale* [Historical Mirror], Christine's source for most of book 3 of the *City*.

1. Cf. Luke 1:38; after the Annunciation by the angel that she would be the mother of Christ, "Mary said, Behold the handmaid of the Lord; be it unto me according to thy word."

will be founded on flat and fertile land, where all fruits and fresh rivers are found and the earth abounds in all good things. Take the pick of your understanding and dig deep and make a great ditch wherever you see my outlines, and I will help you carry away the soil on my own shoulders."

To obey her commands I gingerly got up, feeling, thanks to them, stronger and lighter than before.[2] She went ahead and I behind, and once we had arrived at this field, I began to dig along her marks with the pick of inquiry. And my first piece of work went like this: 15

"Lady, I remember well that you told me earlier, on the subject of why so many men have blamed and continue to blame the behavior of women, that the longer gold is in the furnace the purer it gets: which means that the more wrongfully they are blamed, the greater is the merit of their glory. But I beg you to tell me why and for what reason so many different authors have spoken against women in their books, since I already know from you that they are wrong: is it that Nature makes them do it or do they do it out of hatred, and where does all this come from?"   16

Then she replied: "Daughter, to give you a way of entering more deeply, I will remove this first basketful of soil. You should know that all this does not come from Nature but is in opposition to her; for in this world there is no greater and stronger bond than that of the great love that Nature, by the will of God, forged between man and woman. But the causes that have moved and still move men to blame women are diverse and varied, and the same goes for the authors in their books, as you have found. For some have done this[3] with good intentions: that is, to get men that were led astray away from frequenting vicious and dissolute women, with whom they may be besotted or to keep them from getting besotted in the first place, and so that men avoid a lewd and lascivious life. They have blamed all women in general because they believe that they should all be abominated."

"Lady," I said then, "forgive me if I interrupt your words: have they done well, then, because they were motivated by good intentions? For the intention, so people say, judges the man." "This is badly put, dear daughter," she said, "for one should never excuse gross ignorance. If someone killed you with good intentions moved by crazy thoughts, would this then be well done? Rather, those that act like this, whoever they may be, misinterpreted the law: for to harm and wrong one party in order to help another is not justice, and nor is to blame all feminine behavior in opposition to the truth, as I will demonstrate by this hypothesis: Let us suppose that they did it in order to get fools away from foolish behavior. It would be as if I blamed fire, which is, after all, very good   16a

---

2. These lines seem to echo *Fortune's Transformation*, lines 1336–37 and 1351, where Christine describes her physical transformation into a man. Note that here she achieves the same strength in a female body. "Them": i.e., the ladies.
3. I. e., blame women.

and necessary, just because some people burned themselves, or water because people drown in it. And the same could be said of all good things that can be used well or badly. Nonetheless, one should not blame them just because fools abuse them; you yourself have touched upon this point quite well elsewhere in your texts.[4] But those who have spoken abundantly on the subject, whatever their intentions might be, have cast their net rather widely just to achieve their goal. Just like someone who has a long and wide robe cut from a large piece of cloth that costs him nothing and that no one refuses him: he takes and usurps the rights of others.

"But, as you have said earlier, if these writers had looked for ways and means to get men away from folly and to keep them away by untiringly blaming those women who show themselves to be vicious and dissolute—which is exactly, to tell the straight truth, what an evil, dissolute, and perverse woman does, a woman who is like a monster in nature, a counterfeit far removed from her true natural condition, which must be simple, quiet and honest—if they had done this, then I would agree that they would have built a good and beautiful piece of work. But to blame all of them, when there are so many excellent women, I can assure you that this did not come from me and that whoever does this and whoever follows this approach is making a great mistake. So now throw away these dirty, black, and knobbed stones, for they will never be part of the beautiful edifice of your city.

"Other men have blamed women for other reasons: some have 17 invented blame because of their own vices and others have been motivated by the defects in their own bodies, others through pure envy, and some others by the sheer pleasure they experience from slander. Others, in order to show that they have read many texts, base themselves on what they have found in books and repeat others and cite authorities.

"Those who have invented blame because of their own vices are men 18 who wasted their youth in dissolution and had a great many love affairs with different women, used deception in many instances, have grown old in their sins without repentance, and now regret their past follies and the dissolute life they led in their time. But nature, which does not allow the fulfillment of the heart's desire without sufficient power of the appetite, has grown cold in them. They are mournful when they see that the life that they used to call good times is over for them, and it seems to them that the young, who are now what they used to be, are enjoying the good times. They do not know how to make their sadness go away except by blaming women, believing that in this way they will make them displeasing to others. And one sees commonly such old men speaking obscenely and dishonestly, just as you can see with Matheolus, who admits himself that he was an old man with plenty of will but no

---

4. A reference to Christine's *The God of Love's Letter*, lines 341–47.

potency. Through him you can prove that what I tell you is true, and you can firmly believe that the same holds true for many others.

"But these corrupt old men who are like incurable leprosy, are not   19
the good, valiant men of ancient times whom I made perfect in virtue and wisdom—for not all old men have such corrupt desires, it would be too bad if such were the case—and in whose mouths are, according to their hearts, good, exemplary, honest, and discreet words. And these men hate misdeeds and slander and neither blame nor defame men or women, they hate vices and blame them in general without indicting or charging anyone in particular, they counsel the avoidance of evil and the pursuit of virtue and the straight path.

"Those men who are motivated by the defect of their own bodies are   20
impotent and have deformed limbs but sharp and malicious minds, and they cannot avenge the pain of their impotence except by blaming those women who bring joy to many: and thus they hope to spoil for others the pleasure that they themselves cannot enjoy.

"Those who blame women out of jealousy are those wicked men who   21
have seen and perceived many women of greater intelligence and nobler conduct than they themselves possess, and thus they are full of sorrow and disdain; and for these reasons their great jealousy has made them blame all women, hoping to suppress and diminish their glory and praise, just like I do not know which man who in his text entitled *On Philosophy* makes a great effort to prove that women should not be honored by men, and he says that those men who make so much of women pervert the name of his book: that is to say that out of 'philosophy' they make 'philofolly.'[5] But I assure and swear to you that he himself, through the deduction—filled with lies—of the case he makes there, transforms the content of his book into a true philofolly.

"As for those who are slanderers by nature, it is no wonder that they   22
blame women since they blame everyone. Nevertheless, I assure you that any man who willingly slanders women, does so because of a vile heart, for he acts against reason and nature. Against reason, in so far that he is most ungrateful and ignorant of the great good that woman has brought him, so often and continuously catering to his needs; it is so great a good that he could never pay. her back. And it is against nature, in so far as there is no mute beast anywhere, nor is there a bird who does not by nature dearly love its companion: and that is the female! And thus it is quite unnatural when a reasonable man does the opposite.

"And just as there has never been a work so worthy and made by such   23
a good master that some people did not, and still do not want, to counterfeit it, there are many who want to try their hand at writing poetry.[6]

5. *Sophia* means "wisdom"; *philosophy* is the "love of wisdom." Christine invents the counterpart "love of folly."
6. The word in French is *dicter*. Eustache Deschamps (or Eustache Morel), to whom Christine wrote a letter in 1404 (see p. 109), had written an *Art de dictier* [Art of poetry] in 1393.

And it seems to them that they cannot go wrong, since others have stated in their books what they want to say—or rather misstated, as I well know. Some want to embark on expressing themselves by making poems of water without salt, such as they are, or ballads without feeling, speaking of the behavior of women or princes or other people, while they themselves cannot recognize or correct their own miserable behavior and inclinations. But the simple people, who are as ignorant as they are, say that these poems are the best in the world."

Here Christine Tells How She Dug into the Earth: Which Means the Questions She Asked Reason and How Reason Answered

"Now I have prepared and ordered from you a great work; give some thought to continuing to dig in the ground along the lines I marked." Then, in order to obey her command, I struck with all my force in this way: 24

"Lady, how is it possible that Ovid, who is reputed to be the foremost poet—although some people believe that Virgil should be praised more, and, since you set me straight on this, I now agree with them—blames women so much in many of his works, for example in the book he called On the Art of Love and also in the one he entitled Remedies for Love[7] and in other volumes? Answer:[8] "Ovid was a man skilled in the art of poetry, and he had a very sharp wit and great understanding in what he was doing. However, he let his body slip into vanity and fleshly delights, not just into one love affair, but he abandoned himself to all possible women, he showed no moderation or loyalty, and valued none of the women. And in his youth he led this kind of life as much as he could, for which in the end he got his just deserts: that is, loss of reputation, of his possessions, and of his limbs, for he was exiled for his great lewdness, not only because he himself lived like this but also because of the advice he gave others to lead a similar life.   25

"Similarly, when he was later called back from exile with the help of some powerful young Romans, his followers, he did not keep from committing again the misdeeds for which he had been punished, and he was chastized and disfigured[9] for his faults. This point confirms what I said to you earlier, for when he saw that he could no longer lead the life he used to delight in so much, he began to blame women with his subtle reasoning and tried to make them displeasing to others."   26

"Lady, this is well said, but I saw a book by another Italian author, from the region or the marshes of Tuscany, I believe, who is called   26a

---

7. In the first text Ovid gave advice on how to seduce women, while in the second he gave remedies for falling out of love. The second text is more misogynistic than the first.
8. The present text preserves the structure of question and answer (which evokes both legal proceedings and a scholastic debate) and does not translate *response* by "she answered."
9. Curnow's edition has *chastiez*, which means "chastized." Richards translates this as "castrated," which one also finds in Christine source, Le Fèvre's *Book of Joy*; line 2712 states "someone cut off his two testicles."

Cecco d'Ascoli[1] and who wrote in one chapter abominations one can only marvel at, and they are such that any reasonable person should not repeat them." Answer: "If Cecco d'Ascoli speaks badly of all women, daughter, do not be amazed, for he detested and hated all of them and was annoyed by them. And similarly, because of his horrible wickedness he wanted all men to find them displeasing and hate them. He got what he deserved for this: as a reward for his criminal vices he was shamefully burned to death."

"I saw another small book in Latin, Lady, which is called *On the Secrets of Women*, which speaks of the disposition of women's natural bodies which have great defects." Answer: "You can realize by yourself, without any other proof, that this book was written tendentiously and hypocritically: for if you read it, it should be obvious to you that it is full of lies. And although some people say that it was written by Aristotle,[2] one cannot believe that such a philosopher would have taken it upon himself to fabricate such nonsense. For since women can clearly know by experience that some things he treats are not true but pure nonsense, they can conclude that other specific points he speaks of are straight lies. But don't you remember that he says in the beginning of his book that some Pope, I do not know which one, excommunicated every man who would read it to a woman or who would give it to her to read?" "Lady, I remember it well." "Do you know the malicious reason, given at the beginning of this book, why bestial and stupid men were supposed to believe this nonsense?" "No, Lady, not unless you tell me." "It was done so that women would not know about this book and what it contains: for the man who wrote it knew well that if women read it or heard it read, they would know well that it was nonsense and would contradict it and make fun of it. In this way, the author who wrote it wanted to fool and deceive the men who read it." "Lady, I remember that among other things—after he has spoken at length about the impotence and weakness that are responsible for the formation of the female body in the womb of the mother—he says that Nature seems all ashamed when she sees that she has formed such a body which appears to be something imperfect."[3]

"Ha, sweet friend! Just consider the great folly, the blindness beyond all reason that made him say this. Is Nature, then, who is the handmaiden of God, a greater mistress than her master, from whom she receives her authority, almighty God, who by the power of his thought had created the form of man and woman?

₂₇

_{27a}

1. As Curnow notes, Francesco Stabili, an astrologer at the University of Bologna, was known as Cecco d'Ascoli; see Curnow's edition, 1048. He was the author of the *Acerba* and was burned for heresy in 1327.
2. In fact, this work was most often attributed to the thirteenth-century theologian Albert the Great, although he did not write it either.
3. Aristotle, in his *The Generation of Animals*, argued for the female as a defective male. See Joan Cadden, *Meanings of Sex Difference in the Middle Ages: Medicine, Science, and Culture* (Cambridge, UK: Cambridge University Press, 1993), chap. 1.

When it occurred to His holy will to form Adam from the clay of the earth in the field of Damascus, he led him, after he had created him, to the terrestrial paradise which was and is the most worthy place down here on earth. There he made Adam fall asleep and formed the body of woman from one of his ribs, which signifies that she should be at his side as a companion and not at his feet like a slave, and also that he should love her as his own flesh. If the supreme craftsman was not ashamed to create and form a female body, Nature should be ashamed? Ha, it is the height of folly to say this. Indeed, how was she formed? I don't know if you noticed this, but she was formed in the image of God.[4] Oh, how can any mouth slander something which bears such a noble imprint? But some men are so crazy that they believe, when they hear it said that God created man in His image, that this means the material body.[5] But this is not so, for at that time God had not taken on a human body. Rather, it refers to the soul which is an intellectual spirit and lasts forever, just like the Deity. God created this soul and put completely equal souls, one as good and noble as the other, into the female and male bodies.[6] But to return to the question of the creation of the body: woman, then, was made by the supreme craftsman. And in which place was she made? In the earthly paradise. And of what? Of vile matter? No, but from the noblest matter that had ever been created: it was from the body of man that God made her."

"Lady, according to what I hear from you, woman is a most noble thing; yet Cicero says that no man should serve a woman and that whoever does so debases himself, for no one should serve anyone lower than him." Answer: "That person, male or female, who possesses more virtue is the higher; neither the eminence nor the lowliness of people lies in their bodies according to their sex, but in the perfection of morals and virtues. And happy is he who serves the Virgin who is above all angels."   28

"Lady, one of the Catos,[7] who was such a great orator, says further that if there were no women in this world we would converse with the gods." Answer: "Now you can see the folly of someone whom people consider wise: for it is through woman that man reigns with God. And   29

4. On all of these arguments and their origins see Elaine Pagels, *Adam, Eve, and the Serpent* (New York: Vintage Books, 1989). Boccaccio states in his *Concerning Famous Women* that Adam was created near Damascus.
5. Christine repeats here ideas of St. Augustine. See Kari E. Børresen, "God's Image, Man's Image? Patristic Interpretation of Gen. 1,27 and I Cor. 11,7" and "God's Image, Is Woman Excluded? Medieval Interpretation of Gen. 1,27 and I Cor. 11,7" in Kari E. Børresen, ed., *The Image of God: Gender Models in Judaeo-Christian Tradition* (Minneapolis: Fortress, 1995), 187–235.
6. See Eleanor Commo McLaughlin, "Equality of Souls, Inequality of Sexes: Woman in Medieval Theology," in Rosemary Radford Ruether, ed., *Religion and Sexism: Images of Woman in the Jewish and Christian Traditions* (New York: Simon & Schuster, 1974), 213–66.
7. There were two Catos, both Roman statesmen. The name *Cato* was known through a medieval text of sayings falsely attributed to him. Le Fèvre translated one of the Latin compilations into French.

if anyone claims that he was exiled because of Lady Eve, I reply that he has gained a higher good through Mary than he lost through Eve, when humanity was joined to the Deity, which would have never happened if Eve's misdeed had not occurred. Thus man and woman should be happy about this fault which has brought them such honor. For as low as human nature fell through the created beings, the higher is was lifted up by the Creator. And as for conversing with the gods if woman did not exist, as this Cato said, he spoke truer than he thought: for he was a pagan, and those of this religion believed that gods lived in hell as well as in heaven—that is, the devils whom they called gods of hell—so it makes sense that men would have conversed with these gods had it not been for Mary."

[Christine asks more questions about misogynistic prejudices, for example that women are only interested in dresses, that they are gluttonous and childish. For each reproach Reason offers counterexamples that demonstrate the essential goodness of women. In response to the proverb stating that women are only made for talking, crying, and spinning, Reason proves that women's tears are not signs of helplessness but of piety, which has brought about many miracles. Reason now turns to woman's speech.]

"Similarly, God gave women speech, and praised be He for this, for   34
if He had not given them speech they would be mute. But to refute what is said in this proverb, which someone, I don't know who, made up only in order to level reproach at women, if women's language had been so worthy of reproof and of so little authority, as some men maintain, our Lord Jesus Christ would have never deigned to wish that such a holy mystery as that of His glorious Resurrection should first be announced by a woman, for He Himself ordered the blessed Magdalene, to whom He first appeared on Easter, to tell and announce it to the Apostles and to Peter. Oh, blessed God, may you be praised, you who together with other infinite gifts and favors that You have given to the female sex, wished that a woman should be the bearer of such high and worthy news."

"All those envious people should be silent now, Lady, if they could see the truth," I said. "But I smile at the foolishness that some men utter and I even remember that I heard some foolish preachers say that God first appeared to a woman because He knew well that she could not keep quiet, so that the news of His Resurrection would become known faster." Answer: "Daughter, you have spoken well when you called those people fools who say this: for it is not enough for them to blame women, they even ascribe to Jesus such blasphemy by saying that He wanted to reveal His great perfection and dignity through a vice. And I don't know how a man dares to say this; and though they may say it in jest, God should not be mixed up in such mockery."

[Further examples of the goodness of women's speech follow. And Reason concludes in paragraph 38.]

"As you can understand now, fair sweet friend, God has given language to women to be served by it. Thus they should not be reproached for something from which much good and little evil comes, for one sees rarely that their language does any great damage.   38

"As for spinning, truly God wanted it to be natural for them, for it is necessary for the divine service and it is useful to every reasonable creature, for without this kind of work the affairs of this world would fall into great corruption. Thus it is very bad to reproach women for what should be construed to their great credit, honor, and praise."   39

Christine Asks Reason Why Women Do Not Sit in the Seats of Lawyers; and the Answer

"Most high and honored lady, your excellent arguments completely satisfy me. But tell me still, if you please, the truth about why women do not plead in law courts, know nothing about arguments, and do not render judgments; for these men say that some woman, I don't know who, behaved unwisely in the seat of justice."[8] "Daughter, the things one says about her are frivolous and cunningly invented. But whoever would ask about the causes and reasons of all things, there would be too many answers to give; not even Aristotle, although he explains many of them in his *Problems* and *Categories*, would be sufficient. But as for that question, fair friend, one might just as well ask why God did not ordain that men do the tasks of women, and women those of men. So this question can be answered by saying that just as a wise and well-organized lord arranges his household so that people do different tasks, one person one thing and another person another thing, and what one person does the other does not do, in the same way God has established man and woman to serve him in different tasks and also to help and comfort one another, each one in what he has been given to do, and to each sex He has given the nature and inclination fitting and appropriate for their task.   40

[Reason describes the strength and boldness of men that make them fit for upholding the law by force or in court. Women do not have the same strengths.]

Although there are women to whom God has given great understanding, nonetheless, because of the decency they are inclined to, it would not be appropriate for them to go and appear boldly in court like men,

---

8. A reference to Cafurnia, whose outrageous behavior Matheolus discussed in his *Lamentations* 2.177–200.

for there are enough men who do so. What would be the good of sending three men to lift a load that two can carry easily?

But if anyone wanted to claim that women do not have sufficient   41
understanding to learn the laws, the opposite is evident, as is proven by experience, which shows, and has shown this (as I will tell you shortly) through many women who have been great philosophers and have acquired more subtle and more eminent knowledge than written laws and things established by men. And furthermore, if anyone wanted to propose that women do not have a natural sense for politics and government, I will give you examples of several great female rulers from the past. And, so that you will better understand my truth, I will also remind you of some women of your own time who remained widows whose excellent governing of their affairs after their husbands' deaths clearly shows that a woman who possesses understanding is up to all tasks."[9]

[In paragraph 42 Reason tells the stories of Nicaula, the empress of Aethiopia, and in paragraph 43 of Fredegund, queen of France, who, though crueler than women naturally are, was a skilled ruler. She then lists some more women[1] of the French past and present who ruled nobly.]

More Exchanges and Debates between Christine and Reason

[Christine agrees that Reason proved her case for the excellence of women's minds. Yet, they have weak bodies and some people claim that they are natural cowards. Reason invalidates this argument by showing that Aristotle and Alexander the Great, though ugly and even sickly, were nevertheless great men. Indeed, many strong men are cowardly, while some men who appear weak are bold.]

"But as for boldness and bodily strength, God and Nature have done   52
much for women by depriving them of these qualities, for at least through this pleasant defect they are excused from committing the horrible cruelties, murders, and great and serious crimes, which have been and are being done by force throughout the world. Thus they will never have to suffer the punishment that such cases demand: and it would have been better for the souls of many strong men if they had spent their earthly pilgrimage in weak female bodies. And I truly say, to return to my point, that if Nature did not give great bodily strength to women she has well compensated for this by giving them a most virtuous inclination, that is, to love one's God and to be fearful of transgressing His commandments; and those women who do otherwise act against nature.

[Nonetheless, there are some women who possess both physical strength and daring. In a return to the building imagery Reason now finds that the

9. This is one of the topics of her *Book of the Three Virtues.*
1. Most of the examples in this section come from Boccaccio's *Concerning Famous Women.*

ditch is deep enough and that the first stone can be laid. Christine is ordered to take up "the trowel of [her] pen" and to place the first stone, which is Semiramis, queen of Niniveh. She was a conqueror and founder of cities; she also married her own son, something that was then not forbidden by written law.[2] Next, Reason tells of the Amazons and of other noble queens and military heroines. This section completes the foundations of the City; they can now start on the walls.]

Christine Asks Reason Whether God Has Ever Wanted to Ennoble the Mind of Woman with the Eminence of the Sciences; and Reason's Response

After listening to these things, I replied to the lady who spoke without error: "Lady, God has truly revealed great marvels in the strength of these women of whom you have told me. But help me to become even wiser, if you please, by telling me whether it has ever pleased this same God, who has done so many favors to women, to honor the feminine sex by giving some of them the privilege of the virtue of high understanding and great learning, and whether women have a mind capable of this? I very much want to know this because men claim that the understanding of women is of little capacity." Answer: "Daughter, by what I told you earlier you can conclude that the opposite of their opinion is true and to make it even clearer to you I will prove it by examples. I tell you again, and do not believe that the contrary is true, that if it were the custom to send little girls to school and have them study the sciences, as one does in the case of boys, they would learn just as perfectly and would understand the subtleties of the arts and sciences as boys do. And as it happens there are such women: for, as I touched on earlier, just as women have more delicate bodies than men, weaker and less able to do various things, so they have minds that are more open and sharper in the cases where they apply themselves."

"Lady, what are you saying? May it not displease you to bear with me a little on this point. Certainly men would never admit the truth of this point unless it is explained more fully, for they claim that one commonly sees that men know more than women." Answer: "Do you know why women know less?" "No, lady, unless you tell me." "Undoubtedly it is so because they do not encounter so many different things but stay in their houses, and it is enough for them to run their households; and there is nothing that teaches so much to a reasonable creature as the exercise and experience of many different things." "Lady, since they have minds capable of comprehending and learning things, why do women not learn more?" Answer: "For the reason, daughter, that public life does not need their participation in tasks that men are meant to

82

82a

2. On this story see Maureen Quilligan, *The Allegory of Female Authority: Christine de Pizan's 'Cité des dames'* (Ithaca, N.Y.: Cornell University Press, 1991), 69–85.

perform, as I told you earlier. It is enough that they perform the customary tasks for which they are meant."

[Reason goes on to explain that not natural incapacity but a lack of learning is at the origin of what people might consider savage or unwise customs. Just as for men, some women have better minds than others. She will now tell of some women who have the kind of learning that resembles men's.]

She Begins to Speak of Some Ladies Who Were Enlightened with Great Learning, and First about the Noble Maiden Cornificia

"Cornificia, the noble maiden, was sent to school by her parents— through tricks and deception—with her brother Cornificius, still in their childhood. But this little girl had such a wonderful mind for study that through her learning she began to feel the sweet taste of knowledge. It was not easy to take away from her this pleasure to which she devoted herself at the expense of other feminine tasks. And she spent so much time on this that she became a most excellent poet, and her talent and expertise were not only in the learned craft of poetry but it also seemed that she had been nourished with the milk and doctrine of philosophy: for she wanted to experience and know about all kinds of learning, in which she acquired such mastery that she surpassed her brother, a great poet himself, through her superior learning.

"And she was not satisfied with mere knowledge unless she could put her mind to work and her hands to her pen in the compilation of several very well known books. Her books and poems were much appreciated at the time of St. Gregory[3] and were even mentioned by him. In this context Boccaccio, the Italian, who was a great poet, speaks in praise of this woman in his book: 'Oh, greatest honor to a woman who abandoned all feminine tasks and applied and devoted her mind to the study of the most eminent scholars.'

"Further, Boccaccio speaks—and in this he confirms what I said to you earlier—of the minds of women who despise themselves and their own judgment, and, just as if they were born in the mountains and did not know what is good and honorable, they become discouraged and say that the only thing they are good and useful for is to embrace men and carry and feed children. And God has given them such beautiful understanding to apply themselves, if they want to, to the same things as glorious and excellent men. Whatever subjects they want to study, they will find that they are just as open to them as to men, and through their honest labor they can acquire a name that will last forever, something that is much desired by the most eminent men. Dear daughter, now you can see how this author Boccaccio testifies to what I have told you and how he praises and approves learning in women."

83

83a

3. Boccaccio specifies St. Jerome in *Concerning Famous Women*, 188.

[Reason now tells Christine about the Roman poet Proba, author of the
Cento, which draws on many of Virgil's works; about Sappho, Manto, and
the skills of Medea (without mentioning the murder of her children), and
Circe.]

Christine Asks Reason Whether There Was Ever a Woman Who by Herself Invented a Science Not Known Before

[Christine agrees that Reason has made a good case for the existence of
many learned ladies, but did women ever invent something new? Reason
replies that women have invented many arts and sciences, both theoretical
and practical. A new series of examples begins, as Reason tells of Nicostrata.]

"And first I will tell you about the noble Nicostrata whom the Italians   92
called Carmentis.[4] This lady was the daughter of the king of Arcadia,
named Pallas. She had an extraordinary mind and was endowed by God
with special gifts of knowledge: she was so learned in Greek literature,
spoke so beautifully and wisely, and possessed such praiseworthy eloquence that the poets of her time who wrote about her made up stories
that she was loved by the god Mercury,[5] and that a son she had had by
her husband, and who was extremely learned in his time, was actually
this god's son. Certain changes that occurred in her country caused her
to leave and, in a large ship, she transported her son and a great number
of people who followed her to the land of Italy and arrived at the river
Tiber. There she landed and climbed up on a high hill she named the
Palentine after her father, on which the city of Rome was later founded.
There, this lady with her son and followers built a fortress. And as she
had found that the men of this country were like savage beasts, she
wrote certain laws in which she urged them to live by the order of right
and reason, according to justice. And she was the first to establish laws
in this country which later on became so famous and from which came
and issued all just laws.

"This noble lady knew by divine inspiration and the spirit of proph-   92a
ecy, which together with other graces had been given to her and in
which she was particularly expert, that this country would become in
future times ennobled by excellence and reputation, surpassing all the
countries on this earth. It seemed to her that it would not be proper
that, once the Roman Empire had attained its superiority, its people
should use the strange and inferior letters and characters of another
country. And also, in order to demonstrate her wisdom and the excellence of her mind to future centuries, she labored and studied until she

---

4. On the importance of Carmentis for the creation of a new poetic consciousness in the late
   Middle Ages, see Jacqueline Cerquiglini-Toulet, *La Couleur de la mélancolie: La fréquentation
   des livres au XIVe siècle (1300–1415)* (Paris: Hatier, 1993), 118–25.
5. This is a euhemeristic (historical) explanation of myth—one of the popular ways of interpreting mythological stories in the Middle Ages. See also n.4, p. 29.

came up with her own letters that were completely different from those of other nations: that is, the ABC and the rules for Latin, how letters could be put together, and the difference between vowels and consonants, and all the fundamentals of the science of grammar. She presented and taught these letters and science to the people and wanted to make them widely known. The science invented by this woman was neither unimportant nor useless and one owes her no small amount of gratitude, for the subtlety of this science and the great utility and good it subsequently brought to this world justify our saying that nothing more worthy was ever invented in this world.

"And the Italians were not ungrateful for this benefit, and with good reason; to them, these events were so marvelous that they not only held this woman in greater repute than any man, but considered her a goddess, and for this reason bestowed divine honors on her while she was still alive. And when she was dead, they constructed a temple that they dedicated to her name; it was built at the foot of the hill where she had lived.   92b

[Reason now explains not only how the Romans named their country and important concepts with the words she had invented or even after her (such as Latin *carmen*, which means "song, poem," from Carmentis) but that her language survives to this day. And Carmentis was not the only woman who invented new things.

Reason tells the story of Minerva or Pallas who invented shorthand writing in Greek as well as numbers. Among other skills, she also invented the making of armor and musical instruments. For her accomplishments she was worshiped as a goddess. Ceres invented agriculture and Isis taught people how to plant. Reason and Christine now recapitulate the achievements of these women and the benefits humanity derived from their inventions. Reason then tells the story of Arachne, an expert weaver and the inventor of the cultivation of flax and hemp. All this is very useful for civilization, though some authors seem to object to this view.]

"And nonetheless, some authors, and even the poet Boccaccio who tells these very stories, have said that the world was faring better when people lived on nothing but hawthorn fruits and acorns and did not dress in anything but animal skins than it has fared since people were taught more refined ways of life. But, while appreciating him and those who claim that the world has been worse off because of the things invented for the well-being and nourishment of the human body, I have to say that the more good things, favors, and gifts human creatures receive from God, the better they are obliged to serve Him.[6] And if humans misuse the goods their Creator has promised and granted them   108a

6. On Christine's ideas on the Golden Age see Rosalind Brown-Grant, "Décadence ou progrès? Christine de Pizan, Boccace et la question de 'l'Age d'Or,'" *Revue des langues romanes* 92 (1988), 295–306.

to use well and fittingly and that He made for the use of men and women, it is because of the wickedness and perversity of those who misuse them, and not because the things in themselves are not good and profitable when people use them and avail themselves of them in a lawful manner. Jesus Christ Himself demonstrated this to us in His own person: for He used bread, wine, fish, colored garments, linen, and all necessary things, which He would never have done if it were better to live on hawthorn fruits and acorns. And He bestowed great honor on the science that Ceres invented, namely bread, when it pleased Him to give man and woman such a worthy body in the form of bread so that they could profit from it."[7]

[Reason tells the story of Pamphile who invented a way of getting silk from worms; she then speaks of several painters of antiquity—Thamaris, Irene, and Marcia—who surpassed all others in the world. Christine feels compelled to add a contemporary example.]

Then I said to her: "Lady, by these examples one can see that in ancient times the wise were honored more than at present, and that the sciences were prized much more. But, concerning what you said about women expert in the science of painting, I know a woman today whose name is Anastasia, who is so expert at painting manuscript borders[8] and illustrating landscapes that there is no craftsman in the city of Paris, where the most eminent painters in the world can be found, who surpasses her, nor is there anyone who paints flowers and small details as delicately as she does, or anyone whose work is appreciated more, however rich or expensive the book may be that those people lucky enough to obtain one get from her. And this I know from experience: for she has done some things for me which are considered extraordinary among the manuscript borders of other great craftsmen." Answer: "I certainly believe you, dear daughter; one could find plenty of intelligent women in the world if one were willing to look. And still in this context I will tell you of a Roman woman."

[Reason now tells of Sempronia who possessed an extraordinary memory.]

113

---

7. A reference to the bread equaling the body of Christ used in the Christian ritual of the Eucharist.
8. The French words *vigneteures* ("vines") and *champaignes d'istoires* ("illustrated landscapes") are interesting technical terms that show how expert Christine was in manuscript illumination. We know that she supervised the illustration of several of her manuscripts. Millard Meiss refers to this passage in *French Painting in the Time of Jean de Berry*, vol. 1 (London: Phaidon, 1957), 362, n. 3. See also Jonathan J. G. Alexander, *Medieval Illuminators and Their Methods of Work* (New Haven, Conn.: Yale University Press, 1992) as well as n. 6 on p. 30.

Here Christine Asks Reason if There Is Any Prudence in the Natural Sense of Women; and Reason's Answer to Her

[Christine observes that many scholars show little prudence in their moral conduct, despite their learning. She now wants to know whether there were any women who were guided in their actions by prudence. Reason responds that there are two forces that produce prudence: natural sense and acquired knowledge. Acquired knowledge should be prized more because it can be transmitted and lasts forever. But this question does not directly relate to the building of the City. Reason therefore returns to her examples and begins to tell of prudent women. After citing the Song of Solomon, she speaks of Gaia Cirilla, wife of King Tarquin, who excelled at both governing and in the administration of her household. In a long chapter Reason tells the story of Dido, emphasizing her skill at acquiring land and retaining power.[9] Ops, the Cretan queen, and Lavinia, Aeneas's wife, close book 1 as examples of prudent rulers. Reason now summarizes the points of this book.]

"What else would you like me to tell you, dear daughter? It seems to me that I have produced enough proofs for my points: namely to show you, by quick reasoning and example, that God has never had, nor has, any objections to the feminine sex, or to that of men, as it has become clear and will become even clearer in the depositions of my two sisters who are here. For it seems to me that for now the walls I have built for you as the enclosure of the City of Ladies must suffice; they are finished and covered with plaster. May my two sisters step forward, and with their help and advice may you complete what still remains to be done with this building."   123

Here ends the first part of the Book of the City of Ladies.

Here Begins the Second Part of the Book of the City of Ladies, Which Tells How and by Whom the Houses within the City Walls Were Built and Populated

[Lady Rectitude, the second sister, now approaches Christine and tells her about the ten Sibyls, wise women with prophetic voices.[1] She then tells the stories of more women prophets such as Cassandra; Queen Basine, wife of King Childeric; and Antonia, empress of Constantinople.]

Christine Speaks to Lady Rectitude

"Lady, because I understand and see clearly that women are in the right against the things they are so often accused of, please make me   143

---

9. Christine told Dido's story twice: once in the context of abandoned lovers and once showing Dido as a powerful ruler. Aside from Boccaccio, her story was also known from Virgil's *Aeneid* and Ovid's *Heroides.* See Marilynn Desmond, *Reading Dido: Gender, Textuality, and the Medieval Aeneid* (Minneapolis: University of Minnesota Press, 1995).
1. See n. 3 on p. 40.

comprehend better the injustice of their accusers. And again, I cannot keep quiet about a habit of thought that circulates commonly among men, and even among some women, which maintains that when women are pregnant and give birth to a daughter, the husbands are unhappy and grumble because their wives have not given birth to a son. And their silly wives, who should be overjoyed that God has safely delivered them and likewise thank Him from their hearts, are upset because they see their husbands unhappy. Why, lady, are they so sad about this? Are daughters more trouble than sons, or do they love their parents less or are they more indifferent toward them than sons?"

Answer: "Dear friend, since you ask me about the cause, I can answer you with certainty that the reason is the extreme simplemindedness and ignorance of those who are unhappy about this. However, the principal reason that motivates them is the cost of marrying them, which will require a great part of their possessions. And some worry because they fear the danger of their daughters being deceived by bad advice when they are ingenuous and young.   143a

"But all these reasons amount to nothing when looked at sensibly. For, as far as the fear of their daughters doing something foolish is concerned, all one has to do is to instruct them wisely when they are small and for the mother to serve as an example of decency and good teaching, for if the mother were to lead a disordered life she would be a bad example for the daughter; and she should be kept away from bad company, on a tight rein and respectful, for the discipline maintained over children and young people serves as preparation for a lifetime of virtue. Likewise, as far as the expense is concerned, I believe that if the parents looked more closely at the amount their sons cost them—be it for teaching them knowledge or a profession, or simply for living expenses, and even for superfluous expenses (whether they belong to the high, middle, or lower classes), or for foolish companionship or a lot of silliness—I believe that they will hardly find it more advantageous to have sons than daughters. And if you consider the anger and worry caused by many sons and the fact that they often incite rough and grievous brawls and riots or lead dissolute lives—and all this to the grief and at the expense of their parents—I believe that this easily surpasses the worries they have because of their daughters.

"Just see how many sons you can find who take care of their father   143b
and mother in their old age as gently and humbly as they should.

[Rectitude observes that many parents make gods out of their sons, and then, when the sons are rich and the father poor, the sons abandon the parents. Or, if the father is rich, they cannot wait for him to die so that they can inherit.]

"And on this subject Petrarch spoke the truth when he said: 'Oh foolish man, you desire to have children, but you could not have a more mortal enemy: for if you are poor, they will find you tedious and will desire your death to be rid of you; and if you are rich, they will desire it no less, in order to have what belongs to you.'[2]

"I certainly do not claim that all sons are like this, but there are a lot who are. And if they are married, God knows how eager they are to exploit their fathers and mothers: they could not care less if these weary old people die of hunger, just as long as they get everything. What a family! Or if their mothers are widowed, at the moment when they should comfort them and be the support and help in their old age—these mothers who cherished them so much and brought them up to tenderly are well rewarded for all this: for the evil children believe that everything should belong to them, and if the mothers don't give them everything they want they will not spare them their displeasure. God knows how much respect is observed here! And there is worse, for some have no qualms about bringing lawsuits against their mothers and drag them to court. And this is the reward that many people receive after having spent their lives trying to get richer or advancing their children. There are many sons like this, and it is possible that there are daughters like this as well. But, if you look closely, I think that you will find that there more sons than daughters among these perverse children.

"And let us suppose that all sons were good, one still sees daughters keeping their fathers and mothers company more often than sons, and they visit them more often and give them greater comfort and care in their sickness and old age. The reason is that sons move around the world more, here and there, while daughters keep more quiet and stay closer to their parents, as you can see by your own example: for, regardless of the fact that your brothers were not unnatural children and very loving and good, they went out into the world, while you alone stayed behind to keep your good mother company, which is her greatest comfort in her old age. And for this reason, I tell you in conclusion that those people who are upset and unhappy when daughters are born to them are just too foolish. And since you got me into this subject, I want to tell you about some women, written about among others, who are very natural and show great love to their parents." 143c

[Rectitude tells the stories of Drypetina, Hypsipyle, and Claudine who were good companions to their fathers and even fought for them in battles. Now Rectitude turns to the story of a daughter and a mother in Rome.]

About a Woman Who Breastfed Her Mother in Prison

"Similarly, a woman from Rome showed great love for her mother, as the history books tell. It happened that her mother was condemned to 147

2. Petrarch speaks on these topics in his *De remediis utriusque fortunae* [On the remedies of the two fortunes], i.e., good and bad fortune. Christine's father may have known Petrarch.

die in prison for certain crimes of which she was accused, and no one was supposed to give her anything to drink or eat. Her daughter, moved by great filial love and saddened by this sentence, requested as a special favor from those who guarded her that she be allowed to visit her mother every day, as long as she was still alive, so that she could counsel her to show perseverance. And, to make matters brief, she cried and begged so much that the prison guards took pity on her and gave her leave to visit her mother every day. But before they brought her to her mother, they always searched her very well so that she would not bring her any food.

[This goes on for so many days that the guards begin wondering how the mother can survive so long without food.]

"In fact, one day they spied on the mother and daughter together: and they saw that the unhappy daughter, who had just had a child, gave her teat to her mother until she had drawn all milk from her breasts. And thus the daughter gave back to her mother in her old age what she had taken from her in her infancy. This continuous care and great love of daughter to mother moved the jailers to great pity, and the act was reported to the judges who, moved by human compassion, freed the mother and gave her back to her daughter."

[Griselda is another example of a good daughter.[3] Many more daughters could be listed, but Rectitude decides that she has said enough on this topic.
Rectitude explains that the houses of the City are now finished and that the City needs to be populated. It will be like a new and better Amazon kingdom, for the ladies will not have to leave to give birth in order to perpetuate their realm. Rather, the ladies who will now be put into the City will suffice forever. But only virtuous women of integrity will be admitted. Christine asks Lady Rectitude whether what the books and men say is true, namely that married life is so hard to bear because of women and their great faults. And Rectitude responds and begins to speak of the great love women have for their husbands.]

Then as we were leaving to seek out these ladies by the order of Lady Rectitude, I spoke these words as we were moving along: "Lady, you and Reason have truly found solutions and conclusions to all my questions and queries to which I knew no answer, and I consider myself very well informed on the subject I inquired about. And I have learned from you a lot about how all feasible and knowable things, be they related to the strength of the body or to the wisdom of understanding or to all the

152

---

3. Her story, told by Boccaccio as the last in his *Decameron*, was extremely popular in the Middle Ages. Christine tells it at length later in book 2; see E. J. Richard's complete translation, 170–76. Petrarch wrote a Latin version and Philip of Mézières, to whom Christine once sold some property, wrote the first French version in his book on the sacrament of marriage: Joan B. Williamson, ed., *Le livre de la vertu du sacrement de mariage* (Washington, D.C.: Catholic University of America Press, 1993).

virtues, are possible and easy for women to achieve. But I am still asking you to tell and certify for me whether it is true what men say and so many authors testify to—something about which I am thinking deeply—that for men life within the order of marriage is so filled with and taken over by uproar because of the fault and impetuosity of women and their vengeful bad moods, as it is written in many books? And many people bear witness to this kind of life by saying that women like their husbands and their company so little that nothing else annoys them as much. For this reason many people have counseled wise men not to marry so that they can resist and escape from such inconveniences, and they affirm that no women, or very few of them, are loyal to their partners.

"And in this vein Valerius wrote to Rufinus, and Theophrastus[4] said in his book that no wise man should take a wife, because there are too many worries in women, little love, and an abundance of idle talk, and that if a man marries to be better taken care of and watched over in his sickness, a loyal servant would serve and watch over him better and more diligently and would not cost him as much, and if the woman gets sick the husband languishes and does not dare move away from her. And he says a lot of things like that, which would take too long to recite; therefore I say to you, dear lady, that if these things are true, these flaws are so shameful that all the other graces and virtues women could possess amount to nothing and are canceled out by them."

Answer: "Certainly, friend, just as you yourself said earlier on this topic: whoever brings a lawsuit without opposition, pleads at his own convenience. And I assure you that the books that say this were not written by women.[5] But I have no doubt that whoever were to inquire into the debate on marriage in order to write a new book in accordance with the truth, would find some news! Dear friend, how many women are there, and you yourself know this, who because of their husbands' hard-heartedness spend their weary lives in the bonds of marriage under greater punishment than if they were slaves among the Saracens? Oh, God! How many harsh beatings without cause and reason, how many gross insults, how much nastiness, how many injuries, humiliations, and outrages have many good and upright women suffered of whom not one cried out for help. And what about those women that die of hunger and misery with a house full of children and their husbands go rabble-rousing about town or in taverns, and what about the poor women who are beaten by their husbands upon their return, and they are supposed to count this as their supper—what do you say about that: am I lying? And have you ever seen any of your female neighbors treated like that?"

4. Rufinus was mentioned by Jean Le Fèvre in his *Book of Joy*. Walter Map wrote an antimarriage text in the twelfth century featuring these characters who were mentioned by St. Jerome. See Wilson and Makowski, *Wykked Wyves*, 51–53 and 87–98.
5. Christine made the same argument in her *The God of Love's Letter* (see p. 15).

153

And I said to her: "Certainly, lady, I have seen many, and I pity them 153a
greatly." "I believe you, and to say that men are so saddened by their
wives' illnesses, I beg of you, my friend, where are they? And without
telling you any more, you can well see that this nonsense spoken and
written against women is invented, biased, and untrue. For men are
masters over their wives, and wives are certainly not mistresses over their
husbands: they would never let them have such authority.

"But I assure you that not all marriages are filled with such quarrels,
for there are people who live together in great peacefulness, love, and
loyalty because the partners are good, considerate, and reasonable. And
although there are bad husbands, there are also very good ones, valiant
and wise, and the women who encounter them were born lucky with
respect to the glory of this world, because God pointed them in the right
direction. And you know this very well by your own example: you had
such a husband that, even if you could have had your heart's desire, you
could not have asked for a better one; in your judgment no one surpassed him in goodness, peacefulness, loyalty, and true love, and the
grief over death having taken him away from you will never leave your
heart. And although I am telling you, and it is true, that there are many
good women badly mistreated by their wicked husbands, you should
know nevertheless that there are also wicked and unreasonable women,
for if I were to tell you that they are all good, I could rather easily be
accused of being a liar—but that is the least of it. And I have no business
with those, for such women are like beings removed from their own
nature.

"To speak of good women: as for this Theophrastus who said that a 154
man will be just as loyally and diligently taken care of in his sickness
and worry by a servant as by his wife: ha! How many good women are
there who are so concerned in serving their husbands, healthy or sick,
with a love so loyal as if their husbands were gods? I do not believe one
could find such a servant. And because we have broached this subject
matter, I will give you many examples of the great love and loyalty
shown by wives for their husbands. And now, thank God, we have
returned to our City in the noble company of the beautiful and virtuous
women that we will settle there."

[The first inhabitant of the City is a loyal wife: Rectitude tells of Hypsicratea, the wife of king Mithridates; she dressed like a man to follow him
through war and sweeten his exile. Her devotion refutes the misogynistic
prejudices of Theophrastus.]

Of the Empress Triaria

"Quite similar to the above-mentioned queen's were the circum- 156
stances and the loyal love for her husband of the noble Empress Triaria,

the wife of Lucius Vitellius, emperor of the Romans.[6] She loved him so greatly that she followed him everywhere, and in all battles, armed like a knight, she remained courageously at his side and fought vigorously. One day, at the time of the emperor's fight against Vespasianus for the rulership of the empire, when he attacked a city of the Volscians at night, he managed to enter it and found the people asleep whom he attacked cruelly. But this noble lady Triaria, who had followed her husband throughout the night, was not far off so that, ardently wishing for his victory and fully armed and girded with a sword, she fought fiercely among the troops next to him, now here, now there, in the darkness of the night. She showed no fear or horror, but rather such force that she was praised by everyone for this battle where she had truly done marvels. Thus she demonstrated well, as Boccaccio says, the great love she had for her husband, sanctioning the bonds of marriage that others so strongly object to."

[Rectitude adduces more examples of good wives: Artemisia, queen of Caria; Argia, King Adrastus's daughter, taking care of the body of her husband, Polynice, after the Theban war; the stories of a number of Roman ladies prove that, contrary to what the misogynists say, women can be trusted with secrets and are capable of giving good advice to their husbands. More Roman ladies are cited as well as women from the Old Testament, such as Judith and Esther. This section culminates with the story of the French king Clovis who was converted to Christianity[7] by his wife Clotilda.]

Against Those Who Say That It Is Not Good That Women Should Pursue Learning

After hearing these things, I, Christine, spoke as follows: "Lady, I see well that many good things have come about through women, and if any evil resulted from evil women, it still seems to me that the good things brought about by good women, and also by the wise women and those learned in literature and the sciences I mentioned above, are more numerous. For this reason I am extremely amazed by the opinion of some men who say that they do not want their daughters, wives, or female relatives to study the sciences and that their morals would worsen through this."

Answer: "In this you can clearly see that not all the opinions of men are based on reason and that these men are wrong. For it should not be assumed that knowing the moral sciences, which teach the virtues, would worsen morals, rather, there is no doubt that they improve and

6. Boccaccio states that Triaria was the wife of the emperor's brother; see *Concerning Famous Women*, 217.
7. The conversion to Christianity of King Clovis in 496 was an important part of late medieval national ideology (see also n. 7 on p. 162). See Colette Beaune, *The Birth of an Ideology: Myths and Symbols of Nation in Late-Medieval France*, trans. Susan Ross Huston (Berkeley: University of California Press, 1991), chap. 2.

ennoble them. How is it possible to believe that a person who follows good teaching and doctrine could be the worse for it? Such a thing cannot be uttered or supported. I do not say that it would be good for a man or a woman to study the science of sorcery,[8] or those areas that are forbidden—for the Holy Church did not remove them from common usage for nothing—but that women should get worse by knowing good things is not believable."

[Rectitude tells the story of Hortensia, daughter of the rhetoricain Quintus Hortensius, who through her rhetorical skill supported the cause of women against a tax on jewelry in a time of financial crisis.]

"Similarly, to speak of more recent times, without looking about in ancient histories, Jean André, the solemn legal scholar in Bologna the Fat[9] not quite sixty years ago, was not of the opinion that it was bad for women to be learned. His beautiful and good daughter, whom he loved so much was called Novella. He had her educated in the law to such a high level, that, when he was occupied with some business which prevented him from lecturing to his students, he sent his daughter in his place to present the lectures to the students from his professorial seat. And so that her beauty would not distract the listeners from their thoughts, she had a little curtain in front of her. And in this manner she aided and lightened her father's work. He loved her so much that, to commemorate her name, he gave a notable lecture on a law book he named after his daughter, *Novella*. 185

"So not all men, and especially the wisest, are of the above-mentioned opinion that it is bad for women to be learned. But it is quite true that some men, who are not wise, say this because it would displease them if women knew more than they do. Your father, who was a great scientist and philosopher, was not of the opinion that women were worth less by learning the sciences, rather, as you know, he derived great pleasure from seeing you inclined toward learning. But the feminine opinion of your mother, who wanted to keep you busy with stuff like spinning as is the common custom of women, was the stumbling block that kept you from being thrust further and deeper into the sciences when you were still a child.[1] But, just as the proverb says, 'What Nature gives, no one can take away,' your mother could not put a stop to your feeling for the sciences which you, by natural inclination, had at least gathered in little droplets. I believe that you do not think you are of less worth because of these things, but rather consider it a great treasure for yourself; and there 186

8. The word in French is *science des sors*, literally "drawing lots," i.e., prophecy or sorcery.
9. In French, it is *Boloungne la Grasse*, "Bologna the Fat" or wealthy, a common way to refer to Bologna at the time. Jehan Andry (as Christine spelled it) was Giovanni Andrea (1275–1347), a legal scholar in Bologna. He was mentioned in Le Fèvre's *Book of Joy*, lines 1140–54.
1. On the theme of Christine's inadequate education, see p. xii. "Spinning": the word in French is *filasse* from *filer* ("to spin"); the suffix *-asse* expresses the worthlessness of an activity.

is no doubt that you have grounds to do so." And, I, Christine, responded to all this: "Certainly, lady, what you say is as true as the *Pater Noster.*"[2]

[Christine now addresses the question of whether those men are right who say that there are no chaste women. Rectitude replies with the stories of some biblical women like Susanna, Sarah, Rebecca, and Ruth, as well of Roman women like Lucretia who killed herself after being raped. The next topic is inconstancy: women are not fickle, says Rectitude and proves it through the stories of several ancient ladies. She also demonstrates that there were plenty of men who were inconstant and untrustworthy, like the Roman emperors Nero and Galba. Then she tells the story of Griselda, Florence of Rome, and others.

After Rectitude has told of constant ladies, Christine asks her why so many valiant ladies of the past have not contradicted the books and men that spoke ill of them, and Recitude answers. Why did women not protest against this slander when they knew the men were wrong? Christine asks.]

Answer: "Dear friend, this question is rather easy to answer. You can   216a
see through the things I told you earlier that the ladies whose great virtues I described to you occupied their minds with tasks that differed from one to the other, and not all with the same things. To build this work was reserved for you and not for them[3] for these women's work garnered them enough praise among people of good understanding and true discernment, without their writing anything else. And as for the length of time that has passed without women contradicting their accusers and slanderers, I can tell you that in the long run things come together at the right time. For how is it possible that God permitted heresies against His holy law to exist in this world for such a long time, which were stamped out with such great effort and would still last to this day if they had not been disproved and vanquished? The same goes for many other things that were tolerated for a long time and are then debated and rejected."

[Christine anticipates objections to her work: will people not say that her praise of women is exaggerated? They will only admit that there are some good women and that not all women are good. Rectitude sweeps these worries aside by showing that there were a lot of bad men (like Judas) and that generalizations about women or men serve no purpose.

Rectitude now tells of women faithful in love. She refers to Christine's own works, *The God of Love's Letter* and the *Debate on the Romance of the Rose.* In these works Christine has proved that women are not deceitful. Dido, Medea, Thisbe, Hero, Ghismonda, Lisabetta, Yseut, and others are examplars of constant love.[4] Other stories disprove claims that women are

2. The Lord's Prayer (Latin).
3. Christine is indeed the first woman writer explicitly to address women's role in society.
4. These examples range from ancient literature to almost contemporary literary heroines from Boccaccio's *Decameron.*

flirtatious and greedy. Generosity is indeed the virtue of many French ladies, including contemporary ones like Margaret of Riviere. The City is now filled with houses and inhabitants. But it is not yet perfect: Lady Justice will have to finish the job. Thus ends the second part of the book.]

Here Begins the Third Part of the Book of the City of Ladies, Which Tells How and by Whom the High Tops of the Towers Were Completed and which Ladies Were Chosen to Live in the Great Palaces and High Fortresses

[Lady Justice brings forward the queen, the Virgin Mary, who will reign over all ladies of the City, that is, Christians and pagans alike. Whether the misogynist slanderers like it or not, the Virgin now resides with all women in the City. As examples of constancy Justice now tells of women saints.[5] The first is Catherine of Alexandria, a learned young woman who debated so well with a group of wise pagans that she converted them. She was then cruelly put to death by the Romans and thus became a holy martyr.]

Of St. Margaret

"Let us also not forget the blessed virgin saint Margaret, whose legend is rather well known. It tells how she was born in Antioch of noble parents and was as a young girl introduced to the faith by her nurse, whose sheep she humbly guarded every day. On these occasions Olybrius began to lust after her and he had her fetched to him. And, to make matters brief, because she would not submit to his will and because she confessed to being Christian, he had her harshly beaten and thrown into prison. And in this prison, because she was feeling tempted, she asked God to grant her the sight of the one who was causing her so much wretchedness. And immediately a horrible dragon appeared which frightened her horribly and swallowed her; but she, making the sign of the cross, split open the dragon. And afterward she saw in a corner of the prison cell a figure, black like an Aethiopian. And right away Margaret went boldly toward him and stretched him out under her; she put her foot on his neck and he cried loudly for mercy. The prison filled with light, and she was consoled by the angels. Thereupon Margaret was again brought before the judge, who, when he saw that his admonitions had no effect, had her tortured even more than before. But God's angel came and destroyed the torture machines, and the virgin emerged unharmed and a great many people were converted. And when this deceitful tyrant saw this, he ordered that she be decapitated. But first she said her prayers and prayed for those who would remember her suffering and would ask for her in their tribulations, for pregnant women, and women giving birth. And God's angel appeared,

---

5. These stories come from Vincent of Beauvais. On book 3 of the *City* see Quilligan, *The Allegory of Female Authority*, chap. 4.

who told her that her petition had been granted and that she should go and receive the victory palm in the name of God. And then she stretched out her neck: she was beheaded and the angels carried away her soul.

"This deceitful Olybrius in the same way had the holy virgin Regina, 267 a young girl of fifteen, tortured and beheaded because she would not submit to him and converted many people with her preaching."

[Justice offers other legends as proof of women's steadfastness: saints Martina, Lucy, Benedicta, Fausta, Justine, Barbara, Dorothy, and others. The center of book 3 is occupied by the legend of St. Christine.[6] She is persecuted by her father, who wants her to worship pagan idols, and a series of judges. After many tortures her tongue is cut out. St. Christine throws her tongue into the tyrant's face and thus blinds him. Two arrows finally kill her and make her a martyr. The legend ends with a prayer by Christine to her namesake in which she expresses joy at being able to include the saint's legend in her writings. Justice continues.]

Of Several Saintly Women Who Saw Their Children Martyred before Their Eyes

"Oh, what feelings could be more tender in the world than those of 285 a mother for her child, and what greater pain could her heart suffer than when she sees her child in pain? But, from what I see, faith is an even greater matter, as it is demonstrated by many valiant women who, for the love of Our Lord, offered their own children up to torture: as, for example, the blessed Felicia who saw her seven sons, beautiful young men, martyred in front of her. And the excellent mother comforted them and admonished them to be patient and firm in the faith. Thus the good lady had forgotten her maternal heart, as far as the body was concerned, for the love of God."

[Other stories of such mothers follow. Justice then turns to legends of holy women who disguised themselves as monks.[7]]

Here She Speaks of St. Marina, Virgin

"One could tell about many virgin martyrs, and also about others who 288 lived a holy life in the cloister and in other circumstances. And I will tell you about two in particular, whose legends are very beautiful and again confirm our argument on the constancy of women.

6. On this important figure see Kevin Brownlee, "Martyrdom and the Female Voice: Saint Christine in the Cité des dames," in R. Blumenfeld-Kosinski and Timea Szell, eds., Images of Sainthood in Medieval Europe (Ithaca, N.Y.: Cornell University Press, 1991), 115–35; and Quilligan, The Allegory of Female Authority, 213–22.
7. On cross-dressed saints see John Anson, "The Female Transvestite in Early Monasticism: The Origin and Development of a Motif," Viator 5 (1974), 1–32.

"A layman had an only child, a little daughter named Marina, whom he gave into the care of a relative while he entered a monastery and led a most holy life. But nonetheless, nature drew him to his daughter, and grief about her troubled him greatly. Thus he was weighed down with thought; thereupon the abbot asked him about the cause of his sadness, until he told him that his thoughts were heavily occupied with a son whom he had left behind in the world and whom he could not forget. The abbot told him to go and fetch him and to bring him into the monastery with him. Thus this virgin lived with her father, dressed like a little monk, and she was very good at disguising herself and at observing the discipline. And when she had reached the age of eighteen, being more and more steadfast, her father, who had instructed her in the most holy life, passed away. And she remained alone in her father's cell, leading such a holy life that the abbot and all the others praised her saintly way of life and took her for a man.

"This abbey was three miles away from a market town, and every so often the monks had to go to this market to buy their necessities. On these occasions it sometimes happened that it would be dark before they had finished their business, so that they stayed at an inn in town. And Marina, who was called Brother Marinus, would, when it was her turn, stay in the particular inn where they usually took lodging. At that time it happened that the innkeeper's daughter was pregnant; and because she was forced by her parents to tell who the father was, she blamed Brother Marinus. The parents complained about this to the abbot who summoned him, [8] and the abbot was very much grieved about this matter. And the holy virgin preferred to accept the guilt rather than to reveal that she was a woman in order to excuse herself. She knelt down, weeping, and said: 'Father, I have sinned, pray for me, I will do penance.' Then the abbot, who was furious, had him cruelly beaten and threw him out of the abbey and forbade him to enter. And he threw himself on the ground in front of the door and lay there in penance, and begged from the brothers a single morsel of bread.

"And the innkeeper's daughter gave birth to a son, whom her mother brought to Marinus in front of the monastery and left him there. And the virgin welcomed him; and with the morsel of bread that the people entering the monastery gave her, she fed this child as if it were her own. And some time later, the brothers, moved by pity, begged the abbot to take Brother Marinus back, for mercy's sake—and they could hardly persuade him—for he had already done penance for five years. And when he entered the monastery, the abbot ordered him to perform all the dirty and filthy tasks inside and to bring water to clean their latrines and to serve every one of them. And the holy virgin did all this humbly and gladly.

8. Christine uses the masculine pronoun here, reflecting the point of view of the abbot, for whom Marina was Marinus, the male monk.

"And some time afterward she fell asleep in Our Lord. And when the   288b
brothers had announced this to the abbot, he said to them: 'Although
his sin does not deserve forgiveness, wash him nevertheless and bury
him alongside the monastery.'[9] And when they undressed him and saw
that it was a woman, they began to beat themselves and to cry out in
pain and confusion over the harm they had done without reason to such
a holy creature; and they marveled at her way of life. When this news
was reported to the abbot, he came running and threw himself sobbing
at the feet of the holy corpse, beating his chest for his guilt, crying for
mercy, and begging for forgiveness. And he ordered her tomb to be
placed in a chapel inside the monastery. There all the monks came; one
of them, who had sight in only one eye, bent over the corps, kissing it
with great devotion, and immediately his sight was restored to him. That
same day, the woman who had had the child, lost her mind and cried
out her sin; and she was led to the holy corpse and recovered her health.
And she performed and still performs, many miracles in this place."[1]

[Justice now tells of St. Euphrosyna who also disguised herself as monk to
live with her father; however, she does not reveal her identity to him. Saints
Anastasia, Theodata, Natalia, and Afra (a converted prostitute) lead to the
stories of women who helped and lodged the Apostles. These last will serve
as the gates of the City, which is now finished. The three allegorical ladies
now take leave of Christine.]

The End of the Book: Christine Speaks to the Ladies

My most revered ladies, God be praised, for now our City is all fin-   307
ished and completed, where all of you who love virtue, glory, and praise
may be lodged, ladies from past times just as much as from the present
and future, for it has been constructed and founded for every honorable
lady. And my dearest ladies, it is natural for the human heart to be joyful
when it finds itself to have gained victory in any enterprise and the
enemies are confounded. Thus you have reason to rejoice virtuously in
God and in good comportment when you see this new city perfected,
which can be not only the refuge for all of you, that is, virtuous women,
but also the defense and protection against your enemies and assailants,
if you keep them up well. For you can see that the material from which
it is made is entirely of virtue, indeed it is so resplendent that you can
all mirror yourselves in it and especially in the upper structures built in
this last part, as well as in the other parts that might apply to you.

And, my dear ladies, do not misuse this new heritage, like the arrogant people who become proud when their prosperity increases and
their riches multiply, but rather live by the example of your Queen, the

9. I.e., not in the consecrated ground of the cemetery.
1. Vincent of Beauvais assigns this miracle to St. Euphrosyna, another woman disguised as a
   monk. "She": i.e., Marina.

sovereign Virgin, who, after the great honor of her being the mother of the Son of God was announced to her, humbled herself all the more by calling herself the handmaiden of God. Thus, my ladies, as it is true that the greater the virtues are in human beings the more humble and kind they make them, may this city be the reason for you to have good morals and to be virtuous and humble.

And you, married ladies, do not resent being subject to your hus-   307a bands: for sometimes it is not the best thing for a human being to be free. And the angel of God testified to this to Esdras:[2] Those, he said, who used their free will fell into sin and despised Our Lord and oppressed the just, and for this they were destroyed. And those women who have peaceful, good, and discreet husbands that love them greatly, should praise God for this favor, which is not a small thing, for a greater good in the world could not be given to them. And they should be diligent in serving, loving, and cherishing them with all their heart, as it is fitting, keeping their peace and praying to God that he maintain and safeguard it for them. And those that have husbands in between good and bad should also praise God that they do not have worse ones, and should try to moderate their perverse behavior and pacify them, according to their condition. And those that have husbands who are evil, cruel, and savage should make an effort to endure them so that they can try and oppose their evil ways and lead them back, if they can, to a reasonable and good life. And if the husbands are so obstinate that the wives cannot succeed, at least they will acquire great merit for their souls through the virtue of patience. And everyone will bless them and be on their side.

So, my ladies, be humble and patient; and God's grace will increase   308 in you, and praise will be given to you as well as the kingdom of heaven. For St. Gregory says that patience is the doorway to Paradise and the way to Jesus Christ. And may none of you be obstinate or hardened by holding frivolous opinions that have no basis in reason, or by jealousies, or by a disturbed mind, or by haughty speech, or by outrageous actions. For these are things that corrupt the mind and make a person crazy. Such conduct is improper and unseemly for women.

And you, maidens in the state of virginity, be pure, simple, and peace-   309 ful, without vagueness, for the snares of evil men are set for you. Your gaze should be lowered, few words should be in your mouths, respect should govern all your actions. And be armed with the virtuous strength against the ruses of the deceivers and avoid their company.

And, widowed ladies, may there be modesty in your dress, behavior   310 and speech; piety in your actions and way of life; prudence in your conduct; patience, which is so much needed; strength and resistance in

2. The Book of Esdras is one of the Old Testament Apocrypha, covering similar material as the Books of Ezra and Nehemiah. The quote comes from 2 Esdras 56–58: "For though they had received liberty, they scorned the Most High and despised his Law and forsook his ways."

tribulations and important affairs; humility in your hearts, countenance, and speech; and charity in your works.

And, to make matters brief, all women, whether of the upper, middle or lower classes, be well informed in all things and take care in mounting a defense against the enemies of your honor and chastity. My ladies, see how these men accuse you of so many vices from all sides. Make liars of them all by showing your virtue and prove by your good actions that those who reprimand you are lying, so that you can say with the psalmist: "the wickedness of the evil will fall on their heads." Chase away the deceiving flatterers who use various tricks in their intrigues to try and get that which you should supremely guard, that is, your honors and the beauty of your reputation. Oh, ladies, flee, flee the foolish love with which they beseech you. Flee it, for God's sake, flee: for nothing good can come of it for you.[3] Rather, you can be certain that, with all its deceptive attractions, it will always end badly for you. And do not believe the contrary: for it cannot be otherwise. Remember, dear ladies, how these men call you weak, light-minded, and quickly persuaded; and how, nevertheless, they make a great effort to seek out all sorts of strange and deceptive tricks to catch you, just as one does in trapping animals. Flee, flee, my ladies, and shun the kind of companions under whose smiles are hidden grievous poisons that kill people. And so may it please you, my most honored ladies, to increase and multiply our City through the adherence to virtues and the rejection of vices, and to rejoice and act well. And may I, your servant, be commended to you by praying to God, who by His grace has granted me to live in this world and to persevere in His holy service, and at the end may He be merciful toward my great sins and grant me the joy that lasts forever, which by His grace He may grant you as well. Amen.

Here ends the third and last part of the Book of the City of Ladies.

FROM THE BOOK OF THE THREE VIRTUES

[Christine had built the City of Ladies with the help of three allegorical women — Reason, Rectitude, and Justice — and the city is now complete and populated by virtuous ladies. *The Book of the Three Virtues* (1405) is presented as the continuation, or the "treasury," of the city. The Three Virtues appear once more to Christine and rouse her from bed to drag her back to her desk. But this text's nature and style are quite different. It is a handbook for women in society — not in the idealized society of the city but in the dangerous courts, cities, and countryside of Christine's own time.

3. Christine here mocks the *Romance of the Rose*, where the character Genius repeats the word *flee* six times, advising men to flee the beast, meaning woman, if they wish to preserve their bodies and souls! See Daniel Poirion, ed., *Le Roman de la Rose* (Paris: Garnier-Flammarion, 1974), lines 16577–583.

310a

In its pragmatic and sometimes brutal approach to survival in society it is also quite different from other books offering advice to women, such as *Le Ménagier de Paris* [The Paris Householder],[1] a guide to married life and housekeeping written by an elderly husband for his young wife in late-fourteenth-century Paris. Christine addresses herself mostly to princesses and other noble women but also has advice for the wives of artisans and peasants. One chapter even speaks to prostitutes. There is a strong spiritual current, which points to the afterlife and its rewards. Indeed, for poor people Christine does not offer much hope in this world, but rather consoles them with the next! Other guiding threads are the duty toward one's husband and concern with honor and reputation, both constantly at risk in a society where power and love were closely intertwined. But Christine does not neglect the practical side of life and offers good advice on the keeping of accounts, the supervision of servants, and a noble woman's need to be familiar with finances and warfare. The troubles of widowhood are another important concern for Christine, who was only too familiar with the loneliness and precarious financial situation widows faced at the time.

The book was dedicated to Margaret of Nevers, the daughter of John the Fearless of Burgundy, the same duke who had commissioned Christine to write the biography of his late brother, Charles V. She married the French dauphin Louis of Guienne in 1404 at the age of eleven and was thus expected to become queen one day. Louis died in 1415 before succeeding to the throne, and Margeret was widowed at a young age. In 1423 she married Arthur of Richmont, brother of the duke of Brittany, after he had been released from prison by the English. She proved to be a strong and faithful wife.

As Christine hoped at the end of the book, *The Book of the Three Virtues* was a success. Almost twenty manuscripts survive; it was printed several times, and a Portuguese translation was made in the sixteenth century.

Translated by Renate Blumenfeld-Kosinski from Christine de Pizan, *Le Livre des trois vertus*, ed. Charity Cannon Willard and Eric Hicks (Paris: Champion, 1989).]

Here begins the Book of the Three Virtues, for the instruction of ladies.

Book One

[The first chapter tells how the Virtues, by whose command Christine had written and compiled *The Book of the City of Ladies*, appeared to her again and commissioned her to write this present book.]

After I built the *City of Ladies* with the help and by the commandment of the three Ladies of Virtue, that is, Reason, Rectitude, and Jus-

---

1. See Georgine E. Brereton and Janet M. Ferrier, eds., *Le Ménagier de Paris* (Oxford, UK: Oxford University Press, 1981); it was translated as *The Goodman of Paris* by Eileen Power (London, 1928).

tice, in the form and manner described in the *City*, I remained idle,
seeking some repose, since I was worn out from having accomplished
so much work. My limbs and my body were tired from the long and
continuous effort. Suddenly the three glorious ladies appeared to me
again and lost no time in telling me three things which were of a same
substance and manner:[1] "Studious daughter, have you already put away
and silenced the tool of your intellect, let your ink dry up and abandoned your pen and the labor of your right hand which used to delight
you so much? Will you now listen willingly to the lesson of Laziness,
who will sing it to you if you want to believe her: 'You have done
enough, it is now time for you to rest?' Don't you know that Seneca says
that although the wise man's mind rests after a great effort, he is never
freed from his obligation to good work. You should not be counted
among those who abandon their work when it is half-way done. The
knight who leaves the battle before the final victory should be ashamed,
for the laurel crown belongs to those who persevere. Now, up! Up! Get
your hand ready! Stand up! Do no longer crouch in the ash heap of
idleness!

"Listen to our lectures and you will do good work. We are not yet
completely satisfied with your work as the handmaiden[2] to our virtuous
enterprise. Therefore, we reviewed and discussed it and made some
decisions at the Council of Virtues, following God's example, who at
the beginning of the world He created, saw that it was good and blessed
it; then He created man and woman and the other creatures. Just like
that, our preceding work, the *City of Ladies*, which is good and useful,
may be blessed and acclaimed throughout the world. But so that it will
grow even further, we want you to act like the wise bird catcher who
readies his cage before catching the birds. After the shelter of honored
ladies is built and made ready, we will with your help devise and invent
snares and nets, beautiful with well-made knots of love that we will
supply for you. You will spread them on the ground in those places,
squares, and corners where the ladies, and generally all women, pass
through, so that those who are shy and hard to dominate may be
snapped up and caught in our nets, and so that none who gets into them
can escape and almost all of them will be trapped in the cage of our
glorious City. They will learn the sweet song from those who are already
sheltered there as sovereign ladies and who perpetually sing Alleluia in
harmony with the blessed angels."

Then I, Christine, hearing the sweet voices of my honored mistresses,
joyful and trembling, got up and knelt down in front of them, offering
myself in obedience to their worthy wishes. Then I received the following command from them: "Take your pen and write. Blessed will be

---

1. Christine pursues the idea of the three ladies as the Trinity and, therefore, insists that they
   have the "same substance and manner." See also n. 2 on p. 121.
2. See n. 1, p. 126.

those who will inhabit our City and add to the numbers of its virtuous citizens. Our lesson and sermon of Wisdom are meant for the entire community of devoutly religious women. First of all, for those whose royal or noble state raises them above other wordly estates. By necessity, these women and men whom God has established in high positions of power and domination must be better educated than others, so that their reputation may be enhanced and they can be exemplars and mirrors of virtue to their subjects and those they frequent. Therefore, our first lesson will be addressed to them, that is, to queens, princesses, and noble women. Then, going down the ladder, we will similarly convey our doctrine to all social groups of women so that the discipline of our school may be of value to all."

[In chapter 2, the Virtues emphasize the importance of loving and fearing God.]

Chapter 3. Which Tells of the Kinds of Temptations That Can Confront a High-Born Princess

When the princess or high-born lady wakes up from her sleep in the morning and finds herself lying in her bed between soft sheets, surrounded by rich ornaments and everything designed for her bodily comfort, with ladies and maids-in-waiting around her, intent on catering to her every need, ready to run to her should she sigh ever so slightly or utter a word, poised on bended knee to administer any service and obey any command, temptation may often assail her, singing this song:

"Dear God! Is there in this world a lady greater than you, or more worthy? Whom should you take into account? Do you not take precedence over everyone? This one or that one, though married to a high-born prince, cannot be compared to you. You are richer or of a more exalted lineage, more esteemed because of your children, more feared, more renowned, and have more authority because of your husband's power. Who would dare to cause you any displeasure? Would you not avenge yourself by such or such a powerful act? There is no person grand enough that you would not overpower. Nonetheless, some, both men and women, have shown arrogance toward you and have had the presumption to attack you, and have done this or that to offend and harm you. You will well avenge yourself, when the time is right. And you will be able to do this very well with the support and power you have.

"But what is needed to do all this? No matter how great the person, no one achieves anything or gains respect unless he has money and great financial resources. Therefore, you must strive to amass great treasures so that you will be able to cater to your own needs. Treasures are the best friends and the surest means to any end. Who would dare to disobey you when you give so generously? Let's suppose you give only very little, you will still be well served by those who hope for and expect more, for you will have a reputation for wealth. Only when a woman is dead does she no longer attract hands held out for gain! Whether people like it or not, go ahead and do it. What do you care if people talk? Those who talk cannot harm you. Why should you be worried? You should only think about those things that please you. You have only one life in this world: soon you'll reach your eternal rest. What should you worry about? You will never lack wine and food, you can take your delight in them and in all other delicacies. In short, you have nothing to think about but the joy and pleasures you can enjoy in this world. No one has a good time unless she provides it for herself. You only have to think delightful thoughts to give you pleasure. For whom will I make myself pretty? You must have such dresses, such ornaments, such jewelry, such clothes, made just so: you have nothing yet in this new fashion."

Chapter 4. Which Tells How the Good Princess Who Loves and Fears Our Lord Will Be Able to Resist Temptation through Divine Inspiration

All the things mentioned above, or something like them, are the dishes Temptation offers to any creature living in ease and delights. But what shall the good princess do when she feels herself thus tempted? There will appear to her the love and fear of Our Lord who will sing her a different lesson: "Oh, foolish idle woman, what are you thinking of?"

[The Virtues admonish the princess not to give in to pride by telling of ancient kings who were brought down by pride. They close the chapter by reminding the princess of the Holy Scriptures, which also warn against pride.]

Oh dear God! You who are a simple little woman who has no other strength, power, or authority than the one given to you by someone else,[3] do you believe you can tread on the rest of the world and dominate it just because you are surrounded by luxury and honors?

[Chapter 5 reminds the princess of the pains of Hell and of the joys of Paradise and of the choice she has to make.]

Chapter 6. Which Tells of the Two Holy Ways of Life, That Is, The Active and the Contemplative Lives

Now pay attention to what you have to do if you want to be saved. The Scriptures speak of two paths that lead to Heaven which you cannot

---

3. I.e., God.

enter without following them: one is called the contemplative life, the other the active life. And what does this mean, contemplative and active? The contemplative life is a manner and a state of serving God in which a person loves God so much and so ardently that she completely forgets father, mother, children, everyone, even herself, for the great and glowing devotion she has endlessly for her Creator. She thinks of nothing else, and nothing else means anything to her. There is no poverty, tribulation, or any suffering—by which others could be harmed—that could hinder or preoccupy the truly contemplative heart. Her way of life is to disdain completely the things and the joys of this world, to remain solitary and apart from everyone else, kneeling on the ground, her joined hands raised to Heaven, her heart elevated by such exalted thoughts that she comes before God to contemplate by sacred inspiration the Holy Trinity, the court of Heaven and its joys.

In this state the perfect contemplative is often in such ecstasy that he[4] does not seem to be himself, and the consolation, sweetness, and joy that he feels cannot be told, nor can any earthly joy be compared with them, for he already feels and tastes[5] the glories and joys of Paradise, which means that he sees God in the spirit through contemplation. He burns in his love and is perfectly content in this world, for he desires nothing else. And God comforts him, for he is his servant; and he feeds him the sweet foods of His Holy Paradise, that is pure and holy thoughts of the things that are in Heaven and perfect hope to go there in joyous company: no joy can compare to it.

Those who have tried it, know it, though I am sorry to say that I cannot speak of it any more than a blind man can speak of colors. And that this life is above all others agreeable to God has been demonstrated many times to the world. Thus it is written that several holy contemplatives, both men and women, have been seen to rise high above the ground in their contemplation, by God's miracle, so that it seemed that their bodies wanted to follow their thoughts which had risen to Heaven. I am not worthy to describe adequately this holy life of the chosen or to do it justice, but whoever is interested can find much about it in the Holy Scriptures.

The active life is another way of serving God. The person who wants to follow it will be so charitable that, if she could, she would serve everyone for the love of God. She seeks out hospitals, visits the sick and

---

4. Christine clearly uses the French pronoun *il* ("he"); i.e., she is speaking of contemplatives in general, not just women.
5. Christine alludes here to a controversial subject: Could some particularly blessed people enjoy the Beatific Vision before the Last Judgment? See Caroline Walker Bynum, *The Resurrection of the Body in Western Christianity, 200–1336* (New York: Columbia University Press, 1995), 283–91. Many mystical writers underlined the sensuous aspects of experiencing God. The Carthusian religious writer Margaret of Oingt (d. 1310), for example, speaks of the sweetness and the fragrance of God that people can eat, smell, and drink; see *The Writings of Margaret of Oingt, Medieval Prioress and Mystic*, trans. R. Blumenfeld-Kosinski (Binghamton, N.Y.: Medieval and Renaissance Texts and Studies, 1995), 44.

the poor, helps them with her own money and physical effort for the love of God, as best she can. She has such great pity for the creatures she sees in sin, misery, or tribulation that she weeps as though she suffered herself. She loves the good of her neighbor as she would her own, she always seeks to do good and is never idle. Her heart has the constant ardent desire to do the works of charity to which she devotes herself entirely. Such a person bears all injuries and tribulations patiently for the love of Our Lord.

As you can see, this active life is more useful to the world than the first one we described. They are both of great excellence, but Our Lord decided which is the more perfect of the two when Mary Magdalene, who is a figure of the contemplative life, sat down at His feet as a woman who thought about nothing else and burned with holy love. Martha, her sister, who stands for the active life, and who was the hostess to Our Lord and busied herself around the house to serve Him and the Apostles, complained that her sister, Mary, did not help her. Our Lord excused her by saying: "Martha, you are very diligent, and your work, which is good, is necessary, but nonetheless Mary has chosen the better part." We can understand His pronouncement to mean that although the active life is of great excellence and necessary for the help and succor of many people, the contemplative life, which abandons the whole world and its occupations to devote itself entirely to Him, is of greater dignity and more perfect. For this reason holy men in ancient times founded and established religious orders, which is the state closest to God for those who devote themselves to it. Those who wish to live in contemplation can exist there separated from the world in the service of God and without any other care. And they can please themselves, for God is only too happy if they do their duty there.

Chapter 7. Which Tells of the Path the Good Princess, Counseled by God, Decides to Follow

"You must decide which of the two paths described above you want to follow," the good princess, inspired by God, says to herself. "People commonly say, and it is true, that discretion is the mother of the virtues. And why is she the mother? Because she guides and leads the others. And whoever undertakes something without her will see his work come to nothing and be worthless. This is why I have to work with discretion. But what does discretion mean? It means that undertaking anything I must think about the strength or weakness of my own body and the frailty to which I am inclined. How much submission must I show, according to the state God has called me to in this world? And when I honestly consider these things, I find myself, however willing I may be, too weak of body to suffer great abstinence or pain and too feeble of spirit because of my frailty and inconstancy. And knowing myself to be like that, I cannot presume to be of such virtue. Although God says, 'You will leave father and mother for the sake of my name,' I could not make such a decision and leave husband, children, my worldly condition, and all earthly occupations in order only to serve God in the contemplative life, as the most perfect humans have done. I must not undertake something in which I believe myself unable to persevere.

"What shall I do then? Shall I journey in the active life? Alas, happy are those who can fulfill its demands. Dear God, why did You not put me into this world as a poor woman, so that at least I could serve You perfectly in the active life by administering to your members, that is, the poor, for love of You. Alas, how will I accomplish this? I do not at all feel ready to leave behind my worldly position in order to devote myself to this life. Dear Lord God, counsel and inspire me as to what I must do to save myself. Although I know well that I should not love or desire anything but You alone and that any other joy is nothing, I do not have the strength to abandon the world. I am terrified as to what I should do, for You say that it is impossible for the rich to be saved."[6]

[Holy Inspiration now comes to the princess and explains that the condemnation of the rich applies only to the rich without virtue. You can be rich and still "poor in spirit," that is, humble and virtuous. Holy Inspiration continues.]

"And you can see this for yourself: were there not many kings and princes who are saints in Paradise, such as St. Louis, king of France, and several others, who did not abandon the world but reigned and governed their possessions at God's pleasure? But they lived justly and did not delight in vainglory or take pride in the honors shown to them. They judged that honor was not given to them as individuals but to their estate of which they were God's vicars on earth. And there were also many queens and princesses who are now saints in Paradise, such as the queen who was the wife of King Clovis, and also St. Badour, St. Elizabeth,[7] queen of Hungary, and many others. There is no doubt that God wants to be served by people from all estates, and in every estate people who want to save themselves can do so. And it is not the estate which

6. This passage poses the interesting problem of late-medieval lay sanctity: people were striving for a saintly way of life without leaving behind their families and all earthly possessions. See André Vauchez, "Lay People's Sanctity in Western Europe: Evolution of a Pattern (Twelfth and Thirteenth Centuries)," in R. Blumenfeld-Kosinski and Timea Szell, eds., *Images of Saint-hood in Medieval Europe* (Ithaca, N.Y.: Cornell University Press, 1991), 21–32; and Dyan Elliott, *Spiritual Marriage: Sexual Abstinence in Medieval Wedlock* (Princeton, N.J.: Princeton University Press, 1993).

7. The daughter (1207–1231) of the king of Hungary and the wife of the lord of Thuringia; she became a Franciscan Tertiary and devoted herself to the care of the sick. St. Louis, or King Louis IX, died during a crusade at Tunis in 1270. Queen Clotilda converted her husband, Clovis (481–511), to Christianity; Christine tells her story in *The Book of the City of Ladies*, trans. E. J. Richards (New York: Persea, 1982), 151–52. St. Badour is St. Balthild (d. 680), wife of Clovis II.

leads to damnation, but the fact that a human being does not know how to use it wisely."

"Therefore, in conclusion, since I realize that I do not have the strength to choose and follow one or the other of these paths, I will at least try to follow the middle way, as St. Paul advises, and I will adopt from each way of life as much as I can."

[Chapter 8 speaks of the virtues of humility, patience, and charity.]

Chapter 9. Which Speaks of the Good and Wise Princess's Efforts to Make Peace between the Prince and the Barons if There Is Any Discord

If it happens that any neighboring or foreign prince because of some dispute wishes to wage war against her lord, or that her lord wants to begin a war against someone else, the good lady will consider this problem carefully, thinking of the great evil and infinite cruelties, losses, deaths, and destruction of land and people that result from war whose outcome is often terrible. She will deliberate with all her powers to see whether she can do something, all the while preserving her lord's honor, to avoid this war. To this end she will work wisely, calling God to her aid, and by good counsel she will try to find a way to keep the peace. Or if it happens that one of the princes of the realm or country—or one of the barons, or knights, or other powerful subjects—commits a misdeed, perhaps even against his lord's majesty, or that he is accused of anything, and she sees that to arrest and punish him or to wage war against him could result in great damage to the land, she will seek peace. We have seen such cases many times in France and elsewhere, where the quarrel of an unimportant baron or knight with the king of France, who is such a great lord, has resulted in great harm and damage to the kingdom. The *Chronicles of France* tell of the count of Corbeil, the lord of Monthlehery, and several others. And not long ago a quarrel between the king and Robert of Artois [8] did great harm to the kingdom and helped the English.

Therefore, the good lady, keeping in mind these things and feeling pity for the destruction of the people, will strive to make peace. She will admonish her lord, the prince, and the council to consider everything carefully before embarking on anything, in view of the evil that could result from it, especially since a good prince should strive to avoid shedding blood, in particular that of his subjects. It is never trivial to undertake a new war which should never be started without careful thought and serious deliberations; and it would be better to think about a better way to reach an agreement by any fair means. This lady will not hesitate

8. He was involved in a quarrel with the countess of Artois that contributed to the outbreak of the Hundred Years' War. He made efforts to incite the English king Edward III against the French.

for a moment, but will speak, or have someone speak for her—while safeguarding her own and her husband's honor—to those who have committed the misdeed. She will use the stick and the carrot,[9] saying that the misdeed is great and that the prince has good reason to be offended and would be justified in seeking his vengeance, nonetheless she, who always strives for the good of peace, will make an effort on their behalf, in case they wish to repent or make suitable amends, and she will try to restore peaceful relations between them and her lord.

By means of such words, or similar ones, the good princess will always be as much of a peacemaker as possible, just as in the olden days was Queen Blanche,[1] the mother of St. Louis, who always strove to reconcile the king and his lords, as she did for the count of Champagne and others. This is the right role for a wise and good queen and princess: to be the maker of peace and concord and to work toward an avoidance of war because of the troubles that result from it. And women should particularly devote themselves to peace, for men are by nature more courageous and hot-blooded, and their great desire for vengeance keeps them from considering the dangers and evils that can come from it. But woman's nature is more timid and of sweeter disposition, and therefore, if she is willing and wise, she can be the best means to pacify any man. In this context Solomon says in the twenty-fifth chapter of the Proverbs: "Sweetness and humility assuage the prince and the soft tongue (which means sweet words) bends and breaks his hardness, just as water by its moisture and coldness extinguishes the fire's heat."[2]

How much good have the queens and princesses done to this world by making peace between enemies, between princes and their barons, and between rebellious people and their lords: the Scriptures are full of examples! There is no greater good in the world than a wise princess or noble lady. Fortunate the country that possesses her. I would give some examples, but I have spoken enough about this topic in *The Book of the City of Ladies.*

And what happens to such a princess? All her subjects know her to be of such wisdom and goodness that they flock to her to take refuge, not just because she is their mistress, but because she seems like a goddess on earth in whom they have complete hope and confidence; and she is the cause that peace reigns in the land. Her works are never without charity but they are so worthy that no greater good could be accomplished.

[Chapter 10 speaks of the value of charity.]

---

9. The words in French are *poignant . . . oignant*, i.e., to attack and soothe with ointment.
1. She acted as a regent for her son, who became king in 1234.
2. Proverbs 25:15: "By long forbearing is a prince persuaded, and a soft tongue breaketh the bone."

Chapter 11. Which Begins to Speak of the Moral Teachings Which Worldly Prudence Will Give to the Princess

We have sufficiently spoken of those teachings that the love and fear of Our Lord give the good princess or noble lady. From now on we have to speak of the lessons of Worldly Prudence which are not different from those of God but rather come from and depend on them. We will speak of the wise governance and way of life according to Prudence. Prudence will first of all teach the princess or noble lady that above all other things in this earthly world she must love honor and good reputation. She will tell her that God is not at all displeased with a creature who lives morally in the world, and if she lives morally she will love good reputation, which means honor. St. Augustine testifies to this in his *Book of Correction* which states that two things are necessary for a good life: conscience and a good reputation. The wise man in the Book of Ecclesiasticus agrees when he says: "Take care of good reputation, for it will stay with you longer than any other treasure."[3]

Therefore, the wise princess will say to herself, "Above all earthly goods there is none that is as suitable for noble people as is honor. And which things are necessary," she will say, "for true honor? Certainly, properly speaking, not earthly riches, at least not if they are employed according to the ways common in this world. Indeed, they are the least suitable means for the perfection of honor. And what things, then, are suitable? In truth, good morals. And what end do they serve in this world? They perfect the noble creature and give her a good reputation. There is true honor, for there is no doubt that whatever wealth a princess or any other woman may possess, if she does not lead a life in which by good deeds she acquires a good reputation and praise, she will not deserve or acquire honor, though people will flatter her, and for their own gain they will try to make her believe she possesses honor; but true honor must be without reproach. And how much must a lady love honor? Certainly more than her life, for it would cost her more to lose her honor than her life. There is good reason for this, for whoever dies well is saved, but whoever is dishonored will suffer reproach, dead or alive, as long as there is any memory of her. Oh, what a great treasure is honor to the princess or noble lady! Certainly, there could be no greater treasure, nor could she love or amass a greater one. For common riches are useful only in her narrow circle, but the treasure of good reputation is useful near and far, for it exalts her honor in the whole country. Good reputation is like a wonderful fragrance that comes from a person's body

3. Ecclesiasticus is one of the Apocryphal books of the Old Testament. The quotation is from 41:12–13. As Charity C. Willard points out, Christine found this quotation in the *Manipulus florum*, a collection of sayings of the Church Fathers under the heading *Fama* ("Reputation"); see Willard and Hicks's edition, 233.

and spreads all over the world so that all people can smell it: thus through the fragrance of good reputation, which issues from a worthy person, all people can smell and taste a good example."

These are the three things that Prudence will teach the wise princess. And what shall she do to put them into practice? She will arrange her life principally around two concepts: one pertains to the moral life she wants to lead, and the other to the rules she will follow for her lifestyle. As far as morals are concerned, in addition to the virtues discussed above two qualities are especially necessary for a princess and any noble lady, indeed for any woman who desires honor: one is sobriety and the other is chastity.

Sobriety does not encompass only eating and drinking but everything else that can be useful in restraining and reducing superfluities. This sobriety will keep a lady from being difficult to serve, for she will require no service beyond reason. In spite of her high social position, sobriety will make her be content with those wines and food put before her, for she will not want to have her own way in this and she will not desire more than the necessities of life require. Sobriety will keep her from sleeping too much, because Prudence will tell her that too much rest brings forth sin and vice. Sobriety will also guard her against avarice, for she will be satisfied with a small amount of wealth. Above all, Prudence will forbid her to indulge in superfluous and extravagant clothes, jewels, accessories, and an unreasonable lifestyle.

* * *

This Sobriety will be apparent in all the lady's senses as well as in her actions and clothes, for it will cause her glance to be deliberate, steady, and without vagueness. She will also protect her from too much curiosity about sweet fragrances, which many ladies care too much about and for which they spend a great deal of money. She will tell her not to indulge her body in too many delights and that it would be better to give the money to the poor. Sobriety will correct and rule the lady's speech to keep her from talking too much, which is most unsuitable for a noble lady and indeed for any worthy woman. She will make her hate with all her heart the vice of lying and will make her love truth, which will be so habitual in her mouth that people will believe what she says as they believe a person who never lies. The virtue of truth is more necessary in the mouths of princes and princesses than in other people because one has to be able to trust them. Sobriety will also forbid her to utter words that she has not carefully considered in advance, especially in places where she will be judged and talked about.

Prudence and Sobriety will teach the lady well-ordered speech and eloquence, not cute but serious, quiet and restrained, with a composed face, without gesturing with her hands, body, or grimaces. They will keep her from laughing too much and without cause. Above all, they

will forbid her to speak ill of anyone, not to blame but rather highlighting the good. She will not say anything vague or dishonest, and
even in her amusement she will be modest and discreet.

[The lady must then by example teach her companions and servants the
same virtues].

This lady will gladly read books teaching good morals and sometimes
devotional books. She will detest books about dishonest and lubricious
things and will not have them at her court and will not let them be
brought before her daughter, relative, or lady-in-waiting, for there is no
doubt that examples of good or evil influence the minds of those who
see or hear them.[4]

[The lady will also gladly listen to deeds of chivalry and be a considerate
hostess to devout people.]

Chapter 13

[It tells the lady how to have a harmonious marriage. Her concern for her
husband should take precedence over everything else. But do all husbands
deserve such a good treatment?]

But some ladies may say to us that we tell only one side of the story,
saying that no matter what ladies must love their husbands and show it,
but that we do not consider whether all husbands deserve this kind of
treatment from their wives, for we all know that there are husbands who
treat their wives atrociously and without any sign of love, or hardly any.
To these women we reply that our teaching in the present volume is not
addressed to men, although they could use well such instruction. Since
we speak only to women, we are interested in teaching them how they
can profitably find ways to avoid dishonor, and in giving them good
advice on how to follow a straight path, though some will do the opposite and will profit from both good and evil.

Suppose, then, that the husband exhibits unbelievably perverse, rude,
and unloving behavior toward his wife, no matter what social class he is
from, or is led astray into love affairs with one or more other women.
Here we can see the good sense and the prudence of the wise wife,
when she knows how to bear all this and wisely pretend that she notices
and knows nothing. For if this is the case, there is nothing she can do
about it. She will make these wise reflections: if you speak to him
harshly, you will gain nothing and even if he leads a life that's bad for
you, you would only kick against the spur: he may leave you and people

---

4. Christine had expressed this idea about the influence of books on morals in the *Debate on the
   Romance of the Rose* (see p. 41).

would mock you, adding shame and dishonor, and even worse things may happen. You must live and die with him, whatever he is like.

[The remaining chapters of book one outline the rules for decent behavior in the lady's love life: love your husband and resist seduction. Further, the Three Virtues instruct the princess on the details of governing, warfare, and revenues, which she will have to take over in case of her husband's absence. The widow in particular must be aware of her rights and the dangers confronting them after her husband's death. Book two prescribes good and prudent behavior for ladies at court, emphasizing the dangers of slander and extravagance.]

Book Three

[The Three Virtues state that everything that has been said in the first two books can also apply to the bourgeois women who are the focus of book three.]

Chapter 1. Which Speaks of the Management That a Woman of Position Must Apply in Her Household

* * *

The wise housewife must know everything about her household, even about the preparation of food, so that she can direct and command her servants and so that her husband can always be reassured when he invites people for dinner. If necessary, she herself must go into the kitchen and order how they should be served. She must take care that her house is well kept and that things are in their place and in order; that her children are well taught, and that even when they are small they are not too spoilt or make too much noise: they should be neatly dressed and have good manners, and neither the nurse's cloths nor the children's belongings should be scattered around the house.

[The next two chapters speak of merchants' wives. Like their noble sisters, they should avoid extravagant dress and love affairs. For the merchants themselves, the wives' exaggerated elegance may lead to higher taxes!]

Chapter 4. Which Speaks of Widows Young and Old

To make our work more complete and to the profit of all classes of women, we will speak to the widows of the common people, although we have already spoken of this topic as concerns princesses.

Dear friends, you move us to pity when we see your fall into widowhood by the death that has taken away your husbands, whoever they may have been. In this state you will usually find much anguish and very troublesome business, manifesting itself in one way to those who are rich and in another to those who are not. Rich women are in trouble because people try generally to rob them, and poor and less wealthy women because no one will show pity toward them. So with the pain of having lost your partners, which should really be enough, you—whether rich or poor—will be assailed by three major evils.

The first, which we have already touched on, is that generally you will find harshness and lack of consideration and pity everywhere, and those who used to honor you during the lifetime of your husband, who were officials or men of great importance, will now take little account of you and will no longer show you any friendship. The second evil that assails you are the various lawsuits and demands of various people, concerning debts or claims on your property or income. The third evil is people's malicious talk who will attack you so that you can behave ever so well and people will still malign you. And because in all this you need to be armed with good sense against these plagues and all the others that may happen to you, we want to teach you valuable lessons. Although we have already spoken of these things elsewhere, we want to remind you of them because they are apropos here.

As for the harshness that you generally find in people, which is the first of the three above-mentioned evils, there are three remedies. The first is that you turn toward God who was willing to suffer so much for human creatures. Contemplating this will teach you to be patient— which is a very necessary thing—and if you put your heart into it you will reach a point where the rewards and honors of this world will matter very little to you, for you will learn that the things of this world are changeable. The second remedy is to turn your heart to speaking sweetly and gently, showing reverence to everyone, so that with sweet prayers and humble requests you may conquer and bend the hearts of the evildoers. The third point is that, despite what we just said about your humble and sweet speech and countenance, you must take the advice of good prudence and wise conduct on how to defend yourself against those who want to beat you down: that is, you must avoid their company and try to have nothing to do with them. You must stay in your house and not quarrel with anyone, not a neighbor, not even a servant or chambermaid. Speak gently but look out for your rights. Avoid mingling with people more than is absolutely necessary and you will avoid being injured or exploited by other people.

[Lawsuits should be avoided, since women are not always well served by lawyers, and it is too dangerous for them to have to appear at court at all hours. She may have to give up something, yet she should persist where she is right.]

In order to achieve these goals and to avoid all other troubles if she wants to bring the suit to a conclusion, she must take on the heart of a man. She must be constant, strong, and wise in order to decide on and pursue the best course of action, not crouching like a foolish woman in tears and sobs, without any defense, like a poor dog who cowers in a corner when all the others attack him. For if you behave like this, women, you will find plenty of people who will take the bread from your hand and will call you ignorant and simple, and you will find no pity in anyone. Therefore, you should not work with only your own intelligence and trust only your own good sense but get good advice, especially in those areas you know little about.

[To avoid gossip the widow's household should be discreet.]

And because widowhood means such a hard life for women, as we have in truth seen, it could seem to some people that it would be best for all widows to remarry. This assumption can be answered by saying that if married life were all repose and peace, it would be reasonable for a woman to enter into it again. But since one sees exactly the contrary, women should be warned, although for young women remarriage may be necessary or suitable. But for those who are past youth and who are sufficiently well off so that poverty does not force them to remarry, it would be complete folly, although there are some who say that a woman should not be alone, and they have so little faith in their good sense that they excuse themselves by saying they would not know how to manage their own lives. But the height of folly and the greatest scandal is if an old woman takes a young husband. She will sing a good song only for a short while, and people will not feel sorry for her misfortune—and rightly so.

[The Three Virtues now address themselves to artisans' wives and chambermaids. They also discuss the relationships between old and young women, pleading for tolerance and mutual understanding.]

Chapter 10. Which Contains Teachings for Women Who Lead Immoral Lives

Just as the sun shines on the good as well as on the wicked, we will not be ashamed to extend our teaching even to those women who are foolish, of light morals, and a disorderly life, although there is nothing more abominable. And we should not be ashamed, remembering that the worthy person of Jesus Christ felt no disgust to preach to them in order to convert them. Therefore, for charity and aiming for their good, and so that some of them, if by chance they hear this, can receive and retain of our teachings something that may make them leave their foolish life—for there is no greater gift than to turn away the sinner from evildoing and sin—we speak as follows: Open your eyes to the knowledge that you give yourself to sin and live miserably and dishonestly.

Get out as long as there is daylight and before night overtakes you, that is, before death attacks you and surprises you in sin which will lead you to Hell, for no one knows the hour of his death.

Think about the great filth of your way of life which is so abominable that you attract God's wrath. The world so despises you that every honest person flees your company as if you were excommunicated and turns away his gaze if he meets you in the street. How can your heart be so blind to make you remain plunged in this swamp of abomination? How can a woman, who is by nature honest, simple, and modest be reduced to such baseness that she will endure such indecency: to live, drink, and eat among men more vile than pigs—and not even know another kind of man—who beat her, drag her about, and threaten her and through whom she is daily in danger of being killed? Alas, why have womanly straightforwardness and honesty fallen into such vulgarity? Oh, for the sake of God! You women who bear the name of Christians and who use it for such base purposes, raise yourselves up and get out of this abominable mud. Let your souls no longer be weighed down by the filth committed by your vile bodies; for God is full of pity and ready to receive you in mercy, if you want to repent and cry for mercy in great contrition. Take the example of the blessed Mary the Egyptian, who repented of her foolish life and converted to God; she is now a saint in Paradise. Similarly, take the blessed St. Afra,[5] who offered the very body with which she had sinned in martyrdom for the love of Our Lord. And there are others who have been saved in this manner.

And some of you may want to make excuses, saying that they would gladly do it, but that three reasons prevent them: one is that the dishonest men who frequent them would not permit it; the second reason is that the world who thinks them abominable would reject them and chase them away, and because they are so ashamed they would never dare to be seen among people; the third reason is that they would not know what to live on, for they have no profession. To this we respond that these reasons are not valid, for one can find a remedy for everyone of them.

First, they must know that there is no woman, however common and however involved with various men, who will not be protected by God from those who will want her to slide back into sin, if she truly wants to renounce sin no matter what happens, crying mercy to God, repenting and determined to move closer to Him. But she herself must be careful in her deeds and looks, abandoning her indecent clothes and dressing in long, modest gowns, and she must avoid the places she used to frequent. She must go to church in devout prayer, listen to the sermons, and sincerely and in great repentance confess to a wise confessor. And

---

5. She was believed to have been a martyr killed during the persecutions by the emperor Diocletian in the early fourth century. St. Mary the Egyptian was one of the most popular saints of the Middle Ages; after an immoral life she converted and became a saint in the desert.

to those who accuse her of sin she should answer plainly that she would rather offer her body to martyrdom than fall into sin again: for God has given her the grace to repent and reform herself, and as long as she lives she will not relapse. And if she keeps to this path, calling God to her aid, there is no doubt that she can free herself from any bad person; and if someone is so evil that she cannot get rid of him, let her take her case to court, which would pity and protect her.

As for the second reason, that the world would despise her, she should not believe it or give up because of it, for the truth is exactly the opposite. There is no doubt that good people who see her so converted and contrite over her sinful and foolish life would take great pity on her, calling her to them and saying kind things, and giving her the opportunity to persevere and do good.

*   *   *

The third reason, that she would not be able to earn a living, is also not valid. For if she has a body strong enough to do evil things and to suffer bad nights, beatings and other misfortunes, she would be strong enough to earn her living. For people would gladly take her in to help with the laundry in big households; they would pity her and gladly give her the means to earn money. But she has to watch out that no one ever sees anything filthy or wicked in her. She could spin or take care of women in childbed or the sick. She could live in a little room in a good street and among good people. There she would live simply and soberly, so that one would never see her drunk, or gorging herself, or picking a fight or brawling. She should be careful not to pronounce any indecent or dishonest words, but should always be courteous, humble, and sweet-tempered, and of good service to all good people. And she should make sure that she attracts no man, for then she would lose everything. And in this way she could serve God and earn her living. One penny earned honestly would do her more good than a hundred earned in sin.

[The next three chapters praise a life of chastity and modesty in all women and then address the wives of laborers who often can lead more honest lives than women in high places since there are fewer temptations in simple surroundings. Finally, the Three Virtues speak to the poor and give them hope for the afterlife.]

Chapter 14. The End and Conclusion of the Present Book

The three ladies stopped speaking and suddenly vanished, and I, Christine, remained, pretty exhausted from writing for so long, but rejoicing at the beautiful work of their worthy teachings. As I looked at them written down and reviewed them, they seemed to me more and more profitable for the improvement of virtuous habits, increasing ladies' honor, and good for the whole community of women, now living and those in the future, wherever this work may reach an audience.

Therefore I, their servant, though not always adequate in serving them well (though I always desire to be so), began thinking that I would make many copies of this work and would distribute it throughout the world, no matter what the cost. It would be presented in many different places to queens, princesses, and noble ladies so that it would be more honored and exalted—for it is most worthy—and through them it could be disseminated to other women. Once this idea is executed and my wish fulfilled—and I have already started on this—the work will circulate and be published in all countries, even though it is written in French. But since this language is more common in the world than any other, this work will not remain unknown and useless but will remain in the world without fail in many copies. Many valiant ladies and women of authority will see and hear it in present and in future times, and they will pray to God for their servant Christine, wishing that she should have lived during their lifetime so that they could have known her. May all women keep her in their grace and loving memory and pray that as long as she is alive God may by His pity favor her with ever greater understanding, granting her such light of knowledge and true wisdom that she may use them as long as she lives in the noble labor of study and the exaltation of virtue through good examples for all human beings. And after her soul has parted from her body, may it please these women as a reward for her meritorious service to offer to God on her behalf, Our Fathers, oblations, and devotions so as to ease the pain suffered for her faults, so that she may be presented before God in the world without end, which is promised to you all. Amen.

Here ends the Book of the Three Virtues,
for the instruction of ladies.
Thanks be given to God.

FROM CHRISTINE'S VISION

[Christine's Vision of 1405 is the principal source for her biography. In a moving lament addressed to the allegorical figure of Philosophy in part 3 she lays out for us her changing fortunes from childhood to the moment of writing. But it is important to remember that part 3 follows upon two books that give us a panoramic view of French history, politics, and learning.

The genre is that of a vision, a form that could be filled with all sorts of different themes: a vision of love, of the afterlife or God (in mystical visions), or of the future. In the later Middle Ages many visions had political and moral contents, such as Philippe de Mézières, *Songe du vieil pelerin* [Dream of the old pilgrim].[1] Within her vision Christine engages in a number of dialogues, reminiscent of Boethius's *Consolation of Philosophy* and Petrarch's[2] *Secretum meum* [My secret], an intimate conversation between the poet and St. Augustine. Christine first speaks with the Crowned Lady (France), then with Lady Opinion, representing the world of the universities and learning, and finally with Philosophy.

Christine leads up to her own extended life story by telling us an allegorical version of her own birth (swallowed up by Chaos, she emerges with the help of Nature) and by showing us the origins and current situation of France. Everything she says in the *Vision* has, according to Christine's own preface, three meanings: one as applied to the world at large, one as applied to the individual, and one as applied to the realm of France.[3] In all three areas, things are not going well. For example, just as Christine became a widow and suffered all kinds of troubles, France is depicted as a widow whose former happiness has turned into ruin: the king has increasingly frequent bouts of madness (which Christine blames on Fortune's malevolent influence); the dauphin seems incapable and leads a dissolute life; and the great dukes are at each others' throats.[4]

The *Vision*, then, is a kind of interior journey, where Christine hopes to find meaning for her country and her own life by reviewing past successes and failures with the help of authoritative allegorical figures. Like St. Augustine, she strives to connect temporal history with a higher providential scheme. That Lady Philosophy is recognized to be Lady Theology at the end underlines the ultimately spiritual nature of Christine's quest.

Translated by Renate Blumenfeld-Kosinski from the new edition of the *Avision* by Christine Reno and Liliane Dulac (in preparation). The editor thanks Christine Reno for supplying the manuscript of this edition.]

Here begins the book of Christine's Vision which is divided into three parts. The first part deals with the image of the world and the marvels that she saw there; the second part speaks of Lady Opinion

1. Written between 1386 and 1389. See G. W. Coopland's edition in two volumes (Cambridge, UK: Cambridge University Press, 1969). For an analysis of this text and its relation to Christine's work see Sandra L. Hindman, *Christine de Pizan's 'Epistre Othéa': Painting and Politics at the Court of Charles VI* (Toronto: Pontifical Institute of Mediaeval Studies, 1986), 144–56. On visions, see Kathryn L. Lynch, *The High Medieval Dream Vision: Poetry, Philosophy, and Literary Form* (Stanford, Calif.: Stanford University Press, 1988).
2. One of the greatest Italian poets (1304–1374). Other sources for the *Vision* are the *Grandes Chroniques de France* [Great Chronicles of France] and the *Histoire ancienne jusqu'à César* [Ancient history up to Julius Caesar] for book 1; for book 2 especially, Thomas Aquinas's commentary on Aristotle's *Metaphysics*—translated by John Rowan in two volumes (Chicago: Henry Regnery Co., 1961)—and Guillaume de Tignonville's *Dits moraux des philosophes* [Moral sayings of the philosophers], as C. C. Willard points out in her *Christine de Pizan: Her Life and Works* (New York: Persea, 1984), 77 and 159. Book 3 has many quotations from Boethius's *Consolation of Philosophy*; patristic citations, most likely coming from Thomas Hibernicus's compilation *Manipulus florum* [Sheaf of flowers]; and references to the Bible.
3. This self-interpretation is reminiscent of the *Letter from Othea*. The "Preface" has been edited and translated by Christine Reno in "The Preface to the *Avision-Christine* in ex-Pillips 128," in E. J. Richards, ed., *Reinterpreting Christine de Pizan* (Athens: University of Georgia Press, 1992), 208–27.
4. For a vivid portrait of that troubled period and its society see Bernard Guenée, *Un meurtre, une société: L'assassinat du duc d'Orléans 23 novembre 1407* (Paris: Gallimard, 1992).

and of her shadow; the third part speaks of the consolation of philosophy.[1]

Part One

1. First, Christine Tells How Her Spirit Was Transported

I had already finished half of my pilgrimage[2] when one day, toward evening, I found myself tired of the long journey and desiring shelter. And since I had arrived here by my desire for rest, after having partaken of the refreshment necessary for human life and said grace, I commended myself to the Creator of all things and I went to bed to a troubled rest. And shortly afterward, when my senses were weighed down with sleep, a marvelous vision came to me as a strange prophetic portent, although I am not Nebuchadnezzar, or Scipio, or Joseph[3]—the secrets of the Almighty are not kept from the simple people.

It seemed to me that my spirit left its body and, just as in dreams I often had the impression that my body flew in the air, I thought at that moment that by the blowing of different winds my spirit was transported into a dark region where there was the end of a valley that was floating on several rivers. There the figure of a man appeared to me, of a beautiful shape but of an immeasurable size, for his head pierced the clouds, his feet walked over precipices, and his middle was a wide as the earth. His face was bright and ruddy; countless stars served as ornaments for his head; from his beautiful eyes came a great brightness so great that it illuminated everything and reflected to the very insides of his body. The breaths he took with his great mouth attracted so much air and wind that everything was filled with an agreeable freshness. The figure had two principal conduits: one was the opening of his mouth, through which he received nourishment; the other, below, was the one through which he purified and emptied himself. These two were of different natures, for everything that entered through the upper duct, through which he was fed, had to have a material and perishable body; but

1. This consolation evokes one of Christine's favorite texts, Boethius's *Consolation of Philosophy*; see n. 8, p. 38. In some of the manuscripts of the *Vision*, Christine gives detailed instructions for the interpretation of her own text at this point. The most elaborate can be found in Reno, "The Preface to the *Avision-Christine*."

2. The reference to the halfway point of Christine's earthly pilgrimage evokes the opening of Dante's *Divine Comedy*: "In the middle of the journey of our life I came to myself within a dark wood" (*Inferno* 1.1–2). See *The Divine Comedy*, trans. John D. Sinclair, (New York: Oxford University Press, 1939).

3. Joseph's dreams are recorded in Genesis 37:5–11. Nebuchadnezzar's dream-vision is in Daniel 4. Scipio's dream is the subject of Cicero's *Dream of Scipio*, which was known in the Middle Ages particularly through Macrobius's late antique commentary. Some of the remarks Christine makes later about the soul's descent into the body recall that commentary. See Macrobius, *Commentary on the Dream of Scipio*, trans. W. H. Stahl (New York: Columbia University Press, 1952), 133–37.

through the other duct nothing perishable or tangible passed. The clothing of this creature was of a beautifully patterned silk cloth, very finely worked, rich and durable. Well visible on his forehead there was an imprint of five letters, c.h.a.o.z., signifying his name. Nothing in this figure was badly formed, except that at times his face was sad and tearful, just like a man who suffers various aches and pains in different parts of his body and because of this complains to God with lamentations and crying.

2. Here She Tells of the Way the Said Figure Was Fed

Next to the said figure stood as a helper a great crowned shade in the shape of a woman who looked like a very powerful queen, formed by nature without a visible or tangible body. She was so large that she cast a shadow that completely surrounded the above-mentioned figure; she was especially designated and employed to administer his feeding: that was her job. Around her she had an infinite number of instruments of various shapes and imprints, just like the waffle irons or other similar tools one finds in Paris. And since this lady did not possess the vice of sloth she was continually occupied with tending diligently to her different tasks; for without a break she was mixing mortar which she made congeal. In this mixture she put gall, honey, lead, and feathers. With this matter she filled vases of various kinds and then poured small quantities in the afore-mentioned molds which she closed and sealed well. All this she did not do uniformly but in different ways. She put everything to bake and take shape into the mouth of the above-mentioned large figure which was so wide that it looked like a huge furnace, heated like a stove meant for tempering. There she left them for the appropriate time, one longer than the other, depending on the different shape and thickness of the mold.

When the wise administrator knew that her work had come to perfection, she opened the mouth of this figure so skilfully that she could pull out all those materials that were sufficiently baked and leave the others to bake until their day had come. Little bodies of different shapes. depending on the pattern of the instrument then sprang from these molds. But something very strange happened to them. For as soon as the little figures left their molds, the great figure, in whose mouth they had been baked, swallowed countless numbers of them, all alive, with one gulp into his belly. And thus, night and day the endless work of feeding the great insatiable body through the hands of this lady continued.

3. How Christine Was Swallowed into the Body of the Above-Mentioned Figure

My spirit approached this place, intent on witnessing this marvel. Then the breath of this great figure pulled my spirit toward him until it fell into the hands of the crowned lady. When she had put the mold with all the material into the oven, she took my spirit and stuck it in, and exactly in the way in which she usually gave form to human bodies she mixed everything together. And like this she let me bake for a time until a little human body was made for me. But according to the wishes of her who had made the mixture I received the female sex—because of her and not because of the mold. Suddenly, just like the others, I was swallowed up into the belly of that figure. When I had fallen into it, right away the maid of the afore-mentioned lady arrived holding vials full of a sweet liqueur which she gently gave me to drink; through its strength and continuous action my body began to grow and took on force and vigor. And this wise woman increased and supplemented the nourishment as I grew stronger until I could hold up and feed my body by myself. My understanding grew and I learned about the diversity of the figure's insides on which I walked on my two feet and whose mountains and valleys were made of pebbles and hard rocks, of wood and metals and various materials. But the space enclosed by this figure seemed so far and wide to me that the span of a man's life would not suffice to seek out the different regions that exist within him.

4. How She Moved from One Place to Another

[Fame trumpets the honors of a Crowned Lady (France) and as Christine comes to the second Athens (Paris) she wonders how she can become acquainted with this princess. Since Christine is still young and has not yet perfectly learned the language, which is not her mother tongue, she needs to learn about this lady. Her country is fertile and rich, yet there are some indications of trouble.]

5. The Acquaintance Which She Desired to Have with a Certain Lady

[When Christine is fully grown she finally manages to become acquainted with the Crowned Lady.]

Now, thank God, I was so close to the beloved princess that she did me the gracious favor of revealing to me the secrets of her heart, and she was not afraid to bestow on me, a woman, the honor of making me the scribe of these events. And she desired that through me poems and songs should be made about this. She already knew as much about my feelings as about who I was.

6. The Complaint of the Crowned Lady to Christine

Thus she said to me: "Dear friend, you who are concerned with pre-serving my welfare, since by nature every loving heart deserves to be loved, it is right that your desire should be valued. And since you wished for my acquaintance, I grant your wishes. Friend, whom God and Nature have given the gift of the love of learning beyond the normal level of women, prepare parchment, ink, and pens and write down the words coming from my breast. For I want to reveal everything to you. And I am pleased that you should be the one to prepare written memo-ries of my dignity for your wise and benevolent people."

[Now follows an outline of the history of France, from the Trojan origins [4] to the Hundred Years' War and thus Christine's own time. She praises Charles V, the benefactor of Christine's family who died in 1380. She now speaks of his sons in allegorical terms as birds of prey.]

12. Here She [5] Speaks of Two Noble Birds of Prey

From his [6] entrails emerged two small golden butterflies, very graceful and beautiful, who, as they grew larger together with swarms of wasps, dared to boast that they were the guardians of me and my dwellings. They banded together and because of the ancient renown of their ori-gins, people rightly allowed them to sit at the top of the highest stalks. And just as *About the Properties of Things* [7] says of the phoenix that it first comes forth from the ashes in the shape of a little worm and then grows and gets larger until he surpasses all birds in beauty, these butter-flies grew and got stronger so that they were transformed into the species of noble birds of prey, [8] but with the difference that a certain number of them had crests on their heads like the birds one calls hoopoes.

[The noble birds fly over France.]

Oh Fortune, who is the giver of all troubles, who made you find the means to disturb the peregrine falcon, flying so high that the prospect of his attack made tremble the plundering prey, the target of his fury. Where did you find the adverse wind with which you brought him down when he so proudly made his rounds before attaining his prey? You

4. On the supposed Trojan origins of the French, see Colette Beaune, *The Birth of an Ideology: Myths and Symbols of Nation in Late-Medieval France*, trans. Susan Ross Huston (Berkeley: University of California Press, 1991), chap. 8.
5. I.e., the Crowned Lady, or France. Christine interprets this chapter as the ruin of the Church or the illness of the French king Charles VI. See Reno, "The Preface to the *Avision-Christine*," 219.
6. Most likely Charles's father, Charles V.
7. A reference to an extremely popular thirteenth-century encyclopedia written by Bartholomew the Englishman (Bartholomeus Anglicus).
8. On the image of the falcon see Hindman, *Christine de Pizan's "Epistre d'Othéa,"* 45.

threw him down so violently through your blast that he remained
stretched out, all broken, not just his feathers but his entire body, so that
from then on he had to be fed by the hands of strangers.[9] Oh God, what
a pity for such a noble bird, trained in good behavior, proud and brave
in his flight, with a sweet voice and a lively and pleasant look, who
without fail would have defended all my marshes and rivers from all
greedy and misguided birds. I lamented and wept over him as a particular loss the pain of which does not go away; rather, it is renewed every
day by grievous harm.

[The Crowned Lady now speaks of various revolts that occurred in her
realm.[1] She then castigates the vices that are rampant in France: gluttony,
indolence, cruelty, and fraud. The allegorical figure of Lust is one of the
chief offenders; she brings down the kingdom.]

25. More on the Same Topic

I will again speak of the indecent woman who holds my defenders
and my other officials and likewise my closest relatives and friends in
her chains, together with the other sufferings mentioned earlier. Alas, it
seems that if one possesses only one vice one cannot be happy! But
harm comes to the person who is surrounded and filled with several or
all of them! I cannot be silent about God's great deed in condemning
her[2] vice and the evils that come about through it, today and in the
earliest times, for several kingdoms were destroyed by it. Therefore, I
should be frightened when I see the same thing happening, the same
scourge. For example: Dinah, Jacob's daughter, was ravished by the son
of the king of Shechem, and this was the cause of the destruction of this
kingdom. Amnon pretended to be ill to have his sister, Tamar,[3] and
because of this he was killed by his brother, Absalom. The abduction of
Helen through Paris in Greece was the cause of the destruction of Troy.
A king of France was driven away and exiled because of it, as the chronicles tell. The force that the arrogant Tarquin used against Lucretia,[4] the
chaste Roman lady who committed suicide because of this, was the
reason that he and his sons were disinherited; and because of this event
the Romans swore that there would never again be a king in Rome.
Hannibal, king of Carthage, was a victorious conqueror in the battles
with the Romans and others, and his name was renowned for prowess
as long as he was not acquainted with this indecent woman. But as soon

---

9. A reference to Charles's VI madness, which first appeared in 1392 and got worse over the
   years.
1. For a brief summary, see Mary Louise Towner, ed., *Lavision-Christine* (Washington, D.C.:
   Catholic University of America Press, 1932), 29–31.
2. I.e., Lust's.
3. Her story is in 2 Samuel 12–13. For Dinah, see Genesis 34.
4. A Roman noble lady who was raped by Tarquin. Her story was popular in the Middle Ages.
   The king was the Merovingian Childeric I (ca. 436–481), as Christine states in the preface;
   see Reno, "The Preface to the *Avision-Christine*," 217.

as he began to rest and to surround himself with pleasures, through which he made the acquaintance of this evil woman, he was toppled into the valley of misfortune and after that nothing good happened to him.

[The Crowned Lady could add further examples, but will not do so since this vice is visible everywhere. God once sent the Flood to eradicate this vice, but it nonetheless survived. After many more complaints on this topic the Crowned Lady thanks Christine for her company and understanding. Christine promises to live up to the lady's expectations and be a faithful scribe.]

Here ends the first part of Christine's Vision.

Part Two

1. Here Begins the Second Part of Christine's Vision Which Speaks of Lady Opinion and Her Shadows

After all this I had the urge to inquire further and it seemed to me that I was traveling through the city of Athens[5] until I was in the midst of the schools. Then, overjoyed at having arrived at such a noble university, with my mind eager profitably to drink in their erudition, I stopped among the scholars of the different faculties of learning who were involved in disputations of various questions and arguments.

Then, just as I wanted to approach to listen, my sight was quicker than my hearing. For as I was lifting up my eyes, I saw flying among them a great female shadow without a body, which seemed like a spiritual thing of the strangest nature. And experience proved that she was a supernatural being. For what I saw to be a single shadow had more than a hundred million, indeed countless parts: she produced out of herself some large parts, some small, others even smaller; then the parts of the shadow came together in a great throng, just as clouds do in the sky or birds that fly together in flocks. But there were more of them than any birds that ever flew. These throngs differed one from the other by their colors. They differed by all the colors that ever existed and more. For there was large group that was all white, another red, others blue, others the color of fire, others of water, and so on through all the colors. And those of one color stuck together just as birds of one species do. Nonetheless it happened that sometimes they mingled with others, but each one always returned to its own color. * * * And just as the colors of these shadows differed by group so their forms differed. For there is no body of a human being, or of a strange animal, bird, sea monster, ser-

5. The seat of learning; here it refers to Paris.

pent, or anything ever formed by God—and be it the highest celestial thing or whatever idea could be present to the imagination—that was not among these forms. There were so many strange forms that no one could think of them all. But the forms of giants, of horrible serpents, of beasts or any other mortal thing did not terrify me as much as the horrible, black, disfigured monsters from hell, the memory of which still fills me with fear.

2. Here She Tells What Was the Use of These Shadows

I saw that the clerks disputing in the schools mentioned above were surrounded by these throngs of shadows flying through the air.[6] And before the one who wanted to propose his question could speak, one of these shadows approached his ear as if it were going to tell him what to say. Then, when the other one wanted to answer or respond, another shadow approached him in a similar way. And thus there was no disputant who did not have around his head one, two, three, four, or more of them who all gave him advice. But each branch of learning had its own color of shadows.

[Christine now describes all the different disciplines and wonders about the function of these shadows.]

3. How the Shadow Addressed Christine

Then, as I was absorbed in looking at this marvel, the shadowy creature turned to me and addressed me as follows: "Learned daughter, what brings you here?" And I said to her: "Lady, chance, but your marvels have made me pause; and if I could, I would like to become better acquainted with you." And she said to me: "Don't you know me then?" "Lady, I have no memory of it." And she said to me: "Oh, I see well that ignorance takes away from humans the knowledge of the objects of their work. But to fulfill your wish, I grant that you may know me, and I will be revealed to you through forceful proofs.

"Know that as soon as Adam was formed I was created, and I am the daughter of Ignorance: the Desire for Knowledge engendered me. I made the first man and his wife bite into the apple by my deceitful urging. And after God had condemned him for this misdeed to gain his living by the sweat of his brow, I made him look for and research the properties of herbs and plants, and taught him the methods for cultivating the land; and I made him experience the nature of created things until he understood them. After that I governed humans and made them acquire laws, of which the first was the law of nature. And from these first times on there were some ingenious men whom I made do

6. Christine may have been inspired by some passages in Dante's *Inferno* 3 and 5.

so much research that they discovered philosophy. And then all the sciences and arts were investigated because of me and ways were found to attain them."

[The shadow, Lady Opinion, explains that in this world she is the servant of Philosophy, created by God. The shadow is the means by which all learning and values are transmitted to men. The shadow then speaks of what philosophers think about the origin of the world and about nature. In particular, the shadow details Aristotle's refutation of earlier philosophers (chapter 8). She lists all the things that she was responsible for in the world, such as the Trojan War. At the end of her discourse, the shadow refers to the *Debate on the Romance of the Rose* that she instigated and Christine participated in.]

12. Christine Responds to the Shadow

Then, as I understood clearly who this was who had addressed me for so long, I spoke as follows: "Ah! Powerful and strong Lady Opinion, I should truly know you very well, for I have been acquainted with you since my childhood. And I certainly know and acknowledge that your authority is of great vigor and power. And although you are often blamed, he who makes good use of you cannot fall into error, and it is bad for those in whom you do not exist in a healthy way. But since it has pleased you to honor with the grace of revealing yourself to me so clearly and openly by telling me about your great powers, I ask you not be annoyed and to clarify some more questions for me." And she said to me: "Daughter, say what you please."

"Lady, since, as you said, it is from you that comes the original invention of good or bad human deeds, crude or subtle, according to the disposition of people's minds, please assure me that in the things that you brought forth in me, which I acquired by means of study and such knowledge and understanding that are in my power, and which are laid out in my compilations and volumes, I did not commit any error—for nobody is so wise that he does not ever err. For if this were the case, I would rather correct them late than never."

And she said to me: "Dear friend, be at peace. For I tell you no, although earlier I accused you of wanting to give the sovereign honor to Fortune, and thereby forgetting me though I am the first one, there is no fault in your works, even though because of me many people argue about them in different ways: for some say that learned men or monks forged them for you, and that they cannot come out of the understanding of a woman. But those who say this are ignorant, for they have no knowledge of the writings that mention so many valiant women, wiser and more learned than you, nor of the prophets who lived in past times; and because Nature's power is not diminished this can still happen. Others say that your style is too obscure and that one cannot understand it and that, therefore, it is not enjoyable. And thus in different ways I make some people give praise and others take it away, since it is impossible that a thing should please everyone. But I tell you this: the truth, as is witnessed by experience, does not let blame have any effect on reputation. I therefore advise you to continue your work, for it is right, and do not fear to be in error because of me. For as long as I am in you, based on justice, reason, and true understanding, you will not make any errors in the fundamentals of your work, in those things that seem most true, no matter what the different judgments are, of which some come simply from me and others from Envy. For I assure you, when she and I are together very wrong judgments are often made, and no one is so good that he should be spared. And, therefore, I am dangerous when ruled by Envy. We blind a person who has both of us within him to the things of others and even to his own. We gnaw at his heart, do not let him rest, and give him the desire to do many evil things, which he sometimes does. He who falls into our hands goes in a bad direction. He will never be good or powerful.

"Did we not once forbid the gates of Rome to the valiant Julius Caesar, who returned there so victoriously, and did we not finally succeed in having him killed? We have done many such deeds and no one is so wise that he could protect himself from us. Now I have told you enough of my adventures; it must suffice. For, since I make one person believe that something is good and well done or true, and make another person believe the contrary, which causes many fights and debates, the prolixity of the many stories I told could become boring to readers. And I can prophesy to you that many people will testify to different things regarding their reading of this book. Some will pronounce themselves very differently about your language: they will say that it is not elegant; others will say that the composition of the materials is strange. And those who will understand it will speak well of it. And in future times it will be spoken about more than during your lifetime. For I again tell you that you have come at a bad moment. At present, learning does not have a high reputation; rather, it seems to be out of season. And as proof that this is true you see few people who have risen in the house of Fortune because of it. But after your death, a prince full of valor and wisdom[7] will come who, because of what he has heard about your volumes, will always desire for you to have lived in his time and will ardently wish to have seen you. Now I have described myself to you. Define to me, then, who do you think I am."

And I said to her: "Lady, since your own description defines it for me, I tell you that now I know you perfectly, that you are the daughter of Ignorance, adhering to one side, always distrusting the other. And in this I consider what Aristotle says about you in the first book of his *Prior Analytics*, namely that the person who possesses you always wonders if

---

7. This may be the great poet Charles of Orléans (1391–1465), the son of Louis of Orléans, one of Christine's patrons.

things could be different from what he thinks, since you are never certain. And St. Bernard also says in the fifth chapter of the *Considerations* that you are ambiguous and can be deceived.[8] So I say and conclude that you are the attachment to one side, which attachment is caused by the appearance of some argument that can be proved, whether the person who has this opinion has doubts concerning the other side or not. And about your power I say that because of the ignorance that resides in men the world is governed more by you than by great learning."

Here ends the second part of the book of Christine's Vision.

Part Three

1. Here Begins the Third and Last part of Christine's Vision

[Christine tells how she was escorted through the various buildings of the schools by the nun assisting Philosophy. While Christine's relative lack of learning and her "weak feminine body" keep her from the highest ascent and access to all of Philosophy's treasures, she is given a fair amount that she laboriously carries away. Finally she comes to a little room that reveals a bright light when opened. A sweet voice addresses her that turns out to belong to Lady Philosophy, the same one who had appeared long ago to Boethius. This is why Christine feels confident that she can turn to Philosophy and tell her of her troubles.]

3. Christine's Complaint to Philosophy

Reverend lady, obeisance to your Serenity in the prescribed fashion. May the narration of my fortunes not bother you by their prolixity, and may you deign to extend the help of your counsel to come to the aid of my unworthy thoughts. Oh lady, dear mistress, note how changeable Fortune has always been a bitter stepmother to me, as one says, from my childhood on. For I was born of noble parents in Italy in the city of Venice where my father, born in Bologna the Fat[9] where I was later raised, went to marry my mother, who was born there, whom he had met through the long acquaintance with my grandfather, a licensed clerk and doctor from Forli and a graduate of the University of Bologna. He was a salaried counselor in the city where I was born. Because he was related to him, my father became acquainted with the Venetians and was, because of the high level and authority of his learning, similarly retained as a salaried counselor to the city of Venice, where he resided for a time, enjoying great honor and gaining riches. Now tell

---

8. As Glenda McLeod points out, this is a reference to *Prior Analytics* 89a3. The quotation from Bernard of Clairvaux probably comes from the compilation *Manipulus florum*. See McLeod, trans., *Christine's Vision* (New York: Garland, 1993), 103–04.

9. See n. 9, p. 148.

me, was it not Fortune who shortly after my birth made my father go to Bologna the Fat in order to take care of certain matters and to visit his properties? There he right away heard news and received certain messages, all at the same time, from two excellent kings, who for the great fame of his learned authority had sent for him, and begged him, promising great salaries and gifts if only he came to each of them. One of them was the sovereign Christian king, Charles the Wise, the fifth of this name, and the other was the king of Hungary, who for his deeds and merits later was called the "Good King of Hungary." [1]

Then, since he could not just ignore these messages because of the respect due the dignity of these princes, my father decided to obey one of them, namely the most worthy; and as he also had the desire to see the schools of Paris and the nobility of the French court, he decided to go to the French king.

He planned to see the king for a time, to obey his commands and to visit the above-mentioned schools in the space of a year, and then return to his wife and family whom he had enjoined to stay on his inherited properties in Bologna the Fat. When all this had been done and arranged he left with the permission of the rulers of Venice and came to France, where he was splendidly and honorably welcomed by the wise king Charles. And soon after, in light of the king's experience of his great knowledge and learning, the king made him his special, private, and valued counselor who pleased him so much that he could not give him permission to leave when the year was up. Instead, the said king insisted that at his generous expense my father should send for his wife, children, and family so that they could spend their lives in France close to him; and he promised properties, annuities, and pensions so that they might live honorably. And although my father, still planning to go back, delayed this project for three years, it nonetheless had to be done in the end. And thus, as I said, our move from Italy to France was accomplished.

The wife and children of your beloved philosopher Master Thomas, my father, were welcomed in great style once they arrived in Paris; and the most mild, good, and wise king wanted to see them and receive them joyously. This was done soon after their arrival when they were still wearing their richly ornamented Lombard clothing and headdresses in the style fit for women and children of rank. The said king was in the palace of the Louvre in the month of December when this beautiful and honorable family and their relatives were presented to him; and he received his wife and family with great joy and many presents.

---

1. Louis I of Hungary (1326–1382).

4. Christine Tells of Her Good Fortunes

Fortune was most favorable to us during the lifetime of the said good and wise king Charles.

[Christine now describes the favors and gifts, such as revenues and a castle, King Charles bestowed on her father.]

To come to the highpoint of my fortunes, the time arrived when I was approaching the age when girls are commonly given to a husband. And although I was still very young, nonetheless several knights, other nobles, and wealthy clerks asked for my hand in marriage; and this truth should not be considered to be boasting, for the cause of it was not my own value but the power my father had because of the honor and great love the king bestowed on him. And since my father considered that man the most worthy who combined great learning with a decent way of life, he sought out a young scholar[2] who had already graduated, well born of a noble family in Picardy and who had more virtues than riches. I was given to him whom my father regarded as his own son. In this matter I do not complain about Fortune, for, as I have already said, I could not have done better myself in choosing all the right good qualities. And shortly afterward our good prince, who liked him for his abilities, gave him the office of notary and of his secretary, which was vacant, with a salary and other benefits, and retained him at his court as a beloved servant.

5. Christine Begins to Speak of Her Misfortunes

This prosperity lasted for several years. But as Fortune showed herself envious of our glories, she wanted to shut off the source from which they came. Dear mistress, was it not through her that grievous harm befell this kingdom, and was sorely felt in Master Thomas's household? It was at this time that the good wise prince, not in old age, reached in nature's course, but at the rather young age of forty-four, fell into a rather brief illness from which he died.

Alas! Truly it often happens that good things last only a short time. For even today he would not be very old had it pleased God to let him continue this life that was so necessary to this kingdom whose government and condition are now in such bad shape—so different from what they used to be. At that moment the door to our misfortunes was opened, and I, who was still very young, entered. And, as is usual when powerful men have died, great upheavals and changes come about in the condition of their courts and lands, caused by the clash of many

---

2. I.e., Etienne de Castel; see also p. xi.

opposing wills; and it can hardly be otherwise unless great wisdom prevents it, as it can be seen from what is written about Alexander the Great after whose death great conflicts broke out between the barons, in spite of his dividing up the lands for them.

At that time my father lost his large pensions. He was paid no more than a hundred francs a month, the income from his properties and gifts put together, which was much less than what he was used to. And the expectation my father had had through the king's promise to settle on him and his heirs lands that would yield five hundred pounds a year came to nothing because my father had not reminded the king and then the king died so soon. Nonetheless my father was retained by the governing princes but at a badly reduced and irregular salary. He was already in his old age, and shortly afterward he fell into a long period of decline and illness, bringing him great suffering in which he could well have used all the money he had already spent. And for this reason I believe it a good thing to save prudently in one's youth which can then help a man in his old age.

Being of sound mind until the end and recognizing his Creator like a good Catholic, my father died at exactly the hour he had predicted; for this reason his reputation lived on among the clerks, stating that in more than a hundred years there had not lived a man of such high understanding of mathematics and astrology. The princes and those who knew him mourned his death and missed him because of his true probity, his good deeds, loyalty, truthfulness and other virtues; there was nothing to blame unless one counts the excessive generosity of refusing none of his possessions to the poor, although he had a wife and children. And to prove that I do not say this only because of love, there are still many of his acquaintances, princes and others, who know this for a certainty. He was a man justly mourned and wept over by his family.

6. More on the Same Subject

Then my husband, a young, wise and prudent man, beloved by the princes and everyone who frequented his office, became the head of our household; his wise prudence made it possible to maintain the position of our family. But since Fortune had already put me on the descending side of her wheel and destined me for the evil she wanted to give me by throwing me to the very bottom, she did not want this excellent man to remain with me much longer. Because of Fortune Death took him from me in his prime at the age of thirty-four, just when he was on the brink of ascending to high office, as much through his wisdom as through prudent acquisitions and good administration; and I, at twenty-five, was left behind with the care of three small children and a large household. I had just cause to feel bitterness, missing his sweet companionship and the past joys that had barely lasted ten years for me. When I saw the flood of tribulations rushing upon me I wanted to die rather than live; and not forgetting my vow and the good love promised to him, I decided wisely never to have another husband.

Now I had fallen into the valley of tribulation. For Fortune, once she wants to destroy something, be it a kingdom, city, empire or an individual, gathers far and wide everything that is adverse to the object of her fury in order to lead it to the height of misfortune—and this is what happened to me. For, as I was not present at my husband's death who died unexpectedly in a sudden epidemic—though, thank God he died as a good Catholic—in the town of Beauvais where he had gone with the king and was accompanied only by his servants and followers unknown to me, I could not establish the precise state of his finances. For it is the common habit of married men to say and explain nothing about their financial affairs to their wives, which often causes great harm, as is clear to me from experience; and this does not make sense when the women are not stupid but prudent and good administrators. I know well that I had no clear notion of what he possessed.

Thus I had to set to work, which was something that I who had been brought up in delights and finery had never learned; I had to become the captain of the ship lost in the storm without a master,[3] that is, the desolate household far from its homeland. Then troubles arose from all sides, and, as is the common fare of widows, lawsuits and legal disputes came to me from everywhere. And those who were in debt to me attacked me so that I would not come forward and demand anything from them. And God knows that it is true that one liar claimed that the evidence of papers signed by my husband showed the debt of this fraudulent man as paid; but he lied in his claim, and the testimony of the paper finally confounded him and he dared no longer make a claim and continue his lying. Soon obstacles were put in my way in the matter of a property my husband had purchased. For as it was put into the king's hands, I had to pay rent on it and could not profit from it. And in the Chamber of Accounts I pleaded a lengthy lawsuit against a man who was and still is one of the masters and rulers from whom I cannot have justice; from him I received injustice and great harm, and many people know that this is the manifest truth. Now he has grown old in his sins and still gives no thought to this nor does his conscience bother him.

This was not the only plague. For with my consent the money of my little orphans had been placed by their guardians with a merchant who had the reputation of an honest man, so that their meager means should increase and multiply; and as the investment had grown by half in the space of a year, he was tempted by the devil to pretend that he had been

---

3. This is the allegory Christine used in the first part of *The Book of Fortune's Transformation* to speak of her marriage and her husband's death (see p. 104).

robbed and to flee. Again it was expensive to pursue him and we lost that money.

[Christine now describes further lawsuits and a grave illness she contracted which prevented her from successfully pursuing many of these suits. She finally had to abandon the suits, but her misfortunes did not come to an end. She continues to address Lady Philosophy.]

Oh sweet mistress, how many tears, sighs, complaints, and lamentations do you think I sent forth, how many sharp pains I suffered when I was alone in my retreat, or when I saw around me in my home my little children and poor relatives and thought about the past and the present misfortunes whose floods had so deeply submerged me—and there was nothing I could do about it! In this unhappy situation I grieved more for my loved ones than for myself. Once I replied to someone who said that I had nothing to complain about, since as a single person I was without any responsibilities, that he had not looked at me very closely, for I was three times double; and when he said he did not understand me, I explained to him that I was six times myself.[4] And with all this, dear mistress, don't you think that my heart was heavy with the fear that people might become aware of my financial situation and with the worry that by the way things looked the downfall of my estate—due to my predecessors and not to myself—would become apparent to outsiders and neighbors? And that ignorance made me so bitter that I would have chosen death over bankruptcy? Ah, what a burden and pain for a heart that is so bent on maintaining our former way of life and Fortune does not permit it! There is no pain like it, and no one believes it who has not experienced it himself. And God knows how many troubles have happened and are still happening to many people for this very reason! I assure you that the extent of my troubles was not obvious to others from my appearance and dress. I often shivered under my fur-lined cloak and my fine surcoat that was not often refurbished but kept in good condition; and I spent many bad nights in my beautiful and well-arranged bed. But our meals were modest, as it befits a widow; one has to live somehow. And God knows how my heart suffered when bailiffs took action against me and my dearest things were taken from me. I greatly felt the loss, but even more I feared the shame. When I had to borrow from someone, even if it was in order to avoid greater troubles, dear Lord God, how I was ashamed, how I blushed when I asked for it, even if it was from a friend. And to this day I have not recovered from this affliction, and it seems to me that a bout of fever would pain me less than ever having to do it again.

Ah, when I think of the many winter mornings I spent standing

4. I.e., that she is responsible for three children, her mother, her niece, and herself.

around the palace, dying of cold, waiting for my counselors to remind them or to charge them with my case; or how often I heard there various decisions and strange conclusions that brought tears to my eyes; but worst of all was the expense that was beyond my means. Following the example of Jesus Christ who was willingly tortured in every part of His body in order to teach us patience, Fortune wanted to torture my heart with all kinds of cruel and unpleasant thoughts. What greater evil and unpleasantness can befall an innocent person, what can cause greater impatience than to hear oneself accused without cause, as Boethius testifies in his book *The Consolation?*

Was it not said about me throughout the town that I had lovers? At this point I must insist that Fortune did all this with her blows. For such rumors appear and spread, often unjustly, because people know and frequent each other, or they spread by conjecture, or because they are likely. But I swear on my soul that the man in question did not even know me or even knew who I was, nor was there any man or creature who had ever seen me in public or private, inside or outside in any place where this man was, for my path did not go in that direction, nor did I have any business there, and God be my witness that I speak the truth. And in view of his situation and mine such a thing could not rightly have happened, nor was it likely; and since no one could have had cause to think it, I often wondered where such tales could come from which were passed from mouth to mouth with the comment: "I heard it said." And as an innocent person I was sometimes troubled by what people told me and other times I smiled about it and said: "God and the man in question and I know very well that there is nothing to it."

But my suffering still did not end.

[Christine now describes her efforts to obtain wages still owed to her husband].

You can imagine how difficult it was for me, a feeble and naturally fearful woman, to make a virtue out of necessity and to take on the risk and expense of running after them following their procedures. Then I had to sit around in their courts or antechambers, clutching my bag and and papers, most days without accomplishing anything, or at long last receiving an ambiguous reply for all my waiting. But the wait was very long. Oh God, how many annoying remarks, I had to listen to; how many stupid looks, how many jokes from some fat drunkard did I suffer; and because I was afraid of putting my case at risk and was so dependent on its outcome, I hid my thoughts and turned away without answering or else I pretended that I did not understand and that I took it all as a light joke. And may God reform all evil consciences, for I found some very bad ones!

In the midst of these affairs I could find no help of any great or simple person anywhere, although I did ask several nobles to assist me through their word, hoping that they would feel obliged by the rules of justice to help widows and orphans; but when nothing good came to me of all this one day, disconsolate about all these things, I wrote this ballad in tears:

> Alas! where will they find comfort,
> Poor widows who have lost their possessions,
> Since in France, which used to be their harbor
> Of safety, where exiled women and
> Those without counsel used to flee,   5
> They now no longer find friendship.
> The nobles take no pity on them,
> Nor do the clerks, great or small,
> Nor do the princes deign to listen to them.
>
> From the knights they receive no shelter;   10
> From the prelates they get no counsel;
> Nor do the judges protect them from injustice.
> From officials not a bit of encouragement;
> Often they are harassed by the powerful;
> They would never even get what they asked for   15
> From the nobles—they have to turn elsewhere—
> Nor do the princes deign to listen to them.
>
> Where can they flee, since they have no recourse
> In France, where they are given vain hopes, deadly
> Counsel?   20
> The path to hell is prepared for them
> If they want to believe in confused advice
> And bad counsel, where no one cares about their
> Cause; their friends' help turns to harm;
> Nor do the princes deign to listen to them.   25
>
> Worthy and valiant men, put your virtues
> On alert, or widows are destined for great harm;
> Help them with a happy heart and put faith in what I
> Say: For I see no one who is friendly toward them,
> Nor do the princes deign to listen to them.[5]   30

[After six years Christine finally receives a modest sum from various nobles.]

---

5. This poem also appears as number 6 in *Other Ballads*.

7. Christine Continues Her Complaint

Do you understand now, sweet mistress, in what sweet pleasures I passed the youthful days of my widowhood? Would there have been a reason for me to flirt and to listen to foolish love?

[But Fortune is still not satisfied by Christine's unhappiness.]

As I already said, in the time of my troubles I realized that it makes no sense to reveal one's business and problems to others—and why? Because charity is rare and can quickly turn into servitude. But since it is very difficult to keep one's pain all bottled up without talking to anyone, Fortune could not hurt me so deeply to keep me from having the company of the poets' muses. For although she drove them away from Boethius in the time of his troubles in order to serve him worthier dishes, they induced me to write tearful complaints in rhyme, to lament my dead beloved husband and the good days of the past, as one can see at the beginning of my first works, the One Hundred Ballads. And then to pass the time and to give some cheer to my unhappy heart I began to compose love poems that show other people's happy feelings, as I say in one of my virelais.

8. Christine Speaks of How She Changed Her Way of Life

After all these events, since most of my youth lay already behind me as did a great part of my outside occupations, I returned to the way of life that I naturally liked best: solitude and tranquillity. Then, in this solitude some memories of Latin and of the noble sciences came back to me, along with various learned sayings and refined rhetoric which I had heard in the past from my dear departed friends, my father and my husband, even though I was too frivolous then to retain much. For although I was naturally and from my earliest youth inclined to learning, the preoccupation with the duties common to married women and also frequent child bearing kept me from it. Also, great youth, that sweet enemy of good sense, will often not allow children of even great intelligence to devote themselves to study because of the desire to play— unless the fear of beatings keeps them there. And since I had no such fear, the desire to play so overcame my intelligence and thoughts that I could not apply myself to the labor of learning.

9. Christine Complains of Youth

[She enjoins her readers not to be as foolish as she was when she neglected to drink from the fountain of philosophy in her youth, for ignorance is one of the worst evils.]

Once a man criticized my desire for knowledge by saying that it was not fitting for a woman to possess learning because there was so little of it; I replied that it was even less fitting for a man to possess ignorance because there was so much of it.

10. Christine Tells How She Began to Study

When I had thus arrived at an age that brings with it a certain level of understanding, looking back at my past adventures and ahead to the end of things—just like a man who has passed along a dangerous path looks back in wonder, saying that he will never return there but choose a better path—I began to realize that the world is full of dangerous snares and that there is finally only one single good, and that is the way of truth; I therefore embarked on the path to which nature and the stars inclined me, that is, the love of learning. Then I closed my doors, that is, my senses, so that they would no longer wander around external things, and snapped up your beautiful books with the intention of making up for at least part of my past losses. I was so presumptuous as to tackle the profound and obscure sciences, written in terms that I could not understand; for as Cato says, to read and not to understand is not reading at all.[6] Rather, just like a child whom one first teaches the alphabet, I began with the ancient histories from the beginnings of the world, the histories of the Hebrews, the Assyrians and the origins of kingdoms, proceeding from one to the other all the way to the Romans, the French, the Britons, and many other writers of history;[7] afterwards I turned to those deductions of science I was able to comprehend in the time I had for study.

Then I started to read the books of the poets and as my knowledge kept on increasing, I was glad to have found a style that was natural to me; I delighted in their subtle coverings[8] and noble subject matter hidden under delightful moral fictions and in their beautiful style of their verses and prose, ornamented by polished rhetoric adorned with subtle language and surprising proverbs. For having found this science of poetry Nature rejoiced in me and said: "Daughter, be happy when you have fulfilled the desire I have given you, continue to apply yourself to study, understanding the writings better and better." All this reading was not enough to satisfy my thoughts and intelligence; rather, Nature wanted that new books should be born from me, engendered by study and by the things I had seen.[9] Then she said to me: "Take your tools and hammer on the anvil the matter I will give you, as durable as iron:

6. Cato's Distichs. Christine found this quotation in one of the compilations she used.
7. Christine's major source for ancient history was the thirteenth-century universal history, the Histoire ancienne jusqu'à César [Ancient history up to Julius Caesar].
8. Boccaccio's treatise On Poetry contains theories about the "covering" of allegory.
9. Christine draws on books and on her own experience. On this topic, see R. Blumenfeld-Kosinski, "Christine de Pizan and the Misogynistic Tradition," on p. 297.

neither fire nor anything else can destroy it; from this you should forge delightful things. When you carried your children in your womb, you felt great pain when giving birth. Now I desire that new books should be born from you, which you will give birth to from your memory in joy and delight; they will for all time to come keep your memory alive before the princes and the whole world. Just like a woman who has given birth forgets the pain and labor as soon as she hears her child cry, you will forget the hard work when you hear the voices of your books." [1]

Thus I began to forge pretty things, at the beginning of a lighter nature, and just like a craftsman who becomes more and more skillful the more he works, by studying different subject matters my mind filled more and more with new things, improving my style by more subtleness and nobler subject matter. Between the years 1399 when I began writing and the present year, 1405, during which I am still writing, I have compiled fifteen major works, without counting some smaller works, which together are contained in seventy large-size quires, as one can see clearly. And since no great praise is due for this, for there is little subtlety in my works, I say this, God knows, not in order to boast but to tell about my good and bad fortunes in the right order.

11. The Pleasure That Christine Took in Learning

Now my way of life had changed, but my misfortune had not improved; it was as if Fortune, feeling spite at the pleasure and comfort my scholarly and solitary life brought me, persevered in her malevolence, and not only against me but, to anger me even more, against my nearest and dearest friends, which I see as part of my own adversities.

It is true that word about my way of life devoted to study had already spread even among princes. And because it was revealed to them—although I would have preferred to keep it secret—I made them gifts of some new things from my works on various subject matters, however small and insignificant they were. The princes, benign and gracious as they were, saw them with pleasure and received them joyfully; and I believe this was more for the unusual fact that a woman could write, something that had not happened in quite some time, than for the value they actually had. And thus my books were discussed and circulated in many different regions and lands.

Around that time, as the daughter of the French king was being married to King Richard of England, a noble count named Salisbury came here for that reason. [2] And since this gracious knight loved poetry and was himself a very good poet, after seeing some of my poems, he had

---

1. On the feminine imagery of literary creation, see Sylvia Huot, "Seduction and Sublimation: Christine de Pizan, Jean de Meun, and Dante," *Romance Notes* 25 (1985), 361–74.
2. See James Laidlaw, "Christine de Pizan, the Earl of Salisbury, and Henry IV," *French Studies* 36 (1982), 129–43.

several nobles entreat me until I agreed—though somewhat unwillingly—to let my eldest son, a rather clever child of twelve with a talent for singing, go with him to England to become the companion of one of his own sons who was the same age. And the count's promises were not lies, for he conducted himself well and generously toward my child; as for his further promises for the future, I am sure he meant to keep them, since it was in his power.

Please note, dear mistress, the truth of what I said earlier, how Fortune was contrary to my prosperity by taking away from me my good friends through death. Misfortune, who had already done me so much harm, would not permit me to enjoy this good state of affairs for long, for only a short time later she brought a grievous pestilence down against King Richard in the country of England.[3] The good count, remaining loyal to his rightful lord, was later beheaded, which was a great injustice. Thus the beginnings of my son's worldly fortunes came to nothing, and as he was still young and in a foreign land during a time of great pestilence he had good reason to be terrified! But what happened next? King Henry, who usurped the crown and still is king, saw the books and poems that I had already sent to the count for his pleasure. Thus he learned of the situation and received my child gladly and generously at his court and held him dear. Indeed, he sent two of his men of arms, the heralds Lancaster and Falcon, to me in order to entreat me with generous promises that I should go there as well. And since in view of the circumstances I was not in the least tempted by this offer, I dissembled and thanked the king, saying that I was at his command, all this in order to get my son back.

To be brief, I went to great trouble and sent some of my books so that my son finally got leave to come and accompany me to some place—a trip which I have not yet made. Thus I rejected this opportunity both for myself and him, for I could not believe that someone so disloyal could come to a good end. I was overjoyed to see the child I loved, for I had been without him for three years, and death had left him my only son. But the burden of my expenses grew, which was difficult for me. I feared that the high rank which he had had over there would induce him to want to return there, for children who do not possess great discernment often are inclined toward those things that seem most attractive and comfortable to them. This is why I looked for a great and powerful master for him who by his grace would retain him. But as the modest talents of the young child were not very evident among the multitude of people in the court, I still had to support him financially in his situation, and thus his service brought us no benefit.[4] And thus Fortune robbed me of one of my good friends and of one of my good hopes. But since then she has done even more harm to me.

3. This happened in 1399. Shortly afterward, Richard II was assassinated.
4. I.e., Louis of Orléans did not agree to employ Christine's son.

12. Christine Complains of Fortune Who Took Her Good Friends from Her

As I told earlier, my books had already procured a reputation for me, since they were given as presents to many princes in foreign lands—not by myself but by others—as a novelty devised by a woman. As the proverb says, new things please, and I say this not in order to boast; boasting has nothing to do with this. The first duke of Milan in Lombardy,[5] who heard about this (perhaps in a way that made me seem greater than I am) wanted to attract me to his country and ordered a generous lifetime income paid to me, if only I would go there. And several noblemen, charged with this embassy, can testify to this fact. But Fortune, as is her wont, did not allow that the ruinous state of my finances should be improved. Through death she soon took from me that man who wished me well; not that I would have left France easily, not even for solid prospects in what is after all my native land. Nonetheless, she hurt me when she took away my good friend (which is no small loss), particularly since, as worthy people reported to me, he would have valued me for the merits of my books even if I had remained in France.

13. More on the Same Topic

It remains for me to tell about the death that caused me the greatest loss after the time of the King Charles. The venerable and powerful Prince Philip, Duke of Burgundy, the brother of the wise king just mentioned, had developed some affection for me because of the books I had sent him (for I had not considered them worthy to be opened in the presence of such a wise man). In his benign clemency he found them agreeable (though, I believe, more for the constant effort I had made than for the great subtlety of my works), as became apparent not only in the praise he had for them but also through the generous financial help not only for myself but also for my son whom he retained as his well-liked servant with a good salary. In addition to all his assistance he also deigned to value my learning so much that with own words—a fact I much appreciate—he instructed me to record in a book the noble life and notable deeds of the wise king,[6] so that the memory of his noble name would live on forever in the world as a good example. Alas, shortly afterward, as his good will toward me grew ever greater, Fortune, the disloyal woman, took him away from me through death. Was this not an obvious sign of the hateful jealousy Fortune felt against me? This death renewed the wounds caused by my adversities and was also a grievous

---

5. The duke of Milan, Giangaleazzo Visconti (d. 1402), was the father of Valentina Visconti, the wife of Louis of Orléans.
6. This is the biography of Charles V, *The Book of the Deeds and Good Conduct of the Wise King Charles V*; see p. 113.

loss to the kingdom, as I recount in the sad lamentations in the book he had commissioned but which was not yet finished at that time."[7]

14. Christine Concludes Her Complaint

[Christine states that she did indeed receive some financial help from the French princes, but they gave it reluctantly, thus undoing the merit of their deed. She continues.]

Dear mistress, can you imagine how painful it was for a woman like me, who likes a secluded life and does not care about the lure of money, to have to act against her natural inclination and be forced by her great responsibilities to pursue—and with great effort—these men of finance and to be led on day after day by their empty promises. And thus it goes for widows today, my honored Lady from whom nothing is hidden. You know that I do not care about amassing riches or increasing our fortune beyond what I have inherited; I am foolish to care even about that, knowing full well that all worldly things are like the wind. You also know that I have no hidden desires for superfluous ornaments or for delicate food, but that I act because of the love and the responsibility, pleasant though it is, I have for my good old mother, leaning on me as her only daughter who has not forgotten the great maternal benefits she has received from her. I am disturbed and sad that Fortune will not allow my willingness to help my mother have the desired effect, that is, that a woman of such perfect honor, noble life and good family, as she is and has always been, should live as is appropriate for her. In addition, I am responsible for finding husbands for poor relatives and for other friends. Nowhere do I see Fortune inclined to be helpful.

To pursue the topic of how my sadness adds to all my other burdens: don't you think that I consider myself unhappy when I see other women in the company of their families, brothers, and relatives, living comfortably and joyfully together, and I think of myself, without friends and in a foreign land? My two brothers, wise and worthy men, had to return to Italy to live on the lands inherited from our father, because they were not provided for here. And I, who am loving and inclined to friendship, complain to God when I see a mother without the sons she longs for, and myself without my brothers. And thus you can see, dear mistress, that Fortune has served me contrary to my desires and still perseveres in her evil deeds.

God who is really you and you who are really God know that I speak the truth about these things. And I return to what I said earlier, namely how Fortune has been my adversary and continues her attacks which

7. He died in April 1404. The book was completed in November. It contains a lament for the deceased duke; see Suzanne Solente, ed., *Le Livre des faits et bonnes meurs du sage roy Charles V*, 2 vols. (Paris: Champion, 1936–40), vol. 1, 108–11.

are not trivial for the weak heart of a woman to bear. What grieves me most is that all these activities keep me from my studies. Many times all the troubles I have darken my thoughts so they cannot devote themselves to the understanding of the things that truly delight me—and this is the worst consequence of all my misfortunes.

15. *Philosophy Responds to Christine*

When I finished all my arguments, I kept quiet. Then the excellent goddess spoke as if she were smiling, just as a wise man does when he is presented with the arguments of a simpleminded person. But my ignorance did not prevent me from being comforted by her worthy words. She spoke as follows: "Certainly, dearest friend, I understand from what you say how a foolish disposition deceives you as to the judgment of your own condition. Oh blind creature, who attributes to bad fortune the gifts that God gives you to drink from His own chalice! And why do you complain ungratefully about the gifts you have received?"

[Just as she did for Boethius, Philosophy will now prove to Christine through examples appropriate to her intellect that God has guided Christine's fortunes for the best. Is she not better off in France, far from the fires of civil war burning in Italy? It is folly to attribute bad luck to the powers of Fortune and to see adversities as personal punishment: for it is presumption to see oneself as the center of the universe. Other people suffer even more and even profit from their suffering for it builds character.]

17. *On the Same Topic*

[Philosophy now comes to the positive aspects of Christine's life.]

"I realize that among other good things three joys and glories are particularly highly regarded by you people in the world. And I suppose that without having some or all three of these, there would be no riches that could satisfy man's heart, nor is there any treasure among the goods of Fortune that one would not give in return for having these goods. Two of these are external to one's self, and the other is within.

"The first is being born of noble parents, and by nobility I mean virtue. The second is to have a rather pleasing body, without deformity, healthy, not sickly, and competent in discernment and understanding. The third joy, by no means a small one, is to have beautiful, attractive, and God-fearing children of good intelligence and morals. Oh woman, consider your ingratitude! Are you in fact lacking these wonderful advantages, together with many other favors given you by God? It seems that you have forgotten your true condition when you claim to be so unhappy. Is there any woman that you know today who comes from a family more glorious than your own? Don't you remember the dignity of our noble philosopher, your father, who was such a regular in our schools that we sat beside him in the chair,[8] telling him our secrets and that for his familiarity with our skills he had in his time the reputation of being the most eminent master in the speculative sciences? And with all this, he was always a true Catholic, as became apparent especially at his end, and so virtuous that I call on you to tell me whether meditating on his knowledge (of which some at least remained with you, despite your complaints to the contrary) is not more valuable than any earthly goods. Think about whether you should not be happy with these goods.

"What shall I say of your noble mother? Do you know a more virtuous woman? Do you recall that from her youth to this day she has never neglected the contemplative life in God's service, no matter what her other occupation may have been? I think not! Oh what a noble woman! How glorious is her life, never was she overcome by any tribulations, nor did impatience ever break her courageous heart. And what an example of a virtuous life she sets for you, if you would only imitate it! Just think what a great favor God is doing you by letting such a noble woman, so filled with virtue, live to old age in your company. And how many times has she comforted you and has led you away from your impatience to an understanding of God? And if you complain that you suffer in your heart because you cannot provide for her as is fitting, I tell you that this desire, when coupled with patience, is commendable for both of you. Indeed, her worthy and dignified way of life makes her stand out among women; this is a well-known and blessed fact.

"As for the second among your blessings, did God not give you a rather strong body, well composed according to your needs? Can you ask anything else of Him? Make certain that you use well the understanding He has given—or else it would have been better for you to know less.

"And as far as the third joy is concerned, do you not have beautiful, attractive, and intelligent children? Your first offspring is a daughter, dedicated to the service of God, who by her own desire and divinely inspired—and against your will—entered the Church in the noble order of the ladies of Poissy where, in the flower of her youth and great beauty, she nobly leads a contemplative life of devotion. Hearing about her beautiful life often gives you great comfort, and she herself often sends you very sweet, pious, and wise letters for your consolation in which she in all her youth and innocence persuades and admonishes you to hate the world and despise prosperity.

"Do you not have a son, just as beautiful, attractive and well mannered, and such a student that even before he was twenty years old, from the time he began to study our first sciences, one could not find anyone surpassing him in his natural talent for grammar, rhetoric, and

8. The word in French is *chaiere*, which refers to a pulpit or a professorial chair.

poetry and in his subtle understanding and faculty for sound judgment. And anyone can see by the evidence that I do not lie. I am not saying this to you to lead you to false vanity, but so that you will give thanks to Him from whom all blessings come, who has given you these goods and many others. It is not Fortune who gives them, but He bestows them on whomever He pleases out of His pure grace."

[Philosophy will not comment on Christine's other relatives.]

18. Philosophy Blames Christine for Her Complaints

"When you complain that death took your husband from you at a young age, I tell you that God did no wrong when he wanted to take back his servant in order to elevate him to a higher level. And it pleased Him that you should remain in the valley of tribulation in order to test your patience and purify yourself in virtue."

[Philosophy now quotes St. Augustine and tries to prove that her tribulations are in fact good for Christine. She continues.]

"As you said yourself, there is no doubt that if your husband were still with you today, you would not have acquired that much learning, for the cares of your household would not have allowed you to devote yourself to a life of study, which you consider the highest good after the life that is reserved for the perfect: the contemplative life in which true wisdom is to be found. You will admit that for all the goods of Fortune you would not want to have missed this life of study—however little you have accomplished in it—and the pleasure this life gives you. Therefore you should not consider yourself miserable when you possess of all the things in the world the one thing that delights and pleases you, namely the sweet taste of knowledge."

[Philosophy tries to convince Christine that her trials are actually profitable for her. To this end she cites saints Jerome, Augustine, Gregory, and Bernard. Like a good doctor, she will now prescribe a remedy. But first she asks Christine to know herself. If she had been rich, her life would not have been as satisfactory.]

"So I ask you whether you know any man or woman, be it a prince or princess or anyone else favored by Fortune with power, land, honors, or other noble things (I speak to you of worldly things and omit the noble speculations of the mind), with whom you would have exchanged your simple manner of life, the desire, love, and pleasure you take in learning, and your solitude for the cares and responsibilities of so many different affairs, weighing on your soul and conscience, together with burning greed and other such emotions. And was not your feeble feminine body transformed into a man's[9] so that you could become the person who, as you believe, is more favored by Fortune?"

[Philosophy tells Christine that her duties should be borne with patience. Philosophy adduces the Holy Scriptures as well as Boethius and various Church Fathers to prove that one should disdain worldly goods and seek one's consolation in God. Christine then realizes that Philosophy is Theology and feels consoled. She addresses Philosophy/Theology one last time.]

Dear Lady, what can I say about the good you have done me with your holy nourishment which has satisfied my hunger, has made me realize the ignorance of my misunderstanding, and through which I know my faults as you have explained them to me? So I declare that you, Holy Theology and divinity, are a rich nourishment that contains within it all delights, just like the manna that rained from heaven for the Jews and that tasted in everyone's mouth according to his desires.[1]

Thus I leave my vision, which I have divided in three different parts like three precious stones divided by their qualities. The first is in the shape of a diamond which is hard and sharp; and however clear it is by itself, when it is set in gold it seems to be dark and brown; and nonetheless its great virtue does not vanish. The second is the cameo in which are imprinted various faces and figures; its background is brown and the imprint is white. The third is like the precious ruby, clear and bright and without a blemish, which has the property of becoming more and more pleasing the more one looks at it.[2]

Here ends the book of Christine's Vision.
Thanks be given to God.

FROM THE BOOK OF THE BODY POLITIC

[In *The Book of the Body Politic*, written between 1404 and 1407, Christine approaches the teaching of virtues to a prince somewhat differently than in the *Letter from Othea*. Here she takes up the image of society as a body, popularized by John of Salisbury's *Policraticus* (1159), in which every part has its specific function and duties. Drawing also on Brunetto Latini's *Livre dou tresor* [Book of the treasure]—an encyclopedic work on history, theology, and politics written in the 1260s—and Egidio's Colonna's *De regimine*

---

9. See the description of her transformation into a man in *The Book of Fortune's Transformation* on p. 88.
1. See Exodus 16:14–27.
2. Lapidaries, or treatises on stones, were popular in the Middle Ages. Philip of Mézières, whom Christine knew, deals with the properties of stones in a theological context in his book on the sacrament of marriage: Joan B. Williamson, ed., *Le Livre de la vertu du sacrement de mariage* (Washington, D.C.: Catholic University of America Press, 1993). See also n. 3, p. 144.

principum [On the conduct of rulers] as well as Valerius Maximus,[1] Boethius, and the Bible, Christine constructs a tripartite work in which she addresses first the prince (the head), then the knights and nobles (the limbs), and finally the common people (the feet).

The proper education of the ruling classes is essential, since there is a strong connection between private morals and public conduct. Rulers should be just and authoritative but also humble, when necessary, and not given to a voluptuous life. One of the more interesting parts of the book is Christine's treatment of the responsibilities of the bourgeois toward the lower classes: they can act as their advisors and advocates and keep them from instigating rebellions.

Christine's concern for an orderly and hierarchical society also becomes evident in the passages on the proper clothing for people of each class. Presumptuous desires for fancy dress cannot be tolerated since they undermine the very structure of society. Whether this structure was worth preserving was not a question Christine would have asked herself.

Translated by Renate Blumenfeld-Kosinski from Christine de Pisan, *Le Livre du corps de policie*, ed. Robert H. Lucas (Geneva: Droz, 1967).]

Here begins the Book of the Body Politic,[1] which speaks of virtue and manners and is divided into three parts. The first part is addressed to the princes, the second to the knights and noblemen, and the third to people.

Part 1

1. The First Chapter Describes the Body Politic

If it is possible that vice can bring forth virtue I will gladly speak in this part with the passion of a woman.

Since many men claim that the feminine gender does not know how to be quiet or how to silence their overflowing hearts, let courage now come forward and make visible in several streams the source and inexhaustible fountain of my heart which cannot stanch the flow of my desire for virtue. Oh virtue, noble gift of God, how can I be so presumptuous to speak of you when I know that my mind cannot grasp nor explain you? But it comforts and encourages me to know you so benign that it will not displease you if I speak of you—not of your most subtle aspects, but only of those parts where I can conceive of you and understand you. I will call you forth in my mind as best I can for the construc-

1. See Francis J. Carmody, ed., *Li Livres dou tresor de Brunetto Latini* (Berkeley: University of California Press, 1948). For Egidio Colonna, also known as Giles of Rome, see n. 4, p. 203. Valerius Maximus's work on great men, *Facta et dicta memorabilia* [Memorable deeds and sayings], from ca. A.D. 20, was known to Christine in the French translations and commentaries by Simon de Hesdin and Nicole de Gonesse, finished about five years earlier.

1. The image of the state as a body where each part has a specific function goes back to John of Salisbury's *Policraticus*, written in 1159. See Cary J. Nederman's translation, *Policraticus: Of the Frivolities of Courtiers and the Footprints of Philosophers* (Cambridge, UK: Cambridge University Press, 1990).

tion of good comportment and speak first of the activities and rules of conduct of those above us. I mean the princes, whose majesty I humbly beseech not to take in the wrong way or disdain that such a simple mind as mine and such a humble creature as I am dares to speak of the rules for such a high estate. And may it please them to keep in mind the teaching of the philosopher who says that, however great you are, you should not disdain a lowly person who teaches you a good lesson.[2]

After that, I will with God's help speak of the rules of living pertaining to the nobles and knights, and third to the common people. The three estates should be united in a single commonwealth, just like a living body, as Plutarch[3] said in a letter to the emperor Trajan where he compares public life to a living body, with the prince or princes occupying the place of the head, for they are or should be the rulers and they establish laws, just as from the mind of man come the exterior movements that the limbs make. The knights and nobles occupy the place of the hands and arms. For just as man's arms are strong to sustain labor and pain, so they have the task to defend the right of the prince and the commonwealth. And they are also hands, because just as the hands get rid of harmful things, they have to throw out everything evil and useless. The other, common, people are like the stomach, feet, and legs. For just as the stomach receives the things procured by the head and the limbs, the deeds of the princes and nobles will be for the good and love of the public; and just as the legs and and feet support the actions of the human body, similarly the workers support all the other estates.

[Chapter 2 speaks of the felicity brought about by virtue. For the commonwealth to have a virtuous head, one must educate the princes carefully.]

3. Here She Speaks about the Early Education of the Princes' Children[4]

Since loving God is one of our explicit commandments one should first introduce the prince's child to this love very early on in his development and introduce him to serving God with little, simple prayers,

---

2. Christine makes the same important point in the last section of her *Letter from Othea*, where she explains that what counts is the lesson, not the person giving it, and that, therefore, women can be the teachers of powerful men.

3. Greek biographer and essayist (46?–120); his supposed letter to Trajan is a fiction. Christine here repeats the divisions found in John of Salisbury's *Policraticus*. On the idea of society's division into three orders see Georges Duby, *The Three Orders: Feudal Society Imagined*, trans. Arthur Goldhammer (Chicago: University of Chicago Press, 1980). But Christine's society is more complex: in addition to those who fight, pray, and work the land (the twelfth-century scheme), there are now merchants, artisans, and students who play important roles in urban society.

4. The major source of these educational ideas is Egidio Colonna's *De regimine principum* [On the conduct of rulers], available to Christine in a thirteenth-century French translation. See Diane Bornstein, *The Middle English Translation of Christine de Pisan's 'Livre du corps de policie'* (Heidelberg: Carl Winter, 1977), 15–17. The French translation has been edited by S. P. Molenaer as *Li Livres du gouvernement des rois, a XIIIth Century Version of Egidio Colonna's Treatise 'De regimine principum'* (New York: Macmillan, 1899, rept. 1966).

appropriate for the understanding of a child. For the things one learns in childhood can only be abandoned with difficulty later on. And that this is pleasing to God is clear when the psalmist says that God receives His perfect praise from the mouths of children and babies.[5] Then, when he is older, one must teach him letters and the divine service so that he can praise God, and more than those of other countries the French princes have the praiseworthy custom of teaching their children to hear mass and say their prayers.[6]

One must provide a master for him who is wise and prudent, more in manners than in great science, although in former times the children of princes were taught by philosophers, as it is written about the the the Macedonian king Philip, father of Alexander the Great, who wrote to Aristotle[7] to tell him of the joy of having a son born to him. But he said he had even greater joy that he was born in Aristotle's lifetime, so that he could be instructed and taught by him, which indeed happened later, for Aristotle was the master of Alexander the Great. However, today princes are not so eager any more to be taught the sciences—may it please God that they go back to the way it used to be.

In my opinion it is best to find a master who is a very discreet, wise man, well brought up and loving God, even if he is not the most excellent or subtle philosopher. And though it would be wonderful to find a master who has all perfections, it is still better to give him a well brought up master than a great scholar who is less prudent and less well brought up. The princes must make careful inquiries in this matter, for the good behavior a child sees in his master and his wise words and manners are a lesson and mirror to him. The wise master must lead his life with great prudence in this office. For although a child's nature can only be disciplined by fear, for the child of a prince another method than that of instilling fear by beating is suitable. For if a child that has been delicately brought up and already feels the greatness of rulership through the honors paid to him is punished too harshly, instead of chastized he might feel indignant toward his lessons and his master, which would be detrimental to his discipline and might endanger the master and even the health of the child who has been brought up delicately and gently. So what should the wise master do? He must treat him as one treats a lion. For usually other little children, such as sons of barons, are brought up together with the princes' children; they are all the master's students. He must be harsh to them when they have misbehaved in the same way the prince's son did, and he must beat them accordingly, but he should threaten them more with a harsh face than with beatings. Similarly, he

5. Cf. Psalm 8:2: "Out of the mouth of babes and sucklings hast thou ordained strength."
6. The word in French is *heures*, "hours." The term refers to prayers to be said at specific times of the day. See John Harthan, *The Book of Hours* (New York: Thomas Y. Crowell, 1977), 11–31.
7. See the *Policraticus* 4.6. Aristotle lived from 384 to 322 B.C. and Alexander the Great from 356 to 323 B.C.

must use these threats with the prince's son if he does not correct himself, and sometimes he must make him feel the sharpness of the rod, for like this he will make him ashamed of his bad behavior and fearful and obedient. And the wise master must be careful not to show himself too familiar or intimate with his student, for he would fear him less, and the child should not see him playing silly games, or laugh or talk foolishly, or be too familiar, but he must act as if he were the master of just about everyone.

His countenance should be noble and sedate, and his clothes clean and honorable. In front of his student, he should not say useless but profitable and exemplary things, but nonetheless he should not show a harsh face or say grand things all the time. He should rather draw the child to him with kind words when he has retained well what was taught him or when he does something good. The master should please him by giving him little things that children like and sometimes kindly telling him some children's tales about some trifle to make him laugh, and all this so that he will like his studies as much as his master.

The master must establish a suitable and regular timetable when the child will occupy himself with studies and then give him time to play for a while before his meal which should be regulated and not contain too many delicate or choice foods and wine, which often corrupt the body or make it sick. And when the child studies grammar, the master must begin to use more subtle expressions and lessons, depending on what he considers right for the child's understanding, so that little by little he will give him more and more, just as a nurse increases the nourishment of a child as he grows.

I certainly suppose that the prince wants his child instructed in the letters so that he knows the rules of grammar and understands Latin, and if it pleased God this would be the general custom for all the children of princes now and in the future. For I believe that great good would come from it for them and their subjects, and they would increase in virtue. The children should be taught logic and the prince should have them continue their studies, like the most wise prince the Duke of Orléans who lives in the present time, and on the example of the very wise, good, and virtuous duchess, his wife,[8] who appreciates and honors the goods of learning and science, and takes care, like a prudent mother, that her children are well taught in letters and virtues.

When the child's understanding begins to grow and he is able to comprehend more, the above-mentioned wise master should feed him wise doctrine about good morals by telling him of examples or having him read various arguments in books. And he has to make him understand the difference between good and evil and teach and show him the way to good morals and virtues, as did the valiant, renowned princes,

8. Christine must have written this before November 23, 1407, the day on which Louis of Orléans was assassinated. His wife was Valentina Visconti.

his predecessors, and others. One should show him the great benefits that come from being good and follow those who are good and govern themselves well, and also the opposite, namely the evil that follows bad and vicious people. If the master sees him in any way inclined or talented toward learning, he should show and make him understand the great felicity that resides in knowledge in order to make it more attractive and open him the ways of philosophy, that is, he should give him some feeling for and an understanding of the sciences. Thus, with such a master at the start, the prince's son will be able—if he continues his studies—to attain such learning that as an adult he will reach great virtue and fame.

[Chapters 4 to 8 further elaborate the education of the prince's children. Now Christine turns to the desired result of all these efforts, the just and virtuous prince. The first foundation for a just rule is devotion to God.]

9. How the Good Prince Must Resemble the Good Shepherd

We have touched upon the first point on which the goodness of the prince should be principally based. Now we have to speak of the second point, which is that he must exceptionally well love the common good and its increase more than his own, according to the teaching of Aristotle in his book of *Politics*, who says that tyranny is when the prince seeks his own good over the common good, and that is against the principle of royal rule which must care more for the profit of its people than for its own. We have to consider in which way this love becomes manifest.

The good prince who loves his country will guard his people carefully by the example of the good shepherd. He guards his sheep and takes great care to defend them against wolves and harmful animals, to keep them clean and in good health, so that they can grow and yield profits, give good and thick wool to the farms which nourish and guard them; and the shepherd should be well paid for their fleeces, sheared at the appropriate season. But the rich good shepherd who has many possessions needs to procure good and suitable help, for he cannot guard all his flocks by himself. He takes on good and and careful servants, knowledgeable in their profession and diligent, whom he knows to be loyal and wishing for his profit. He will order these servants to be provided with good, strong dogs with iron-studded collars, whom they have well trained by taking them out into the fields frequently to chase the wolves. At night they leave them untied in the sheepfold so that if robbers come to steal the sheep, they will attack them. By day they keep them tied up by their leashes and close to them, while the sheep graze peacefully in the fields. But if it happens that the servants sense an attack of wolves or dangerous animals coming from the woods or the mountains, they will untie the dogs and let them run and urge them on often. And to give them greater boldness they go all out and run after them with iron-studded staffs, attacking the wolf or dangerous beast. Or if it happens that a sheep gets lost and leaves the flock, the dogs that are trained for this purpose will run after him, and will bark at him without doing him harm and bring him back to the flock. And in this way the wise servants defend and guard them so well that they can render a good account to the head shepherd who watches over everything closely.

For our present purposes we can say that thus it is with the good prince who cares for the defense and safeguard of his country and people but for whom it is impossible to be in person in all the necessary places and offices. He procures very good assistants for matters pertaining to knights and other things, that is, very valiant captains whom he knows well and whom he knows to be good and loyal and who love him, such as constables, marshals, admirals, and others, whom he charges to be equipped with very good men of arms, well trained and experienced in warfare, whom they keep bound to them by oaths, and who cannot absent themselves without their leave, and who are always near so that if necessary they can sally forth against the enemies, so that the country will not be conquered or the people killed or pillaged. That does not mean that the men of arms should themselves devastate and pillage the country as they are doing at present in France, which they would not dare do elsewhere and which is a great evil; it is a perversion that those who are there for the defense of the people should themselves pillage, devastate, and rob them. Indeed, there are some who are so cruel that short of killing the people and setting their houses on fire, the enemies could do no worse.

This is not the right way to wage war, which should be just and without extortion. Otherwise, the men of arms and the princes who sent them to fight are in great danger that the wrath of God will fall on them and punish them severely, for there is no doubt that the curses of the people, justly uttered because of their great oppression, can induce God to send many evil events, as one can read in Holy Scripture in several places, for everyone should know that God is just and that all this evil comes from the bad ordering of things. For if the men of arms were well paid, one could and should pass an edict forbidding them under threat of punishment to take anything without paying, and like this they would get food and everything they need plentifully and cheaply.

It is amazing that people can live under an order where there is no compassion for their pitiful lives. May the Holy Spirit, father of the poor, visit them. And in connection with what we said above, if a shepherd had a dog that attacked his sheep, he would hit him right away with his stick. This is not something a good prince who loves God and his people should allow, and as one keeps the dogs untied at night in the sheepfold to guard against thieves, the captains should keep guards and spies at the borders and send them far away so that the country and the people are not secretly surprised by any ruse, and so that they know the plan of the enemies. The men of arms should have another duty which is, just as the good dog brings back the sheep that loses its way, they must, if they see common people or others who because of fear or some ill will want to rebel or side with the enemy, bring them back to the right path, either by threats or by arresting them.

And because it may displease and amaze some that I compare the noble office of arms to the nature of the dog, I can say without fault that the dog has truly many qualities on which the good man of arms could model himself and which he could imitate. The dog loves his master very much and is loyal to him. The good man of arms must be the same way. He is bold and exposes himself to death to defend his master, and when he is charged with guarding a place, he listens very carefully and awakens quickly in order to attack evildoers and thieves. He does not bite his master's friends, but sniffs them as is his nature; nor does he bite the neighbors or those who live in the house where he was brought up as best as possible, but he protects them. He is very bold and fights courageously. He has great understanding and knowledge and is very friendly to those who show him friendship. All of these qualities the good men of arms should possess as well.

[Christine pursues this topic in the next chapter and then turns to the question of taxes.]

11. On the Love the Good Prince Should Have for His Subjects

Now we have to consider briefly the legal rights of the prince and ask whether the prince can levy any new charges or subsidies from his people on top of the existing ones if some unexpected event occurs. It seems to me that the laws permit him to do this in some cases, though he has to do it as late as possible, for example to defend his country when it is attacked by enemies and he needs to hire soldiers for the country's defense. Also, in order to marry his children or to get them out of prison, should they be captured.[9] In these special cases the king can, without breaking the law, require new taxes from his subjects that go beyond the normal rates.

But this must be done compassionately and with discretion; the poor should not be charged more than necessary, and the money should not be used for superfluous things rather than for the war or other appropriate purposes. In this case, the rich should support the poor, and the

---

9. Demanding ransom for captured prisoners was common at the time. One of the most famous cases was the capture by the English of the French king John II after the battle of Poitiers in 1356. The ransom was initially set at four million pieces of gold. Of course, the amount depended on the rank of the prisoner.

rich should not be exempt, as it is the custom today, while the poor are taxed more. This is a strange law, if I may say so—and may it not displease anyone, by your grace—that the rich and the high officers of the king and of the princes who hold their high and powerful positions from the king and the princes and can very well pay taxes should be exempt, while the poor who receive no income from the king are required to pay. And why should it be that if I do a lot of good to one of my servants and give him a great livelihood and position, and I need his help in some matter, that he should not be more willing to help me in my need than the person who has never received a favor from me? This is a strange custom which governs the tax rates in our country today. But if one wanted to break this custom one would have to do it uniformly, and it should not be that some pay high taxes and the others none, for this causes jealousy, for those who pay would feel despised and in servitude, but if it were uniform there would be no reproach.

Nonetheless, I do not say that those who go to war in the defense of the country should be exempt, and what I say of the poor I say out of compassion for the bitter tears and sighs they show those who come to collect the money they owe. Afterward, they and their whole household have to go hungry, and to sell their beds or poor possessions at the market and they get nothing for them.[1] May it please God that the king and princes should be well informed about this. There is no doubt that there is so much goodness in their noble blood that they could not condone such harshness. But it often happens that the tax collectors are getting fat and rich from these collections and not all taxes are used for the purpose for which they are established. God knows, others do the same thing.

[Christine continues in the same vein and cites Greek and Roman examples to buttress her arguments. She continues.]

Saying these things does not please bad officials who have enriched themselves and who will blame me. I can tell them without arrogance that what the great poet Euripides answered the people of Athens who asked him to remove a sentence from a tragedy he had written. A tragedy, says Valerius,[2] is a manner of writing which blames those things that are badly done in politics and the commonwealth or by the princes. He[3] said that he did not write his plays to be blamed or to blame but rather to present a better way of life. And Valerius also says of this poet that he did not want to lower himself to such a degree that he would submit to the judgment of the people and leave aside his own.

1. Cf. what Christine says about the anguish she felt when a bailiff confiscated her belongings in *Christine's Vision*; see p. 173.
2. I.e., Valerius Maximus; see n. 1 to the headnote, p. 202. On the justification Christine gives for using his book, see chapter 13.
3. I.e., Euripides.

[Christine closes by praising the persistence of those who support a just cause. Examples from antiquity occupy chapter 12. She now turns to her principal source for this book.]

13. Here She Explains the Reason Why Valerius Is Cited So Often in This Book

I cite the great Valerius more than any other author because in his book on the deeds of the Romans he gives me subject matters to speak of and prove by example my pure intention, which is important to me and which is to move hearts to virtue and a good life; this applies to princes as well as knights and nobles and the common people. For the same Valerius states that examples make people desire honor and valiance more than simple words, and Aristotle testifies to this in the tenth book of his *Ethics*. For this reason I follow the style of the noble author Valerius in order to move the hearts of those who listen to these lessons to virtuous deeds through which one acquires true honor. This is my motivation for using various examples of events that happened to several magnificent men of the past whose deeds are commemorated in this book. Listening to them has inspired pleasure in many noble hearts and has given them the desire to aspire to the kind of honors virtue makes desirable. For we see that worthy and excellent things, such as great courage or knowledge or another virtue, are considered honorable. And although I call these courageous, valiant Roman conquerors whom I mentioned princes, some people could have the impression that they were not princes because they did not rule over vast lands and riches. But according to Valerius, the Romans saw a man's greatness in his courage and virtue and not in his possessions, for he does not merely call them princes but calls them emperors in his book, as one can see in various chapters where he speaks of Scipio Africanus, Pompei the Great, Sulla,[4] and others. But they certainly did not have the title of emperor.

[The rest of part 1 deals with the qualities and behavior of the ideal prince, who should be guided by philosophers and who is even allowed some recreation, provided it is reasonable and does not involve any voluptuous or illicit pursuits.]

Here begins the second part of this book which addresses itself to the noble knights.

---

4. Roman general (138–78 B.C.) who drove Mithridates's armies back to Asia. There were two Scipio Africanuses: the Elder (236–184 B.C.) and the Younger (185–129 B.C.). The Younger was praised by Cicero as the model of a statesman and philosopher. The Punic Wars, in which they were active, ensured Rome's domination over Carthage (modern Tunisia) and the western Mediterranean. Pompey (106–48 B.C.), a Roman general, was Julius Caesar's rival and became part of the Triumvirate in 60 B.C. He was assassinated in Egypt after losing the battle of Pharsalia.

Part 2

1. The First Chapter Explains How These Nobles Are the Arms and Hands of the Body Politic

We continue our subject after having finished the first part where we urged a moral life on the princes whom we consider the head of the living image of the body politic, which Plutarch describes as we indicated above. In the second part of the present book we will keep our promise and speak of the arms and hands of this image which mean, as Plutarch understands it, the nobles, the knights, and others of their estate. In the same manner as above we have to treat their introduction to virtue and good morals, especially as concerns the profession of chivalry which is in charge of protecting the public, as the authors say. And although all of them—simple and noble knights and princes alike—need the same virtue and can profit from it, there is a difference in their way of life, the company they keep, and their activities; and we must therefore differentiate in what we are saying. For a prince must do things a simple knight or a noble does not do, and vice versa. But there is no doubt that as far as the above-mentioned virtues are concerned one can say the same things to the nobles and the princes. That is, they must love and fear God above all else, take care of the public good which they are charged to protect through their love of justice. Like the princes they should be humane, generous, and merciful; love wise and good men and govern themselves by their counsel; and possess all the other virtues which I will not repeat in relation to them because it is enough that I told about them once. This applies to all estates of the body politic and to each individual as far as the soul and virtues are concerned. I will therefore not pursue this way of presenting things. Without further ado I can say how everyone should do what God has ordained for him in the order He has established: the nobles should act as nobles should, the people as they should, so that all are part of one body politic and live together in peace and justice as it should be. And by what I just said I mean to admonish them to a moral life. Now I will begin my subject and will speak in this first part about the education of noble children in the same way I spoke about the education of the princes' children.

[Numerous examples from Roman history illustrate the ideal comportment of the knights' children and finally of the knight himself.]

Here begins the third part of the book which addresses itself to the people.

Part 3

[A call to unity opens part 3. The people should love, obey, and revere their prince. Christine then briefly surveys different forms of government, such as elected emperors, government of ancient lineages or even of burghers, as in Bologna.[5] Christine concludes that none of these forms can be as good as the government of a wise prince, as Aristotle states in book 3 of his *Politics*.]

4. Here She Begins to Speak of the Three Estates of the People, and First of the Scholars Studying the Sciences

The people consists of three estates, especially in Paris and other cities: the clerks,[6] the burghers and merchants, and then the common people like craftsmen and laborers. Now we have to take care to say things that provide useful examples for everyone to live according to their different estates. And because the clerical estate is among all the highest and the most honorable, I will first speak of this estate, that is, of the students at the University of Paris and elsewhere.

Oh, well-counseled and happy people, I address you, the disciples of the study of wisdom, who through God's grace and good fortune or by nature are devoted to the search of the high and brilliant joyful star, that is, science, take this treasure diligently, drink from this clear and healthy fountain, fill yourself with this pleasant food that can be so valuable to you and elevate you. For what is more worthy of a human being than science and high learning? Certainly, you who desire and practice it, you have chosen a glorious life. For through it you can understand that you must choose virtue and eschew vice, for learning encourages you to the one and forbids the other.

[Christine cites many examples from Valerius that confirm that the lover of learning must shun earthly glory. Knowledge must be shared in order to be worthwhile. But the scholar must also stop working from time to time and devote himself to recreation. She ends chapter 5 with the following.]

Continuous mental work breaks the strength of the scholar and brings forth madness; and for this reason nature gave men the inclination to play and have fun occasionally. And for the same reason those who established the laws ordered certain holidays to be celebrated so that people could get together publicly to have fun and to stop working. In this context says Socrates, to whom no aspect of learning was unknown, that he was not ashamed when Alcibiades made fun of him when he found him playing with small children, for he did it so that after this recreation his understanding would be clearer and sharper for his stud-

---

5. Cf. what Christine says in the *Book of Peace*; see p. 229.
6. This term can refer to the clergy or simply scholars.

ies. And for this reason he began to play the harp when he was already very old.

6. Of the Second Estate, That Is, of the Burghers and the Merchants

I have said before that the second estate of the people are the burghers and the merchants in the cities. Burghers are those who have ancient lineages in the cities, a proper surname and ancient coats of arms. They are the principal inhabitants in the cities, provided with inherited houses and manors, which give them an honest living. Books that speak of them call them citizens. Such people must be honorable, wise and of good appearance, dressed in suitable clothes, without any exaggeration or anything fancy. They must be truly honorable men, people of faith and of discreet speech; being a citizen is a fair and profitable estate. And in some places they are called noble if they have for a long time held a high estate and reputation. One should praise the good burghers and citizens of towns everywhere.

It is a good and honorable thing when there are notable burghers in a town, and it is a great honor for the country and means great riches for the prince. These people are responsible for the activities and needs of the city where they live and see to it that the trade and public affairs are well ordered. And because generally the common people have no prudence when it comes to saying and doing things touching on politics—and they should not get involved in any ordinances established by the prince—the burghers and upper-class people should take care that those things done for the common good are not hindered and that no evil conspiracy arises against the prince or the council. These conspiracies and machinations of the common people usually turn against those who have something to lose. It is never to their advantage but always comes to a bad and unhappy end, and for this reason, in case they are aggrieved over some issue, they should from among them assemble the wisest and most discreet in deed and speech and go to the prince or the council and present their complaint in all humility and state their case frankly and not permit any harm to come to the common people, for that would mean the destruction of the towns and the land. The burghers should as best they can appease the complaints of the people, for bad things could ensue in many different places. And they should protect themselves even more than others. For the upper classes are in the most danger.[7]

And although sometimes the princes' and the council's ordinances may seem to their judgment not quite just, they should not interpret this in the worst possible way but rather think of the good intentions

---

7. This last phrase comes from Bornstein, *The Middle English Translation*, 178.

with which the ordinances were made and for which the reasons may not be apparent to everyone. And thus there can be danger in foolish complaints. On the subject of being wisely quiet, Valerius says that what the philosopher Socrates said was good and praiseworthy: one day he found himself in a place where several people spoke of the princes' ordinances and they complained about them. One of these complainers asked Socrates why he alone was quiet when all the others were speaking. "Because," he said, "I regretted many times what I said but never what I kept silent." It is a good thing not to say anything that can result in evil and never in good, as the wise man says. And for this reason the wise Cato says that the first virtue is to restrain one's tongue. He who can keep silent following the teachings of reason is close to God. And Seneca says in book five of his last text that whoever wants to be a disciple of Pythagoras must be silent for five years, for he said that like this one would learn the things one should say.[8]

[Christine repeats that the burghers must keep the people in check and then speaks of the merchants without whom neither the princes nor public life would function. Those who cheat are not worthy of being called merchants. Trade is the base for the prosperity of princes and cities; merchants have, therefore, a grave responsibility. To close her book Christine now turns to the third estate, the people.]

9. Of the Third Estate of the People

After [the merchants] comes the third estate of the people, who are craftsmen and laborers of the land, which we call the last part of the body politic, namely the legs and the feet. Plutarch says that one must protect them with the greatest care that they hit no obstacle, for this could dangerously affect the body. They have to be all the more protected and provided for more because they walk on the earth for the good of the body; that means, the diverse labors that the craftsmen do and that are necessary to the human body and which it could not do without, just as a human body could not do without the feet, for without them he would drag his body along painfully and uselessly on his hands. Just like this, he says, it would be for the commonwealth if you took away the laborers and craftsmen—it could not stand up. Thus everything would break down, including the craftsmen whom the clerks call artists, and whom some people appreciate little, but they are good and necessary, as we said. And with all the other goods we find there, this estate should be praised more than the other worldly estates for it is closest to the sciences. For they apply what the sciences have prepared for them, as Aristotle says in his *Metaphysics*,[9] for their work is the result of science, such as geometry, which is the science of measures and pro-

8. All this (starting from "Valerius says") is in Valerius Maximus.
9. Book 1, chapter 1.

portions and without which no profession could exist; and the same goes for other sciences.

[Christine now describes the importance of science for construction. As far as the craftsmen's morals are concerned, they should stay away from lechery and taverns.]

10. Of the Simple Laborers

I can say of the estate of simple laborers—although many people despise them and trample on them—that of all the estates they are the most necessary, for they are the cultivators of the goods that feed all human creatures and without which the world would perish in a short time. And truly, those that treat them so badly do not pay attention to their function, for every reasonable creature who considers this well would feel beholden to them. It is a sin to be ungrateful for all the services they do for us. And truly, they are the feet which sustain the body politic, for they sustain through their labor the body of each person. That they should not be despised and that God considers this job acceptable is apparent firstly because the two principal heads of the world, from whom descended the entire world, were laborers of the earth. The first head was Adam, the first father, of whom it is written in the second chapter of Genesis that God took the first man and put him in the delightful paradise so that he would work, cultivate, and preserve it.

From this Scripture one can derive two arguments to prove the worthiness of labor. The first is that God ordained it and that it is the first of all professions. And the second is that this profession was made in a state of purity and innocence. The second head of the world was Noah, from whom after the deluge the entire world is descended. Of him is written in the ninth chapter that Noah, who was a laborer, began after the deluge to work the earth and to plant vines. And thus our ancient patriarch fathers were cultivators of the earth and herdsmen of animals. But I won't speak more of them for the sake of brevity. In ancient times [agriculture] was not a lowly or despised profession.

[Christine gives some examples from Roman history to buttress her arguments. In any case, she states, great people are usually more unhappy than simple laborers who often lead a purer life.[1]]

Here Christine concludes her book.

Now, thank God, I have come to the intended end. That is, I have finished this present book which I began with the head of the body, as

---

1. This kind of romantic view of the life of laborers echoes views of a simpler "Golden Age" before too much civilization, although in *The Book of the City of Ladies* (see p. 116), Christine had debunked such views.

Plutarch describes it, namely the part of the policy that is represented by the princes whom I ask humbly—and first of all the head of all, the king of France and then the princes and all those of noble blood—that the diligent labor of the writings of the humble creature Christine, for the present text as well as her other works, such as they are and will be, may be agreeable to them. And if she is at fault through ignorance—for she is not a very knowledgeable woman—may she be forgiven and may her good intention be appreciated since it aims for nothing but the positive effect of her work. And I would like to ask for a reward from the living and their descendants, most noble kings and other French princes, who through the memory of my writings will remember my name in times to come, when my soul will be separated from my body, that by their devout prayers, either by them or offered by them.[2] May they ask God for indulgence for me and for the remission of my faults. And likewise I ask knights and noble Frenchmen and all people wherever they may be, who may read or hear my little writings with pleasure and will remember me, that they say an Our Father as a reward for me. And may the universal people do the same, the three estates which God may by His holy mercy maintain and increase more and more perfectly both in soul and in body. Amen.

Explicit.

FROM ONE HUNDRED BALLADS OF A LOVER AND A LADY

[In *One Hundred Ballads*, finished by 1402, Christine had written a series of twenty-three poems that chronicled a love story between a knight and a lady. In *One Hundred Ballads of a Lover and a Lady*, written between 1405 and 1410, she elaborates this idea and writes the full one hundred ballads in the voices of a knight and a lady who fall in love, enjoy a brief period of happiness, and then part. The last poem takes us to the lady on her death bed.

This cycle of poems dramatizes Christine's strong critique of the conventions of courtly love. All the major themes are there: the lover's burning love and his entreaties to the lady to grant him her love, which he considers ennobling; the initial reluctance of the lady, aware of the pitfalls of illicit love and the risks to her honor; her yielding to his seductive words; his ever more frequent departures and the growing suspicions as to each partner's faithfulness; gossip mongers who threaten their relationship; and finally the collapse of their love for each other, brought about as much by external as by internal pressures. Christine shows clearly that relationships which seem

2. A reference to prayers one could pay to have said for the departed.

to follow the ideals of courtly love are in reality destructive of people's honor and lives.

The dialogue form allows readers to draw their own conclusions as to the truth of each lover's speeches and behavior. There is no narrator to guide us. The lovers themselves often seem to communicate rather badly, and we need much ingenuity to construct and interpret the "true" story, which finally may remain elusive.

Translated by Renate Blumenfeld-Kosinski from Christine de Pizan, *Cent ballades d'amant et de dame,* ed. Jacqueline Cerquiglini (Paris: Union Générale d'Editions, 1982).]

One Hundred Ballads of a Lover and a Lady

Although at the present time I had neither the
intention nor thought to write love poems—
for my inspiration now lies elsewhere—by
the command of a person[1] who should be
agreeable to everyone I have undertaken to   5
write of a lover and his lady together, one
hundred ballads about amorous feelings in
order to obey and comply with the wishes of
this other person.

And all about how they spent their days   10
occupied with love which caused them many ills
and many joys intermingled with pain, trouble,
and contretemps, I must tell everything,
without hesitation, in this book where I will
presently write about joy and its opposite one   15
hundred ballads of amorous feelings.

I pray to God that I won't get tired, for I'd
rather occupy myself with other business, with
more learning, but a sweet and noble person
requires me to write this to make up for what   20
I said about noble ladies and what amorous
thoughts do to them. Thus I must compose one
hundred ballads of amorous feelings.

Prince, I see well that it would be better to
be silent than to speak unwillingly. Here is   25
how I must pay a voluntary fine: one hundred
ballads of amorous feelings.

1. It is not clear who commissioned the poem. In *Christine's Vision* 3.10 (see p. 193) she describes the evolution of her style and the switch to different, more intellectual, subjects.

1. *The Lover*

I can no longer hide from you the great love
with which I love you, my unsurpassed beauty,
and which I have carried within me for a long
time, without saying anything or complaining.
But today I realize that my strength is   5
declining through my excessive love; it will
attack and kill me unless you comfort me
without delay.

I am forced to speak—though I am in great
fear—so that I will be healed by you, for   10
blood, life, and humor[2] are failing me, and
though I have suffered many a year, now the
hour has come where I can no longer escape
from death, unless you comfort me without
delay.   15

I beseech you, most beautiful lady, in whom my
heart resides entirely, that you will show me
mercy, may it not tarry, for be it evening or
morning, I can no longer endure this pain. May
your great harshness come to an end or I must   20
weep in mourning, unless you comfort me
without delay.

Oh, sweet being, refined by goodness, may you
grant me your sweet love, for my heart will be
as dark as a blackberry, unless you comfort me   25
without delay.

2. *The Lady*

I never knew what love meant, nor did I want
to learn about it, my ambitions lie elsewhere.
Thus your expectations are in vain. I am
telling you, stop thinking about it, this does
not interest me nor is such a love suitable   5
for a lady who loves honor. Do not be
offended, for, to make it brief, I will love
neither you nor anyone else.

---

2. I.e., in the medical sense. According to ancient and medieval humoral theory, each person
was governed by different humors, such as phlegm and bile. A person's well-being depended
on the correct balance of the humors.

And I certainly intend to defend myself
against such a love. Thank God, I will not be   10
ensnared in Love's nets which I see and saw so
often do harm to others. I've watched it for a
long time but it has not gotten me—whoever
may speak to me of it, or write a letter or a
note. To make it brief, I will love neither   15
you nor anyone else.

I cannot give you another answer, don't speak
of it anymore, I'm tired of listening. Go
elsewhere for here your request has been
denied. Whoever comes here is mad, for I will   20
have nothing to do with such love. No one
would succeed here. To make it brief, I will
love neither you nor anyone else.

Don't think about it anymore. To make it
brief, I will love neither you nor anyone   25
else.

[The lover insists that it is a question of life or death for him. The
lady responds that all men are liars and that she will not fall for men's
tricks. The lover complains to the god of Love who now addresses the
lady.]

10. Love to the Lady

Your vanity is crazy, sweet and fair girl. Do
you believe that Love will let your youth go by
without your devoting yourself to the pleasures
of love which distribute things in many cases:
sometimes joy, sometimes pain?   5

This was not your desire, but Love certainly
does not agree. I tell you that your young and
joyful heart must feel the arrow of Love which
will send you thoughts of desire in many
different ways, sometimes in joy, sometimes in   10
pain.

And if your are forced, whether you like it or
not, to accept a frank, sweet glance, without
waiting too long, what's the use of being so
slow and langorous? I send you sighs, more than   15
thirty, some in joy, some in pain.

Little sweetheart, who sings so well, do you
think you can escape from the happy times that
are approaching, sometimes joyful, sometimes
painful?   20

[The lover keeps pursuing the lady who torments herself with doubts and
concerns over her honor. The lover focuses only on the more and more
promising glances she gives him and does not notice her torment. But he
does promise to protect her honor. Finally she yields, though she is aware
of male tricks and verbal deceptions.]

24. The Lady

If you will promise me and swear loyally on the
saints that you will always love me, as you say,
and if you do not just feign your harsh
suffering, I will accord you the love you ask
for. But honor must be protected, do not think   5
otherwise.

For I tell you clearly, and you can be certain of
it, that for nothing that could ever happen would
I do anything that could diminish me, I swear
this on the saints. I will no longer refuse the   10
request you are making. But honor must be
protected, do not think otherwise.

This is my intention, if possible, may it make
you happy, but not before I see you put your
hands on the book and swear—you must do no   15
more and no less—that I will not be deceived
and that you give yourself to me entirely. But
honor must be protected, do not think otherwise.

I have given you my love, if you will agree. But
honor must be protected, do not think otherwise.   20

[The lover swears on the saints to be true to her and she considers him the
best of men. Their love seems perfect but gossip begins to circulate.]

38. The Lady

Come to me, sweetest friend, at the usual hour,
do not fail to come, for the gossip mongers want
to attack our love, which makes me tremble with
fear. Beware of them, be wise, for they are
determined to hurt us, I am sure of it. We have   5

to be very careful, I have heard all about their
ways. They will harm us, may hell fire burn them!

And don't make the mistake of coming too late or
too early, for I will not fall asleep. God help
me, I desire you with the loyal heart of a lover.   10
And if you feel the same desire put on a brown
habit and cloak to disguise yourself, I beg you,
so that you will deceive the guard they have put
around me, this is not a joke. They will harm us,
may hell fire burn them!   15

I am so impatient, sweet friend that I am crying.
May I be with you in an hour and a half, I know
and ask for no other good, without you I feel
dazed. Watch out for what "they" do before you
leave, for my reputation will suffer if one sees   20
you, and so, though I am impatient, I am afraid
of being found out by them. They will harm us,
may hell fire burn them!

Oh, sweet friend, I would be so reassured if I
were in your arms. I am such a coward in face of   25
the gossip mongers and their false designs. They
will harm us, may hell fire burn them!

39. The Lover and the Lady

Now I have come to you my sweet and loyal
mistress. Alas, who made me come here, my blond
beauty? You alone are my riches, by my soul, I
have no other possession! Put on a happy face for
me. How are you faring? Kiss me, my dear sweet   5
love.

Dear friend, have you forgotten me? Tell me why I
see you less often and for a shorter time? Have
you made promises to another woman or why is it?
Or is it because you are afraid one might blame   10
me? Let's move over into the light and embrace
me, no one is here. Kiss me, my dear sweet love.

Lady, I have not returned to you earlier and this
caused me great distress. But I restrained myself
because of the gossipy tongue of someone I know   15
and who hurts me, for I am afraid you may be

defamed. For this reason I kept a bit away from
you. I ask your forgiveness. Kiss me, my dear
sweet love.

Sweet friend, my heart faints in your arms. Your   20
breath smells sweeter to me than balsam. Kiss me,
my dear sweet love.

[The lady believes the lover's excuses. She alerts him that they have been
found out. He decides to leave for a while and goes off to war. They correspond and yearn for each other. On his return they have a joyful reunion.
But soon doubts appear. Without any special provocation the lover doubts
his lady.]

74. The Lover

Believe me, lady, I feel very uncomfortable. I
don't know why I would hide it from you, for I
believe that another man pleases you, or begins
to please you, more than I do. For I have the
impression that you are changing a little   5
toward me and don't look at me—at least
that's what I'm thinking—the way you used
to. You will kill me, my dear sweet lady.

If it were so I'd be as troubled as are jealous
people who have no joy or happy times—and   10
I'm already in this state, I cannot calm myself
and I will not be reassured until I see you
behave differently. I don't know whether you're
trying to test me, this method seems too
dangerous to me. For no one could be as   15
sorrowful as I. You will kill me, my dear sweet
lady.

And it seems to me, though I don't say anything
about it, that I see another man who likes to
busy himself around you, and it does not calm   20
me that you don't seem to mind, as far as I
know. Thus I may, without any wrongdoing on my
part, lose the thing I love best. While I am
serving you as best I can, you will kill me, my
dear sweet lady.   25

For God's sake, let me see you again soon, for
if you make it difficult for me I must believe
that you don't care. You will kill me, my dear
sweet lady.

[The lover leaves again for the battlefield, and the lady reassures him of her love. He returns and comes to her house by the back door, as instructed; and they have a sweet reunion. But soon the lover comes less often. The lady suspects he is seeing another woman.]

90. The Lady

I will never believe that a lover who loves his
lady perfectly would stay away for a month and
not see her without a serious obstacle— he'd
rather be killed. But those do it who don't give
two nuts whether they're loved or not, they don't   5
care, they go around asking for love, first two,
then three. But their hearts do not care about
anything.

I'm saying this for you, friend, certainly, for I
have not seen you a single time in over a month,   10
and you seem to think that with sweet talk and a
happy voice you can blind me so that I will
believe you. Now I know whether you love me or
not. Without fail, this is how the false lovers
act who have abandoned the rules. But their   15
hearts do not care about anything.

Oh! God knows that your staying away keeps my
poor heart in the grip of painful sorrow, for
deeds show better than words how much you love
me; this weighs on me so much that I die of   20
grief, but you don't care in the least. I did not
think that you were of the same kind as those who
cry while their hearts do not care about
anything.

Oh, sweet friend, are those your deeds? Do men   25
love with a swiftly burning love, do they pretend
to be tormented by love, but their hearts do not
care about anything?

[The lover retaliates by accusing the lady of loving elsewhere, which she denies vehemently. She believes he has betrayed her and he complains that false reports have destroyed their love. The lady becomes grievously ill.]

100. The Lady

I am lying in my sick bed, trembling with a high
fever, because I was too intent on loving, which
now oppresses me and seems more poisonous than

hemlock. I die of it, without ever going outside
again, for my heart is already failing me.   5

Adieu, you who seduced me and kills me
treacherously. I will be avenged, for you have
deceived me badly, but all ladies should learn
about this example so that their hearts will not
be swayed by such a love, for my heart is already   10
failing me.

Adieu, Love. I am close to death because of you,
I'm already sweating its sweat, and I am
transfixed in this place. May my soul not be lost
but received by God. Adieu, world, adieu, honor,   15
my eyes are losing their sight, my voice is
becoming silent, for my heart is already failing
me.

Pray, that I may be received by God. Adieu,
brothers and sisters, I am leaving without delay,   20
for my heart is already failing me.

[To these one hundred ballads Christine added the "Mortal Lay of the
Lady" (284 lines), in which the lady speaks of the destructive power of love,
recounts once more her experience with a lover she believed to be treacherous, and describes the suffering leading to her death. The last word is *cendre*,
i.e., the ashes into which her body will soon turn.]

THE LAMENTATION ON THE EVILS THAT
HAVE BEFALLEN FRANCE

[Christine's involvement in the politics of her time finds a strong expression
in the lamentation addressed to all French princes and in particular to the
duke of Berry, the last remaining brother of the admired Charles V. The
situation in France had deteriorated in 1410 when Charles, duke of
Orléans, formed an alliance, the league of Gien, with the dukes of Berry,
Bourbon, and Brittany and several counts. This party, called the "Armagnacs" after Charles's father-in-law, the duke of Armagnac, opposed the ambitious duke of Burgundy, John the Fearless. This alliance was ready to move
on Paris, and it must have been the terror felt at the prospect of a full-blown
civil war that would pit the Burgundians against the supporters of the king
led by Armagnac that moved Christine to write the *Lamentation* on August
23, 1410.
    Translated by Renate Blumenfeld-Kosinski from Angus J. Kennedy, ed.,
La Lamentacion sur les maux de la France de Christine de Pisan, in
Mélanges offerts à Charles Foulon (Rennes, 1980), 177–85.]

Whoever possesses any pity should put it to work now. Now is the time when it is needed!

Alone and apart, I hold back with great difficulty the tears that obscure my vision and run like a fountain over my face, so that I will be able to write this sad complaint; the pity for the great misfortunes causes me to erase my writing with bitter drops. I am stunned and cry out plaintively: "Oh, how is it possible that the human heart can turn a man into a devouring and cruel beast, even if Fortune behaved strangely toward him? Where is Reason that gives him the name of a 'reasonable animal'? How can it be in the power of Fortune to change man so much that he is transformed into a serpent, the enemy of human nature? Alas! Here is how it can happen, noble French princes! And may the question not displease you: where is at present that sweet natural blood among you that from time immemorial used to stand for the utmost kindness in this world, and which true history books recorded from ancient times on, and about which Fame used to sing her songs throughout the entire world? What has become of the clear-eyed noble understanding that by nature and custom made you work, following the counsel of worthy men of good conscience? Are you now blinded, you fathers of the French community whose ancestors used to keep safe and well nourished the many children of this land that was once blessed? Now the land is changing to desolation if pity does not intervene. What harm did those people who used to adore you like God do to you; these people who in all lands gathered fame to your honor and whom you now treat not like your children but like mortal enemies, for the discord among you gets them nothing but harm, war, and battles?

For God's sake! For God's sake! Most noble of princes, open your eyes for a vision of what will be the result of your taking up arms! There you will see ruins of cities, destroyed towns and castles, fortresses razed to the ground! And where? In the very center[1] of France! The noble knights and youth of France, united by nature, who, conjoined like soul and body, used to be the defense of the crown and public life have now come together in a shameful battle, one against the other, father against son, brother against brother, relatives against each other, covering the pitiful fields with blood, dead bodies, and severed limbs! Oh, what a dishonorable victory for whoever may gain it! What kind of glory can his reputation bring him? Will this victory result in a laurel crown? Alas, no. It will rather be surrounded by shameful black thorns, for it will not regard itself victorious but rather a killer of its own blood for which it should be clad in black clothes, as one wears for the death of a relative.

Oh, you knight who comes from such a battle, please tell me what kind of honor do you gain there? Will the records of your deeds bring you honor when they say that on that day you were on the winning side?

1. Christine uses *nombril* ("navel"), evoking the image of the country as a body, as she did in her *The Book of the Body Politic*.

But even though you escaped from this dangerous situation, it will be weighed against your other, more noble, deeds—for such a shameful day does not deserve praise. Oh, if men would only agree, for God certainly does, not to take up arms, neither for one side nor for the other!

And what in God's name are going to be the consequences? Famine because of the inevitable plundering and destruction of all goods; non-cultivation of the fields which will cause rebellions by the people who are brutalized and robbed by the military, oppressed and pillaged from all sides; uprisings in the cities because of the outrageous taxes that will be levied on the citizens and inhabitants in order to raise money; and above all the English who are waiting in the wings and will check mate us if Fortune lets them; and finally, dissensions and mortal hatred will take root in many hearts and will bring about treason. Is this the purpose? It certainly seems so!

Cry therefore, cry, ladies, maidens, and women of the French realm, clap your hands with great cries as did the sorrowful Argia with the ladies of Argos in similar circumstances.[2] For the swords are already sharpened that will turn you into widows and rob you of your children and relatives! Oh, Sabine women,[3] we would need you in this situation, for the danger and strife between your relatives was not any greater than it is here when you intervened with great circumspection in order to bring peace, when a large group of you rushed dissheveled onto the battlefield, clutching your little children and crying: "Have mercy on our dear friends and relatives and make peace!"

Oh, crowned queen[4] of France, are you asleep? Who keeps you from snatching the reins and stopping this deadly enterprise? Do you not see that your noble children's inheritance hangs in the balance? You mother of France's noble heirs, respected princess, who else can do anything in the matter but you? Who would dare to disobey your power and authority, if you truly want to intervene for the sake of peace?

Come, come together with your queen, wise people of this kingdom! What good are you, even you members of the King's council? Let everyone lend a hand! In the past you intervened even in minor matters. What good are all these wise heads France is so proud of if they do not find a way to protect her, the fountain of wisdom, from destruction? Where are now your spirit of enterprise and your wise reasoning? Ah, clergy of France, will you thus let Fortune have her way? Why do you

---

2. A reference to the story of Thebes and the fratricidal war between Oedipus's sons Polynices and Etheocles. Argia was the daughter of Adrastus, king of Argos, and the widow of Polynices. Christine also tells this story in her *Le Livre de la mutacion de Fortune* [Book of Fortune's transformation]; see Suzanne Solente's edition (Paris: Picard, 1959–66), 2.319–28, lines 13087–306. The Theban story was known through the twelfth-century *Roman de Thèbes* and the thirteenth-century *Histoire ancienne jusqu'à César* [Ancient history up to Julius Caesar].

3. They made peace between warring men in early Roman history. Christine told their story at length in the *Mutacion*, Solente's edition, 3.183, and *The Book of the City of Ladies*, trans. E. J. Richards (New York: Persea, 1982), 147–50.

4. Isabeau of Bavaria, wife of Charles VI, to whom Christine had addressed a letter in October 1405.

not have processions with devout prayers? Don't you think it necessary? For already our situation seems to be that of Niniveh[5] which God had condemned to perish because it had attracted God's wrath by the grievous sins that were plentiful there. Our cause is in grave danger, if the sentence is not revoked through the intercession of devout prayers.

Try to prevent this, people, devout women, cry with pity for this grievous storm! Oh, France, France, once a glorious kingdom! Alas, what else can I say? The most bitter and endless of tears run like a stream onto my paper, so that there is no dry place left where I could continue to write the painful lament that my overflowing heart wants to utter because of the great pity it feels for you. My tired hands are busy putting down the pen with which I write and restoring sight to my troubled eyes by wiping away the tears which with their abundance moisten my chest and lap, when I think of what your future reputation will be. For will you not be compared from now on to strange nations where brothers, cousins, and relatives kill each other like dogs out of envy and greed? Will they not say by way of reproach: "Here you go, you French, boasting of the gentle blood of your princes, not tyrants, and you berate us Guelfs and Ghibelins[6] for our customs! Now these same customs are born in your country. The seed has germinated, everything is complete and your provinces have now come to the same point. Now you can lower your horns, for your glory is destroyed! Alas, sweetest France! Is it true, then, that you are in such peril? Yes, certainly! But something can still be done, for God is merciful! Not everything is lost yet, however long it has been exposed to danger.

Oh, Duke of Berry, noble prince, excellent ancestor of the royal children, son of a French king, brother and uncle, forebear of the entire French lily![7] How is it possible that your merciful heart can allow you to find yourself, on a certain day, in the midst of a deadly battle against your nephews?[8] I do not believe that the memory of the great natural love you had for their fathers and mothers, your beloved dead brothers and sisters, would not cause nature to let tears run down your face like a fountain and make your heart feel as if it were split in two by the pain you feel. Alas, how painful it is to see the noblest of the uncles that are still alive, uncle of three kings, six dukes, and many counts, ready to do mortal battle against his own flesh and blood, and the nephews who should revere such a noble uncle like a father, in battle against him!

---

5. The repentance of the people of Niniveh (Jonah 3) is also told in *Mutacion*, Solente's edition 1.152–53.
6. In Italy, the Guelfs were supporters of the pope and the Ghibelines, of the emperor. The conflicts between these two parties lasted from the twelfth to the fifteenth centuries. Christine also spoke of this in the *Mutacion*, Solente's edition 2.14–18, as did Dante in *Purgatory* 26.
7. On the significance of the lily see Colette Beaune, *The Birth of an Ideology: Myths and Symbols of Nation in Late-Medieval France*, trans. Susan Ross Huston (Berkeley: University of California Press, 1991), chap. 7. John, duke of Berry (1340–1416), was the brother of Charles V and the uncle of Charles VI.
8. I.e., Charles VI and John the Fearless, duke of Burgundy.

Oh, noble blood of France, without reproach! How can you, noble nature, endure that such shameful things should be able to happen (oh, may the day never come!); that those who should be the pillars of faith, supporters of the Church, through whose virtue, power, and wisdom it has always been sustained peacefully, and who among all nations are called the most Christian peacemakers, friends of concord, should arrive at such an impasse?

Oh, come, come noble Duke of Berry, most excellent prince, follow the divine law that calls for peace! Take the bridle forcefully and stop this disgraceful army, at least until you have spoken with the different factions. Come into Paris, your father's city where you were born, which cries out to you with tears, sighs, and weeping; it asks for you and needs you! Come soon to comfort the city in pain, come to your children speaking to them like a good father who wants to correct his children who have done wrong. Bring peace to them even while reproving them, as is your function, explaining to both sides that whatever may be the reason for their discord, they have to be the pillars, defenders, and supporters of the noble crown and shield of the kingdom that has never done them any harm, and that this is more important than anything they may want from each other. They should not destroy the kingdom!

For Gods' sake! Noble duke, alert them that although there is much talk of each party expecting victory in this battle for itself—they say things like "We will win and this is how we'll do it"—, this is just crazy boasting. For we cannot ignore that the outcome of every battle is unknown to us. For whatever man may propose, it is Fortune who disposes. What good was it to the Theban king in ancient times who left the battle victorious with only three of his knights, leaving behind all his men dead on the battlefield, lying among his many enemies, decimated by the swords of his relatives and princes? God, what a victory! It was too painful! And the king of Athens[9] mortally wounded in battle, what good did his victory do him? What profit have many other people derived from such circumstances? Was not Xerxes[1] destroyed who had so many men that valleys and mountains were all covered with them? Is it worth it, then, to fight for a rightful and just cause? If it were so, then the King Saint Louis who had won so many beautiful victories would not have been defeated at Tunis by the infidels.[2] What better example is there for us to recognize God's wonderful disposition to let a battle run its course, where the evil consequences are certain and any good that may come from it more than doubtful? And above all,

9. I.e., King Codrus, the last king of Athens. He was mentioned in her biography of Charles V, *Le Livre des fais et bonnes meurs du sage roy Charles V*, 2 vols., ed. Suzanne Solente (Paris: Champion, 1936–40), 1.186–87.
1. King of ancient Persia (d. 465 B.C.), whose fleet was destroyed in the battle of Salamis in 480 B.C. See *Mutacion*, Solente's edition 2.242–56.
2. Louis IX died at Tunis in 1270 during a crusade. His biography was written by the historian Joinville.

although wars and battles are always full of danger and difficult to wage, there is no doubt that between such close relatives, conjoined by nature through a common bond of love, they are most perverse, dishonorable, and blasphemous. They can never come to a good end. Alas, if it is true—and it is—that wars are undertaken for all sorts of motives and disputes, there is a much stronger and better reason to stay away from them and avoid them, and to seek peace instead.

May virtue now triumph over vice! May a way be found to lead back to peace these friends by nature who have become enemies by accident. Alas, may it please God that the efforts and strategies that are at present expended could be as devoted to the search of peace as they are to the search of its opposite! I believe that this could be achieved with less expense, and that with a common will and true unity this army could be converted into one fighting our natural enemies; this is how our good loyal Frenchmen should occupy themselves—not with killing each other. God, what a joy that would be, and what a great and eternal honor to the kingdom!

Oh, most honored, noble Duke of Berry, please listen to this, for there is nothing too great for the human heart to undertake, particularly if it is done with good intentions, that it will not achieve. And if you work toward this goal from now on, you will be called father of the realm, preserver of the crown and the most noble lily, custodian of the noble lineage, protector against the killing of the nobles, comforter of the people, guardian of noble ladies, widows, and orphans. May the blessed Holy Spirit, bringer of all peace, give you the heart and courage to put an end to all this! Amen. And to me, poor voice crying in this kingdom, desiring peace and good for you all, your servant Christine, moved by the best of intentions, may it be given to see that day. Amen.

Written on the twenty-third day of August, in the year of grace 1410.

FROM THE BOOK OF PEACE

[The composition of *The Book of Peace* reflects the troubled political climate of the time. Christine began writing it on September 1, 1412, when peace between the Armagnacs and the Burgundians seemed to be established and stopped on November 30 because of the failed peace. After another (equally futile, it would turn out) peace treaty at Pontoise in September 1413, Christine took up her pen again to write books 2 and 3, which she finished on January 1, 1414.

In the *Lamentation* of 1410 she had appealed to the duke of Berry not to let France fall into total civil war. A truce had indeed been concluded in 1412, but it did not last long. A full-blown civil war was now inevitable.

In one of the complicated developments of the Hundred Years' War, the Armagnacs began to ally themselves with the English, who later were successfully courted by the Burgundians. Meanwhile, the duke of Burgundy declared himself the defender of the King Charles VI and the dauphin Louis of Guienne, to whom *The Book of Peace* is dedicated. It is another "mirror" of princes that reuses parts of her biography of Charles V and *The Book of the Body Politic*. Again, Christine speaks of the role of the people whom she considers irresponsible and incapable of making a true contribution to government. In the spring of 1413 a revolt broke out, led by the butcher Simeon de Caboche (who gave his name to the "Cabochien" revolt) and supported by the duke of Burgundy, which brought chaos to Paris until the summer. Various concessions promised to the rebels were annulled because they were said to have been imposed on the king.[1] These events polarized relations between the Armagnacs (who were strengthened by the defeat of the Cabochiens) and the Burgundians even more.

Christine refuses to take sides, since she considers the good of France to lie in unity and concerted opposition to the English. She had connections to both factions, having had as patrons the dukes of Burgundy, Orléans, and Berry as well as members of the royal family. The dauphin Louis, then, is the "child," as she puts it in the opening section who is destined to bring peace to the war-torn country. To this end, Christine speaks of the virtues necessary for a prince and his responsibilities toward all parts of society. Again she calls on his ancestor Charles V as well as on celebrated men from antiquity as exemplars. The major source was Brunetto Latini's *Livre dou tresor* [Book of the treasure]. Written in the 1260s during his exile in France, it was a very successful encyclopedic work on theology, sacred and profane history, natural sciences, ethics, rhetorics, and politics. As in the *Book of the Body Politic* she draws on Egidio Colonna's *De regimine principum* [On the conduct of rulers] and also cites Aristotle, Seneca, Valerius Maximus, Vegetius, Ovid, and of course Boethius.[2]

The book is an eloquent plea for peace, but for France it was already too late. The following year Henry V invaded France, and after the disaster at Agincourt, Christine moved from futile exhortations to peace to a consolation for the families of the victims.

Translated by Renate Blumenfeld-Kosinski from Charity Cannon Willard, ed., *The 'Livre de la Paix' of Christine de Pisan* (The Hague: Mouton, 1958).]

Here begins the table of contents of the *Book of Peace* which addresses itself to the noble and excellent prince, Monseigneur the Duke of Guienne, the eldest son of the King of France, begun on the first day of September after the peace treaty sworn between our lords of France in the year of grace 1412.[1]

This book is divided into three books: the first book is an exhortation addressed to the said lord of Guienne, dealing with the virtue of pru-

---

1. See Edouard Perroy, *The Hundred Years War,* trans. W. B. Wells (London: Eyre & Spottiswoode, 1951).
2. For more details see Willard's edition of *The Book of Peace,* 40–45.
1. See the headnote to this selection for details.

dence and what it requires of a prince who governs. The first part was finished on the last day of November, and I left the rest unfinished because of the broken peace. I began work again on the second book on the third day of September, after peace agreements had again been sworn to in the town of Pontoise and our lords of France assembled with great joy in Paris in the year 1413. The second book praises and speaks of the good things brought about by peace and is meant to exhort the said lord of Guienne and to encourage the princes to love and chivalry, based on the three virtues of justice, magnanimity (also called greatness of heart), and strength, by giving examples from the life of his ancestor, Charles V.[2] The third book tells how to govern the people and public affairs well, based on another three virtues, namely clemency, generosity, and truth.

Book 1

1. The First Chapter Praises God for Peace

Out of the mouth of babes and sucklings [you receive perfect praise.]
Psalm 8:2[3]

Truly from the mouth of children and babies, Our Lord God, heavenly all-powerful king who takes away at His pleasure the misery of the world, it pleases you to receive perfect praise, as it has become manifest many times, for example when You opened the childish lips of Daniel for the good Susanna, wrongly accused, and saved her from death, when he said: "I am cleansed by the blood of her etc."[4] For this You were praised by all people. Oh glorious Trinity, one inseparable God whom the angels praise ceaselessly, whoever does not trust in You is truly crazy, for did You not also powerfully show your great strength when the three young men, Azana and his companions, were put into the burning furnace by the king of Babylon and praised you with melodious songs, without feeling any pain, and said: "Blessed be the name of God etc."[5] It also pleased you, dear Lord God, to be blessed by the mouth of children on the day of Your solemn entry into Jerusalem when they cried

---

2. Christine reuses a number of passages from her *Book of the Deeds and Good Conduct of the Wise King Charles V*, written in 1404 at the command of the duke of Burgundy, Charles's brother (see p. 113).

3. Each chapter head is followed by a Latin quotation. The translations of the biblical passages are based on the King James version, though Christine used the Latin Vulgate, in which the verse numbers are often different. Here, the Vulgate differs from the King James version; the translation reproduces Christine's quotation.

4. Christine quotes only the beginning of the verse and then adds "etc." Readers were expected to fill in the rest of the quote, as was common the Middle Ages. In the *Livre de la paix* manuscript edited by Charity C. Willard further words of the biblical quotes were added in the margins. Susanna's story is in Daniel 13 in the Greek version of the Bible, but this chapter is not included in the King James version. Susanna was spied on by two old men who wanted to rape her. When she escaped, they falsely accused her of immorality with a young man. She was saved by the child Daniel, who pronounced her innocent.

5. Daniel 2:20–49.

in loud voices: "Hosanna to the son of David: Blessed is he that cometh in the name of the Lord."[6] And sweetest God, full of goodness and infinite pity, although one could tell of many instances when it pleased You to demonstrate Your divine grace and strength in many different forms through innocent and simple children, we must now be silent about this subject and praise and magnify Your name with the affection of all our hearts, because together with all Your past goodness you have now decided to help us again in a similar way, to be with us and comfort us in our great affliction through a child, inspired in speech and deed by Your Holy Spirit.[7]

Having listened to the voice of true prayer, in Your great pity, it has pleased You through him to bring peace in order to cure and heal the mortal wound of vicious hatred and horrible bloodshed suffered by Your Catholic kingdom of France where everything perished. For this goodness we praise You, dearest Jesus Christ, who sits in glory at the right side of God with the Holy Spirit; we bless and glorify You, thanking You, our true God and sole Creator, for this great gift, You, our good shepherd, just judge, wise master, powerful helper, helping physician, bright light, and our life. You, king of glory, please hear our just prayers for our victorious duke Louis, whose deeds can tell the French people: "O sing unto the Lord a new song; for he hath done marvellous things."[8] May it please You to give him perfection in grace, knowledge of virtue, good sense of government, and infinite glory. Amen.

2. Praise and Benediction for Our Lord of Guienne through Whom Peace Was Made Possible and Promoted

Glory, honor, reverence, and all obedience be given to you, most excellent and respected prince Louis, eldest son of the king, in line for the crown by God's grace, Duke of Guienne and dauphin of the Viennois. Eminent and noble prince, may your great magnificence not disdain the writings of your servant and humble subject, moved by goodwill and pure affection for the good of your worthy person; may the great clemency of your noble heart rather receive them willingly. In saying this, prince of the highest excellence, I appeal to your kind humility that you will not resent my addressing you in the singular,[9] for your good sense, already steeped and trained in learning, knows that according to the rhetorical usage this is the most proper style in which to write to emperors and kings.

6. Matthew 21:9.
7. Christine emphasizes here the continuity between biblical and contemporary history. As the children in the Bible testified to God's greatness, so the young duke of Guienne should be an example of piety doing God's will.
8. Psalm 98:1.
9. *Vous* would be the more formal address. She also explains her use of the informal *tu* in her letter to Eustache Deschamps (see p. 109).

Most excellent lord, the great joy which is at present so abundant in my heart because of the new peace brought about by you through God's mysterious workings does not permit me to wait any longer to take up the pen to write a new book about glorious things in your praise. For it is not only me, simple and ignorant woman, who possesses no erudition and has no other knowledge than that expressed in her writings in a rural and vulgar[1] style, but also all the other eminent and learned persons, wise orators, expert in the rhetorical style, in law and reasoning, who feel obliged to sing about you in verse and prose, so that your memory will be preserved forever. For are you not the one who by God's grace at the young age of fifteen has brought peace to those of your blood, whose wars had long laid waste the kingdom? You did this by divine inspiration, without any other means, in spite of the enemy from hell who is against the good of peace, and who by various countermoves hoped to prevent it; and you did this not like an easily influenced and lighthearted child but like a mature, wise man, deliberate in his work and deeds. And you have brought together those of your blood who were torn apart by horrible hatred, you have reunited and pacified them, you have created new love between them through loyal bonds, worthy and to be praised; have they not sworn their true loyalty in your presence and without accusing anyone?

Oh, child born in a favorable hour, blessed be you forever in heaven and on earth whence you were inspired to undertake such a great task, which everyone claimed to be impossible. Did not the motivation come from you without fault (as from the one without whose vigilance the city's guard is worth nothing), when on the eve of the feast of St. John the Baptist of this year 1412—as I was informed by trustworthy people who heard it—you, hearing during mass the passage of the Scripture where it is said of St. John: "And many people rejoiced in his birth," you turned around with a joyous expression, suddenly moved, and said to your confessor: "Oh, may it please God that on this glorious day we could unite in peace and joy the two warring Johns"—meaning on the one hand John, Duke of Berry, and John, Duke of Burgundy, on the other. But you said this so that beginning at this moment we could initiate, execute, and finish a good treaty with God's help; and it is good that a beautiful mass with all solemnity should be celebrated in the chapel of St. John which is nearby and toward which the two above-mentioned men feel great devotion. Oh, noble prince, this has not come about without a miracle, considering the disputes and great conflicts when you assembled the great army in front of Bourges together with your father the king; there, there was no talk of peace, not even in jest. The miracle is that you were then inspired in the matter of peace and that you have persisted in this enterprise and stuck to your purpose

1. Willard suggests that Christine may have used this expression based on the *Proverbes ruraux et vulgaux*; see Willard's edition, 184.

from that moment on, whatever the substantial obstacles may have been, working constantly until peace was concluded.

But even though this inspiration came to you from God, you deserve praise, for He has made you worthy of receiving such a great benefice, for which we should give thanks now and ever more. You, God's vassal, approved by Him, are you not the one who restored, repaired, and comforted all of France? You have transformed war into peace, mourning into joy, death into life, hatred into love, bloodshed into healing, lack into abundance, and everything bad into good. Oh, glorious things are said about you, which from now on will always cause you to be called "Louis given by God," and you will persist in doing good. May you be blessed for your present goodness by the divine essence and by all good heavenly and earthly things where God has placed His goodness, you who give us cause to chant in strong voices: "Glory to God in the highest and on earth peace among men of good will." Luke 2:14.

[In chapters 3 to 5 Christine still addresses the duke of Guienne and points out that discord has brought down powerful kingdoms. By citing Scripture and ancient philosophers like Cicero she urges the duke to help preserve the peace. Virtue has to be the duke's guide. First, she speaks of the virtue of prudence (citing Seneca, St. Augustine, and others) who governs the other virtues. Past deeds, she insists, can serve as examples of virtue.]

6. Here She Proves by Arguments That It Is More Urgent for Princes Than for Anyone Else to Know Many Things and Begins to Give Examples from the Life of King Charles V[2]

Apropos of what is said in the preceding chapter, most noble prince, please understand why I have so lengthily described Prudence and have insisted on her authority, for it is for no man more necessary to know more and better things than it is for a prince, because his prudence and well-ordered way of life can profit and be valuable for his subjects, as much in exemplary value as in being governed well. And to this end, so that your authority may now and in future times be shining throughout the world not only for your great nobility but even more for your virtue and wisdom, you should make use of this virtue of Prudence and use her to plan all your deeds with circumspection, which for the wise man comes before all action, as one says. At first I was thinking of giving you examples of the valiant ancients like the valorous Julius Caesar, Pompei, Scipio,[3] and other very worthy men, who all put their efforts into gaining

2. This chapter begins with a Latin quote from Vegetius's *Art of Warfare* (fourth century), the basis for Christine's own *The Deeds of Arms and Chivalry* (1410). See Publius Flavius Vegetius, *Epitome of Military Science*, trans. N. P. Milner (Liverpool, UK: Liverpool University Press, 1993).
3. Roman statesmen. Julius Caesar (100–44 B.C.) conquered most of Europe for the Roman Empire. He was assassinated by his own followers. See also n. 4, p. 210.

knowledge and wisdom before their actions and decided on their great undertakings based on this; and it served them very well to be governed by great wisdom rather than by the force of arms.

But it will be enough to give you the example of your good ancestor, the wise King Charles, fifth of that name, whom you resemble by God's grace. Thus you will never lack in whatever one may require of a perfect and wise prince. Oh, who could speak of anyone more prudent than he, better educated and more perfect in all things? For from his early youth, by God's grace, knowing through his great prudence that it is necessary for a prince, however young he may be, to have a mature heart and to know what to do and what not to do, he gave up the way of life of young people and devoted himself to everything that wisdom teaches. Once he had made this decision, and in order to put into action his wishes, he removed from his entourage all those whom he thought capable of making him do things contrary to his good intentions; and from everywhere he wanted to attract wise people, noble men with a good education. And these were the people he looked for and he retained them at great honor and profit in all sorts of functions. In spiritual matters, which are the most important, he wanted to be well taught by solemn and worthy theologians, as for example Jean de Chaleur,[4] and others to whom he wanted to listen frequently; and he often heard on certain days and during certain hours lessons of wisdom whose teachings he followed so that he could serve God and fear and love Him above all else. Thus he did good works, as much in giving to the poor as in building churches, saying prayers and practicing devotion throughout his life, as is still visible in many places.

Similarly, in order to well administer his kingdom, he wanted to have around him notable expert jurists, so that through their advice, based on the rules of law, he could well plan all his actions. The result was that as long as he reigned he followed the customs that a well-organized royal order requires and governed his kingdom with great magnificence; and its prosperity increased and improved through the perfect exercise of justice and well-ordered chivalry that was never idle but engaged in appropriate activities; the clergy had their privileges and rightful order; he held his bourgeois in esteem; merchants, whether foreign or native, were held to the rules; the people were in peace, not required to labor and exercise their professions more than good management required, nor were there extortions or suffering imposed on them.

Furthermore, so that his kingdom would be well defended and would grow in prosperity, he wanted to assemble around him the flower of chivalry from everywhere where good people could recommend them; and of the best he made commanders with great honor and salaries, as it should be done, and as many people who are still alive know well.

---

4. Chancellor of Notre Dame of Paris from 1370 on. He died in 1380 or 1381.

And as to what resulted from all this, certainly, noble lord, it is obvious that his prowess still resides in you and will forever, if it pleases God, reside in the crown through his merit and high reputation.

7. Here She Tells How a Prince Should Conduct Himself According to the Wise People, and She Gives the Example of the Above-Mentioned King

The multitude of the wise is the salvation of the world and a prudent king is the stability of the people.

Wisdom 6:24

In the quote cited above Solomon wants to say that through many wise people all lands and countries can be secure. And be not deceived into believing that wise necessarily means that these people have acquired vast book learning, although this is part of it, and when they also possess prudence and circumspection they do indeed surpass all others. But nonetheless, one often sees the most learned men say frivolous things, and the truth is that they are not the wisest as far as matters of government and policy are concerned, and not even in what they say, although learning teaches and demonstrates these skills. And it is true that these people could very well express ideas and use arguments drawn from books, but there are many who have great difficulty in applying this knowledge to their tasks and are little skilled in worldly things. For this reason we say that he is wise who wisely does good work, and not the one who only knows about it but does not know how to apply his knowledge. And although Aristotle says that he who does not know anything about all things cannot be called wise, those who only have book learning must be called knowledgeable but not wise. And for this reason one can count among the wise men also lay people, those who have good understanding and know how to prudently use for their work their experience: for example, wise knights or others who have experienced many things and seen different events, be it in the practice of arms or in the government of the lands; through this experience they have gained knowledge by example and discern through good circumspection the remedies most suitable for present difficulties, and they know how to plan for the future.

But to return to the first topic, we say, following the authorities, that wisdom is so appropriate for a king that such a king represents the security and the firm support of all his subjects and his people. And for this reason, on the subject of the wise king, most honored prince, it is a fact that wisdom reveals itself, as we have said, only in good work. In order to show this, examples that explain the causes of things usually make more of an impression than a mere listing of reasons.

I therefore see no better way of teaching you to govern under the

appropriate direction of Prudence than again to tell you of your ancestor. Since you are so closely related to him, you should enjoy hearing
about his noble deeds and to imitate them by taking them as an example; and although I have treated his deeds in another book[5] and have
spoken about them more fully, it is necessary in the present volume to
recall his deeds especially for you; may you not reproach me for this or
make me fearful. Oh, sweet God, most noble lord, imagine for a
moment, if you will, what an astonishing difference it would be for you
to see the state of affairs then, compared to what it is now. Oh, how well
everything was arranged, what a good pontificate, what good sense, what
government, how well the prince showed himself, what abundance,
what eloquence he had and what respect he commanded! He did not
spend an hour or a moment without good work, that is, he devoted
himself to everything that had to do with the prosperity of public affairs;
most of all, the affairs of the Church were important to him, as were his
dealings with foreigners and military matters, or any other appropriate
business. You should have seen his diligence in getting up in the morning to hear mass, to attend to the canonical hours[6] at length and serve
God well, then to go to the council at the appropriate hour, where, I
assure you, there were no people who should not have been there
because they were unworthy in their lack of judgment to be part of the
prince's council. And whoever made the best suggestions did not do so
in vain, for he[7] was there and understood and took note of what they
said. Then the good prince sat down to dinner at the appropriate time,
and afterward, until the afternoon meal, he made time for all people to
present their business to him and listened to them very graciously. And
similarly, after his sleep, which never lasted very long, and also when,
to get some fresh air, he was walking back and forth in his gardens of
St. Paul, which he had kept in such good order, he attended to his
duties. But do you think everything took as long then as it does today?
He found it too annoying to be burdened with one thing for too long,
whatever it may have been, and he could not have attended to so many
tasks if he had not speeded things up.

Thus he did not tarry over anything and did not put off those things
that he could finish quickly. But if you could have seen around him his
noble brothers, the other barons of his family and others, or his valiant
knights who were waging his wars, or foreigners who came to him—
how well he knew how to receive them, to speak with them, to enjoy
himself with them and to entertain them. Surely, with such good order,
and a manner at the same time elevated and humble, many people
praised him and everyone was content. And at his various celebrations

---

5. Her biography of Charles V; see p. 113.
6. The prescribed hours of prayer, such as matins, terce, and vespers (usually around 6:00 P.M.).
   Louis, by contrast, had the reputation of sleeping all day and partying all night.
7. I.e., the king.

and feasts, such rich ornaments, such buffets, such rich tableware, how well his chambers were decorated, and how generously people were served; one no longer feasts like this! Oh, noble prince, look at this wisdom and what impression it makes on those who recognize it in someone.

It is true that although the king was gracious to all princes of this world and had a friendly face for everyone and was never seen to be rude to anyone, nonetheless the display of his prudent behavior and beautiful generosity made him so respected that no one, however great he may have been, dared to contradict him in anything, not even his brothers, who served him at great festivities, or any great foreign lords who were present.

[Christine now describes, based on the account of eyewitnesses, the magnificent sight of Charles V on horseback, surrounded by his knights, and the beautiful sight of the queen and her attendants. The king's premature death put an end to this glorious period. Chapters 9 to 15 deal with the qualities required in a prince's counselors and the signs by which one can recognize bad counselors.]

Book 2

1. The First Chapter Speaks of the Great Joy of Peace and Addresses Itself to the Lords

They that sow in tears shall reap in joy.

Psalm 126:5.

More than I can say, I cannot stop or wait to express the great joy that fills my heart at present because of the glorious peace now concluded between the French princes who, through an evil spirit envious of the prosperity of this realm, had been enemies for a long time. Through this discord France had come to ruin, but the prophecy of the psalmist has come true, by God's grace: we, the good subjects of France, desiring the end of these torments, sowing our prayers with tears and crying, now assemble in joy by God's strength. That is, our loyal wishes have been fulfilled when we see this peace which we celebrate trembling with the greatest joy and almost beside ourselves. There is no human heart, full of loyal faith and love of his prince, desiring the good of public affairs, full of pity toward past disasters, brotherly and charitable toward his neighbor, who does not at this moment express its joy and great consolation.

Oh God, and who would not express it, when we see that the killing has ended, the great cruelties, the destruction, the rebellions, the boastfulness of vile and low people, the mad rule of the lowly and bestial people, the subjection of the king, the lack of respect for the nobles—

in short, the infinite disasters and disgusting torments that have made their way worse than ever in this current year?

Oh, good French princes, enlightened by God, royal branches issued from the crown, members of the head all joined together in one body,[8] loudly proclaimed more noble than any other lineage, generous, good and of mild blood, very humane, without cruelty, settled and reasonable, of Catholic faith and very Christian, may peace be preserved in you forever, without your forgetting the bad things that happened and that could happen again because of a conflict. May the pity felt over such destruction keep you from giving your consent to such a war—no matter what may happen. May your labors and good counsel reconstruct the ruins of this beaten-down kingdom to the benefit of the crown and increase in public good, so that henceforth we can live in the manner we deserve, with the order of rightful justice well maintained. And if in these respects you keep peace in this world, you will gain God's grace and that of the world; everyone will praise you and the right order will be reestablished in all parts of society which had been so alienated from their rightful condition by various events. The nobles will devote themselves to the defense of the crown and public affairs, as is their duty; the clergy to laws and sciences; the bourgeois to their affairs; the merchants to their trading; the workers to their jobs; the laborers to their labor; and thus everyone will be in his rightful rank, without one group encroaching on the other more than is necessary. And thus public policy will flow in its rightful channel after having been deviated too much outside of its prescribed course. May God let you accomplish all this by His grace. Amen.

[Chapter 2 praises the duke of Guienne, and chapter 3 specifies that Louis will need two things in order to prevent another outbreak of the fighting: the memory of the disasters brought about by war and the willpower to keep his relatives from engaging in renewed acts of war.]

4. Here She Accuses the Cruelty That Is the Cause of War

[Christine first lists authorities like Seneca, Cicero, and St. Gregory, who speak against cruelty and force. In order to guard against war, one has to understand its causes. There are four possible causes that exist, either alone or in various combinations.]

[These causes are] hatred, envy, vengeance, and greed. [War comes about] through some particular hatred or enmity that has some reason, such as the woman Herod kept, who was his brother's wife, something which St. John the Baptist reproached him with; for this reason she succeeded in having his head cut off. An example of envy is when Cain

---

8. The image of the body politic comes from John of Salisbury's *Policraticus* (1159), which was translated by Denis Foulechat in 1372; see also n. 1 to *The Book of the Body Politic*, p. 202.

killed Abel because he was better; and also the envy of Joseph's brothers. An example of vengeance is when Jacob's children killed the king who had raped their sister. Greed was when Ahab condemned Naboth to death in order to get his vineyard, or when David wanted to have Uriah's wife and made him die through flattery.[9] The following events were also caused by greed: when the false servants of King Dares killed him (because they wanted to please King Alexander) and wanted to have a reward; or those who killed the valiant knight Pompei in order to please Caesar.[1]

Although such evil deeds are sometimes done in response to certain rumors circulating in the world and done for justice—or made to look as if they were done for justice—one should not give in to such desires. For Seneca says that a man overcome by anger, hatred, or greed sees and hears nothing, does not think or say anything, except through his madness; he pays no heed to his conscience or any danger. And Cato spoke the truth when he said that anger and greed blind a man to such an extent that he does not see the law, but the law sees him very well; that is, he does not see the risk he takes with regard to justice when he translates his evil intentions into deeds. These are horrible faults in those that give themselves over to them, and especially for true princes, not tyrants, who should possess true nobility and to whom Ovid says: "Be victorious over your heart, you man who wants to conquer everything." And similarly Seneca says: "You who want to subdue everything, submit first to reason, and when reason rules you, you will be the ruler; but when your will governs you, you will be ruled over."[2] We will now define what true justice is.

[Chapters 5 to 18 deal with justice and judges. King Charles V again appears as an exemplar who not only was just but also realized that a king cannot govern alone but must surround himself with good counselors. He also must be generous.]

Book 3

[Chapter 1 praises the virtue of clemency in France.]

2. Here She Tells How the People Must Be Part of the Peace

> Mercy and truth are met together; righteousness and peace have kissed each other.
>
> Psalm 85:10

9. Christine means that David gave Uriah a high-ranking but dangerous position in battle; see 2 Samuel 11. For Herod, see Matthew 14:1–11. For Cain, see Genesis 4:1–15. For Joseph, see Genesis 37–45. For Jacob, see Genesis 34. For Ahab and Naboth, see 1 Kings 21.
1. The story of Alexander was known through the twelfth-century *Romance of Alexander*. Roman history was known primarily through a thirteenth-century compilation called the *Faits des Romains* [Deeds of the Romans].
2. All this comes from Christine's source, Brunetto Latini. See his *Li Livres dou tresor*, ed. Francis J. Carmody (Berkeley: University of California Press, 1948), book 2.

> Peace is the perfect product of virtue and the purpose of all labors.
> Peace moves the stars and all earthly things.
>   Prudentius, *Book of the Battle between the Vices and the Virtues*[3]

As we speak of the virtue of clemency we can come to the matter of the capacities and conditions of the people. As far as peace is concerned, we can say that it is an impossibility to keep it when many of them through simplicity, bad advice, or otherwise, follow a bad course, in view of human nature which by itself tends toward all vices when understanding and reason do not prevent it. There is generally not much reason among the lower classes, because it takes much effort to teach virtuous things and the difference between good and evil, and they were not taught all this in their time; and thus one can see quite a few among them who are hardly better than beasts. As for reason, it is necessary. Just as when a good doctor is employed in order to heal the body of a sick man in all its parts and omits to heal the legs or the feet or other small members, one would never call this cure good or the entire body healed. And similarly it is with the universal body politic of this kingdom of which the king is the head;[4] in the cure of the glorious peace we must include with the others the cure belonging to the people, although it is true that they, at the instigation of some of them, unjust and thus deserving of punishment, had received bad counsel (at least a part of them did), foolishly believed it and committed some deeds against your reverence. But nonetheless, for the good of the whole body, the moment of what David said in the quote cited at the beginning in Latin has come: that pity and truth have come together, that justice and peace have kissed each other, which means in this context that although many deeds worthy of punishment have been committed, it is nevertheless fitting that pity should encounter this truth. This means that pity should appeal to the rigor that applies in these matters, and this is why it is said afterward that justice and peace kissed each other. Oh, this kiss should be blessed! And since peace is necessary to us, we can say, following the authority, that peace is the fullness of all virtue and the end and culmination of all our deeds and labors. The stars have their movements regulated by good proportion, concord and peace, and so do the elements and lowly things. For this reason it is obvious that without peace we cannot live properly or according to virtue. Therefore, since all our labors are directed toward peace, as we said, we should make all efforts to preserve it amongst us, reasonable creatures, just as it exists in the other things God has created.

[Chapters 3 to 5 speak of the importance of French unity and the consequences of bad rulership. The next chapters describe the good treatment of

---

3. Prudentius's text, generally referred to as *Psychomachia*, dates from the fourth century. It depicts an allegorical battle between the vices and virtues. The quotation comes from lines 769 and 771.
4. See n. 1 to *The Book of the Body Politic*, p. 202.

a people by its ruler. Christine then addresses herself directly to the people to dissuade them from rebellion. In chapter 11 she argues that common people should not be given public office because they have no experience and can be led like sheep by anyone with evil intentions. They murder and rob people without remorse.]

12. Here She Speaks of the Danger of Giving the Common People More Authority Than They Should Have

Oh noble hearts and simple, beware of treacherous blades.

Ovid, *Fasti* 2.226

A noble prince, says Ovid, should always guard against criminals. For this reason I want to return to the common people. I could endlessly speak about their evil deeds committed in fury, but I do not want to recall them in order to harm them or to put them in the bad graces of the king or you, good prince; nor do I want to accuse them to those who, when in future times these things are forgotten or peace has been made, will read or listen to this book. God knows, my only motivation is to bring peace and all good things and to avoid war. I have written this according to my little understanding in order to demonstrate how such people should be governed with great wisdom so that the dangers I described above or similar ones will not reappear; for a wise man says that he who does not want to get into trouble must have a grip on things.

Certainly, there is no doubt that even among simple artisans there are good people who do not want to rebel because of some rumors they hear, and I know several who were very upset about what happened; we should praise those who listen to good sense. Therefore, for the reasons I laid out in the previous chapter, common people should not hold public office. And if some want to say that the opposite is true because some cities in Italy and elsewhere, such as Bologna and others, are governed by the common people, I respond that they are, but that I have heard nothing to indicate that they are well governed or that they are at peace for very long. And if someone may want to say that in the past Rome governed itself very well without a lord, I say that it was not the common people that governed, but the nobles, just like today in the city of Venice, and they have always done so and with very good rulership. But these were the old families of notable bourgeois in the city, and they call themselves noble and would never admit one of the common people to their councils. Such governments can last for a long time, but I do not think that a wise man would ever approve of one of the commoners. And Catilina, whom Sallust mentions, spoke of this matter.[5] He said that the poor people in the cities always envy the rich, and for that reason they like to rebel and to get rid of the bad people; they want to have new rulers and all sorts

---

5. Also from Brunetto Latini, *Li Livres dou tresor*, book 2. Sallust (86–34 B.C.), Roman politician and historian, who wrote on the conspiracy of Catilina.

of changes. And nothing is ever sufficient for them; how ever good their government is, they always want things in the city to change.

And recent experience teaches us that this is true. For although these people are poor and indigent and own nothing except what they earn in their daily labor, they still always want war, and in particular civil war, so that they can attack the rich people. They see that there are more of them than the rich people and there is nothing else that would give them any authority or, once there is war, the licence to rob and kill. While before they'd be afraid and would hide out in the woods, they now commit their murders and robberies brazenly in public and out in the open against those who are not poor, so that the rich will become poor like them.

There is no greater folly for a prince who wants to be able to rule freely and in peace, if I may say so, than to give permission to the common people to carry arms. And as experience teaches us, whoever does this is like the person who himself cuts the stick with which he will be beaten.[6] I dare say, that if they get used to bearing arms, it will not be easy to keep them from rebelling. And even their lord will be in danger of losing his rule because they are so changeable and always want new things. And a wise duke of Athens knew this well, for when he had barely subjugated the people of Lacedemonia he ordered them to exercise their professions and not to bear arms any more. In view of the reasons listed above, and others that I could mention, I conclude (and perhaps someone wants to correct me) that if a prince does not have enough nobles and soldiers in his country to use in a war, he should rather hire foreign soldiers, as it is done in Italy and some other countries. And some may say the opposite because they believe that native soldiers would be more fierce and proud in the defense of their country and in the support of their lord than would be foreign soldiers. But I say that all this counts for nothing, for as Vegetius says,[7] there is no defense or any other force in war equal to that of the men whose profession is war, that is, excellent fighters. And because common people provide no security whatsoever and will only be interested in their advantage and in looting one should not use them in warfare.

[The next two chapters insist that nobles should always be well trained in arms and remind readers of the recent civil war.]

15. Here She Speaks of the Way in Which a Prince Should Deal with the Common People in Order to Keep Them from Presumption and Grounds for Rebellion

> Only when the desire for different things ends, can enemies become friends.
>
> Seneca

6. See Morawski, *Proverbes antérieurs au XVe siècle* (Paris, 1925), nos. 1154 and 2335.
7. See n. 2, p. 234.

But I want to finish what I began earlier—for sometimes one has to postpone conclusions in order to explain matters more fully—namely about the way a prince should govern in order to keep his people in peace. We can interpret the above-cited authority to mean that evil deeds will not cease until the desire and wishes for certain things come to an end, and then those who were enemies become friends. Certainly the common people have desires for certain things, as we mentioned, but so that their vague desires come to an end and so that the evil deeds of the past will not occur again, it seems good to me that the prince should govern them suitably and with good justice; principally to do his duty toward God but also so that the people should have no reason to grumble and to be malcontent. He should not let them be mistreated or plundered by the military or anyone else; he should defend them diligently against all enemies, just as the good shepherd does for his sheep. He should see to it that nothing is taken from them or their labors accepted without satisfactory payment, for the wise man says, "Do not keep the salary of a laborer from the evening till the next morning so that no curse will harm you; nor should you withhold an extra sum for yourself." The prince should not impose taxes or other charges beyond what is necessary to wage lawful wars; he should keep them in peace and let no one oppress or harm them so that they will have no reason to stir up trouble or to occupy themselves with anything but their labors and their professions. He should be kind and mild in his speech if it happens that they speak to him, and he should favor their just petitions and show no cruelty toward them for he should want them to be treated kindly. And when he walks through the town or elsewhere where they may come to encounter him and greet him, he should salute them with a mild and friendly face.

Further, he should order that they not wear outrageous outfits and only those clothes that are appropriate for their status, without adopting the dress of noblemen, embroidery or emblems, for such pride can be harmful and has perhaps already done some harm.[8] And so that they learn to behave better, he should forbid under the threat of punishment these curses, blasphemy and outrageous swear words using the name of Our Lord. He should forbid this generally so that nobles, common people, and courtiers will all be punished equally. And so that everyone will be appreciated according to his true worth and to avoid any grumbling by the common people, those who misbehave should be punished with moderation. These crazy parties and meetings that take place in various houses without any reason whatsoever should be forbidden. Further, because free time is often the reason why young people get into all kinds of trouble and crazy conspiracies, certain people should be appointed in all justice to look out for and prevent any uproar that may brew in

---

8. Christine addressed this question also in her *Book of the Three Virtues*. For her, the social hierarchy must be safeguarded by appropriate dress. The sumptuary laws of the later Middle Ages were meant to prevent people from wearing too-outrageous costumes.

the town, and they should not tolerate any longer that these idle men-
about-town go about here and there and into the taverns without doing
anything. They should be questioned as to what they are up to, and they
should be imprisoned if they do not go to their jobs on working days.
Likewise, one should forbid these crazy partisan rumors that have circulated—and still do—and that can cause great harm; those that use them
to get back at others should be punished.

In brief, in these general ways and through other good ordinances
that could be applied to these cases the prince can keep his people in
peace to their great advantage, for they would no longer waste their time
as is their habit; rather, everyone would do his appointed job and they
would be content with their prince because he rules them in peace and
good justice, and they could prosper so that they would be in a better
position to help him should the need arise. And like this, the people
would live gloriously under a good ruler.

[Chapters 16 to 18 again present Charles V as the exemplar of the good
king. He loved learning and had translated into French a number of
important texts, such as St. Augustine's *City of God*, Aristotle's *Ethics* and
Politics, and John of Salisbury's *Policraticus*.]

19. Here She Tells of Examples of the Punishment Sent by God to Cruel Princes

> The good ruler is slow to punish and quick to reward. And it grieves
> him if he is forced to be cruel.
>
> Ovid, *Ex ponto* 1.2.121–23

As I explained above, it is therefore advisable for a prince to be mild,
humane, and friendly; cruelty is not suitable for him. And in this, say
the wise men, one sees the difference between a natural prince and a
tyrant. The natural prince moves among his subjects like a father among
his children or like a shepherd who is ready to risk his life in the defense
of his pasture; the tyrant is like the ravishing wolf among sheep. The
authority quoted above says that a prince should not delay, that is, in
meting out punishment, and always be ready, that is, in giving rewards.
And he should be careful that every time he is obliged to be harsh to
someone he should not seem cruel.

[Christine now gives examples from the Bible of the terrible fate that befell
tyrants.]

Nero[9] and others died miserably, and so we can say in conclusion
that such cruel tyrants really persecute themselves in persecuting others,

---

9. Roman emperor from A.D. 54 to 68; he committed suicide when his Praetorian guard revolted
against him. He had his wife and mother murdered; had large parts of Rome burned; and
started the first persecutions of the Christians, blaming them for the fire. It is believed that
among his victims were Saints Peter and Paul.

and they start out on hell in this world, but they would get there in any case! Juvenal says that fear engenders hatred, hatred conspiracy, and conspiracy death. And Horace says about the misery of those who want to make the whole world tremble by their outrageous deeds, that there is no one who lives in greater fear, or with less peace of mind. Since they have done evil to everyone, they trust no one and are always fearful of the traps laid by those they have intimidated by force. And this is why Boethius said: "Do not believe that the man who always has guards with him is powerful, for he fears those that he wants to scare. And this is why it is said of Denis[1] the tyrant that he feared his barber's razor so much that he burnt off his beard himself."

[Chapters 20 and 21 pursue the theme of punished pride. Then Christine turns to the virtue of generosity and the vice of greed. Charles V is again presented as an exemplar. Chapters 32 to 36 deal with the eloquence necessary for a prince. He should be eloquent but not talk too much. Christine then turns to questions of sex or "carnal delights."]

37. Here She Blames Voluptuousness in a Prince and Too Much Abandonment to Carnal Pleasures

> If you devote time to Bacchus and Venus, though you subdue all else, you have come beneath the yoke.
>
> Walter in Alexandreis[2]

In order to treat all things that are suitable for a prince and so that our work should be complete, we shall, in the context of blaming vices and praising virtues, touch in the conclusion of our work on something which, if someone is involved in it, can harm the esteem in which a great lord and any other noble person is held. I mean physical pleasures and everything related to voluptuousness, because the involvement in such activities is vain, illicit, and dishonorable; it endangers and disrupts all the good things in a person who amuses himself with these activities. It does great harm if this vice is within a man who has great governmental duties, such as a prince, for they should give all their care and solicitude to the public domain which they have to maintain well, and it is not an easy job to devote oneself to all the duties this entails.

We can see that this is so when the above-mentioned author addresses Alexander in the Latin words cited earlier and which can equally well apply to all princes: "You who subjugate and rule men, if you give yourself over to wine and luxuriousness you lower yourself." The same goes

---

1. Dionysius the First, tyrant of Syracuse. The story about his fear of barbers is in Brunetto Latini, Li Livres dou tresor 2.302.
2. Walter of Chatillon wrote his Alexandreis between 1176 and 1202. The quotation is from the English translation by R. Telfryn Pritchard (Toronto: Pontifical Institute of Mediaeval Studies, 1986), 40. Bacchus and Venus stand for wine and love, respectively.

for all superfluous physical luxuries, for infinite harm can ensue. I could name any number of examples of various princes and very notable men who in this manner lost soul, body, honor and even their rulership. But I will not elaborate on this, since I have treated this topic already in my *Book of the Body Politic*, also dedicated to you.

[Christine then cites various authorities to confirm the harmful effects of a dissolute life.]

38. On the Same Topic, with Praise of the Order of Marriage

A mind becomes petty and sick through voluptuousness.
                                        Juvenal, *Satires* 13.190

On this same topic, it is not suitable for a prince, who should be grander than anyone else, to get too involved and preoccupied with physical pleasures. And we see that this can be very negative for him, for the Latin cited above says that voluptuousness and sensual delight are a sign of a small and weak heart. And for this reason Virgil says: "Occupy yourselves with great things, you who want to rule." [3]

[Christine cites further authorities to buttress her argument. Finally she turns to the idea of marriage.]

In truth, in order to avoid the inconveniences of sin and in order to appease the flesh when it feels carnal desires there is a licit means. And also so that the human race may continue through rightful generation marriage was instituted, an estate to be honored, and eleven principal reasons for this are is stated in the treasure of a book: [4] the first is that God established marriage; the second because of the dignity of the place were it was established, namely the earthly paradise; the third, because it is an ancient institution; fourth, because Adam and Eve were clean of all sin when God united them; fifth, because God saved the institution of marriage from the deluge through Noah's ark; [5] the sixth reason is that Our Lady was married; the seventh, because Our Lord honored the marriage feast by attending with his mother and disciples the wedding of St. Archdeclin. The eighth reason because He turned water into wine as a sign of the great good that comes from marriage; the ninth, because the children born in marriage are legitimate heirs and without reproach; the tenth, because marriage is one of the seven sacraments of the

---

3. From Brunetto Latini, *Li Livres dou tresor*, book 2.
4. This is a rather roundabout reference to Brunetto Latini's *Li Livres dou tresor*. St. Paul says in 1 Corinthians 7:9 that chastity is best, but that for those who cannot practice abstinence "it is better to marry than to be aflame with passion." On the idea of marriage as a remedy for carnal desires, see Pierre Payer, *The Bridling of Desire: Views of Sex in the Later Middle Ages* (Toronto: University of Toronto Press, 1993).
5. See Genesis 7:1–5, where God orders Noah to take pairs of animals with him in the ark.

Church; and the eleventh, because of the sin one avoids through marriage,[6] and also because many other good and profitable things come to those who live in marriage as they should.

[In chapters 39 to 47 Christine returns to vices such as laziness, flattery, and the virtues of charity and friendship.]

48. The Last Chapter and End of the Book

[Here Christine addresses Louis of Guyenne and hopes he will read and profit from this book.]

Here ends the Book of Peace.

FROM THE LETTER ON THE PRISON OF HUMAN LIFE

[One of the greatest disasters for the French during the Hundred Years' War was the battle of Agincourt on October 25, 1415. In approximately three hours the flower of French chivalry was either killed or imprisoned by the English who now occupied Normandy and Paris. The Burgundians were on the side of the English, while the Armagnacs supported the mad Charles VI. Mary of Berry, to whom Christine addressed the *Letter* (finished on January 20, 1418), had lost a number of family members at the battle. Christine intended her *Letter* as a consolation: earthly life, she insisted, is nothing but a prison, as the twelfth-century religious writer St. Bernard put it. Through death human beings are released from this prison into eternal life. She draws heavily on the Scriptures, the Church Fathers, an author known as Pseudo-Seneca, and many other classical sources.[1]

This is one of Christine's most spiritual and edifying texts, offering philosophical and Christian arguments in order to console grieving ladies, but it is also one where her hopelessness for the situation in France begins to reveal itself. It was that same year, 1418, that Christine had to flee from Paris, never to return.

Translated by Renate Blumenfeld-Kosinski from Christine de Pizan, *The Epistle of the Prison of Human Life with an Epistle to the Queen of France and Lament on the Evils of the Civil War*, ed. and trans. Josette A. Wisman (New York: Garland, 1984).]

Here begins the letter on the prison of human life and the comfort one can find facing the death of friends and patience in adversity.

In order somehow to find a remedy and medicine for the grievous illness and infirmity caused by bitterness of heart and sadness of thought which

6. See n. 4, p. 247.
1. For details see Wisman's edition, xxvii–xxx.

could stem the flood of the tears—unprofitable to either body or soul—
which has flown and still does flow (which is a great pity) among
queens, princesses, baronesses, ladies, and maidens of the noble royal
blood of France, and more generally among so many honorable women
struck by this pestilence in our French kingdom, by so many deaths or
captivity of those close to them, such as husbands, children, brothers,
uncles, cousins, and other relatives and friends, some of them killed in
battle, others dead from natural causes in their beds, and by so many
other misfortunes and misadventures that have unjustly occurred for a
while: I am thinking whether it might be helpful to propose or recall
anything that may have some use or value in bringing comfort. Among
those who mourn for these reasons are you, most honored princess, my
lady Marie of Berry, Duchess of Bourbon and Auvergne.[1] To my sorrow,
you have not been exempted. Because of the merits of your generous
charity which you extended to me in this time of great affliction, where
friends have failed me and your help has aided me greatly in my humble widowed state, may God reward you for it; and because I am also
grateful for other good deeds on your part and desirous to serve you in
any way possible, this letter of mine will be addressed to you, the first of
the princesses of this realm (although this letter was first suggested to
me by someone else,[2] and I hope that it will also be of value to all those
who have suffered from similar troubles.

[Christine proposes to the recently bereaved Marie of Berry, and to other
women similarly saddened, to cull stories and sayings from history and the
Scriptures that may comfort them.]

As to my first point, most noble lady, since words coming from me may
not be strong enough in face of your great sorrow, in showing you and
reminding you of the subject of patience, may it please you to give
credence to the Holy Scriptures and to what the glorious doctors and
many wise authors have said: we must have patience in face of the adversities Fortune metes out by various means and in view of the glory and
blessedness of those who die in grace. Among those who died well, my
most revered lady, we can, by the evidence and true beliefs of the Catholic faith count those above-mentioned men whom you mourn with natural fraternal and filial pity. For this reason I can ask you the following
question: what would you choose? Should these men still be among the
living in this world as long as you live or even longer but destined to be
imprisoned for the rest of their lives and be in mortal danger every day,
spending their lives in various troubles, risks, dangers, and torments? Or
should each one of them be elected emperor of a world where it is

---

1. Mary's husband and son were taken prisoner. Her father, John, duke of Berry, died in 1416.
   Three cousins were killed at Agincourt, while another was taken prisoner.
2. Perhaps John, duke of Berry, as Suzanne Solente suggests in *Bibliothèque de l'Ecole des
   Chartes* 84 (1924), 270–71.

possible they should never die but rather live in all prosperity, power, joy, tranquillity, and peace? Certainly, my lady, I do not doubt that you would prefer for them the way you would choose for yourself: that is, the second of the two choices. Oh, revered lady, shall we not believe the Holy Scriptures and believe in the true God, without which faith no one can please God or be saved, as St. Paul says.[3]

And on this topic St. Bernard says that this mortal life can be figured for all of us by a prison,[4] for just as the enclosure of a prison holds back the prisoner so tightly that he cannot use his will or accomplish his desires, but rather must generally do the opposite, so the rational soul, which is the noblest part of man, without which the body is nothing but dust and rot, is held a bound prisoner in the body as long as it is in it; it is so constrained and hindered by the weight and coarseness of this vessel that it does not have the power, except in a very small way, to make use of its own inclinations and desires, but rather has to assent most of the time to the opposite of what it wants. And in this context the wise Albert[5] says: when a man dies his soul is set free and delivered from prison. So it is true that every man alive in this mortal world — where we are all equal, whether high-born, middle or lower class — must consider himself in this respect a prisoner. Now it remains to be seen whether in this prison any man, no matter what his estate,[6] can be assured of all comfort, and run no risk. Oh, how great would it be to possess rulership, power, fame, riches, and how wonderful it would be to acquire them, if by these means we could avoid and escape from the mortal dangers and various snares of false Fortune and from the harsh torments and painful trials the world offers us! But whether worldly greatness can serve this purpose or not, we can learn from many examples, and here are some of them.

Alas, what was his great power worth to Alexander[7] under whose hand the entire world trembled? Was it of use to him when the traitors and even his own servants quickly killed him with poison? His joy at the end of his great achievement of conquering the world was quickly over, for it lasted not three days. And what shall we say of Julius Caesar? Did he put his efforts to good use when, after so many labors and perils, having suffered wounds and troubles in many diverse battles, he conquered a great part of the world? When Fortune placed him on top of her wheel and when he thought he could triumphantly reign in peace as emperor, he would hardly have believed that any man or Fortune would harm

---

3. Hebrews 11:6: "But without faith it is impossible to please him: for he that cometh to God must believe that he is, and that he is a rewarder of them that diligently seek him."
4. In *De virtute oboedientiae et septem ejus gradibus* [On the virtue of obedience and its seven levels]. See Wisman, p. 7, n. 5.
5. Albert the Great, thirteenth-century theologian, who among many other texts wrote *De arte moriendi* [On the art of dying]. See Caroline Walker Bynum, *The Resurrection of the Body in Western Christianity, 200–1336* (New York: Columbia University Press, 1995), chap. 6.
6. On social classes in the afterlife see Bynum, *The Resurrection of the Body*, chap. 6.
7. Alexander the Great (356–323 B.C.), king of Macedon and conqueror of much of Asia.

him, who had escaped so many perils. But was he not quickly stabbed
to death by his own citizens in his private council among his barons?

* * *

In brief, I could recall many examples of various dangers and troublesome events which always occur in this dolorous prison of human life I
described above. And, what is even more important, just as when the
weather is stormy and a tempest runs through the air, strengthened by
various winds, it will more likely encounter and beat down the tops of
high towers and shake them than the floors in the middle and at the
bottom. Similarly, the blasts of Fortune, when she is against someone,
bear down more dangerously on highly placed people than on those of
the middle and lower ranks. And for this reason Boethius[8] says in his
second book that bad Fortune is more profitable than good Fortune, for
good Fortune blinds with the prosperity she gives and makes people feel
secure, but perverse Fortune makes clear the truth of her mutability and
that one must not trust her.

[The lengthy letter continues to speak of the brevity of life and the joys of
Paradise, given to those who have died well and escaped from the prison of
human life. To support her points, Christine calls on both Christian authors
and pagan philosophers.]

The End and Conclusion

* * *

My revered lady, it seems to me that I have fulfilled my promise to
demonstrate to you the difference between the present life and the life
those who have died in grace enjoy in the other world. In conclusion I
repeat that through the above-mentioned proofs you can see clearly that
there are no grounds to mourn or complain about the death of your
friends who died by God's grace and who, as I believe, ended their lives
in salvation. They can profit more from alms, prayers, and good deeds
than from your tears. Consider the great good they may expect, namely
the glory of Heaven, to which God will lead them and also you, God
who is the beginning and creator of all things, and who may protect
you!

Written in Paris by me, Christine de Pizan, your humble and obedient servant, who humbly begs you not to take it amiss or think less of
me because you have not received this letter from me sooner. May your
kindness receive it with pleasure; my excuses for having taken so long
(though I had thought of sending it to you for a long time) are various
great worries and my troubled heart which, because of the many
unpleasant things that have happened to me since I began this letter

8. In his *Consolation of Philosophy* (sixth century); see also n. 8, p. 38.

long ago, have hindered my poor understanding with all kinds of sad imaginings and thoughts, so that it was not in my power to finish it earlier than on this twentieth day of January, 1417.[9]

THE TALE OF JOAN OF ARC

[After Christine fled Paris she took refuge in an abbey, most likely the abbey of Poissy, where her daughter was a nun. Her son, Jean de Castel, died probably in 1425, and around that time Christine wrote a religious meditation, *Les Heures de contemplacion sur la Passion de Nostre Seigneur* [The hours of contemplation on our Lord's Passion]. But toward the end of her life, Christine had occasion to rejoice, for it seemed that salvation had come to France in the shape of a simple young girl from Lorraine, Joan of Arc.

Born around 1412 in the little village of Domremy, Joan began hearing the voices of saints Michael, Catherine, and Margaret when she was thirteen, urging her to save France. In 1429 she managed to persuade Robert de Baudricourt, captain of the royal garrison, to support her cause and provide an escort to the dauphin's court. She was examined by theologians and then given the command of an army that managed to raise the siege of Orleans in May 1429. On July 17 she succeeded in having the dauphin crowned as King Charles VII in Rheims. Only two weeks later Christine composed her *Tale*. But Joan's good fortune did not last. After the unsuccessful attack on Paris in September 1429 and a truce with the Burgundians, Charles abandoned Joan when she was taken prisoner in May 1430 and sold by the Burgundians to the English. Her male dress and her claims to divine inspiration provided the pretext for her trial on charges of witchcraft. She was finally burned at the stake on May 30, 1431.[1] In the nineteenth century she was rediscovered as a French national heroine, and in 1920 she was canonized.

Christine probably died before Joan's fall from grace and could thus celebrate her success at the moment of her greatest triumph. In the figure of Joan, two of Christine's aspirations found their fulfillment: a woman, worthy of living in the City of Ladies, has come forward to drive the English from France and unite the country.[2] Christine saw Joan's mission as ordained by Providence and evoked various prophecies that over the centuries had predicted the coming of a saviorlike figure. The celebration of Joan's accomplishments was a fitting end to Christine's career.

Translated by Renate Blumenfeld-Kosinski from Christine de Pisan, *Le Ditié de Jehanne d'Arc*, ed. Angus J. Kennedy and Kenneth Varty (Oxford, UK: Society for the Study of Mediaeval Literatures and Language, 1977).][3]

---

9. I.e., 1418 by modern dating; see n. 1 to the headnote, p. 109.
1. Twenty-five years later her sentence was annulled by Pope Calixtus III. For her biography see Marina Warner, *Joan of Arc: The Image of Female Heroism* (New York: Knopf, 1981). Her trial records were edited by Jules Quicherat in *Procès de condamnation et de réhabilitation de Jeanne d'Arc, dite la Pucelle*, 5 vols. (Paris: Renouard, 1841–49).
2. See Kevin Brownlee, "Structures of Authority in Christine de Pizan's *Ditié de Jehanne d'Arc*" on p. 371.
3. Christine wrote this piece as a poem, though it has been translated here as prose.

1

I, Christine, who have wept for eleven years in a closed abbey, where I have lived ever since Charles (what a strange thing!), the king's son, fled, if I dare say it, in haste from Paris,[1] enclosed here because of this treachery, I begin now for the first time to laugh.

2

I begin to laugh frankly with joy because winter is departing when I used to stay sadly in my cage. But now that the good weather is back . . .[2] I will change my language from weeping into singing. I have well endured my share.

3

In 1429 the sun began to shine again. It brings back the good new season which we had not really seen for a long time, which made many people live in sorrow. But I no longer grieve over anything, for now I see what I desire.

4

But things have changed from great sorrow to new joy since the time I came here to stay, and, thank God, the lovely season I so desired, the one called spring where everything renews itself, has turned dry land green.

5

All this because the cast-out child of the legitimate king of France,[3] who has suffered for a long time great troubles and who now approaches, rose up like one who goes to prime, coming as a crowned king, in wonderful and great power, wearing spurs of gold.

6

Now let us celebrate our king! May he be welcomed on his return! Rejoice at his noble appearance, let us all go, great and small—may no one hold back—and joyfully greet him, praising God who has protected him and loudly shout "Noel."

1. When the Burgundians took Paris in 1418, the dauphin fled; see also p. xiv.
2. At this point there is a gap in the manuscript.
3. In the 1420 treaty of Troyes, Charles VI had to disinherit his son and recognize Henry V, husband of his daughter Catherine, as the heir to the French throne.

7

But now I want to tell how God has done all this by His grace. I pray to Him to give me guidance so that I won't omit anything. This should be told everywhere, for it is worthy of memory and of being written down—no matter who may be displeased—in chronicles and history books!

8

Now listen, throughout the world, to something more marvelous than anything! See if God, in whom all grace abounds, does not support in the end that which is right. This fact is noteworthy, in view of the case at hand! May it be of value to those who are disappointed, those whom Fortune has beaten down.

9

And note that no one should be dismayed by misfortune, when he sees himself unjustly despised and attacked by everyone! See how Fortune, who has harmed so many people, is always changing. For God, who takes a stand against all wrong deeds, raises up those in whom hope lives on.

10

Who, then, has seen something so extraordinary occur—which should be noted and remembered in all regions—that France, who in everyone's opinion was defeated, has, by divine command, changed from evil to such great good,

11

and truly through such a miracle that, if the matter were not so well-known and obvious in every way, no one would believe it? This is well worth remembering: that God has wished to bestow His grace on France—and this is true—through a tender virgin.

12

Oh, what an honor given to the French crown by this divine proof! For by the grace He gives it it is obvious that he supports it and that more than anywhere else He finds faith in the royal estate of which I read—and there is nothing new in this—that the Lilies of France never erred in the faith.

13

And you Charles, French king, seventh of that noble name, who waged a great war before things changed for the better for you: But now, by God's grace, see how your renown is exalted by the Maid, who has subjugated your enemies under your flag—and this is something new—

14

in a short time; people thought that it was impossible that you would ever get back your country which you were losing. Now it is clearly yours, for against all those who harmed you, you have recovered it! And through the clever Maid, who thank God has done her share!

15

I firmly believe that God would not bestow on you this grace if it were not ordained by Him that you should, in the course of time, bring to fruition and a good end a great and solemn task, and if it were not destined for you to be the leader of the greatest events.

[Christine pursues the idea that there was a prophecy predicting the current events and appeals to the king to be worthy of his great mission. She thanks God for His mercy and then turns to the maid, Joan of Arc.]

21

And you blessed Maid, should you be forgotten in all this? For God has honored you so much that you undid the rope that held France tightly bound. Could one praise you enough when you have given peace to this country humiliated by war?

22

You, Joan, were born at a propitious hour, blessed be He who created you! Maid, ordained by God, in whom the Holy Spirit (in whom there was and is the greatest generosity with noble gifts) poured His great grace and never refused any of your requests, how can we ever reward you?

23

How could one say more of anyone else or of the great deeds of the past? Moses, on whom God in His generosity bestowed many blessings and virtues, by a miracle led his people out of Egypt, without tiring of it. In the same way you have led us from evil, elected Maid!

24

When we reflect on your person, you who are a young maid, to whom God has given the strength and power to be a champion who gives to France her breast of peace and sweet nourishment and cast down the rebels. See how this goes beyond nature!

25

For if God performed so many miracles through Joshua[4] who conquered so many places and rousted so many enemies—he was a strong and powerful man! But after all, a woman, a simple shepherdess, braver that any man ever was in Rome! For God, this was an easy thing to do.

26

But for us, we never heard tell of such a great marvel, for all the brave men from the past cannot measure up in prowess against this woman who strives to cast out our enemies. But this is God's doing who counseled her, who from Him received more courage than any man.

27

We make much of Gideon,[5] who was a simple laborer, so the story goes, God made him fight, none could hold out against him, he conquered everything. But whatever orders He gave him, He never did such a clear miracle as He did in our case.

28

I have learned about Esther, Judith, and Deborah,[6] worthy ladies, through whom God restored His people which was so oppressed, and I also learned about many others who were brave, but there was none through whom He has performed a greater miracle than through the Maid.

29

She was sent by divine command, guided by God's angel to the king, in his support. Her deeds are not an illusion, for she was well

4. He vanquished the Amorites when the sun miraculously stood still (Joshua 10:12–14).
5. See Judges 6–7.
6. As Kennedy and Varty point out, Joan was often linked to these Old Testament heroines, for example, by Jean Gerson in his text about Joan, *De quadam puella* [About a certain maid], written in the spring of 1429 in support of Joan's mission. They suggest that the *Tale* may have been inspired by Judges 5, the "Song of Deborah"; see *Le Ditié*, 67. Christine also mentioned these women in the *Book of Fortune's Transformation* and the *City of Ladies*.

tested in a council (we conclude that a thing is proved by its effect),

30

and before one wanted to believe her, and before it became known that God sent her to the king she was led before clerks and wise men and was well examined to see whether she spoke the truth.[7] But one found in history books that she was destined for these deeds.

31

For more than five hundred years ago, Merlin, the Sibyl, and Bede[8] foresaw her in their minds and put her into their writings and made prophecies about her as the remedy for France. They said she would carry the banner in French wars and they exactly predicted her deeds.

32

And her life in beauty, by my faith, shows that she is in God's grace, and therefore one accords more faith to her deeds. For whatever she does, she always has God before her eyes, whom she calls to, serves and prays to in deed and word; nowhere does she let her faith decrease.

33

Oh, how clear was this at the siege of Orléans[9] where her power first appeared! No miracle, I believe, was ever clearer, for God helped His people so much that the enemies were as helpless as dead dogs. There they were captured and put to death.

34

Oh, what an honor to the female sex! That God loves it is clear with all these wretched people and traitors who laid waste the whole kingdom cast out and the realm elevated and restored by a woman—something a hundred thousand men could not have done! Before, one would not have believed it possible.

7. Joan was interrogated during March and April 1429 in Poitiers.
8. To link these three prophets may appear strange to a modern reader, since Merlin was a magician connected to the Arthurian tradition, Bede an English historian (d. 735), and the Sibyl one of the prophetic women of antiquity. But in the Middle Ages the three were often linked. At the time, their prophecies were interpreted as referring to Joan of Arc. For details see Kennedy and Varty, Le Ditié, 68–69, and Andrew Lang, The Maid of France (London: Longmans Green, 1909).
9. It was raised May 8, 1429.

35

A young girl of sixteen years (is this not something beyond nature?), to whom arms seem weightless, she seems to have been brought up for this, she is so strong and hardy. And the enemies flee before her, not one can last in front of her. She does this, with many eyes looking on,

36

and rids France of her enemies, recapturing castles and towns. Never was there such great strength, not in a hundred or a thousand men. And she is the supreme leader of our brave and skilled people. Neither Hector nor Achilles[1] had such strength! But all this God does who guides her.

37

And you, trusty men-at-arms who do the deeds and prove yourselves good and loyal, one should certainly mention you (you will be praised for it in all countries!) and speak of you above all else, and of your courage,

38

you who in such harsh pain risk blood, body, and life for justice and dare to go forward in such great peril. Be constant, for I promise you, for this you will receive glory and praise in heaven. For I dare say, whoever fights for justice will win Paradise.

39

And so you English, lower your horns, for you will never find good game! Don't carry on with your nonsense in France! You are check mated, something you wouldn't have thought possible recently when you seemed so threatening; but then you were not yet on the path where God cuts down the proud.

40

You thought you had already conquered France, and that she would be yours forever. Things have turned out differently, you false people! You'll have to beat your drums elsewhere if you do not want to taste death like your companions whom the wolves may well devour, for they lie dead in the fields.

---

1. Heroes of the Trojan War.

41

And may it be known that she will cast down the English, there will be no getting up, for this is the will of God who hears the voices of the good people whom they wanted to harm! The blood of those forever dead cries out against them. God will no longer stand for this, but condemn them as evil—this is decided.

42

In Christendom and the Church harmony will reign through her. She will destroy the unbelievers one talks about and the heretics with their vile ways,[2] for thus it is prophesied; she will have no pity for any place where one speaks ill of God.

43

She will destroy the Saracens, by conquering the Holy Land.[3] There she will lead Charles, whom God may protect! Before he dies he will make this trip, he is the one who will conquer it. There she will end her life, and both will gain glory. There things will be fulfilled.

44

Therefore, above all the brave men of the past she must wear the crown, for her deeds show clearly that God has given her more courage than all those men one talks about. And she has not finished yet! I believe that she is God's gift to those of us on earth, so that through her deeds peace may be made.

45

And destroying the English is the least of her worries, for her desires lie rather elsewhere: to guard against the destruction of the Faith. As for the English, whether one laughs or cries about it, they are done for. One will mock them in times to come. They have been vanquished!

2. Christine writes in the aftermath of the Great Schism (1378–1417), during which two popes had reigned and had thus divided Europe. Johan Hus was burned as a heretic at the Council of Constance in 1415. Christine probably refers to his followers, the Hussites.
3. Joan seems to have had plans for a crusade. In two letters, to the king of England and to the duke of Burgundy, she spoke of fighting the Saracens. To the duke she suggested that it would be more useful to make peace with the French king and fight the Saracens than continue the internal strife. For details, see Kennedy and Varty, *Le Ditié*, 70.

46

And all you lowly rebels who make common cause with them,[4] now you can see that you should have gone forward rather than backward and become the serfs of the English. Watch out that nothing else will happen to you (for you have been tolerated long enough), and think well about the end result!

47

Don't you realize, you blind people, that God has a hand in this? Those who don't see this are truly stupid, for how could this Maid have been sent to us in this way, she who strikes all of you down dead? You do not have sufficient strength! Do you want to go into combat against God?

48

Has she not led the king with her hand to his coronation? Greater things were not done before Acre.[5] There as well, were many obstacles. But in spite of everyone he was received there gloriously and duly anointed, and there he heard mass.

49

With great triumph and display of power was Charles crowned at Rheims. In the year 1429, without a doubt, he was there safe and sound, in the midst of many men-at-arms and barons, right on the seventeenth day of July. His sojourn there was five days,

50

and he stayed with the little Maid. As he returns through his lands, no city, castle or small town remains unconquered. Whether he is loved or hated, whether the inhabitants are overwhelmed or reassured, they all surrender. No need to attack, they fear his power so much!

[Stanzas 51 and 52 emphasize the pointlessness of trying to resist the maid's assault.]

---

4. I.e., the Burgundians.
5. Acre was captured in 1191 by the French king Philip Augustus and the English Richard the Lionheart during the third crusade.

53

I don't know if Paris will hold up[6] (for they have not arrived there yet), nor whether it is prepared for the Maid. But if it makes her its enemy I'm afraid she will attack it harshly, as she has done elsewhere. If they resist for an hour, or even half an hour, they will be in trouble, I believe,

54

for [the king] will enter it—whether they like it or not! The Maid has promised him that much. Paris, do you think the Burgundians will keep him from entering? They won't, for he does not present himself as their enemy. No one has the power to prevent it, and you and your presumption will be subdued!

55

Oh, Paris, you have received bad advice! Foolish inhabitants without confidence! Would you rather be cast out than make peace with your prince? If you don't watch out your great contrariness will surely destroy you! You'd be much better off if you humbly begged for mercy.[7] You are making a mistake!

56

I am speaking about the bad [inhabitants], for there are also many good ones, I have no doubt. But they don't dare to speak out. I am sure that it displeases them that one has cast down their prince like that. These people will not have deserved the punishment Paris is heading for, where many will lose their lives.

57

And you, all you rebel towns, and you people who have rejected your lord, you men and women who have renounced him for another, may everything be settled in peace, with you seeking his forgiveness. For if you are subdued by force, his generosity will come too late for you.

6. Paris was then in the hands of the English and the Burgundians.
7. As it turned out, the attack on Paris (September 8, 1429) did not succeed.

58

And to avoid killing and wounding people he waits as long as he can, for it saddens him to spill blood. But, finally, if people won't give up peacefully what is rightfully his, if he recovers it by force and bloodshed, he does well.

59

Alas, he is so generous that he wants to pardon everyone. And the Maid, following God's commands, makes him do this. Give yourselves and your hearts to him as loyal Frenchmen! And when the news are spread, you will not be blamed by anyone.

60

I pray to God that He will put it in your hearts to act this way, so that the cruel tempest of these wars will be obliterated, and that you can spend your lives in peace, under your supreme ruler, and that you may never offend him, and that he may be a good lord to you. Amen.

61

This poem was finished by Christine in the above-mentioned year 1429, on the day that ends July. But I understand that some people will not be satisfied with its contents, for if one's head is lowered and one's eyes are heavy one cannot look at the light.

Here ends a most beautiful poem written by Christine.

CRITICISM

JACQUELINE CERQUIGLINI

The Stranger †

Christine de Pizan is not the first woman poet of the French Middle Ages, but she could well be, in a strict sense, the first woman writer, the first to have written professionally, always reflecting on her profession. Christine de Pizan made herself into a writer of her own volition, motivated initially by something that was lacking in her life and that in the course of her life took on different aspects and realized itself in various specific ways. Indeed, it is striking to observe how her writing is constructed based on an experience, how, laying claim to this link between writing and feeling, she transforms an event into a text, the negative into the positive, how she in effect rewrites her life as a book. Does she not say in the *Livre de la Mutacion de Fortune* [Book of Fortune's Transformation],[1] rethinking and commenting on the proverb "bad luck is good for something":

> For this reason it is right to argue
> That bad luck is sometimes a good thing,
> For it always teaches you something.

The daughter of the Bolognese astrologer is the writer of distance, of overcome distance: distance from her mother tongue, her country, from others, from herself. I believe that it is this concept that allows us to understand the portrait she sketches of herself as a writer.

Christine de Pizan comes from elsewhere: first of all, from another language. She arrives at the French court at the age of four, and French is the language of her symbolic father who, as she says at the end of her *Livre des fais et bonnes moeurs du sage roy Charles V* [Book of the deeds and good conduct of the wise king Charles V],[2] has "nourished her with his bread." We note that this "father" is very interested in questions of translation, in particular that from Latin to French, and that Christine several times analyzes the motivations that push him into commissioning such works: "Because he had less command of Latin than French, perhaps because of the force of its subtle terminology, he had several theological works of Saint Augustine and other Doctors of the Church translated."[3] Translation, or "translacion" as she calls it, is not a neutral subject for Christine. She will never write in Italian, but her native

---

† First published in *Revue des langues romanes*, 1988. Translated with permission by Renate Blumenfeld-Kosinski.
1. *Le Livre de la Mutacion de Fortune*, ed. Suzanne Solente, 4 vols. (Paris: Picard: 1959–1966); vol. 1 (1950), 11, 43–46.
2. Ed. Suzanne Solente, 2 vols. (Paris: Champion, 1936 and 1940), pp. 437–44. Rept. Geneva: Slatkine, 1977. Quote in vol. 2, p. 193.
3. *Livre des fais et bonnes meurs*, vol. 2, p. 13. See also the chapter devoted to Charles V's love of books and to "the beautiful translations he commissioned" (vol. 2, pp. 42–46).

language exists within her like a source or a potential resource. One knows of her admiration for Dante, "Dante of Florence, the valiant poet."[4] Thanks to the studies on Christine's Italian culture we can understand better and better her direct or indirect knowledge of works like those of Boccaccio, Petrarch, and Francesco da Barberino.[5] The biographic event which at first was significant only in the constitution of her psyche is taken up by Christine and elevated to the rank of a literary event and presented as a "translacion." Christine transforms the anecdote into a design for her life and into her destiny.

Born in Italy like Minerva in the euhemeristic interpretations, she will be a new Minerva: "Oh Minerva, goddess of arms and chivalry! . . . I am like you an Italian woman."[6] Having come from Italy to France, she embodies, through this trajectory, the movement of the *translatio studii*[7] from the east to the west. She will be, must be, knowledge in movement. From this perspective, we must keep track of one particular female figure in Christine de Pizan's works: that of Carmenta. Having come from Greece to Italy *(translatio)*, a founder of a city, bringer of civilization, Carmenta, whose name means song, "carmen," invents Latin writing.[8] Christine de Pizan as well, playing as she does with song (that is, lyric poetry) and didacticism, invents a kind of writing, that of women, also new, following upon the writing of the mother country, Italy. Christine perceives very well the strangeness of this new place of writing, the place of women: first of all through the denial that her writings attract at first. Thus she recalls in the *Avision Christine* [Christine's vision] the remarks Lady Opinion made when speaking of her works: "For there are some who say that clerks or monks have forged your works and that they could not issue from a female sensibility."[9] Further, through her very success, which she attributes less to the intrin-

---

4. *Le Livre de la Mutacion de Fortune*, ed. Solente, vol. 2, ll. 4,645–46. On the relationship between Christine de Pizan and Dante see entries numbered 155 to 165 in Angus J. Kennedy, *Christine de Pizan: A Bibliographical Guide* (London: Grant and Cutler, 1984), pp. 43–45.

5. For some recent studies see Carla Bozzolo, "Il *Decameron* come fonte del *Livre de la Cité des dames* di Christine de Pizan," in *Miscellanea di studi e ricerche sul Quattrocento francese*, ed. Franco Simone (Turin: Giappichelli, 1967), pp. 3–24; Liliane Dulac, "Inspiration mystique et savoir politique: les conseils aux veuves chez Francesco da Barberino et chez Christine de Pizan," dans *Mélanges à la memoire de Franco Simone: France et Italie dans la culture euro-péenne, vol. 1: Moyen Age et Renaissance* (Geneva: Slatkine, 1980), pp. 113–141; on the Italianisms of Christine de Pizan see the paragraph Solente devotes to this question in her study of Christine in *Histoire littéraire de la France*, vol. 40, *Suite du quatorzième siecle* (Paris: Imprimerie Nationale, 1974), p. 418.

6. *Livre des fais d'armes et de chevalerie*, Bibliotheque nationale, ms. fr. 603, fol. 2v. [The abbreviation means French manuscript number 603. Euhemerus, an ancient Greek writer, interpreted the myths as historical events, hence the term "euhemeristic interpretations." Editor]

7. A reference to the transfer of learning from Greece to Rome to France. [Editor]

8. See *Le Livre de la Cité des Dames*, 2 vols., ed. M. C. Curnow, Ph.D. dissertation Vanderbilt University, 1975, vol. 2, pp. 735–39. For example, pp. 735–37: "This lady left her country because of certain changes that happened in her land. . . . She worked and studied so hard that she invented letters quite different from those of other nations: that is, a.b.c. and the structure of Latin." [All translations from this text are by the editor.]

9. Ed. Sister M. L. Towner (Washington: The Catholic University of America, 1932), p. 143.

sic quality of her works than to the strangeness of this kind of writing coming from a woman.[1]

Finally, a third biographical element is taken up by Christine to transform it into an element for the construction of her writerly personality: her loneliness as a widow. In this work of mourning there are two aspects that make her take up her pen: a folding in on herself, a retreat, and a transformation: socially speaking, she becomes a man. Christine evokes this alchemy in the *Livre de la Mutacion de Fortune*. There she presents the death of her husband allegorically as the death at sea of the "captain of her ship." At the end of the prologue she writes:

> I will tell you how I who
> Speaks to you, became from a woman a man
> Through Fortune who wanted it thus;
> She transformed my body and my will
> Into a perfect natural man. (ll. 141–45).

Through the first attitude, that of retreat, Christine makes herself into a stranger to others and creates the conditions that make her writing possible in its specific variations. We should note that through this process she meets up with one of the tendencies that characterize literary creation in the fourteenth and fifteenth centuries. The author poses as a writer who needs solitude for his creations or else he justifies the fact that he writes because of his solitude. The bustling of the courts, social intercourse hinder his creation. Guillaume de Machaut affirms this in his *Voir Dit* [True Tale] in the form of an excuse he makes after being reproached by his lady:

> My lord the Duke of Bar and several other lords were at the house; there was so much coming and going, and I went to sleep so late and got up so early, that I could do nothing about your book, not even a little, which weighs heavily on me.[2]

The author of *La Cour de May* [The May Court] suggests this as well. The figure of courtesy speaks to the poet as follows:

> Go and begin your ballads,
> It is time to get on with it;
> We will leave you all alone here.[3]

Similarly, the author of the *Pastoralet* [Pastoral] remarks on the decision of the shepherds who take part in a competition of writing rondels:

1. *L'Avision Christine*, pp. 164–65.
2. Guillaume de Machaut, *Le Livre du Voir-Dit*, ed. Paulin Paris (Paris: Société des bibliophiles françois, 1875), letter 35, p. 262. I cite from the forthcoming edition by Paul Imbs. [De Machaut (1300–1377) was a famous poet and composer. Editor]
3. *La Cour de May* in *Oeuvres de Froissart. Poésies*, ed. Auguste Scheler, vol. 3 (Brussels: Devaux, 1872), ll. 1551–53. [Jean Froissart (ca. 1337–after 1404) was a historian and poet acquainted with Christine. Editor]

> In order to work better and be quiet,
> The shepherds went off by themselves and withdrew.[4]

All the prisoners whom their confinement pushes toward writing emphasize this catalyst represented by their solitude in order to justify their entry into literature. From Jean de Garencières the Young to Jean Regnier or Geoffroy de Charny:[5]

> If you are imprisoned you are a locked-up man, . . .
> Then you can compose ballads, rondels, and songs,
> For you will have little else to do.

The most beautiful example, and also the richest and most complex, is certainly that of Charles d'Orléans.[6] Left "all alone," Christine de Pizan gladly puts herself into a cage in order to shed her old feathers. This is the transformation prison causes in those it holds, whether they are human beings or birds. Let us recall the words of the lady whose lover is a prisoner of the Turks in the *Livre du Dit de Poissy* [Book of the Tale of Poissy]:[7]

> For when I think of the harsh prison,
> Where my love has been kept in moulting
> for many a season.

Let us also think of the beginning of the *Livre des Trois Vertus* [Book of the three virtues]:[8]

> "And just like the wise bird catcher readies his cage before he catches any birds. . . ."

This is how the three virtues, Reason, Rectitude, and Justice, think of the *Cité des Dames* [City of Ladies] constructed by Christine: the creation of another place, both protected and protecting.

She is also a stranger to others in her mourning:

> I was disconcerted by this sharp pain
> And became a recluse,
> Beaten down, mournful, alone, and weary,

she confides in the *Livre du Chemin de long estude* [The Path of long study].[9] Christine de Pizan becomes a prisoner of herself, of her *estude* [learning or study], in the two senses that the medieval language assigns

---

4. *Le Pastoralet*, ed. Joel Blanchard (Paris: Presses Universitaires de France, 1983), ll. 447–49.
5. See Arthur Piaget, "Ballades de Guillebert de Lannoy et de Jean de Werchin," *Romania* 26 (1897): 324–68, specifically p. 325. Jean Regnier, *Les Fortunes et Adversitez*, ed. Eugénie Droz (Paris: Champion, 1923). *Le Livre de Messire Geoffroi de Charny*, ed. A. Piaget, *Romania* 26 (19897): 394–411, ll. 244–45 and 249–51.
6. The son of Louis d'Orléans and one of Christine's patrons (1394–1465). He was one of the best known poets of the late Middle Ages. [Editor]
7. *Oeuvres poétiques de Christine de Pisan*, 3 vols., ed. Maurice Roy (Paris: Didot, 1886–96), vol. 2, ll. 1886–88.
8. Ed. Charity Cannon Willard (Paris: Champion, 1989).
9. Ed. Robert Püschel (Berlin: Hettler, 1887; rept. Geneva: Slatkine, 1974), ll. 119–21.

to this word. She is a prisoner of the material place, her cell—this is the beginning of the *Livre de la Cité des Dames* [1]—where she locks herself in and which is evoked so frequently in the illustrations to her works: she is a prisoner of her desire for knowledge. She presents herself like this in the *Avision:*

> Then I closed my doors, that is, my senses, so that they would not wander toward exterior things and snatched up these beautiful books and volumes of tales so that I could make up for some of my past losses. [2]

Christine closes her senses, shuts out the outside world, but she does so in order to garner new knowledge which her status as woman had kept from her, [3] the knowledge of the clerks, given by books: "I can say truly that there is nothing I love more than learning and a solitary life," she notes in a letter to Master Pierre Col, [4] and she elaborates on this in the *Livre de la Mutacion de Fortune:*

> I have chosen for all my joy
> (no matter what else there may be), such is mine,
> Peace, voluntary solitude,
> And a withdrawn and solitary life. (ll. 23632–636).

Through this devotion to learning, this bulimic, even man-eating relationship to knowledge, Christine takes the place of dead men, of her fathers, all learned and wise men: Charles V, the revered king; Thomas, the admired father; Etienne, the beloved husband. Christine engineers her transformation. She thus becomes, as she indicates indirectly in the

1. Ed. Curnow, p. 616: "These are my habits and the way I spend my life: studying literature. One day, doing just that, I was sitting in my study surrounded by several volumes on a variety of topics." From these first lines Christine shows herself barricaded behind her books. See also the end of her letter to Eustache Morel, that is, Eustache Deschamps, where Christine notes: "Written all alone in my study" (ed. *Oeuvres poétiques*, ed. Maurice Roy, vol. 2, l. 205) and the beginning of the *Livre du Chemin de long Estude:* "One day I joyfully retired into a little study" (ed. Püschel, ll. 171–73). [For the letter to Morel, see p. 109. Editor]
2. Christine already mentioned this closing of the doors represented by the five senses in a passage of her *Epistre Othéa* [Letter from Othea]. She writes: "And Saint Augustine says that the soul must be guarded like a chest full of treasures, like a castle besieged by enemies, and like the king who takes a rest in his secluded chamber. And this chamber must be closed with five doors, which are the five senses of nature." (Ed. Halina D. Loukopoulos, Ph.D. dissertation, Wayne State University, 1977, pp. 220–21.) Jean Gerson in another similarity with Christine shows himself in the identical attitude evoked by Christine in the *Avision* in his *Sermon sur le retour des Grecs à l'unité* [Sermon on the Greeks' return to unity] (1409): "I would like to tell how I recently retired into the secret chamber of my thoughts by closing the door and windows of the corporeal senses in order better to consider and weigh what I had to say" (ed. Galitzin, p. 27). Let us also think of Charles d'Orléans. [For the *Letter from Othea*, see p. 29. Jean Gerson (1363–1429) was a celebrated theologian and chancellor of the University of Paris. Editor]
3. Christine offers a very fine analysis of this distance to learning that characterizes the status of woman in three of her works: the *Mutacion de Fortune*, the *Livre de la Cité des Dames*, and the *Avision Christine*. Based on her own experience she highlights three obstacles: custom, the natural inclination of children toward play which makes a young girl who is not forced to study turn toward games, her position as a married woman.
4. *Le Débat sur le Roman de la Rose*, ed. Eric Hicks (Paris: Champion, 1977), p. 148, lines 1076–77.

Livre de la Mutacion de Fortune, the son of her father; all the manuscripts support this reading:

> I was the son of a noble and renowned
> Man, who was called a philosopher. (ll. 171–72).

In this way Christine becomes a stranger to herself, inventing an interior other place, her "heart of a man," from which her voice can come
forth with a new legitimacy.[5]

This twofold movement of retreat and transformation defines the
activity of the poet. Christine always circumscribes a margin where she
places herself, and from this modest and remote place she creates a
center. This center may derive from the question of filiation (she turns
herself into a son instead of a daughter); from her relationship to the
court (to be accepted as a clerk, that is, to receive commissions from the
great nobles for learned works of literature);[6] or from her relationship
to herself: to constitute herself as subject: "I, Christine." This is the
beginning of the *Ditié de Jehanne d'Arc* [*Tale of Joan of Arc*] which is a
typical illustration of the movements we analyze here:[7]

> I, Christine, who has cried
> Eleven years in a closed abbey.

Christine evokes the idea of retreat but concludes the strophe with a
new opening: "Now I finally begin to laugh." She is one of the first to
celebrate the victory of Joan of Arc. Therefore, as she says at the end of
the *Ditié* (ll. 486–88), she can "look into the light," contrary to those
whose "heads are inclined and whose eyes are heavy."

Christine de Pizan constantly plays with transgression. But not in
moral terms; for her it is never a question of bravado, this would be
nonsensical. We must think of transgression in ontological terms. It is
in a very real sense a displacement, the creation of new places. A daughter from elsewhere has become the son of herself, that is, she has constituted herself as a writing subject. We recall the remark she addresses as
an excuse to Eustache Deschamps:

> I supplicate you that you may not
> Be displeased if I choose to address
> You in the singular, for I learned this
> Through the clergical style which those
> Use who spend their time with learning.[8]

5. On the expression *cuer d'omme* ("heart of a man") characterizing Christine's heroic women,
   see Liliane Dulac, "Sémiramis ou la veuve héroïque," in *Mélanges de philologie romane offerts
   à Charles Camproux* (Montpellier: Centre d'Etudes Occitanes de l'Université Paul-Valéry,
   1978), vol. 1, pp. 317–43, specifically p. 326.
6. See how she presents the circumstances of Philip of Burgundy's commissioning the *Livre des
   fais et bonnes meurs* from her (ed. Solente, Prologue, pp. 4–6).
7. Ed. Angus J. Kennedy and Kenneth Varty (Oxford: Society for the Study of Mediaeval Languages and Literature, 1977), ll. 1–2.
8. *Une epistre à Eustace Morel*, ed. Maurice Roy, *Oeuvres poétiques* vol. 2, ll. 17–22.

Christine de Pizan is always shifting shapes. There are many examples from very diverse areas. The most remarkable is the way in which the writer enters into each of her works. She always presents herself as uneasy and disturbed, since her spirit or her heart was occupied with other things. This is particularly clear for her lyric writings, but it goes beyond what one could call the constraint of the court. It is true that for most writers at the fourteenth- and fifteenth-century courts—and particularly for Christine who has no other income than from her pen—works were commissioned. But this tension between constraint and personal engagement is for Christine her mode of being. She is never where she is desired, where she is expected and nonetheless decides to occupy the place assigned to her. Let us consider the case of her first collection of *Cent Ballades* [One hundred ballads].[9] There is a distance between the desires of the courts ("Some people ask me to compose some beautiful poems," ballad 1, ll. 1–2) and Christine's present *sentement* [feeling]:

> But I do not have feeling nor inclination
> To compose poems of solace and joy;
> For my pain, surpassing all others,
> Derails all my joyous sentiments. (Ballad 1, 11.9–12)

Her solution is to "laugh in tears" which, contrary to what this will mean for François Villon,[1] is not the sign of a divided self but the indication of a voluntary acceptance of a commission that has little relationship to her personal experience or feelings:

> And if I have to, in order to silence people,
> To laugh while crying bitterly
> And with a heavy heart sing joyously.[2]

In her second collection of a hundred ballads, the *Cent Ballades d'amant et de dame* [One hundred ballads of a lover and a lady],[3] the contradiction is no longer between different shadings of lyricism (the court desiring songs of joy, Christine wanting to cry over her pain), but between the court commissioning a lyric work celebrating amorous feelings ("A hundred ballads of amorous feeling," as the refrain of the prologue ballad says) and the learned preoccupations of the author:

> For my thoughts are *elsewhere*.
> For I'd rather concentrate on *something else*,
> Of greater learning, she specifies. (Prologue ballad, ll. 3, 18–19)[4]

9. Ed. Maurice Roy, *Oeuvres poétiques*, vol. 1 (Paris: Didot, 1886).
1. The last great poet of the Middle Ages (b. ca. 1430). He wrote several poems on the theme "I laugh in tears." [Editor]
2. See Rondeau 11, ed. Maurice Roy, *Oeuvres poétiques*, vol. 1, ll. 10–12.
3. Ed. Jacqueline Cerquiglini (Paris: U.G.E., 1982).
4. Emphasis added.

The solution proposed by Christine is always of the same order: acceptance but without giving up, or what she calls in this ballad "l'amende volontaire" [voluntary acquiescence; l. 27]. She transforms the courtly command into a didactic work on the dangers of love which in no way contradicts the book it was meant to correct: *Le livre du duc des vrais amants* [The book of the duke of true lovers].[5] Christine is present and absent, she accepts and escapes. In a fascinating and characteristic mirror effect the lady of the *Cent Ballades d'amant et de dame* is also presented as occupied *elsewhere*:

> I never knew what love was, nor do I
> want to learn it; my thoughts are *elsewhere*. (Ballad 2, 11. ll. 1–2)

And she asks her lover to love elsewhere: "go *somewhere else*" (l. 19). It is only due to an outside intervention, that of the god of love (ballad 10) that the lady embarks on the adventure of love, from which Christine draws a lesson. The parallelism is obvious. On one side of the mirror, a god, described by the lover as "god and prince" (poem 9, l. 25) at the end of the complaint he addresses to her, orders the lady who is "lassée" [weary] to love; on the other side the princes order Christine, who fears to be "lassée" (prologue ballad, l. 17), to write of love. In both cases the ladies obey but also escape: Christine by the very act of writing, by the liberating act of her pen, and later by the prayer and voluntary retreat in an abbey; the lady escapes through death. This is a radical elsewhere, often evoked by Christine:

> But I have the desire to be taken from my body,

she writes in a ballad of her first collection.[6] The body is a prison, as her analysis in her *Epistre de la prison de la vie humaine* [The letter on the prison of human life] shows, from which the soul has to liberate itself.[7] Christine de Pizan is a stranger in her interior being.

This attitude of the elsewhere occurs again, identically, in the presentation of her learned works. Here the author also puts forward the distance that always seems to be the impetus of her writing. Take the prologue to the *Livre des fais et bonnes meurs* [of Charles V]:

> I, Christine de Pizan . . . undertake a new compilation written in prose and quite different from the other things I have written in the past." (Ed. S. Solente, vol. 1, p. 5)

Or take the mise en scène of the *Cité des Dames* where Christine turns away from her learned work only to return to it:

---

5. Ed. Maurice Roy, *Oeuvres poétiques*, vol. 3.
6. Ed. Maurice Roy, *Oeuvres poétiques*, vol. 1, ballad 5, l. 14.
7. Ed. Angus J. Kennedy (University of Glasgow: French Department, 1984). [For *The Book of the Deeds and Good Conduct of the Wise King Charles V*, see p. 113. Editor]

I was wondering whether I should leave alone for now these subtle problems and enjoy myself by looking at some cheerful poetry. (Ed. M. C. Curnow, p. 616),

and then, speaking of the book of Matheolus whose reading had been interrupted by supper and taken up again the next day:

I put it down in order to devote myself to the study of higher and more useful things. (Ed. Curnow, p. 617).

This image of distance appears to me to constitute the manner in which the writer in the fourteenth and fifteenth centuries seeks to announce his status, historically, sociologically, and ontologically. This distance can be exterior. The narrator presents himself obliquely with regard to the scene he retraces. He is concealed, hidden, listening or observing secretly. This is the figure of the narrator "lying in wait," which I analyzed in the works of Guillaume de Machaut, and which one can observe in many texts of the fourteenth and fifteenth centuries.[8] The distance can be interior, this is the pose of the melancholic or of the naive, a stranger to himself, which I am currently studying for Alain Chartier.[9] Of course, the two attitudes can exist simultaneously. It is in the distance from the world and from himself that the subject constitutes himself. It is this feeling of being different that the authors of the fourteenth and fifteenth centuries turn into a sign of election. Here as well, Christine de Pizan is, in her own voice, a privileged witness. In her *Livre de la Cité des Dames*, Reason justifies her arrival at Christine's:

For although we are not common to many places and our knowledge does not come to all people, nonetheless you, because of the great love you have for inquiring into the truth of things by long and continuous study, for which reason you are solitary and withdrawn from the world, you have earned to be with us as a dear friend and to be visited and consoled in your trouble and sadness. And so that you should have a clear vision into the things which contaminate and trouble your heart . . ." (Ed. Curnow, p. 628).

A new pride of the writer.[1]

Stranger by birth, stranger by her gender (the similarity with Marie

---

8. See Jacqueline Cerquiglini, 'Un engin si soutil.' *Guillaume de Machaut et l'écriture au XIVe siècle* (Paris: Champion, 1985), pp. 107–116 and " 'Le Clerc et le Louche': Sociology of an Esthetic," *Poetics Today* 5:3 (1984): 479–91; "L'écriture louche. La voie oblique chez les Grands Rhétoriqueurs," in *Actes du Ve Colloque international sur le Moyen Age Français* (Milan: Vita et Pensiero, 1985), vol. 1. See also Pierre-Yves Badel, "Le Chevalier, le Clerc et le Prince dans les débats des XIVe et XV siècles," presented at the colloquium "Images de l'écrivain aux XIV et XVe siècles," Orleans, June 1, 1985.
9. The poet was born between 1385 and 1395 and died in 1430. [Editor]
1. See Agostino Paravicini Bagliani, "Les Intellectuels et le pouvoir au Moyen Age. Réflexions sur l'imaginaire social," *Etudes de Lettres* (University of Lausanne), 1984:1: 21–48.

de France[2] in this respect is not without interest), Christine de Pizan manifests her alterity through her name. We know of the importance she, like other writers of her time, accords to her signature (I, Christine) and of the role of her anagrams.[3] In her name there two rare letters that we should meditate on: the X, by which she writes the first syllable of her name, *Christ*, thus using the symbol that designates the son of God. Christine has transformed herself into a son and makes herself a son literally, through this letter. The z is unusual as well, designating the Pizzano of her origin, the birth place of the paternal family. It is not insignificant that posterity has rubbed out this sign of the elsewhere beginning in the sixteenth century, taming it into an s. To give Christine de Pizan's strangeness its due is perhaps to recognize how she transformed herself into a writer. The pen tempers her misfortune.

BEATRICE GOTTLIEB

The Problem of Feminism in the Fifteenth Century †

A number of women who lived in earlier times have been called feminists, and among them is Christine de Pisan, the prolific writer of French verse and prose who lived from 1364 to about 1430 and did most of her work in Paris. Christine could not, of course, be called a feminist before the word existed. As a matter of fact, she was virtually unknown before the time of the French Revolution. It was then that she was discovered by a kindred soul, a learned and prolific writer and translator named Louise de Keralio, who between 1786 and 1789 issued a 14-volume edition of works by women.[1] This marked the first appearance in print of many of Christine's works, but as interest in medieval and Renaissance literature intensified, Christine became better known. As early as 1838 her contributions to the polemical literature on women were recognized,[2] although she was most often regarded as one of those *monuments historiques* of which the French are so proud. I do not know who first labeled her a feminist, but in 1886 a politically liberal literary critic in Great Britain called her a 'woman's rights person' in an article

2. A poet in the second half of the twelfth century. She may have been a French writer working at the court of the English king Henry II. Her best-known work is a collection of tales called the *Lais*. [Editor]
3. See my analysis of the power of the name in Christine's works in the introduction to my edition of the *Cent Ballades d'amant et de dame* (as in note 3 above), pp. 22–23.
† Reprinted by permission from *Women of the Medieval World: Essays in Honor of John H. Mundy*, ed. Julius Kirshner and Suzanne F. Wemple (London: Basil Blackwell), 337–64.
1. Mlle de Keralio (ed.), *Collection des meilleurs ouvrages français composés par des femmes* (14 vols, Paris, 1786–9).
2. Raymond Thomassy, *Essai sur les écrits politiques de Christine de Pisan* (Paris, 1838).

entitled 'A champion of her sex'.[3] A few years later he would probably
have said 'feminist'; the Oxford English Dictionary reports that the word
first appeared in print in 1894.[4] A scholarly edition of her poetry meanwhile began to appear, and is still the most authoritative available presentation of her work.[5] Her reputation as a feminist was based on her
prose works, however, which remained, for the most part, in manuscript.
As scholars, especially women scholars, read them, they kept being
struck by something they characterized as feminism. Christine's feminism is a commonplace today. The author of a recent biography for a
general audience may be somewhat cautious: 'That kind of feminism
which claims that women are the equal of men in every way was far
from her. Her ideas on the subject were much more reasonable'.[6] But
an even more recent article names her as the first of the 'early feminist
theorists' who resisted 'the cultural and social colonization of women by
men'.[7]

Interesting questions are raised by this application of a modern term
to a fifteenth-century person. Feminism is not easy to define in spite of
its free use by its present-day proponents and attackers. Though it is
sometimes used today to refer to a general sensitivity about women and
a concern with their plight, many who share that sensitivity and concern
shy away from the label. This has been true from the word's first appearance. French dictionaries say it was first used by the Utopian Socialist
Charles Fourier, and it has never completely lost its radical associations.
Almost the whole history of women's movements in the nineteenth and
twentieth centuries can be written in terms of those who took a radical
stance, thinking of themselves as feminists, and those who did not. It is
a complicated history because notions about what is radical have
changed over the years. Broadly speaking, radical proponents of wom-
en's rights in the nineteenth century (those most likely to call themselves feminists) believed in the complete equality of men and women
and wanted to end what they regarded as the demeaning restriction of
women to the domestic sphere. Less radical activist women spoke not
of equality but of women's special qualities, qualities they believed
should be recognized and used to benefit all of society. One curious
feature of this history is that the demand for suffrage began as an

3. William Minto, 'A champion of her sex', Macmillan's Magazine, LIII (February, 1886), pp.
264–75.
4. The Oxford English Dictionary (Oxford, 1933) gives only an early and 'rare' use of 'feminism'
as 'the quality of females'. Its Supplement, however, catches up with the late nineteenth century, stating that the word is no longer rare and that, by way of French féminisme, means 'the
opinions and principles of the advocates of the extended recognition of the achievements and
claims of women; advocacy of women's rights.' The earliest reference for the word 'feminist' is
an 1894 newspaper article about a political group in France.
5. Oeuvres poétiques de Christine de Pisan, ed. Maurice Roy (3 vols, Société des Anciens Textes
Français 24, Paris, 1886–96; reprinted New York and London, 1965).
6. Enid McLeod, The Order of the Rose; the Life and Ideas of Christine de Pizan (Totowa, NJ,
1976), p. 73.
7. Joan Kelly, 'Early feminist theory and the Querelle des Femmes, 1400–1789', Signs, VIII
(1982), p. 28.

extremely radical issue and gradually became absorbed into the program of the non-radicals. Feminism, if not perfectly easy to define, was in those early days a movement, and it had a program.

Today the label of 'feminist' may be more widely accepted, but its meaning seems to have become more diffuse. There are self-styled feminists who still hold something very similar to the radical nineteenth-century women's-rights position. They are concerned about equal pay for equal work, the Equal Rights Amendment, affirmative action, the availability of legal abortions and a number of other essentially political matters. They no longer think of themselves as terribly radical, of course. Those who now call themselves radical feminists have moved into different areas. They have taken up matters connected with domestic arrangements and sexual identity, some even suggesting that heterosexuality is inherently oppressive to women. Equality with men is almost beside the point for them. Somewhere in the middle are feminists who support the generally agreed upon political positions but have a 'raised' consciousness of the larger implications of being a woman in our society and see some value in recognizing male and female differences. It is probably still true that to regard oneself as a feminist of whatever stripe it is not enough to think certain thoughts: one needs a sense of sharing those thoughts with others, of being part, even if not a particularly active part, of a movement.

I cannot claim to have exhausted the subject of modern feminism. On the contrary, the subject has almost exhausted me. 'Feminism' has too many interests and factions to be briefly defined, except in rather reductionist terms. If it has a common shared meaning, it is that it is the opposite of 'not feminism', which is not a movement, of course, even if some of us are convinced we could paint a picture of it. Feminists are opposed to a wide variety of ideas and conditions, not a single enemy, and they are committed to a fairly wide variety of remedies. Here, then, is a complex concept belonging to our age, and there is a fifteenth-century woman. Is there any justification for bringing the two together?

There is an obvious danger in doing so, a danger that Lucien Febvre went so far as to call a sin. The name of the sin (the cardinal sin for a historian, he said) is anachronism. I have just spent some time translating Febvre's *Problem of Unbelief in the Sixteenth Century*,[8] the book in which he makes his most eloquent and elaborate attack on this sin, using what he regards as the only effective procedure for a historian. He amasses detail upon detail of the context in which the ideas under scrutiny existed. The question he deals with is whether it is appropriate to call Rabelais an atheist and, beyond that, whether atheism, as we usually understand the term, could even have existed in Rabelais' time. It was

---

8. Lucien Febvre, *The Problem of Unbelief in the Sixteenth Century; the Religion of Rabelais,* trans. Beatrice Gottlieb (Cambridge, Mass., 1982); original: *Le Problème de l'incroyance au XVIe siècle; la religion de Rabelais* (Paris, 1942).

only natural that, being immersed in Febvre's approach to the mental life of the past, I would respond to Christine de Pisan's alleged 'feminism' with some sensitivity to the possibility of anachronism.

What follows is an attempt to do in very modest terms something analogous to what Febvre did for the problem of atheism in the sixteenth century. Unlike his *magnum opus*, what I can produce on this modest scale is only a first foray into the problem of feminism in earlier times. It suggests some appropriate questions and possible answers. Febvre's basic axiom was that the changes over the past centuries have been considerable and it is therefore dangerous to assume that words carried the same load of meaning in the sixteenth century as in the twentieth. Utterances of the past should never be taken at face value, because 'face value' more often than not means current value, the value derived from a twentieth-century context. As historians we are prepared to find modes of thought in the fifteenth century that are no longer with us. For example, a tendency to think in hierarchical terms, to see both the physical world and society as naturally existing in layers arranged in something like a pyramid, a tendency to explain things by what we call supernatural causes (whether emanations or sympathies or miracles), and a tendency to think allegorically and use symbols not as arbitrary literary devices but as expressions of a real correspondence between different spheres of being. It is not a world we can be truly at home in, even if we are trained historians. We have to put on a pair of fifteenth-century eyeglasses (as Febvre would say) and make a special effort to keep them on. We have to be prepared to deal with dead literary conventions that can easily tax our patience, at the same time trying to imagine them striking contemporary listeners as fresh, natural and compelling. Their listeners, of course, not their readers. Even after the introduction of printing, as Febvre loved to point out, most information came through the ears, not the eyes. In the end, we have to ask how much is a matter of surface style and how much a reflection of something very deep that we have to reckon with.

There is one obvious difference between the problem of atheism and the problem of feminism. The word feminism did not exist, while the word atheism did, and was used a great deal. Some may consider this to be the end of the discussion: there is no problem, feminism is clearly an anachronism and it is foolish to waste time. Of course, there was no term for anything remotely resembling feminism, but that is not really where the problem lies. The problem is linked to the larger problem of women's history. Our history, the history of the history books, has until very recently been one from which women have been absent. They have been absent much as peasants have been absent. Women and peasants could be fitted into 'larger' events and structures, but they were not themselves considered worth focusing on. Now that our eyes have been opened to the fact that women were not absent (opened very slowly, I would say), we see that all history has to be rewritten. The contributors to this volume have been rewriting history, most of them having gone back over 'womanless' material and found that there were women there all along if only they had had the eyes to see them. The problem of feminism in the fifteenth century is not the simple-minded one of whether Christine de Pisan had the same ideas as Gloria Steinem. That would be what Febvre called a *question mal posée*. The problem is more complex. How was it possible to think about women and how in fact did women think about themselves in the fifteenth century? For a serious historian, furthermore, this does not mean a search for heroines and inspiring precursors, years ahead of their times. Precursors, as Febvre demonstrated, are dubious historical personages. Let us be content if we can see what women were like in their own times. I hold this to be a goal of self-evident importance. But reaching it is not easy.

For a woman to write for a wide audience (as audiences went) and to deal specifically with the subject of women was extremely rare in the fifteenth century. Christine de Pisan dealt with the subject many times. Her *Book of the City of Ladies* was entirely devoted to demonstrating the worth and talents of women, and its sequel, *The Book of the Three Virtues*, was a sort of instruction manual for women. Her other works contain frequent references, both direct and indirect, to the situation of women. There is no doubt that she gave the subject a lot of thought. As a remarkable woman herself, who had managed to establish herself as a literary craftsman with a distinguished patronage, she also thought about her own situation and related it to that of women in general.

Most of her explicit utterances about women were defenses against attacks and abuse. She saw these as coming from two sources, misogynistic books and men's behavior. In addition, in comments on her own life and in some passages in *The City of Ladies* she made the particular point that women had at least as much capacity for learning as men did.

The strain of misogyny is strong in the Western literary tradition, and although it is often glibly referred to as Christian, Christine apparently saw it as older and not distinctively Christian. She particularly took Ovid to task. Juvenal was perhaps a likelier target among the ancients, but she was clearly concerned with what her contemporaries might be reading and hearing, and Ovid, who was widely available in vernacular translations, was known for his advice on seduction. She referred in a general way to a multitude of nameless misogynistic 'clerks', but singled out for special mention two works, *The Romance of the Rose* and *The Lamentations of Matheolus*. Jean de Meun and Matheolus, the authors of these popular works, were almost proverbial in Christine's time as denigrators of women.

What did misogyny mean to Christine? What exactly was she

defending women against? We can get an answer from a poem, 'L'Epistre au dieu d'amours', from the letters she contributed to the war of
words over *The Romance of the Rose*, and from the introduction to *The
Book of the City of Ladies*. In brief, misogynists called women lascivious,
fickle and incompetent. They complained that women could not keep
faith and could not be trusted with confidences. Women were depicted
either as evil seductresses or as passive quarry for sexual predators, an
inconsistency of outlook that Christine seems to have enjoyed pointing
out. Inferior is hardly the right word: women were seen as utterly vicious
and worthless, an afterthought in cosmogony and a mistake in biology.
'A great unhappiness and sadness welled up in my heart, for I detested
myself and the entire feminine sex, as though we were monstrosities in
nature . . .'[9]

Christine does not cite chapter and verse, and we may not feel that
she has to. But since she chose to refer by name to Jean de Meun and
Matheolus, it may be useful to take at least a cursory look at what disturbed her.

The Lamentations of Matheolus, written in Latin around 1300 and
translated into French some 70 years later, seems to be the impassioned
outpourings of an unhappy husband. To a modern reader it is likely to
convey more passion than sense, in spite of the impressive array of
authorities it cites. The writer bewails the fact that when younger and
vulnerable he fell in love with a widow and married her; as a result, he
is now saddled with a wife who is no longer attractive, who has burdened him with children and household cares, and who is a constant
nuisance. On top of that, by marrying a widow he has lost the privileges
and prospects he used to have as a member of the lower orders of the
clergy. The message of the poem at first glance seems to be that marriage is a trial and women are to be avoided—a plea for chastity, in other
words, for those lucky enough to be able to manage it. But no, at second
glance it appears that women should not be avoided. Men are inevitably
going to be attracted to them, and others must simply try to avoid falling
into the same trap as Matheolus. Poor Matheolus. I think I might have
been able to sympathize with him if he had only stuck to his own case.
But instead he reaches out in all directions for stories and sayings about
the failings of women in general. It may have been some comfort to
him that such material existed in abundance. At any rate, it was no
doubt for marshalling and recounting it with such zest that he gained
the reputation of being a hater of women.[1] Christine did not go into
any detail about Matheolus, but her choice of an example of misogyny
seems uncannily perceptive if, as may be the case, the impulse toward

9. Christine de Pizan, *The Book of the City of Ladies*, trans. Earl Jeffrey Richards (New York, 1982), p. 5.
1. For the text of the *Lamentations* and much other information, see A. G. Van Hamel (ed.), *Les Lamentations de Mathéolus et le Livre de Leesce de Jehan le Fèvre, de Resson* (2 vols, Paris, 1892, 1905).

misogyny arises from the inability of men to come to terms with their own sexuality.

Jean de Meun is better known but more difficult to understand. Literary scholars today treat him with great respect as a master of subtle irony, and the misogynistic passages tend to get explained away. Since *The Romance of the Rose* is a tissue of speeches by the various allegorical personages who populate the work, we are told to be wary about assuming that any of them speaks for the author. Among the passages that excoriate women are a speech within a speech, the words of a jealous husband to his wife, quoted by the character Friend to the Dreamer who narrates the poem. Written shortly before *The Lamentations of Matheolus*, it goes over some of the same ground ('Ah! If I had believed Theophrastus, I would never have married a wife . . . By Saint Denis! Worthy women, as Valerius bears witness, are fewer than phoenixes. . . .')[2] Another passage is the speech of The Old Woman, who says that since all men are sensualists who betray and deceive women, women should be deceivers in return.[3] And there is a passage in which Genius, starting with references to Virgil, Solomon and Livy, shows how women cannot be trusted, especially with secrets. ('Fair lords, protect yourselves from women if you love your bodies and souls'.)[4] The whole poem, of course, is about how to win over a woman, but its literary merit is said to lie in complex levels of meaning and a panoramic view of contemporary life and learning. One side in the early fifteenth-century debate on the poem seems to have agreed with this assessment. A modern French scholar feels that misogyny may actually be held up to ridicule in the poem, and an American woman, writing in 1917, said that Jean de Meun was 'in many ways . . . in advance of his times in his attitude towards women . . . The most abusive passages . . . are put in the mouth of those whose cavil is slight reproach.'[5] I am willing to grant a work of literature its complexity, and I do not know enough about this particular giant of a work to enter the debate on its meaning, but it must be pointed out that the cumulative effect of all those passages was to convince many fifteenth-century readers that Jean de Meun had a low opinion of both women and sexual morality.

As I have said, Christine wanted to defend women not only against what was written about them but also against how men treated them. She started where The Old Woman in *The Romance of the Rose* did, with a conviction that many men wanted only to trick women into sleeping with them. They lied to these women, and if they were unsuc-

---

2. Guillaume de Lorris and Jean de Meun, *The Romance of the Rose*, trans. Charles Dahlberg (Princeton, 1971), pp. 157, 159.
3. ibid., pp. 229ff.
4. ibid., p. 279.
5. Daniel Poirion (ed.), *Le Roman de la Rose* (Paris, 1974), preface; Mary Morton Wood, *The Spirit of Protest in Old French Literature* (New York, 1917; reprinted 1966), p. 182.

cessful they told lies about them. Men were promiscuous as a matter of course and falsely accused all women of being the same. They boasted of their conquests after having promised to guard their mistresses' honor. In 'L'Epistre au dieu d'amours', Christine says such behavior was readily observable in France.

Christine's defense against both literary attacks and shabby treatment was, first, to deny the truth of what was said. She could see with her own eyes that women were not what they were said to be. If some women were vicious, it was unjust to say that all were. The bad examples found in books were isolated cases, and they could be countered with at least as many good examples. *The Book of the City of Ladies* is essentially a long list of such examples. She implied that men's judgement was warped because they were slaves to lust and, even worse, poor losers. Her defense also moved onto another plane, where in effect it became an attack, in which she claimed that women had special qualities that made them superior to men. They were gentle, sweet, kind and by their very nature loyal. Women did not cause wars and mayhem, as men did. And they had a monopoly on one of the most wonderful things in the world, motherhood. Men, she said, should try to be loyal, considerate and truthful to women because they were 'elles de qui tout homme est descendu', and there was no joy for men in this world without women: 'C'est sa mere, c'est sa suer, c'est s'amie.'[6]

On the subject of education, Christine also took the stance of a defender. Not allowing women to study implied a lack of capacity that she denied. Again, she used examples, among them herself by implication. The fact is that she had few enough real examples, so she resorted to fable. She is more interesting when she occasionally gives up argument and demonstration and falls back on observation. Her father had educated her, and she had learned to love books as much as any man could. She looked around and saw women who seemed to possess all the mental ability that was needed. Her most moving passages are those in which she seems to plead for a fair chance, as in her dialogue with the allegorical figure of Reason, who assures her that 'if it were customary to send daughters to school like sons, and if they were then taught the natural sciences, they would learn as thoroughly and understand the subtleties of all the arts and sciences as well as sons . . . [Women] have minds that are freer and sharper whenever they apply themselves.' Christine pretends that she cannot believe her ears. 'My lady, what are you saying?' she cries. 'Certainly men would never admit this answer is true, unless it is explained more plainly, for they believe that one normally sees that men know more than women do.' Reason does explain: 'Without the slightest doubt, it is because they are not involved in many

6. 'Epistre au dieu d'amours', ll. 725, 733, in Maurice Roy (ed.), *Oeuvres poétiques*, II, pp. 23–4. ['Those from whom every man is descended.' . . . 'She is his mother, his sister, his friend.' Editor]

different things, but stay at home, where it is enough for them to run
the household, and there is nothing which so instructs a reasonable
creature as the exercise and experience of many different things.'[7]
Christine's advice in *The Book of the Three Virtues* is kept within cautious bounds. In the exercise of ordinary housewifely duties, she suggests, an educated mind is no hindrance, and a knowledge of literary
graces and practical skills is a great help in running a noble household.
There is even more urgency for widows to have the great treasure of
education, not only for the consolation it could provide (here she is
autobiographical) but also for its practical value in protecting themselves from being defrauded and mistreated (also probably autobiographical).

In the light of all this, I can detect in Christine what we today would
call a feminist consciousness. Here was a woman who, pained and outraged by reading and hearing that women were inferior and evil, refused
to suffer in silence. She did not defend herself as an individual but made
common cause with all women. She thought about women's lives and
how they might be improved. We have no idea whether she talked about
any of this with other women since there are few hints in her writing or
in any writing of the period of what women said to each other, but it is
tempting to think that she did, even that women had been saying such
things to each other for a long time. 'Such things' were not a modern
feminist program. There were no demands for equal rights or political
power, there was no hint of women forming organizations, there was
not even a modest proposal that regular schooling be available for
women. Still, to see that women as a group shared common problems
that not only differed from men's problems but also somehow stemmed
from men's defects, and to refuse to accept insults and contempt in
silence—this is a plausible kind of feminism. There is too much that is
recognizable in it for us to ignore it.

There is much more to say about Christine de Pisan. She had many
sides, and we need to see what they were before we can understand this
plausible feminism more fully.

She was perhaps the closest thing to a career woman in the fifteenth
century. I have already suggested that what she had achieved in her own
life was one of her implicit arguments when she wrote about women's
capacities. She had shown that a woman who had been married at 15
and had had several children could at 25, when her husband died, galva-
nize her energies and resources to support herself and her family without any loss of dignity or respect. She must have been a strong and
enterprising person, to say nothing of her intelligence. She did what had
to be done to be a successful writer in those days. That is, she gained

7. *The City of Ladies*, p. 63.

patrons by cultivating her acquaintance among the rich and highly placed, some of whom were women. She seems to have been very good at keeping her patrons, both by being personally ingratiating and by producing works that pleased them. Her reputation as a writer was excellent, and she was admired for her personal qualities. A fifteenth-century manuscript of one of her poems refers to her as 'a lady distinguished for her birth and her character'.[8]

Her output was tremendous and astonishingly varied. She wrote more than a hundred poems, on many subjects. She was the official biographer of Charles V and wrote a long work on warfare *(The Book of Feats of Arms)* that later so impressed Henry VII of England he asked William Caxton to translate and publish it. She wrote works of moral counsel, political theory, patriotic exhortation and philosophical reflection. All in all, it was a prodigious display of literary energy and versatility that would have been equally impressive in a man.

She seems to have played the role of woman of letters to the hilt, even initiating a controversy that has become famous as probably the first literary *querelle*. This was the famous debate on *The Romance of the Rose*, which Christine apparently triggered by a letter to a distinguished scholar who had written in praise of the *Romance* after reading it for the first time. A number of other people entered the fray later, most notably Jean Gerson, who shared Christine's dislike of Jean de Meun. It was Christine who was most responsible for pursuing and preserving the debate, since she collected the letters that were exchanged and had them published in a single manuscript. It is a complicated story. Scholars disagree about the sequence of events and what the fight was really about, but the episode's main interest may be that it shows the different ways in which educated readers of the time responded to immorality and sexual explicitness in literature. Christine and Gerson both felt that the *Romance* was disgustingly lubricious, an inducement to adultery and fornication. We know that Christine thought it was particularly insulting to women, but that was not the focus of the debate, although she herself pursued the point. It is also true that Christine was not treated with much respect by the brothers Gontier and Pierre Col, the chief defenders of Jean de Meun, and that she vigorously defended the right of a woman to participate in such a discussion. Still, it is not clear whether she thought that Jean de Meun's chief offense was against women or against propriety. As far as the merits of the arguments go, modern critical judgements of the *Romance* tend to agree with Christine's antagonists, who believed that words were not in themselves lascivious or immoral and that a work had to be seen in its entirety. Gerson's *Treatise Against the Romance of the Rose*, which supported her side of

---

8. 'Domina praeclara natu et moribus.' See Christine de Pisan, *Ditié de Jehanne d'Arc*, ed. Angus J. Kennedy and Kenneth Varty (Oxford, 1977), p. 2.

the debate, was a strict moralist's indictment of love literature as frivolous, hedonistic and destructive of the institution of marriage (he did
not say anything about its being demeaning to women). From the distance of so many centuries we have no way of knowing what he thought
of Christine's love poetry.

As a writer, Christine's favorite voice, especially as she grew older, was
that of moralist and patriot. She frequently bewailed the decline of
moral standards, especially in the relations between men and women.
She saw this moral decline as part and parcel of France's perilous condition. She lived in turbulent times (the midpoint of the Hundred Years
War), and eventually, when the Burgundians occupied Paris in 1418,
when she was about 54 years old, she had to leave her home and her
whole way of life, effectively ceasing to be a writer. Eleven years later
she broke her silence with her last work, a poem in praise of Joan of
Arc's triumphs over France's enemies. One of her preoccupations in all
her writings was individual morality, how to live a virtuous, useful and
honorable life. Her method of handling the subject, as she dealt out
advice to her son, to statesmen, to young men in general, to women at
all levels of society, to princes and to soldiers, was the approved medieval
one of combing the authorities and restating what had already been said
and had stood the test of time. We should not expect her to be an original thinker on all these subjects, and we can only guess which attitudes
reflected her deepest convictions. But if frequent repetition means anything, she thought life was a serious matter and that doing one's duty
was more important than personal enjoyment. Princes and rulers were
the guardians of order, and to rebel against authority was to destroy the
fabric of society. After all, she had before her very eyes the spectacle of
a legitimate king defied, with dire results for France. The morality she
expressed was the conventional morality of her day, and she wrote much
more about the plight of France than she did about the plight of women.

Christine also had another voice, that of a fashionable court poet,
especially at the beginning of her career. For some modern scholars,
this is the most interesting part of her work; it was certainly what caught
the fancy of nineteenth-century Frenchmen. She turned out ballades,
virelays and rondeaux by the dozen, with what looks like considerable
skill at rhyming and meter. The subject matter of her poems was precisely what these verse forms were normally associated with: the beauty
of spring, the power of love, praise of the beloved, the sorrow of lovers'
parting, the capriciousness of Fortune, pleas for reassurance. She had
begun by writing some particularly sorrowful poems about the loneliness and misery of widowhood, but she soon shifted to the more conventional melancholy of lovers' addresses. There has been some
speculation whether these were poems addressed to a real lover, but for
our purpose this hardly matters. Whether the lover was real or imagined,
the language and outlook came from the courtly love tradition, the tradi-

tion of Guillaume de Machaut before her and of her contemporaries Alain Chartier and Charles d'Orléans.

What emerges from a consideration of Christine's life and work as a whole is a picture of a strong person who was not a rebel, who succeeded by applying her talents to activities that, while unusual for a woman, were considered admirable, and who conformed to the dominant values of the world around her. Her ideas about women should be seen in this light. They were the ideas of an upper-class fifteenth-century woman about fifteenth-century women. To focus on her outrage and concern without seeing the context of values that underlay them is to miss an opportunity to get a little closer to what things were really like for women then.

Christine de Pisan wrote poems that placed love in a special realm with its own rules and values. It was a realm that often seemed to exist only in literature and the imagination, but its influence was none the less great for that. Everyone familiar with the secular literature of the Middle Ages knows what I am talking about, and I shall not attempt to describe it fully or minimize its complexities and contradictions. One of its characteristics was surely the high place it gave to women. According to the rules, women were in command and men existed to serve and honor them. The complaint to Cupid in Christine's 'Epistre au dieu d'amours' was that too many men were no longer doing this, that they pursued women to satisfy their lust and that they made their conquests, real and pretended, a matter of public knowledge instead of preserving the silence that the rules of love required.

The Book of the Duke of True Lovers, a long poem by Christine, depicts the special realm of love in a particularly uncompromising form. It is one of several long poems she wrote exploring the nature of love, but it seems more definitive than the others, claiming as it does to tell the story of someone who is without irony called a True Lover.[9] He is depicted as a paragon of a lover of a married woman. He falls in love when he reaches a point in his life when the desire to be in love overcomes him, as though in love with love itself. He then thanks the god of love for providing him with a lady to serve, a lady who is again and again called 'perfect'. There follows a long narrative about letters, go-betweens, secret meetings, a jealous husband, etc. Suffice it to say that this perfect love affair continues for ten years as a demanding and absorbing relationship in which nothing more physical than a kiss passes between them. At one point a startling, jarring note is sounded when the lady receives a letter from an older woman friend advising her to avoid the snares of such love affairs. 'Consent not, for the sake of any foolish pleasure, to be forgetful of your souls and of your honour,' she

---

9. Christine de Pisan, *The Book of the Duke of True Lovers*, trans. Alice Kemp-Welch, with verse trans. by Laurence Binyon and Eric R. D. Maclagan (London, 1909).

cautions, saying that lovers' promises to behave honorably cannot be trusted and that even innocent behavior can lead to loss of honor. 'From such faithless rascals keep you free,' is the refrain of the ballade appended to the letter. The lady is deeply disturbed, but the True Lover is equal to the challenge. Assuring her that it would be impossible for him ever to give up his total dedication to her, he offers to 'go beyond the seas to end my days'. This makes her see she was wrong to doubt him, and before long the affair resumes its perfect and honorable course, ending only when the inevitable slander—though they have still not given any carnal expression to their love—becomes too great.

As we read this story we may very well think it is simply too ridiculous to be taken seriously. Yet it is imbued with a deeply serious, quite passionate tone. We may therefore understandably resort to the kinds of exclamations and questions Febvre peppered his writing with. This is astonishing! Did people think such behavior was possible? Did they admire it? Why do we find a criticism of love in the middle of a work that seems to be celebrating it? Why was love a god anyway? What did Christine really think? And what does it tell us about her thoughts on women?

These questions go to the heart of important differences between the fifteenth century and the twentieth century. Final answers are impossible, but let us engage in a little speculation, based in part on two distinguished works of scholarship, Huizinga's *The Waning of the Middle Ages* and Febvre's *Amour sacré, amour profane*, his book about Margaret of Navarre (see the references at the end of this chapter for both of these books).

Love was a god because he wielded power over people. This was an inescapable conclusion based on the observation of human behavior. He took possession of men and women and inspired them to acts of passion, unreason, brutality—and incredible selflessness. He was a god of a sweet and bitter mystery, impossible to ignore and difficult to come to terms with. The religion of love that formed the subject of court poetry was one way of dealing with this importunate deity. It was an elaborate structure for taming a force often perceived as uncontrollable. In its obsession with rules and refinements it was clearly disjunctive with the rest of fifteenth-century life. Everyone knew that. It contradicted the experience of most men and women in their sexual encounters, and it contradicted the precepts of the Christian church. The fifteenth century confronted the god of love with a mixed legacy of attitudes.

Christine was aware of these contradictions. The letter from the perfect lady's friend shows that. What is more, Christine later used the letter again in almost the same form in a prose work of advice to women, *The Book of the Three Virtues*. And yet she apparently remained attached to the values of love's religion. She thought some men misused the rules to imperil women's immortal souls, but the rules could bring out the best in men, encouraging them to treat women with proper respect. Christine was an enthusiastic supporter of the new chivalric orders that required their members, among other things, to adhere to the rules of the courtly religion of love. She wrote an approving poem, 'Le Dit de la Rose', about such an order, dedicated, so she said, to the honor of 'the female sex'. Her main complaint in 'L'Epistre au dieu d'amours', remember, was that too many men in France were unmindful of the old codes of behavior and no longer seemed to know how to act toward ladies. She cared as much as anyone of her time about 'honor', a value intimately associated with chivalry. Much ink has been spilled on the subject of honor, but I suspect there is more to be said, now that historians are asking new questions about women. Christine, at any rate, accepted the prevalent notion of honor as good reputation achieved at almost any cost. She said, for example, that a maid had such an overriding duty to guard her mistress' honor that if the lady strayed from virtue and bore an illegitimate child the maid should claim the child as her own.

I doubt whether Christine ever resolved the contradictions connected with the god of love. *The Book of the Duke of True Lovers* can be seen as an attempt, one that I find interesting for all that it is feeble and far-fetched. The scorn expressed for the chivalric code in the letter to the True Lover's lady bears a slight resemblance to the scorn of Jean de Meun for those who do not recognize the earthy reality behind lovers' fine words, but it really comes out on the side of Jean Gerson, who emphasized the huge gap between the demands of Christian morality and the concerns of love's devotees. The True Lover makes himself almost blameless in Gerson's terms, even though he devotes his life to loving a married woman. He does not threaten her virtue because he never tempts her to actual adultery. His love is totally pure, almost saintly in its spiritual magnificence. His conduct is a most reassuring fantasy, a lovely daydream in which Cupid and Christ are reconciled.

Did Christine think the story was ridiculous? Did it occur to her that all this idealizing of ladies might be denigrating to women? We have no way of knowing, but she seems to have liked what I would regard as an exaggerated veneration of women. It certainly could have been welcome as a refuge and relief from the harsh denigrations of the everyday world and the painful attacks in misogynistic literature. Did women belong on a pedestal? Christine's answer might have been, 'Why not?'

In the everyday world most men and women were husbands and wives, and the realm of marriage was very different from the realm of love. The connection between love and marriage is another complex subject, which again I will only touch on. Broadly speaking, there were two opinions. Either love was a force too powerful to be contained by marriage (with its requirements of fidelity, its involvement in the trivia of ordinary living and its subordination of free choice to financial and

political considerations) or it was too ephemeral and unreliable a basis
for a permanent relationship on which both Church and society made
heavy demands. The married state as described in the writing of Christine's time is a far cry from perfection. It is often a battlefield or a vale
of tears. Christine herself said a great deal about married women,
including herself. She tells us that she loved her husband very much,
but in her advice to women she says that marrying for love is a bad idea.
An admirable husband inspires love to develop in his wife. As for a
husband who is not admirable, his wife has a duty to care for him tenderly and try to improve him with tact and gentleness. Of cruel and
unfaithful husbands she wrote that their wives needed to learn how to
cope with them. They might, after all, eventually repent, if only on their
deathbeds, and leave them well provided for as widows.

As Christine knew, and not only from her own experience, one of
the commonest consequences of marriage was widowhood. Therefore a
woman needed an education, not only because she often helped her
husband to run household and estate but also because the day might
come when she would be left to deal with these matters alone in a
hostile world. Christine said she had known nothing about her husband's financial situation before he died. Learning to fend for herself
had turned her into a man, and she had had to remain so ever since.
Are there, by the way, feminist implications in such a statement? At the
very least it suggests that widowhood revealed resourcefulness in women
that was ordinarily hidden, and that only outside their tightly confined
'normal' roles could women find opportunities to develop wider skills.
It is a suggestion some of us are likely to fasten on, but I think we
should not overlook Christine's tone. It is ambiguous, if not downright
sorrowful. Turning into a man (whatever that means) was a misfortune.
On the other hand, Christine urged widows not to remarry. This may
have been a conventional Christian attitude or a deep conviction about
the opportunities of widowhood—she only said remarriage was not necessary for survival.

There was a conventional ideal picture of marriage, which played
down conflict and omitted passion. It highlighted the virtues of loyalty
and obedience, just as the chivalric code did, except that the lines of
authority ran in almost exactly opposite directions. The head of the
household was the man, and the wife owed him complete obedience.
This was a view Christine never directly opposed (we can speculate
whether anything in her love poems implied opposition). She praised
women's capacity for humility, which was a kind of moral superiority,
related to women's natural gentleness and other maternal qualities. It
was the wife who guarded the peace of the household and its honor
(that is, its reputation, even if it meant covering up a husband's miscon-
duct). The ideal view of marriage included loyalty, kindness and wisdom on the man's part, but Christine implied that it was women's

responsibility to make marriage what it should be. There is an exaggerated depiction of the ideal wife's virtues in the story of patient Griselda, which Christine retold with as much loving attention to the details of the poor heroine's sufferings at the hands of her capricious husband as did Chaucer and other male writers.

This ideal view of marriage embodied Christian values. Christine, who was not what could be called a religious poet, was nevertheless mindful of religion at every turn. Her ideas on women at their most explicit were suffused with religious ideas and feelings. She said women's characteristic virtues were those most highly valued in Christianity: humility, fidelity, charity. Her response to the attacks on women's lustfulness was to say that men blamed women for a problem that was their own, and that in fact most women were naturally chaste. The crowning 'argument' in *The City of Ladies* is that God chose the Virgin Mary as his spouse 'from among women' and therefore 'not only should men refrain from reproaching women but should hold them in great reverence'. This did not mean that women should succumb to the sin of pride. Christine urged them to:

> . . . follow the example of your Queen, the sovereign Virgin, who, after the extraordinary honor of being chosen Mother of the Son of God was announced to her, humbled herself all the more by calling herself the handmaiden of God . . . So, my ladies, be humble and patient, and God's grace will grow in you, and praise will be given to you as well as the Kingdom of Heaven.[1]

The goal of an individual on this earth was to live a Christian life, not to pursue happiness or self-fulfillment. Needless to say, any improvement in women's conditions that met Christine's approval would have to be in harmony with Christian virtues.

Not only did Christine inevitably look to God for the moral basis of life but she also saw the hand of God in most social and political arrangements; hence her acceptance of a hierarchical structure in the state and the family and her belief that men and women have separate spheres of activity ordained by God. Like so many of her contemporaries, Christine welcomed hierarchical rank as a guaranty of order, regarding rebellion against authority as a form of sinful self-indulgence with no possible redeeming value. This was, after all, long before democracy stopped being a term of disapproval. Her thinking about women took place in this hierarchical framework with its religious sanction. 'God has . . . ordained man and woman to serve Him in different offices and also to aid and comfort one another, each in their ordained task, and to each sex has given a fitting and appropriate nature and inclination to fill their offices,' she says in the book that comes closest to being her feminist manifesto. 'Though God has given women great understand-

---

1. *The City of Ladies*, pp. 218, 254–5.

ing—and there are many such women—because of the integrity to which women are inclined, it would not be at all appropriate for them to go and appear so brazenly in the court like men, for there are enough men who do so.'[2]

One of the things that made Christine so much a person of her time is the feeling she conveys of being on good terms with God. She was in awe of His power, but she was not afraid of His justice and she relied on His mercy. She believed that the learned men who cited chapter and verse to defame women were simply wrong about God's intentions. They either misread God's works or they followed the opinions of evil men. When Christine defended women from misogynistic attacks she usually went back to the same authorities used by the misogynists, and it was in Christian texts that she found the greatest consolation. Though her works do not especially sparkle with wit, there is an amused irony in her triumphant display of the ways in which God evidently approved of women much more than his creature, man, did. The best example of this is her poem on Joan of Arc. At first glance it seems to be a poem in praise of an outstanding woman, and has been called part of her 'defence of the feminist cause.'[3] Read a little more skeptically, it is an expression of love for France and praise to God. What was remarkable about Joan was that she was a mere girl—not only a woman but also young and lowly—and God miraculously transformed her into a warrior more triumphant than any man. It was something only God could have done, since it was 'chose fors nature'.[4] In a way, Christine agreed with Joan's prosecutors, but they gave the credit to the devil. Christine said that, in exalting Joan, God demonstrated his love for France—and, of course, his love for women. 'What an honor for the female sex!' Christine exclaims.[5] Some feminist irony is surely there. But the praise goes to God, who guides every victor, whether male or female. The example of Joan was an encouragement to religious and patriotic fervor, not to acceptance of women's aptitude for the military arts.

Christine's thinking about women can hardly begin to be understood without reference to her period's attitudes toward love and religion. Her ambivalence about love and sexuality was not unlike that of her contemporaries, and it colored her view of women as both refiners of manners and innocent victims. Her concern with the relationship of women to God, while low-keyed, was constant. It was impossible for her to speak of moral values without referring to God, and she found consolation for her sex in the fact that it had always been assumed by Christians that the arrangements of the City of Man ultimately did not matter. Each soul, even if downtrodden on earth, was in touch with God.

2. ibid., p. 31.
3. *Ditié de Jehanne d'Arc*, p. 16.
4. ibid., p. 34 (1.274).
5. ibid. (ll. 265–6).

The Book of the City of Ladies may have started the *querelle des femmes*, a series of loosely related texts to which many European writers, mostly male, contributed in the course of the fifteenth and sixteenth centuries, and even to some degree into the eighteenth century. An individual writer usually took up a position on one side or the other: women were bad or women were good. The many-sided debate on women in Castiglione's *Courtier* is sometimes considered part of the *querelle* because it makes use of familiar arguments from both sides. The method of argument was almost always the same, and Christine de Pisan had shown the way: examples and authorities, organized by topics. Except for the interspersed conversations between Christine and the allegorical visitors who instruct her, her book is a list of names and an anthology of exemplary tales. There is a pervasive tone of hyperbole. To modern tastes the genre is repellent. This should make us wonder why it was so popular, and I am sure an investigation of this would be a real contribution to the history of *mentalité*. For our present purposes it is enough to recognize that with an obsolete literary form we can never be sure we are reading it correctly. We cannot tell whether Christine's marshalling of examples from every kind of source and her uncritical inclusion of goddesses and mythical characters were intended to convince by force of authority or to overwhelm by force of numbers. Or was her aim to charm and amuse, making a serious point along the way? I know I am not alone in finding the method unconvincing. The argument seems forced, even desperate, no matter how much a modern reader may share her conviction about women's worth. To be sure, the inhabitants of Christine's *City of Ladies* have much in common with the guests at Judy Chicago's *Dinner Party*,[6] so a potpouri of legend, fiction and history may not be as out of date as I think. Out of date or not, it is none the less hyperbolic and naive.

Christine was undoubtedly sincere when she said that women were unfairly maligned, and the vices of a few did not apply to all, that the distinctive qualities of women were admirable and that there have been outstanding women in past and present. Whether the later contributors to the *querelle des femmes* were equally sincere is another question. No difference in tone is detectable when a man argues that women are inferior to men and another man argues that men are inferior to women. It is all too easy to assume that men only meant it when they said men were better. Furthermore, one and the same man often took both positions in the *querelle*. The translator of the terrible Matheolus, Jehan le Fèvre, wrote a work in typically fulsome praise of women, called *Le Livre de Leësce*, as a kind of answer to Matheolus. Its method was not unlike Christine's. The *querelle* ran its zigzag course through the fifteenth century. To mention a few of the works that have survived:

6. A recent multimedia art work consisting of a dinner table of huge proportions with distinctive place settings for 39 famous women from many periods and spheres of activity.

John Lydgate translated *De coniuge non ducenda* into English; an anonymous author wrote *La Malice des femmes*; another wrote the sardonic *Quinze joyes de mariage*; on the other side were Martin le Franc's *Champion des dames*; Pierre Michault's *Procès d'honneur fémenin*; and Philippe Bouton's *Miroir aux dames*. The *querelle* picked up steam at the beginning of the sixteenth century with Cornelius Agrippa's *Nobility and Excellence of Womankind* and continued on its way, including among its productions an English poem with the all-encompassing title *In Praise and Dispraise of Women*. For purposes of political polemic, John Knox borrowed from the *querelle* for his *First Blast of the Trumpet Against the Monstruous Regiment of Women*, but most of the contributors were literary men. The *querelle* was an approved means for displaying learning, ingenuity and writing skill, and we are probably right to be suspicious that so many of the praisers of women were seeking the patronage of women rulers. In a word, it was a literary game, a game with a popular subject and one that was capable of turning serious. It was not till the end of the seventeenth century that the form of the argument changed and both hyperbole and traditional authorities disappeared. Poulain de la Barre called his 'Cartesian discourse' *De l'égalité des deux sexes*. The title alone says a great deal. Its aim was to reason dispassionately, and its unflamboyant conclusion was that neither sex was better or worse.

But that was in the distant future. The first hundred years of the *querelle* showed little movement, going over the same ground again and again. We can get a sense of how familiar it was to literate people when we read the Third Book of *The Courtier*. When women are praised it is always for 'womanly' qualities of sweetness, beauty and chastity, and they are said to be capable of learning, which is to be put to 'womanly' uses. If we think we detect a plausible feminism in Christine de Pisan, can we detect it in male writers who sometimes wrote the same sorts of things she did? If not, what is the difference? The answer would seem to lie only partly in the writing itself. It is true that the sense of outrage that comes through in Christine's writing is mostly absent from the others. But the fact that a woman was doing the writing, that she was speaking for herself and for other women, conditions the effect of what she wrote.

If other women had written about women in that period would the effect have been the same? That is a hard question to answer, since we have almost nothing to go by. If we wait for about a hundred years to pass, however, we come upon a woman of equal literary stature who had something to say on the subject.

Although Margaret of Navarre never wrote a full-dress defense of women as Christine did, I find striking similarities in their attitudes. Margaret has also been called a 'feminist', and it is interesting to compare the two. The most obvious difference is that Margaret did not quote authorities or tell exemplary tales drawn from history and legend, although the *querelle des femmes* was flourishing when she lived. She adopted instead the manner of the Erasmian dialogue, something unknown to Christine a century earlier, and her reflections emerge from the freewheeling conversations of the storytellers about the stories told and heard in her *Heptameron*.

What concerns Margaret in these conversations are the private relations between men and women. The answer Margaret gives to any general condemnation of women is the one Christine gave: all women should not be judged for the evil of a few. Like Christine, Margaret complains that men deceive and betray women to achieve sexual gratification. Chivalric ideals are a front for seduction, and a truly loyal 'servant of love' is almost never found. Men who commit adultery are outraged if their wives do the same; like Christine, Margaret says that men condemn women for their own failings. Margaret's advice to women was similar to Christine's. Since women were naturally more chaste, they could help refine the behavior of men and make relations between the sexes less brutal. As wives they had a right to be loved and cared for, but if their marriages were unhappy they still had a duty to preserve the peace and stability of the home. Women had always to be on guard to keep their honor (the same honor Christine wrote about). Above all, women needed to exercise great patience and accept the conduct of bad husbands with resignation.

Like Christine, Margaret was abundantly aware of the power of God. Unlike Christine, she wrote religious poetry and carried on a correspondence with distinguished theologians. In the *Heptameron* her strong religious feeling plays an interesting counterpoint to her depiction of a world in which the god of love holds everyone in thrall. Love—and Margaret was less reticent than Christine in showing that love was inseparable from sexual passion—is part of the human experience, causing both men and women to behave irrationally and sinfully. Only God could rescue them. He could help them avoid the temptation of that other powerful deity, and His justice, not human vengeance, was to be relied on when a lover or a wife was betrayed or abused.

Margaret was probably not influenced by Christine. She was simply reflecting on similar subjects a hundred years later, when things had not changed very much with regard to those subjects. She was as sensitive as Christine to the plight of women, although she was perhaps less outraged by it because of her deeper acceptance of human fallibility. She thought men always tended to deceive women, and she had no nostalgia for some chivalric code that men supposedly used to follow. We can almost hear Christine and Margaret talking to each other across the chasm of years. The poet and the queen had a lot in common. They were both well-educated, both had been buffeted by fate, both had been widowed when young. They shared a yearning for better treatment of women by men and a sense of their own superiority to many men, which they expressed indirectly in their writing but might have talked about openly if they had come face to face, the remarkable accomplishments of the one reinforcing those of the other. As the scene unfolds in my imagination, I wonder whether it would have culminated in the laughter and tears of newly founded comradeship or with Christine and Margaret on their knees before God.

If feminism means thinking about women and feeling that they deserve better in the world, then Christine was a feminist, Margaret was a feminist, and I have no doubt that many mute women whose thoughts we will never know were feminists. So were the men who sang the praises of women in the *querelle des femmes*, if we are to judge from what they wrote. But if feminism means a belief in the equal capacities of men and women, if it means wanting sweeping changes, if it means demanding equal opportunities for women to be educated and trained for careers, if it means women organizing to get what they want, if it means having *any* kind of program—well, then feminism obviously did not come into existence until the nineteenth century. That does not have to be proved.

The questions that are raised when we look for the glimmerings of feminist consciousness in earlier centuries are not about similarities but differences. We know—or we should know—that women were not worse off in the nineteenth century than in the fifteenth. If suffering alone caused revolutions there would have been a radical feminist movement in the fifteenth century. The nineteenth-century women's movement did not come into being because things had become more and more unbearable. On the contrary, one of the preconditions of all revolutions is an atmosphere of rising expectations. I leave it to others to delineate the atmosphere of the late eighteenth and early nineteenth centuries. We need to remind ourselves why it may have taken so long to develop.

There were important changes between 1400 and 1800 in politics, economic conditions and thought. Certain key notions of the fifteenth century had faded considerably by the nineteenth century. Conversely, it is easy to recognize that many of the notions most taken for granted today were absent in the fifteenth century. They include the belief in equality, in the autonomy of the individual and in the right to self-government. Could anyone, much less women themselves, have thought it possible to change the conditions of their lives before they learned to be familiar with the idea of political action? The idea of inalienable human rights in the secular realm came before the idea of women's rights, and the idea that all men were equal came before the idea that men and women were equal. There is no need to labor this, but the danger of anachronism lurks in an unwillingness to recognize the role played by this cluster of ideas. Those embryonic feminists of the past may have smarted at the injustices done to women, but they issued no calls to action. They issued instead what may seem to us like calls to inaction. What we find in Christine and Margaret is something akin to quietism or stoicism. An individual woman was to make her own peace with the world by doing what the world was supposed to admire most profoundly: living a good Christian life. Historical research has shown that women were engaged in all kinds of enterprises and that widows in particular sometimes achieved considerable independence. But these facts were hardly mentioned by the writers we have been talking about, and never as models or goals. For them the ideal woman was a competent, virtuous, devout wife, whose merits they wanted to be recognized. Beyond that, they suggested that the greatest consolation to women should be the fact that they had no less an inside track to God than men did. If we are looking for an element of subversion in a supposed early feminism, it is hidden in the religious message. The traditional church made the male priest the intermediary between God and the rest of the population, just as men were the intermediaries between secular authorities and the members of their families, but at the same time women could pray directly to God, and the experience of women saints and mystics showed that God did not always communicate through men. Christine often reminded her readers of this, and it is a large part of the message of her poem about Joan of Arc. Margaret, in her less flamboyant, evangelical way, said something similar.

What did women really talk about? We wish we knew, since we have good reason to believe they took comfort from each other, even if they never organized for action. The topics discussed by Christine and Margaret offer some clues. They may have talked about the travails of love, about their resentment of their husbands' petty tyrannies and about the unfairness of misogyny. Did they also talk about their secret feelings of superiority, especially their special aptitude for Christian living? Did they consciously see religious devotion as a wonderful opportunity for women, in the perspective of the values they held most dear? A long line of fifteenth- and sixteenth-century women mystics and martyrs suggests that women took advantage of the opportunity. Reform movements seemed to offer particular promise, as one woman wrote in a letter to Margaret of Navarre, urging women to be active in the Reformation, partly to support a worthy cause, partly to vindicate women, 'hoping to God that from now on women will not be so despised as in the past'.[7]

To want to know about women in the past is a feeling all historians — if they are motivated by curiosity about humanity's endless variety and

---

7. 'Esperant en Dieu que doresnavant les femmes ne seront plus tant mesprisées comme par le passé.' In a letter of 1539 by Marie Dentière, wife of Antoine Froment, cited in Emile Telle, *L'Oeuvre de Marguerite d'Angoulême, reine de Navarre, et la querelle des femmes* (Toulouse, 1937; reprinted Geneva, 1969), pp. 377–8.

resourcefulness—should share. To know them piecemeal, however, is not enough. Historians cannot understand the past if they admit only the bits and pieces of information that correspond to their present concerns, even if their questioning of the past necessarily begins with those concerns. Avoiding anachronism is always hard when historians care deeply about an issue, but they have an overriding commitment to be fair to the people of the past, to stretch their own vision to take in what may no longer matter but used to matter very much. Women historians may very well feel a special obligation to the women of the past, but that is all the more reason to be fair and to shun anachronism. At the same time, we should also be fair to ourselves. For what we have to do as women in the second half of the twentieth century we do not need women of the fifteenth century, as embryonic feminists or as anything else. We should give ourselves credit for recognizing our own problems, which are not the same as theirs, partly because the world has changed and partly because perceptions have changed. We are dealing with different conditions and different options. If we need fifteenth-century women, it is not for guidance or inspiration, but simply because history is a poor thing without them.

REFERENCES

Agrippa of Nettesheim, Henry Cornelius, *Of the Nobilitie and Excellence of Womankynde*, trans. David Clapham (London, 1542).
Bell, Susan Groag, 'Christine de Pizan (1364–1430): humanism and the problem of a studious woman', *Feminist Studies*, III (1976), pp. 173–84.
Castiglione, Baldesar, *The Book of the Courtier*, trans. Charles S. Singleton (New York, 1959).
Chafe, William H., *The American Woman; Her Changing Social, Economic and Political Roles, 1920–1970* (New York, 1972).
Degler, Carl N., *At Odds; Women and the Family in America from the Revolution to the Present* (New York, 1980).
Favier, Marguerite, *Christine de Pisan; muse des cours souveraines* (Lausanne, 1967).
Febvre, Lucien, *Amour sacré, amour profane; autour de l'Heptaméron* (Paris, 1944).
———— *The Problem of Unbelief in the Sixteenth Century; the Religion of Rabelais*, trans. Beatrice Gottlieb (Cambridge, Mass., 1982).
Golenistcheff-Koutouzoff, Elie, *L'Histoire de Grisélidis en France au XIVe et au XVe siècle* (Paris, 1933).
Hicks, Éric (ed.), *Le Débat sur le 'Roman de la Rose'* (Bibliothèque du XVe Siècle, XLIII, Paris, 1977).
Huizinga, Johan, *The Waning of the Middle Ages*, trans. F. Hopman (New York, 1949; paper 1954).
Kelly, Joan, 'Early feminist theory and the *Querelle des Femmes*, 1400–1789', *Signs*, VIII (1982), pp. 4–28.
Keralio, Mlle de (ed.), *Collection des meilleurs ouvrages français composés par des femmes* (14 vols, Paris, 1786–9).
Knox, John, *The First Blast of the Trumpet Against the Monstruous Regiment of Women*. In *The Works of John Knox*, ed. David Laing (6 vols, Edinburgh, 1846–64), IV, pp. 363–420.
Laigle, Mathilde, *Le Livre des trois vertus de Christine de Pisan, et son milieu historique et littéraire* (Bibliothèque du XVe Siècle, Paris, 1912).
Langlois, Ernest, 'Le traité de Gerson contre *Le Roman de la Rose*', *Romania*, XLV (1918–19), pp. 23–48.
Lorris, Guillaume de and Jean de Meun, *Le Roman de la Rose*, ed. Daniel Poirion (Paris, 1974).
———— *The Romance of the Rose*, trans. Charles Dahlberg (Princeton, 1971).
McLeod, Enid, *The Order of the Rose; the Life and Ideas of Christine de Pizan* (Totowa, NJ, 1976).
Marguerite de Navarre, *L'Heptaméron*, ed. Michel François (Paris, 1967).

Matheolus, *Les Lamentations de Mathéolus et le Livre de Leesce de Jehan le Fèvre, de Resson*, ed. A. G. Van Hamel (2 vols, Bibliothèque de l'Ecole des Hautes Etudes, Sciences Historiques et Philologiques, XCV, XCVI, Paris, 1892, 1905).

Minto, William, 'A champion of her sex', *Macmillan's Magazine*, LIII (February 1886), pp. 264–75.

Phillips, James E. jun., 'The background of Spenser's attitude toward women rulers', *The Huntington Library Quarterly*, V (1941–2), pp. 5–32.

Pisan (or Pizan), Christine de, *The Book of the City of Ladies*, trans. Earl Jeffrey Richards (New York, 1982).

────── *The Book of the Duke of True Lovers*, trans. Alice Kemp-Welch, with verse trans. by Laurence Binyon and Eric R. D. Maclagan (London, 1909).

────── *Ditié de Jehanne d'Arc*, ed. Angus J. Kennedy and Kenneth Varty (Medium Aevum Monographs, New Series IX, Oxford, 1977).

────── *Oeuvres poétiques de Christine de Pisan*, ed. Maurice Roy (3 vols, Société des Anciens Textes Français 24, Paris, 1886–96).

Richardson, Lulu McDowell, *Forerunners of Feminism in French Literature of the Renaissance; from Christine de Pisan to Marie de Gournay* (The Johns Hopkins Studies in Romance Literature and Language, 12, Baltimore and Paris, 1929).

Rigaud, Rose, *Les Idées féministes de Christine de Pisan* (Neuchâtel, 1911; reprinted Geneva, 1973).

Seidel, Michael, 'Poulain de la Barre's *The Woman as Good as the Man*', *Journal of the History of Ideas*, XXXV (1974), pp. 499–508.

Telle, Emile, *L'Oeuvre de Marguerite d'Angoulême, reine de Navarre, et la querelle des femmes* (Toulouse, 1937; reprinted Geneva, 1969).

Thomassy, R., *Essai sur les écrits politiques de Christine de Pisan* (Paris, 1838).

Utley, Francis Lee, *The Crooked Rib; an Analytical Index to the Argument About Women in English and Scots Literature to the End of the Year 1568* (Columbus, Ohio, 1944).

Wood, Mary Morton, *The Spirit of Protest in Old French Literature* (Columbia University Studies in Romance Philology and Literature, XXII, New York, 1917; reprinted 1966).

RENATE BLUMENFELD-KOSINSKI

Christine de Pizan and the Misogynistic Tradition †

In a by now famous scene at the beginning of the *Book of the City of Ladies*, Christine de Pizan describes how she came, by chance, upon a book that someone had lent her. When she sees that it is by Matheolus, she smiles for

> oncques ne l'avoye veu et maintes fois ouy dire avoye qu'entre les autres livres celluy parloit bien a la reverence des femmes, me penssay qu'en maniere de solas le visiteroye (616–17).

> (. . . though I had never seen it before, I had often heard that like other books it discussed respect for women. I thought I would browse through it to amuse myself, 3).[1]

† Reprinted by permission from the *Romanic Review*, 81, no. 3 (1990). Copyright by the Trustees of Columbia University in the City of New York.

1. All French quotations come from Maureen Curnow, ed., *The Livre de la Cité des Dames of Christine de Pisan: A Critical Edition*, 2 vols. (Dissertation Vanderbilt University, 1975). For the translation I used *The Book of the City of Ladies*, trans. Earl Jeffrey Richards (New York: Persea Books, 1982). When page numbers are given in the text, the first number refers to Curnow, the second to Richards. Unless otherwise indicated, all other translations are my own. In order to clarify my analysis of textual parallels between the *Chemin de long estude* and the *Cité*, I suggest to translate "en maniere de solas" as "to seek solace," not as "to amuse myself."

Before she can do so, however, her mother calls her to supper, and it is only the following morning that Christine returns to the book and finds to her dismay that it contains many unpleasant things about women; but because it was written by a notable clerk, Christine muses, the book must contain some truth—particularly since it reiterates what countless philosophers and poets had said before, namely that "les meurs femenins [sont] enclins et plains de tous les vices" (618) (that the behavior of women is inclined to and full of every vice, 4). And although Christine's experience tells her that the misogynistic charges found everywhere are untrue, she begins to despair: the written tradition seems overwhelming in its condemnation of women. When Christine has reached a low point in her lamentations, three ladies appear to her, not in her sleep, she insists—in a clear opposition to the opening scene of the *Roman de la Rose* and some of her own earlier works—but in a waking state.

The first figure, Lady Reason, consoles her by suggesting that it is possible to reinterpret the misogynistic tradition through various methods: she claims that many authors speak by antiphrasis (meaning the opposite of what they say) or in a veiled manner ("en maniere de fable"), for otherwise what they say would be pure heresy. Also, Lady Reason insists, experience tells us that husbands like the Jaloux of the *Roman de la Rose* are rather unlikely constructs. Reason concludes her initial admonition by telling Christine that simplicity has caused her current distress, that she should come to her senses and shed her ignorance or intellectual blindness.[2]

This opening scene is crucial for our understanding of Christine's reception of the misogynistic tradition. The elements framing this reception are the following: Christine turns to books for solace; she seems to have a misconception regarding the contents of Matheolus' book; her mother interrupts her at a crucial point, that is, before she can find out what Matheolus is really about; her reading conflicts with her experience; she is saved by Reason / reason who presents her with hermeneutic tools; and she is finally charged to build her own written tradition in praise of women's achievements.

These elements can be divided into two groups which circumscribe the two fronts on which Christine is prepared to fight the misogynistic tradition as well as the means she intends to use: the bookish tradition, represented by the *auctores*, and the realm of experience, represented by individual women. In this second area, I will concentrate on Christine's image of her mother and the concept of the "natural woman" she develops in her *Book of the City of Ladies*.

2. Curnow, 624–25; Richards, 6–8.

Christine and the Authors

For Christine de Pizan, the misogynistic tradition was first and foremost a written one. This becomes clear in the earliest work where Christine directly addresses this unfortunate tradition. In the *Epistre au Dieu d'Amours* (Cupid's Letter) of 1399 she puts the following accusation into the mouth of the god of love:

> Si se plaignent les dessusdites dames
> De pluseurs clers qui sus leur mettent blasmes,
> Dittiez en font, rimes, proses et vers
> En diffamant leurs meurs par moz divers. (vv. 259–62)

(Thus the above-mentioned ladies complain about several learned men who heap blame upon them. They write narratives about this, in rhyme, prose and verse and thus diffame their behavior with many different words.)

Like the Wife of Bath, Christine knows that

> Mais se femmes eussent les livres fait
> Je sçay de vray qu'autrement fust du fait,
> Car bien scevent qu'a tort sont encoulpées,
> Si ne sont pas a droit les pars coupées,
> Car les plus fors prenent la plus grant part,
> Et le meilleur pour soy qui pieces part. (vv. 417–422)

(But if women had written the books, I know for sure that things would be quite different; for they know well that they have been falsely blamed. Things are not divided up evenly, for the strongest ones take the biggest part, and the one who cuts up things takes the best part for himself.)

From the outset, then, Christine defines her task: to rectify a tradition riddled with mistakes and slander and to turn the conditional "eussent fait" into an affirmative: "ont fait."

Was Christine equipped for this task? Although she repeatedly describes her education as nothing but picking up the crumbs of learning that fell from her father's table,[3] she had a grasp of the most important authors of her time. The countless quotes in her works of classical authors, church fathers, poets, and historical writers indicate a

3. In the prologue to the *Epistre d'Othéa* (1400; ed. Halina Loukopoulos, diss. Wayne State University, 1977), Christine describes her education as sitting beneath her father's table, waiting for some crumbs to fall down. Speaking of her father's wisdom compared to her own, she says: ". . . n'en ce cas ne resemble/Mon bon pere, fors ainsi com l'en emble/Espis de ble glanant en moissons/. . ./Ou mietes cheans de haulte table/. . ./ Autre chose n'en ay je recueilli/De son grant sens, dont il est assez cueilli" (p. 151, vv. 14–20); and in the *Mutacion de Fortune* (1400–1403; ed. S. Solente, 4 vols., Paris 1959–66) Christine says: "Y (=learning) avoie inclinacion/De ma droite condicion/Et pour mon pere ressembler;/Ne me poz je tenir d'embler/Des racleures et des paillettes,/Des petits deniers, des maillettes/Choites de la tres grant richesce,/Dont il avoit a grant largece," (vv. 449–56).

familiarity with the learned tradition that goes way beyond "crumbs" from her father's table. Christine knew how to select her materials from the many *compendia* and *specula* available in her time. The *Mutacion de Fortune*, for example, draws intelligently on the *Histoire ancienne jusqu'à César*, while the one hundred mythological stories of the *Epistre d'Othéa* testify to an intimate knowledge of Ovid via the *Ovide moralisé*. The question whether Christine knew Latin probably has to be answered affirmatively. Her remarks on Aristotle's *Metaphysics* (known in a Latin but not in a French translation at the time) in the *Lavision Christine* constitute the first French commentary on that work.[4] Thus her relationship to her *auctores* was an informed and at times even an intense one, as we can see at the beginning of the *Chemin de long estude*.[5]

In an opening scene similar to that of the *City*, Christine here recounts how on October 5, 1402 she was looking about her study for something to read but could not find anything "qui me peust donner confort/ D'un desplaisir que j'avoie" (which could give me comfort for the uneasy feeling I had; vv. 180f.). Finally, "me vint entre mains/Un livre que moult amay" (a book I loved very much came into my hands; vv. 202f.). This book is Boethius' *Consolation of Philosophy*, a text she knows well and loves because it helps her in her *desolacion* (v. 205). But even Boethius cannot comfort her completely, and before falling asleep she muses on the disasters of this world. Eventually, *after* falling asleep she as an "estrange vision/Ce ne fu pas illusion" (a strange vision, this was not an illusion; vv. 453f.): the Sibyl of Cumae appears to her and takes her on a celestial journey which ends up at a great debate on who is the proper ruler for this earth torn by strife. Christine is chosen as the messenger to return to France where, it is hoped, this perfect ruler can be found. But before she gets there, her mother, surprised at "tant de gesir" (v. 6391), or so much laying about, knocks on her door and wakes her.

The *Chemin* played a crucial role in Christine's literary and ideological development.[6] On one level, it dramatizes her entry into the world of learning, shown here as an allegorical dream journey: by using this form (and by writing in verse), Christine makes it clear that her learning flows in traditional channels, in fact she uses the very form the *Roman de la Rose* had made almost *de rigueur* for showing a subjective personal experience infused with vast amounts of encyclopedic learning.[7] The configuration of her learning experience is extremely complex, con-

---

4. See *Lavision Christine* (1405; ed. M. L. Towner, Washington, 1932), p. 159.
5. 1402–1403; ed. Robert Püschel, Berlin/Paris, 1881/1887.
6. On the development of Christine's thought in the first few years of the fifteenth century, see the excellent article by Joel Blanchard "Christine de Pizan: les raisons de l'histoire," *Le Moyen Age* 92 (1986): 417–36.
7. Cf. Michel Zink, "The Allegorical Poem as Interior Memoir," in K. Brownlee and S. Nichols eds., *Images of Power. Yale French Studies* 70 (1986): 100–26.

taining echoes of both Virgil's *Aeneid* and Dante's *Commedia:* by being guided by the Sibyl, Christine posits herself as another Aeneas and by writing about it as another Virgil. At the same time, her journey to the celestial spheres likens her to Dante who was guided there not by Virgil (as in the *Inferno* and the *Purgatorio*), but by Beatrice and Saint Bernard. The Sibyl, an extremely important figure throughout Christine's works,[8] is thus "contaminated" by these two saintly figures, while Christine herself follows in Dante's footsteps. Her attitude towards her *auctores* is not exactly modest, and this brief description of the *Chemin* will help us understand the position from which Christine is able to deal with the misogynistic authors who constitute the underbrush on the building site of the City of Ladies.[9]

Boccaccio is mentioned close to twenty times in the *City*, usually in a neutral or positive manner:[1] in his case, Christine's rewriting takes implicit forms. As for Ovid, although he is praised in the *Chemin de long estude* as one who "bien et bel en [= of Phaeton's chariot] a escript" (who wrote of it well and beautifully; vv. 1977f.), in the *City* he is the first victim of Christine's pick axe: "frappay sus a tout mon pié en tel maniere: 'Dame, dont vint a Ovide . . .'" (647) (I struck with all my force in the following way: "My lady, how does it happen that Ovid . . . ;" 21). Christine's question, represented here as an attack by pick axe more than suggestive of an act of castration, concerns Ovid's reputation as a great poet which is a puzzle to her, since he wrote so badly of women. The figural castration at the beginning of this passage is literalized a bit farther on when Reason explains that he "fu par ses demerites chastiez et diffourmez de ses membres" (was castrated and disfigured because of his faults; 648, 21). For Christine, there are two Ovids, the good one, her *auctor* and source (most often via the *Ovide moralisé*) for much mythological material, and the bad one, the misogynist.

Jean de Meun as well, plays a mostly negative role in Christine's writings, and his works have even fewer saving graces than Ovid's. The first attacks against Jean de Meun's part of the *Roman de la Rose* were launched in the *Epistre au dieu d'amours* (1399) and pursued in the debate on the *Roman de la Rose*. The most important accusations leveled against Jean were his badmouthing of all women (in other words, his irresponsible generalizations) and his pretense of wanting to teach

8. For an overview of the Sibyl's role in Christine's works, see pp. 140–43 in Kevin Brownlee, "Structures of Authority in Christine de Pizan's *Ditié de Jehanne d'Arc*," pp. 131–50 in Kevin Brownlee and Walter Stephens, eds., *Discourses of Authority in Medieval and Renaissance Literature* (Hanover/London, 1989). Look to page 371 in this edition.
9. This clearing of the "misogynistic underbrush" is represented in manuscripts of the *City of Ladies*. See, for example, the beautiful illumination reproduced by Maureen Quilligan in "Allegory and the Textual Body: Female Authority in Christine de Pizan's *Livre de la cité des Dames*", *Romanic Review* 79 (1988): 222–48, fig. 3 (London, Ms Add 20698, f. 17).
1. On Christine's reworking of Boccaccio's *De claris mulieribus* (Concerning Famous Women), see the detailed study by Patricia A. Phillippy, "Establishing Authority: Boccaccio's *De claris mulieribus* and Christine de Pizan's *Livre de la cité des dames*", *Romanic Review* 77 (1986): 167–94.

through negative *exempla*, a doomed enterprise, according to Christine.[2] Pierre Col's excuse in one of his letters in the *Débat sur Roman
de la Rose* that Jean de Meun is speaking through personages, i.e., allegorically, and hence cannot be blamed for what he says, does not convince Christine.[3] She continues her disapproval of Jean de Meun in the
City, although not in as forceful a manner as in the *Débat*: here he is
mentioned only in the context of the foolish advice some writers give,
i.e., that one should not tell secrets to one's wife. But implicitly the
Roman de la Rose is present throughout the *City*, where the walled
impregnable city of virtuous ladies contrasts sharply with the surrender
of the Rose castle and the obscene plucking and impregnation of the
rose. At the end of the *City*, there is a sarcastic echo of Genius' warning
against women "Fuiez, fuiez, fuiez, fuiez,/fuiez enfant, fuiez tel beste:"[4]
while Genius refers to woman *(tel beste)*, Christine refers to treacherous
men when she exclaims "O! mes dames, fuyes, fuyes la folle amour
dont ilz vous admonnestent. Fuyez la! Pour Dieu fuyez!" (1035) (Oh
my ladies, flee, flee the foolish love, the foolish love they urge on you.
Flee it, for God's sake, flee! 256). The *City*, having begun with a pitiful
complaint triggered by one misogynist, thus ends with a forceful and
comical reversal of another. How did Christine arrive at this position?

In the *Chemin*, Boethius provides consolation. In the *City*, it is Christine who will have to provide her own consolation. The allegorical
ladies state their mission clearly as "toy consoler" (622) (to console you;
6), and they will do this by having Christine display her learning in the
service of revisionist history. We saw that the immediate cause for her
unhappy thoughts and consequently for the arrival of the comforting
ladies was a book, Matheolus' *Lamentations*.[5]

Who was this Matheolus or "Mahieu" as he is sometimes called?
Although he was the proverbial misogynist, Christine says that his book
"entre les livres n'a aucune reputacion" (618).[6] She may just mean that

2. For the accusation against generalization see the *Epistre au Dieu d'Amours* (in *Oeuvres poétiques de Christine de Pisan*, ed. Maurice Roy, 3 vols. [Paris, 1886–91], vol. 2, pp. 1–27), vv.
   184–191, 345–48, 741f.; the *Débat sur le Roman de la Rose* (ed. Eric Hicks, Paris 1977), pp.
   18 and 22. Significantly, Jean de Meun's defender in the debate, Pierre Col, picks up on
   exactly that point when he says in reference to Jean's method, "Par Dieu! ce n'est pas blasmer
   tout le sexe femenin!" (p. 103).
3. Pierre Col claims that ". . . maistre Jehan de Meung en son livre introduisy personnaiges, et
   fait chascun personnaige parler selon qui luy appartient" (*Débat*, p. 100). The author, Col
   argues, does not necessarily agree with what his figures say. She refutes his arguments on p.
   132 of the *Débat*.
4. Vv. 16552f., vol. 2, ed. Lecoy (Paris, 1973). (Flee, flee, flee, flee, flee, child, flee such a beast.)
   Christine had already singled out for criticism this exhortation by Genius in the *Débat*, pp. 17
   and 21.
5. This work was edited by Anton-Gérard van Hamel in its original Latin and in the French
   translation by Jean le Fèvre de Ressons whose *Livre de Leesce* occupies the second volume of
   van Hamel's edition. See *Les Lamentations de Matheolus et le Livre de Leesce de Jehan le Fèvre
   de Ressons*, 2 vols., Paris, 1905).
6. It is very likely that Christine knew of more this book than she indicates here. Pierre-Yves
   Badel states that the *Lamentations* was a veritable "bestseller" in the fourteenth century. See
   Le Roman de la Rose au XIVe siècle: Etude de la réception de l'oeuvre (Geneva, 1980), p. 182.

it "had a bad name anyway" (4), as Richards translates this phrase. But she may also use her supposed ignorance of the contents of this book as a rhetorical ploy: her shock at reading Matheolus is all the greater because his slanderous remarks on women are so unexpected. Undoubtedly, Christine's supposed unfamiliarity with Matheolus is necessary to dramatize her passage from intellectual blindness to the kind of "clairvoyance" or clear understanding demanded of her by Reason: "Et que tu soyes faite clerveant es choses qui contaminent et troublent ton couraige en obscurté de pensee" (628) ("so that you might also see clearly, in the midst of the darkness of your thoughts, those things which taint and trouble your heart"; 10). Her initial misunderstanding of Matheolus and the despair resulting from reading his book are what brings the three allegorical ladies into her chamber: Christine most effectively builds the opening passages of the *City* around the acts of reading and misreading.

Matheolus's *Lamentations,* a lengthy (9844 lines) complaint in four books by a "bigamous clerk," as he calls himself, was written around 1290 and translated into French by Jean le Fèvre de Ressons around 1370.[7] The work as a whole is tedious and repetitious, assembling misogynistic common places and relating them to the author's own unhappy marriage. Matheolus poses as a "martyr" of marriage (I, v. 10) who failed to read the *Roman de la Rose,* a work that would surely have warned him against marriage (I, vv. 19–26)![8] The method of generalization, so odious to Christine in the context of Jean de Meun's misogynistic tirades, is used here as well. Matheolus often generalizes, then applies this generalization to his own wife. In book 2, for example, he says

> *La femme* est toujours rioteuse,
> Jangleuse, dure, despiteuse;
> La pais par elle est bannie,
> A rebours dit la letanie,
> La parole Dieu et la messe.
> Souvent maudit en sa promesse.
> *Ma femme* les tenebres chante,
> "Ve" et lamentacio[n]s hante;
> Elle maudit a chascune heure,
> Ou elle tance et elle pleure. (vv. 41–50; emphasis added)

7. The date for the *Lamentations* (1290) is given by Badel in *Le Roman de la Rose,* p. 178. Matheolus refers to himself as "bigamous" because at the Council of Lyon, called by Pope Gregory X in 1274, the rules for clerical marriage were redefined. A clerk who married a widow would now be guilty of bigamy and lose his clerical benefits. This was the situation of Matheolus. (See van Hamel, vol. 2, pp. CXII–CXVIII.)

8. The prologue from which I quote here does not appear in the Latin text. But since Christine most likely knew the *Lamentations* in their French translation, she must also have known this prologue. Matheolus' own prologue is purely classical: "Parve, nec invideo, Morini, liber ibis in urbem" (l. 1), translated by Le Fèvre as "Va t'en, petit livre, va t'en/En la cité, plus n'y atten!" (vv. 83f.).

(Woman is ever riotous, gossipy, hard, and full of spite; through her all peace is banished, she says the litany, the word of God and mass backwards. Often she curses in her promise. My wife's tune is only gloom, she utters only maledictions and lamentations; she constantly curses, or fights and cries.)[9]

Note the passage from the general to the particular here: *la femme—ma femme*. The excerpt just quoted represents the tenor and method of his entire text which, finally, is nothing but one unmitigated attack on women. Why did Christine think, then, that this book spoke well of women? It may be that she was thinking of the *Livre des Leesce* (Book of Joy), Jean le Fèvre's work in praise of women that often appeared in the same manuscripts as the *Lamentations*. But it may also be that she sets the reader up: she leaves us in suspense as to the true nature of Matheolus' book, for the moment she opens the book for the first time her mother interrupts her with a call to supper. The timing of this interruption is extremely important, for it links the moment of Matheolus with the moment of the mother.

Christine and Her Mother

Christine's mother appears in a number of her works and in each case she seems to represent Christine's ambiguous view of traditional medieval womanhood and its functions in society and the world of learning.

Christine's conflicted attitude towards her mother becomes evident in the *Mutacion de Fortune* when she begins the section "Ci devise de sa mere" (Here she speaks of her mother) as follows:

> Ma mere qui fu grant et lee
> Et plus preux que Panthasellee
> . . .
> En tout cas, mon pere passa
> De sens, de puissance et de pris,
> . . .
> Et fu royne couronnee,

(vv. 339–345)

> . . .
> On l'appelle dame Nature.
> Mere est celle a toute personne.

(vv. 366f.)

---

9. For the idea of "woman as riot" (and the relationship of misogyny and language) see R. Howard Bloch, "Medieval Misogyny," *Representations* 20 (1987): 1–24. I have investigated Jean le Fèvre's use of the term "riot" (as applied to male discourse) in his *Livre de Leesce* in a detailed analysis of this text: "Jean le Fèvre's *Livre de Leesce*: Praise or Blame of Women?" *Speculum* 69 (1994): 705–25.

(My mother who was great and joyful and more valiant than Penthesilea . . . surpassed my father in everything: sense, power and achievement. . . . She was a crowned queen. . . . One calls her lady Nature, and she is the mother of everyone.)

Christine's real mother appears only in the next section ("Here she speaks of how she gathered nothing but scraps from her father's treasure"). Christine insists that she resembles her father in everything but gender. But she was dearly loved by her mother:

> Si fu comme fille nommee
> Et bien nourrie et bien amee
> De ma mere a joyueuse chiere,
> Qui m'ama tant et tint si chiere
> Que elle meismes m'alaicta,
> Aussitost qu'elle m'enfanta
>
> (vv. 406–406)

(Thus I was named as a girl and nourished and well loved by my joyful mother, who loved me so much and held me so dear that she herself breastfed me as soon as she had given birth to me.)

Although love and affection for her mother permeate this passage, one cannot deny that Christine posits Nature as her real mother here, Nature who surpasses Penthesilea, an amazon praised highly in many of Christine's works,[1] and even her father to whose achievements she had just dedicated hundreds of lines. The function of her physical mother that is highlighted here is just that: physical, that is, breastfeeding.[2] Thus while her father's heritage is a permanent one of erudition and scholarship, what her mother gave her is as valuable but less durable.

The opposition between the father's and the mother's ambitions for their daughter is dramatically expressed in a chapter on the benefits of education for women in the *City of Ladies* when Lady Rectitude tells Christine that

> "Ton pere, qui fu grant naturien et phillosophe, n'oppinoit pas que femmes vaulsissent pis par science apprendre, ains de ce qu'encline te veoit aux lettres, si que tu sces, grant plaisir y prenoit. Mais l'oppinion femenine de ta mere, qui te vouloit occupper en fillasses selonc l'usaige commun des femmes, fu cause de l'empeschement

---

1. For an examination of the role of Penthesilea in Christine's works see Kevin Brownlee, "Hector and Penthesilea in the *Livre de la Mutacion de Fortune:* Christine de Pizan and the Politics of Myth," in Liliane Dulac and Bernard Ribémont, eds., *Une Femme de Lettres au Moyen Age: Etudes autour de Christine de Pizan* (Orléans: Paradigme, 1995), 69–82.
2. Despite the many connotations breastfeeding had in the context of mystical writing, I believe that the breastfeeding should be taken literally here, emphasizing the closeness of mother and daughter in an age when many mothers gave their children to wet nurses to be breastfed.

que ne fus en ton enffance plus avant boutee es sciences et plus en parfont." [875])

("Your father, who was a great scientist and philosopher did not believe that women were worth less by knowing science; rather as you know, he took great pleasure from seeing your inclination to learning. The feminine opinion of your mother, however, who wished to keep you busy with spinning and silly girlishness, following the common custom of women, was the major obstacle to your being involved in the sciences.") (154f.)

The complaint that she was prevented in her youth to delve more deeply into her father's well of learning also appears in the *Chemin*. When Christine and the Sibyl approach two kinds of ladders that lead up to the firmament, the Sibyl agrees that Christine is indeed authorized to ascend but not on the path they had originally contemplated:

> Le chemin ou premierement
> Entrasmes, ne t'y menra mie,
> Mais par cestui yras, amie;
> Monter au firmament te fault,
> Combien qu'autres montent plus hault,
> Mais tu n'as mie le corsage
> Abille a ce: toutefois say je
> Que de toy ne vient le deffault
> Mais la force qui te deffault
> Est pour ce que tart a m'escole
> es venue. . . .
>
> (vv. 1670–80)

("I will not lead you along the path that we first entered, but you will go along this one, dear friend; you must ascend to the firmament. But although there are others who ascend even further, you yourself do not have the stature appropriate for this: however, I know that this is not your fault, but that you are lacking strength because you started instruction in my school late.")

Christine insists here that it is impossible to catch up, once she has lost the advantage of the early education her father had wanted for her. Consequently her mother's objections to learning will forever keep her from making the highest ascent. While this accusation against her mother remains implicit in the *Chemin*, it is spelled out in the *City of Ladies*: it is there that the mother appears in the most negative light as the prime obstacle to Christine's education.

An interesting contrast to this negative depiction is Lady Philosophy's praise of Christine's mother in *Lavision Christine*. Just as Christine is about to despair while enumerating the bad luck Fortune has dealt her, Lady Philosophy comforts her by listing all the good Christine has in her life: her children, her mother and good health. Here is Philosophy's praise of Christine's mother:

> "Que diray ie de ta tres noble mere? Sces tu point femme plus vertueuse? Remembre toy depuis ta jonece jusques au iour duy sa vie contemplative constamment au service de dieu. . . . O quel noble femme! Comme sa vie est glorieuse." (173)[3]

> ("What shall I say of your noble mother? Do you know a more virtuous woman? Remember—from your youth until today—her contemplative life, always in the service of God. Oh, what a noble woman! How glorious her life is.")

Lady Philosophy emphasizes the piety and patience of Christine's mother, in other words, the most traditional female virtues, those Christine highlights again and again in the *Livre des trois vertus*.

Thus the image Christine presents of her mother is double-edged: nurturing and consoling in Christine's childhood as well as in her adult life (after all, in the *City* she calls her daughter to a supper which the writer did not have to prepare), she was a stumbling block in Christine's youth, the decisive period of her education. This double function is dramatized in the two scenes of interruption in the *Chemin* and the *City* I mentioned earlier. We saw that the *Chemin de long estude* marked an important step in Christine's artistic and philosophical development. In it Christine first articulates the new serious intent of her work as well as her personal political mission centering on France's unity and strength. But before she can accomplish this mission, her mother wakes her, that is, Christine is still hampered by what her mother represents: "real" life and its concerns, traditional women's roles. Similarly, the mother's interruption at the *beginning*—significantly not at the end as in the *Chemin*—of the *City* dramatizes Christine's position in face of the misogynistic tradition: just as she is about to get to the bottom of it, she is called to supper; and it is only after this irruption of the domestic and traditional woman's lot that she returns to the book and learns its truth. In each case, then, the mother's function is a disruptive one, but in the *City*, unlike in the *Chemin*, it is not a definitively disruptive function, since here Christine manages to go on with her mission.[4]

The mother's role is emblematic of the difficulties Christine perceived in her own career: how to combine a serious literary intent with

3. I added punctuation to the edition by M. L. Towner.
4. The interruptions also have to be considered in the context of the waking vs. sleeping (dreaming) pattern. In his *Le Roman de la Rose au XIVe siècle*, Pierre-Yves Badel distinguishes three types of conclusions to dream visions: *conclusions internes, externes* and *immotivées* (p. 336). Christine's waking at the end of the *Chemin* is clearly an external conclusion. I would suggest that in the *City* Christine transfers the mother's interruption to a waking state, thus highlighting implicitly what she spells out explicitly later on: that this vision is not a dream vision as the *Chemin* had been. Here one sees a tendency on her part to "correct" her own work throughout her career: the form of the dream vision was too close to the *Roman de la Rose*, a text she rejects and rewrites in the *City*.

being a woman in a society that valued nurturing, piety and passivity in women above all else. This type of misogyny is more subtle than Matheolus' tirades, but it is nonetheless present and powerful. To conquer it was Christine's goal and she admirably shows in the *City* how this subliminal misogyny can be overcome; for she returns to the book she had picked up and uses it as the starting point for her own enterprise. And this time her mother will not interrupt her.

"Unnatural" and "Natural" Women: Books and Experience

As we saw earlier, the function of the three allegorical ladies in the *City* is to console Christine. On a first level, Christine's complex relationship with her authors is bound up with the question of consolation; consolation is an achievement that requires Christine's active participation: the correct evaluation of her own experience, the shedding of her blindness, and finally, writing. We also saw that the principal means for Christine's consolation in the *Chemin* and the *City* are books. In the later *Lavision*, on the other hand, her children and mother are sources of strength, her consolation can be found in the realm of her own experience. How do the two areas of books and experience relate to each other? And what role does Reason play in all this?

Interestingly, these three concepts correspond to what Jean de Meun describes as the three ways to perfect understanding at the end of the famous passage in the *Roman de la Rose*, generally referred to as "l'excusacion de l'auteur:"[5] texts (*escrit*), experience and reason. Although it was this very passage that Christine singled out for criticism in the *Débat* (where she shows that Jean's "excusacion" is in fact a "lame excuse") she seems to appropriate it here. In Christine's writings the *Roman de la Rose* is ever present as a kind of foil or counterpoint; she frequently sets off her own opinions against those of Jean de Meun. Here, characteristically, Christine adopts Jean's methodology only up to a certain point: she shows us how reason/Reason came to her aid; she shows us how to use texts in the defense of women. But when it comes to experience, Christine departs from Jean de Meun: where he offers us the "experiences" of the likes of Jaloux, Christine offers us her own experiences as a "natural woman." What does it mean to be a natural woman, a *femme naturelle* (618)?

At the beginning of the *City* Christine presents herself as a *femme naturelle* (618) who examines her own experience. This leads her to oppose the positive concept of the natural woman to the bookish misogynistic tradition. Character and conduct are the elements that constitute the natural woman. From both perspectives—encompassing the internal and the external—Christine finds, women do not in the least corre-

---

5. "Onc riens n'en dis, mien esciant/conmant qu'il m'aut contrariant,/qui ne soit en escrit trové/ et par experimant prové,/ou par reson au mains provable . . ." (ed. Lecoy, vv. 15262–67).

spond to the images painted of them in the misogynistic tradition.[6] And yet, Christine is still the victim of a misleading bookish tradition: although contradicted by her own experience, this tradition seems unchangeable, graven in stone.

In this initial passage Christine does not give us a definition of the character and conduct of the natural woman. This definition emerges only when the natural woman is contrasted with the unnatural woman, the latter being the "counterfeit" of the former:

> ". . . il ne soit chose en ce monde qui plus face a fouyr, a droite verité dire, que fait la mauvaise femme dissolue et perverse si comme monstre en nature, qui est chose contrefaitte hors de sa propre condicion naturelle qui doit estre simple, coye et honneste. . . ." (642f.)

> (". . . there is nothing that should be avoided more than an evil, dissolute, and perverted woman, who is like a monster in nature, a counterfeit estranged from her natural condition, which must be simple, tranquil and upright . . ."; 18).

and

> "Et de celles qui telles sont, je ne me mesle, car telles femmes sont comme chose hors de sa nature." (819)

> ("I will not meddle with evil women, for such women are like creatures alienated from their own nature"; 120)

Right after this passage, Christine mentions Theophrastus, another proverbial misogynist. The first passage, as well, had been placed into the immediate context of refuting the misogynistic tradition. It is this tradition, then, that equates "unnatural" with evil women. But not all "unnatural women" are evil, as Christine shows when she contrasts the "natural woman" with her own *concrete* examples of "unnatural women." It is here that Christine makes the decisive step in her enterprise: she expands and redefines what is "natural" and "unnatural" in a woman, and she does so by exploiting the bookish tradition (from which she draws almost all her examples) in light of her own experience. The realm of experience enables Christine to arrive at a judicious evaluation of the misogynistic and misogamous traditions. She does not simply try to turn this tradition against men, but she shows that as there are good and evil women so there are good and evil men. Lady Rectitude reminds Christine of her own husband:

> "Et quoyqu'il soit des mauvais maris, il en est tres bons, vaillans et sages. . . . Et ce puez tu bien sçavoir par toy meismes, qui tel l'avoyes. . . ." (819)

6. Pp. 618f.; 4.

> (And although there are bad husbands, there are also very good
> ones, truly valiant and wise. . . . You know this perfectly well from
> your own experience, for you had such a good husband . . . ; 119)

Thus Lady Rectitude demonstrates the correctness of Christine's personal experience and—since it deals with good *men*—proves its unprej-
udiced nature. She thus authorizes Christine's use of that experience in
her defense of women.

In the depiction of women like Queen Fredegund, who may at first
sight appear "unnatural," Christine fuses her book learning with an evaluation based on experience:

> "En France fu la royne Fredegonde, laquelle fu femme du roy
> Chilperic. Celle dame, nonobst[ant] fust elle cruelle oultre loy
> naturelle de femme, toutesvoyes, aprés la mort de son mary, gouv-
> erna le royaume de France par grant sçavoir." (668)

> ("In France there was once a queen, Fredegund, who was the wife
> of King Chilperic. Although she was cruel, contrary to the natural
> disposition of women, following her husband's death, with great
> skill this lady governed the kingdom of France." 33)

And Fredegund appears once more later where, speaking to her subjects, she says:

> ". . . car j'ay pourpenssé un barat par quoy nous vaincrons . . . Je
> lairay ester toute paour femenine et armeray mon cuer de har-
> diesce d'omme." (713)

> (". . . for I have thought up a ruse by which we will conquer . . . I
> will abandon all feminine fear and arm my heart with a man's
> boldness"; 59)

Fredegund is, in the final analysis, not "unnatural" but rather represents
an expansion of the notion of the natural woman. Although Fredegund
may represent an extreme, she also reenacts Christine's own experience
of overcoming female nature, described so dramatically in the *Mutacion
de Fortune*. What warfare was for Fredegund, writing is for Christine.

Looking at the many women who appear in the *City of Ladies* we
find few—except Griselda and some of the saints—who correspond
completely to Christine's initial definition of the "natural woman" as
simple, coye and *honeste* (642). Of course, the women are upright, but
are they simple and tranquil? The ideal conduct for women described
in the *Livre des trois vertus* is much more in line with the qualities
initially listed by Christine in the *City*, for here it is a question of "real"
life. She realized very well that in the real world only a skilful combina-
tion of strength with simplicity and tranquility can guarantee a woman's

survival and success. As the *City of Ladies* progresses, however, it becomes clear that women's achievements are of a different nature: active learning, prowess and even active martyrdom are the hallmarks of the women there.[7]

In the course of the *City of Ladies*, then, Christine—by joining her experience as a woman to her learning—offers a redefinition and expansion of the concept of the "natural woman." The consolation offered by Reason, Rectitude and Justice involves reinterpretation: not only the reinterpretation of the misogynistic tradition—although this is the starting point and guiding thread of the entire book—but also a reinterpretation of the received concept of what makes a "natural woman." Christine herself and her mother offer interesting paradigms in this context. Christine, like Fredegund, is transformed after her husband's death: she turns into a man and, until the beginning of the *City* reluctantly remains one. At that moment, of course, Lady Reason begins to instill pride in Christine, pride for her female body and her female intellect. While before she had been an "unnatural" albeit effective woman, she now no longer needs her male disguise since she will be in the company of the most excellent and successful women of her own creation. Her mother, on the other hand, from the outset and consistently, conforms to the definition of the "natural woman"; her goodness is profound, but it is passive and sometimes even obstructive. Linked to the new positive view of her own womanhood found in the *City*, the favorable valuation of the mother we find in the later *Lavision* confirms that Christine has so successfully redefined women's roles and achievements that she can now clearly see her mother's consoling role as one necessary piece in the vast mosaic of women's diverse functions.

Returning to the three roads to perfect understanding outlined above—reason, experience, and writing—we can see how Christine uses these three means for a refutation of the misogynistic tradition. Reason, in the form of Lady Reason, first comes to her aid and incites her to reinterpret received notions about women. Experience lets her see the foolishness of misogynistic texts and allows her to adduce counterexamples. Writing—and reading—that is, her vast learning, forms the basis for her entire enterprise: examples of feminine virtue and valor were plentiful in books, they only had to be unearthed and reinterpreted; what is "natural" and "unnatural" in women had to be redefined: finally, then, it is the long road of learning paved with reason and experience that leads to the city of ladies.

---

7. For the idea of active martyrdom see Kevin Brownlee, "Martyrdom and the Female Voice: Saint Christine in the *Livre de la cité des dames*," in R. Blumenfeld-Kosinski and Timea Szell, eds. *Images of Sainthood in Medieval Europe* (Ithaca, N.Y.: Cornell University Press, 1991), pp. 115–35.

SHEILA DELANY

"Mothers to Think Back Through": Who Are They? The Ambiguous Example of Christine de Pizan †

My title comes from Virginia Woolf, who claims in the sixth chapter of *A Room of One's Own* that "a woman writing thinks back through her mothers." The book attempts to revive the tradition of the writing woman and to explore some of the special problems of that tradition. Woolf's notion of "mothers to think back through" poses a problematic of its own which I address in this essay, using as my test case the late-medieval French courtly writer Christine de Pizan. The problem of antecedents has begun to be explored by contemporary gender-oriented scholars stimulated as much by the work of Harold Bloom as by that of Virginia Woolf. In *The Anxiety of Influence* (1973) Bloom advances a more or less Freudian and Oedipal theory of poetic history as a history of influence in which the strong poet "corrects" or completes the work of precursors. The poet does so through "strong misprision": a misreading or misinterpretation that is actually a complex defense mechanism permitting the poet to absorb and transcend the influence of the powerful precursor. Gender-oriented scholars have both appropriated and criticized Bloom's theory. Sandra Gilbert and Susan Gubar write that their well-known study of nineteenth-century female writers, *The Madwoman in the Attic* (1979), "is based in the Bloomian premise that literary history consists of strong action and inevitable reaction" (p. xiii). Simultaneously they point out that the female poet does not experience anxiety of influence as her male counterpart would do, for she experiences something much more fundamental: "anxiety of authorship," the fear that she cannot become a precursor. "The creative I AM cannot be uttered if the 'I' knows not what it is" (p. 17).

The consensus among those who have used Bloom's thesis, whether they are pro or con,[1] appears to be that Bloom's theory itself requires a strong "creative misprision," a rewriting that will free it from the male-

† Reprinted by permission from *Medieval Texts and Contemporary Readers*, ed. Laurie A. Finke and Martin B. Schichtman (Ithaca, NY: Cornell University Press, 1987). Copyright © 1987 by Cornell University.

1. See, for instance, Annette Kolodny, "A Map for Rereading; or, Gender and the Interpretation of Literary Texts," *New Literary History* 11 (Spring 1980), 451–67; Joanne Feit Diehl, " 'Come Slowly-Eden': An Exploration of Women Poets and Their Muse," *Signs* 3 (Spring 1978), 572–87; S. Delany, "Rewriting Woman Good: Gender and the Anxiety of Influence in Two Late-Medieval Texts," in *Chaucer in the Eighties*, ed. Julian Wasserman (Syracuse: Syracuse University Press, 1986). Also on the question of the experience of the woman reader or writer, see Judith Fetterley, *The Resisting Reader: A Feminist Approach to American Fiction* (Bloomington:

oriented Oedipal perspective and allow the notion of influence or models to operate in the context of female experience. Such a rewriting must
restore the social dimension that seems marginal in Bloom's project but
that, as Virginia Woolf stresses, has profoundly molded the woman artist's relation to her work. It must recognize as a primary component of
female experience the fact of exclusion—exclusion, often, from production and consumption of the means of culture; more generally, exclusion from that range of experience which writers write about, including
the experience of personal and institutional power.

One of the aims of contemporary gender-oriented scholarship has
been to acquaint us with our antecedents and to provide role models—
"mothers to think back through"—by rehabilitating women writers
whose work has been neglected. Thus we have learned, to mention only
a few examples from my own period of specialization, about Hrotswitha,
the tenth-century German nun and playwright; about some two dozen
trobairitz (women poets of courtly love) in twelfth- and thirteenth-century France; about the women humanist scholars of quattrocento Italy;
about women poets of the Renaissance; and about the early fifteenth-
century courtly writer Christine de Pizan.[2] This rehabilitation is a valuable effort, and not only for women. Everyone needs to know what
women have done and what they have not done, and the reasons why;
for as the utopian socialist Charles Fourier long ago declared, the condition of women in any society is an index to the advancement and limita-
tions of that society as a whole.

Paradoxically, however, the very effort to reconstitute a full understanding of women's participation in cultural history can result in a
skewed perception of individual contributions and of history at large.
This need not happen, but it can happen and has happened when we
do not firmly anchor the figure in question in her own historical milieu.
If we desire the full equality and genuine liberation of women, then we
desire the transformation of social life; we cannot afford an inaccurate
view of past or present, for that would condemn us to ineffectuality. If
we do not wish to maintain a falsified history, then we have to assess

---

Indiana University Press, 1978); Margaret Homans, *Women Writers and Poetic Identity*
(Princeton: Princeton University Press, 1980); Ellen Moers, *Literary Women* (Garden City, N.Y.:
Doubleday, 1976); Suzanne Juhasz, *Naked and Fiery Forms: Modern American Poetry by Women:
A New Tradition* (New York: Octagon, 1976); Mary Jacobus, ed., *Women Writing and Writing
about Women* (London: Croom Helm, 1979).
2. Ann L. Haight, ed., *Hroswitha of Gandersheim: Her Life, Times and Works* (New York: Hroswi-
tha Club, 1965); Meg Bogin, *The Woman Troubadours* (New York: Paddington, 1976); Patricia
LaBalme, ed., *Beyond Their Sex: Learned Women of the European Past* (New York: New York
University Press, 1980); Margaret King and Albert Rabil, eds., *Her Immaculate Hand . . . The
Women Humanists of Quattrocento Italy* (Binghamton: Center for Medieval and Early Renaissance Studies, 1983); Albert Rabil, *Laura Cereta, Quattrocento Humanist* (Binghamton: Center
for Medieval and Early Renaissance Studies, 1981); Ann Jones, "Assimilation with a Difference:
Renaissance women Poets and Literary Influence," *Yale French Studies* no. 62 (1981), 135–153;
E. Jeffrey Richards, trans., *The Book of the City of Ladies: Christine de Pizan* (New York: Persea,
1982).

every rehabilitated woman writer in relation to her social context. Without a rounded and balanced analysis of this kind, the search for "mothers to think back through" becomes simply a scholarly version of that
"sisterhood" which the revived women's movement in our era has confronted as one of its basic theoretical and political questions. In this
essay I challenge the idea that the act of writing by itself suffices to
qualify an early woman writer as a feminist, a radical, a revolutionary, or
a model for us. We have, in short, to *select* the mothers we wish to think
back through.

Christine de Pizan has a place-setting in that powerful and controversial monument to "sisterhood," Judy Chicago's installation *The Dinner
Party*. One criterion for inclusion in *The Dinner Party* was ability to
"present a role model for the future," and this criterion gave the artist a
moment of doubt. "As I worked on research for *The Dinner Party*," she
writes, "and then on the piece itself, a nagging voice kept reminding me
that the women whose plates I was painting, whose runners we were
embroidering, whose names we were firing onto the porcelain floor,
were primarily women of the ruling classes." [3] But Judy Chicago shies
away from the difficult implications of this nagging voice with the truism that "history has been written from the point of view of those who
have been in power. It is not an objective record of the human race."
Are we then to reject the notion of ruling class or to reject all historical
data recorded by men? Chicago's evasion implies a total skepticism that
would render any historical understanding impossible, including that
of *The Dinner Party*, which reveals a strongly biased (and inaccurate)
conception of history. The nagging voice that Chicago dismissed is the
one to which I pay attention, arguing that we need not clasp every
woman writer to our collective bosom merely because—as Virginia
Woolf remarked of the eighteenth-century novelist Eliza Haywood—
"she is dead, she is old, she wrote books, and nobody has yet written a
book about her." [4]

Christine de Pizan requires a hard historical look because of the large
claims that have been made for her. Jeffrey Richards, for example, translator of Christine's *Livre de la Cité des Dames*, adopts a tone nearly
hagiographical, in which the vocabulary of "mothers to think back
through" is very pronounced. We are told of "the experimental and
innovative nature of her prose" (p. xxi), "her enormous range" (p. xxii),
"her participation in the intellectual currents of her age" (p. xxvi).
Christine is "revolutionary . . . profoundly feminist," completely dedicated "to the betterment of women's lives and to the alleviation of their
suffering" (p. xxviii). This appreciation, which seems to me wrong on

3. This and the following quotation are from Judy Chicago, *The Dinner Party: A Symbol of Our
Heritage* (New York: Doubleday, 1979), p. 56.
4. "A Scribbling Dame," in *Virginia Woolf: Women and Writing*, ed. Michele Barrett (New York:
Harcourt Brace Jovanovich, 1979).

every count, is one of the most extreme, and particularly odd because the view of Christine as protofeminist is not a new one.[5] The notion emerged and was debated a century ago, in the heyday of the international feminist movement; it was laid to rest as early as 1912 by Matilde Laigle in her study of Christine's *Le Livre des Trois Vertus.* Later I suggest some reasons for the latter-day revival of this "querelle de Christine."

My purpose in presenting a cautionary dossier on Christine is to show that she was not, even by the standards of her own day, a reformer or protofeminist; that she is at best a contradictory figure, admirable in some respects, deplorable in others. I approach Christine as a reader and a writer who has been moved by Christine's account of her own "anxiety of influence" at the beginning of *Cité des Dames,* where she confronts head-on the literary tradition of medieval clerical misogyny. I believe I have understood her subversive propagandistic effort to "rewrite woman good" in that text.[6] I have been charmed by some of her lyrics, impressed by her determination to educate herself and above

5. Earlier versions of Richards's position were put forward by Rose Rigaud, *Les idées féministes de Christine de Pisan* (1911; rpt. Geneva: Slatkine, 1973), who writes of "cette femme 'moderne,' féministe convaincue . . . 'précurseur' " (p. 25) and of "la théoricienne du féminisme moderne" (p. 142); also by Léon Abensour, *La femme et le féminisme avant la Révolution* (Paris: Leroux, 1923), who claims that Christine "élabore un corps de doctrine féministe . . . avec la même méthode que les modernes défenseurs des droits de la femme" (p. v). Though Lulu M. Richardson begins her book on *The Forerunners of Feminism in French Literature of the Renaissance* (Baltimore: Johns Hopkins University Press, 1929) with a chapter on Christine, she nonetheless concludes that there is nothing in Christine's work that "could give any one any grounds for calling Christine a radical feminist" (p. 33); and even Rigaud is circumspect enough to place Christine "à la droite du mouvement actuel" (p. 143).

More recently, Angela Lucas sees Christine as "dedicated to championing women's interests in her society," *Women in the Middle Ages* (New York: St. Martin's, 1983), p. 169; Joan Kelly characterizes Christine as a feminist who "defined what was to become the modern feminist sensibility," in "Early Feminist Theory and the *Querelle des Femmes,* 1400–1789," *Signs* 8 (Autumn 1982), 4–28. Jean Rabant describes her as "la première féministe connue," *Histoire des féminismes français* (Paris: Stock, 1978), p. 19; and two militants of the French women's movement have taken the names of two women whom they obviously consider precursors and role models: Annie de Pisan and Anne Tristan, *Histoires du M.L.F.* (Paris: Calmann-Lévy, 1977). The irony is that neither Christine nor Flora Tristan was a feminist if by feminist we mean someone who draws the sex line before the class (or race) line. Christine was loyal first and foremost to the French aristocracy, Flora Tristan to the international proletariat.

Recent scholars who have seen Christine as conservative or even reactionary include F. Douglas Kelly, "Reflections on the Role of Christine de Pisan as a Feminist Writer," *sub-stance* no. 2 (Winter 1972), 63–71; Joseph L. Baird and John R. Kane, *La Querelle de la Rose: Letters and Documents* (Chapel Hill: University of North Carolina Press, 1978), p. 18; Judith M. Davis, "Christine de Pisan and Chauvinist Diplomacy," *Female Studies* VI (Old Westbury, N.Y.: Feminist, 1972), 116–22. In 1975 Charity C. Willard warned against using Christine for ideas that she did not really express, observing that Christine's role in the *Roman* quarrel does not bear out the recent view of her as forerunner of modern feminists: "A Fifteenth-Century View of Women's Role in Medieval Society: Christine de Pizan's *Livre des Trois Vertus,*" in *The Role of Women in the Middle Ages,* ed. Rosemary T. Morewedge (Albany: SUNY Press, 1975). This reverses an earlier opinion, for in the introduction to her edition of the *Livre de la Paix* (The Hague: Mouton, 1958), Professor Willard had urged us to see Christine as "precursor . . . of the whole feminist movement" (p. 14).

6. See "Rewriting Woman Good." The two texts are Christine's *Cité des Dames* and Chaucer's *Legend of Good Women.* In *Writing Woman: Women Writers and Women in Literature* (New York: Schocken, 1983), I offer a sympathetic view of Christine in the last chapter, "A City, A Room: The Scene of Writing in Christine de Pisan and Virginia Woolf."

all by her will to write. Yet I have also been terminally bored by the tedious, mind-numbing, bureaucratic prose of *Cité des Dames*, imitated from the style of royal notaries and civil servants.[7] I have been angered by Christine's self-righteousness, her prudery, and the intensely self-serving narrowness of her views. I have been repulsed by the backwardness of her social attitudes, attitudes already obsolescent in the early fifteenth century when she lived and wrote. If in this essay I emphasize the negative axis of my response to Christine de Pizan, it is to bring into the foreground the kind of historical interrogation that is necessary in selecting the literary mothers we wish to think back through.

We know a good deal about Christine's life, much of it from her own pen.[8] She was Italian by birth, the daughter of a prominent physician-astrologer who took up residence at the French court under Charles V. Christine was born about 1365, educated at home by her father, happily married to one Etienne de Castel (a notary in the royal service), widowed at twenty-five with three children and a mother to support. With small inheritance and only a little land, Christine eventually turned to writing as her profession, maneuvering skillfully among the murderous rivalries that plagued the French ruling houses. She was a prolific author with a substantial reputation among the French and English aristocrats whose patronage was her livelihood. The *oeuvre* on which her reputation rests was mainly produced over some fifteen years. Later, for more than a decade (1418–29), Christine withdrew to a convent at Poissy, outside Paris, and evidently wrote only a single work, a religious contemplation of the Passion. She was one of many courtiers who followed the dauphin into "exile" upon the Burgundian invasion of Paris in 1418. Her last work, a patriotic poem honoring Charles VII and Joan of Arc, was produced in 1429.[9] We do not know Christine's response when Charles betrayed La Pucelle the following year, nor exactly when Christine died, except that she was dead by 1432. Until 1600 or so her reputation flourished, with translations of her works into several languages.[1]

Those who are not familiar with the period of transition from feudalism to capitalism—Christine's period—are often surprised by its radical

7. See Maureen Curnow, "The Livre de la Cité des Dames of Christine de Pisan: A Critical Edition" (diss. Vanderbilt University, 1975), vol. 1, chap. 5. For a different perspective on Christine's style, see E. J. Richards, "Christine de Pizan and the Question of Feminist Rhetoric," *Teaching Language through Literature* 22 (1983), 15–24.
8. There is autobiographical material in *Cité des Dames*; in the *Mutacion de Fortune*, ed. Suzanne Solente (Paris: Picard, 1959–66), 4 vols. in Société des Anciens Textes Français (SATF); and in *Lavision Christine*, ed. Sister Mary L. Towner (New York: AMS, 1969). The two most recent of several full biographies are by Enid McLeod, *The Order of the Rose* (Totowa, N.J.: Rowman & Littlefield, 1976), and Charity C. Willard, *Christine de Pizan: Her Life and Works* (New York: Persea, 1984).
9. Christine's "Ditié de Jehanne d'Arc" has been edited by Angus J. Kennedy and Kenneth Varty in *Nottingham Mediaeval Studies*, 18 and 19 (1974, 1975).
1. On the later fortunes of Christine, see Gianni Mombello, "Per un'edizione critica del' 'Epistre Othea' di Christine de Pizan," *Studi Francesi*, 8 and 9 (1964, 1965), 29–55 and 53–76.

aspects, for it was a self-consciously modern age that had begun in theory and in practice to attack traditional ideas and institutions. What
was the social context in which Christine lived and wrote? What would
"radicalism" actually mean in early fifteenth-century Europe?[2]

To begin with, the Catholic church was in crisis. Clerical abuses and
high living had generated a tradition of anticlerical sentiment on both
scholastic and popular levels. (At the latter level one would include, for
instance, German polemical poetry, French *fabliaux* and the *Roman de
Renart*, and several of Chaucer's *Canterbury Tales*.) Simultaneously
there flourished, from the eleventh century on, a network of popular
heresies that, despite the variety of their origins and programs, challenged the church by practicing pacifism or apostolic poverty, denying
the sacramental nature of marriage, and advocating the right of laymen
to administer the sacraments, the right of women to preach, or salvation
through women. The church was sufficiently worried about the appeal
of such heresies that it founded not only the Inquisition to combat them
but also the orders of preaching friars. Moreover, a low-level but wide-
spread skepticism about the efficacy of prayer and priestly ministration
was probably inevitable: the Crusade movement failed, the Black Death
invaded Europe in 1348, and the Great Schism in the church from
1378 to 1417 produced the unedifying spectacle of rival popes excom-
municating one another. Reinforcing these centrifugal tendencies was
the consolidation of national monarchies and, in Italy, of city-states or
communes governed by elected councils of the high bourgeoisie. Mon-
archs and republicans had their theoreticians—the corpus of lawyers,
scholars, and theologians, such as Marsilius of Padua, Pierre DuBois,
John Quidort, and William of Ockham—whose task was to rationalize
the dismantling, or at least the limiting, of ecclesiastical power in the
temporal sphere. The English Protestant Reformation was still more
than a century in the future when Christine de Pizan died, but already
in the thirteenth century the nobles of France had formed a society for
the disendowment of the church.

On the intellectual scene, philosophers of the *via moderna*—the revolutionary new "nominalistic" logic—were well established at the universities of Europe and nowhere more firmly or more notoriously than at
the University of Paris. They challenged the certainty of orthodox doctrine on such basic questions as creation *ex nihilo* and transubstantia-
tion. The goodness of God and even His existence were interrogated as
logical propositions and found wanting. In science the diurnal rotation

---

2. There is a vast bibliography on the topics summarized in these paragraphs. Two convenient
surveys of the period, with ample bibliographical references, are Barbara Tuchman, *A Distant
Mirror: The Calamitous Fourteenth Century* (New York: Knopf, 1978), and William C. Jordan,
Bruce McNab, and Teofilo Ruiz, eds., *Order and Innovation in the Middle Ages* (Princeton:
Princeton University Press, 1976). See also G. de Lagarde, *La naissance de l'esprit laïque au
déclin du moyen âge* (Paris: Béatrice, 1934–46), 6 vols., and A. C. Crombie, *Medieval and
Early Modern Science* (New York: Doubleday, 1959), vol. 2.

of the earth was already proposed by Nicolas Oresme, economic adviser to Charles V and a colleague of Christine de Pizan's father. Yet while Tommaso da Pizzano stuck with astrology, the work of Oresme in physics and astronomy anticipated that of Copernicus and Galileo.

Socially, feudalism was dying, stifled by the efflorescence of international commerce and the political and economic demands of the urban bourgeoisie. The order of the day was social mobility both vertical and horizontal: that is, changes in social rank and travel. Symptomatic of these changes were major revolts in every European country and involving every social class: peasants, artisans, bourgeois, university intellectuals, even aristocrats. I list a few of the best-known of these insurrections to give the flavor of the period, but each is only the tip of an iceberg, preceded and followed by decades of struggle that often erupted into strikes and lockouts, sit-ins and occupations, armed confrontation and guerrilla warfare. There was the great antifeudal revolt of English peasants and artisans in 1381, which nearly took London. There was a workers' government in Florence for six weeks during 1378 when textile workers—the Ciompi—demanded reform of labor legislation and the right to participate in municipal government. There was the people's militia in Flanders led by the wealthy merchants Jacob van Artevelde and his son Philip, who twice during the fourteenth century ousted the count of Flanders. There was the guildsmen's overthrow of the city government of Freiburg in Germany in 1388.

In France—mother of revolutions—the normal tensions of the transition period were exacerbated by war with England and by a ruling elite whose self-indulgence turned every holiday into a national financial disaster. The country was in a constant turmoil that during the lifetime of Christine de Pizan coalesced into several nationwide insurrections. The Jacquerie, the great national peasant revolt of 1358, linked up with dissatisfied bourgeois in many cities who were already organizing general strikes against royal fiscal policy. The Maillotin insurrection of 1382 brought to a head months of tax riots by bourgeois and artisans in major cities, taking its name from the police mallets seized by the rebels. During 1383 and 1384 guerrilla warfare was carried on throughout the south by bands of dispossessed peasants and urban poor, the so-called Tuchins.

Christine herself witnessed and wrote about one of the most important of these insurrections, the 1413 Cabochian revolution, centered in Paris.[3] Here, a multiclass coalition (today we would call it a

3. The standard study is by Alfred Coville, *Les cabochiens et l'ordonnance de 1413* (Paris, 1888; rpt. Geneva: Slatkine, 1974). 4. In "Le debat du heraut, du vassault et du villain," the *vilein* interrupts the other two to present the views of the peasantry on the state of society; J. C. Laidlaw, ed., *The Poetical Works of Alain Chartier* (Cambridge: Cambridge University Press, 1974). Deschamps is cited by Tuchman, *A Distant Mirror*, pp. 396–97. Kenneth Varty makes the point about criticism of government in his edition of Christine's *Ballades, Rondeaux and Virelais* (Leicester: Leicester University Press, 1965), p. 164.

popular front) developed around a program of fiscal reform. The bloc was led by Jean Sans Peur, duke of Burgundy and Christine's long-time patron, who saw the reform movement as a convenient anti-Orléanist weapon. His main bloc partner was the pro-Burgundian University of Paris, official thinktank of the day. The muscle of the coalition was the working population of Paris—artisans, apprentices, servants, shopkeepers, guildsmen—headed by the wealthy guild-corporations of skinners and butchers, whose leader, Simon Caboche, gave his name to the rising. The rebels placed under house arrest princely advisers and courtly hangers-on, including fifteen of the queen's ladies-in-waiting. They forced the king to "dis-appoint" (désappointer) officials and replace them with the rebels' university allies; they made the king establish a committee of inquiry into abuses and proclaim a series of reform ordinances. The rebels achieved, in other words, a short-lived period of dual power. But it is typical of cross-class blocs that the threat of force, while effective, alienates the ruling-class partners, and so the nobles and the university dumped their embarrassing allies along with the reforms already won. A new coalition was formed, its slogan of "Peace at all costs" appealing to the high or "respectable" bourgeoisie who had no particular desire for fiscal reform. (It was this new party that won the sympathy of Christine de Pizan.) The reform ordinances were revoked, the corporations of butchers and skinners destroyed, and the country returned to the *status quo ante* just as the rebels had warned: civil war and economic disaster.

Such was the tenor of the Parisian life that Christine observed. Even at court, though, there was a long tradition of criticizing government and royalty, continued by—among others—Christine's fellow poets and courtiers Eustache Deschamps and Alain Chartier. Deschamps sympathized with the poor whose labor produced the country's wealth:

> This grain, this corn, what is it but the blood and bones of the poor folk who have plowed the land? Wherefore their spirit crieth on God for vengeance. Woe to the lords, the councillors and all who steer us thus, and woe to all who are of their party, for no man careth now but to fill his bags.

Chartier went so far as to give voice to the peasant directly.[4] To be a courtier, clearly, one did not have to suspend all critical faculties.

The last aspect of medieval society I refer to is the role of the urban middle-class woman, which changed, like other aspects I have men-

---

4. In "Le debat du heraut, du vassault et du villain," the *vilein* interrupts the other two to present the views of the peasantry on the state of society; J. C. Laidlaw, ed., *The Poetical Works of Alain Chartier* (Cambridge: Cambridge University Press, 1974). Deschamps is cited by Tuchman, *A Distant Mirror*, pp. 396–97. Kenneth Varty makes the point about criticism of government in his edition of Christine's *Ballades, Rondeaux and Virelais* (Leicester: Leicester University Press, 1965), p. 164.

tioned, to reflect the radical social changes of the epoch.[5] From the eleventh century, expanding mercantile and manufacturing capital had called more and more women into the labor force and given them numerous legal and social rights (to be lost during the Renaissance). In Christine's day the bourgeois woman owned, inherited, and bequeathed property independent of her husband; she sued and was sued in court; she lobbied Parliament; in some cities she held minor public office, in others voted in municipal elections. She apprenticed, worked in, owned, and operated virtually any trade or profession, from apothecary to shoemaker, brothel-keeper to weaver. The huge food and textile industries were often staffed and controlled by women, who also joined the guilds of their craft. Though women were not admitted to university, they could receive education at home or at church or public schools. Some Italian women scholars gave public orations or lectures at university. The ideal of the educated woman penetrated even the literary romances of the day: some of them present a heroine skilled in languages, literature, and science.

In the late Middle Ages, in sum, dissent from received norms was neither impossible nor unusual. Radical ideas and practices were current in this pluralistic and seethingly modern society—but not in the work of Christine de Pizan.

She was, of course, a courtier and a foreigner. In an age of international marriages, alliances, and cultural exchange, many Italians lived and worked in France. Few can have been so intensely loyal to their employers as Christine, who—the Rosemary Woods of her day—praises her corrupt and fratricidal patrons as the most benign and humane nobility in the world.[6] When Christine, "plus royaliste que le roi," asserts it is literally a sin to criticize king or nobles—"Je dy que c'est pechie a qui le fait"[7]—she is very much in the rearguard of social thought of the period. Christine seems to think little of parliaments, councils, cabinets, or any of the institutional means whereby a ruler might consult the ruled. Republican government with rotating administration, which already existed in Bologna and elsewhere, she rejects. The principle of electoralism frightens her deeply: why, if a ruler can

---

5. For information in this paragraph, see Frances and Joseph Gies, *Women in the Middle Ages* (New York: Crowell, 1978); A. Abram, "Women Traders in Medieval London," *Economic Journal* 26 (1916), 276–85; Alice S. Green, *Town Life in the Fifteenth Century*, 2 vols. (Boston 1894; rpt. New York: Blom, 1971); Sylvia Thrupp, *The Merchant Class of Medieval London* (Chicago: University of Chicago Press, 1948); Georges Renard, *Guilds in the Middle Ages* (1918; rpt. New York: Kelley, 1968); Barbara Kanner, ed., *The Women of England from Anglo-Saxon Times to the Present: Interpretive Bibliographical Essays* (Hamden, Conn.: Archon, 1979). On the Italian women scholars see LaBalme, *Beyond Their Sex*, and King and Rabil, *Her Immaculate Hand*. In *The Court of Richard II* (London: Murray, 1968), Gervase Mathew lists at least a half-dozen well-educated romance heroines (p. 193).
6. *Le Livre du Corps de Policie*, ed. Robert H. Lucas (Geneva: Droz, 1967), III, vii. Further citations to this work will appear in my main text, as will references to *Le Livre de la Paix*, ed. Charity Cannon Willard (The Hague: Mouton, 1958).
7. In Varty, *Ballades*, no. 118, or in the *Oeuvres Poétiques*, ed. Maurice Roy (Paris: Didot, 1886), I:263, as no. XLIX.

be elected, he can also be deposed (*Policie*, III, ii)! For the Parisian reformers and their project Christine shows nothing but hatred and contempt. The *Livre de la Paix* is filled with her execrations against "le vile et chetive gent, le fol gouvernment de menu et bestial peuple" (*Paix*, II, i) who flout the will of God in their dissatisfaction with the nobility (*Paix*, III, ix and x). Even an Italian despot is better than such people, who should keep silent "de ce de quoy ne leur apertient a parler" (*Policie*, I, iii). Her sketch of a political meeting—"celle diabolique assemblee" (*Paix*, III, xi)—is nothing short of vicious. For Christine, social justice and harmony consist in each rank fulfilling its divinely appointed duties according to its divinely determined nature (*Paix*, III, x and xi). By the fifteenth century this model was sadly outmoded, completely out of touch with late-medieval social life and political theory. The image that comes to mind is of King Canute trying to beat back the tide with a broom; so Christine tries to beat back the tide of social change, of protest and nascent democracy, with her little broom of pious anecdotes and exhortations gathered from the Bible and other ancient authorities. In a time when even courtiers and clerics wanted change, Christine continues in her quiet neo-Platonic hierarchies and her feudal nostalgia.

It is not inconsistent with a static, neo-Platonic world view that Christine should consider rural laborers the most necessary social group of all and advise us to be grateful for their services. She merely repeats the truisms of classical and Christian rhetoric: Adam and Noah tilled the soil, so did some famous Romans, therefore we ought not to have contempt for those who till the soil. Besides, a life of poverty is the most morally perfect of all (*Policie*, III, x). Christine herself did not, of course, aspire to this particular form of perfection but strove mightily to avoid it. In fact her brief, edifying reflections on rural life consist of a set of literary *topoi* echoing the pastoralism then in vogue with the French nobility.[8] Perhaps Christine was among the retinue of Queen Isabel when the latter retreated, as she often did, to her farm-estate, Hostel des Bergeries, the gift of her fond husband Charles VI, "pour esbattement et plaisance."

What about Christine as champion of women? Surely this is the arena in which, for feminists, her credentials as protofeminist are decisive. The *Cité des Dames* is usually cited as the strongest evidence of Christine's dedication to he cause of women. Here Christine offers

---

8. As for the urban poor, her treatment is equally literary. Brian Woledge calls attention to passages in the *Mutacion* in which Christine writes vividly of the suffering of city dwellers who have been reduced to poverty by misfortune: "Le thème de la pauvreté dans la *Mutacion de Fortune* de Christine de Pisan," in *Fin du Moyen Age et Renaissance: Mélanges . . . offerts à Robert Guiette* (Antwerp: Nederlandsche Boekhandel, 1961). On medieval poverty and attitudes toward it, see C. Lis and H. Soly, *Poverty and Capitalism in Pre-Industrial Europe* (London: Harvester, 1979); M. Mollat, *Les pauvres au moyen âge* (Paris: Hachette, 1978); David Aers, "*Piers Plowman* and Problems in the Perception of Poverty: A Culture in Transition," *Leeds Studies in English*, n.s., 14 (1983), 5–25.

models of female courage, intelligence, and prudence to show that women are indeed capable of these virtues and to bolster women in a positive self-image undermined by clerical misogyny. The aim is laudable, but it is surely minimal given the already prominent role of women in medieval social life. Moreover, in several ways the text subverts its own "subversion." We are told of ancient warriors, queens, goddesses, and scholars, and of a few present-day noblewomen said to be of surpassing virtue. But for all the book's valorization of female strength and ingenuity, we hear of no modern working woman, whether rich or poor. The sole exception is a painter, Anastasia, who illuminated some of Christine's manuscripts (CD, I, chap. xli). France was full of strong, clever, industrious, and ambitious women, but one would never guess it from Cité des Dames. The reason, I suspect, is that these women were of a class that Christine had little affection for — they were, after all, the realm's trouble-makers, and the considerable virtues of the bourgeois or artisan woman were lost on our arch-courtier. In the same text Christine's *porte-parole*, Dame Rayson, justifies the exclusion of women from public office on the grounds that it is not their God-given place (I, xi). Though many women were their husbands' partners, both domestically and commercially, Christine fears the implicit egalitarianism of such an arrangement, advising the married woman to submit humbly to whatever comes her way (III, xix).

In *Le Livre des Trois Vertus*, Christine ignores the independent woman of her day, presenting her only in relation to a husband's "professional conscience." It is the wife's duty to ensure her husband's honesty, especially if the husband should be a rural laborer:

> If your husbands work land for others, they should do it well and loyally, as if for themselves, and at harvest they should pay their master in wheat ... and not mix rye with the grain. ... They shouldn't hide the best sheep with the neighbors to pay the master the worst ones ... or make him believe the sheep have died by showing him the hides of other animals, or pay the worst fleeces or give short count of his goods or fowl. (Laigle, p. 300, my trans.)

Thus Christine sees woman as domestically "the angel in the house," socially an agent of control on behalf of the ruling elite.

Christine is sometimes mentioned as an early crusader for the education of women. The notion is far from the truth. In reality Christine argues merely the standard Catholic truism that women are *capable* of learning. Despite her own thirst for knowledge, though, she does not recommend education for women generally, her point being that most women do not require an education to fulfill their social obligations. They need neither Latin nor scholarly texts such as Christine herself knew: vernacular romances and saints' lives will do for most girls, and only as much arithmetic as will enable them to keep household accounts (Laigle, pp. 173–86). One need not wonder what Christine's countrywoman, the learned Laura Cereta, would have thought of such a limited program. We know what her countryman Giovanni Boccaccio thought, for he denounced the narrow domestic aspirations of women — who "have in common the ability to do those things which make men famous." We know, too, how highly the fourteenth-century French theologian Pierre DuBois valued the capacities of women, for he proposed to the pope a scheme for sending a large corps of educated women into the Muslim East, to regain by propaganda and fraternization what the Crusades had lost.[9] By contrast with such ideas of her contemporaries, Christine's proposals seem timid at best.

The last aspect of Christine's career I consider here is her part in the well-known debate on the *Roman de la Rose*, one of the most popular, influential, and durable works of the entire Middle Ages.[1] It is not difficult to see why the *Roman* has often been interpreted as a subversive text. The poem denounces numerous social ills, among them clerical hypocrisy and the perversion of justice by wealth. It propounds a rationalistic — though by no means unorthodox — Christianity threatening to conservative churchmen such as Jean Gerson, chancellor of the University of Paris and Christine's ally in the debate. It offers a fictional representation of fornication — that is, sex without benefit of the marriage sacrament — which implicitly removes sexuality from the ecclesiastical control to which it had been subjected in the ecclesiastical reforms of the eleventh and twelfth centuries: a campaign that also established clerical celibacy, persecuted homosexuality, and intensified clerical misogyny.[2]

9. Boccaccio, *De Claris Mulieribus*, trans. by Guido A. Guarino as *Concerning Famous Women* (New Brunswick: Rutgers University Press, 1963), p. 188 (Chap. 84, Cornificia); see also p. 220 (Chap 95, Proba). This text was a primary source for Christine's *Cité des Dames*. Pierre's scheme is mentioned by Shulamith Shahar, *The Fourth Estate: A History of Women in the Middle Ages* (London: Methuen, 1983), p. 155. A similar program was in fact established by the Bolsheviks after the Russian Revolution of 1917 in order to bring literacy and other social benefits to Muslim areas; see Gregory J. Massell, *The Surrogate Proletariat* (Princeton: Princeton University Press, 1974). Christine's failure to recommend advanced learning to her contemporaries is addressed by Susan Groag Bell, "Christine de Pizan (1364–1430): Humanism and the Problem of a Studious Woman," *Feminist Studies* (Spring/Summer 1976), 173–184. Bell seems to agree with Christine's view that "it is woman's work to keep the fabricsociety intact," and the three reasons she offers for Christine's limited educational policy do not convince me: that Christine had in mind the necessity of repopulation during a period of war; that she realized most women had insufficient time to study anyway; that as a writer — an isolated woman doing "man's work" — Christine "outgrew her female friends and became estranged from the essential female network of her society." These strike me more as excuses than as reasons. See also Astrik L. Gabriel, "The Educational Ideas of Christine de Pisan," *Journal of the History of Ideas* 16 (1955) 3–21.
1. See Eric Hicks, *Le débat sur le Roman de la Rose* (Paris: Champion, 1977); Baird and Kane, *La Querelle*; and Pierre-Yves Badel, *Le Roman de la Rose au XIVe Siècle* (Geneva: Droz, 1980).
2. See Georges Duby, *Le chevalier, la femme et le prêtre: Le mariage dans la France féodale* (Paris: Hachette, 1981). I am not suggesting that Jean de Meun advocated fornication — indeed, I tend to agree with John V. Fleming's interpretation of the work in *Le Roman de la Rose: A Study in Allegory and Iconography* (Princeton: Princeton University Press, 1969), though Fleming ignores the social context of "sexual politics" which Duby illuminates and which surely affected response to the *Roman*.

If we can speak of a Phyllis Schlafly of the Middle Ages, surely that title belongs to Christine. Her main complaint against the *Roman* is that its author talks dirty. In a discussion of the nature of justice, Jean de Meun has Dame Raison recount the story of Saturn's fall. Raison's narration includes a reference to "les secrez membres" — specifically the "coilles" (testicles) — of Saturn, whose castration by his son Jupiter ended the Golden Age. Raison argues (as did many defenders of the *Roman*) that because all creation is good, such naming is permissible. Christine refutes this justification of obscene language: as the beauty of creation is a paradisal condition, to name the genitals is to deny the polluting effects of original sin, and hence it is an act not only socially offensive but also virtually heretical. Nor may we excuse an author because a fictional character spoke: Christine insists that an author take full responsibility for every word written. Luckily Christine did not explicitly apply this criterion to her contemporaries: Geoffrey Chaucer, for one, would scarcely have passed muster with his apologias for plain speaking (*Canterbury Tales*, General Prologue 725–46 and Fragment A 3167–86). French popular literature must have been agony for Christine: such words as "con," "foutre," "merde," "vit," and "pet" were quite common in *fabliaux*, riddles, jokes, and popular songs, even finding their way occasionally into the *chansons de geste* and other courtly literature.[3] It was not, by and large, a prudish age.

After castigating the book's use of obscenity, Christine objects to the *Roman*'s potential influence. As human nature is already inclined to evil, the *Roman* will encourage abominable behavior and dissolute living through its portrayal of unmarried love. It is a dangerous book, and all the more so for being well written. Finally, the author or his characters (for Christine, the same thing) slander women by portraying in certain episodes their love of gossip and their ability to deceive a jealous husband. (Curiously, Christine ignores numerous examples of virtuous women in the text.)

Christine's solution to the *problème de la Rose* is simple: burn the book. She proposes it not only in her letters but in a *balade*, where she self-righteously compares herself to Aristotle and Socrates, who had also been attacked for telling the truth. "Le Roman," she writes, "plaisant aux curieux, / de la Rose — que l'en devroit ardoir!" Interestingly, Jean Gerson, the most influential of the several parties to the debate, seems virtually obsessed with fire: the imagery of fire recurs constantly in his letters, in proverbs and metaphors as well as in actual recommendations. Gerson demands the flames not only for the *Roman* and for the letters of those who defend it but also for the works of Ovid, for popular songs,

---

3. See the collection of riddles and jokes in Bruno Roy, ed., *L'érotisme au moyen âge* (Montreal: Aurore, 1977); Charles Muscatine, "Courtly Literature and Vulgar Language," in *Court and Poet*, ed. Glyn S. Burgess (Liverpool: Cairns, 1982); Betsy Bowden, "The Art of Courtly Copulation," *Medievalia et Humanistica* n.s., 9 (1979), 67–85; Philippe Menard, *Le rire et le sourire dans la littérature courtoise* . . . (Geneva: Droz, 1969).

poems, or paintings that incite to lubricity, for homosexuals or those who practice any other "vice against nature" (which for Gerson included sodomy, oral copulation, and abortion). "Justice les arde!" "Au feu! bonnes gens, au feu!" he writes, in the exalted hysteria of Crusade rhetoric. Gerson's recommendations would have decimated the ranks of the church and society at large, as well as a good deal of medieval literature and art.[4] Fortunately neither the ecclesiastical nor the civil powers were as committed as Gerson to the salubrious ministrations of the flames.

Censorship was a genuine issue in Christine's day, and burning—of books and of people—was its most extreme expression, not common but possible. Need we recall that many of the heretics burned before and during Christine's lifetime were women, that most of the witches who would later go to the stake were women, and that Christine's heroine Joan of Arc met her death by fire? Political censorship was not unknown at the French court. In 1389 Christine's colleague Philippe de Mézières proposed a ban at court on all poets except those using moral or religious themes, and in 1395 Charles VI forbade all poets and balladeers to mention the pope or the schism. Burning had been rare in France since the extermination of the Cathars in 1330, but at the time of the *Roman* debate Jean Gerson was engaged in polemical struggle against a sect of which a group had been burned in Paris in 1372 for heresy. As Pierre-Yves Badel has shown, there was for Gerson a close association between the errors of the *Roman* and those of the heretics, particularly on the subject of sex.[5] Christine does not go so far as to demand the burning of individuals, not even Jews: she merely denounces them, endorsing Fortune's continual punishment of them, though such uncompromising hostility was neither the "official" position nor held by all educated laymen and clerics.[6] Yet Christine's advocacy of book-burning has a logic of its own that should give us pause: Gerson's intervention in this seemingly innocuous literary debate was motivated by no chivalrous gallantry but by the most conservative of political interests. And although I do not doubt Christine's sincerity any more than I do Gerson's, I do not forget that she first publicized what began as a private literary discussion and thereby effectively enhanced her career at court.

<hr/>

4. On homosexuality and the evolution of ecclesiastical attitudes toward it, see John Boswell, *Christianity, Social Tolerance, and Homosexuality* (Chicago: University of Chicago Press, 1980); for methods of and attitudes toward contraception, John T. Noonan, *Contraception: A History of Its Treatment by the Catholic Theologians and Canonists* (Cambridge: Harvard University Press, 1965).

5. Badel, *Le Roman de la Rose*, pp. 447–61.

6. *Mutacion*, 8413–42. For this reference I am indebted to the unpublished dissertation of Nadia Margolis, "The Poetics of History: An Analysis of Christine de Pizan's Livre de la Mutacion de Fortune" (Stanford University, 1977). Though Margolis claims Christine "was no more antisemitic than any other Christian living in France or Italy at that time" (p. 205), see to the contrary Richard Schoeck, "Chaucer's Prioress: Mercy and Tender Heart," in *The Bridge; A Yearbook of Judaeo-Christian Studies*, 2, ed. John M. Oesterreicher (New York: Pantheon, 1956), and reprinted in *Chaucer Criticism*, 2 (Notre Dame: University of Notre Dame Press, 1960), 245–58.

Christine's role in the *Roman* debate shows her once again less the friend of woman than of the powers that be, at their most oppressive: a position no more inevitable in her time than in ours. If Christine stood in advance of her day, it was in anticipating the prudish moralism of nineteenth- and twentieth-century literary censorship. If Christine was correct on the *Roman de la Rose*, then so were the censors of James Joyce, Henry Miller, and D. H. Lawrence. If Christine was correct, then we should not read Djuna Barnes or Anaïs Nin either. In fact it was Christine's opponents, the defenders of the *Roman*—male, clerical, arrogant, and patronizing though they were—who made the arguments that today permit us to read some of the most interesting writers, male and female, of our own time.

This completes my short dossier on Christine de Pizan, and I return now to the late twentieth century and to gender-oriented criticism. The kind of overestimation that I have tried in this chapter to correct is not limited to Christine. I note it, for instance, in some scholarship on the American feminist Charlotte Perkins Gilman, who shows interesting parallels with Christine and whom I have elsewhere characterized as "representative of a day that was drawing to a close rather than as harbinger of a day that was dawning."[7] Phyllis Rose, a biographer of Virginia Woolf, has warned against imbalanced appreciation of women writers. "Recent feminist biography," she notes, "has been challenging in exciting ways our accepted notions of major and minor. But just because an artist has been underappreciated does not mean her work is major. . . . This partisanship, this absence of perspective produces some outrageous statements."[8] Nor is the phenomenon limited to literary studies. In reviewing two books about activist women, the sociologist Berenice Fisher writes that "it is especially important that we do not incorporate role models uncritically. We need to examine carefully our portrayal of women as models, to ask ourselves what message these images convey." Fisher goes on to call for "the radical social analysis that shows the objective constraints under which individual women have achieved."[9]

I believe that the data assembled here are conclusive with respect to Christine's conservatism. What doubtless remains open for some, though, is interpretation. Was Christine's view of things inevitable or predictable precisely because of "objective restraints?" Bluntly, was she forced into ultraconservatism by complete dependence on royal patrons, a dependence created by lack of opportunities for women? If so, ought we not to sympathize rather than to judge? The first is primarily a histor-

---

7. "Two American Feminist Utopias," in *Writing Woman*.
8. *New York Times Book Review*, June 26, 1983.
9. "The Models Among Us: Social Authority and Political Activism," *Feminist Studies* 7 (Spring 1981), 100–112.

ical question, the second moral. To treat them fully would require another long paper, but I shall address what seem to me the major problems with this approach.

Historically, the position is less tenable for Christine's epoch than for those preceding and following it. The tenth century, or the sixteenth, might offer more convincing evidence, but the high and late Middle Ages did in fact open significant opportunities to women. Moreover, ultraconservatism is only one possible response to constraint; many medieval women found others. Thus women participated in the rebellions of the time, joined heretical sects, banded together in collectives to do good works (the Beguines), ran businesses, petitioned Parliament for legislative change in their industries, and regularly disobeyed the church's teachings on contraception, abortion, and sexuality.

Nor was Christine herself without resources. She might have remarried. She might have chosen to live at a convent (as in fact she would do later in life), there to continue her scholarship and social life, as was normal for well-placed convent boarders. She might have retired to the Château de Mémorant, a property given her father by King Charles V and which Christine eventually sold to Philippe de Mézières. She might have gone into business as a bookseller, a notary, or a copyist, or in some other branch of the burgeoning book industry. She might have accepted invitations from Henry IV to take up residence at the English court, where her son was companion to the young prince, or from the duke of Milan to grace his court. These invitations and refusals were made in 1400 and 1401—"even before she had begun to produce her major works," as Charity Willard points out.[1] In France she was supported by many members of the royal family, male and female. All this suggests that the search for patronage was considerably less urgent a matter for Christine than it must have been for many another courtly writer.

Despite the opportunities available to urban women in general, and to Christine in particular, even an exceptional woman had neither complete freedom nor complete equality with men. Nor do we today, and there can be no doubt that the special oppression of women deforms consciousness. Nonetheless, to adduce special oppression, then or now, in mitigation of reactionary social attitudes strikes me as condescending, naive, and ultimately irresponsible.

Condescending, because it implies that we should exempt women from moral or political polemic because of their gender. About Christine it implies that her stated opinions were insincere. Indeed, in its effort to exculpate Christine from the unfashionable charge of conservatism, the defense from sheer economic necessity (besides being inaccurate) paradoxically reduces her to a completely unprincipled and

---

1. Willard, *Life and Works*, p. 165.

hypocritical opportunist. I prefer to think that she understood the choices available to her and chose as she believed. To think so preserves at least her dignity.

Naive, because the position implies that an individual can hypothetically be removed from her social environment and inserted into an ideal, ahistorical existence, one in which special oppression no longer deforms her consciousness and in which therefore her "true," "authentic" opinions can be known or guessed. In literary terms this is a version of the old sincerity fallacy. For better or worse, though, all we have is the text, and all we have is individuals in their social context.

Irresponsible, because although any opinion surely has both personal and social determinants, these do not, in my view, justify the denial or abdication of choice. Here I mean both Christine's choice and ours. To take an extreme instance: in our day the woman fascist or the woman racist can be understood; the special oppression of women is doubtless relevant to her position; but then what? or even so what? If we do not accept a passive-deterministic attitude toward life, then we ought not to gloss over reactionary views, though they be voiced by a woman and in the name of womanhood.

What I find interesting about the revival of Christine's reputation as proto-feminist is that it seems to reflect a much more conservative feminism than was typical of the women's movement two decades ago: a backlash, if you will, observable in academic life, among the organized left, in the labor movement, in national electoral politics. It is a telling sign of the times that Jeffrey Richards can adduce, as Christine's fellow so-called revolutionary, the humble pacifist Martin Luther King, whose slogan "If there is blood in the streets, let it be ours" was rightly denounced twenty years ago by activists of both races and varying political persuasions. But if King is your idea of a revolutionary, then the leap to Christine de Pizan is not hard to make. If the censorship of pornography strikes you as progressive social action—as it does some feminists today—then to see Christine as progressive will not be hard. If you cannot imagine any alternative to the institution of the family as it now exists, then you may well endorse Christine's admonitions to women. And if you believe that the special oppression of women—even the exceptional woman—foredooms women to conservatism, then Christine's conservatism will appear perfectly "natural."

But I suggest another model in keeping with the metaphor of "mothers to think back through" with which I began. We learn from our mothers in various ways, not exclusively by imitation.[2] We also learn by struggling against them, by coming to terms with our ambivalence about them, by making the effort to understand historically their success and their failure.

2. My thanks for this perception to Sandra Gilbert, who heard an earlier version of this paper.

PATRICIA A. PHILLIPPY

Establishing Authority: Boccaccio's *De Claris Mulieribus* and Christine de Pizan's *Le livre de la cité des dames* †

Christine de Pizan wrote during the Quarrel of the Rose:

> Mais se femmes eussent les livres fait
> Je scay de vray qu'autrement fust de fait
> Car bien scevent qu'a tort sont encoulpees.[1]
> (*Epistre au Dieu d'Amour* [The God of
> Love's letter], 417–419)

Le Livre de la cité des dames [Book of the city of ladies], written in 1405, continues the program of rewriting those books, which Christine began in the debate on Jean de Meung's view of women in the *Roman de la Rose*.[2] In building her city of ladies as a challenge to the books of men, however, Christine turned to the work of a male writer for her source, Boccaccio's *De Claris Mulieribus*.[3] The relationship between the two writers is complicated by Christine's paradoxical reliance on Boccaccio's text, and his authority as a male author, in her attempt to refute the traditional representations of women by male authors and write a history of women from her unique and revolutionary perspective as a woman. Christine's "radical break with all previous historiography" [Richards, xxviii] positions itself, by means of the reference in the work's title to Augustine's *City of God*, within the tradition of Christian political history, and, by means of her conscientious self-positioning in relation to her Italian predecessors, within a traditional understanding of the project of writing in the vernacular and the responsibility of the writer to his, or her, "mother tongue." While Dante writes, "E però sappia ciascuno, che nulla cosa per legame musaico armonizzata si può

---

† Reprinted by permission from the *Romanic Review*, 77, no. 3 (1986). Copyright by the Trustees of Columbia University in the City of New York.

1. "But if women had written the books, I know for certain they would have done it differently. For they know well that they have been wrongly blamed." [Editor]

2. See D. Kelly, "Reflections on the Role of Christine de Pizan as a Feminist Writer," *Sub-stance*, vol. 2 (1972), pp. 63–71.

3. Curnow has argued convincingly that Christine was using the 1401 translation of *De Claris Mulieribus*, *De cleres et nobles femmes* by Laurent de Premierfait, rather than the Latin original, though it was available to her. She adds, "In her use of this work as a source, Christine de Pizan follows the basic goal of Boccaccio: both of them are teaching moral principles and illustrating them with historical examples" (147), and thus assumes that the version by de Premierfait faithfully translated both Boccaccio's substance and ideology. Laurent de Premierfait's acquaintance with Jean de Montreuil, Christine's principal [adversary] in the Quarrel of the Rose, and Gontier de Col, her chief adversary in the debate, further complicates her revisionary project in dealing with the texts of men. This relationship, however, is beyond the scope of this paper. It appears that Christine used the original versions of Boccaccio's *De Casibus Virorum Illustrium* and *Decameron*.

della sua loquela in altra trasmutare, senza rompere tutta sua dolcezza e armonia"[4] (*Il Convivio* [The banquet], 1.7; Busnelli and Vandelli, p. 43), Christine, involved in a program of making her adopted French language the vehicle of her own literary autobiography, and the basis of her approach to the education and history of women, makes use of the Italian debate on the 'illustrious vernacular' to thematize the problem of translation between languages within a polemic on the possibilities of translation between the sexes, and on the language unique and natural to women and to their city. If, as Pézard has argued, Dante's condemnation of Brunetto Latini to the circle of the sodomites in Canto XV of *Inferno* reflects his condemnation of the "blasphemy" involved in turning away from one's natural tongue to write in a foreign tongue, Christine's French version of Boccaccio's Latin text at once capitalizes on the unnaturalness of Boccaccio's decision to write in Latin, and seeks to point to the natural language of women, in opposition to the blasphemous charges of male writers; a language necessarily distilled from the available language of the male tradition, and thus necessarily an act of translation. Thus while she uses Boccaccio as a source, and invokes him by name as a witness in support of her claims, she is equally involved in a revision and correction of his views on women and their capabilities. Out of a tradition which she seeks to assimilate and revise, Christine establishes not only her own authority and poetic program, but also the position of women in society, which she believes has been obscured and misrepresented by that tradition. Thus her 'revision' is linked to the male literary tradition, on the one hand, in its desire to uncover and return to the correct relationship between men and women which has been confused in the past, and, on the other hand, involves a turning away from traditional authorities toward experience, and toward a future for women which has been denied them in the past. These interests inform her handling of *De Claris Mulieribus* [Concerning famous women] and result in a reappropriation of Boccaccio's text which reflects this two-sided relationship of textual dependence and ideological independence.

The overall designs of the two works, their prefatory and concluding apparatus, and stated intentions indicate differences between the two authors' treatment of their materials which will permeate the texts. Boccaccio states proudly in his Preface that "the merits of pagan women . . . have not been published in any special work up to now, and have not been set forth by anyone" (xxxix), and he states his purpose as a didactic one: "Nor will the reading have been in vain, I believe, if by emulating the deeds of ancient women you spur your spirit to loftier

---

4. "Everyone should recognize that no writing fashioned into a harmonious unity by its musical form can be translated from its original language without all its sweetness and harmony being destroyed." Dante, *The Banquet*, trans. Christopher Ryan (Saratoga, Calif.: Stanford French and Italian Studies 61, 1989), 26. [Editor]

things" (xxxiv). The exemplary function of the stories to follow parallels Panfilo's statement at the close of Day IX of the *Decameron*, "Queste cose, e dicendo a valorosamente adoperare accendera. . . ."[5] (IX,x: 594), and in *De Claris Mulieribus*, the natures of the morals to be drawn from the exempla are as complex, though for different reasons, as they are in the tales of Day X. While Boccaccio does not leave the morals of the stories in *De Claris Mulieribus* to the reader to supply, but states them overtly (and sometimes, for example in the life of Medea (B.16), at greater length and with greater energy than he has afforded to the tale itself), the application of these morals is complicated by the dedication of a work written in Latin to women, raising the question of the capabilities of most women to read the work, thus of its intended audience. Boccaccio states,

> Lest it seem that according to ancient custom I have touched only on the high points of what I could learn from trustworthy authors, I have lengthened them and broadened them into more extensive histories because I think it both useful and necessary that the accomplishments of these women please women no less than men. (xxxviii)

The statement, while inviting a female reading audience, nonetheless suggests that this audience is secondary to the work's male readers. Boccaccio's equation of his work with Petrarch's *De Viris Illustribus* [Concerning famous men] and his statement in the Conclusion that ". . . I ask, for the glory of honorable studies, that wiser men tolerate with kindly spirit what has not been done properly" (251), suggest that the work appears not as a book of exempla for women, but as part of the scholarly discourse of humanism. Accordingly, the nature of many of the morals themselves, as advice to men to avoid the trickery of women (Iole, B.21), or as to how young girls ought to be raised (Europa, B.9), and so on, further disrupts a perception of the work as providing exemplary figures for contemporary women to follow.

The didactic function of the text, moreover, is covertly challenged by Boccaccio's exclusion of Christian women from the work. He explains:

> . . . this was done because it seemed that they (pagan and Christian women) could not very well be placed side by side and that they did not strive for the same goal. In order to attain true and eternal glory Hebrew and Christian women did indeed steel themselves to endure human adversities, imitating the sacred commandments and examples of their teachers. But these pagans through some natural gift or instinct, or rather spurred by desire for this fleeting glory, reached their goal not without great strength of mind and

---

5. "The telling and hearing of such things will assuredly fill you with a burning desire . . . to comport yourselves valorously." Trans. G. H. McWilliam (Harmonsdworth, UK: Penguin Books, 1972), 731. [Editor]

often in spite of the assaults of Fortune, and they endured numerous troubles. Moreover, not only do Christian women resplendent in true, eternal light, live on, illustrious in their deserved immortality, but we know that their virginity, purity, saintliness, and invincible firmness in overcoming carnal desire and the punishments of tyrants have been described in special books, as their merits required. (xxxviii–xxxix)

If Christian women are excluded for the sake of originality, Boccaccio's work seems more obviously to be intended for a male audience of the literati. If, on the other hand, they are excluded because they aim at different goals than those of pagan women, then the morals to be derived from the lives of pagan models would be irrelevant to contemporary women readers. Boccaccio's statement in the Conclusion that "I have reached the women of our time, in which the number of illustrious ones is so small that I think it more suitable to come to an end here rather than proceed farther with the women of today" (251) supports the supposition that the virtues of antiquity are beyond imitation by women of Boccaccio's era, and troubles the easy connection between the exempla and the world beyond.

The moral which Boccaccio affixes to the life of Dido (B.40), however, indicates the kind of exemplum the tales of pagan women can provide for Christian women: in a lengthy invective against lasciviousness in widows, Boccaccio states:

> Let those who consider Dido's dead body be ashamed then, and, thinking of the reason for her death, let them bow their heads, and let Christian women grieve at being surpassed in chastity by that woman who was a limb of Satan. Let them not think that by mourning and dressing in black they have fulfilled all their duties to the dead. Love must be kept whole until the end if they want to fulfill the duties of widowhood, and they must not think of adulterously contracting another marriage. . . . (91–92)

A similar moral, this time addressed to men, is drawn from the life of Epichrasis (B.91):

> And so I think men should be ashamed to be surpassed by a woman who was lewd but also very constant in the endurance of difficulties. For if we are stronger because of our sex, is it not proper that we be stronger in bravery? If this is not done, we rightly seem to have exchanged characters with them and become effeminate. (210–11)

As Christian women ought to be superior to pagan women, by virtue of their faith, and thus be shamed by the good examples of pagan women, so men ought to maintain their superiority over women, by virtue of their sex, and be shamed by the example of a virtuous woman.

For Christine, these incongruities initiate a revisionary treatment of

Boccaccio's text, in which the lives of famous women are edited and reorganized within a framework dictated by Christine's didactic purposes. Three quarters of Christine's exempla come from Boccaccio, but not all are included.[6] The notable additions to Boccaccio's text are Christine's inclusion of examples of virtuous women drawn from her own era and experience, thus positing a historical continuity between the examples of pagan virtues and their contemporary applications which, she feels, Boccaccio denies; and the inclusion of the third book of the *Cité des dames*, drawn from Vincent de Beauvais, in which the city is populated by the Virgin and thirty saints, thus affirming the connection between pagan and Christian virtues which her feminine city, founded by the secular virtues of Raison, Droitture and Justice, seeks to establish.[7] In the first pages of her work, Christine thematizes the method which she will employ throughout the text. Reading Matheolus' attack on women, Christine says, "me sourdi une grant desplaisance et tristesce de couraige en desprisant moy meismes et tout le sexe feminin" (1c). This was because, "m'en rapportoye plus au jugement d'autruy qu ad ce que moy meismes en sentoye et savoye" (1b).[8] It is in putting the book down, and turning away from this literary tradition, however, toward her own experience as a "femme naturelle" [natural woman] (1b), that the figures of Raison, Droitture and Justice are permitted to appear to her, and the truth can be revealed.[9] Marcus points out that the efficacy of the exemplum relies on the connection between concrete experience and a transcendent truth beyond, and in Christine's text, these two factors of the genre are embodied in Christine's participation as the voice of experience, and the presence of the three Virtues as the truths beyond (Marcus, 12). Moreover, this 'ground situation' of the narrative invokes the theoretical position which Christine will occupy: while men have erred in their mistreatment of women by "se fondent sur ce qu'ilz ont trouvé en livres et dient après les autres et aleguent les autteurs"[1] (17), Christine, as peripheral to this tradition, set apart by her sex and yet privileged to this discourse by virtue of her education, is best qualified to reestablish the reputation of women, who are themselves marginal in a man's world.

6. See A. Jeanroy, "Boccace et Christine de Pisan: Le *De Claris Mulieribus* principale source du *Livre de la cité des dames*," *Romania*, vol. 48 (1922), pp. 147–154.

7. C. Reno sees virginity as the structural and thematic principle governing Christine's text. See "Virginity as an Ideal in Christine de Pizan's *Cité des dames*," *Ideals for Women in the Works of Christine de Pizan*, ed. by D. Bornstein, pp. 69–90.

8. "A great unhappiness and sadness welled up in my heart and I despised myself and the entire feminine sex." . . . "I relied more on the judgment of others than on what I myself felt and knew." [Editor]

9. Richards points out that Christine's emphasis on the realism of her vision stands in opposition to Jean de Meung's "dream vision" of Amant in the *Roman de la rose*, thus asserts the truth of the arguments to follow as refutations of de Meung's derogatory treatment of women. See Richards, pp. 259–260.

1. "Basing themselves on what they found in books and repeat after others and cite the authors." [Editor]

Christine's perception of the marginality of feminine society is further suggested by the scope of her *Livre du corps de policie* [Book of the body politic] written as an explanation of the body politic of men, with no mention of women's roles, and the separate *Livre des trois vertus*, the body politic of women. While the *Cité des dames* offers examples of secular and Christian virtues, the *Livre des trois vertus* [Book of the three virtues] emphasizes the practical knowledge necessary for women to maintain their households and themselves, and fulfill the roles allotted to them in the most efficient, and least obstrusive, way. For example, she recommends:

> Ainsy, la sage dame usera de ceste discrette dissimulation et prudent cautelle, laquelle chose ne croie nul que ce soit vice, mais grant vertu, quant faitte est a cause de bien et de paix. (qtd. in Curnow, 218–19)[2]

The distinction is between liberal and moral education, as defined by Italian humanism:

> Moral philosophy . . . teaches us that man is free, like Hercules at the crossroads, to choose the path of virtue or that of vice; it teaches us self-knowledge, practical wisdom, and our duties to God, family and friends, country, and ourselves . . . History gives us concrete examples of the precepts inculcated by philosophy. The one shows what men should do, the other what men have said and done in the past and what practical lessons we may draw from them for the present day. (qtd. in Willard, "Trois vertus", 102)

While Christine advocates liberal education for men, and as we shall see, for herself, her concern in establishing the body politic of women is in moral studies. Christine's "corps du policie" is based upon John of Salisbury's *Policraticus*, and follows that text's conception of the organic metaphor closely, while adopting its tenets to the situation of France at the time of Christine's composition. The body politic of women, however, departs from the model in ways which parallel and illuminate the *Cité des dames*. John's organic metaphor assumes not only the exclusion of women from the body politic, but also the "natural," pre-ordained and static character of this conception of the commonwealth. For Christine, as a woman writing to advise men in the *Livre du corps de policie* and to advise women in an alternative conception of the body politic in the *Livre des trois vertus*, these assumptions require redefinition, not only in order to establish her own authority as advisor, but also to point out the conventionality of this "natural" concept, and thus to clear a space for the body politic which is "natural" to women. Christine's city

---

2. "Thus the wise lady will use discreet dissimulation and prudent caution, and no one will consider this a vice but rather virtue when it is done for a good cause and for the sake of peace." [Editor]

is built alongside the city of man, on foundations which emerge from the male tradition but which are distinct from it, and with an exemplary purpose distinguished from Boccaccio's by Christine's concluding invitation to women in all classes to live in the city and "faittes les tous menteurs par monstrer vostre vertu et prouvés mencongeurs ceulx qui vos blasment par bien faire"[3] (310a). The image of the sealed fortress at the end of the *Cité des dames* distinguishes Christine's work from the *City of God* by utilizing the traditional Christian evaluation of virginity in women above all other virtues, but by redefining the concept of virginity itself:

> . . . the ideal of virginity she [Christine] sets forth is metaphorical as well as literal. Virginity implies, in addition to sexual purity, the freedom from any sort of involvement with men that might hamper women's pursuit of her particular goals. Moreover, Christine's focus in the *Cité* is not the spiritual reward of a more perfect state of eternal bliss that the Church held out to the celibate, but rather a triumph that could be measured primarily in terms of the standards of this world. (Reno, 70)

Though the two worlds are worlds apart, exchange is obviously necessary, and the *Livre des trois vertus* offers sound advice to women to manage this exchange most profitably. For Christine, as an intermediary figure between the two worlds, the terms of this exchange need to be established in the works themselves; and this commonwealth, as it is established in the *Cité des dames*, and clarified in the *Livre des trois vertus*, consists in Christine's equation of the body politic with the body poetic, her relationship to and manipulation of her own femininity; and in this project she has in mind the works of Dante, particularly *De Vulgari Eloquentia* [On vulgar eloquence].

In *De Vulgari Eloquentia*, Dante sets out a portrait of the 'illustrious vernacular,' in which Italy is anatomized and defined in terms of its language (I, 10–15; Marigo, pp. 75–132). The Italian vernacular is superior to Latin, and to other vernacular languages, according to Dante, because it is "natural":

> Est et inde alia locutio secundaria nobis, quam Romani gramaticam vocaverunt. Hanc quidem secundariam Greci habent et alii, sed non omnes; ad habitum vero huius pauci perveniunt, quia non nisi per spatium temporis et studii assidutatem regulamur et doctrinamur in illa.
>
> Harum quoque duarum nobilior est vulgaris: tum quia prima fuit humano generi usitata; tum quia totus orbis ipsa perfruitur, licet in

---

3. "Make liars of them all by showing your virtue and by your good deeds prove those wrong who blame you." [Editor]

diversas prolationes et vocabula sit divisa; tum quia naturalis est nobis, cum illa potius artificialis existat. (I,1.3–4; Marigo, pp. 6–8)[4]

The emphasis Dante places on the naturalness of the mother tongue becomes the grounds for revision by Christine. Dante points out that, since language is the faculty which distinguishes men from the lower animals, the first words spoken in Genesis were Adam's speaking the name of God. However, he confronts the awkward fact that "ubi de primordio mundi sacratissima Scriptura pertractat, mulierem invenitur ante omnes fuisse locutam, scilicet presumptuosissimam Evam"[5] (I,iv,2; Marigo, p. 20), a possibility he rejects, since, "rationabilius tamen est ut hominem prius locutum fuisse credamus; et incovenienter putatur tam egregium humani generis actum non prius a viro quam a femina profluxisse. Rationabiliter ergo credimus ipsi Ade prius datum fuisse loqui ab eo qui statim ipsum plasmaverat"[6] (I,iv,3; Marigo, p. 20). It is tempting to speculate as to Christine's reaction to the passage, especially in light of her attempt to bring to the fore an alternative understanding of what is "natural" to the sexes and to humankind. Certainly her revision of world history, and of the figure of Eve,[7] attempt to establish the role of women in founding civilization and languages alike. The conception of the mother tongue as natural and generational (DVE, I, vi; Marigo, pp. 30–38) (thus maternal in a real sense, which Christine turns to her advantage) results in the possibility of rejecting the mother tongue and writing in a foreign vernacular, and of such a decision constituting a rejection of God's natural order, thus constituting blasphemy. Pézard has written on the placement of Brunetto Latini in the circle of the sodomites in Inferno XV, and pointed out that in writing in French, Latini, for Dante, turned away from his natural language to the artificial French tongue, a turning away which parallels the unnatural desire of sodomy. Christine's decision to write in her adopted tongue, when viewed in light of Dante's judgment on Latini, can be seen as a movement which at once emphasizes the unnaturalness of male language

---

4. "From this we have also another, secondary language, which the Romans call grammatical. This secondary language the Greeks and others also have, but not all; indeed few attain to its use, since not without much time and assiduous study are we trained and taught in it.

   "And of these two the nobler is the vernacular—as well because it was the first to be used by mankind, as because the whole world makes use of it, although divided into different endings and words, as because it is natural for us, whereas the other is instead artificial." [Editor]

5. "In the beginning of the world we do find, as the Holy Scripture says, that a woman spoke before anyone else, namely that most presumptuous Eve." [Editor]

6. "Still it is more reasonable for us to believe that a man spoke first, and it is not fitting to think that so noble an act of the human race did not issue from a man rather than from a woman." Based on W. Welliver, trans., Dante in Hell. The De Vulgari Eloquentia: Introduction, Text, Translation, Commentary (Chapel Hill: University of North Carolina Press, 1981). [Editor]

7. Christine redeems Eve with the example of the Virgin Mary, attempting to prove that "woman was formed by God, in his spiritual image" (Curnow, 235), and that in the Christian tradition as well as in that of secular history, women's roles have been indispensable in the foundation of culture.

toward and for women, and revises Dante's estimation on his own terms, according to and alongside Christine's revision of the sexual relationship between men and women during the Quarrel of the Rose. If Dante inveighs against the blasphemy of using a foreign tongue, Christine, in a foreign tongue, inveighs against blasphemy against women. The languages of countries becomes recast as a problem of the languages of the male and female bodies politic. Recognizing the distinctions between the two, and their grounding in custom rather than nature, Christine attempts a revision of the *translatio studii* in terms of her personal authority. In her brief reference to Boccaccio's story in *Decameron* IV, 9 of the wife of Guiglielmo Rossiglione, Christine writes simply "d'une autre racompte Bacace, a qui son mary fist mengier le cuer de son amy, qui oncques puis ne mengia"[8] (227), omitting the French origin of the tragedy and presenting it as an example of women "que trop on amé de grant amour sans varier"[9] (227).

The reception of Christine's work, however, frustrates her revisionary purpose, and points to the ambivalent situation of the text, positioned between being a translation of Boccaccio's work and a revision of that book, along with other books of men: with the complete translation of *De Claris Mulieribus* in the mid-15th century, copying of the *Cité des dames* ceased.[1] It appears that, in spite of Christine's intentions of correcting Boccaccio's text, her work was accepted as a faithful translation of Boccaccio. Within Christine's corpus, however, its position is exemplary of her poetic purpose as a whole. Christine writes in the French vernacular not only to distinguish her text from Boccaccio's Latin work, and thus assure its accessibility to women and assert its audience more strongly than does Boccaccio's work, but also as a part of her self-conceived mission of continuing the Virgilian, and Dantesque, poetic in the vernacular. As she says in *Le Livre du chemin de long etude* [The path of long study]:[2]

> Dant de Florence recorde
> En son livre qu'il composa
> Ou il moult beau stil posa
> Quante en la silve fu entrez
> Ou tout de paour ert oultrez.
> Lors que Virgile s'aparu
> A lui, dont il fu secouru
> Adont lui dist par grant estude

8. "Boccaccio tells of another woman whom her husband forced to eat her lover's heart; after that she ate no more." [Editor]
9. "Who have loved with too much steadfast love." [Editor]
1. Richards, p. 267. See also C. C. Willard, "The Manuscript Tradition of the *Livre des trois vertus* and Christine de Pizan's Audience," *JHI*, vol. 27 (1966), pp. 433–444.
2. See also Dante, *Inferno* I, 82–7: O de li altri poeti onore e lume,/ vagliami 'l lungo studio e 'l grande amore/ che m'ha fatto cercar lo tuo volume./ Tu se' lo mio maestro e 'l mio autore/ tu se' solo colui da cu' io tolsi/ lo bello stile che m'ha fatto onore."

> Ce mot: 'Vaille moi lonc estude
> Qui ma'a fait cercher tes volumes
> Par qui ensemble accointance eumes.'
> Or cognois a cele parole
> Qui ne fu nice ne frivole
> Que le vaillant poet Dant,
> Qui a lonc estude ot la dent,
> Estroit en ce chemin entrez
> Quant Virgile y fu encountrez,
> Qui le mena par mi enfer
> Ou plus durs lieus vid que fer.
> Si dis que je ne'oublieroie
> Celle parole: ains la diroie
> En lieu d'avvangile ou de croix
> Au passer de divers destrois
> Ou puis en maint peril me vis.[3]
>   (lines 1120–1143)

Thus Christine draws upon the examples of her male countrymen to justify her position as an Italian woman writing in the French vernacular, simultaneously rejecting the tradition, and language, these writers provide and drawing upon it as the basis of her own authority.

Christine's position as an Italian writer producing works for French patrons on topics of French politics and culture involves, on the one hand, her readaption of Italian authors into the French language and cultural context, and on the other, challenges her authority as a spokesperson for her adopted country. This authority is defended by Christine in *L'Avision-Christine* [Christine's Vision], and the defense provides an analogue to that of her peripheral position as a female writer, a foreigner in the world of male discourse. In *L'Avision*, the personified figure of France says to Christine, "o ma bonne nourrice et chiere amie compaigne de mon dueil tout ne soies tu mie du fruit de ma terre mais ton cuer de noble nature non ingrat des biens que y as receus pleures avec moy par vraye amistie piteuse de veoir les iours de ma tribulacion,"[4] (86), and following her complaint of the troubles of the country, reaffirms Christine's mission as her spokesperson:

---

3. "Dante of Florence records in the book he composed in such a beautiful style that when he had entered the wild wood and was completely overcome by fear, at the moment when Virgil appeared who helped him, he [Dante] exclaimed with great enthusiasm: 'May the long study now avail me which has made me pore over your volumes through which we first came to know each other.' At that point I knew that with these words, neither silly nor frivolous, the valiant poet Dante, whose taste for learning was fierce, had embarked upon this path when he encountered Virgil, who led him into Hell, where he saw chains much stronger than iron. I thereupon declared that I would not forget this phrase, but would use it instead of the Gospel or the sign of the cross when I encountered various dangers and perils." [Editor]

4. "Oh my dear nurse and companion of my sadness, although you were not born in my country, your noble heart is grateful for the things it received there and cries with me in true sympathetic friendship when it sees the days of my tribulations." [Editor]

O quel plaisir et quel alegement est de dire et descouvrir a son loial ami ou amie les pesenteurs de ses pensees . . . Si te mercy ma bien amee en fin de mes paroles de ta loial amour et compagnie/la quelle to pry que ne me faillejusques a la fin non obstant que dial-leurs tu soies requise/et que de moy des miens tu ayes petiz esmolu-mens/mais ton bon courage ne vueille delaissier la nourriture de son enfance/si demeure constante avec moy ou gracieux labour de tes dittiez duquel maint plaisirs encour feras a moy et mes enfans. lesquelx ie te pry que me salves/et que leur segnefies les plaines de mes clamours/et que comme loyaulx et vrais enfans vueillent avoir pitie de leur tendre mere de qui encor le laitt leur est necessaire et doulce nourriture/mais vueillent se espargner ses doulces ma-melles quilz ne la succent jusques au sang.[5] (107–8)

This defense is interesting in relation to Christine's self-defense during the Quarrel of the Rose. When Gontier de Col condemns Christine's "error and folly" which her "overweening presumption as a passionate woman" has incurred, her defense rests on the virtues and learnedness of exemplary women of the past. And in reply to Col's condemnation, "O words hastily and thoughtlessly uttered by a woman's mouth to con-demn a man of such high understanding," Christine points out that it is cowardly of him to attack the weakest opponent, when such learned men as the Chancellor of the University of Paris take her side of the debate. "Car ie repute mon fait et mon savoir chose de nulle grandeur . . ." she writes to Col, ". . . puet bien estre que q'i ay cuelli des basses flouretes du jardin delicieux, non pas monté sur les haulx arbres pour cueillir de ce beau fruit odorant et sauoureux, non mie que l'appetit, et la volenté n'y soit grant, mais foiblece d'entendement ne le me sueffre, et mesmes pour l'odeur des flourettes, dont j'ay fait grais les chappellez."[6] Thus her position as 'foreign,' an Italian in France or a woman in scholarship, is for Christine a double-edged sword, which she can use in excuse and in defense of the novelty of her opinions, and at the same time invoke as the objective view, from the outside looking in, from which she derives her authority.

Accordingly, in turning to Boccaccio's work as a source, Christine

5. "Oh what a pleasure and relief it is to tell and reveal to one's loyal friend one's heavy thoughts. . . . I thank you, dear one, at the end of speech for your loyal love and company which I ask you to preserve for me even if you are called elsewhere and even if you have received little from me. But a true heart will not leave behind its childhood. Please remain steadfast with me through the gracious labor of your texts with which you give me and my children great plea-sure. May you save them for me and make my complaints known to them so that like loyal and true children they will take pity on their tender mother whose milk and sweet nourish-ment they still need, and may they spare the tender breasts so that they won't suck them all the way to the blood." [Editor]
6. See Ward, ed., *The Epistles of the Roman de la Rose and Other Documents of the Debate* (Chicago: University of Chicago Press, 1911), p. 110. ["For I do not think much of my deeds and knowledge . . . It is possible that I picked the lower flowers in a delightful garden and have not climbed up on the high trees in order to pick some of these fragrant and savory fruits: and not because of a lack of appetite or will power but because my weak understanding will not permit it in spite of the odor of the flowers with which I made rich garlands." Editor]

begins building her city by clearing the "champ des escriptures" [field of letters] on which it will stand (14). Raison explains that the condemnation of women by male writers is contrary to Nature, "car il n'est ou monde nul si grant ne si fort liain comme est celluy de la grant amour que Nature, par voulente de Dieu, met entre homme et femme"[7] (16). Though men sometimes say that they write against women with good intentions, to warn men away from the evils of women, Raison points out that this is absurd: "est aussi que se je blasmoye le feu, qui est elle-ment tres bon et tres neccessaire pourtant, se aucuns s'y bruslent, et aussi l'iaue pource se on s'y noye. Et semblebalement se pourroit dire de toutes bonnes choses de quoy on / puet et bien et mal user"[8] (16a). Thus Christine begins her work by echoing Boccaccio's conclusion to the *Decameron*, "Le quali chenti che elle si sieno, e nuocere e guivar possono si come possono tutte l'altre cose, avendo riguardo allo ascolta-tore"[9] (678); but women themselves, as they appear in tales like Boccaccio's, are the good things used badly by men, according to Christine. Boccaccio's life of Medea (B.16), and Christine's rewrite of it, are revelatory of this notion. For Boccaccio, the story leads to a lengthy admonition against succumbing to the temptations of the eyes:

> . . . we must not give too much freedom to our eyes, because as we look we perceive beauty, become envious, and are attracted to concubines. By means of the eyes audacity is aroused, beauty is praised, squalor and poverty are unworthily condemned, and since they are not learned judges, the eyes believe only in the outward appearance of things. Often they place the shameful ahead of the sacred, the false ahead of the true, and impropriety ahead of bless-ing. . . . Certainly, if powerful Medea had closed her eyes or turned them elsewhere when she fixed them longingly on Jason, her father's power would have been preserved, as would her brother's life, and the honor of her virginity would have remained unblemished. All these things were lost because of the shame-lessness of her eyes. (37)

As the figure of Medea herself can be read as a dangerous and tempting image, her story can equally be read, as Boccaccio does, as an example of those dangers and thus as a morally edifying exemplum. Christine's version of the story of Medea rejects the possibility that the heroine could at once succumb to the dangers of visual seduction and present, in the story itself, the potential exemplum of such a seduction: rather,

---

7. "For there is in the world no greater bond than that which Nature by God's will establishes between man and woman." [Editor]
8. "It is just as if I blamed fire which is in itself is good and necessary when some people burn themselves, or water because one can drown in it. And similarly one could speak of all good things which one can use well or badly." [Editor]
9. "Like all other things in the world, stories, whatever their nature, may be harmful or useful, depending on the listener." Boccaccio, *Decameron*, trans. McWilliam, 830. [Editor]

she purifies Medea, saying that her only sin was that she "ama de trop grant et de trop ferme amour Jason"[1] (221)

Women, in Christine's estimation, are inferior to men by custom rather than by nature: "se coustume estoit de mettre les petites filles a l'escolle et . . . suyvantment on les faist aprendre les sciences, comme on fait au filz, elles appren/droyent aussi parfaittement et entendroyent les soubtilletez de toutes les ars et sciences comme ilz font" (82).[2] Thus at the heart of Christine's work is a program of education for women. While in Le Livre des trois vertus that education is in the practicalities of women's lives in a society without civil rights, in the Cité des dames the education of women is in the secular virtues and in their own capabilities. Though Raison explains that the occupations of men and women are ordained by God, and thus "il souffit qu'elles facent le commun office a quoy sont establies"[3] (20c), nonetheless it is the purpose of the Cité to show that women are capable of conquering the 'male' arts and sciences:

> Mais se aucuns vouloyent dire que femmes n'ayent entendement souffisant pour apprendre les loys, le contraire est magnifest par preuve de experience qui appert, et est apparue, de plusieurs femmes, si que sera dit cy aprés, qui on esté tres grandes philosophes et ont aprises de trop plus soubtilles sciences et plus haultes que ne sont lois escriptes et establissements d'omnes.[4] (41)

The basis of this proof is Christine's own experience, as it is reflected in her reading of Boccaccio, and in the course of the work, her own erudition becomes an exemplum, though a problematic one, of the erudition of women at large.

Christine's reorganization of De Claris Mulieribus displays her dual purpose of connecting the pagan virtues with those of her contemporaries, and of presenting herself as a model, like those whose lives Boccaccio related. In Raison's argument against men who say that women ought not to be educated (183–186), Christine begins with Boccaccio's example of Hortensia (B.82), and provides an example of her own acquaintance, that of Novella, the daughter of Giovanni Andrea, a law professor at Bologne. Novella, she says,

> fist apprendre lettres et si avant es loys, que, quant il estoit occuppez d'aucun essoine par quoy ne povoit vacquier a lire les leçons a

1. "Loved Jason with too great and steadfast a love." [Editor]
2. This custom is attacked by Christine in other works, especially in autobiographical passages. See L'Avision-Christine, Bk. III, and Le Livre de la mutacion de Fortune, vol. 1, lines 413–427. ["If it were customary to send little girls to school and . . . have them learn the sciences as one does with boys, they would learn just as well and would understand the subtleties of all the arts and sciences just as boys do." Editor]
3. "It is enough that they do their assigned tasks." [Editor]
4. "But if someone wanted to say that women do not have enough understanding for learning the laws, the opposite can be proved by the experience of several women, of whom we will speak later, who were great philosophers and who have mastered more subtle and elevated sciences than are the laws and rules of men." [Editor]

ces escolliers, il envoyoit sa fille en son lieu lire aux escolles en chayere. Et adfin que la beauté d'elle n empeschast la penssee des ouyans, elle avoit une petite courtine au devant d'elle.[5] (185)

Raison then concludes with the example of Christine herself:

Ton pere, qui fu grant naturien et phillosophe, n'oppinoit pas que femmes vaulsissent pis par science apprendre, ains de ce qu'en-cline te veoit aux lettres, si que tu sces, grant plaisir y prenoit. Mais l'oppinion femenine de / ta mere, qui te vouloit occupper en fil-lasses selonc l'usaige commun des femmes, fu cause de l'emp-eschement que ne fus en ton enffance plus avant boutes es sciences et plus en parfont.[6] (186)

The same method provides the basis of Christine's reorganization of Boccaccio's stories of Cornificia (B.84), Proba (B.95), Sappho (B.45) and Leontium (B.58), which are grouped together early in her work, as examples of learned women, in order to establish Christine's position as inheritrix of their legacies. The changes she makes in Boccaccio's accounts of these women's lives are as startling as the overt appeals to his authority in these passages, and are prompted by the same desire to valorize the position of the "studious woman."[7] While Boccaccio's Cornificia is the equal of her brother (188), Christine's heroine "voulst sentir et savoir de toutes sciences qu'elle apprist souverainement, en tant que son frere, qui tres grant pouette estoit, passa en toute excellence de clergie"[8] (83). She omits Boccaccio's statement that "with her genius and labour she rose above her sex" (188),[9] and says instead that "Bocace l'Italien, qui fu grant pouette, en louant ceste femme dist en son livre:"

'O! tres grant honneur a femme qui a laissié son engin aux estudes des tres haulx clers.' Dist oultre celuy Bocace, certifiant le propos que je te disoye, de l'engin des femmes qui se deffient d'elles meismes et de leur entendement, lesquelles, ainsi que se elles fus-sent nees es montaignes sans savoir que est bien et que est hon-neur, se descouraigent et dient que ne sont a autre chose bonnes

5. "Was so educated in the law that, when he was occupied with some other task and could not devote himself to presenting his lectures to his students, he sent his daughter in his stead to lecture to the students from his podium. And so that her beauty would not distract the listeners, there was a little curtain in front of her." [Editor]

6. "Your father, who was a great scientist and philosopher, was not of the opinion that women were worth less by studying the sciences, rather, as you know, he derived great pleasure from seeing you inclined toward learning. But the feminine opinion of your mother, who wanted to keep you busy with stuff like spinning, as is the common custom of women, was the stumbling block that kept you from being thrust further and deeper into the sciences when you were still a child." [Editor]

7. For a discussion of the humanist debate on the studious woman, and Christine's relationship to that tradition, see S. G. Bell, "Christine de Pizan: Humanism and the Problem of the Studious Woman," *Feminist Studies*, vol. 3 (1975), pp. 173–184.

8. "Wanted to experience and know all the sciences which she learned effortlessly, so much so that she surpassed her brother, who was a great poet, in excellence of learning." [Editor]

9. Boccaccio's denigrations of 'woman's work' are frequent occurrences in *De Claris Mulieribus*. See, for example, the lives of Semiramis (2), Martesia and Lampedo (11), Arachne (17), Iole (21), Nicaula (41), Thamyris (54), Marcia (64), Cornificia (84), and Proba (95).

ne prouffitables fors pour acoller les hommes et porter et nourir les enffans. Et Dieu leur a donné le bel entendement pour elles apliquer, se elles veullent, en toutes les choses que les glorieux et excellens hommes font. Se elles veullent estudier les choses, ne plus ne moins leur sont communes comme aux hommes, et pueent par labour honneste acquerir non perpetuel, lequel est aagreable a avoir aux tres excellens hommes. Fille chiere, si puez veoir comment celluy auteur Bocace tesmoigne ce que je t'ay dit, et comment il loe et appreuve science en femme.[1] (83a)

Proba's life, too, is subject to simultaneous acts of revision and of appeal to Boccaccio's authority. She quotes Boccaccio's opinion that "it is certainly astonishing that such a lofty plan came into a woman's mind, but more marvelous is the fact that she fulfilled it" (219; *Cité* 84), though the suggestion that this fact is remarkable because of the natural inferiority of woman's mind is tempered by Christine's suggestion that Proba surpassed Virgil in her reorganization and Christianization of his works:

> ... sans y faillir, ordenoit tant magistraument que nul homme ne peust mieulx. Et par tel maniere des le commencement du monde fist le comencement de son livre, et ensuivant de toutes les hystoires de l'Ancien Testament et du Nouvel vint jusques a l'envoyment du Saint Esperit aux Apostres, les livres de Virgille a tout ce / concordans si ordenement que qui n'avoit congnoissance de ceste composicion cuideroit que Virgille eust este prophette et evvangeliste ensemble. Pour lesquelz choses, ce dit meismes Bocace, grant et louenge affiert a ceste femme. ... Et nonobstant que le labour de celle oeuvre, pour sa grandeur, deust souffire a la vie d'un homme, a y vacquier ne s'en passa mie a y tant, ains fist plusieurs autres livres excellens et tres louables.[2] (84–84a)

---

1. "Boccaccio, the Italian, who was a great poet, speaks in praise of this woman in his book:

   "Oh, greatest honor to a woman who abandoned all feminine tasks and applied and devoted her mind to the study of the most eminent scholars. Further, Boccaccio speaks—and in this he confirms what I said to you earlier—of the minds of women who despise themselves and their own judgment, and, just as if they were born in the mountains and did not know what was good and honorable, they become discouraged and say that the only thing they are good and useful for is to embrace men and carry and feed children. And God has given them such beautiful understanding to apply themselves, if they want to, to the same things as glorious and excellent men, whatever subjects they want to study, they will find that they are just as open to them as they are to men, and through their honest labor they can acquire a name that will last forever, something that is as much desired by the most eminent men. Dear daughter, now you can see how this author Boccaccio testifies to what I have told you and how he praises and approves learning in women." [Editor]

2. "Without fault she arranged things that no man could do better. In this way, she began with the beginning of the world for the opening of her book, and then all the stories from the Old Testament and the New until she came to the sending of the Holy Spirit to the Apostles, and she adapted Virgil's books so well to this that someone who knew only her work would believe that Virgil had been both a prophet and an Evangelist. Because of these facts Boccaccio says that this woman deserves great praise. ... And although the labor required by this work through its grandeur, would have been enough to fill a man's lifetime, she did not spend that much time on it and also composed several other excellent and praiseworthy books." [Editor]

Thus Proba's relationship to Virgil becomes a model for Christine's relationship to Boccaccio, and Proba's act of Christianization becomes, as
it does in Christine's use of Dante's definition of blasphemy, the basis
of Christine's feminization of Boccaccio, based on the realignment of
relationships, and languages, between the sexes to their natural orders.

As for Sappho, Christine follows Boccaccio closely, but for the purposes of emphasizing the erudition of the poet, she adds the fact that
"quant Platon, le tres grant phillosophe qui fu maistre de / Aristote, fu
trespassé, on trouva le livre des dittiez de Sappho soubz son chevet"[3]
(85a). Boccaccio's Sappho is an exemplary poet, who "was born of honorable and noble parents, for no vile soul could have desired to write
poetry, nor could a plebeian one have written it as she did" (99), a
definition of the poet's character which recalls Boccaccio's comments
in the *Genealogy of the Gentile Gods:* "It (poetry) proceeds from the
bosom of God, and few, I find, are the souls in whom this gift is born;
indeed so wonderful a gift it is that true poets have always been the
rarest of men" (XIV: 7; Osgood, 39). Yet in Boccaccio's account, the
explanation of Sappho's greatness lies in her unrequited love. He writes,

> But, if the story is true, she was as unhappy in love as she was happy
> in her art. For she fell in love with a young man and was the prey
> of this intolerable pestilence either because of his charm and
> beauty or for other reasons. He refused to accede to her desires,
> and, lamenting his obstinate harshness, Sappho wrote mournful
> verses. (99)

Christine excludes Boccaccio's report of Sappho's tragic love, in an
attempt to further align Sappho's poetic with her own, occurring in and
initiated by chaste widowhood, as well as stressing the innate skill and
genius of the poet, free from recourse to explanation (or excuse) through
the failed love affair. Christine quotes Boccaccio's praise of Sappho:

> . . . she ascended the slopes of Parnassus and on that high summit
> with happy daring joined the Muses, who did not nod in disap-
> proval. Wandering through the laurel grove, she arrived at the cave
> of Apollo, bathed in the waters of Castalia, and took up Phoebus
> plecturn. (99; *Cité* 85)

But Christine includes within this quotation the further point that "s'en
entra en la forest de lauriers plaine de may, de verdure, de fleurs de
diverses couleurs, odeurs de grant soueftume, et de plusieurs herbes,
ou reposent et habitent Grammaire, Logique et la noble Rettorique,
Geometrie, Arismetique"[4] (85), again recalling the *Genealogy*'s require-

---

3. "When Plato, the great philosopher who had been the master of Aristotle, died, people found
   the book with Sappho's poems under his pillow." [Editor]
4. "She entered the forest of laurel trees, full of May foliage, greenery, and flowers of different
   colors, fragrances of great sweetness and many herbs, where reside at their leisure Grammar,
   Logic, noble Rhetoric, Geometry, and Arithmetic." [Editor]

ment that the poet "know at least the principles of the other Liberal Arts, both moral and natural . . ." (XIV:7; Osgood, 40). The addition, presented as Boccaccio's own words, serves at once to bring the elevated praise into the context of Christine's own experience, emphasizing the liberal arts in which she herself is learned, and at the same time, to better qualify Boccaccio as an authority in support of Christine's argument.

Christine's rewriting of the life of Leontium (B.58) displays her striking departure from Boccaccio's authority in order to establish her own. In direct contradiction to Boccaccio's statement that "she dared to write against and criticize Theophrastus, a famous philosopher of that period, moved either by envy or womanly temerity" (132), Christine writes that Leontium was "si tres grant phillosophe que elle osa, par pures et vrayes raisons, reprendre et redarguer le philosophe Theophaste, qui en son temps tant estoit renommez"[5] (87). The correction recalls Christine's self-defense during the Quarrel of the Rose of her serious and impartial correction and attack on Jean de Meung, and sets the stage for her own attack on Theophrastus in the *Cité des dames*:

> Theofrascus en son livre dit que nul saige ne doit prendre femme, car trop a en femmes de cures, pou d'amour et foyson jangleries, et que se l'homme le fait pour estre mieulx servy et gardé en ses maladies, que trop mieulx serviteur, et ne luy coustera pas tant. . . . A dire des bonnes: pour ce que celluy Theofrascus, dont tu as parlé, dit que aussi loyaulment, autant songneusement sera un homme gardé en la maladie ou essoine par son servant que par sa femme: ha! quantes bonnes femmes sont autant songneuses de leurs maris servir, sains et malades, par loyal amour que ce fussent leur dieux? . . . Et pour ce qu'entree sommes en ceste matiere, je t'en donray mains exemples de grant amour et loyaulté de femmes portee a leurs maris.[6] (153–154)

The examples Droitture brings forth "contre ce que le phillosophe Theoffrastus dit touchant ceste matiere"[7] (155a), are Boccaccio's examples of Hypsicratea (B.76), Triaria (B.94), Artemesia (B.55), and Argia (B.27); she concludes, Boccaccio "approuvant le lian de mariage qu autres veullent tant reprouchier"[8] (156). So the Boccaccio who seems

5. "Such a great philosopher that she dared, by clear and true reasoning, to correct and attack the philosopher Theophrastus who was so famous in her time." [Editor]
6. "Theophrastus says in his book that no wise man should take a wife, for women only bring trouble, little love, and plenty of idle talk, and that a man can be better taken care of in his sickness or trouble by a servant than by his wife, and it will be less expensive. . . . To speak of good women: as far as this Theophrastus is concerned of whom you spoke and who says that a man will be taken care of in his sickness or trouble by a servant as loyally and carefully as by his wife—ha! How many good women are there who are so devoted to serving their husbands, healthy or ill, with such loyal love as though their husbands were gods? And since we have taken up this subject matter, I will give you many examples of the great love and loyalty women have shown toward their husbands." [Editor]
7. "Against what this philosopher Theophrastus says on this subject." [Editor]
8. "Approved the bond of marriage that others want to vilify." [Editor]

to side with Theophrastus against Leontium (whom, he adds, "threw away womanly shame and was a courtesan, or rather, a harlot" thus "bringing Philosophy, the queen of all human pursuits, among panderers" (132) is refuted by the Boccaccio who could only marvel at the conjugal constancy of such ladies as he himself describes.

At several points in her work, Christine directly contradicts Boccaccio's statements in *De Claris Mulieribus*, while at other points her revision rests on a program of qualification by use of the examples of contemporary women. For example, Boccaccio's life of Nicaula (B.41) occurs in Christine, as in Boccaccio, as an example of the political and military achievements of women, but it is immediately followed in the *Cité* by examples of the ladies of contemporary France, of all classes (43–49). Similarly, Christine groups together Boccaccio's lives of Juno (B.4), Europa (B.9), Jocasta (B.23), Medusa (B.20), Polyxena (B.31) and Helen (B.35) as examples of women who have achieved notoriety "by coincidence," and opposes to these examples those of women who have achieved fame through virtue. She uses Boccaccio's example of Busa (B.67) as a classical example of the "inffinies largesces, courtoysies et liberalités des femmes"[9] (245), omitting Boccaccio's observation that "women have habitual, or even innate frugality and very little generosity" (151). The rehabilitation of Busa is followed by examples of ladies of Christine's own time (246–258), and Book II closes with this revised understanding of fame as grounded not on accident but on essential virtue, providing the bridge to Book III's account of Christian models of virtue.

Christine is equally deft at using the unabridged statements of Boccaccio in support of arguments which she imposes on those passages. For example, in his life of Carmenta (B.25), Boccaccio praises Carmenta's contribution in inventing the Latin alphabet and grammar, and enters into a panegyric on Latin (Italian) language and culture:

> By means of these inventions an infinite number of books have been written on all subjects: the accomplishments of men, and the great deeds of God, which are preserved perpetually for mankind, so that through their help we may know things which we cannot see ... Regardless of what has happened to other things through our fault or through an act of Fortune, neither the rapacity of the Germans, nor the fury of the Gauls, nor the wiles of the English, nor the ferocity of the Spaniards, nor the rough barbarity and insolence of any other nation has been able to take away from the Latin name such great, marvelous, and rightful glory, so that they have never said or dared say that the first letters were found through their own talents, and much less that they invented grammar. (54–5)

---

9. "The infinite generosity, courteousness, and liberality of women." [Editor]

Christine turns Boccaccio's words to support the role of women as founders of men's culture, and ironically, of the language men use to condemn women:

> Or se taissent, or se taisent d'or en avant, les clers mesdisans de femmes, ceulx qui en ont parlé en blasme et qui en parlent en leurs livres et dittiez, et tous leurs complices et confors, et baissent les yeux de honte de ce que tant en ont osé dire a leurs diz, considerant la verité qui contredit a leur diz, voyant ceste noble dame Carmentis, laquelle par la haultesce de son entendement les a apris comme leur maistresce a l'escolle—ce ne pueent ilz nyer—la leçon de laquelle savoir se treuvent tant haultains et honnourez: c'est assavoir les nobles lettres du latin![1] (106)

In the same way, Minerva (B.6), Isis (B.8), and Ceres (B.5) provide the foundations of the arts of chivalry and land-owning. Raison states:

> Mais que dirent les nobles et les chevaliers dont tant y a, et c'est chose contre droit, qui mesdient si generaulment de toutes femmes? Refraignent leur bouche d'or en avant, advisant que le usaige des armes porter, faire batailles et combatre en ordenance, duquel mestier tant s'alosent et tiennent grans, leur est venu et donné d'une femme. Et generaulment tous hommes qui vivent de pain et qui civillement vivent es cités par ordre de droit, et aussi ceulx qui cultivent les guaignages, ont ilz cause de blasmer et debouter tant femmes, comme plusieurs de eulx font, penssant ces grans benefices? Certes non, et que par femmes, c'est assavoir, Minerve, Cerés et Ysis, leur sont venus tant de prouffis, lesquelz benefices ont leur vie a honneur et s'en vivent, et vivront, a tousjours.[2] (106a)

Moreover, Christine's identification with these female founders of male culture is suggested in her Preface to *Le Livre des faits d'armes et chivalrie* [The book of the deeds of arms and chivalry], where, in calling on Minerva to guide her in her treatment of the 'male' topic of arms, Christine adds, "For I am, as you were, an Italian woman" (7).

1. "Let them be quiet, let them be quiet from now on, the scholars who malign women, those who have blamed them in their books and poems, and all their accomplices and supporters. May they lower their eyes in shame over what they dared to say in their writings in view of the truth that contradicts them when we look at the noble lady Carmentis who by the superiority of her intelligence taught them like a school mistress—which they cannot deny—the lesson through the knowledge of which they have become so superior and honored: namely the noble language of Latin." [Editor]

2. "But what are these nobles and knights saying—of whom there are so many—who against any justice malign women? May they restrain their tongues from now on, seeing that the custom of carrying arms, waging battles and combating in ranks, of which profession they boast and because of which they consider themselves great, was given to them by a woman. And generally all men who live from bread and live civilly and lawfully in cities, and also those who cultivate the land, do they have cause to blame and rebuff women so much, as some of them do, in view of these great benefits? Certainly not, because through women, that is, through Minerva, Ceres and Isis, they have received such great advantages which give them great honor and they live and will live by them forever." [Editor]

While Christine thus appropriates Boccaccio's own words to her purposes, she is equally interested in correcting those opinions which seem
to qualify his praise of women's achievements, or to degrade them. In
Boccaccio's tale of Ceres (B.5), his ambivalence toward her achievement in inventing the art of agriculture, as at once paving the way to
civilization and signalling the end of the Golden Age, leads him to the
paradoxical equation of Ceres with Eve, the woman by whom the
Golden Age was lost forever (12–13). Christine, on the other hand, has
only praise for this Orphic figure, and rejects Boccaccio's suggestion of
the decline of civilization *through* civilization, which in turn suggests
the decline of feminine virtue (99–99a). In many of the lives of *De
Claris Mulieribus*, Boccaccio's fear of women's encroachment on men's
rights and position, because of the very achievements he describes, leads
to morals which are aimed at men, to the purpose of keeping women in
their place. The story of Iole and Hercules, for example (B.21), leads to
a warning to men of the deceitfulness of women and the unnaturalness
of submission to them (46–7). Christine omits the story altogether, and
states simply, in the voice of Droitture, "quant est ad ce qu'ilz dient que
si decepvables soyent, ne sçay a quoy plus t'endiroye. Car toy meismes as
assez souffisantment traitté la matiere, tant contre celluy Ovide comme
contre autres, et ton *Epistre du dieu d'Amours* et es *Epistres sur le Rommant de la Rose*"[3] (219a). This reference to the works of the debate
suggests that the omission of the story of Iole, and Boccaccio's conclusion, reflects Christine's agreement with Boccaccio as to the unnaturalness of the subordination of men to women, since in these works she
does not advocate the usurpation of men's roles by women, but rather
she exhorts men to govern women properly. Yet Boccaccio's traditional
condemnation of women's faults is repugnant to Christine: rather, she
emphasizes men's faults in failing to fulfill their role as the natural governor of women, according to the tenets of reason.

The omission of the life of Iole parallels Christine's omission of those
of Flora (B.42), Pope Joan (B.99), and particularly Niobe (B.14): in
each case Christine feels the need to suppress the possibility of domination of men by women, and these are figures of feminine usurpation
(grounded on stereotypical feminine qualities such as deceit and pride),
who gain power by abusing the balance of power between the sexes. In
all these cases, though—Pope Joan's manipulation of rhetoric, Flora's
manipulation of history, Iole's castration of Hercules by the abuse of the
feminine art of spinning, and Niobe's presumption against the gods—
the heroines gain power through their outstanding knowledge, beauty,
or ingeniousness, and Boccaccio's statement that Niobe's sin involves
her pride in "surpass[ing] the boundaries of her weakness" as a woman

---

3. "When they say that they are so deceiving, I do not know what I should say to this. For you
   yourself have sufficiently dealt with this topic against Ovid and others in your *Letter from the
   God of Love* and in *The Letters on the Romance of the Rose*." [Editor]

(32) presents a threat to Christine's program of education for women which the *Cité des dames* cannot abide. Boccaccio's invective against Niobe's pride recalls Col's charges against Christine (and Boccaccio's against Leontium). While Leontium can be contained, Niobe presents a dangerous figure for Christine's poetic and city, the darker side of feminine strength and wisdom. While it is necessary to put down these figures, and the possibility of deception by the female figure (and by extension, by Christine herself), it is equally pressing that Christine establish the grounds for distinguishing between their manipulation of knowledge and language and her own project. In the *Cité des dames*, built by and for women, these examples disturb the possibility of alignment between the two sexes according to the rule of reason, and present images of the "manly woman," who, in Christine's understanding of the term, distort the correct relationship between the sexes as do the men who govern women irrationally. The rule by women in the city seeks not to overcome but to correct men. Thus when Boccaccio complains that Veturia's achievement led to the disgraceful custom of allowing women to receive inheritances, and concludes "but what can I say? The world belongs to women, and men are womanish" (121), Christine uses Boccaccio's life of Lucretia (B.46) to argue for greater legal rights for women: "Et a cause de cel oultraige fait a Lucresce, comme dient aucuns, vint la loy que homme mourroit pour prendre femme a force; laquelle loy est couvenable, juste, et sainte"[4] (195a). This is, predictably, a detail not found in Boccaccio's treatment of Lucretia. Moreover, while *De Claris Mulieribus* provides only one direct condemnation of the actions of men (the example of Danaus in the life of Hypermnestra, B.13), Christine looks outside the work to Boccaccio's own *De Casibus Virorum Illustrium* [On the fall of famous men] to bring forth examples of men's inconstancy and fickleness in the face of women's constancy, the epitome of which, for Christine, is the Patient Griselda.

Christine's treatment of Boccaccio's Semiramis (B.2) is of particular interest in illuminating her relationship to the exempla which she derives from the *Decameron*, since her revisions in Semiramis' story parallel the treatment this woman receives in the preface to Philippe de Mézières' translation of Petrarch's Griselda tale, Christine's source for her version of the story.[5] Boccaccio's Semiramis is praised for her military and political achievements (the virtue Semiramis exemplifies in Christine's work), but Boccaccio points out that her success was based on "feminine wiles" and "deceit," and she undertook her "marvelous subterfuge" of playing the role of her own son, "as if she wanted to show that in order to govern it is not necessary to be a man, but to have

---

4. "And as some people say, it was because of the outrage done to Lucretia that the law was created that a man who took a woman by force must die; this is a fitting, just, and sacred law." [Editor]

5. See Golenistcheff-Koutouzoff, *L'Histoire de Griseldis en France au XIVᵉ et au XVᵉ siècle* (Paris, 1933), pp. 167ff.

courage" (5). As praiseworthy as this deceit was, however, Semiramis' exchange of roles with her son leads to the sin of incest, portrayed by Boccaccio as the unnatural domination of women over men. She is further attributed with the invention of chastity belts, "which she forced all her court ladies to wear" (7), and thus the "manly woman," a term of the highest praise in Boccaccio, becomes the enemy of natural feminity. She is, appropriately, killed by her son.

Christine, on the other hand, omits these unsettling conclusions, stressing that Semiramis "fonda et ediffia de nouvel plusieurs cités et fortes places, et parfist plusieurs autres grans faiz, et accompli tant, que de nul homme n'est point escript plus grant couraige ne plus de faiz merveilleux et dignes de memoire"[6] (55b). She further rejects the anachronism of Boccaccio's condemnation of Semiramis' incest by pointing out that:

> ... ycelle noble dame fait aucunement a excuser pour ce que adonc n'estoit encores point de loy escripte: ains vivoyent les gens a loy de nature, ou il loisoit a chacun sans mesprendre de faire tout ce que le cuer luy apportoit: car n'est pas doubte, que se elle penssast que mal fust ou que aucun blasme luy en peust encourir, qu'elle avoit bien si grant et si hault couraige et tant amoit honneur, que jamais ne le faist.[7] (56)

The centrality to the text of this vindication of Semiramis is demonstrated by Raison's statement immediately following her story, "Mais or est assise la premiere pierre ou foundement de nostre cité"[8] (56a).

The assertion of Semiramis' unstained courage is crucial to the treatise that follows because of Christine's inclusion of contemporary examples of virtue in her city, and this relationship is illuminated by Mézières' reading of Semiramis' life. His translation of the Griselda tale appears in a manuscript entitled "Le Miroir des dames marieés," [The mirror of married ladies] thus adopting Petrarch's understanding of the exemplary function of the tale,[9] and his preface contains several points which have bearing on Christine's use of this tale, and of Boccaccio's corpus, in her work. First Mézières asserts the truth of the tale to follow, "et est la dict histoire publique et notoire en Lombardie en par especial en Pieumont et ou marquise de Saluce est reputée pour

---

6. "Founded and constructed several new cities and fortified places, and accomplished other great deeds and did so much that about no man are written more courageous nor more marvelous things that are worthy of being remembered." [Editor]
7. "This noble lady does not need to be pardoned for this because at that time there was no written law: rather, people lived according to the law of nature, which allows everyone to do what his heart inclines him to do, without any blame. For there is no doubt that had she thought that what she was doing was wrong or blameworthy her great and superior heart and her love of honor would not have permitted her to do it." [Editor]
8. "Now the first stone or the foundation of our city has been laid." [Editor]
9. See Richardson and Rolfe, *Petrarch: The First Modern Scholar and Man of Letters* (NY: Greenwood Press, 1968), pp. 191–6.

vraye,"[1] an assertion which strengthens his conclusion that Griselda's behavior is not only capable of being imitated by his female readers, but ought to be imitated: "Les dames donques marieés pour estre contentes et conforteés a leur pooir et par grace se doivent enforcier en aucune maniere d'ensuir la marquise de Saluce et de plair premierement a leur espous immortel, et aprés a leur mari mortel" (qtd. in Golenistcheff-Koutouzoff, 154–5).[2] Secondly, Mézières includes in his preface the example of "les IX. preux," [the Nine Worthies] and particularly the example of Semiramis:

> Les anciennes histoires, a l'example des IX. preux, font grant mention des IX dames qui par aucunes sont appellées preux, lesquelles dames, selonc les histoires, furent de grant vertu et firent en ce monde choses moult merveilleuses et quant au monde digne de memoire, entre lesquelles dames Semiramis, royne des Assiriens et espouse du roy Ninus; aprés la mort de son mari, elle en personne et par bataille conquist a l'espee toute Inde et Ethyope, ce que son mari en son temps n'avoit peu faire. . . . Mais qui vaudra bien peser a la balance, qui rent a chascun le pois de sa valour, la grant vertu du corage invincible de la noble marquise de Saluce. . . . Qui bien vaudra considerer comment la noble marquise vainqui soy meismes et demoura victorieuse! Par aventure sa proesse porra equipoller ou en vray vertu surmonter la force de corage d'aucunes des IX dames preux, cy dessus proposees, qui vainquoyent les autres et se laissoyent vaincre.[3] (qtd. in Golenistcheff-Koutouzoff, 153–4)

This continuity between the pagan virtue of courage, exemplified by Semiramis, and the Christian virtues of constancy and fidelity reflects

---

1. "And this story is well-known in Lombardy and especially in Piedmont where the story of the marquise of Saluce is held to be true." [Editor]
2. The question of the imitability of Griselda's example is problematized in Boccaccio's tale by Dioneo's concluding statement, "Chi avrebbe, altri che Griselda, potuto col viso non solamente asciutto ma lieto, sofferire le rigide e mai più non udite prove da Gualtieri solamente fatte?" (*Dec.* 674), and the issue is again raised by Petrarch, who writes, "my object in rewriting your tale was not to induce the women of our time to imitate the patience of this wife, which seems to me almost beyond imitation, but to lead my readers to emulate the example of feminine constancy and to submit themselves to God. . . ." (qtd. in Richardson and Rolfe, p. 195). ["In order to be content and comforted, married ladies should therefore strive by their efforts and by grace to imitate the marquise of Saluce in many ways and to please their immortal spouse first of all and after that their mortal spouse." The "immortal spouse" is Jesus Christ. Editor]
3. "Modeled on the Nine Worthies, the old histories speak of nine ladies whom some call worthies. These ladies, according to the histories, were of great virtue and did marvelous things in this world which are worthy of being remembered, and among them was Semiramis, queen of the Assyrians and wife of King Ninus. After the death of her husband she herself in battle with a sword conquered all of India and Aethiopia, which her husband in his time had not managed to do. . . . But whoever wanted to weight the scale which gives to everyone the weight of his valor, the great virtue of the invincible heart of the marquise of Saluce. . . . Who would well consider how the marquise of Saluce conquered herself and remained victorious! It could be that her prowess could equal or by its true virtue even surpass that of some of the Nine Worthy Ladies that were mentioned above and who conquered others and were conquered themselves." [Editor]

Christine's understanding of the historical continuity of the virtues in the city, and the characteristics of Mézières' handling of the Griselda tale—the explicitly exemplary function, the emphasis on the tale's truth and imitability, and the Christianization of the allegory to reflect the relationship of the soul to God—begin to explain Christine's reasons for using his translation, in spite of the fact that she had the *Decameron* before her as she wrote, and used the stories of the wife of Bernarbó (II,9), Ghismonda (IV,1), Lisabetta (IV,5), and the wife of Guiglilemo Rossiglione (IV,9) in the *Cité des dames*. The context in which the Griselda story occurs, however, suggests that as eager as Christine is to emphasize the saintly virtues of Griselda, as presented by Petrarch and Mézières, she is equally eager to present Gualtieri as an example of men's tyranny and inconstancy (the equivalent of Nero, Galba, and the other examples drawn from *De Casibus Virorum Illustrium* which directly precede the Griselda tale), suggesting that she had Dioneo's condemnations of Gualtieri in her mind as she wrote (*Dec.* X,10; 665, 674). Throughout her version of the tale, Christine emphasizes that Gualtieri is "moult estrange de meurs" [has very strange customs] (209), and in his reunion with Griselda, Christine's Gualtieri states, "Et croy qu'il n'a homme soubz les cieulx qui par tant d'espreuves ait congneue l'amour de mariage comme j'ay fait en toy"[4] (212), recollecting Droit-ture's discussion of marriage earlier in Book II, and thus linking the tale to Christine's autobiography and her condemnation of Theophrastus:

> Et quoyqu'il soit des mauvais maris, il en est tres bons, vaillans et saiges, et que les femmes qui les encontrent nasquirent de bonne heur quant a la gloire du monde de ce que Dieux les y adreça. Et ce puez tu bien scavoir par toy meismes, qui tel l'avoyes qu'a fin soulhaid ne sceusses mieulx demander et qui, a ton jugement, nul autre homme de toute bonté, paisibleté, loyaulté et bonne amour ne le passoit duquel les regraiz de ce / que mort le te tolly jamais de ton cuer ne partiront. Et quoyque je te dis, et il est voir, que il soit moult de bonnes femmes moult malmenees par leurs divers maris, saiches pourtant que il en est de moult diverses et sans raison, car se je te disoye que toutes fussent bonnes, je pourroye assez de legier estre reprouvee mentaresse[5] . . . (153a)

---

4. "And I believe that no man under the skies has known married love through so many trials as I have known it with you." [Editor]
5. "And although there are bad husbands, there are also very good, valiant, and wise ones, and the women who encounter them were born lucky with respect to the glory of the world because God pointed them in the right direction. And you know this very well yourself for you had such a husband that, even if you could have had your heart's desire, you could not have asked for a better one. In your judgment no other man surpassed him in goodness, peacefulness, loyalty and true love, and the regrets over his death will never leave your heart. And although I am telling you, and it is true, that there are many good women badly mistreated by their wicked husbands, you should also know that there are also wicked and unreasonable women, for if I were to tell you that all women are good, I could easily be accused of being a liar." [Editor]

For Christine, the Pauline understanding of marriage as the figuration of the ordering of reason over the appetites in the rule of the husband over the wife has been perverted by the unnatural tyranny of husbands over wives.[6] The tale of Griselda, then, displays not only Griselda's triumph, but also Gualtieri's failure.

Immediately following the tale of Griselda are Christine's versions of the story of the wife of Bernarbó, Ghismonda, and Lisabetta, and a reference to the tale of the wife of Guiglilemo Rossiglione. C. Bozzolo points out several tendencies which mark Christine's treatment of the tales from the *Decameron*. First, since the tales are harnessed to the purposes of exempla, of women's constancy and loyalty in love, everything in Boccaccio's stories which is not relevant to the virtue of the protagonist is excluded. Secondly, Christine tends to rationalize the exotic or extreme elements of Boccaccio's tales, in order to make them more accessible to her audience as exempla: thus there is in Christine a lengthy explanation of why the wife of Bernarbó allows the chest containing Ambrogiuolo to be placed in her chamber (*Dec.* 146, *Cité* 215a). The grotto in Tancredi's palace in Boccaccio's tale, by which Guiscardo gains access to Ghismonda (*Dec.* 250) becomes simply Ghismonda's "chambre" [room] in Christine's tale (*Cité*, 224). While Boccaccio's Lisabetta has a premonition foretelling her lover's fate (*Dec.* 279), Christine's heroine,

> . . . se trouvast seulle ou jardin ou Laurens gisoit mort, en regardant partout vid la terre soulevee de nouvel, la ou le corps estoit. Adonc a tout un pic que elle avoit porté, fouy la terre et fist tant que le corps trouva. Adonc, le corps embracant par gratn destresçe, fist dueil oultre mesure. Mais pource que bien savoit que la ne povoit mie estre longuement, de paour que apperceue fust, le corps recouvry de la terre, et prist la teste de son amy que ses freres avoyent trenchee.[7] (226a–226b)

Thirdly, the environments in which the tales take place are idealized by Christine: the world of merchants in the tale of Lisabetta (*Dec.* 227–8) becomes the world of Courtly Love in which the stilnovistic belief that virtue is unconnected to class is stressed (as it is in Christine's tale of Ghismonda). Boccaccio's "canna" (*Dec.* 250), the Galeotto between Ghismonda and Guiscardo, becomes in Christine a lengthy dialogue between the two incorporating the clichés of Courtly Love (224b).

Christine's treatment of the tale of the wife of Bernarbó continues the

---

6. See Mazzotta, "The *Decameron:* The Literal and the Allegorical," *Italian Quarterly*, vol. 18 (Spring, 1975), p. 67.
7. ". . . found herself alone in the garden where Laurent had lain dead, and looking around she saw the soil freshly overturned where the body had been. Then, with a pick ax she had brought she dug into the earth until she found the corpse. Then, kissing the corpse in great distress she mourned him beyond any measure. But since she knew very well that she could not remain there much longer for fear of being seen, she covered the corpse again with soil and took her lover's head which her brothers had cut off." [Editor]

strategy of shaming men by the example of women which the Griselda tale began. Christine is explicitly critical of "Ambrose," whom she calls "un oultragieux" [an outrageous man] (215), and she takes great pleasure in proving that his opinion that "le maleureux homme [Bernarbó] en occist sa famme; mais il avoit mieulx desservy pugnicion que elle: car homme doit savoir que toute femme est fraille et de legier vaincue, sy n'y doit avoir tel fiance"[8] (215d) is wrong on both counts. Rather, Bernarbó's fault lies in "moult a louer sa femme de biauté, de scens, de chasteté sur toutes riens et de toutes vertus"[9] (215), as opposed to Boccaccio's Bernarbó's 'mercantile' praise (Dec. 143), and then failing in the kind of constancy his wife displays. "Vous estes digne de mort," Saragut tells him, "car vous n'aviez mie preuve / soubffisant" against his wife (215f), thus "s'en rapportoye plus au jugement d'autruy qu' ad ce que soy meismes en sentoye et savoye."[1]

The tale of the wife of Bernarbó is followed by De Claris Mulieribus' lives of Leaena (B.58), Medea (B.16), Thisbe (B.12), and Dido (B.40), and the set of lives in conjunction with the tale of Ghismonda which follows, constitutes a second definitive group in which Christine's understanding of her poetic and her self-portrayal is exposed.

Boccaccio's moral to the life of Thisbe parallels Guiscardo's statement in Decameron IV,1 of the law, or tyranny, of love which dictates the actions of the three protagonists: "Amor può troppo più che ne voi ne io possiamo" (Dec. 242).[2] Boccaccio affixes to the life of Thisbe the lesson:

> Certainly, the ardor of the young should be curbed slowly, lest by wishing to oppose them with sudden impediments we drive them to despair and perdition. The passion of desire is without temperance, and it is almost a pestilence and fury in youth. We should tolerate it patiently, because, the nature of things being as it is, when we are fully grown we are spontaneously inclined to bring forth children, so the human race may not come to an end through delaying intercourse until old age. (27)

It is a lesson which is echoed by Christine's Ghismonda, whose words and acts she copies faithfully, without omission, from Boccaccio's tale:

> Mais de ceste chose qui vous muet a si grant yre contre nous, n'avez cause de vous prendre que a vostre meismes coulpe: car

---

8. "The unhappy man [Bernabo] killed his wife because of this; but he deserved more punishment than she: for a man must know that every woman is weak and easily conquered, and he should not trust her like this." [Editor]
9. "To praise his wife's beauty, intelligence, chastity, and virtue above everything else." [Editor]
1. "You merit death . . . for you do not have sufficient proof" . . . "you relied more on the judgment of someone else than on what you yourself felt and knew." [Editor]
2. For a discussion of the interrelation of tyranny and tragedy in this tale, see Marcus, An Allegory of Form, pp. 44–63. ["Neither you nor I can resist the power of love." Trans. McWilliam, 335. Editor]

vous qui estes de char, ne penssiez vous avoir engendree fille de
char et no pas de pierre ou de fer? Et souvenir vous devoit, tout
soyés vous envielly, quelle et comment grant est la moleste de
jeunesce vivant en delices et ayse, et les aguillons fors a passer quy
y sont. Et, puisque je vy que vous aviez deliberé de n'y jamais me
marier, et me sentant jeune et stimulee de ma joliveté, m'ana-
mouray de cestuy[3] . . . (225a)

Christine omits Guiscardo's comment, softening the justification of
Tancredi's tyrannical behavior, and shifting the charges against him
from Guiscardo's mouth to that of his daughter. Christine's direct translation of the figure of Ghismonda from her source suggests her great
empathy for and fascination with this woman, and her juxtaposition of
the story of Dido with the tale of Ghismonda suggests a link between
Christine herself and these figures of loyalty in love. Boccaccio's life of
Dido, as noted above, is followed by a lengthy exhortation to widows to
remain chaste in their widowhood: "O inviolate honor of chastity! O
venerable and eternal example of constant widowhood! O Dido, I wish
that widows would turn their eyes to you, and especially those that are
Christian would contemplate your strength. . . ." (89–90). Marcus has
pointed out the centrality of Ghismonda's widowhood to Boccaccio's
tale: "to a medieval reader . . . the implications of Ghismonda's short
acquaintance with conjugal life would not be lost. Widows were notorious in the Middle Ages for their desire to resume the carnal delights of
their previous marital state" (Marcus, 45). Boccaccio, in the *Genealogy*,
explains that Virgil's "second purpose" in relating the tale of Dido "was
to show with what passions human frailty is infested:"

> so he introduces Dido, a woman of distinguished family, young,
> fair, rich, exemplary, famous for her purity, ruler of her city and
> people, of conspicuous wisdom and eloquence, and lastly, a widow,
> and thus from former experience in love the more easily disposed
> to that passion. (Osgood, 68)

For Christine, the problems of widowhood are a frequent theme in
her writings, as is the often repeated fact that her own widowhood
prompted her life of scholarship. Her own position as a widow is central
to both her prescriptions for the behavior of women, and her role as a
writer. In *L'Avision-Christine* and *Le Livre des trois vertus*, she complains
of the lawsuits which plagued her for fourteen years after her husband's
death, and of the dangers to which widows are exposed, unprotected

3. "But in this matter that enrages you so much against us you only have to blame yourself: for
you who are made of flesh did you believe that you did not engender a daughter made of flesh
and not of stone? And you should have remembered, though now you are old, how troublesome is youth when one lives in delights and luxury, and the stings that assail people and must
be overcome. And since I realized that you had decided never to marry me to anyone, and
because I felt young and attractive through my beauty, I fell in love with this man. . . ." [Editor]

and without rights in a man's world.[4] Of her own experience, however, she says that Fortune came to her and gave her "un cuer d'homme" [a heart of a man]:

> Plus ne me tins en la parece
> De plour, qui croissoit ma destrece.
> Fort et hardi cuer me trouvay,
> Dont m'esbahi, mais j'esprouvay
> Que vray homme fus devenu[5] . . .
> (*Mutacion*, I: 51–2)

Thus she turned to writing and entered into her new career in the world of men. As for other women, Christine's advice is, above all, pragmatic: avoid romantic liaisons and ostentation, for they can cause slanders to arise; rely only on the counsel of friends or one's own reason; avoid alienating those whom you need for support; be chaste, prudent, turn only to God for comfort.[6]

While Christine omits Boccaccio's exhortation to widows in her life of Dido, nonetheless her treatment suggests her approval of Boccaccio's conclusion, and some reasons for her disapproval of it as well. She writes,

> Et a tant vint la frequentacion que Amours, qui soubtilment scet cuers soubtraire, les fist enamourer l'un de l'autre. Mais selonc ce que l'experience se monstra, moult fu plus grande l'amour de Dido vers Eneas que celle de/luy vers elle: car nonobstant que il luy eust la foy baillee que jamais autre femme que elle ne prendroit et qu'a tousjours mais sien seroit, il s'en parti aprés ce que elle l'ot tout reffait et enrichi d'avoir et d'aise, ses nefs refraischies, reffaictes et ordonnees, plain de tresor et de biens, comme celle qui n'avoit espargné l'avoir la ou le cuer estoit mis. S'en ala sans congié prendre de nuit en recelle traytreusement, sans le sceu d'elle; et ainsi paya son hoste. Laquelle departie fu si grant douleur a la lasse Dido, qui trop amoit, qu'elle voulst renoncier a joye et vie.[7] (220–220a)

---

4. See *Le Livre des trois vertus*, Bk. II, ch. 22–4, and *L'Avision-Christine*, Bk. III.
5. "I no longer remained in the lethargy of tears which had been increasing my grief. I found my heart strong and bold, at which I rejoiced and was amazed, and I felt that I had become a true man." [Editor]
6. *Le Livre des trois vertus*, Bk. II, ch. 24; see also Laigle, *Le Livre des trois vertus et son milieu historique et littéraire* (Paris, 1912), pp. 300–305.
7. "And they met so often that Love, who skillfully conquers hearts, made them fall in love. But as experience showed, Dido's love for Aeneas was greater than his love for her: for although he swore that he would never take another woman as his wife than her and that he would belong to her forever, he left her after she had helped him to recover, had given him riches and luxuries, his ships newly outfitted, rebuilt and equipped with many treasures and goods, like a woman who spared none of her riches for the one her heart belonged to. He left treacherously and secretly in the night without saying good-bye, without her knowledge; and this is how he paid back his hostess. This departure caused the sad Dido, who loved too much, such great pain that she wanted to give up on all joy and even her life." [Editor]

Thus the stories of Dido and Ghismonda are paralleled in Aeneas' treachery and Tancredi's tyranny, and in the inescapable force of love which overcomes both heroines. One further detail links the story of Dido to Christine's treatment of all the tales she adapts from the *Decameron*, and to her own autobiographical alignment with these women: Dido, she says, "trop amoit," [loved too much] a recantation which is echoed in Christine's conclusion to this section of the *Cité*:

> Mais ses piteux exemples et assez d'autres que dire te pourroye ne doivent mie estre cause d'esmouvoir les couraiges des femmes de eulx fichier en celle mer tres perilleuse et dampnable de folle amour: car tousjours en est la fin mauvaise a leur grant prejudice et grief en corps, en bien et en honneur et a l'ame, qui plus est. Si feront que saiges, celles qui par bon scens la saront eschever et non donner audiance a ceulx qui sans cesser se travaillent d'elles decepvoir en telz cas.[8] (228)

Like Dido, whose name Christine explains means "virago," and whom Boccaccio says "cast aside womanly weakness", and Ghismonda, who bears her fate "par tres affermé couraige et constant chiere, sans gitter larme" (225a), exchanging the masculine role with Tancredi, Christine bears the trials of widowhood with loyalty and a "cuer d'homme". She rejects these models, however, as exempla for her peers: the virtues of womanhood which she wishes to display in the city are not Boccaccio's "manly" virtues transferred to the female sex; rather, they represent a sharpening of essentially feminine virtues, distinct from the masculine ones.

This distinction is reflected in the lives of Leaena, Medea, Dido and Griselda, as well, and in the nature of the stories Christine chooses from the *Decameron* for inclusion in her translation of *De Claris Mulieribus*. The striking parallelism of form and meaning in the tales of Medea, Dido and Griselda epitomizes the dual nature of Christine's role as author: the three stories are the only divided biographies in the *Cité des dames*, and the divisions of these lives elucidate Christine's revisions of and relation to the figures. Both Dido and Medea, we are told, "trop amoit", in their appearances as examples of constancy in love. But both appear earlier in the text, without reference to their tragic loves, as examples of the capability of women to master and discover knowledge and arts. Thus severed from the taint of excessive love and deceit of Jason, Medea is revised to free her as an example worthy of emulation. While in *De Claris Mulieribus* she is a figure of discord in the body politic, and as noted above, a figure of the dangers of imagery and

---

8. "But these pitiful examples and others I could tell you about should not move women's hearts to throw themselves into this perilous and damnable sea of foolish love: for it always ends badly and does them great harm in their bodies, their possessions, and in the honor of their souls, which is the most important. Those act wisely who know how to avoid it and do not listen to those who ceaselessly strive to deceive them." [Editor]

poetry, Christine liberates Medea from her role in the liaison with Jason and presents her as one of the women who constitute and maintain the fabric of society. Dido too first appears in her role as the virtuous ruler of Carthage (119–120b), later in connection with Aeneas (219–220a); and similarly Griselda, whose transformation from the *Decameron's* heroine was noted above, initially appears as an example of filial devotion (148), joining Medea and Dido as figures who, within their unfortunate couplings, represent threats to Christine's position and poetic, and are given lives of their own beyond the notorious affairs. They reflect Christine's own transformation from wife to widow, from submissive partner to independent writer with a "cuer d'homme." Leaena, too, reflects this change: in Boccaccio she is an ambivalent example of feminine virtue, a courtesan who proves above all else that "the person who said that women keep silent only about what they do not know did not know Leaena" (107–8). Boccaccio concludes with the paradoxical comparison: "Certainly, first with her silence and then by biting off her tongue, she gained no less glory than Demosthenes gained among his people with his florid eloquence" (108): the eloquence of women thus rests in her silence. In the *Cité des dames*, Leaena is cleansed of the suggestion of prostitution, and becomes a figure of feminine constancy and the eloquence of women which, quietly, speaks volumes (216).

Christine's reading of the *Decameron* as a source of exempla is justified since, as Guarino points out, there are similarities between the morals of many of the lives of *De Claris Mulieribus* and the tales of the *Decameron*.[9] But she cannot have been blind to the fact that the explicitly 'exemplary' day of the *Decameron*, Day X, the only one to suggest in the frame tale the didactic function of the tales to follow, provides no examples of feminine magnificence but that of Griselda. And, as noted above, Christine rejects Dioneo's problematic exemplum for the more clear-cut reading of Petrarch. Thus Boccaccio's work written in the vernacular for the pleasure of ladies is, for Christine, in need of revision.

9. The conclusion to the life of Rhea Ilia, for example, reads, "So when I consider this woman and see the bands and sacred vestments of nuns hiding furtive love, I cannot help laughing at the madness of some people. There are even men, who, like misers, take away from their daughters their pittance of a dowry; under the pretext of devotion, they confine—or should I say condemn?—their daughters to nuns' cells . . . This is ridiculous and foolish. They do not know that an idle woman serves Venus and that these nuns greatly envy public prostitutes, whose chambers they think preferable to their own cells . . . (97), while *Dec.* III, 1 begins with Filostrato's comments, "Bellissime donne, assai sono di quegli uomini e di quelle femine che si sono stolti, che credono troppo bene che, come ad una giovane e sopra il capo posta la benda bianea et indosso messale la nera cocolla, che ella piu non sia femina ne piu senta de' feminili appetiti se non come se di pietra l'avesse fatta divenire il farla monaca: e se forse alcuna cosa contra questa lor credenza n'odono, cosi si trubano come se contra natura grandissimo, e scellerato male fosse commesso, non pensando ne volendo avere reipetto a se medesimi li quali la piena licensa di potere far quel che vogliono non puo saziare, ne ancora alle gran forze dell'ozio e della sollecitudine" (166). Christine excludes the life of Rhea Ilia, and Boccaccio's libertine conclusion, and rewrites the founding of Rome, in the life of Lavinia (122) without reference to the "sin" of Rhea Ilia, stressing instead Lavinia's role in establishing culture. Compare also the life of Paulina. (B.92) with the tale of Lisetta (*Dec.* V,2) and Flora (B.52) with the tale of Ser Chiappelletto (*Dec.* I,1).

To effect this, she turns to the *Decameron*'s 'tragic' day, Day IV, and uses these tales not as innocent exempla of feminine virtues, but as indictments of the frailties and cruelties of men, Boccaccio included, toward women. The women in these stories are not only beyond imitation, they ought not to be imitated, for such treatment ought not to occur. Christine turns to the *Decameron* partially because *De Claris Mulieribus* provides few examples of men's mistreatment of women, while the tales she selects reflect this mistreatment and thus belong in a text which is concerned with eradicating the abuses of women on all levels—social, conjugal, legal, as well as historical and literary.

The ambivalence of Christine's position as a woman in the man's world of letters, involved in a program of 'clearing the Field of Letters' to make room for her own voice and her uniquely feminine city, is reflected in her self-identification with the figures of Boccaccio's corpus, and in her relationship to her male source in general. By means of her identification with Proba, Sappho, Cornificia and Leontium, she derives from Boccaccio's authority an authority of her own, and establishes her autobiography as an exemplum to her contemporaries. At the same time, though, her identification with Boccaccio's "manly woman," Dido and Ghismonda especially, marks the basis of the disqualification of her own model as an exemplum to her peers. The "manly woman" is reflected in Droitture's discussion of Christine's education, noted above: there Christine calls the usual occupations of women "fillasses," "spinning and silly girlishness" (Richards, 155), aligning herself with Boccaccio's denigrations of women's work in *De Claris Mulieribus*, such as his comment in the life of Proba, "If we consider the ways of women, the distaff, the needle, and weaving would have been sufficient for her had she wanted to lead a sluggish life like the majority of women" (220).[1] Elsewhere in her text, however, beyond the autobiographical passages, Christine is eager to point out that,

> Quant est du filler, voirement a Dieux voulu que ce leur soit naturel, car c'est office necessaire au service divin et a l'ayde de toute creature raisonnable, sans lequel ouvraige les offices du monde seroyent maintenus en grant ordure. Si est grant mauvaistié de rendre en reprouche aux femmes ce que leur doit tourner a tres grant gré, honneur, et loz.[2] (39)

The education by which Christine is enabled to guide women and to correct Boccaccio and other male writers paradoxically aligns her with these writers to such a degree that her abilities become problematic as examples for her contemporaries to follow. She establishes 'woman's

---

1. See also the lives of Rhea Ilia (43), Leaena (48), Europa (9) and Medea (16).
2. "As far as spinning is concerned, God truly wanted this to be natural for women, for it is necessary for the divine service and to the benefit of any reasonable creature, and without this work things in this world would be in terrible disorder. It is very bad to reproach woman with something that should bring them great thankfulness, honor, and praise." [Editor]

work' as the thread which keeps society intact, presenting, for example, the model of Penelope as a woman who is both beautiful and chaste (191), especially in the context of the court, a model of particular relevance in light of the intrigues of the French court which threatened, in Christine's view, the stability of the state.[3] Yet her relation to the potent figures of Medea and Dido prompts a sometimes uncomfortable recognition of the dangers of Christine's own position and its untenability as a model for her contemporaries. As Arachne in Boccaccio is a figure of usurpation, vanity and presumption (B.17), in Christine she necessarily becomes the founder of "science plus necessaire" (108), and thus a guarantor of culture.

The act of translation, for Christine, is a complicated and at times inconsistent one, and the problems involved in translating men's works into a feminine context, pagan examples into a Christian context, or Italian authorities into the French vernacular are topics of extreme self-consciousness in Christine's works, which are subtly thematized throughout *Le Livre de la cité des dames*. Her attraction to Boccaccio's *De Claris Mulieribus* is apparent in her faithful transcription of many of his lives in her own work, but at the same time, her need to establish her own authority as a female writer, from that of a male author, leads to revisions of Boccaccio's text which, Christine hopes, can expand to become revisions in the world beyond. In a sense, Boccaccio's life of the painter Marcia (B.64) and Christine's translation of it, stand as a synecdoche for the city she builds. Boccaccio's Marcia's chastity forbids her painting male subjects, "for in antiquity figures were for the greater part represented nude or half nude, and it seemed to her necessary either to make the men imperfect, or, by making them perfect, forget maidenly modesty. To avoid both these things, it seemed better to her to abstain from both" (145): the feminine world of creation is truly a world apart. In the *Cité des dames*, this restriction is lifted, and Marcia's example is followed by the example of Christine's contemporary, the Parisian painter Anastasia (113). Yet the world of Marcia's art, like the *Cité*, is a sealed fortress, set apart from the world of men:

> A tout dire, elle surmonta et ataigny le comble de tout quanque on puet savoir d'icelle science, selonc ce que disoyent les maistres. Ceste Marcia adfin que memoire demourast aprés elle entre ses nottables oeuvres fist un table par grant art ou elle paigni as figure, en se regardant en un mirouoir, si proprement que tout homme qui la veoit la jugoit estre vive. Laquelle table fu puis longtemps tres souverainement gardee et monstree aux ouvriers comme un tresor de sollempnité.[4] (112)

---

3. See C. C. Willard, "Christine de Pizan's *Livre des trois vertus*: Feminine Ideal or Practical Advice?" in Bornstein, ed., pp. 99–101.
4. "As everyone said, she attained and surpassed the highest level of what one can know in this science, according to the masters. So that people would remember her, this Marcia made

Works Cited

Bell, S. G. "Christine de Pizan: Humanism and the Problem of the Studious Woman," *Feminist Studies*, vol. 3 (1975), pp. 173–184.

Boccaccio, G. *Concerning Famous Women (De Claris Mulieribus)*. Trans. by G. Guarino. New Brunswick: Rutgers University Press, 1963.

———. *Il Decameron*. Ed. by A. Ottolino. Milan: Ulrico Hoepli, 1938.

Bornstein, D., ed. *Ideals for Women in the Works of Christine de Pizan*. Medieval and Renaissance Monograph Series, I. Michigan Consortium for Medieval and Early Modern Studies, 1981.

Bozzolo, C. "Il Decameron come fonte del *Livre de la cité des dames* di Christine de Pisan," in *Miscellanea de studi e ricerche sul quattrocento Francese*. Ed. by F. Simone. Torino: Università degli studi, 1967, pp. 3–24.

Byles, A. T. P., ed. *The Book of Fayttes of Armes and Chivalrye of Christine de Pisan*. London: 1932.

Curnow, M. The *"Livre de la cité des dames of Christine de Pisan: A Critical Edition*. Ph.D. Dissertation, Vanderbilt University, 1975.

Dante Alighieri. *De Vulgari Eloquentia*. Ed. by A. Marigo, in *Opere di Dante*, ed. M. Barbi. Firenze: Felice le Monnier, 1934, vol. 6.

———. *Il Convivio*. Ed. by G. Busnelli and G. Vandelli, in *Opere di Dante*, ed. M. Barbi. Firenze: Felice le Monnier, 1934, vol. 1.

Eargle, B. *An Edition of Christina de Pizan's "Livre du chemin de long etude*. Ph.D. Dissertation, University of Georgia, 1973.

Golenistcheff-Koutouzoff, E. *L'Histoire de Griseldis en France au XIVe et au XVe siècle*. Paris: Librairie E. Droz, 1933.

Jeanroy, A. "Boccace et Christine de Pisan: Le *De Claris Mulieribus* principale source du *Livre de la cité des dames*," *Romania*, vol. 48 (1922), pp. 93–105.

Kelly, D. "Reflections on the Role of Christine de Pizan as a Feminist Writer," *Sub-stance*, vol. 2 (1972), pp. 63–71.

Laigle, M. *Le Livre des trois vertus de Christine de Pisan et son milieu historique et littéraire*. Paris: 1912.

Marcus, M. J. *An Allegory of Form*. Stanford: Stanford French and Italian Studies, vol. 18, 1979.

Mazzotta, G. "The Decameron: The Literal and the Allegorical," *Italian Quarterly*, vol. 18 (Spring, 1975), pp. 53–73.

Osgood, C. *Boccaccio on Poetry*. Princeton: Princeton University Press, 1932.

Pézard, A. *Dante sous la pluie de feu*. Paris: Librairie Philosophique J. Vrin, 1950.

Pizan, Christine de. *L'Avision-Christine*. Ed. by M. L. Towner. NY: AMS Press, 1932.

———. *Le Livre du corps de policie*. Ed. by R. H. Lucas. Geneva: 1967.

———. *Le Livre de la mutacion de Fortune*. Ed. by S. Solente. 4 vols. Paris: 1959–1966.

Richards, E. J., trans. *The Book of the City of Ladies*. [Foreword] by M. Warner. NY: Persea Books, 1981.

Robinson, J. H. and Rolfe, H. W. *Petrarch: The First Modern Scholar and Man of Letters*. NY: Greenwood Press, 1968.

Roy, M., ed. *Oeuvres poétiques de Christine de Pisan*. 2 vols. Paris: 1891.

Ward, C. W., ed. *The Epistles of the Roman de la Rose and Other Documents of the Debate*. Chicago: University of Chicago Press, 1911.

Willard, C. C. "Christine de Pizan's *Livre des trois vertus*: Feminine Ideal or Practical Advice?" in Bornstein, ed., *Ideals for Women in the Works of Christine de Pizan*. Medieval and Renaissance Monograph Series, I. Michigan Consortium for Medieval and Early Modern Studies, 1981, pp. 91–116.

———. "The Manuscript Tradition of the *Livre des trois vertus* and Christine de Pizan's Audience," *JHI*, vol. 27 (1966), pp. 433–444.

among the notable works she accomplished an artful painting where she painted herself by looking into a mirror so accurately that every man who saw her believed her to be alive. This painting was for a long time safely kept and shown to the workers like a solemn treasure."
[Editor]

JOEL BLANCHARD

"Vox poetica, vox politica": [1] The Poet's Entry into the Political Arena in the Fifteenth Century †

At the end of the Middle Ages power becomes a subject for poetic activity. One can observe a convergence between a certain kind of poetry and a certain political practice.[2] This convergence is evident in a discourse that not only addresses the prince in a new way but makes an effort to define the royal virtues indispensable in the exercise of power.

This discourse takes shape at a moment when the monarchy becomes a state and when the conditions of the exercice of power are being transformed:[3] through the establishment of a bureaucratic system of counselors which belong to the *curia* [court], who help the king in his administration; through the creation, already in the twelfth and thirteenth centuries, of a veritable den of ideologues who compose normative treatises for the king; and through the transformation of royal ideology. One passes from the idea of the feudal contract to that of the biological reciprocity of the social body, inspired by the organic conception of the body politic:[4] sin circulates in the social body, attacking even its head, the king, and thus justifies an appropriate pedagogical approach, the presence of a counselor who must tell the prince the truth, thus assuring a perfect equilibrium. This truth telling began much earlier, in the mirrors of princes. The Carolingian mirrors and especially those of St. Louis[5] treat the structures and practices of power, but the beginnings of a rational reflection on royal power do not really take shape before the reign of Charles V, the Aristotelian king, and the introduction of the new Aristotle via Saint Thomas, William Ockham, and especially Giles of Rome. A new taxonomy of virtues and a new way of presenting political and social facts seems to impose new expressions on the discourse of power.

---

1. The poetic voice, the political voice. [Editor]
 † First published in *Etudes littéraires sur le XVe siècle* (Milan: Università Cattolica del Sacro Cuore, 1985), 39–51. Translated with permission by Renate Blumenfeld-Kosinski.
2. On the beginnings of a political literature at the end of the Middle Ages see Janet Coleman, *Medieval Readers and Writers, 1350–1400* (London, 1981); Pierre-Yves Badel, *Le Roman de la Rose au XIVe siècle. Etude de la réception de l'oeuvre* (Geneva, 1980), pp. 379–409 and a collection of articles *Culture et politique en France à l'époque de l'Humanisme et de la Renaissance* (colloquium, Turin, 1971, directed by Franco Simone) (Turin, 1974). For a semiology of political discourse in the Great Rhetoricians (1470–1520) see Paul Zumthor, *Le masque et la lumière. La poétique des grands rhétoriquers* (Paris, 1978).
3. See P. Lewis, *La France à la fin du moyen âge. La société politique* (Paris, 1977); Bernard Guenée, *L'Occident aux XIV et XVe siècles. Les Etats* (Paris, 1978).
4. E. H. Kantorowicz, *The King's Two Bodies. A Study in Mediaeval Political Theology* (Princeton, 1957), pp. 193–231; J. Barbey, *La fonction royale d'après les 'Tractatus' de Jean de Terrevermeille* (Paris, 1983), pp. 157–268.
5. Reigned 1226–70. [Editor]

Critics have studied this discourse from the point of view of contents and have concluded that the moral divisions are always the same, the same vices are opposed to the same virtues. But the textual strategies of the new moralists of the fifteenth century, the way they have equipped themselves and the order of their arguments have not been studied, nor has their tactical integration been highlighted: under which circumstances, in the midst of what commotions, does the speech of the ideologue—which intends to influence the course of history—come forth?

The historical circumstances linked to its appearance are the first years of the fifteenth century: a troubled period, marked by the political vacuum caused by the madness of Charles VI, the fights between rival factions. Three privileged witnesses to these events, Jean Gerson, Alain Chartier,[6] and Christine de Pizan, address themselves to the prince and define what in their opinion must be the prince's conduct in these troubled circumstances.[7]

This taking up of positions, different but close in time, leads us to interrogate not so much the forms of discourse as the act of the discourse itself which is constituted by this speaking to the prince: in which form does the poet establish himself as a subject telling the truth to the prince? Which manner of being does this truth telling impose on the subject uttering this discourse? All truth telling must be considered as a praxis, as a test which forces the poet to consider whether he is right. This is at the same time a legitimation of poetic activity and of the treatise on the prince in question. Here I will address primarily the first question.

The poet's entry into the political arena proceeds along a series of ritual processes of truth telling. The emergence of the truth implies as a preliminary that the person who tells the truth should be qualified to do so. Therefore the poet creates an area of qualification where he constitutes himself as a truth-telling subject by evoking the authority he possesses and which gives him the privilege to speak. Thus in the *Quadrilogue Invectif* [An invective in four voices] there is a whole set of preliminaries which preceded the debate between France and the three estates, her children. The *Acteur* [actor, author] wakes up from a long sleep; he "sees in his imagination the painful fortune of the House of France."[8] Then he falls back asleep and dreams the dream which is the subject matter of the *Quadrilogue*.

Contrary to what normally happens in this type of text, Chartier has doubled the function of sleep to show, in this passage situated before

6. A very productive poet; he was born between 1385 and 1395 and died in 1430. Gerson (1363–1429) was a well-known theologian and the chancellor of the University of Paris. [Editor]
7. I will refer to the following texts (in parenthesis the abbreviation under which the texts will be cited): Jean Gerson, *Oeuvres complètes*, ed. P. Glorieux, vol. 7 (Paris, 1968) (Gerson); Alain Chartier, *Le Quadrilogue invectif*, ed. E. Droz (Paris, 1950) (Chartier); Christine de Pizan, *Le Livre de la Mutacion de Fortune*, 4 vols. ed. S. Solente (Paris, 1959–1966) (Mutacion).
8. Chartier, p. 6.

the second sleep, the direct relationship of the poet to history which exists in the moment of waking between the first and second sleep. Preceding the telling of the dream proper there is a rich monologue. The author dramatizes himself here, and his thoughtful relationship to the world is essential. Of course, there is the fiction of waking up, but "the debate between hope and despair,"[9] which torments his spirit while he is awake, shows the personal situation of the poet. He spoke in the prologue on the spreading and decadence of earthly empires, of the "potter," the Creator, who makes on his wheel "from the same matter diverse pots of different shapes and sizes, and breaks the big ones and tears them up."[1] Where is the poet situated? He has his place in history, in time. The necessity to situate the poet, to reveal who he is, is a manner of constructing an absolute beginning, to link the "little invective treatise" to an origin. This is not yet the allegory; it is a discourse about himself. In creating this intermediary space, where a reflective move can take place, Chartier creates the origin of his speech, its institution. He authorizes himself to speak. It is the second sleep that is presented as fiction. If in most texts of the period the author is, within the fiction, asked to speak by allegorical figures he meets in the course of his journey, Chartier posits himself from the very beginning as authorized to speak. This is a much more willful way of proceeding. It is not something he heard in his dream that encourages him to speak, but his practical experience. The poet situates himself in face of the events that surround him. This situating is part of the strategy that makes him speak about the world.

Same setup for Gerson: before the relationship of the poet to the prince he investigates the relationship of the poet to the prince he investigates the relationship of the poet to himself. In his sermon *Vivat rex* [Long live the king],[2] given before the court on November 7, 1405, there is a whole passage which gives the qualifications of the speaker. Beyond Gerson there is the University, the "king's daughter," but also the "good eye put into this kingdom . . . like a watchman put on the top of the tower in order to see that nothing bad happens."[3] In addition to this privileged relationship, the University watches over the king's body along the three lines of "corporeally, civilly, and spiritually."[4] This coexistence is fundamental. It justifies that "the daughter subjected to the father" has the right to speak out.[5] Reciprocally, if the University is the watchman of the kingdom, the king has the duty to protect it. Before an

9. Chartier, p. 7.
1. Chartier, p. 2. The same image appears in the *Livre de l'Espérance*, ed. F Rouy (Brest, 1967), prose VI, 1.146–48.
2. Gerson, pp. 1137–85.
3. Gerson, p. 1145.
4. Gerson, p. 1137. For the three "lives" of the king see *Sermo Adorabunt eum*. There it is a question of the king's three "kingdoms," the "personal, the temporal, and the spiritual" (Gerson, pp. 520–38), and *Sermo Rex in Sempiternum vive* (Gerson, pp. 1005–30).
5. Gerson, p. 1145.

enumeration of the royal virtues comes the highlighting of a speaker who hides behind the authority of the University in order to speak to the king. A game of mirrors, a delegation of authority which give to the last in the series a universality he can exploit in order openly to challenge the powers in all liberty and to convey to them "the good doctrine of preaching."[6]

The establishment of the poet is further underlined in Gerson by the allegorical mise en scène, a kind of interior dramaturgy that recalls the prologue to the *Quadrilogue*. The preacher is beleaguered in his very being. "First speaks Dissembling,"[7] who counsels him to remain quiet, to suppress his impulses to a speech which risks to create a scandal. Then "Cruel Sedition" addresses the speaker with a furious scream and urges him to denounce without waiting any longer the evil of which the country suffers. Discretion intervenes at the end in order to calm the debate and lay out the middle ground. Cut off as it is from the address proper to the king—as was Chartier's reflection in the *Quadrilogue* from the telling of the dream—the discourse interrogates itself about its own legitimacy.

When the poet begins a solemn discourse before the court and the king we see first of all a way to link poetic activity to an absolute origin, to a precise event. This process can be found in Christine de Pizan, when she evokes this turning point in her poetic inspiration, her *mutacion* [transformation].[8] The "strange case" she evokes in the *Livre de la Mutacion de Fortune* [Book of Fortune's Transformation] is the genesis of the poet's mediating function. It represents the transformation, of the author as she turns her back on personal lyricism and opens herself up to universal history.[9] The *mutacion* illuminates in light of a myth—that of Tiresias—the birth of a serious spirit, the changing poetic inspiration. The gifts which make up the "garland of virtues" given to her by Nature at her birth—and dormant until then—suddenly develop. An irreversible transformation, an indication that she will no longer do what she had done before; a definitive gender change corresponds to a new orientation of her imagination. The gifts that develop rapidly (Discretion, Consideration, Recall, and Memory) inspire a speculative poetry which intends to give its meaning to the events of humanity. This prodigious realization of the power of mediation marks the beginning of a function which consists in interrogating the world, to seek out the meaning of events. The establishment of the poet, illuminated by means of a myth, is meant to underline the origin and the new status of the intellectual charged with taking stock of the events. Christine possessed these virtues from her birth, she specifies in the *Livre de la Mutacion de Fortune*,

6. Gerson, p. 1151.
7. Gerson, p. 1152.
8. Mutacion, ll. 1159–1460.
9. Joel Blanchard, "Christine de Pizan: les raisons de l'histoire," *Le Moyen Age* 92 (1986): 417–36.

because she was Christine de Pizan. Thus there is a part of herself which remains identical to what she used to be, the first virtues. But what is still missing is that great lucidity which is needed for an articulation of history. This is the sense of the transformation: a qualitative leap. The intellectual, instead of reflecting on himself, reflects on universal things. Hence the falling back on history and the call to the great people of this world. This certainly is an establishment, the beginning of a poetic destiny the representation of which precedes the actual discourse addressed to the princes. She justifies herself: it is this dramatization of the slow path toward the truth in Christine's heart that one finds in the *Livre de la Mutacion de Fortune*, the *Livre de Chemin de Long Estude* [The Path of Long Study], and in the *Avision* [Vision].

For the first time the poet poses in an allegorical and dramatic form the problem of an object which exists outside of herself, not the impulses of her heart, but the gaze directed toward that which is not herself, leaving behind a passivity of the spirit: the very male resolution to give shape to the world. The relationship of the poet to a reality in the face of which she cannot remain passive, the misfortunes of her time, lead her to seeking out the truth and addressing the great people of her time in the form of a truth telling which takes the varied forms of addressing the prince in the *Lamentacion sur les maulx de la guerre civile* [Lamentation on the evils of civil war] and in the *Lettre à Isabelle de Bavière* [Letter to Isabeau of Bavaria]; or of a pedagogy in the mirrors of princes, the *Livre des fais et bonnes meurs du sage roy Charles V* [The book of the deeds and good conduct of the wise king Charles V], the *Livre du corps de policie* [Book of the body politic], and the *Livre de la Paix* [Book of Peace]. But in all these works Christine says that she is pushed by a necessity, by the urgency to express herself. Urgency and necessity differentiate her words from those of a flatterer. She acts moved by a necessity which is imposed on her by common interest. The search for truth distinguishes the poet from the flatterer or even from the panegyrist. In the *Livre des fais et bonnes meurs du sage roy Charles V* Christine reflects on her own discourse and distinguishes "praise" from "flattery":[1] "flattery" motivates the flatterer who expects a reward from the king for the praise he bestows on him; "praise," by contrast, means lauding a positive example. The poet's speech is the refusal of any attempt to flatter. Chartier and Gerson take the same position, either directly by addressing the prince, or indirectly when they advise the prince to get rid of the flatterers among his counsellors. While the flatterer speaks for his own profit, the poet offers a text presented as an interpretation of other people's truth. The flatterer makes speeches to the prince that please him and establishes some obligation between himself and the addressee. By denouncing the flatterer's discourse with

1. *Le Livre des fais et bonnes meurs du sage roy Charles V*, 2 vols., ed. Suzanne Solente (Paris, 1936 and 1941; rept. Geneva: Slatkine, 1977), vol. 1, pp. 181–84.

its tricks, the poet wants to expose the maneuvers of the bad counsellor and gives a foundation of truth to a discourse that must proceed differently: the poet's discourse is linked to the truth by what it is not, by its difference from the language of the counselors who "pretend to speak the truth when it seems convenient."[2] It is not *logos* [word] but proof. The poet's discourse freely addresses the prince by words which are risky and under these conditions does not care about possible reproaches. The poet is stubborn, sometimes even rebellious. In the formula at the beginning of the *Lamentation sur les maulx de la guerre civile*, "alone and separate,"[3] we see that the poet is willing to situate herself in a confrontation with power, risking a brutal and violent unveiling of the truth.

This problematic, pitting the flatterer against the truth-telling poet, shapes the political discourse of the first years of the fifteenth century. The flatterer speaks out of self-love, for his profit, and he can expand his discourse as he wishes. Truth telling, by contrast, comes forth under the pressures of history. The poet only speaks for special occasions. Misfortunes cause him to leave his ordinary functions. In other times, the established counselors of the king speak. Gerson insists on this point several times, affirming that he will not impinge on the prerogatives of the king's council, that is, the *Grand Conseil* [Great Council].[4] The poet's intervention is an event. His qualifications do not oblige him to address or counsel the king. To address the king is not an ordinary matter, open to anyone interested in royal activity.

The pressure of extraordinary events, the misfortune of the country, menaces from abroad, pressing dangers, these are the conditions that make the intellectual of the fifteenth century take the political stage. This situation is illustrated very well by Gerson's attitude: he does not hesitate to repeat the *Vivat rex!* which begins his address to the king and is a rallying cry meant to be heard by the prince himself and all his dignitaries and counselors. But evil threatens to cover up the cry of the person who possesses and tells the truth. Christine has a nightmarish vision of this in the *Avision*. The poet evokes the "masses of shadows" of different forms and colors that surround "the clerks involved in disputes."[5] We are in the realm of Opinion which Christine certainly does not mistake for the kingdom of Error. Opinion works on the discovery of truth but she is felled by circumstances. The desire for knowledge becomes violent and transforms, for each of the discussants, the search for truth into an obstinate passion. Opinion reigns over a world about to explode. The authen-

---

2. Gerson, p. 1166. These are the "false alchemists" Philippe de Mézières takes aim at in the prologue of the *Songe du Viel Pelerin*, ed. C. W. Coopland (Cambridge, 1969), vol. 1, pp. 103–104.

3. *La Lamentacion sur les maux de la guerre civile* in R. Thomassy, *Essai sur les écrits politiques de Christine de Pizan, suivi d'une notice littéraire et de pièces inédites* (Paris, 1838), p. 141. [A better edition is the new one by Angus J. Kennedy in *Mélanges Charles Foulon* (Rennes, 1980), vol. 1, pp. 177–85. Editor]

4. Gerson, p. 1151.

5. *Lavision-Christine*, ed. Mary-Louis Towner (Washington, 1932), p. 109.

tic words of the poet, by contrast, strive for unity. This is why the poet's words refuse a discourse of factions while remaining an invective. They have the ambition to proclaim the urgency of the events brought about by Fortune: common misfortunes, war, death. Truth telling shows all this without being apocalyptic: it is flaming virtue.

But what sustains this discourse? The first care of the poet is to think of a living, not an abstract, principle. *Vivat rex!* recalls the king's life in a sermon which evokes the threefold incarnation of the king: "carnal, political, and spiritual." Gerson insists on the king's survival. Here is a tangible reality which awakens the poet from a long rhetorical "sleep." Normally the poet writes about the perceptions of his own being. Here, by contrast, misfortunes put into the center of things the living person of the king, because the destiny of the citizens can only be conceptualized starting with the happy or unhappy destiny of the carnal king. The disasters of the times become inseparable from the physical person of the king and shake up the poet: the two destinies, that of the poet and that of the prince, are conjoined. They come close through a convergence, a homophony, without ever coinciding: the truth telling of the poet which is always true, no matter what the circumstances, and the well-being of the king. At the point of convergence a discourse takes shape, showing in its different modalities the ways by which the poet enters the political arena: in Chartier and Gerson this consists in a denunciation of morally dissipated lives; for Christine it means the elaboration of a political project.

Here our analysis shows nuances, different strategies in our three authors. First, the trigger: a spontaneous reaction precedes a plan of conduct, clear and distinct in the poet's consciousness. This is the first necessary stage in the search for truth. Chartier has perhaps the most violent reaction. A military image evokes the outcry, the drumbeat of words hitting "unnatural children."[6] In the *Quadrilogue* there is no place for the elaboration of a system of royal virtues as we find it in Christine de Pizan, for example in the *Livre de la Paix*. The *Quadrilogue* ends with the image of the prince's misfortunes. Violent criticism has no place for a system of virtues. The Golden Age is banished from the representation of the world. Rather we find a sociological approach that makes the different estates speak in seemingly haphazard ways in response to the urgent present problems.

This strategy also exists in Christine de Pizan. In the *Livre de la Mutacion de Fortune*, after having gained access to the castle of Fortune, where she sketches out a quick study of man and society, she sends forth more and more stinging allusions against the political society of her time.[7] One could multiply the examples in her works. But while Chartier's frank speech aims, via the citizens, to describe the dislocation of

6. Chartier, p. 11.
7. *Mutacion*, 11. 4273–6518.

the social body—not open to redemption or salvation—Christine puts together the elements of an agreement and attaches them to a dream of universality. Chartier accused the Estates, which by trying to legitimate themselves, ruined the kingdom. Christine, by contrast, offers the body politic a principle of legitimation which will protect it from a final dissolution. This principle of truth is what Christine calls the "garland of royal virtues" in the *Livre de la Paix*.[8] Disparagement thus does not exhaust the discourse by sterile repetition, but opens itself up to a moral system where the king's survival is at stake. The poet is no longer an unbearable accuser but the pedagogue who constructs wisdom for the king. Christine de Pizan, unlike Alain Chartier, supplied the prince with means to lay the foundations for a world. Such a project presupposes the fictional elaboration of a model which finds its most perfect form in Christine's last mirror of princes, the *Livre de la Paix*. This model is the product of the web represented by the relations between the different royal virtues organized into a system. This is the sense of the image of the "garland of royal virtues" which represents each virtue as "coming forth from another." This system has a reasonable foundation: the metaphysical base is illustrated by the first of the virtues, Prudence, the "daughter of God." Then come Justice, Magnanimity, Force, Clemency, Liberality, and Truth. Each virtue calls forth the following virtue according to a logical and dense argument that can be reconstructed in its different stages by the reader. Each virtue has its correspondence in a characteristic of the prince whose portrait thus emerges in different layers. We can see that in the *Livre de la Paix* Christine proceeds inversely to what she does in the *Livre des fais et bonnes meurs du sage roy Charles V*: in the latter the poet tries to give a name to each of the manifestations of the late king's virtuous behavior; in the *Livre de la Paix* the concept of each virtue and its name are given first, while Charles V can be cited as an example without necessarily being the point of departure for the system.

If the king's portrait comes together according to the order in which the different traits appear in the "garland of virtues," these traits can only designate the king's activities in relation to his subjects. The emphasis is on the prince's exercise of virtues and their impact on the body politic. Christine underlines the movement which carries the prince toward the social body, insisting on the organic relationship between the king and the subjects or "members." As a result she is led to a kind of phenomenology centered on the person of the king whose characteristics slowly emerge. We find no longer the institutional and functional identity of the head in the body politic but the concrete description of the king's gestures, looks, and words. This constitutes the force of this model, its power of representation. This is no longer an inert model but a memora-

---

8. *The 'Livre de la paix' of Christine de Pisan*, ed. Charity Cannon Willard (The Hague, 1958), p. 64.

ble figure. Here, in order to make this quasi-carnal aspect of the king even more lively Christine proceeds by contraries. In order better to show how the head animates the body politic she describes the gestures of the tyrant, the opposite of the benign and friendly king: vengeance, cruelty, abusive language, impulsive behavior, noncontained violence. A character study of the tyrant supports the opposing representation of the "merciful and courtly" prince." What else is Christine doing but making a list of clinical cases where royalty does not function? It is a kind of political semiology. This recourse to the opposing figure of the tyrant is a part of the text's general strategy. For each member of the body politic Christine highlights some deformities, extortions, and it is on the basis of these perversions that she discovers the foundation of just acts; for she believes that to be just which corresponds to each person's essence. By starting with a designation, then showing how people go astray, she considers the foundation of the prince's virtues just: that is, the virtue of virtues, reason that creates justice.

The elaboration of a fictional model makes all the difference between Alain Chartier and Christine de Pizan. Chartier's entire discourse meant to show that there was no possible construction. By contrast, Christine de Pizan creates a political perspective: she gives shape to a model, even if indirectly, and invites the prince to conform to this model or reject it. In this space—realization or rejection—Christine's political project and its attractions inscribe themselves. A priori there was no relationship between the discovery of a political practice and poetic activity. This is why Christine multiplies her sketches and rough drafts. The relationship between the poet's truth telling and the king's well-being is a lucky coincidence. The literary work guarantees a truth it had not expected to find.

In conclusion we can say that the relationship between discourse and truth sheds new light on the question of power in the first years of the fifteenth century. If the wise man silently considers being and nature, the poet risks an ethical discourse, he pronounces himself on the value of behaviors, denounces moral turpitude and directs his glance toward unique situations. His task is to speak. The idea of an eruptive and violent mode of speaking the truth is inseparable from the poet's entry into the political arena.

We saw that this is not only a discourse of truth but also a proof with which the poet addresses himself to power. The initial self-representation of the poet is a proclamation of the strategic position he occupies in his relationship to power. It is a distanced, externalized relationship. If the prince is the poet's other, the poet experiences the reality of his philosophical practice in this alterity. This discourse serves as proof to the speaker and to the addressee. Up to now the tradition of the mirror dealt with the conditions that would allow the subject to have access to the truth, while the addressee was driven back into the universal. Now there is a place for the ideologue to emerge who unmasks himself by breaking with power, justifying himself, articulating his own worries before telling the king the duties incumbent on his office.

All these ways of truth telling point to a crisis in the monarchy which needs for its establishment the privileged speech of the poet who exists in order to recall for him the principles of the social contract. The king's discourse is an egotistical discourse. The king is always on the way to becoming a tyrant or nothing. To bring about this consciousness in the king is the goal of poetic speech whose truth telling is opposed to the wasteful speech, the evasions of the flatterer. The poet has the capacity to reestablish—thanks to his clairvoyant eyes, as Christine de Pizan puts it—a new *logos*. That is his profession and without the poet, the prince is relegated to the immanence of his personal condition.

This role of the ideologue will become more and more important in the course of the fifteenth century. Now, next to and even above the power of the royal council, one generally sees the rise of an intellectual authority which had no place in the traditional institutions of the royal establishment. These are interlopers who make themselves heard, conscious of the need for them, using their writings as political instruments. A new power emerges in the margins, capable of openly making its existence known. At the very end of the century, when Charles VIII has his first entry into Rouen in 1485, a commoner, Pinel, takes advantage of the royal entry[9] to put his name next to the king's and the city's names.[1] He comes forward incongruously and yet he is part of the spectacle. This is a striking demonstration of the waking of a political function, the *vox poetica* which plays a part in determining the limits of power, and whose first bursts could be heard at the beginning of the century.

KEVIN BROWNLEE

Structures of Authority in Christine de Pizan's *Ditié de Jehanne d'Arc*†

On July 31, 1429, Christine de Pizan completed her final work, the *Ditié de Jehanne d'Arc*. Medieval France's greatest woman writer thus ended her long literary career with a celebration of medieval France's greatest woman hero. It is important for the modern reader to under-

---

9. A public feast, involving processions and other rituals to mark the arrival of the king in a given town. [Editor]

1. Joel Blanchard, "Les entrées royales: pouvoir et représentation du pouvoir à la fin du Moyen Age," *Littérature* 50 (1983): 3–14; and "Une entrée royale," in *Le temps de la réflexion* 5 (1984): 353–74.

† From *Discourses of Authority in Medieval and Renaissance Literature*, eds. Kevin Brownlee and Walter Stephens (Dartmouth, N.H.: University Press of New England, 1989). © 1989 by Trustees of Dartmouth College. Reprinted by permission of University Press of New England.

stand that the *Ditié* was a celebration, for the poem was written at the moment of Joan's greatest triumph, as a brief recall of its immediate historical context makes clear. Joan's abrupt appearance on the main political stage of the Hundred Years War was a very recent event. She had first presented herself to the beleaguered Charles VII at Chinon on February 23, 1429, claiming a divinely inspired mission to save the French monarchy. During March and April, she was interrogated at Poitiers by a learnèd committee of theologians who authenticated her claims. On May 8 she raised the siege of Orléans, a spectacular military success with great symbolic as well as strategic value. The French cause was saved from what had appeared to be imminent disaster. A series of triumphant advances followed in the Loire valley and in Champagne, culminating in the surrender of Rheims on July 16. On the following day, Joan anointed and crowned Charles king in Rheims cathedral, thus annulling "the deposition illegally pronounced by the Treaty of Troyes [1420] and [restoring] to the Valois the legitimacy which had been questioned for the past nine years"[1] On the morrow of his coronation, Charles received the submission of Laon, and he and Joan entered Soissons together in triumph on July 23. By July 29, the King and the Maid were at Château-Thierry, with Paris as the final objective of their advance. Success seemed imminent; Charles received fresh capitulations from all sides; Joan appeared to be unstoppable. Her extraordinary accomplishments seemed to be quite literally miraculous: a direct intervention by God in contemporary French history. This, then, was Christine's perspective when she composed her poem; these were the historical givens of her understanding of the phenomenon of Joan of Arc.

The question of authority is central to this understanding, both in historical and in literary terms, and it is this question that I propose to explore in the present essay by means of a close reading of the text of the *Ditié*. I will be focusing on three issues: (1) Christine's authority as speaking subject; (2) Joan's authority as historical actant; and (3) the complex relation between these two figures in terms of authority, identity, and authorization.

Before turning to the *Ditié* itself, however, some preliminary remarks are necessary. Christine de Pizan was the first French literary figure explicitly to incorporate her identity as a woman into her identity as an author.[2] Fundamental problems of authority were necessarily involved here as Christine sought to effect an innovative first-person conflation

---

1. Edouard Perroy, *The Hundred Years War* (New York: Capricorn, 1965), pp. 284–85.
2. For an insightful recent consideration of Christine's identity as medieval woman author and the implications of her "feminism" in this context, see Sylvia Huot, "Seduction and Sublimation: Christine de Pizan, Jean de Meun and Dante," *Romance Notes* 25 (1985):361–73. For further discussion of Christine's feminism, see Douglas Kelly, "Reflections on Christine de Pizan as a Feminist Writer," *Sub-Stance* 2 (1972):63–71; Mary Ann Ignatius, "A Look at the

of the learnèd clerk and the self-conscious feminist. To authorize this radically new kind of poetic voice, Christine established an authoritative "alternative" genealogy for herself, an anterior line of authoritative female ancestors, exemplars of superlative achievement in politics, science, scholarship, literature, and religion. It was in the *Livre de la Cité des Dames* of 1405 that this project of feminist self-authorization was most explicitly and most elaborately undertaken. For our reading of the *Ditié de Jehanne d'Arc*, two aspects of the *Cité* are of fundamental importance. First, the taxonomic hierarchy of female exemplarity that Christine establishes in the *Cité* privileges absolutely the figure of the female Christian martyr. While exemplary female warrior figures are systematically valorized, there is no overlap of the component "warrior" with the component "Christian." The heroism of exemplary Christian women is fundamentally passive. Second, Christine's concept of history in the *Cité* consistently links the glorious past to the living present. As E. Jeffrey Richards has pointed out, this is one of the most striking aspects of Christine's transformative rewriting of Boccaccio's *De Mulieribus Claris*, the primary model text for the *Cité*.[3] Christine consistently collapses Boccaccio's radical gap between present and past. Within the allegorical plot line of the work, Christine the character repeatedly "complements" the examples of illustrious past women, adduced by Reason, Rectitude, and Justice on the basis of clerkly, bookish authority, with equally valid examples drawn from her own experience of contemporary history. Indeed, the figure of "je, Christine" is largely defined by this first-person experience and the kind of authority that it implies.

With these points in mind, let us turn now to the text of the *Ditié de Jehanne d'Arc.*

The *Ditié* is composed of sixty-one stanzas (huitains), and its overall structure is as follows: The first twelve stanzas constitute a Prologue, which establishes the identity of the first-person speaking subject and the status of her literary enterprise. The main body of the poem (stanzas 13–60) is structured around a series of apostrophes, as Christine addresses, in turn, Charles VII, Joan herself, their loyal French troops, the English enemy, and, finally, the French allies of the English. These direct addresses are punctuated by three narrative passages in which Christine recounts the story of Joan of Arc (past, present, and future), and by a series of "glosses" in which she reveals the significance of Joan's achievements. The relationship among these three discursive modes is

---

Feminism of Christine de Pizan," *Proceedings of the Pacific Northwest Conference on Foreign Languages* 29 (1978):18–21; and Joan Kelly-Gadol, "Early Feminist Theory and the Querelle des Femmes, 1400–1789," *Signs* 8 (1982):4–28.
3. Christine de Pizan, *The Book of the City of Ladies*, trans. E. Jeffrey Richards (New York: Persea, 1982), pp. xxxv–xxxviii.

dialogic: gloss "completes" narrative; narrative authorizes apostrophe; apostrophe confirms and advances narrative.[4] At the same time, Christine's authoritative identity is progressively elaborated by means of her discursive practice and its relationship to history.

The Prologue begins with the words, "Je, Christine,"[5] and the first five stanzas define this *je* in terms of lyric constructs transposed into a historical time that is both private and public. After a long winter, springtime returns: the "bon temps neuf" (v. 19), the "tresbelle / Saison" (vv. 28–29). The poet's grief turns to joy: from "grant dueil en joie nouvelle" (v. 25); and she is moved to song: "Mais or changeray mon langage / De pleur en chant" (vv. 13–14). The lyric "temps yvernage" (v. 9), however, is the real, historical time that has elapsed since May 1418, when the Burgundians captured Paris, forcing both Christine and Charles VII to flee. For Christine, these eleven years have been years of exile in a "walled abbey" ("en abbaye close," v. 2); eleven years of political disappointment and literary silence. The poet's lyric present is the real, historical year 1429. And the cause of her deeply personal joy is a political event: the triumphant approach of the newly crowned Charles VII. This event is what moves her to sing with the stylized intensity and the experiential authority of a lyric lover.

Her song, however, will be combined with a narrative "explanation" of this event:

> Mais or vueil raconter comment
> Dieu a tout ce fait de sa grace,
> A qui je pri qu'avisement
> Me doint, que rien je n'y trespasse.
> Raconté soit en toute place.
> Car ce est digne de memoire,
> Et escript, à qui que desplace,
> En mainte cronique et hystoire!
>
> (vv. 49–56)

But now I wish to relate how God, to whom I pray for guidance lest I omit anything, accomplished all this through His grace. May it be told everywhere, for it is worthy of being remembered, and may it be written down—no matter whom it may displease—in many a chronicle and history-book!

Christine's first-person lyric voice, then, will also be that of the chronicler: she is to be clerkly witness to a sequence of historically factual

---

4. For the structure of the *Ditié* see Christine de Pisan, *Ditié de Jehanne d'Arc*, eds. Angus J. Kennedy and Kenneth Varty (Oxford: Society for the Study of Mediaeval Languages and Literature, 1977), pp. 9–10. See also Therese Ballet Lynn, "The *Ditié de Jeanne d'Arc*: Its Political, Feminist and Aesthetic Significance," *Fifteenth Century Studies* I (1978):150–51; and Liliane Dulac, "Un écrit militant de Christine de Pizan: Le *Ditié de Jehanne d'Arc*" in *Aspects of Female Existence*, eds. Birte Carlé et al. (Gyldendal, Denmark, 1980), pp. 118–20.

5. All citations and translations (with selective emendations) from the *Ditié* are from the excellent edition of Kennedy and Varty.

events that constitute a "miracle" (v. 81). Her authority derives from the truth of history itself, guaranteed, underwritten, by God. And the miracle is the story of Joan:

> Chose est bien digne de memoire
> Que Dieu, par une vierge tendre,
> Ait adès voulu (chose est voire!)
> Sur France si grant grace estendre.
> (vv. 85–88)

It is a fact worthy of remembering that God should now have wished (and this is the truth!) to bestow such blessings on France, through a young virgin.

Christine begins the body of the *Ditié* with an extended direct address to Charles VII (stanzas 13–19) in which she calls upon the king to bear witness to the miracle of Joan. It is important to note that the king is treated as passive subject and the Maid as active object:

> Et tu, Charles, roy des François,
> . . . or voiz ton renon
> Hault eslevé par la Pucelle,
> Qui a soubzmis soubz ton penon
> Tes ennemis (chose est nouvelle!)
>
> En peu de temps; que l'on cuidoit
> Que ce feust com chose impossible
> Que ton pays, qui se perdoit,
> Reusses jamais. Or est visible—
> Ment tien . . .
> C'est par la Pucelle sensible,
> Dieu mercy, qui y a ouvré!
> (vv. 97, 101–109, 111–12)

And you Charles, King of France . . . now see your honor exalted by the Maid who has laid low your enemies beneath your standard (and this *is* new!) in a short time; for it was believed quite impossible that you should ever recover your country which you were on the point of losing. Now it is manifestly yours . . . And all this has been brought about by the intelligence of the Maid who, God be thanked, has played her part in this matter! (emphasis mine)

It is only the authorization conferred upon Charles by Joan that leads Christine to associate him, somewhat tentatively, with prophecies of a future imperial destiny for a chosen king of France. This first prophetic moment in the poem is linked to standard advice on how to be a virtuous ruler. Christine seems to regard continued divine favor for Charles as conditional, in some sense dependent upon exemplary royal behavior. The section ends with an injunction to Charles to thank, serve, and fear God for the bounty bestowed upon him. As if to provide the king with a discursive model, Christine's stanza 20 is an inscribed prayer of praise and thanks addressed directly to God.

It is at this point that Christine turns to consider the significance and the implications of Joan's achievement in detail, in the longest section of the poem (stanzas 21–36). The opening direct address to Joan explicitly and emphatically affirms her status as God's chosen instrument in France's salvation:

> Et toy, Pucelle beneurée
> . . . Dieu t'a tant honnoré
> Que as la corde desliée
> Qui tenoit France estroit lié . . .
>
> Tu, Jehanne, de bonne heure née,
> Benoist soit cil qui te créa!
> Pucelle de Dieu ordonné,
> En qui le Saint Esprit réa
> Sa grant grace . . .
>   (vv. 161, 163–65, 169–73)

And you, blessed Maid . . . God honored you so much that you untied the rope which held France so tightly bound . . . You, Joan, born in a propitious hour, blessed be He who created you! Maiden sent from God, into whom the Holy Spirit poured His great grace . . .

In the sequence of six stanzas that follows (23–28), Christine systematically compares Joan to heroic Biblical figures, both male and female, who saved God's chosen people. It is here that the radical newness of Joan's heroic identity is most explicitly linked to her status as woman. Because she is a woman, her achievement is by definition greater than that of her male Biblical models, Moses, Joshua, and Gideon. Joan is thus valorized in terms of the Christian paradox of "low equals high" in the context of divine revelation in human events. At the same time, part of the miracle of Joan is her absolute superiority in military virtue:

> . . . Car tous les preux au long aler
> Qui ont esté, ne s'appareille
> Leur prouesse à ceste qui veille
> A bouter hors noz ennemis.
> Mais ce fait Dieu, qui la conseille,
> En qui cuer plus que d'omme a mis.
>   (vv. 203–208)

. . . for all the prowess of all the great men of the past cannot be compared to this woman's whose concern is to cast out our enemies. This is God's doing: it is He who guides her and who has given her a heart greater than that of any man.

At the same time, Joan surpasses all previous female exemplars of salvific heroism:

> Hester, Judith et Delbora,
> Qui furent dames de grant pris,
> Par lesqueles Dieu restora
> Son peuple, qui fort estoit pris,
> Et d'autres plusers ay apris
> Qui furent preuses, n'y ot celle,
> Mains miracles en a pourpris.
> Plus a fait par ceste Pucelle.
>
> (vv. 217–24)

I have heard of Esther, Judith and Deborah, who were women of great worth, through whom God delivered His people from oppression, and I have heard of many other women, all full of prowess, through whom He performed many miracles, but He has accomplished more through this Maid.

We have here an implicit figural presentation of Joan of Arc in terms of authoritative Biblical models of active heroism in a politico-religious context. Joan's identity transcends previously operative gender distinctions in this context: she is simultaneously warrior and woman, *"le champion"* who has the "force et povoir" to "ruer jus la gent rebelle" [cast the rebels down] and "celle/Qui donne à France la mamelle/De paix et doulce norriture" [she who nurses France with the sweet milk of peace] (vv. 188, 187, 191, 188–90). She is a kind of conflation of Deborah and Gideon (Judges 4–5 and Judges 6–8). In regard to Christine's earlier models of exemplary female heroic conduct in the *Cité des Dames*, Joan's military prowess combined with her divinely sanctioned mission conflates the Amazon (I.16–19) and the Christian martyr (III.3–11). A radically new category of female heroism is thus established: the bellatrix-crusader (cf. Acre reference v. 379). Further, this category is established not through abstract speculation but historical fact: it is *incarnated* by Joan. According to Christine's concept of history and of feminism, this heroic model represents the ultimate standard, the sole authority. And Joan's literal, historical *success* (in striking contradistinction to the failure of the earlier, exemplary bellatrices Penthesilea and Camilla, *Cité de Dames* I.19 and I.24)[6] is thus an inherent part both of her identity and of her authorization.

Thus the narrative account of Joan's life to which Christine now turns is simultaneously presented as proof of her divine sanction. The story

---

6. The extended narrative of Penthesilea's glorious but tragic death in Part 6 of the *Livre de la Mutacion de Fortune* (1403) is also relevant here (vv. 17561–17896 in the edition of Suzanne Solente, 4 vols. [Paris: Picard/SATF, 1959–1966]). The *Ditié's* reference to Joan of Arc as more powerful than "Hector n'Achilles" (v. 287; the poem's only mention of exemplary female warriors from the classical tradition) should perhaps be seen in part as involving a corrective Christian evocation of Penthesilea's noble pagan failure as bellatrix. [female warrior. Editor]

is told in appropriately Biblical terms, for Joan's life has in effect over-written contemporary French political history with a Biblical signifi-cance:

> Par miracle fut envoiée
> Et divine amonition,
> De l'ange de Dieu convoiée
> Au roy, pour sa provision . . .
>
> O! comment lors bien y paru
> Quant le siege ert devant Orliens,
> Où premier sa force apparu!
> Onc miracle, si com je tiens,
> Ne fut plus cler, car Dieu aux siens
> Aida telement, qu'ennemis
> Ne s'aiderent ne que mors chiens.
> Là furent prins et à mort mis.
>   (vv. 225–28, 257–64)

She was miraculously sent by divine command and conducted by the angel of the Lord to the King, in order to help him . . . Oh how clear this was at the siege of Orléans where her power was first made manifest! It is my belief that no miracle was ever more evi-dent, for God so came to the help of His people that our enemies were unable to help each other any more than would dead dogs. It was there that they were captured and put to death.

It is in this first sequential narrative of the events of Joan's life in the *Ditié* that Christine first explicitly utilizes the discourse of prophecy to authorize the unfolding present. Significantly, this prophetic authoriza-tion is itself part of an episode in Joan's story: her interrogation by the "royal committee" of theologians acting on behalf of King Charles dur-ing March and April of 1429.

> Son fait n'est pas illusion,
> Car bien a esté esprouvée
> Par conseil (en conclusion,
> A l'effect la chose est prouvée),
> Et bien esté examinée
> A, ains que l'on l'ait voulu croire,
> Devant clers et sages menée
> Pour ensercher se chose voire
> Disoit, ainçois qu'il fust notoire
> Que Dieu l'eust vers le roy tramise.
> Mais on a trouvé en histoire
> Qu'à ce faire elle estoit commise;

Car Merlin et Sebile et Bede,[7]
Plus de V cent ans a la virent
En esperit, et pour remede
En France en leurs escripz la mirent,
En leur[s] prophecies en firent,
Disans qu'el pourteroit baniere
Es querres francoises, et dirent
De son fait toute la maniere.
(vv. 229–48)

Her achievement is no illusion for she was carefully put to the test in council (in short, a thing is proved by its effect) and well examined, before people were prepared to believe her; before it became common knowledge that God sent her to the King, she was brought before clerks and wise men so that they could find out if she was telling the truth. But it was found in history-records that she was destined to accomplish her mission; for more than 500 years ago, Merlin, the sibyl and Bede foresaw her coming, entered her in their writings as someone who would put an end to France's troubles, made prophecies about her saying that she would carry the banner in the French wars and describing all that she would achieve.

Three overlapping kinds of authorization are at issue here. First, Joan's achievements are guaranteed by clerkly authority, by writing as authoritative medium, and by historiography as authoritative genre. The clerkly testimony to Joan's life that Christine had called for in stanza 7 is here shown in stanzas 30–31 to have antedated the Maid's birth. Her present deeds have *already* been recorded—in a written history of the future. Second, these prophecies authorize Joan's mission within the

---

7. In terms of historical chronology, it seems that Christine is privileging the Sibyl by including her here. The relevant prophecies attributed to Merlin and to Bede clearly antedate the composition of the *Ditié*. With regard to Merlin, it is a question of two passages in Book 7 *(De prophetiis Merlini)* of Geoffrey of Monmouth's *Historia Regum Britanniae:* (1) "Ad hec ex urbe canuti nemoris eliminabitur puella . . ." and (2) "Ascendet virgo dorsum sagittarii. & flores virgineos obfuscabit" (ed. Acton Griscom [London, 1929], pp. 390–91 and p. 397). With regard to Bede, it is a question of an incorrectly attributed chronogram widely circulated in France during the spring of 1429 and supposed to indicate that year: "Vis comulcoli. bis. septen. se sotiabunt/Galboni. pulli. bella. nova. parabunt./Ece. beant. bela. tunc. fert. vexila. puela." See the *Chronique d'Antonio Morosini*, 4 vols., ed. L. Dorez et G. Lefèvre-Pontalis (Paris: Renouard, 1898–1902), vol. 3, pp. 126–127 and vol. 4, pp. 316–27. See also Kennedy and Varty, pp. 68–69; and Deborah Fraioli, "The Literary Image of Joan of Arc: Prior Influences," *Speculum* 56 (1981):817–18. The Sibyl, however, was not associated with prophecies concerning Joan before the composition of the *Ditié*. As Fraioli notes, "The view that Joan of Arc had been heralded in sibylline literature was not articulated until the summer of 1429 in a treatise written by a cleric of Speyer, entitled *Sibylla francica*" (817–18). Indeed, the text of this treatise as found in Jules Quicherat, ed., *Procès de condamnation et de réhabilitation de Jeanne d'Arc*, 5 vols. (Paris: Renouard, 1845–1849), 3:422–68, gives the date "juillet–septembre 1429" (422). An important literary precedent for the association of the Sibyl with Merlin and Bede in political prophecies of French victory in the Hundred Years War is to be found in a ballade of Eustache Deschamps written c. 1385–1386 (number 26 in the edition of Queux de Saint-Hilaire and Gaston Raynaud, 1:106–107).

inscribed narrative episode of her examination by the council. Her learnèd interrogators are convinced, and are, of course, meant to serve as models for Christine's reader in this respect. At the same time, their belief operates reciprocally to lend authority to the prophecies as such. Third, Christine as writer and the *Ditié* as *écriture* are simultaneously authorized by the articulation and incorporation of these prophecies. Christine's present discursive treatment of the present events of Joan's life is authoritatively "doubled" by these past predictions of the same events. Christine's voice is doubled by the prophetic voices whose authority she is simultaneously invoking and confirming. In this context the figure of the sibyl has a privileged status, for her appearance here is, as it were, overdetermined as a result of her singular importance in Christine's earlier works.

The sibyl's role as an exemplar of authoritative female discourse in Christine's *oeuvre* goes all the way back to the *Epistre d'Othea a Hector* of 1400. The one hundredth (and final) chapter of this work recounts how the Cumean sibyl announced the coming of Christ to the emperor Augustus. What is stressed is that the revelation of the most important event in history to the greatest temporal ruler of antiquity is made by a woman: "que Cesar Augustus, qui prince estoit de tout le monde; apprist a congnoistre Dieu et la creance d'une femme."[8] In the *Livre du chemin de long estude* of 1403, the role of the Cumean sibyl is central, for she functions as Christine's guide on an allegorical journey through earth and heaven. The Dantean model for this journey is explicitly evoked in Christine's text (vv. 1125–52) in such a way as to foreground her substitution of the sibyl for Virgil as guide for the first-person protagonist. This ironic "restoration" of Aeneas's guide involves, however, an important remotivation of the sibyl in Christine's new—and radically feminized— narrative context. It is the sibyl's identity as female authority figure that authorizes her to be the mentor of Christine qua female protagonist. At the same time, the sibyl confirms and valorizes Christine's literary vocation within the context of the *Chemin's* plot line. In the course of their allegorical journey, the sibyl repeatedly identifies Christine as a member of "nostre escole" (e.g., vv. 1588, 6288); and her first speech to her protégée contains the promise that

> . . . ains que vie te decline,
> En ce [l'amour qu'as a science] t'iras tant deduisant
> Que ton nom sera reluisant
> Apres toy par longue memoire,
> Et pour le bien de ton memoire

8. Halina D. Loukopoulos, *Classical Mythology in the Works of Christine de Pisan, with an Edition of L'Epistre Othea from MS Harley 4431*, diss. Wayne State University, 1977, p. 289. See also Charity Canon Willard, *Christine de Pizan. Her Life and Works* (New York: Persea, 1984), p. 99. For Christine's global strategy of feminist rewriting of clerkly sources in the *Epistre*, see Christine Reno, "Feminist Aspects of Christine de Pizan's *Epistre d'Othea a Hector*," *Studi Francesi* 71 (1980):271–76.

Que voy abille a concevoir
Je t'aim et vueil faire a savoir
De mes secres une partie,
Ains que de toy soie partie.

(vv. 494–502) [9]

. . . before your life is over you will delightfully pursue your love of
learning so far that your name will be remembered long after your
death; and because of your excellent memory and your keen conceptual faculty I love you and I want you to know a portion of my
secrets.

In the *Livre de la Cité des Dames* (1405), the figure of the sibyl plays
an important role in structuring Christine's feminist polemic. At the
beginning of Part II of the *Cité*, the allegorical character Rectitude steps
forward to help Christine continue building the city by supplying her
with "belles reluysans pierres plus precieuses que autres nulles"[1] [beau-
tiful shining stones more precious than any other];[2] that is, with illustrious examples of female achievement. The very first of these exemplars
are the sibyls:

> Entre les dames de souveraine dignité sont de haultesce les tres
> reamplies de sapience, saiges sebilles, lesquelles, si que mettent les
> plus auttentiques autteurs en leurs institucions, furent dix par nom-
> bre . . . Quel plus grant honneur en fait de revelacion fist oncques
> Dieux a prophete, quel qu'il fust, tant l'amast, qu'il donna et
> octroya a ces tres nobles dames dont je te parle? Ne mist il en elles
> saint esperit de prophecie tant, et sy avant, que il ne sembloit mie
> de ce qu'elle disoient que ce fust pronosticacion du temps a venir,
> ains sembloit que ce fussent si comme croniques de choses passees
> et ja avenue[s], tant estoyent clers et entendibles et plains leurs diz
> et escrips? Et meesmes de l'advenement Jhesu Crist, qui de moult
> longtemps vint aprés, en parlerent plus clerement et plus avant que
> ne firent, si qu'il est trouvé, tous les prophettes. Ycestes dames user-
> ent toute leur vie en virginité et desprisierent polucion. Sy furent
> toutes nommees sebilles; et n'est mie a entendre que ce fust leur
> propre nom, ains est a dire sebille, ainsi que sçavant la pensee de
> Dieu. Et furent ainsi appellees pour ce qu'elles prophetisierent si
> merveilleuses choses que il cou/venoit que ce qu'elles disoyent leur
> venist de la pure penssee de Dieu . . . Et nonobstant que ces sebil-
> les fussent venues et nees des payens, toutes reprouverent la loy

9. *Le Livre du Chemin de Long Estude*, ed. Robert Püschel (Berlin: Damköhler, 1887), my translation. Other related points: (1) The Sibyl thus will play the role of the learnèd female teacher
to Christine the protagonist, especially during the first part of the journey. This female configuration is important. (2) Within the plot line, Christine attains future knowledge and thus, in
a sense, becomes a sibyl herself (pp. 92–95).
1. Maureen Curnow, *The "Livre de la Cité des Dames" of Christine de Pisan: A Critical Edition*,
diss. Vanderbilt, 1975, p. 786. All citations are from this edition.
2. Richards, p. 99. All translations from the *Cité* are from this edition.

d'iceulx et blasmerent aourer plusieurs dieux, disant qu'il n'en
estoit fors un seul et que les ydolles estoyent vaines. (pp. 787–89)

Foremost among the ladies of sovereign dignity are the wise sibyls,
most filled with wisdom, who, just as the most credible authors
note in their manuals, were ten in number . . . What greater honor
in revelation did God ever bestow upon any single prophet, regardless of how much God loved him, than He gave and granted to
these most noble ladies whom I am describing to you? Did He not
place in them such a profound and advanced prophecy that what
they said did not seem to be prognostications of the future but
rather chronicles of past events which had already taken place, so
clear and intelligible were their pronouncements and writings?
They even spoke more clearly and farther in advance of the coming
of Jesus Christ, who came along afterward, than all the prophets
did, just as can be seen from their writings. These ladies abhorred
pollution and spent their entire lives as virgins. They were all
called sibyls, but it should not be taken that this was their own
name, for saying "sibyl" means "knowing the thinking of God."
Thus they were so called because they prophesied such marvelous
things that what they said must have come to them from the pure
thinking of God . . . Even though these sibyls were all born pagans
and lived among pagans, they all attacked pagan religion and
assailed the pagans for worshipping many gods, declaring that there
was only one God and that the idols were useless (pp. 99–101).

Two of the ten sibyls receive more elaborate treatment by Rectitude:
both are explicitly presented as superior to their male counterparts, and
both are exalted as examples of God's high love for women. Both are
also, it should be noted, poets, writing their prophecies in "vers rimés"
(p. 793), in "dittiez" (p. 790). Erythrea's prophecies are more exclusively
religious: she foretold the entire story of Christ's life, from the Incarnation to the Crucifixion, as well as his coming on the Day of Judgment.
The prophecies of Almathea, the Cumean sibyl, are more exclusively
political: she foretold, at the time of King Tarquin, the entire future
history of Rome. It is this latter achievement that prompts Rectitude to
emphasize Almathea's status as a feminist exemplum for Christine the
character:

> Or prens cy garde, doulce amye, et vois comment Diex donna si
> grant grace a une seulle femme que elle ot scens de conseiller et
> adviser non mie seullement un empereur a son vivant mais si
> comme tous ceulx qui le monde durant estoyent a avenir a Rome
> et tous les faiz de l'empire. Sy me dy, je t'en pry, ou fu oncques
> hommes qui ce faist? Et tu, comme folle, te tenoyes naguaires mal-
> comptent d'estre du sexe de telz creatures, penssant que Dieu l'eust
> si comme en reprobacion. (p. 794)

Now, pay attention here, dear friend, and consider how God bestowed such great favor on a single woman who possessed the insight to counsel and advise not only one emperor during his lifetime but also, as it were, all those who were to come in Rome as long as the world lasts, as well as comment upon all the affairs of the empire. Tell me then, please, where was there ever a man who did this? A short while ago, like a fool, you considered yourself unlucky to be a member of the sex of such creatures, thinking that God held this sex in reprobation (p. 104).

In Christine's earlier works, then, the sibyl's function as authoritative female figure of religious and political prophecy is deeply linked to Christine's sense of her literary vocation, and of her identity as a woman in this context. There is thus an added significance to the sibyl's role in the *Ditié* as one of the prophets of the coming of Joan of Arc, for the figure of the sibyl, embodying authoritative female discourse—poetry and prophecy—underwrites the figure of Christine as she speaks in the *Ditié*. A powerful female configuration—or, better, genealogy—of authority is thus suggested at the very midpoint of the poem, for the inscription of the names of Joan's three prophets occurs in the first line of the *Ditié's* central stanza (number 31).[3]

What follows is the poem's most explicit and emphatic celebration of Joan's female identity (correctly understood as a mark of divine favor) in words that recall Rectitude's feminist explanation of the sibyl to Christine in the *Cité*:

> Hee! quel honneur au femenin
> Sexe! Que Dieu l'ayme il appert,
> Quant tout ce grant peuple chenin,
> Par qui tout le regne ert desert,
> Par femme est sours et recouvert,
> Ce que C mille hommes [fait] n'eussent,
> Et les traictres mis à desert!
> A peine devant ne le creussent.
>
> (vv. 265–72)

Oh! What honor for the female sex! It is perfectly obvious that God has special regard for it when all these wretched people who destroyed the whole Kingdom—now recovered and made safe by a woman, something that 100,000 *men* could not have done—and the traitors [have been] exterminated. Before the event they would scarcely have believed this possible. (emphasis mine)

The implications of this extraordinary *fact*, God's public inscription of female preeminence in the book of contemporary history, are of

---

3. It is suggestive to note in this context that Christine's name appears twice in this poem, at the beginning (in the first line of the first stanza) and at the end (in the first line of the final stanza).

course directly applicable to Christine, even as she writes. The authority of her poetic voice is strengthened by virtue of her shared female identity with her heroic subject.

Her apostrophes to the French and English troops (in stanzas 37–38 and 39–40, respectively) are thus commands, positively and negatively marked, which simultaneously presuppose and confirm her position as authoritative speaker vis-à-vis her addressees. In terms of discourse analysis, Christine incorporates into her very identity as speaking subject the appropriateness condition of the illocutionary act of commanding.[4] Further, this authority now allows her to speak from the privileged position of a prophet. Old Testament and *chanson de geste* elements are combined in the context of contemporary history as crusade.

Christine thus addresses the French troops as follows:

> Et vous, gens d'armes esprouvez,
> Qui faites l'execution,
> Et bons et loyaulx vous prouvez . . .
>
> Soiés constans, car je vous jure
> Qu'en aurés gloire ou ciel et los!
> Car qui se combat pour droiture
> Paradis gaigne, dire l'os.
> (vv. 289–91, 301–304)

And you trusty men-at-arms who carry out the task and prove yourselves to be good and loyal . . . Be constant, for this, I swear to you, will win you glory and praise in heaven. For whoever fights for justice wins a place in Paradise—this I do venture to say.

To the English, on the other hand, Christine says:

> Si rabaissez, Anglois, voz cornes
> Car jamais n'aurez beau gibier!
> En France ne menez voz sornes! . . .
> Vous irés ailleurs tabourer,
> Se ne voulez assavourer
> La mort . . .
> (vv. 305–307, 316–18)

And so, you English, draw in your horns for you will never capture any good game! Don't attempt any foolish enterprise in France! . . . Go and beat your drums elsewhere, unless you want to taste death . . .

Christine's identity as prophet only becomes fully realized, however, when she speaks of the future achievements of Joan of Arc in stanzas 41–45. A universal significance is revealed for Joan's mission as God's

---

4. See Mary Louise Pratt, *Toward a Speech Act Theory of Literary Discourse* (Bloomington: Indiana University Press, 1977), p. 82: "The illocutionary act of commanding . . . has an appropriateness condition requiring that the speaker be in a position of authority."

chosen vessel. Not only will she definitively defeat the English (stanza 41), but she will reform the Church and reconquer the Holy Land, where she will establish Charles as emperor (stanzas 42–43):[5]

> En Christianté et l'Eglise
> Sera par elle mis concorde.
> Les mescreans dont on devise,
> Et les herites de vie orde
> Destruira, car ainsi l'acorde
> Prophecie, qui l'a predit . . .
>
> Des Sarradins fera essart,
> En conquerant la Saintte Terre.
> Là menra Charles, que Dieu gard!
> Ains qu'il muire, fera tel erre.
> Cilz est cil qui la doit conquerre.
> Là doit-elle finer sa vie,
> Et l'un et l'autre gloire acquerre.
> Là sera la chose assovye.
>
> (vv. 329–34, 337–44)

She will restore harmony in Christendom and the Church. She will destroy the unbelievers people talk about, and the heretics and their vile ways, for this is the substance of a prophecy that has been made . . . She will destroy the Saracens by conquering the Holy Land. She will lead Charles there, whom God preserve! Before he dies he will make such a journey. He is the one who is to conquer it. It is there that she is to end her days and that both of them are to win glory. It is there that the whole enterprise will be brought to completion.

By this point in the *Ditié*, Christine has become a new, Christian sibyl with regard to Joan. She speaks with the voice of an authoritative — and authentic — female prophet. In the unfolding both of Christine's text and of Joan's life, a kind of continuity is involved here: the sibyl had predicted Joan's arrival and accomplishments up to the historical and textual present; Christine "takes over," in her own voice, for the narra-

5. Christine is here utilizing the so-called Second Charlemagne Prophecy, current in France since at least 1382. See Kennedy and Varty, *Ditié*, pp. 63–65; and Marjorie Reeves, *The Influence of Prophecy in the Later Middle Ages. A Study in Joachimism* (Oxford: Clarendon, 1969), pp. 320–31. See also Fraioli's astute consideration of the role of the later medieval tradition of political prophecy in contemporary perceptions of Joan of Arc (811 ff.). In terms of the *Ditié*, what is of capital importance is the fact that Christine's tentative and conditional associations of Charles VII with the Second Charlemagne Prophecy (in stanzas 16–18) only become certain and definite when linked to prophecies of Joan of Arc's future achievements (in stanzas 42–43). In this case, as in so many others in the *Ditié*, it is Joan who "authenticates" Charles. It is important to note that this authentification involves a strategic rewriting (and reinterpreting) of the Second Charlemagne Prophecy as it had previously existed. "A blend of several different prophetic strains, this prophecy made promises that had little or nothing to do with Joan's mission as she announced it. It is Christine de Pizan who applied these promises to the mission of Joan of Arc" (Fraioli, 827).

tive of Joan's future. Past, present, and future converge in Christine's feminist reading of Joan's historico-political significance; God's active agent is a woman:

> Donc desur tous les preux passez,
> Ceste doit porter la couronne,
> Car ses faiz ja monstrent assez
> Que plus prouesse Dieu lui donne
> Qu'à tous ceulz de qui l'on raisonne.
> Et n'a pas encor tout parfait!
> Si croy que Dieu ça jus l'adonne,
> Afin que paix soit par son fait.
>
> (vv. 345–52)

Therefore, in preference to all the brave men of times past, this woman must wear the crown, for her deeds show clearly enough that God bestows more courage upon her than upon all those men about whom people speak. And she has not yet accomplished her whole mission! I believe that God bestows her here below so that peace may be brought about through her deeds.

Christine's discourse as woman prophet figure, as new sibyl, is authorized by Joan's appearance in history as a new kind of woman hero: a divinely sanctioned military leader with a mission that is at once religious and political.

In the final section of the *Ditié* (stanzas 46–60), it becomes clear that Christine's discursive act is also a political act, an attempt to influence the course of events in which Joan is involved,[6] for Christine's apostrophes to the French allies of the English are designed to effect an extratextual transformation, to change these present enemies into the loyal French subjects they all potentially are—to effect, in other words, a (politico-religious) conversion. Her direct address to "vous, rebelles rouppieux . . . gent aveugle" (vv. 361, 369) [you base rebels . . . you blind people] is intended to convince them of Joan's divine backing. Once again, it is the simple, historical narrative of Joan's miraculous past deeds that is presented as proof of her status as God's chosen one:

> N'a el le roy mené au sacre,
> Que tousjours tenoit par la main?
> Plus grant chose oncques devant Acre
> Ne fu faite . . .

---

6. See in this connection Dulac's excellent discussion of the *Ditié*'s "militancy": "son rapport étroit avec *l'actualité* et surtout la volonté qui s'y manifeste d'intervenir dans le cours des événements" (127 ff.). Also relevant is Jean-Claude Muhlethaler's analysis of Christine's utilization of the stance and discourse of Old Testament prophecy in "Le Poète et le prophète: Littérature et politique au XVe siècle," *Le Moyen Français* 13 (1983):37–57.

> A tresgrant triumphe et puissance
> Fu Charles couronné à Rains.
> L'an mil CCCC, sans doubtance,
> [Et XXIX, tout] sauf et sains,
> Ou gens d'armes et barons mains,
> Droit ou XVIIe jour
> De juillet. [Pou plus ou pou mains,]
> Par là fu V jours à sejour,
>
> Avecques lui la Pucellette.
> > (vv. 377–80, 385–93)

Has she not led the King with her own hand to his coronation? No greater deed was performed at Acre . . . It was exactly on the 17th day of July 1429 that Charles was, without any doubt, safely crowned at Rheims, amidst great triumph and splendor and surrounded by many men-at-arms and barons; and he stayed there for approximately five days, with the little Maid.

At this point, the historical present and the textual present merge, for the triumphant advance of Charles and Joan through the French countryside (narrated in stanzas 50–52) is taking place as Christine is writing. The emphasis is on Joan's invincibility—not as desired result but as imminent historical reality:

> En retournant par son païs,
> Cité ne chastel ne villete
> Ne remaint . . .
> . . . N'y a si forte
> Resistance qui à l'assault
> De la Pucelle ne soit morte.
> > (vv. 406–408)

As they return through his country, neither city nor castle nor small town can hold out against them . . . No Matter how strong the resistance offered, it collapses beneath the Maid's assault.

The cumulative effect of Christine's rhetorical strategy here is very powerful, and she uses it to focus on the immediate object of the French military advance: the city of Paris. The key question at the time of writing is: Will Paris resist the royal army under Joan and Charles? Christine's fundamentally polemical purpose at this crucial point in her text is to convince Paris to yield. To this end, she threatens, warns, and advises, exploiting the authority established thus far in the *Ditié* both for her own voice and for the figure of Joan:

> Ne sçay se Paris se tendra
> (Car encoures n'y sont-ilz mie),

Ne se la Pucelle attendra,
Mais s'il en fait son ennemie,
Je me doubt que dure escremie
Lui rende, si qu'ailleurs a fait.
S'ilz resistent heure ne demie,
Mal ira, je croy, de son fait,

Car ens entrera, qui qu'en groigne!
—La Pucelle lui a promis . . .

O paris tresmal conseillié!
Folz habitans sans confiance!
Ayme[s]-tu mieulz estre essillié
Qu'à ton prince faire accordance?
Certes, ta grant contrariance
Te destruira, se ne t'avises!
Trop mieulx te feust par suppliance
Requerir mercy . . .
                    (vv. 417–26, 433–40)

I don't know if Paris will hold out (for they have not reached there
yet) or if it will resist the Maid. But if it decides to see her as an
enemy, I fear that she will subject it to a fierce attack, as she has
done elsewhere. If they offer resistance for an hour, or even half an
hour, I believe that things will go badly for them, for [the King]
will enter Paris, no matter who may grumble about it!—The Maid
has given her word that he will . . . Oh Paris, how could you be so
ill-advised? Foolish inhabitants, you are lacking in trust! Do you
prefer to be laid waste, Paris, rather than make peace with your
prince? If you are not careful your great opposition will destroy you.
It would be far better for you if you were to humbly beg for mercy.

In the final apostrophe of the *Ditié*, Christine elaborates, in a strategi-
cally inclusive way, the target audience of her poem's polemical intent.
Her focus widens from the specific and immediate political objective
(the surrender of Paris) to the global context—the reestablishment of
the French kingdom under its legitimate sovereign:

Et vous, toutes villes rebelles,
Et gens qui avez regnié
Vostre seigneur, et ceulx et celles
Qui pour autre l'avez nié,
Or soit après aplanîé
par doulceur, requerant pardon!
Car se vous este[s] manié
A force, à tart vendrez au don.
                    (vv. 449–56)

And as for you, all you rebel towns, all of you who have renounced your lord, all of you men and women who have transferred your allegiance to another, may everything now be peacefully settled, with your beseeching his pardon! For if force is used against you, the gift [of his forgiveness] will come too late.

Just as it is Joan who guarantees the threat of Charles's use of force, so it is also Joan who guarantees the offer of royal pardon:

> [Charles] est si debonnaire
> Qu'à chascun il veult pardonner!
> Et la Pucelle lui fait faire,
> Qui ensuit Dieu.
> (vv. 465–68)

[Charles] is so magnanimous that he wishes to pardon each and everyone. And it is the Maid, the faithful servant of God, who makes him do this.

In her final exhortation, Christine articulates the transformation that the militant strategy of the *Ditié* as a linguistic act is meant to effect in its audience:

> . . . Or ordonner
> Vueillez voz cueurs et vous donner
> Comme *loyaulx François* à lui!
> (vv. 468–70; emphasis mine)

Now as *loyal Frenchmen* submit your hearts and yourselves to [your king].

The inscribed prayer with which Christine closes is part of this militant strategy, relying for its effect on the extraordinary authority the *Ditié* has conferred upon her:

> Si pry Dieu qu'il mecte en courage
> A vous tous qu'ainsy le faciez,
> Afin que le cruel orage
> De ces guerres soit effaciez,
> Et que vostre vie passiez
> En paix, soubz vostre chief greigneur,
> Si que jamais ne l'offensiez
> Et que vers vous soit bon seigneur. Amen.
> (vv. 473–81)

And I pray to God that He will prevail upon you to act in this way, so that the cruel storm of these wars may be erased from memory and that you may live your lives in peace, always loyal to your supreme ruler, so that you may never offend him and that he may be a good overlord to you. Amen.

This prayer as speech act, contextualized and given full meaning by the poetico-political context of the poem as a whole, is Christine's final tribute to Joan. As such, the prayer and the *Ditié* that contains it must be seen as an act of *collaboration* between Christine, the woman poet, and Joan, the woman hero, for the poem that celebrates Joan's career in history is also meant to advance that career, to function, in a real sense, as part of that career, to help fulfill Joan's mission. Christine's *Ditié* thus becomes part of the very historical process to which she is authoritatively bearing witness. At the same time, Joan of Arc qua historical fact authorizes, validates, not only the literary enterprise of the *Ditié*, but Christine's entire previous literary career, her very identity as female *auctor*, her self-created *je, Christine*.

Selected Bibliography

HISTORICAL AND IDEOLOGICAL BACKGROUND

Fowler, Kenneth. *The Age of Plantagenet and Valois: The Struggle for Supremacy, 1328–1498.* New York: Putnam, 1967.

Guenée, Bernard. *Un meurtre, une société, L'assassinat du duc d'Orléans, 23 novembre 1407.* Paris: Gallimard, 1992. [A fascinating portrait of the society and politics at the time of Christine de Pizan.]

Jordan, Constance. *Renaissance Feminism. Literary Texts and Political Models.* Ithaca, NY: Cornell University Press, 1990.

Perroy, Edouard. *The Hundred Years War.* Trans. W. B. Wells. London: Eyre & Spottiswoode, 1951.

Seward, Desmond. *The Hundred Years War. The English in France, 1337–1453.* New York: Atheneum, 1978.

Shahar, Shulamith. *The Fourth Estate: A History of Women in the Middle Ages.* Trans. Chaya Galai. London: Methuen, 1983.

GENERAL WORKS ON CHRISTINE DE PIZAN AND BIBLIOGRAPHIES

Bornstein, Diane, ed. *Ideals for Women in the Works of Christine de Pizan.* Michigan Consortium for Medieval and Renaissance Studies, 1981.

Brabant, Margaret, ed. *Politics, Gender, and Genre: The Political Thought of Christine de Pizan.* Boulder, Colo.: Westview Press, 1992.

Dulac, Liliane and Bernard Ribémont, eds. *Une femme de lettres au Moyen Age: Etudes autour de Christine de Pizan.* Medievalia 16. Orleans: Paradigme, 1995.

Kennedy, Angus J. *Christine de Pizan: A Bibliographical Guide.* Research Bibliographies and Checklists 42. London: Grant & Cutler, 1984. [Updated to 1987 in Richards, ed. *Reinterpreting Christine de Pizan,* 285–98.]

McLeod, Enid. *The Order of the Rose: The Life and Ideas of Christine de Pizan.* Ottawa: Rowan & Littlefield, 1976.

McLeod, Glenda, ed. *The Reception of Christine de Pizan from the Fifteenth through the Nineteenth Centuries: Visitors to the City.* Lewiston, Queenston, Lampeter: Edwin Mellen, 1992.

Richards, Earl Jeffrey, ed., with Joan Williamson, Nadia Margolis, and Christine Reno. *Reinterpreting Christine de Pizan.* Athens: University of Georgia Press, 1992.

Willard, Charity Cannon. *Christine de Pizan: Her Life and Works.* New York: Persea, 1984.

Willard, Charity Cannon, ed. *The Writings of Christine de Pizan.* New York: Persea, 1993.

Yenal, Edith. *Christine de Pizan. A Bibliography,* 2nd ed. Metuchen, N.J.: Scarecrow Press, 1989. [An annotated bibliography containing 841 items, including references to all available editions and translations.]

Zimmermann, Margarete and Dina De Rentiis, eds. *The City of Scholars: New Approaches to Christine de Pizan.* Berlin: Walter de Gruyter, 1994.

STUDIES OF SPECIFIC THEMES AND WORKS

Bell, Susan Groag. "Christine de Pizan (1364–1430): Humanism and the Problem of the Studious Woman." *Feminist Studies* 3 (1976), 173–84.

Blanchard, Joel. "Compilation and Legitimation in the Fifteenth Century: *Le Livre de la Cité des Dames.*" In E. J. Richards, ed. *Reinterpreting Christine de Pizan.* Athens: University of Georgia Press, 1992, 228–49.

Brownlee, Kevin. "Discourses of the Self: Christine de Pizan and the *Rose.*" *Romanic Review* 79 (1988), 199–221.

Brownlee, Kevin. "The Image of History in Christine de Pizan's *Livre de la Mutacion de Fortune.*" In Daniel Poirion and Nancy Freeman Regalado, eds. *Contexts: Style and Values in Medieval Art and Literature. Yale French Studies* [special issue] (1991), 44–56.

Brownlee, Kevin. "Martyrdom and the Female Voice: Saint Christine in the *Cité des dames.*" In R. Blumenfeld-Kosinski and Timea Szell, eds. *Images of Sainthood in Medieval Europe.* Ithaca, N.Y.: Cornell University Press, 1991, 115–35.

Hindman, Sandra L. "With Ink and Mortar: Christine de Pizan's *Cité des Dames* (An Art Essay)." *Feminist Studies* 10 (1984), 457–83.

Hindman, Sandra L. *Christine de Pizan's 'Epistre Othéa': Painting and Politics at the Court of Charles VI.* Toronto: Pontifical Institute of Mediaeval Studies, 1986.

Kelly, Joan. "Early Feminist Theory and the *Querelle des Femmes.*" In *Women, History, and Theory. The Essays of Joan Kelly.* Chicago: University of Chicago Press, 1984, 65–109.

Kolve, V. A. "The Annunciation to Christine: Authorial Empowerment in *The Book of the City of Ladies.*" In Brian Cassidy, ed. *Iconography at the Crossroads.* Princeton, N.J.: Department of Art and Archaeology, 1993, 171–96.

Laidlaw, James. "Christine de Pizan—An Author's Progress." *Modern Language Review* 78 (1983), 532–50.

Margolis, Nadia. "Christine de Pizan: The Poetess as Historian." *Journal of the History of Ideas* 47 (1986), 361–75.

Mombello, Gianni. "Quelques aspects de la pensée politique de Christine de Pizan d'après ses oeuvres publiées." In Franco Simone, ed. *Culture et politique en France à l'époque de l'humanisme et de la Renaissance.* Turin: Accademia delle Scienze, 1974, 43–153. [The fundamental study of Christine's political thought.]

Paden, William D. "Christine de Pizan as a Reader of the Medieval Pastourelle." In Keith Busby and Norris Lacy eds. *Conjunctures: Medieval Studies in Honor of Douglas Kelly.* Amsterdam: Faux Titre, 1994, 387–405.

Quilligan, Maureen. *The Allegory of Female Authority: Christine de Pizan's 'Cite des Dames.'* Ithaca, N.Y.: Cornell University Press, 1991.

Reno, Christine. "Feminist Aspects of Christine de Pisan's *Epistre d'Othéa à Hector.*" *Studi Francesi* 24 (1980), 271–76.

Reno, Christine. "Christine de Pizan: 'At Best a Contradictory Figure'?" In Margaret Brabant, ed. *Politics, Gender, and Genre: The Political Thought of Christine de Pizan.* Boulder, Colo.: Westview Press, 1992, 171–91. [Argues against Delany's article reprinted in this volume, p. 312.]

Richards, Earl Jeffrey. "Christine de Pizan and the Question of Feminist Rhetoric." *Teaching Language through Literature* 22 (1983), 15–24.

Schibanoff, Susan. "Taking the Gold out of Egypt: The Art of Reading as a Woman." In Elizabeth A. Flynn and Patrocinio P. Schweickart, eds. *Gender and Reading.* Baltimore: Johns Hopkins University Press, 1986, 83–106.

Willard, Charity Cannon. "A Fifteenth-Century View of Women's Role in Medieval Society: Christine de Pizan's *Livre des Trois Vertus.*" In Rosemarie Thee Morewedge, ed. *The Role of Women in the Middle Ages.* Albany: State University of New York Press, 1975, 90–120.